Why choose the **CARE** approach?

Development: Infancy through Adolescence
offers students an authoritative, integrated, and chronologically organized perspective on child and adolescent development unique to the field today. With its distinctive and effective combination of **cutting-edge research**, **applications**, **readability**, and **essential knowledge**, the text helps students understand and appreciate the processes by which today's scientists study child development, what they are discovering about child development, and how this knowledge can be used to improve the lives of infants, children, and adolescents around the world.

Unfold the page to learn more about the benefits of the **CARE** approach!

roach benefit students?

Readability

▶ Points and concepts are clarified and illuminated by many real-world examples, many drawn from the authors' broad and extensive experiences as researchers, teachers, and experts in their respective areas of study.

▶ The authors' engaging writing style distinguishes this book from the dry and encyclopedic presentation of material characteristic of most textbooks.

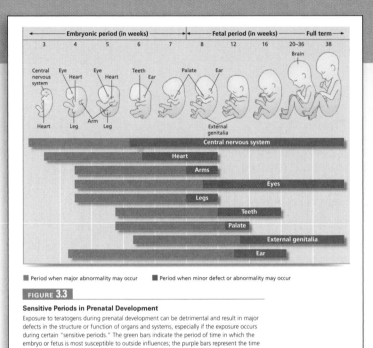

■ Period when major abnormality may occur   ■ Period when minor defect or abnormality may occur

FIGURE 3.3

Sensitive Periods in Prenatal Development

Exposure to teratogens during prenatal development can be detrimental and result in major defects in the structure or function of organs and systems, especially if the exposure occurs during certain "sensitive periods." The green bars indicate the period of time in which the embryo or fetus is most susceptible to outside influences; the purple bars represent the time in which teratogenic effects might be less serious. Several structures, like the central nervous system and the eyes, remain sensitive to outside influences for most of prenatal development (Moore, 1998).

INTERIM SUMMARY 1.1

Why Study Development?

Goals of Developmental Research	■ To *describe* what people are like at different ages and how they change over time. ■ To *explain* what causes developmental change. ■ To *predict* what an individual will be like at a later point in development based on past and present characteristics. ■ To *intervene;* that is, to use this knowledge to enhance the quality of children's lives.
Defining Development	**Development** is relatively *enduring* growth and change that makes an individual better *adapted* to the environment, by enhancing the individual's ability to engage in, understand, and experience more *complex* behavior, thinking, and emotions.
Basic Questions	1 Which aspects of development are universal, and which vary from one individual or group to the next? 2. Which aspects of development are continuous and which are not? 3. Which aspects of development are more or less fixed and difficult to change, and which are relatively malleable and easy to change? 4. What makes development happen?
Guiding Principles	1. Development results from the constant interplay of biology and the environment. 2. Development occurs in a multilayered context. 3. Development is a dynamic, reciprocal process. 4. Development is cumulative. 5. Development occurs throughout the lifespan.

Essential knowledge

◀ One of the text's most important features is, in fact, its lack of distracting features. If a topic wasn't important enough to appear in the main body of the text, it wasn't important enough to include in the book—resulting in a strong primary narrative that stands uninterrupted.

◀ Summaries and part reviews at the end of each chapter and section offer students a succinct overview of the material they've just covered while setting the stage for what lies ahead.

How does the CARE app

Cutting-edge research

▶ Students will discover the best of today's cutting-edge research—including extensive coverage of new research in developmental neuroscience.

▶ This book is the product of a collaboration among three active scientists who study different periods of development: infancy, childhood, and adolescence, each of whom has more than thirty years of teaching and research in child development.

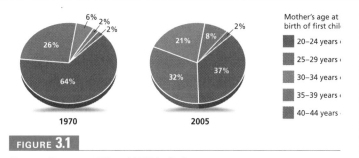

FIGURE 3.1

Changes Between 1970 and 2005 in the Age When Women Have Their First Child

In 1970, the majority of women (64%) were ages twenty to twenty-four years old when they had their first child; however, in 2005, fewer than 40 percent of women had their first child in their earlier twenties. Moreover, between 1970 and 2005, the percentage of women who had their first child at age thirty or older tripled from 10 percent to 31 percent.

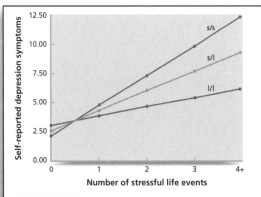

FIGURE 2.6

Environmental Influences on Gene Expression

This figure demonstrates how experience can influence the phenotypic expression of our genes. The 5-HTT gene plays a role in producing brain chemicals associated with depression, and there are three different versions of the gene whose allele pairs vary in length (short/short, short/long, and long/long). A group of researchers found that individuals who had experienced very few stressful life events all reported low levels of depressive symptoms. But among people who experienced multiple stressful life events, the level of depressive symptoms varied based on the type of 5-HTT gene they carried. Individuals with the short/short 5-HTT genotype were most affected by stressful life events and reported higher levels of depressive symptoms than individuals with the short/long or long/long genotype who were exposed to comparable levels of stress.

Applied developmental science

◀ In every chapter, the authors emphasize the application of developmental psychology to real world problems, focusing on the ways in which knowledge of child development can inform social policy and practice in the fields of child care, education, mental health, and family life.

◀ The combined expertise of the authors enables them to raise examples throughout the text that resonate with students from different backgrounds and fields of study, and with different occupational goals in mind.

Who created the **CARE** approach?

Laurence Steinberg

Laurence Steinberg is the Distinguished University Professor and Laura H. Carnell Professor of Psychology at Temple University. Since receiving his Ph.D. from Cornell in 1977, Dr. Steinberg's research has focused on a range of topics in the study of contemporary adolescence, including parent-adolescent relationships, adolescent employment, high school reform, and juvenile justice.

Dr. Steinberg is a former President of the Division of Developmental Psychology of the American Psychological Association as well as the Society for Research on Adolescence. The recipient of numerous honors recognizing his contributions to the field of human development, Dr. Steinberg has also been recognized for excellence in research and teaching by the University of California, the University of Wisconsin, and Temple University. He is the author or co-author of several hundred articles on growth and development during the teenage years, as well as several successful books, including the textbook **Adolescence** (soon to be published in its 9th Edition).

Deborah Lowe Vandell

Deborah Lowe Vandell is the Chair of the Department of Education at the University of California, Irvine. After receiving her Ph.D. in psychology from Boston University, Dr. Vandell began conducting extensive research on the effects of early child care on children's development, as well as the effects of after-school programs, extracurricular activities, and self-care during middle childhood and adolescence. Dr. Vandell has been recognized for excellence in teaching and research by the University of Texas and by the University of Wisconsin. She has served on advisory boards and panels for the National Academy of Sciences, the National Institutes of Health, the U.S. Department of Education, the Charles Stewart Mott Foundation, and the National Institute for Early Education Research. She works with national, state, and local officials to translate research into effective policies to support children's development.

Marc H. Bornstein

Marc H. Bornstein serves as Senior Investigator and Head of Child and Family Research at the Eunice Kennedy Shriver National Institute of Child Health and Human Development and as Editor of *Parenting: Science and Practice*. He received his Ph.D. from Yale University, and has since focused on studying aspects of cognitive, emotional, and language development across the lifespan and on parent-child relationships in cross-cultural contexts. He has held academic appointments at several prestigious universities around the world, including Princeton University, New York University, University College London, and the Sorbonne. Dr. Bornstein is the author of several hundred articles on infant development and parent-child relationships as well as the textbooks **Development in Infancy** and **Developmental Science: An Advanced Textbook**.

Development

Development
Infancy Through Adolescence

Laurence Steinberg
Temple University

Deborah Lowe Vandell
University of California, Irvine

Marc H. Bornstein
National Institute of Child Health and Human Development

WADSWORTH
CENGAGE Learning™

AUSTRALIA • BRAZIL • JAPAN • KOREA • MEXICO • SPAIN • UNITED KINGDOM • UNITED STATES

Development: Infancy Through Adolescence
Laurence Steinberg, Deborah Lowe Vandell,
Marc H. Bornstein

Editors: Jane Potter, Jon-David Hague

Development Editors: Shannon LeMay Finn,
Jeremy Judson

Assistant Editor: Rebecca Rosenberg

Editorial Assistant: Kelly Miller

Technology Project Manager: Mary Noel

Marketing Manager: Tierra Morgan

Marketing Communications Manager:
Talia Wise

Project Manager, Editorial Production: Holly
Rudelitsch

Creative Director: Rob Hugel

Art Director: Vernon Boes

Print Buyer: Karen Hunt

Permissions Editor: Katie Huha

Production Service: Graphic World Inc.

Text Designers: Susan Gilday, Jeanne Calabrese

Art Editor: Jessyca Broekman

Photo Researcher: Ann Schroeder

Copy Editor: Laurie McGee

Cover Designer: Roycroft Design

Cover Image: Jim Scherer

Compositor: Graphic World Inc.

For product information and technology assistance, contact us at
Cengage Learning Customer & Sales Support, 1-800-354-9706

For permission to use material from this text or product,
submit all requests online at **cengage.com/permissions**
Further permissions questions can be emailed to
permissionrequest@cengage.com

Library of Congress Control Number: 2009935600

Student Edition:
ISBN-13: 978-0-618-72155-9
ISBN-10: 0-618-72155-X

Advantage Edition:
ISBN-13: 978-0-840-03307-9
ISBN-10: 0-840-03307-9

Wadsworth
20 Davis Drive
Belmont, CA 94002
USA

Cengage Learning is a leading provider of customized learning solutions with
office locations around the globe, including Singapore, the United Kingdom,
Australia, Mexico, Brazil, and Japan. Locate your local office at:
international.cengage.com/region

Cengage Learning products are represented in Canada by Nelson Education, Ltd.

For your course and learning solutions, visit **academic.cengage.com**

Purchase any of our products at your local college store or at our preferred
online store, **www.ichapters.com**

Printed in Canada
1 2 3 4 5 6 7 13 12 11 10 09

To our families

About the Authors

Laurence Steinberg is the Distinguished University Professor and Laura H. Carnell Professor of Psychology at Temple University. Since receiving his Ph.D. from Cornell in 1977, Dr. Steinberg's research has focused on a range of topics in the study of contemporary adolescence, including parent-adolescent relationships, adolescent employment, high school reform, and juvenile justice.

Dr. Steinberg is a former President of the Division of Developmental Psychology of the American Psychological Association as well as the Society for Research on Adolescence. The recipient of numerous honors recognizing his contributions to the field of human development, Dr. Steinberg has also been recognized for excellence in research and teaching by the University of California, the University of Wisconsin, and Temple University. He is the author or co-author of several hundred articles on growth and development during the teenage years, as well as several successful books, including the textbook *Adolescence* (soon to be published in its 9th Edition).

Deborah Lowe Vandell is the Chair of the Department of Education at the University of California, Irvine. After receiving her Ph.D. in psychology from Boston University, Dr. Vandell began conducting extensive research on the effects of early child care on children's development, as well as the effects of after-school programs, extracurricular activities, and self-care during middle childhood and adolescence. Dr. Vandell has been recognized for excellence in teaching and research by the University of Texas and by the University of Wisconsin. She has served on advisory boards and panels for the National Academy of Sciences, the National Institutes of Health, the U.S. Department of Education, the Charles Stewart Mott Foundation, and the National Institute for Early Education Research. She works with national, state, and local officials to translate research into effective policies to support children's development.

Marc H. Bornstein serves as Senior Investigator and Head of Child and Family Research at the Eunice Kennedy Shriver National Institute of Child Health and Human Development and as Editor of *Parenting: Science and Practice.* He received his Ph.D. from Yale University and has since focused on studying aspects of cognitive, emotional, and language development across the lifespan and on parent-child relationships in cross-cultural contexts. He has held academic appointments at several prestigious universities around the world, including Princeton University, New York University, University College London, and the Sorbonne. Dr. Bornstein is the author of several hundred articles on infant development and parent-child relationships as well as the textbooks *Development in Infancy* and *Developmental Science: An Advanced Textbook.*

Brief Contents

Contents

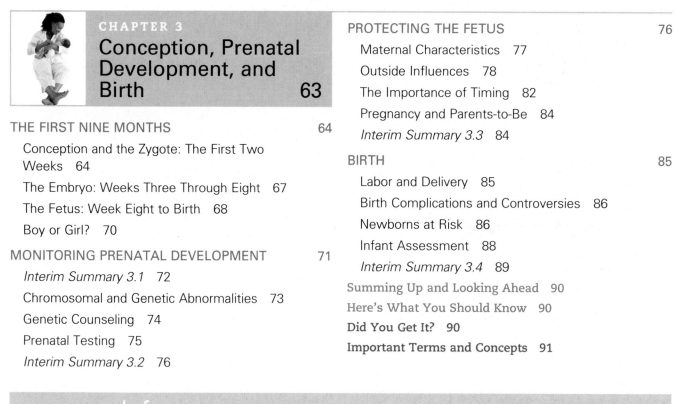

Part Three: Early Childhood

Part Four: Middle Childhood

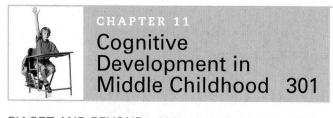

Part Five: Adolescence

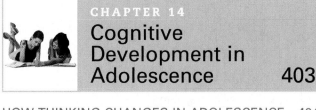

CHAPTER 13
Physical Development in Adolescence   372

CHAPTER 14
Cognitive Development in Adolescence   403

CHAPTER 15
Socioemotional Development in Adolescence   435

Preface

This book grew out of our shared belief that a change in the way we teach students about the study of child development was long overdue. What distinguishes this text from other titles can be sumarized with an acronym: CARE.

Cutting-edge research
Applied developmental science
Readability
Essential knowledge

Some books share one, maybe two, of these features. But none has all four. And it is our view that students need the full combination to really understand and appreciate both how children develop and how scientists study this process.

Simply put, students should know what today's scientists are discovering about child development and how this knowledge can be applied in the real world. This information also needs to be presented in a style that is contemporary and engaging and that is free from the distractions of fluff and filler. These have been our overarching aims.

CUTTING-EDGE RESEARCH

There is no better way for a textbook author to keep up with the latest developments in the field than to be an actively engaged specialist in his or her own research. **Specialists are often the most knowledgeable about the science that is defining, and redefining, the field.** This book is the product of collaboration among three active scientists who study different periods of development: Marc H. Bornstein specializes in infancy, Deborah Lowe Vandell in childhood, and Larry Steinberg in adolescence. All of us have been teaching and doing research on child development for more than thirty years, and all of us have occupied prominent positions in the field's major organizations and on the field's most important editorial boards.

APPLICATION THROUGH LUCID EXAMPLES

The authors of this book come at the study of development from different disciplinary perspectives: Marc was trained in developmental science, Deborah in education, and Larry in human development and family studies. One of us has taught elementary school (Deborah), another has done clinical work with children and families (Larry), and another has conducted research all over the world (Marc). **Our combined expertise allows us to raise examples that resonate with students from different backgrounds and fields of study, and with different occupational goals in mind.** All three of us have made strong commitments in our professional careers to the application of developmental science in the real world, whether through the design of legal and social policy, the dissemination of information about children through television and film, the development of educational and after-school programs, or the authoring of books and articles written explicitly for parents, teachers, and health care practitioners. Our commitment to the profession has enabled us to write a textbook that is full of examples and illustrations that permit students not simply to understand and appreciate the scientific study of child development, but to **see how this knowledge can be used to improve the lives of infants, children, and adolescents around the world.**

READABILITY WITH A GOAL TOWARD COMPREHENSION

We strongly believe that there is no reason that a textbook has to be boring. We find the study of child development exciting, and we've tried to communicate this excitement to students in the way this text is written. Although each of us is an accomplished and well-published author, we worked closely with Ann Levine, a professional writer who has written several successful textbooks and trade books, to keep the writing lively and engaging, and to ensure that the book has a strong and common voice that cuts across chapters. And we worked closely with the design team to create an interior look that is coherent, contemporary, and attractive.

As soon as you start to read, you will see that the writing is more conversational than is usually the case. **The combination of cutting-edge research coverage and conversational writing gives students comfortable access to core concepts.** In this way, each chapter tells a story. We think that students are more likely to retain information that they have really read—not just scanned and memorized.

ESSENTIAL KNOWLEDGE THAT PROVIDES FOCUS ON CORE CONCEPTS

As we set out to write this book, we asked ourselves, "What do students *really* need to know?" And, "What content can students probably do without?" We know that there are topics that are mainstays in developmental textbooks not because they remain useful or important, but because they just have always been there.

We began our work by listing, for ourselves, every conceivable topic that might be covered in an introductory developmental textbook. Like a brain producing synapses during infancy, we deliberately overproduced. And then, as is the case during childhood and beyond, we pruned. If a topic was essential, we kept it on the list. If it wasn't, we said goodbye. We elected to cover fewer, more important topics in depth rather than create an encyclopedia that was shallow and superficial. **The result is a book that focuses more on core concepts and good explanations of those concepts.**

We also decided to eliminate the fluff—the boxed inserts that students never read because they know they won't be covered on the exam, the cartoons and comics that take up valuable real estate in a book, and the imaginary children invented to tell stories about development. We knew that we could illustrate our points with real-world examples, so why make them up? Our rule was that if a topic wasn't important enough to include in the main body of the text, it wasn't important enough to include in the book. Every photo, figure, and table was selected to illustrate a very specific, substantive point. Our decision to eschew boxes had the added benefit of giving the interior design a clean, crisp feel.

Organization and Learning Aids

As we noted earlier, this book is organized in a way that will be familiar to instructors who teach child development and follow a chronological organization.

The book is divided into five parts, each comprising three chapters:

- The first part introduces the scientific study of development with a chapter on theory and research design, a chapter on nature and nurture, and a chapter on prenatal development and birth.
  - The coverage of theory in Chapter 1 departs from the usual, in that we place less emphasis on classical theorists—Freud, Erikson, and Piaget—and give more attention to more contemporary views, including sociocultural, ecological, behavioral-genetic, evolutionary, and dynamic systems perspectives.
  - Chapter 2 (Nature with Nurture) combines our discussion of genetics and our discussion of the context of development, culminating in a contemporary view of how nature and nurture work together.
  - Chapter 3 begins at conception, covers prenatal development, and concludes with the birth of the baby.

- Each of the remaining parts of the book focuses on a specific developmental period—Infancy, Early Childhood, Middle Childhood, or Adolescence—and contains separate chapters on Physical Development (including brain development), Cognitive Development, and Socioemotional Development.

Within each chapter we have included interim summaries (one following each major subsection) and a running glossary in the margin, as well as three concluding pedagogical devices that we hope students will find helpful:

- A brief section called "Summing Up and Looking Ahead," which reviews the chapter's main themes and piques students' interest in the next chapter;
- A section called "Did You Get It?" which tells students what they should have come away with after reading the chapter
- A list of "Important Terms and Concepts," which provides page numbers for each of the glossary terms so that students can quiz themselves on them.

Supplements

Instructor's Resource Manual: Save time, streamline your course preparation, and get the most from the text by preparing for class more quickly and effectively. The *Instructor's Resource Manual* contains: learning objectives, chapter outlines, lecture and discussion topics, and student activities and handouts.

Test Bank: Containing over 1500 questions, the test bank contains both multiple-choice and essay questions. Each question is tied to a learning objective and marked with the main-text page reference to help instructors efficiently create quizzes and tests.

PowerLecture® with ExamView® and JoinIn™: This one-stop lecture and class preparation tool contains ready-to-use PowerPoint® slides and allows you to assemble, edit, publish, and present custom lectures for your course. PowerLecture lets you bring together text-specific lecture outlines and art from the text along with videos or your own materials, culminating in a powerful, personalized media-enhanced presentation. The CD-ROM also includes the JoinIn Student Response System that lets you pose book-specific questions and display students' answers seamlessly within the PowerPoint® slides of your own lecture in conjunction with the "clicker" hardware of your choice, as well as the ExamView assessment and tutorial system, which guides you step by step through the process of creating tests.

Book Companion Website: Full of resources for both instructors and students, the website contains chapter outlines, learning objectives, chapter quizzing, a glossary, flash cards, and more! To access the website, go to www.cengage.com/psychology/steinberg.

Study Guide: The study guide contains learning objectives, chapter outlines, key terms with fill-in-the-blank exercises, applied learning and critical thinking exercises, multiple-choice quizzes, and a quiz review.

ACKNOWLEDGMENTS

We deeply appreciate the contributions of all those who have supported this text's evolution, including the following colleagues:

Heather Alvarez, Ohio University Main Campus

Melissa Atkins, Marshall University

Elmida Baghdaserians, Los Angeles Valley College

Byran Bolea, Grand Valley State University

Stacie Bunning, Maryville University

Melinda C. R. Burgess, Southwestern Oklaoma State University

Krista Carter, Colby Community College
Claudia Cochran, El Paso Community College
Melanie A. Conti, College of Saint Elizabeth
Caroline Cooke Carney, Monterey Penninsula College
Sheridan DeWolf, Grossmont College
William Fisk, Clemson University
Ross Flom, Brigham Young University
Pamela Flores, Nassau Community College
Belinda Hammond, Los Angeles Valley College
Dee Higley, Brigham Young University
Suzy Horton, Mesa Community College
Maria Ippolito, University of Alaska–Anchorage
Lauri A. Jensen-Campbell, University of Texas–Arlington
Marygrace Kaiser, University of Miami
Karen Kwan, Salt Lake Community College
Deborah J. Laible, Lehigh University
Judy Levine, Farmingdale State College
John Lindstrom, Virginia Commonwealth University
Kevin MacDonald, California State University, Long Beach
Ashley Maynard, University of Hawaii
Camille Odell, Utah State University
Wendy Orcajo, Menifee Valley Campus (Mt. San Jacinto College)
Randall E. Osborne, Texas State University–San Marcos
Judith (Lyn) Rhoden, University of North Carolina–Charlotte
Sarita Santos, Santa Monica College
Pamela Schuetze, Buffalo State
Jack J. Shilkret, Anne Arundel Community College
David Shwalb, Southern Utah University
Elizabeth Soliday, Washington State University
Lisa Stein, Atlantic Community College
Kaveri Subrahmanyam, California State University, Los Angeles
Ada Wainwright, College of DuPage
Lois Willoughby, Miami Dade Community College

Producing *Development: Infancy Through Adolescence* and its supplements was a formidable task. We are especially indebted to each of the following individuals for their contributions to this project:

Sean Wakely	Lauren Keyes
Michelle Julet	Holly Rudelitsch
Vernon Boes	Kelly Miller
Kim Russell	Aileen Mason
Jeremy Judson	Shannon LeMay Finn
Rebecca Rosenberg	

It has been a pleasure to work with such a gifted group of professionals and many others at Cengage and at Houghton-Mifflin. We would especially like to express our deepest gratitude to our publisher, Linda Schreiber; editors Jon-David Hague and Jane Potter; and developmental editor, Rita Lombard.

Finally, we are indebted to Ann Levine, whose final editing and voicing of each chapter helped produce a book that is not only informative, but also a pleasure to read.

Laurence Steinberg
Deborah Lowe Vandell
Marc H. Bornstein

part one

Foundations

The Study of Child Development

© Christina Renee/Getty Images

The study of child development begins with observing children. You can do this yourself almost anytime, anywhere. While you are taking this class, why not make "child watching" a habit?

The next time you walk by a school playground, stop and watch the action. What age(s) do you think the children are? What games are they playing? Do some children seem to be at the center of the action, while others remain on the outskirts? If the children are from different ethnic groups, are they playing together or with "their own kind"? Try to figure out which children are popular and which less so, which are at the top of their class and which near the bottom, and which are "model" students and which are troublemakers.

What were you like at their age—say, nine years old (about the fourth grade)? How would you describe yourself then—for example, as easygoing or high-strung, mostly quiet and subdued, or energetic, even a little wild? What were you interested in? How did you do in school? Did you have a lot of friends, or were you more of a loner? Are you similar now? If you had to name three of your current characteristic that have *not* changed, what would they be?

A central question for scientists who study child development is, What traits are relatively stable over the course of child development (and perhaps into adulthood)? For example, shy children tend to remain shy as adolescents. Notice that we said *tend* to: Many shy children overcome their fear of being noticed. Likewise, outgoing children *tend* to remain sociable and uninhibited as they grow up. Developmentalists are also interested in what traits tend to go together. For example, children who are above average in intelligence usually are outgoing and well liked. Contrary to the stereotype of "geeks" or "nerds," research shows that children who are above average in intelligence are popular. They have social as well as scholastic smarts (Hartup, 1983; Jarvinen & Nicholls, 1996).

Here's another informal assignment. When you are in a shopping mall, sit down for a while and watch parents with babies and small children. If you catch a child's eye and smile, does the child smile back? Do some small children seem curious and excited, whereas others appear bored or irritable? Take note of the parents, too. Are they paying attention to their child(ren)? If a child acts up, how do they respond? The impact of different styles of parenting is another central issue for developmentalists.

Last, think about what you were like at age sixteen. (Some of you may be only a few years older than age sixteen; others, twice that age or more. Regardless, most of you remember being sixteen.) Are you the same person as you were then? What experiences kept you on the same track or influenced you to change? Could people who knew you at age sixteen (or age nine or in infancy)—including your family and close friends—have predicted what you are like now? Would *you* have predicted what you are like now?

© Laura Dwight

© Laura Dwight

Some traits, such as the ability to focus sustained attention on a task, are highly stable over time.

Everyone has ideas about what makes individuals turn out the way they do. Some think it's all in the person's genes, that who we are is more or less biologically determined. (As the old saying goes, "The acorn doesn't fall far from the tree.") Others think what matters most is how someone was treated at home, by parents or other caregivers. ("Her parents were so busy with their own lives, they didn't have time to be parents.") Some place a lot of weight on experiences outside the family—with friends, in school, or around the neighborhood. ("She grew up in Beverly Hills. Of course she's 'stuck up'.") Others think that what's most important is the culture in which someone has been raised. ("That's the way Americans are; we Asians are different.") Commonsense explanations are not necessarily "wrong," but they are simplistic—based on stereotypes and isolated observations.

The science of child development is more reliable, more informative, and—we believe—far more interesting than everyday "theories." Common sense is largely speculation. Science is based on **empirical evidence**—information obtained through systematic observations and experiments. Scientific theories about how and why people develop as they do are accepted, modified, or rejected on the basis of research.

The study of child development uses scientific methods to describe and explain the ways in which people grow and change over time—from birth through adolescence. Although much of the research on child development has been conducted by psychologists, the study of development is an interdisciplinary enterprise, one that draws not

empirical evidence Information obtained through systematic observations and experiments.

only from psychology, but also from education, sociology, anthropology, biology, and medicine, to name just a few. Experts who study development—regardless of their training—are referred to as **developmental scientists**.

This chapter focuses on three main questions:

- What distinguishes developmental science from popular, commonsense ideas about children?
- How do developmental scientists think?
- How do developmental scientists work?

Before we get to these questions, here's an overview of this book.

WHAT LIES AHEAD?

This book is organized chronologically and divided into five age periods: the **prenatal period**, from conception to birth; **infancy**, from birth to about age two; **early childhood**, approximately ages two to six; **middle childhood**, about ages six through eleven; and **adolescence**, ages eleven through twenty.

These time periods reflect major developments. The term *infancy* comes from the Latin for "unable to speak." Early childhood used to be called "the preschool years." However, today so many "preschoolers" go to daycare, nursery school, and kindergarten ("children's garden" in German) that this term no longer applies. Puberty, the period in which young people reach sexual maturity and are capable of reproduction, marks the end of childhood and beginning of adolescence.

The age boundaries for each period are only approximate. Some children begin speaking at eleven months, others after fourteen months. (Reportedly, Einstein did not start speaking until he was two years old—proving that it's all relative!) Not only does the age at which individuals enter puberty vary (from as early as eight to as late as sixteen), but also, for more than a century, the average age of puberty in Europe and North America has been declining (Steinberg, 2008). Last, the age at which young people see themselves, and are recognized by others, as adults varies widely around the world. In some cultures, boys and girls are expected to marry and assume adult responsibilities a few months after puberty. In the United States and other Western societies, teenagers are thought to be emotionally immature, though they may physically tower over their parents and act as their parents' "computer tutor."

Within age periods, we've divided our discussion into three broad categories or *domains*: physical, cognitive, and socioemotional development.

- **Physical development** entails changes in size, shape, outward appearance, and inner physical functioning; changes in physical capabilities (locomotion, perception, and sensation); and changes in the structure and function of the brain.
- **Cognitive development** involves changes in intellectual abilities, including memory, thinking, reasoning, language, problem solving, and decision making.
- **Socioemotional development** covers changes in feelings and motivation, temperament and personality, and relationships with others.

Separating these domains is also somewhat arbitrary. The borders between them are not hard and fast. Indeed, it can be difficult to decide what goes where. Is brain development "physical" or "cognitive"? That is, does physical maturation lead to more advanced thinking, or the reverse; that is, does the more mature thinking that comes with experience cause physiological changes in the brain? The answer is, both. Is temperament "physical" or "social and emotional"? Are some individuals sensitive and others calm by nature (as a result of heredity) or is temperament acquired (as a result of early interactions)? Again, the answer is both (see the chapter on socioemotional development in the "Infancy" part). What impact does puberty (physical development)

developmental scientists Experts who study development—regardless of their disciplinary training.

prenatal period The period of development from conception to birth.

infancy The period of development from birth to about age two.

early childhood The period of development from about ages two to six.

middle childhood The period of development from about ages six to eleven.

adolescence The period of development from about age eleven to age twenty.

physical development The domain of development that includes changes in size, shape, outward appearance, and inner physical functioning; changes in physical capabilities; and changes in the structure and function of the brain.

cognitive development The domain of development that involves changes in intellectual abilities, including memory, thinking, reasoning, language, problem solving, and decision making.

socioemotional development The domain of development that includes changes in feelings and motivation, temperament and personality, and relationships with others. Sometimes referred to as *psychosocial development*.

have on peer relations (social development)? It depends. (See the chapter on physical development in the "Adolescence" part.)

Ultimately, however, developmentalists are concerned with the "whole person," with how physical, cognitive, and social and emotional development work together as individuals move along the path from conception and birth to adolescence and beyond.

WHY STUDY DEVELOPMENT?

Why study development? Every individual developmentalist has his or her own answer. (So, no doubt, do you.) Some developmentalists are drawn to the field by the opportunity to study change, whether on a neurobiological or microgenetic level, or on the much wider evolutionary scale. Developmental science covers the entire spectrum of human thinking, feeling, and behavior; a scientist whose main interest is the brain, perception, or nonverbal communication, to pick just a few examples, might find a perfect niche. Others are more interested in the cultural aspects of development—how ideas about development vary from one culture to another, how the experience of development varies in relation to the context, and what impact globalization and other twenty-first-century trends might have on development. Still others are concerned about children's futures—in our own society and around the globe. The mass media have brought home pictures and stories of child soldiers, child prostitutes, child laborers, even child slaves—conditions we once believed we had left behind more than a century ago—as well as tell stories about and show pictures of children who live in substandard conditions in our own society. And some developmentalists, of course, are simply fascinated by how young people develop.

The Goals of Developmental Research

Whatever their personal motivations, experts who study child development have four related goals:

1. *To describe* what people are like at different ages and how they change as a result of age (or in some cases as a result of specific experience—entering daycare, starting school, or going through puberty).

2. *To explain* what causes developmental change. Some explanations deal with universal developments, such as language. All healthy children begin to talk at about the same age, and in the same sequence, whether they are growing up in a wealthy family in Boston, the *favelas* or slums of Rio De Janeiro, or a hill tribe in the Himalayas. We also seek to explain the origins of individual differences. Why does one baby develop into an introverted child whereas another develops into an extravert?

3. To *predict* or forecast what an individual will be like at a later point in development based on past and present characteristics. Is an infant who begins to walk at an early age likely to be athletic in childhood? Is an aggressive toddler destined to become an aggressive teenager?

4. To *intervene*, that is, to use this knowledge to enhance the quality of children's lives by giving parents, teachers, public policy makers, and others who influence children advice. How can we facilitate positive development, prevent problems, or correct problems that already exist? Does an intensive early education program, like Head Start, help prevent disadvantaged children from falling behind their peers when they start elementary school? Does incarcerating juvenile offenders make it less likely that they will commit crimes in the future, or does it have the unintended consequence of increasing their chances for criminal activity after they are released?

Defining Development

Development is a word we frequently use but rarely stop to define. The meaning is obvious . . . or is it?

On the simplest level, development is growth and change over time. In infancy, a baby grows bigger and stronger. His proportions change as his body begins to "catch up" with his head. We would describe this as physical development. As preschoolers become elementary school children, they become capable of using logic. Certainly we would describe this as cognitive development. As children become teenagers, they often begin to develop an interest in romantic relationships. Undoubtedly, we would describe this as social development.

But development is more than growth and change. When an adult gains weight, his or her body *grows* bigger, but this is not development. Likewise, becoming a vegetarian, moving across the country, or learning how to throw a fastball may be significant *changes*, but they are not development. Development differs from simple growth and change in three main ways (Overton, 2006; Valsiner, 2006):

1. *Development makes an individual better adapted to the environment*. Consider language. A baby has no way to tell his mother what he wants; all he can do is cry and hope that she knows why. By age three and a half or four, a child can *say* what he wants and how he feels, *describe* something that happened to someone who wasn't there, and *ask* questions. Thus the development of language enables a child to become a more active participant in his or her world.

2. *Development proceeds from the relatively simple and global to the more complex and specific*. Language development begins one word at a time, with "Mama, "Bye," "Aw'gone," and the like. Between ages two and three, children begin putting two words together, as in "Baby cry," "My ball," and "Bad doggie." To understand, the listener depends on the context and the infant's inflection (a rising tone is a question, "My ball?"; a descending tone, a command: *My ball!*). By age five children's conversation is more detailed and specific, as they fill in sentences ("Billy school" becomes "Billy goes to school"), learn verb tenses and concepts (or mental categories), and expand their vocabulary.

3. *Development is relatively enduring*. Change can be permanent, but it can also be fleeting. Once a child begins to talk there is virtually no stopping her (which may drive her parents crazy). Without formal instruction, she becomes increasingly fluent in her native tongue. Barring a severe brain injury, she will never forget or "unlearn" language, nor will she revert to "baby talk."

Thus, **development** is relatively enduring growth and change that makes an individual better *adapted* to the environment, by enhancing the individual's ability to engage in, understand, and experience more *complex* behavior, thinking, and emotions.

development Relatively enduring growth and change that makes an individual better adapted to the environment, by enhancing the individual's ability to engage in, understand, and experience more complex behavior, thinking, and emotions.

Basic Questions

Much as developmentalists share a precise definition of development, so they are united by four basic questions about the *nature* of development.

1. *Which aspects of development are universal, and which vary from one individual or group to the next*? To what can we attribute differences between individuals in their interests, skills, and abilities? Do infants in China develop language along the same timetable as infants in the United States? Are the factors that contribute to high self-esteem in one ethnic group (Latino Americans) the same as those that boost self-esteem in another (Russian Americans)? For boys and girls?

Is there a link between the quality of individuals' early relationships and the quality of their later ones? One question asked by developmental scientists is whether different aspects of development are continuous or discontinuous.

© Charles Gulling/Getty Images

2. *Which aspects of development are continuous and which are not?* This question looks forward and backward. How much can we predict about a child's future development from information about his or her present state? Are aggressive toddlers likely to grow up to be aggressive children? Can we link a child's present state to his or her previous patterns of development? Did an adolescent who achieves high scores on intelligence tests demonstrate above-average intelligence as a young child?

3. *Which aspects of development are more or less fixed (like marble) and difficult to change, and which are relatively malleable (like clay) and easy to change?* For example, research shows that, across cultures, children who have authoritative (firm but responsive) parents are more cooperative than are children whose parents are authoritarian (dictatorial) or permissive (Bugental & Grusec, 2006). Can parent training improve children's behavior? (The answer is yes; see Collins et al., 2000). As early as age three, children "know" that trucks, guns and hammers, and rough-and-tumble play are for boys; dolls, pots and pans, and playing house are for girls. They expect males in storybooks and on TV to be strong and brave and females to be soft and gentle. Can these early gender stereotypes be changed? (The answer here is more complex, a maybe; Ruble, Martin, & Berenbaum, 2006).

4. *What makes development happen?* What factors influence the course of development, and how do they do so? Is the development of language due solely to the maturation of the brain, or does it depend on input from the environment, or is it a product of the two? To what extent is the development of interest in romantic relationships in adolescence an inevitable outgrowth of the physical changes of puberty, and to what extent is it culturally determined?

Whether stated explicitly or not, most scientific research attempts to discover the following: whether the aspect of development studied is universal or variable; whether development is continuous or not; whether development is fixed or pliable; and what factors influence patterns of development over time.

Guiding Principles

Last, the study of child development, like all sciences, rests on the following set of shared principles about which all developmentalists (or almost all) agree:

1. *Development results from the constant interplay of biology and the environment.* All children come into the world with the set of genes they inherit from their parents, but only a few traits (such as eye color and blood type) are genetically "determined." The characteristics a child develops are the result of interaction between genetic and environmental influences over time (Gottlieb, Wahlstein, & Lickliter, 2006). A child may inherit a genetic tendency to be inhibited, for instance, but whether this leads to painful shyness or quiet confidence depends on the child's experiences.

2. *Development occurs in a multilayered context.* Children are profoundly affected by their *interpersonal* relationships, the *social* institutions that touch their lives, their *culture*, and the *historical* period in which they are developing (Bronfenbrenner & Morris, 2006).

3. *Development is a dynamic, reciprocal process.* Children are not passive recipients of environmental influence. They actively shape their own development: by selecting the contexts in which they participate (for example, choosing their friends); by

imposing their subjective appraisal on the context (children who believe that their parents love them have fewer mental health problems than those who feel unloved, even if their parents' behavior is the same); and most of all by affecting what takes place in the context (the way parents or peers behave toward a child is affected by that child's behavior toward them) (Lerner, 2006; Magnusson & Stattin, 2006).

4. *Development is cumulative.* Development builds on itself. To understand an individual at one point in the lifespan, we need to look at earlier periods (Baltes, Lindenberger, & Staudinger, 2006). The quality of the infant's relationships at home lays the groundwork for the relationships she forms with school friends, which in turn shapes relationships she develops with intimate friends and lovers, and so on. Psychologists call the pathway that connects the past with the present and the future a **developmental trajectory** (Nagin & Tremblay, 2005). A child who has poor early relationships is not destined to have bad relationships throughout life, but one who is launched on a healthy trajectory clearly has an advantage.

5. *Development occurs throughout the lifespan.* The belief that the first years of life are a critical period in development has become part of our popular culture, or what "everyone knows." In reality, no one period of development overrides all others. Although this book stops at the brink of adulthood, we believe that development continues from birth to death, and change is almost always possible, in infancy, childhood, adolescence, adulthood, and old age (Baltes et al., 2006; Elder & Shanahan, 2006).

Development occurs over the entire lifespan. This father and son are both influenced by their interactions with each other.

In brief, virtually all developmentalists agree that development involves constant interplay between biology and the environment, occurs in a multilayered context, is cumulative, and continues throughout life. As the next section illustrates, however, developmental scientists are not "of a single mind." Some find one theory or approach more useful than others, sometimes to the exclusion of different points of view. (For a summary of the reasons to study development, see "Interim Summary 1.1: Why Study Development?")

THEORIES OF DEVELOPMENT

In everyday conversation, we often dismiss an idea by saying, "It's only a theory" or "That's good in theory, but it won't work in practice." By implication, a theory is an opinion based on speculation, not concrete evidence or hard facts. In science, however, theories hold weight.

A scientific **theory** is a set of ideas and principles based on empirical findings that explain related natural phenomena. Members of the scientific community accept a theory because it stands up under testing, fits the known facts, and continues to be refined in response to new scientific discoveries.

developmental trajectory
A pathway of developmental change that connects the past, present, and future.

theory A set of ideas and principles based on empirical findings that explain related natural phenomena.

INTERIM SUMMARY **1.1**

Why Study Development?

Goals of Developmental Research	■ To *describe* what people are like at different ages and how they change over time. ■ To *explain* what causes developmental change. ■ To *predict* what an individual will be like at a later point in development based on past and present characteristics. ■ To *intervene;* that is, to use this knowledge to enhance the quality of children's lives.
Defining Development	**Development** is relatively *enduring* growth and change that makes an individual better *adapted* to the environment, by enhancing the individual's ability to engage in, understand, and experience more *complex* behavior, thinking, and emotions.
Basic Questions	1 Which aspects of development are universal, and which vary from one individual or group to the next? 2. Which aspects of development are continuous and which are not? 3. Which aspects of development are more or less fixed and difficult to change, and which are relatively malleable and easy to change? 4. What makes development happen?
Guiding Principles	1. Development results from the constant interplay of biology and the environment. 2. Development occurs in a multilayered context. 3. Development is a dynamic, reciprocal process. 4. Development is cumulative. 5. Development occurs throughout the lifespan.

A theory is a scientist's map. Theories help scientists to organize their thinking, to decide which phenomena are significant, and to generate new questions and ideas. Developmental science covers a vast array of topics. Without theories, scientists would be lost. Imagine trying to put together an 800-piece jigsaw puzzle without the image on the box lid for guidance. But theories are not engraved in stone. The history of science is one of widely accepted theories being replaced by new approaches.

Classical Theories

Through most of the twentieth century, the study of development was guided by what we might call "classical theories": overarching visions that sought to explain every aspect of development from birth to adulthood (and sometimes beyond). Although less influential now than they were fifty years ago, classical theories laid the foundation for today's science of development.

psychoanalytic theory The theory of human behavior and development, first articulated by Sigmund Freud, that focuses on the inner self and how emotions determine the way we interpret our experiences and thus how we act.

Psychoanalytic Theory **Psychoanalytic theory** focuses on the inner self and how emotions determine the way we interpret our experiences and therefore how we act. Many emotions are irrational. A popular child lives in fear of being rejected by his peers. A student with a 3.8 grade point average panics before every exam, certain she will fail. After rave reviews of his latest film, an actor slips into depression. Where do these emotions come from? Why are they so persistent? According to psychoanalytic theory, they come from our early experiences, mainly in the family.

Sigmund Freud (1856–1939), the founder of psychoanalytic theory, is one of the best-known but most controversial figures in the history of psychology. Freud, who began his career as a physician specializing in nervous disorders, came to believe that his patients' symptoms were psychological, not neurological (or physiological) in origin. This led him to a revolutionary image of human nature. In Freud's view, we are not as rational as we think; indeed, often we do not understand the reasons for our own behavior (Freud, 1910).

Freud believed that infants are born with powerful sexual and aggressive urges—to suck, to defecate, to experience pleasure, and to avoid discomfort or pain. Babies want what they want now, not later! But the infant's insistence on immediate gratification collides with reality. The nipple is not always available; parents do not "give in" to the infant's every wish (at least in modern Western societies). As the infant matures, parents expect increasing self-control. The child's desires and wishes inevitably clash with his or her parents' rules and restrictions. How these conflicts are resolved—or *not* resolved—leaves a lasting imprint. According to Freud, a child's basic emotional outlook is set by age five or six.

Freud's theory of psychosexual development Freud divided psychosexual development into stages, named for the zone of the body a child finds most arousing at a given age: the *oral, anal, phallic,* and (after a period of latency) *genital* stages. In each stage, the child must learn to gratify his desires in socially approved ways. Parents declare, "Thou shall not." Initially the child protests; later he complies out of fear of being punished or (worse) losing his parents' love. Over time, his parents' commands are internalized as a conscience: The child forbids himself to do what his parents and culture condemn.

According to Freud, the key to healthy development is the emergence of the *ego*—the rational, adaptive part of the self—in middle childhood. The ego's job is to mediate between persistent sexual and aggressive urges, which originate in what Freud called the *id;* the demands of the *superego* (or conscience); and the demands of reality. Ideally, the ego becomes increasingly skilled at balancing the id, the superego, and reality during childhood and adolescence. But even with the development of the ego, childhood conflicts are never fully resolved, once and for all. They remain active in the *unconscious,* a reservoir of secret cravings, unspeakable memories, and suppressed rage too dangerous to admit even to oneself. Although hidden from waking awareness, unconscious wishes often overpower conscious intentions.

Erikson's theory of psychosocial development The developmental emphasis in Freud's theory was on the individual's progression through psychosexual stages. In contrast, Erik Erikson, a follower of Freud, described a different sort of progression. Erikson's ideas about development would come to have a far greater impact on the field than Freud's.

Erikson (1902–1994) studied *psychoanalysis* (the term for the application of psychoanalytic theory to the treatment of psychological problems) before moving to the United States when he was in his thirties. Erikson's own ethnic identity was ambiguous. His Danish parents divorced soon after he was born, his mother remarried, and he was raised as a German Jew. He changed his last name from Homburger back to Erikson when he became an American citizen. This multicultural background and personal identity confusion clearly influenced his thinking.

Erikson used psychoanalytic theory as a scaffold, but his theory of **psychosocial development** differs from Freud's in two important ways. Erikson disagreed with the idea that personality is fixed in early childhood. To the contrary, he held that development continues over the entire lifespan, from infancy to old age, "cradle to grave" (Erikson, 1959). He believed that just as children go through stages, so do adults. An

psychosocial development See *socioemotional development.*

individual's emotional disposition is not fixed at any one stage, but always subject to revision. Each of our lives, at every age, is "a work in progress."

Like Freud, Erikson believed that development takes the form of a series of predictable stages, each centered on a different challenge or crisis. But Erikson saw these problems as psycho*social*, not psychosexual; the result of social interaction, not inner conflict. As the individual develops new abilities and interests, society imposes new codes of conduct and offers new opportunities. What matters is that individuals find a niche—a position or activity that fits their talents and inclinations—in society.

Erikson emphasized that the transition from one stage to another depends on the society and culture in which the person lives. For example, many traditional societies have *initiation rites* to mark the transition from childhood to adulthood (Cohen, 1964; Schlegel & Barry, 1991). These rites may be physically brutal or psychologically terrifying, but the child emerges as a "certified" adult. In these societies, the young adult's future is often predetermined; for example, all men herd cattle and all women tend sheep and goats, as their parents and grandparents did before them. The rights and responsibilities of adulthood are clearly defined. In Western societies, the transition to adulthood is gradual and the point at which a child becomes a full-fledged adult is ambiguous. Faced with a wide array of possible occupations and lifestyles, each adolescent must create his or her own identity. According to Erikson, these conditions contribute to the "identity crisis" of adolescence (Erikson, 1959, which we discuss in the chapter on socioemotional development in the "Adolescence" part).

Psychoanalytic theory's most important contribution to how we think about development today is the idea that childhood experiences can affect adult emotions, thoughts, and behavior, sometimes in ways of which we are not consciously aware. Freud was the first influential theorist to propose that individuals move through qualitatively different stages of development in a predictable sequence, and to emphasize that an individual's current psychological functioning builds on development in previous stages. Erikson pioneered the study of development throughout the lifespan, and he mapped out a sequence of psychosocial "crises" that individuals must resolve successfully in order to develop in healthy ways. Erikson's ideas about what issues are important at different periods of life remain highly influential.

Learning Theory In psychoanalytic theory, emotions are central to development. In contrast, **learning theory** stresses the role of external influences on behavior. Learning theorists argue that it isn't necessary to speculate about what is going on inside the child's head to explain development. Nor is it necessary to consider the child's wider social and cultural environment. Rather, the way individuals behave is a consequence of their experiences in the *immediate* environment. All behavior is learned—including love, fear, laughter, generosity, shyness, and confidence, as well as knowledge and skills. Moreover, the basic principles of learning are the same, regardless of who is learning and what they are learning—whether a dog learning to obey a command to "Sit!" or a student learning to program computers.

Behaviorism Pioneered by the Russian scientist Ivan Pavlov, the behaviorist approach found its widest audience in America and a champion in psychologist J. B. Watson (1924), who led an academic rebellion against "introspective psychology."

Watson was primarily interested in the simplest form of learning, **classical conditioning**, which is based on associations. In a famous experiment, "Little Albert" was introduced to a white laboratory rat, which he liked. On their next encounter, as Albert reached out to touch the rat the experimenter hit a steel bar with a hammer. Frightened by the sound, the little boy cried and buried his face in his blanket. Watson repeated

learning theory The theory of human behavior, based on principles of classical and/or operant conditioning, as well as observational learning, that stresses the role of external influences on behavior.

classical conditioning A process of associative learning by which a subject comes to respond in a desired manner to a previously neutral stimulus (e.g., the sound of a steel bar being hit with a hammer) that has been repeatedly presented along with an unconditioned stimulus (e.g., a white furry object) that elicits the desired response (e.g., fear).

this procedure several times. Soon the sight of the rat alone made Albert cry—a conditioned or learned response. He developed a *generalized* fear of anything white and furry: a rabbit, a coat, even Santa Claus's beard.

—**Operant conditioning**, studied extensively by B. F. Skinner (1953), refers to behavior that is acquired as a result of its prior consequences, rather than its associations with specific stimuli (as is the case in classical conditioning). Simply put, people are likely to repeat behavior that has positive consequences (the behavior is *reinforced*) and unlikely to repeat behavior that has negative consequences (the behavior is *punished*). A girl hits a winning home run; her teammates jump up cheering and carry her off the field. She begins to practice batting every day, striving to be a hero again. A boy rides his bike down a hill, falls, and badly scrapes his knee; he doesn't ride down that hill again.

Operant conditioning can be intentional—parents reward a toddler for using the "potty" with candy or punish a child for hitting her brother—or *unintentional*. A seventh-grader acts up in class, not for the first time. The teacher warns, "One more time, Tony!" When she turns to the blackboard, he gets up and imitates her, to the class's giggling amusement. "Out!" she shouts, marching him to the door and ordering the hall monitor to take him directly to the principal. Does Tony learn to behave in class? No, he learns that misbehaving wins attention. A better way to change Tony's behavior would be to quietly walk him into the hall and talk there. Without his audience, Tony will not be rewarded for showing off. Over time, behavior that is not reinforced fades away; in behaviorist terminology, it is *extinguished*. **Behavioral therapy** (an attempt to change behavior through the deliberate use of rewards and punishments) has proven successful in programs and therapy for troubled children (and their families), as well as a means of changing undesirable habits (smoking) and overcoming phobias (such as fear of flying).

Social Learning Theory A more contemporary version of learning theory, developed by Albert Bandura (Bandura & Walters, 1959) and others, fills in the gaps left by behaviorism. One problem with behaviorism is that it doesn't explain the sudden appearance of complex behavior. Out of nowhere, a four-year-old marches around the room, singing the jingle from a television commercial. How did she learn this? If children had to learn everything through conditioning, parents and teachers would have to spend every waking hour shaping children's behavior. Learning everything through trial and error would be time-consuming, dangerous—and probably ineffective. According to **social learning theory,** children also learn by watching what other people (*models*) do and imitating their behavior. **Observational learning** is most likely when the model is someone powerful or admired, like a parent, an especially popular peer, or a celebrity (real or cartoon); when the child perceives the model as similar to him- or herself; and especially, when the child sees the model rewarded for the behavior he or she is watching. Social learning theory is the basis for numerous preventive programs, such as workshops on peer pressure in which young people watch models refuse cigarettes, alcohol, or sex, then practice or role-play saying "No!" themselves.

Learning theory called attention to how much children's development is shaped by the people around them. Whether studying the impact of parents, teachers, peers, or the mass media, contemporary developmentalists frequently invoke the concepts of reinforcement, punishment, and modeling. In particular, social learning theory led to research about what children see—on television, for example—and whether they imitate what they see.

operant conditioning
A process of learning in which the likelihood of a specific behavior is increased or decreased as a result of reward or punishment that follows.

behavioral therapy An attempt to change behavior through the deliberate use of rewards and punishments.

social learning theory A theory of human behavior that emphasizes the ways in which individuals learn by observing others and through the application of social rewards (e.g., praise) and punishments (e.g., disapproval).

observational learning A process of learning based on the observation of others.

© Laura Dwight

According to social learning theory, children learn by watching what other people do and imitating their behavior.

cognitive-developmental perspective A perspective on human development that emphasizes qualitative changes in the ways that individuals think as they mature, mainly associated with the work of Jean Piaget.

sensorimotor stage In Piaget's theory, the stage of cognitive development from birth to about age two, during which infants learn by relating sensations to motor action.

preoperational stage In Piaget's theory, the stage of cognitive development from approximately ages two to seven, during which children acquire a mental storehouse of images and symbols, especially spoken and written words.

concrete operational stage In Piaget's theory, the stage of cognitive development from approximately ages seven to eleven, during which children make giant strides in their ability to organize ideas and think logically, but where their logical reasoning is limited to real objects and actual experiences and events.

Cognitive-Developmental Theory Cognitive-developmental theory is concerned with what goes on in people's minds: how we learn, reason, solve problems, understand language, explain ourselves and our experiences, and form beliefs. (*Cognition* comes from the Latin for "getting to know.") The **cognitive-developmental perspective** emphasizes changes in the way children think about their physical and social world as they move from infancy through adolescence. Behaviorism is essentially *non*developmental. Behaviorists explain complex adult behavior as an accumulation of simple behaviors, or changes in the *quantity* of associations. Cognitive-developmental theorists see development as the result of new levels in the organization or structure of thought, or *qualitative* changes.

The Swiss scientist Jean Piaget (1896–1980) was a pioneer in the field of cognitive development. An amateur naturalist (whose first article was published when he was age ten!), Piaget earned a degree in natural science, worked at a psychiatric clinic in Zurich, and then became an instructor at the Sorbonne. There he met Alfred Binet and Theodore Simon, the inventors of the IQ test. Dissatisfied with the "right-or-wrong" format of intelligence tests, he used psychiatric techniques from his clinical experience to interview test subjects. He came to believe that children's mistakes revealed distinct changes in how children reason at different ages. Ultimately he concluded that the best way to understand development in general was to learn how children think at different ages (Piaget, 1952).

Piaget identified four stages of cognitive growth. In the **sensorimotor stage** (birth to age two), infants learn by relating sensations to motor action. In the **preoperational stage** (ages two to seven), children acquire a mental storehouse of images and symbols, especially spoken and written words. As a result, they can think about things that are not physically present. But they cannot retrace their thoughts, imagine how an object looks from different angles, try out different ways of solving a problem, or perform other *operations* in their head. In the **concrete operational stage** (ages seven to eleven), youngsters make giant strides in their ability to organize ideas and think logi-

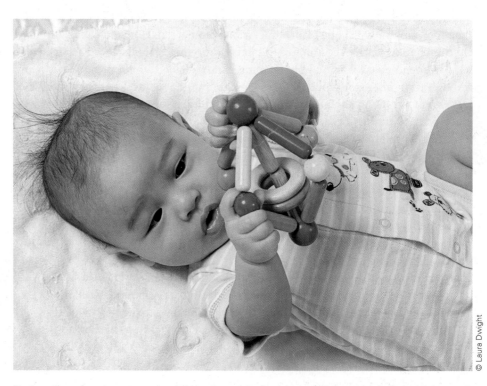

© Laura Dwight

During the sensorimotor stage, infants learn about the world by manipulating objects and experiencing them with their senses.

cally, but their thinking is limited to the concrete, physical world; that is, to real objects and people and actual experiences and events. In the **formal operational stage** (ages eleven and beyond), children break free from the here-and-now of concrete experience and are able to think about the world in hypothetical, symbolic, abstract terms, transcending space and time.

Piaget's theory is not limited to the kind of intellectual achievements we associate with school. Just as the ability to understand mathematics develops over time, so does the ability to understand what other people are thinking or feeling. Small children do not even realize that other people *have* different thoughts and emotions than they do. When her father is injured on the job and stays in bed the next day, a four-year-old brings him her favorite toy for comfort. The cognitive capacity to see different points of view also affects the way children play with one another. One reason that toddlers often quarrel over toys is that they don't yet have the ability to understand what another child may be thinking or feeling when they try to grab *his* favorite toy.

Piaget saw cognitive development as a form of adaptation. When children encounter new information, they attempt to fit the information into their existing way of thinking, a process called **assimilation**. Thus a child may call all four-legged, furry animals "doggie." When this way of thinking is challenged—her mother tells her that this "doggie" is really a cat—a child adapts by developing a new understanding, a process called **accommodation**. She creates a new mental category for cats, and in time a general category for "animals," which includes cats, dogs, and perhaps horses and cows. Through the reciprocal processes of assimilation and accommodation, children develop a more advanced understanding of the world.

Piaget's chief contribution to the study of development was to envision the child as an active organism who strives to make sense out of his or her world. In other words, development is self-motivated. Contemporary researchers have found that Piaget overemphasized the existence of clear-cut stages; cognitive development does not take the form of sudden leaps forward, but consists of many small and uneven steps in that direction. Still, Piaget is widely credited for changing the ways in which developmental scientists think about cognition, as well as for describing patterns of thinking at different ages.

Contemporary Theories

Ideas from the classical theories remain in contemporary scientists' library, like reference books, available for use as needed. The guiding principles, introduced earlier, still apply. But new approaches have expanded the range of developmental science. Here are some of the most influential.

The Ecological Perspective Ordinarily, we think of "ecology" as a branch of biology that deals with the complex interactions between living organisms and their natural environment, whether in a drop of pond water or on the African savannah. But the term applies equally well to the multilayered relationships between human beings and their social environment. In this perspective, the word *ecology* refers to the interconnected network of immediate and broader social and cultural settings in which children develop, as well as the physical environment.

The **ecological perspective** on development holds that we can never fully understand development without taking into account the *context* in which it occurs (Bronfenbrenner, 1979). This means studying not only the child's immediate environments (like the home or school), but also the network of different relationships and settings children encounter as they grow older; the institutions that influence children, directly or indirectly (such as the world of work, the education system, and the mass

formal operational stage In Piaget's theory, the stage of cognitive development that emerges approximately at age eleven, during which individuals develop the ability to apply logical reasoning to abstract phenomena.

assimilation In Piaget's theory, the child's attempt to fit new information into his or her existing way of thinking.

accommodation In Piaget's theory, the child's adaptation of an existing way of thinking in response to new information.

ecological perspective A perspective on human development that emphasizes the contexts, both proximal and distant, in which development occurs, often associated with the work of Urie Bronfenbrenner.

media); and the cultural values, economic conditions, and other forces that shape a society. Figure 1.1 illustrates this ecological model of development.

The ecological perspective broke barriers between academic disciplines. "Before Bronfenbrenner, [developmental psychologists] studied the child, sociologists examined the family, anthropologists the society, economists the economic framework of the times and political scientists the structure. . . . The concept of the ecology of human development [brought together] these environments. In this perspective all of these—from the family to economic and political structures—were viewed as part of the life course, embracing both childhood and adulthood" (*American Psychological Society*, 2005, p. 28). We look more closely at this influential viewpoint in the chapter on nature and nurture.

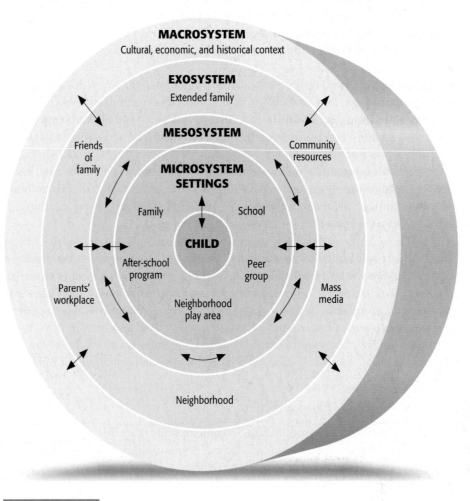

FIGURE 1.1

An Ecological Model of Human Development

To fully understand human development, the contexts in which it occurs must be taken into account. As depicted in this figure, children both influence and are influenced by their immediate "microsystems," environments like school, family, and peer groups. In addition to the bidirectional influences between a child and his or her immediate contexts, the "mesosystem," or network of connections *between* the environments, is also important.

At a broader level, the "exosystem," which is composed of contexts in which a child does not directly participate—like a parent's place of employment or community resources—can still be influential, as is the "macrosystem," which refers to the overarching cultural context in which development takes place.

Source: Kopp, C./Krakow, J., *Child development in a social context,* © 1982. Reprinted by permission of Pearson Education, Inc., Upper Saddle River, New Jersey.

The Sociocultural Perspective Culture is a pervasive presence in all of our lives, so much so that we take it for granted. Yet everything we do—and many things we don't—are based in culture: where we sleep, what we eat, whom we admire, how we see ourselves, and, of course, what we think of as "normal" development.

In the past, developmentalists used cross-cultural studies mainly to identify universal patterns of development. Today, we see culture itself as a key contributor to development: There is much to learn from studying development in different cultures in their own right. The study of cultural influences provides a window on how development takes place.

The **sociocultural perspective** on development is similar to the ecological approach, in that both insist that we examine development within the specific context in which it occurs. But the ecological perspective gives

Development is influenced by the cultural context in which it takes place.

equal weight to all aspects, all levels, of the child's environment, whereas the sociocultural perspective stresses that development must be seen as adaptation to specific *cultural* demands (Shweder et al., 2006). For example, children in societies with little formal education tend to do poorly on standardized tests of math. But they perform complicated mathematical computations in the marketplace—transactions that children with book learning alone would find extremely difficult (Saxe, 1991). As this example shows, concepts of "healthy" or "successful" development cannot be separated from the requirements of a particular cultural setting.

sociocultural perspective
A perspective on human development that stresses the ways in which development involves adaptation to specific cultural demands.

Behavioral Genetics Obviously people inherit physical traits from their parents: the color of their eyes, the shape of their face, and perhaps certain gestures. But do we also inherit *behavioral* traits? Is intelligence hereditary? Generosity? Aggressiveness? Homosexuality? (Of course, everyone has intelligence; the question is whether some individuals inherit high intelligence and others, average or below-average intelligence.) The fact that we even ask these questions is due in part to the growing influence of **behavioral genetics**, the study of the inherited bases of behavior. We will say more about this field in the chapter "Nature with Nurture." Here, let's focus on what it is *not*.

Contemporary behavioral geneticists do *not* study which behavior is "genetically determined" and which is not. Virtually all scientists today agree that development is a result of *reciprocal* influences between biology and experience, genes and environment (Gottlieb et al., 2006). And although it was once common in developmental science to try to estimate how much of a behavioral trait is genetic and how much is environmental, this question is rarely asked today. Human behavior is not a cocktail, "Mix two parts heredity with one part context and shake."

Neither is behavioral genetics abstract or speculative. Thanks to remarkable advances in the study of genetics over the past two decades, culminating in the map of the human genome (i.e., a map of all the human chromosomes), scientists are beginning to study inheritance directly. As we will explain in "Nature with Nurture," scientists can now look at the actual processes through which the chemicals that code genetic information influence patterns of development and behavior.

behavioral genetics The study of the inherited bases of behavior.

© Gerald Hinde/Getty Images

Developmental scientists do not restrict their research to studies of humans. Much has been learned about human development from studies of other species.

One of the main contributions of behavioral genetics is that scientists who study development today—whether they are interested in personality traits, social relationships, family contexts, or cultural dynamics—cannot ignore possible genetic influences.

The Evolutionary Perspective Behavioral geneticists are primarily interested in the origin of individual differences; evolutionary psychologists are mainly interested in the universals in human development. Psychologists who take an **evolutionary perspective** on development look at changes in the child's behavior over the course of development in light of the evolution of the human species (Bjorklund & Pellegrini, 2001). How was the appearance of a certain pattern of behavior at a certain point in development *adaptive* for the human species during the course of our evolution? What advantage did it give our ancestors over their competitors?

To answer these questions, evolutionary psychologists sometimes study behavior patterns in other animals, especially our nearest kin, the great apes (chimpanzees, gorillas, and orangutans). The reason is not that human beings are descended from monkeys and apes (a common misperception), but rather that we are all descended from a common ancestor. We humans became a distinct species "only" about 5 million years ago, a mere blip on an evolutionary time scale. Today, we share more than 95 percent of our genes with apes (and almost 99% with chimpanzees). What does their behavior tell us about the evolutionary origins of, say, attachment, the close bond that infants form with their caregivers (usually mothers) during the first year of life (see the chapter on socioemotional development in the "Infancy" part)?

The existence of similar patterns of behavior and development in species who share our ancestry indicates that these patterns were probably a part of the human developmental repertoire before we became a distinct species. The evolutionary perspective has been applied to a wide range of developmental patterns, from the infant's early preference for looking at faces, to parents and children bickering during early adolescence (Collins & Steinberg, 2006).

The Dynamic Systems Perspective By tradition, scientists have divided the study of development into separate age periods or stages, different domains of development, and different social contexts. In fact, most developmental scientists have become so specialized that they study one aspect of development, during one developmental period, in one specific setting (e.g., the influence of the peer group on the development of self-esteem in elementary school students, or the contribution of daycare to language acquisition during late infancy). In short, the study of development has become fragmented and specialized. Some developmental scientists have declared, "Enough!"

Dynamic systems theory looks at the many facets of development as part of a single, dynamic, constantly changing system—including multiple levels of human functioning (e.g., genes, cells, organs, systems, whole persons), multiple domains of development (e.g., physical, cognitive, social and emotional), and multiple levels of context (e.g., interpersonal, institutional, social, cultural) (Thelen & Smith, 2006).

evolutionary perspective
A perspective on human development that emphasizes the evolved basis of human behavior.

dynamic systems theory
A perspective on human development that views the many facets of development as part of a single, dynamic, constantly changing system.

Central to dynamic systems theory is the idea that any change in one context or domain of development can disrupt the entire system, prompting a reorganization that leads to more adaptive functioning. Thus, changes in a specific context (e.g., the classroom) that stimulate changes in a young adolescent's cognitive development do not merely affect academic achievement, but may provoke a change in the child's social behavior (e.g., extra attention from a teacher following a dramatic improvement in the child's school performance boosts her confidence), which may provoke a change in the child's relationships in an entirely different context (e.g., she is in a much better mood at home, which leads to her parents spending more time conversing with her), which may provoke a further change in the child's thinking (e.g., the extra time with her parents stimulates further cognitive development), and so on.

What's important is that from a dynamic systems perspective, it is impossible to understand one domain of development in isolation from any other, impossible to study one level of context in isolation from any other, and, of course, impossible to study the child in isolation from the context in which he or she lives.

In sum, new theoretical approaches have expanded the scope of developmental science. Ecological and sociocultural theories require developmentalists to look more closely at the developing child's social and cultural surroundings. In different ways, behavioral genetics and evolutionary psychology direct attention to the impact of genes on behavior. Dynamic systems theory calls for a more integrated approach to studying development.

The different theories we have introduced draw different conclusions about the nature of child development. Some place more weight on biology and others on the environment. Among the environmental approaches, some emphasize one context (early family experiences) more than another (the broader culture). How do scientists decide which features of what theories are correct, and which aspects are not? How do we decide whether early experience in the family truly is especially important, or whether children actually do model what they see on television, or whether what happens in the classroom really does spill over into the home environment? The answer is research. (For a summary of developmental theories, see "Interim Summary 1.2: Theories of Development.")

THE SCIENTIFIC STUDY OF DEVELOPMENT

"Trust yourself. You know more than you think you do."

This is the opening of Dr. Spock's *Common Sense Book of Baby and Child Care*, first published in 1946. For decades, Dr. Spock's advice was "the gospel" on child rearing for middle-class American parents. Indeed, his book sold nearly 50 million copies, second only to the Bible on all time bestseller lists (Garner, 1998). But common sense—that mixture of folk wisdom, gut feelings, counsel by relatives and strangers, advice gleaned from books and magazines, and vague memories of one's own upbringing—is often wrong, and certainly not a sound basis for making decisions that will affect children's lives. To be fair, when Dr. Spock wrote "Trust yourself," the study of child development was in its infancy. Neither pediatricians like Dr. Spock nor parents had a body of concrete, reliable research on why children develop in certain ways.

Today, the study of child development (including the impact of different styles of parenting) is a science. Systematic research allows developmentalists to test elements of the different theories, to put their own ideas to the test, and to gather information that can be used to guide public policy and practice.

INTERIM SUMMARY **1.2**

Theories of Development

Theory	Major Concept
Classical Theories	
■ Psychoanalytic theory	Focuses on the inner self and how emotions determine the way we interpret our experiences and therefore how we act.
	Key theorists: Freud, who emphasized psychosexual stages of development and the dynamic struggle among the id, the ego, and the superego; and Erikson, who stressed the psychosocial crises we face over the entire lifespan.
■ Learning theory	Stresses the role of external influences on behavior.
	Key theorists: Behaviorists, such as Pavlov, Watson, and Skinner, who emphasized the role of classical and operant conditioning in learning; and social learning theorists, such as Bandura, who emphasized the importance of learning through observation and imitation of the behaviors displayed by others.
Classical Theories	
■ Cognitive-developmental theory	Concerned with development of thinking.
	Key theorist: Piaget, who described the child as an active organism striving to make sense out of his or her world and who proposed four stages of cognitive development: sensorimotor, preoperational, concrete operational, and formal operational
Contemporary Theories	
■ Ecological perspective	Context is key to understanding development.
■ Sociocultural perspective	Stresses that development must be seen as adaptation to specific *cultural* demands.
■ Behavioral genetics	Studies the inherited bases of behavior.
■ Evolutionary perspective	Looks at changes in the child's behavior over the course of development in light of the evolution of the human species.
■ Dynamic systems theory	Looks at the many facets of development as part of a single, dynamic, constantly changing system.

The Scientific Method

scientific method A systematic, step-by-step procedure for testing ideas.

hypothesis A prediction that can be tested empirically and supported or rejected on the basis of scientific evidence.

The scientific study of child development follows the same principles that govern other sciences. The **scientific method** is a systematic, step-by-step procedure for testing ideas (see Figure 1.2). The main steps are:

1. Formulate a question based on theory, past research, or an applied issue. For example, Are mothers more likely to discipline boys than girls for disobedience?

2. Develop a **hypothesis**—a prediction that can be tested empirically and supported or rejected. For example, mothers are more likely to discipline boys than girls.

3. Conduct a study that tests the hypothesis. A researcher might give mothers of boys and mothers of girls a questionnaire on how they handle disobedience.

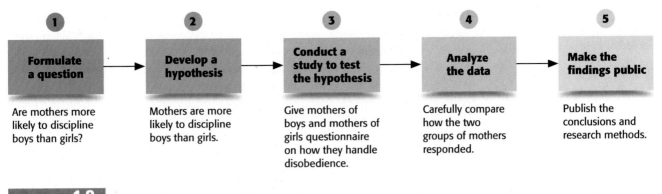

FIGURE **1.2**

The Scientific Method

When investigating new questions, psychologists and other researchers use the scientific method to systematically test their ideas. In many cases, the findings from one investigation lead to new questions and hypotheses about human development, and so the process of scientific inquiry continues.

4. Analyze the data, carefully comparing how the two groups of mothers responded, and decide whether to accept or reject the hypothesis.

5. Make the findings public. Scientists publish their conclusions *and* their research methods so that other scientists can evaluate their findings or replicate the study. **Replication**—a repetition of the study using the same methods, but by another researcher and with different subjects—may verify or challenge the original.

Obviously scientists cannot question *every* mother of girls or boys. Rather, they study a **representative sample**, a group of participants who represent the larger population the scientists want to describe. If all of the participants were mothers whose children attended the same school, or lived in the same city or state, the results might not apply to the entire country. Social scientists often use census data to determine the proportions of individuals from different socioeconomic and ethnic groups who are members in the population of interest and select participants for their research accordingly. Note that the goal of sampling isn't always to identify a group that represents an entire country— just one that accurately reflects the particular population of interest for that study (e.g., eight-year-old girls attending public school in Toronto; infants born to teenage mothers in rural Alabama; junior high school students in New York State).

To illustrate how developmental researchers conduct research, we will focus on one main example. Suppose we are interested in how different styles of parenting affect child development—a broad topic. To narrow the subject, we decide to study the impact of "punitive parenting": parents using threats, punishment, and physical force (grabbing, pushing, or hitting) when a child does not obey them. Then we generate a hypothesis: Children of punitive parents have difficulty regulating their emotions; they are easily upset and slow to calm down.

We begin this section by describing the research methods or "tools" developmentalists use to collect data, using our study of punitive parenting and children's emotional development as a recurring example. Then we will explain why different types of questions call for different research designs.

Research Methods

The first step in all scientific research is to collect empirical data (i.e., evidence from an observation or experiment). Researchers use basically three ways to gather information about people: observe them, ask them, or test them.

replication The repetition of a study using the same methods.

representative sample A group of participants in a research study who represent the larger population the scientist wants to draw conclusions about.

naturalistic observation
A method of data collection in which the researcher observes individuals in their everyday settings.

Observational Research Observing children is a mainstay of developmental research. In **naturalistic observation**, researchers observe individuals in their everyday settings; for example, parents with small children in a shopping mall. The researcher usually does not interact with the people she is observing, but simply watches. Typically she has a check sheet with predetermined guidelines—in this case, about what parental behaviors to note as "punitive" (e.g., yelling, hitting, being sarcastic) and what children's behavior to record as indicators of poor emotional control (such as crying for three minutes or more, having a temper tantrum, or hitting the parent in frustration). The researcher may carry a stopwatch, so that she can record not just what she sees, but also how long it lasts.

© Laura Dwight

In some cases, the observer *does* interact with the people she is watching, a method called **participant observation**. For example, one of the authors had a student who was interested in the way that adolescent girls talked about food, and the implications of this for understanding why so many girls dieted (Sugarman, 2001). To study this, she sat at the same junior high school girls' cafeteria table, every day, for an entire semester. She ate with the girls; took notes on their conversation, behavior, and what they ate; and interviewed them.

An obvious advantage of naturalistic observation is that it allows researchers to see behavior in the actual contexts where people live. The major disadvantage is time, especially if what the researcher is hoping to observe does not occur very often: An observer interested in the impact of harsh parenting on children's development might sit for hours and see only one example of punitive parenting, if that.

Observation is one of the developmental scientist's most important tools.

participant observation
A method of data collection in which the researcher observes and interacts with individuals in their everyday settings.

structured observation
A method of data collection in which the researcher creates a setting and tasks that are likely to evoke a behavior of interest.

In **structured observation**, researchers create a setting and tasks that are likely to evoke the behavior they want to observe. For our example, we might ask mothers to bring their four- to five-year-old child to an observation room equipped with a number of toys and interesting objects and a one-way mirror that allows us to watch the child and parent without their seeing us. We then chat with the pair for a short time to put them at ease, tell the child that everyone gets a prize when the experiment is over, and leave the room. We have assigned the mother-child pair various tasks. For example, we asked the mother to encourage the child to play with some building blocks, and then to ask the child to clean up (which will allow us to see whether the mother uses punitive or other strategies to get her child to cooperate).

To measure emotion regulation, we need to devise a situation that will allow us to see how well children manage their feelings. Here's our plan: At some point while the mother and child are playing, the researcher reenters the room with a tray holding ten items, some of which children this age like (whistles, bubbles, and stickers) and some they do not like (such as socks, a baby rattle, and a broken pair of sunglasses). We then ask the child to rank these objects from best to worst by placing them in slots marked one through ten on the tray.

Near the end of the session, we use a "disappointment task," designed to study how children control negative emotions (Cole, Zahn-Waxler, & Smith, 1994). We bring in a large, brightly wrapped gift box, give it to the child, and leave the room. However, the package contains the item the child had ranked tenth, or worst. We observe the child's reaction to the "prize" through the mirror, recording how upset the child becomes, how long the child takes to recover, and what role the mother plays in this scenario. After a short time we come back into the room with another gift box for the child and explain there had been a "terrible mistake." This box holds the child's first choice. Note that the disappointment task is mildly upsetting to some children; giving the child his or her favorite gift is intended to relieve whatever distress this test might have caused. A research review committee, which is responsible for ensuring that scientists use ethical procedures and do not cause participants in a study harm or distress, must approve the procedure before the experiment begins. (We'll say more about ethics and research later in the chapter.)

Structured observations like this enable researchers to make sure that the behavior they want to study actually occurs. This method also allows researchers to eliminate factors that might interfere with a naturalistic study, such as whether a mother is directing the way her child ranks the objects on the tray during the disappointment task, or whether the child is hungry (which might make the child more easily frustrated than usual). The main drawback is that participants may not behave naturally in an unfamiliar setting. Knowing that they are being watched, the mother may be on her "best behavior" and instruct her child to "be good," with a promise of ice cream after the session.

Self-Reports Another way to gather information is to ask individuals about themselves, or collect **self-reports**. This can be done by giving research participants questionnaires or by interviewing them face-to-face. Both interviews and questionnaires can be open-ended ("Tell me how you usually discipline your child") or structured ("Which of the following methods of discipline did you use in the previous week: [a] time-outs; [b] spanking; [c] taking away something my child enjoys; [d] yelling").

self-report A method of data collection in which the researcher asks individuals about themselves, either through questionnaires or interviews.

Well-constructed self-report measures are an important and widely used tool for developmental researchers. For our study, researchers might combine questions about routine discipline ("What do you do when your child ignores you?" and "When do you think it is necessary to hit a child who is misbehaving?") with questions about the parent's child ("When your child is upset, does it take him/her a long time to calm down?").

As in this case, surveys or interviews include questions about different aspects of the topic researchers are studying, and they often combine answers to a series of questions to make a measure or "score." For instance, at the end of a semester most colleges and universities ask students to complete an evaluation form that has many different items to measure the quality of an instructor (e.g., how well organized he or she was, how engaging, how responsive to questions). The instructor's ratings on these different measures are combined to create an overall rating of the instructor's performance.

Self-report measures allow researchers to collect a large amount of data in a much shorter time and at a lower cost than is possible when conducting observations. But relying on self-reports has several drawbacks. First, we are dependent on respondents answering our questions accurately. Sometimes people simply do not tell the truth, although this is not as common as you might think. More frequent sources of inaccuracy are misremembering or misinterpreting the question. Promising that responses will remain anonymous, careful wording of questions, and, in interview situations, establishing rapport with the individual can help minimize these problems. Asking mothers, "When do you think it's necessary to punish a child?" is more likely to elicit honest answers than asking, "Do you beat your child?" Asking the same questions in different ways—"Have you ever smacked your child?" and, twenty questions later, "Do you agree with the saying, 'Spare the rod and spoil the child'?"—can reveal patterns or inconsistencies.

standardized tests
Measures that are generally accepted by other scientists as reliable and valid, often with norms derived from their prior administration to large and representative samples.

reliability The extent to which a measure yields assessments that are consistent, or the degree to which an instrument measures something the same way each time it is used under the same condition with the same subjects.

validity The extent to which a measure assesses what it is supposed to measure rather than something else; also can be used to refer to the truth or accuracy of a conclusion drawn from a scientific study.

case study An intensive study of one or a small number of individuals or families.

Standardized Tests Developmental researchers also use a variety of **standardized tests** to measure intellectual level (whether general intelligence or a specific ability, such as memory), psychological characteristics (such as temperament or self-esteem), or an individual's physiological state (heart rate, patterns of brain activity, or hormone levels). In our example, we might want to measure the child's level of stress hormones before, during, and after a disappointment task to see how much the child's hormone levels fluctuate and how quickly he or she becomes stressed (e.g., Boyce, 2006).

Standardized tests have norms—average scores based on previous studies of large groups of individuals—so it is possible to compare a child with other children who have been studied by other researchers. In addition, the tests have been carefully developed and they are generally accepted by other scientists as having **reliability** (i.e., the test provides measurement that is consistent, like a ruler that yields the same result when used to measure the same object over and over again) and **validity** (i.e., the test measures what it is supposed to measure rather than something else). A measure of self-esteem that yielded markedly different scores from one day to the next or that was uncorrelated with other measures of how highly people thought of themselves wouldn't be very useful.

However, in many cases there is no standardized test that measures exactly what the scientist is interested in. Many tests are long and many are expensive to administer, because the researcher has to purchase the test or equipment (rather than writing his or her own questions).

This, then, is the developmental scientist's basic tool kit: naturalistic and structured observations; interviews and questionnaires; plus standardized and newly developed tests. Which tools a researcher uses depends on what questions he or she wants to answer.

Research Design

Another decision researchers must make concerns how the study is going to be designed. Most developmental research uses one of three research designs: a case study, a correlational study, or an experiment.

Case Studies A **case study** is an intensive study of one or a small number of individuals or families. In contrast to the other methods we have described, case studies allow a researcher to improvise. He or she is not limited to a particular set of observations or predetermined questions, but can follow up on an ambiguous answer, let the participant "ramble," conduct unobtrusive, naturalistic observations one day and structure situations the next, and interview neighbors, relatives, and others connected to the family. In short, case studies are open-ended. Typically, the researcher sees the individual or visits the family many, many times and records all observations and conversations in a journal. Some case studies last several years (e.g., a case study of an adolescent making the transition to adulthood); others last several months (e.g., a case study of classroom dynamics over the course of a semester); others may be even briefer (e.g., a case study of a hyperactive child's initial response to a new medication).

For example, Alex Kotlowitz (1991) devoted two years to a case study of Lafeyette and Pharaoh Rivers, two young boys growing up in Chicago's Henry Horner Housing Project. The project was an isolated enclave where children lived in hand-to-mouth poverty and witnessed crime and violence daily. Keeping alive—something better-off children rarely think about—was a priority. The boys talked about what they wanted to be *if* (not *when*) they grew up. When Kotlowitz told the boys' mother that he wanted to write a book about her sons and other kids in the neighborhood, she liked the idea but paused and then said, "But you know, there are no children here. They've seen too much to be children." Kotlowitz used *There Are No Children Here* as the title of his book.

An important role of case studies in developmental psychology is inspiration. Freud's theory of psychosexual development was based on case studies of his patients. Likewise, Piaget's theory of cognitive development was based on intensive interviews and observations of a small number of children, including his own. No other research method provides as rich detail, intimate revelations, or complete pictures. Often, case studies generate hypotheses that can be systematically tested in a larger sample. But case studies have built-in limitations.

In addition to observation, developmental scientists often gather information by interviewing research participants.

Because a case study is unique, the findings cannot be *generalized* or applied to others. (In evaluating all research, not just case studies, you should always ask how far the findings can be generalized beyond the specifics of the study.) Because a case study is intensive and long term, it is difficult for the researcher *not* to become personally involved with the subjects. He or she may ask leading questions, "fill in" gaps in participants' self-descriptions, or interpret what individuals do and say as upholding a favored theory. Because a case study is freeform, it's difficult to compare with other case studies or to verify results with other types of research.

Correlational Studies Often, developmentalists want to "connect the dots." In a **correlational study**, researchers examine two or more variables to see if they are linked in any way. A *correlation* is a relationship or connection between two things. The "things" might be age, income, grade-point average, or marital status—anything that (a) varies or changes and (b) can be counted, scored, rated, or measured in some way. Two variables are correlated if they change together.

Correlations can be positive or negative. In a **positive correlation**, two variables change in the *same* direction: High levels of one variable are associated with high levels of the other, and low levels of one are associated with low levels of the other. For example, parents' and children's IQ scores are positively correlated (Scarr & Weinberg, 1983). If parents score above average (or below average) on IQ tests, their children usually score above (or below) average on IQ tests. Note that we said "usually": Correlations are rarely perfect; some parent-child scores differ widely. In a **negative correlation**, two variables are linked in the *opposite* direction; the higher the level of one variable, the lower the level of the other. For example, a high level of watching television is correlated with low school grades (Roberts, Henriksen, & Foehr, 2004) as shown in Figure 1.3. Correlations range from –1.0 (reflecting a very strong negative correlation) to +1.0 (reflecting a very strong positive correlation). In developmental science, a correlation of .2 (or –.2) is considered mild; of .5 (or –.5) moderate; and of .8 (or –.8) strong.

correlational study A study in which the researcher examines two or more variables to see if they are linked in any way.

positive correlation When two variables are correlated such that high levels of one variable are associated with high levels of the other, and low levels of one are associated with low levels of the other.

negative correlation When two variables are correlated such that high levels of one variable are associated with low levels of the other, and low levels of one are associated high levels of the other.

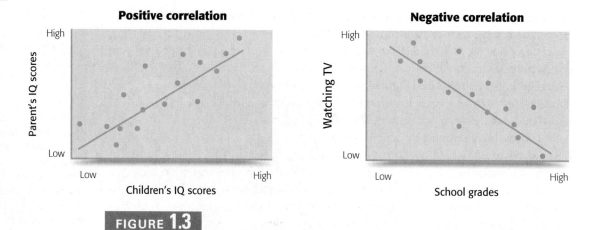

FIGURE **1.3**

Positive and Negative Correlations

These scatterplots represent correlations between two variables. Each point on the graph represents an individual pair of scores, one for each of the variables. The scatterplot on the left shows a positive correlation; parents with a high IQ tend to have children with a high IQ, whereas lower parental IQ is associated with lower child IQ. The scatterplot on the right shows a negative correlation; a high amount of TV-watching time is associated with *lower* grades in school, whereas children who watch less TV have higher grades. Keep in mind, however, that just because two variables are correlated, we still cannot determine if there is a cause-and-effect relation between them.

Developmentalists might look at the correlation between popularity and self-esteem in middle school, or between watching television and IQ scores. They frequently examine correlations between some aspect of development and chronological age (e.g., the number of words in a child's vocabulary and his/her age). Findings from correlational studies are useful in establishing whether phenomena are related to one another, but limited by the fact they cannot establish cause and effect. Nevertheless, correlational research is by far the most commonly used research design in the study of child development.

The difference between correlation and causation is important to understand. Popularity and self-esteem in middle school are correlated: If one is high, the other is usually high, too (Hartup, 1983). But this could be because the first causes the second (being popular causes children to feel better about themselves), because the second causes the first (feeling good about oneself leads to popularity), or the result of a third, unmeasured factor (coming from a wealthy family causes both popularity and high self-esteem). One of the more common mistakes in interpreting and reporting research in the mass media is confusing correlation with causation. A study finding that children who play violent video games are more aggressive does not prove that watching violent games *causes* aggression (as many may interpret the finding), because it is probably the case that aggressive children are more likely than nonaggressive ones to choose to play violent games. Readers *beware!*

Despite the fact that correlational studies cannot by themselves demonstrate cause and effect, an important step in proving cause and effect is showing that, at a minimum, the presumed "cause" and the presumed "effect" are related. If we did a study on parental punitiveness and children's emotional regulation and found that they weren't even correlated, further investigation of whether one caused the other would be a waste of time.

Experiments Experiments are the only reliable way to establish cause and effect. In an **experiment**, researchers are in control. Instead of simply observing behavior or collecting data, they do something that might change the participants' behavior and study the consequences. The researchers' hypothesis is, "If we do X (feed children sugary soft drinks for a year), the subjects in the study will do Y (become obese)." X, the element the researchers introduce or manipulate, is called the **independent variable** (in this case, whether the child did or did not receive the soft drinks). Y, the consequence the researchers want to measure (here, the child's weight), is called the **dependent variable** (it *depends* on the researchers' actions). Ideally, every aspect of the experiment is the same for all participants except for the independent variable.

One way of testing the hypothesis that parental punitiveness leads to problems in emotion regulation is to manipulate the former and see what happens to the latter. But it would be unethical to try to *make* parents behave in a way that we think is bad for children. What do we do? Suppose we try to teach parents *non*punitive ways of handling their children, such as reasoning and distraction, by enrolling them in a program designed to educate parents, and then see if children's emotion regulation *improves* as a result. The hypothesis is, if punitive mothers take part in this program (X, the independent variable), they will be less dictatorial and severe with their child, and the child's ability to control his or her emotions will improve (Y, the dependent variable).

The first step is to identify a sample of punitive mothers, perhaps from a structured observation, and ask them to participate in the educational program. A month after the program ends, we ask the mothers to participate in another round of structured observations with new tasks. If the mothers act differently than they did during the first observation, and their children are calmer, the researchers can conclude that the program *caused* the change. Their hypothesis was supported and the program was successful. (And if the mothers and/or children do not behave differently, we know the program did not work as hoped.)

There's one hitch, though: We need to make certain that the experience of participating in the experiment, by itself (e.g., just the mere fact that one is being observed by researchers could affect a person's behavior), or some other influence we did not anticipate—not the educational program—wasn't the cause of this change. The most common way to guard against this is to divide the participants into two groups: the **treatment** (or **experimental**) **group**, who participate in the education program, and the **control group**, who go through the two structured observations but do not participate in the education program. To select these groups, we use **random assignment**: Mothers are assigned to one group or the other by a flip of a coin (or another method that depends on chance). Only if we find a significant difference between mothers in the treatment and control groups (and their children) can we conclude that the education program caused a change. By the way, you might be interested to know that research has shown that such programs can teach parents to change their parenting style (Collins et al., 2000).

The obvious advantage of experiments is control. But like other research methods, experiments have drawbacks. Because researchers design and control all phases of an experiment, the situation in which data are collected may be artificial and unfamiliar, and the results may not apply to real-life situations. Suppose you were asked to participate in a study on dating with people you had not met before; would you behave the same way you would at a party or in a local hangout? Some participants might be intimidated by a university setting and a scientist ("*Dr.* Jackson") in a lab coat, both symbols of authority. In our example, mothers may use techniques they learned in the parenting program when they know that they are being observed, but not in their ev-

experiment A research design in which the researcher controls conditions in the hopes of drawing conclusions about cause and effect.

independent variable In an experiment, the element the researcher introduces or manipulates in order to examine its effects on one or more outcomes of interest; in nonexperimental research, this can refer to variables that are used to predict outcomes of interest.

dependent variable In an experiment, the outcome of interest; in nonexperimental research, this can refer to variables that are predicted by other factors.

treatment (or experimental) group In an experiment, a group of participants who receive a predetermined program, intervention, or treatment and who then are compared with a control group and/or other treatment groups.

control group In an experiment, a comparison group of participants who do not receive the predetermined program, intervention, or treatment received by the treatment group.

random assignment In an experiment, the practice of assigning participants to treatment or control groups on a random basis, to attempt to limit any observed differences between them to the presence or absence of the treatment.

eryday settings. In addition, many questions simply cannot be studied experimentally because it would be unethical to deliberately try to do something that might be harmful to a participant. We can't do experiments to learn how infants' brain development is affected by not having adequate social stimulation, how children are influenced by peer rejection, or how poverty affects adolescent substance abuse. These are all important questions, but ones where a traditional experimental design would be unethical.

Natural experiments are one way of overcoming some of the limitations of laboratory experiments. Instead of calling for volunteers, researchers study groups that already exist in the real world. For example, we could identify a parent education program in the community that teaches nonpunitive parenting and compare the children of parents who were in the program with the children of parents from the same community who were not. In this case, we have our "treatment" group (program participants) and our "control" group (nonparticipants), but we also have a big problem: We don't know if the parents who choose to enroll in parenting programs are different from those who do not in ways that might affect their child's development. Perhaps the program participants were more motivated to raise their children in positive ways and treated their children differently because of that, even before they started the parenting program. Perhaps some parents enrolled in the program because they had a child who was difficult to discipline. Because this would be a natural experiment, it is impossible to conclude that any differences between the groups were *caused* by the parenting program.

Studying Change Over Time

Developmental researchers face a special challenge in research design: assessing consistency and change over time. The three basic strategies for studying development over time are longitudinal research, cross-sectional research, and accelerated (or cross-sequential) research (see Figure 1.4).

Longitudinal Studies In a **longitudinal study**, researchers follow the same individuals and assess them at regular intervals. This type of study can be done with one group (to see how emotional control develops over a period for children in general) or with several groups (to see how children from punitive versus nonpunitive homes compare emotionally over this age span). Researchers may use these findings to chart *developmental trajectories*, which show the pattern of development over time for one or more groups (Nagin & Tremblay, 2005). The longitudinal approach can also be used to assess stability in characteristics like temperament, extraversion, or aggression.

The advantage of longitudinal studies is that they allow researchers to study change or stability *directly*. Because they study the same people, usually in the same setting (a laboratory or the participants' homes) and with the same tools (observation, interviews, tests, or some combination of these), researchers can be reasonably sure that changes in what they are studying are the result of the passage of time.

On the downside, longitudinal studies are time-consuming and costly. In long-term longitudinal research, researchers may be required to commit ten years or more to a study—and therefore wait ten years or more for results. Individuals may decide to quit the study or simply drift away. Furthermore, participating in a long-term study may alter behavior. Being tested and retested might make people feel "special" or "different," self-conscious or bored, which will be reflected in their behavior and answers. Knowing that they will see the researchers again (and again) may make participants especially eager to cooperate or present themselves in a positive light. And, of course, there is always the possibility that some event that occurs during the course of the study could change the outcome. Suppose that you tracked the emotional development of children in New York City in a study that started in 1999 and ended in 2002. It is quite possible that any change you observed in children's emotional functioning was due to the events of September 11, 2001, and not the fact that they grew older.

---

natural experiment A research design that takes advantage of naturally occurring events that affect some individuals but not others, or that makes use of an opportunity to measure development before and after a naturally occurring event has occurred.

longitudinal study A study in which researchers follow the same individuals over time and assess them more than once.

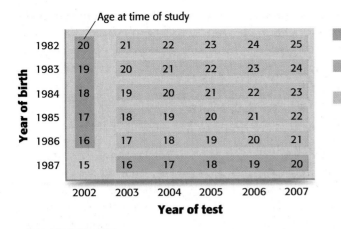

FIGURE 1.4

Research Designs for Studies of Development

Developmental scientists often have to make decisions about how to study whether some aspect of development changes with age. This figure illustrates three common approaches. In *longitudinal* studies, the same group of individuals is followed over a period of time. The purple shaded area shows a group of individuals who were originally tested in 2003 when they were sixteen years old and then again every year until 2007 when they were twenty. In *cross-sectional* studies, individuals of different ages are studied at one point in time. For example, the area shaded in blue shows a study conducted in 2002 that tested individuals who ranged in age from sixteen to twenty. Finally, in *accelerated longitudinal* (also called *cross-sequential*) studies, individuals from multiple age groups are selected and studied over time simultaneously. The orange shaded areas show that groups of participants who were seventeen, eighteen, nineteen, twenty, or twenty-one in 2003 were all studied for five years.

Cross-Sectional Studies In a **cross-sectional study**, researchers study individuals of different ages at the same time. For example, they might place mothers with a child who is two, four, or six years old (one age group at a time) in an observation room where there are more toys than children, and record the consequences. Instead of showing development over time (a developmental trajectory), a cross-sectional study measures average behavior at different ages.

The advantages of cross-sectional studies are that they are less expensive than longitudinal studies, yield immediate results, eliminate the effects of repeated testing, and, if well controlled, rule out alternative explanations of what seem to be age differences. But there are disadvantages as well. Unless the age groups are carefully matched on characteristics that might affect the outcome (e.g., their family circumstances, gender, intelligence, etc.), any differences between them may reflect personal and social differences, as well as age. Usually, a researcher makes sure that the age groups are comparable on these and other relevant characteristics.

The results of a cross-sectional study may also be skewed by the **cohort effect**: People of different ages grew up in different eras and had different experiences. Barring an event like 9/11, this is not a problem when the groups are very close in age (e.g., if we are comparing three-, four-, and five-year-olds) but could be a substantial factor in a study comparing ten-year-olds and twenty-year-olds. People born ten years apart belong to different generations, which may have a significant effect on their personalities, values, skills, and beliefs. If we found, for example, that a sample of ten-year-olds born in 1998 scored higher on a measure of educational ambition than a sample of twenty-year-olds born in 1988, we could not tell whether this was due to an increase

cross-sectional study   A study in which researchers compare individuals of different ages at the same time.

cohort effect   The influence of the fact that people of different ages grew up in different eras and had different experiences, which complicates drawing conclusions about age differences found in cross-sectional studies.

in educational ambitions with age or to social and cultural changes in the quality of education, attitudes toward education, the economy, or some other difference in the circumstances that the two cohorts experienced as children.

Accelerated Longitudinal Design An alternative is an **accelerated longitudinal study** (sometimes referred to as a *cross-sequential study*), which is both cross-sectional *and* longitudinal: The researchers follow different age groups over time. Usually the age groups are chosen so that they will overlap during the study. In a three-year study of four-, seven-, and ten-year-olds, for example, the four-year-olds are followed to age seven, the seven-years-olds to age ten, and the ten-years-olds to age thirteen. This permits researchers to chart development over nine years (ages four to thirteen) in a study lasting just three years, and it also allows the researchers to compare children who are the same age (e.g., the four-year-olds during the last year of the study, when they are seven, and the seven-year-olds, during the first year of the study, who also are seven) but who are from different cohorts. But as in cross-sectional studies, matching study participants on socioeconomic level, family situation, and other variables may be difficult. An accelerated longitudinal study also takes more time than a cross-sectional one, but depending on the age range studied, it is much faster than a longitudinal study.

accelerated longitudinal study (sometimes referred to as a *cross-sequential study*) A study that is both cross-sectional and longitudinal, in which the researcher follows different age groups over time and assesses them more than once.

Research Ethics

Remember Little Albert, the boy we discussed earlier in the chapter who was conditioned to fear white, furry things in an experiment? Watson and his colleague (Watson & Rayner, 1920) could have used behavior modification to extinguish his fears, but they lost track of the child. For all we know he lived in terror of white dogs, shaggy white rugs, and who knows what else for the rest of his life, never knowing why—or that he was a famous figure in the history of psychology! But that experiment was conducted nearly 100 years ago, before scientists uniformly adhered to a common code of ethics.

Today developmental scientists judge themselves—and one another—by a strict ethical code. The following is a summary of the ethical standards published by the Society for Research in Child Development (1993).

Rule 1: Nonharmful Procedures. Researchers should not use any procedure that might harm a child, physically or psychologically. For this and other reasons, all colleges, universities, and other research organizations have review committees that must approve scientists' research plans.

Rule 2: Informed Consent. First and foremost, researchers must obtain the child's voluntary willingness to participate in the study by describing the study in terms the child can understand or, with infants, paying attention to any signs of distress. Under virtually all circumstances, researchers also must obtain the parents' written consent (one exception is if the research is part of a school's normal educational program). In addition, researchers must inform parents, teachers, and others who might be affected by a study about any feature of the research that might affect their willingness to participate. When researchers feel that a degree of deception is necessary, they must justify this to ethics committees. If, at any point, they suspect that a study may jeopardize the child's well-being or have unanticipated consequences, they must inform the child's parents or guardians and attempt to correct the situation.

Rule 3: Confidentiality. Researchers must conceal the identity of participants, in their records and informal discussions as well as in published reports.

Rule 4: Debriefing. Immediately after the study, researchers should inform participants of any deceptions they employed and of the study's purpose. In addition, researchers must keep in mind that because their conclusions might have a powerful impact on participants, they must exercise caution in their public statements or private advice.

Rule 5: Implications. In publishing research and making public statements, researchers must consider the social and human implications of their findings. This does not mean that they should hesitate to publish controversial results, but rather that they should make every effort to ensure that their results are not misinterpreted or their statements misquoted in the media.

Rule 6: Misconduct. Universities and other institutions that employ researchers are required by law to have review boards that monitor the practices of their scientists to make sure they are in compliance with the rules of ethical conduct. These boards review proposed research before it is conducted and investigate any allegations of misconduct in research that is under way or that has been completed.

Researchers who do not comply with review boards or who engage in professional misconduct (fabrication of data, plagiarism, and the like) or personal misconduct (violation of university codes or criminal law) face severe consequences, which may include losing their job, their ability to receive public funding for their work, or in some cases, criminal penalties. (For a summary of this section, see "Interim Summary 1.3: The Scientific Study of Development.")

DEVELOPMENTAL SCIENCE IN THE REAL WORLD

Developmental science can have a powerful impact on how we view children—as parents, as professionals, and as a society. The study of child development provides advice to the following:

- *Parents:* First-time parents, especially, may feel frustrated, angry, and depressed because they do not know what to expect from a child at a given age and see the child's behavior as reflecting on their skill as parents (or lack thereof). Indeed, unrealistic expectations sometimes contribute to child abuse. Developmental science provides parents with information on what behavior is normal at a given age, what behavior is not normal and suggests that they should consult a professional, and what effects different approaches to parenting have on childen. For example, a punitive approach might be effective in dangerous situations (the child runs into the street), but it creates problems when it is the only form of discipline parents use.

- *Teachers:* Knowing what children at a given age can understand and what they cannot helps teachers to develop age-appropriate lesson plans and the most effective ways of dealing with misbehavior. If a teacher recognizes a gifted child in his class, how can he stimulate that child intellectually without isolating the child socially? Should he recommend the child be moved to a special program?

- *Health care practitioners:* Similarly, knowing what is normal and what is atypical for children at different ages helps in diagnosis of problems and the design and delivery of treatment. For example, understanding how children of different ages think about illness helps pediatricians better explain to their patients why they need to treat their problem in a particular way.

- *Program developers:* Professionals who design programs for "special children," or afterschool programs for toddlers, children, and adolescents, need to know what their young clients need. Today we take for granted Head Start, a program designed to bring poor children up to the level of their better-off peers before they start first grade. When initiated in 1965, however, it was considered a radical departure from standard schooling.

- *Policymakers:* Elected and appointed government officials write and enforce laws regarding juveniles and decide which programs for children should be funded

INTERIM SUMMARY 1.3

The Scientific Study of Development

The Scientific Method	
	1. Formulate a question.
	2. Develop a **hypothesis**.
	3. Conduct a study that tests the hypothesis.
	4. Analyze the data.
	5. Make the findings public.

Research Methods	
■ Observational research	Conduct naturalistic, participant, or structured observation.
■ Self-reports	Ask individuals about themselves using questionnaires or interviews.
■ Standardized tests	Administer an established test that has norms.

Research Design	
■ Case studies	Intensive study of one or a small number of individuals or families.
■ Correlational studies	Examination of two or more variables to see if they are linked in any way.
■ Experiments	Manipulations of one variable and observation of the effect of that manipulation on another variable, while holding all other factors constant.

Studying Change Over Time	
■ Longitudinal studies	Researchers follow the same individuals and assess them at regular intervals.
■ Cross-sectional studies	Researchers study individuals of different ages at the same time.
■ Accelerated longitudinal design	Both cross-sectional *and* longitudinal: Researchers follow different age groups over time.

Research Ethics	
	■ Rule 1: Nonharmful Procedures
	■ Rule 2: Informed Consent
	■ Rule 3: Confidentiality
	■ Rule 4: Debriefing
	■ Rule 5: Consider Implications
	■ Rule 6: Monitor Misconduct

and which should not. Although policymakers may not interact directly with children outside their family and social circle, their impact on children is powerful. Here's one example: In recent decades, public concern—and political debate—about juvenile crime has escalated. Should the courts treat juveniles who commit serious crimes as adults, subject to adult penalties? Science cannot decide what is "right" or "wrong." But developmental scientists can provide decision makers with advice based on research, not on political considerations or popular opinion. In our legal system, individuals accused of a crime must be "competent to stand trial"—that is, capable of understanding the trial process and contributing to their own defense. A recent study found that sixteen- and seventeen-year-olds are just as competent to stand trial as adults, but that this is not the case for juveniles fifteen and younger (Grisso et al., 2003).

© Beryl Goldberg Photographer

Findings from scientific studies of development often have practical implications for teachers and other individuals who work with children.

- *Business and industry leaders:* Young people are one of the largest categories of consumers in our society. Although they may not pay for items themselves, they influence decisions on purchases of everything from breakfast cereals, to athletic shoes and jeans, to video games, iPods, and other high-tech goods. From a marketing point of view, it's important to understand how children think and what motivates them. (For a summary of this section, see "Interim Summary 1.4: Developmental Science in the Real World.")

SUMMING UP AND LOOKING AHEAD

In this chapter, we've introduced you to the study of child development, including the sort of questions that developmentalists ask, their theoretical approaches, how they investigate questions scientifically, and how the knowledge gained from this research might be used. As noted earlier, one of the questions that has long fascinated

INTERIM SUMMARY 1.4

Developmental Science in the Real World

Developmental Science Has Practical Implications for

- Parents
- Teachers
- Health care practitioners
- Program developers
- Policymakers
- Business and industry leaders

For further information go to http://www.apa.org/topics/psychologycareer.html

experts who study development is, What makes development happen? In the next chapter, we'll look at what probably is the longest-running controversy in the history of child development: whether development is mostly a product of nature (our genes) or mostly due to nurture (the environment).

The answer may surprise you.

HERE'S WHAT YOU SHOULD KNOW

Did You Get It?

After reading this chapter, you should understand the following:

- The main reasons scientists study development, and the types of questions they ask
- How development is defined
- The five basic principles of development
- The main theories of development, and the people and ideas associated with them

- The methods, designs, and types of studies that developmental scientists use
- The ethical guidelines that scientists who study children must follow
- Some ways in which the results of developmental research are applied in the real world

Important Terms and Concepts

accelerated longitudinal study (p. 30)
accommodation (p. 15)
adolescence (p. 5)
assimilation (p. 15)
behavioral genetics (p. 17)
behavioral therapy (p. 13)
case study (p. 24)
classical conditioning (p. 12)
cognitive development (p. 5)
cognitive-developmental perspective (p. 14)
cohort effect (p. 29)
concrete operational stage (p. 14)
control group (p. 27)
correlational study (p. 25)
cross-sectional study (p. 29)
dependent variable (p. 27)

development (p. 7)
developmental scientists (p. 5)
developmental trajectory (p. 9)
dynamic systems theory (p. 18)
early childhood (p. 5)
ecological perspective (p. 15)
empirical evidence (p. 4)
evolutionary perspective (p. 18)
experiment (p. 27)
formal operational stage (p. 15)
hypothesis (p. 20)
independent variable (p. 27)
infancy (p. 5)
learning theory (p. 12)

longitudinal study (p. 28)
middle childhood (p. 5)
natural experiment (p. 28)
naturalistic observation (p. 22)
negative correlation (p. 25)
observational learning (p. 13)
operant conditioning (p. 13)
participant observation (p. 22)
physical development (p. 5)
positive correlation (p. 25)
prenatal period (p. 5)
preoperational stage (p. 14)
psychoanalytic theory (p. 10)
psychosocial development (p. 11)
random assignment (p. 27)
reliability (p. 24)

replication (p. 21)
representative sample (p. 21)
scientific method (p. 20)
self-report (p. 23)
sensorimotor stage (p. 14)
social learning theory (p. 13)
sociocultural perspective (p. 17)
socioemotional development (p. 5)
standardized tests (p. 24)
structured observation (p. 22)
theory (p. 9)
treatment (or experimental) group (p. 27)
validity (p. 24)

Nature with Nurture

© Mascarucci/Corbis

human genome The complete set of genes for the creation and development of the human organism.

In February 2001—to much acclaim—scientists published a map of the **human genome**, the complete set of genes for building and operating a human body (IHGSC, 2001; Venter et al., 2001). For the first time ever, a species could read its own instruction manual (Ridley, 2003)! The goal now is to determine which genes influence which characteristics. The hope is that the genome will provide insights into even complex behavior and enable us to prevent or reverse diseases with a genetic component. Since 2001 discoveries about human genes have escalated. New findings are published almost every month. But the headlines that accompany popular articles about this research are often misleading.

Nothing as complex as human intelligence is "determined" by a single gene, or even multiple genes. The same is true of mental health, the aging process, and even many aspects of physical appearance. Scientists used to think that genes were stable, fixed units of heredity, passed from generation to generation. New research has revealed that genes are more variable and complex than anyone imagined twenty-five years ago. Almost inevitably, and ironically, these revelations led scientists to "rediscover" the environment. Genes do not act in a vacuum (Plomin, 2004). One cannot understand genes without considering their surroundings—at the cellular level, in a living organism, and from a broader sociocultural perspective.

The early part of the twenty-first century has been a remarkable "age of discovery" for developmental scientists. New lines of research and new insights have led us to reexamine not only our explanations of development but also the questions we ask. This chapter introduces current thinking about "what makes development happen." We focus on four main questions:

- How have ideas about nature and nurture changed?
- What are genes? What exactly do they do?
- What is the "environment"?
- How do the genetic code and environmental contexts interact in development?

PERSPECTIVES ON NATURE AND NURTURE

For centuries, scientists and philosophers have debated how and why people turn out the way they do. How can it be that each person is like all other humans in some ways and yet unique? What roles do nature and nurture, heredity and experience, play in who we become? Over time, four main views have been put forward:

1. Development is driven by nature.

2. Development is driven by nurture.

3. Development is part nature, part nurture.

4. Development results from the interaction of nature with nurture.

All of these views are still alive in popular culture—for example, in how we think about intelligence. Ask yourself this: Why are some children exceptionally quick, other children slow, and most children bright but not brilliant? Many people believe intelligence is innate; thus, some children are simply born smart (the nature view). Some people hold that intelligence is more a result of experience, of having well-educated parents, going to good schools, being encouraged to ask questions and find answers, and making friends whose families hold similar values (the nurture view). Others feel that intelligence is a little bit of both; that is, brains plus upbringing contribute (the nature + nurture position). We'll look at these perspectives, and then introduce the fourth—and newest—view, that genes and environment are in constant interplay.

Development Is Driven by Nature

The idea that intelligence and other characteristics are innate or inborn, not acquired or learned, called **nativism**, has a long history (Spelke & Newport, 1998).

Preformationism In the seventeenth century, biologists and others took the concept of inborn traits quite literally. The prevailing view was that the embryo was *preformed*, a miniature adult whose future anatomy and behavior were already determined (Ariès, 1962). Some held that the "little person" was in the father's sperm; others, that he or she was in the mother's egg (see Figure 2.1). But preformation was assumed; the man or woman who eventually emerged was already present at the time of conception—or perhaps even before—just bottled up and miniaturized, waiting to grow into a full-sized adult. Well into the seventeenth century, paintings portrayed young children as miniature adults—with adult-like features, in adult clothes and adult poses.

The belief in **preformationism** was accompanied by beliefs about human nature. In general, Western culture has viewed children as innately bad (Clarke-Stewart, 1998). This outlook comes from the biblical concept of "original sin," the belief that all human beings are descended from Adam and Eve and inherit the weakness that led them to disobey God and eat fruit from the Tree of Knowledge. As a result, they and their descendants were expelled from the Garden of Eden. All humans inherit this original sin.

The Puritans, for example, believed that children were, by nature, evil and vulnerable to temptation. Parents had an obligation to teach children morality, by whatever means necessary. This meant keeping a constant, watchful eye on the child and punishing transgressions, for the child's own good. A parent's main role in development was "beating the devil" out of his or her children, sometimes literally. The idea that children are trouble waiting to happen—in adolescence if not before—remains part of Western folk wisdom.

Rousseau's Innocent Babes The French philosopher Jean Jacques Rousseau (1762/1911) was an exception. He rejected both preformationism and the idea that children, like wild horses, needed to be broken. Rather, he believed that children are innocent at birth and develop according to nature's plan, much as a flower develops. A tulip bulb is not a little flower, nor does it have a tiny little tulip inside of it—it is something entirely different. But the development of a tulip from a bulb is predetermined, in the sense that it is directed by nature and influenced only slightly by the environment. Depending on the weather and soil—and the gardener—the flower may be strong and sturdy or weak and short-lived. Thus the environment matters, but nature plays the leading role. Under no circumstances will a tulip bulb develop into a crocodile or even a rose bush.

Rousseau saw child development in much the same way. Infants are not miniature adults; neither are they rife with temptation. Children are innocent at birth, and development follows nature's plan. Like flowers, with proper nurturing children grow up into beautiful beings. A parent's job is to protect the child from harmful interference

FIGURE 2.1

Preformationism
Preformationists believed that the adult who would ultimately emerge was already present at the time of conception—or perhaps even before.

nativism The idea that human characteristics are innate or inborn, not acquired or learned.

preformationism The seventeenth-century theory of inheritance that hypothesized that all the characteristics of an adult were prefigured in miniature within either the sperm or the ovum.

and let the child's development unfold. The expression "innocent as a baby" comes from Rousseau. So did the open school movement, carried forward today by Montessori schools, which hold that children should follow their own interests and not be bound by rigid curricula.

Genetic Determinism and Eugenics Genetics was the cutting edge of science at the beginning of the twentieth century, much as it is today. Unlike today, however, early genetics was largely speculative. Scientists could study patterns of heredity only indirectly, and they did not know how or why they occurred.

genetic determinism The idea that human qualities are genetically determined and cannot be changed by nurture or education.

A number of scientists (and nonscientists) came to believe in **genetic determinism**: the idea that human qualities are genetically determined and cannot be changed by nurture or education. Preformationism and genetic determinism share a central assumption. Internal (natural, genetic) factors control development, and external (nurturing, environmental) factors have little impact. Thus, the complete individual is already present in the fertilized egg—literally, according to preformationism—or locked in genes, and development is merely a process of growing.

Carried to an extreme, genetic determinism led to one of the most disturbing chapters in early-twentieth-century science, the eugenics movement (Rutter, 2006). ("Eu-" comes from the Greek word for "good," so **eugenics** means "good genes.") Eugenicists advocated the use of controlled breeding to encourage childbearing among people with characteristics considered "desirable" and to discourage (or eliminate) childbearing among those with "undesirable" traits, often members of ethnic minority groups.

eugenics A philosophy that advocates the use of controlled breeding to encourage childbearing among individuals with characteristics considered "desirable" and to discourage (or eliminate) childbearing among those with "undesirable" traits.

Farmers practice selective breeding all the time, to improve the quality of their livestock. Eugenicists sought to apply this idea to *human* populations. The best-known example was Hitler's effort to "purify" the Aryan race by exterminating Jews, gypsies [or Romany], Poles, homosexuals, and other "undesirables" in Nazi Germany during World War II. But there were advocates of forced sterilization of people who were mentally challenged and other groups in the United States as well.

Perhaps because of this shameful history, the study of genetic influences on *normal* child development fell into disrepute among developmental scientists and was not revisited until the latter part of the twentieth century (Rutter, 2006). Even today the idea that some characteristics are genetically determined remains strong. Think how often we say someone is a "born musician" or a "born athlete." Likewise Americans, especially, tend to hold that some people are "born smart" and others, not so smart (Holloway, 1988).

Development Is Driven by Nurture

At the opposite extreme were those who believed that external forces are entirely responsible for development. *Environmentalists* hold that the newborn is unformed, like a lump of clay, and the individual's characteristics are entirely the product of experience, upbringing, and learning.

The Blank Slate The English philosopher John Locke (1690) introduced the environmentalist view in a highly influential essay, "Concerning Human Understanding." At the time, it was assumed that human nature was predetermined. Philosophers and religious thinkers may have disagreed about whether human nature was good or evil, but they agreed that it was fixed by the time the child was born, and impossible to alter. Locke had a radically different idea.

tabula rasa ("blank slate") The notion, usually associated with the philosopher John Locke, that nothing about development is predetermined, and that the child is entirely a product of his or her environment and experience.

Locke argued that the infant's mind is a **tabula rasa**, or "blank slate." In his view, *nothing* about development was predetermined; *everything* the child becomes is a product of his or her environment and experience. Childhood is a formative period, and parents have responsibility for teaching children reason, self-restraint, and respect for authority. Whatever successes—or failings—children exhibit are the result of their experiences.

The idea that nurture was the driving force behind development dominated nineteenth-century thinking and spilled over into the twentieth century. One social consequence was the mental hygiene movement (Rutter, 2006). Until this time, the "insane" were believed to be possessed by demons, and they were locked up in asylums, chained, beaten, and generally treated no better than animals. Their psychological condition was considered irreversible—and threatening. Advocates of mental hygiene, in contrast, took an environmentalist view. They held that insanity was an illness that, like other illnesses, could be treated and cured. The first step was "cleaning up" the environment in which disturbed people were housed.

Watson's Behaviorism In academic circles, the two dominant views of development during the first half of the twentieth century—learning theory and psychoanalytic theory—saw development primarily as the product of experience, not nature. (See "The Study of Child Development.") Watson's theory of behaviorism was, in effect, a revival of Locke's *tabula rasa*, a strict, "fundamentalist" version of environmentalism. In an often quoted statement, Watson (1930) declared:

> Give me a dozen healthy infants, well-formed, and my own specified world to bring them up in and I'll guarantee to take any one at random and train him to become any type of specialist I might select—doctor, lawyer, artist, merchant-chief, and, yes, even beggarman and thief, regardless of his talents, penchants, tendencies, abilities, vocations, and race of his ancestors (p. 104).

By extension, anyone can become intelligent if he or she is rewarded (reinforced) for studying and learning and for solving problems with intellect rather than emotions. Nurture is everything.

Development Is Part Nature, Part Nurture

By the mid-twentieth century, many developmental scientists were dissatisfied with both the nativist and environmentalist views. Evidence collected in many fields convinced them that both nature *and* nurture were critical to development. The central question changed from whether nature or nurture drove development, to *how much* each contributed to different traits. This in turn led to attempts to measure their relative contributions.

Heritability Developmentalists began attempting to calculate the degree to which different traits were influenced by genetic factors, or the **heritability** of the trait. This measurement was called the *heritability quotient*. For example, right- or left-handedness has a very high heritability quotient. People do not learn to be right- or left-handed; indeed attempting to override natural handedness is exceedingly difficult. In contrast, speaking fluent Spanish has a very low heritability quotient. It depends on being exposed to Spanish as a young child, usually by growing up in a Spanish-speaking family and society, or by making a determined effort to study and learn Spanish as an adult.

Studies of heritability employed one of several research designs. The most common, **twin studies**, took advantage of a "natural experiment" (see "The Study of Child Development"). **Identical twins** are born when a single fertilized egg divides, resulting in the birth of two individuals whose genetic makeup is identical. **Fraternal twins** are born when two separate egg cells are fertilized, and so they are no more alike genetically than other brothers and sisters. If identical twins are more alike than fraternal twins on a trait such as intelligence, this trait is likely to be genetic in origin and have a high heritability quotient (Elkins, McGue, & Iacono, 1997). (See Figure 2.2.) Additional evidence comes from studies of identical twins who were separated at birth and raised in different families. Presumably their similarities are genetic and their differences reflect the environment.

In **adoption studies**, researchers looked at children who were adopted soon after birth and raised by parents to whom they were not genetically related (e.g.,

heritability The extent to which a phenotypic trait is genetically determined.

twin studies A method for estimating heritability in which the degree of similarity in a trait that is observed among identical twins is compared with that observed among fraternal twins.

identical twins Twins born when a single fertilized egg divides, resulting in the birth of two individuals whose genetic makeup is identical.

fraternal twins Twins born when two separate eggs are fertilized, who are therefore no more alike genetically than other brothers and sisters.

adoption studies A method for estimating heritability in which similarities between children and their adoptive parents are compared with similarities between children and their biological parents.

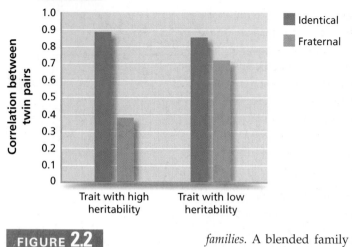

FIGURE 2.2

Heritability of Traits in Twins

In twin studies, the difference in magnitude between the resemblance of identical twins (who share all the same genes) versus fraternal twins (who only share, on average, half their genes) is used to measure heritability. The trait displayed on the left has a high heritability coefficient, which means that variation in that trait is largely influenced by genetic factors. As you can see, the correlation is much stronger between identical twins than between fraternal twins. The trait on the right of the figure has a low heritability coefficient, which means that less variation is due to genetic differences and relatively more variation is due to aspects of the shared and nonshared environments. Therefore, the correlation of scores on that trait between identical twins will be more similar to that between fraternal twins.

family relatedness studies A method for estimating heritability by comparing the similarity of children who vary in their genetic relatedness (e.g., siblings, half-siblings, and stepsiblings).

shared environment In behavioral genetics, the environment that siblings have in common.

nonshared environment In behavioral genetics, the environment that siblings do not have in common, such as the peers with whom they are friends.

Abrahamson, Baker, & Caspi, 2002; Deater-Deckard & Plomin, 1999). Were they more like their birth parents or their adoptive parents? Several studies found that, at least with respect to intelligence, adopted children resemble their biological parents more than their adoptive ones, but that the quality of the adoptive family environment also matters—children who are adopted into more affluent families show more advanced intellectual development than children from similar origins, but who are adopted into less advantaged homes (Scarr & Weinberg, 1983).

In **family relatedness studies**, developmentalists also studied families that combined children from prior marriages and remarriage, sometimes referred to as *blended families*. A blended family might include stepsiblings (from the mother or father's previous marriage), half-siblings (a child born to the new couple and thus half related to stepsiblings, on the mother or father's side), and full siblings (two or more children born after the new marriage). What's interesting here is that children with different degrees of relatedness live in the same family and thus grow up in the same general environment. Studies of blended families thus provide another means to examine the relative contributions of nature and nurture to different aspects of child development. Generally speaking, studies of individuals growing up in blended families have shown that children who are more closely related biologically (i.e., who share more genes in common) are more similar in personality, attitudes, abilities, and behavior than children who grow up in the same family but whose genetic backgrounds are dissimilar (e.g., Hetherington, Henderson, & Reiss, 1999).

Research on heritability produced some tantalizing results about both nature and nurture. On the one hand, twin, adoption, and family relatedness studies have shown conclusively that virtually all human traits—whether physical (e.g., handedness, athletic ability), intellectual (e.g., verbal ability, intelligence), social (e.g., shyness, aggressiveness), or emotional (e.g., self-esteem, anxiety)—have substantial heritability quotients (Plomin, 2004).

At the same time, however, studies of twins, adopted children, and siblings of different degrees of relatedness have also revealed that these very same traits are also influenced by the environment. Ironically, then, behavioral genetics studies have taught us just as much—some might say even more—about nurture as they have about nature. In some cases, for instance, the aspect of nurture that matters most is the environment that children growing up in the same household have in common—what developmentalists call the **shared environment**. If two siblings are similar not because they share genes in common, but because they have been both exposed to the same sort of parenting, that would point to a shared environmental influence. In other cases, however, the aspect of nurture that matters most is the environment that children growing up together do not share—the **nonshared environment** (Plomin & Daniels, 1987). For example, siblings are often different from each other not just because they have different genes, but because they have different experiences either inside the home (e.g., siblings are treated differently by their parents) or outside the home (e.g., siblings run with very different types of crowds). What heritability studies made clear is that, for virtually all human characteristics, nature and nurture both matter.

Heritability studies—and the idea that it is possible to accurately estimate how much of a trait is due to genes and how much is due to the environment—have been criticized, however, on three main counts (e.g., Collins et al., 2000). First, genetic and environmental influences often work hand in hand. Bright children ask bright questions and usually get adult-level answers. Slow children ask more basic questions and usually get simpler answers. Thus their genetic potential and experiences are matched.

Second, as we discuss later in this chapter, the idea that genes have the same impact in all environments is questionable. For example, the impact of genes on intelligence is stronger in high-quality environments (which let genes "shine through") than in low-quality environments, where children do not receive much stimulation and curiosity is discouraged. Their innate intelligence remains dormant.

Finally, heritability estimates do not consider malleability. Even a trait that is largely inherited can change. Your hair color, which is almost entirely determined by your genes, can become lighter if you spend a lot of time in the sun. We know that intelligence has a large genetic component. (Scientists may argue about the *extent* to which intelligence is genetically determined, but no one debates the fact that genes play *some* role.) But we also know that an adopted child reared in an enriched environment usually becomes "smarter" than his or her biological parents. Moreover, even genes are flexible, as described later.

In a nutshell, both nature and nurture count (Gottlieb, Wahlstein, & Lickliter, 2006; Rutter, 2006; Turkheimer, 1998). Think about it. Knowing that intelligence or another trait is 75 percent inherited, as opposed to 50 percent inherited, or 20 percent inherited, or even 5 percent inherited, is not terribly useful. Why? Because this also means the trait is 25 percent environmental (or 50% . . . and so on), and that therefore the context in which the individual develops matters.

Although heritability studies have been criticized, they contributed to a major shift in how scientists view development. Most scientists were convinced by heritability research that studying genetics was a necessary part of understanding child development. We no longer debate whether development is mostly (or entirely) the result of nature or mostly (or entirely) nurture. Instead, contemporary developmental scientists accept the idea that every aspect of development—that's right, every aspect—is the product of *both* biological and environmental factors. Today the question has become, How do genes and environments affect each other and, together, guide development?

Development Results from the Interplay of Nature and Nurture

The contemporary view of nature and nurture emphasizes interaction, an important concept. Interaction is more than combination. For example, a teaspoon of vinegar and a teaspoon of baking soda are, by themselves, motionless. But if you mix them together, you produce a fizzing, bubbling volcano (try it and see for yourself). Thus the result of the interaction between them is something quite different from the initial ingredients.

So it is with development. Measuring genetic and environmental influences doesn't tell the full story. The key to development is how genes and their environments *interact.* This idea is not a new one but rather one that has been revived in light of new discoveries in genetics and studies of the environment. It began with Darwin's theory of evolution.

Darwin's Influence Charles Darwin (1809–1882) is surely the most famous interactionist in Western history. Darwin was not primarily interested in individual development, although he kept detailed diaries of his own children's development. Rather, he was a naturalist who devoted his life to understanding the complexity of nature. Yet his ideas have had a profound effect on how we view development today.

Like others before him, Darwin believed that living plants and animals, including humans, were descended from earlier, simpler forms. But what caused these changes?

Darwin's **theory of evolution** rests on two main ideas: **survival of the fittest** and **natural selection**. In nature, most organisms do not survive long enough to reproduce. Few seedlings become trees, for example, and a small percentage of tadpoles become frogs. Individual variations—found in every species and every generation—provide the raw material for natural selection. Only the "fittest"—those best adapted to their environment—survive. Through reproduction, these individuals pass their adaptive traits to their offspring, who in turn survive to reproduce. And so, over time, adaptive traits become more common in the species and maladaptive traits die out.

Environments are not stable. When the climate changes, the number of predators increases, or the availability of reliable food sources declines, some traits become more or less adaptive than before. This accounts for the emergence of new traits in a species and for the survival of some species and extinction of others (such as dinosaurs). Natural selection is nothing more or less than the outcome of interaction between members of a species and their environment.

Epigenesis Today most developmental scientists view development as **epigenesis**: a gradual process of increasing complexity due to interaction between heredity (genes) and the environment (Gottlieb et al., 2006). In this view, nothing—or very little—is *pre*determined, just as in evolution no species' survival is guaranteed. Even identical twins—who share the same genes—differ in size, weight, hardiness, and brain patterns at birth, because of slight variations in the prenatal environment they shared (Finch & Kirkwood, 2000).

Epigenesis is rooted in embryology on the one hand, and in the theory of evolution, on the other. By the beginning of the nineteenth century, embryologists had charted the progress of the human embryo and fetus, month by month, stage by stage, in a timed sequence of changes in structure and function. In four days a single cell, the fertilized egg, becomes a cluster of dozens of cells; at four weeks the embryo has a distinct heart, digestive tract, and tail (which disappears); at four months the fetus can kick, turn its head, make a fist, squint, and swallow (see "Conception, Prenatal Development, and Birth"). Biologists could *see* that the embryo was not a miniature adult. Molecular genetics lay far in the future. But it was clear that prenatal development was a form of biological self-assembly.

Soon after Darwin published *The Origin of Species* (1872/2003), some scientists began to apply the theory of evolution to development—including G. Stanley Hall (1844–1924), the first president of the American Psychological Association. Hall held that the early life of an individual resembled the evolutionary history of the species— in other words, that the development of the individual repeats the evolution of a species over time. This specific theory was later rejected, though. The human embryo does not go through a "fish stage," "a reptilian phase," and so on. From the beginning, the embryo is distinctively human. But Darwin's central concept—change through interaction with the environment—remains a powerful principle in the contemporary study of development.

Stem cells illustrate epigenesis. **Stem cells** are primitive, undifferentiated cells or "precells," found in large numbers in the embryo (and small numbers in adults) (see Figure 2.3). These cells are the raw material of prenatal development. Each stem cell has a full set of chromosomes and the potential to become anything the body needs. During embryonic development, they become increasingly specialized, eventually de-

theory of evolution Typically refers to the variant of the model of evolution formalized by Charles Darwin, which asserts that organisms evolve and change through the process of natural selection.

survival of the fittest Within Darwin's theory of evolution, the notion that organisms that are best equipped to survive in a given context are more likely to reproduce and pass their genetic material on to future generations.

natural selection Within Darwin's theory of evolution, the process through which adaptive traits that are heritable become more common while maladaptive traits that are heritable become less so.

epigenesis The gradual process through which organisms develop over time in an increasingly differentiated and complex fashion as a consequence of the interaction between genes and the environment.

stem cells Primitive, undifferentiated cells or "precells," found in large numbers in the embryo.

veloping into blood cells, nerve cells, muscle cells, and so on, and assembling themselves into functioning organs and tissues. We do not yet know exactly why this happens, just that it does. This biological process gives us a model for looking at other levels of development.

At birth, many traits are—by analogy, not literally—like stem cells. Intelligence, for example, is almost entirely a potential (inherited from the baby's parents, as modified by the prenatal environment). As the baby matures, her brain develops, her senses become more finely tuned, her actions (or motor skills) turn more coordinated, and her intelligence begins to take shape. Her experiences in the world and her relationships with others are part of this process. So are nutrition, health, and her physical setting. This process continues through childhood and adolescence, indeed throughout life.

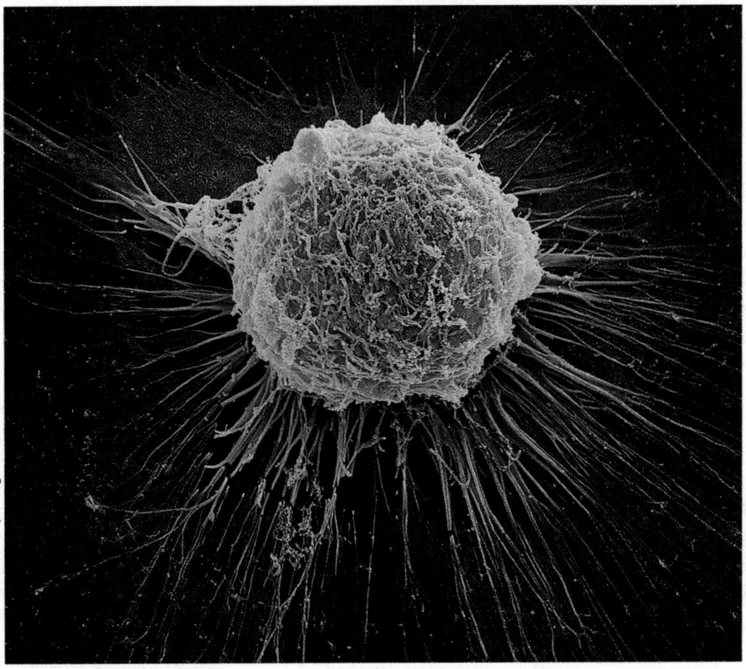

We started this section with the old idea that development is predetermined (preformed), which later resurfaced as genetic determinism—the belief that genes are destiny. Then we looked in the opposite direction—to the environmentalist view that children come into this world unformed, and that experience is everything. We saw the first attempts to restore genetics to the study of development, by calculating what proportions of different traits were innate or acquired. And, finally, we arrived at epigenesis, which puts nature and nurture back together again as active copartners in development. (See "Interim Summary 2.1: Perspectives on Nature and Nuture.") We'll return to the subject of gene-environment interactions at the end of this chapter. First, though, we need to explain what genes are and how they work.

FIGURE 2.3

A Human Embryonic Stem Cell

Stem cells are the raw material of prenatal development. Each stem cell has a full set of chromosomes and the potential to become any kind of cell that the body needs.

WHAT ARE GENES, AND WHAT DO THEY DO?

Genes provide the continuity that makes us human, generation after generation. They direct the cells of an embryo to become a human being, not an armadillo or an apple tree. They help to establish our common modes of thinking, feeling, acting, and communicating. At the same time, genes contribute to the wide diversity within the human species—in appearance, abilities, health, and even happiness.

Thus the study of human genetics deals with two different, related questions. First, how do genes make us human and distinct from other species? Second, within this human pattern, how do genes influence individual differences?

Becoming Human

All human beings have some traits in common: for example, walking upright on two feet, or **bipedalism**. Our upright posture and gait are the result of natural selection; these characteristics made our ancestors better adapted to their environment than their competitors. Our closest cousins, the great apes, are capable of bipedalism and sometimes walk upright, but only humans are routinely, habitually bipedal. Walking upright on two feet freed our ancestors' hands to make and use tools and weapons and to carry food and other goods back to a home base. Bipedalism is one of the defining

bipedalism Being able to stand and walk on two feet.

INTERIM SUMMARY 2.1

Perspectives on Nature and Nurture

Development Is Driven by Nature	The view that genes alone determine the course of development is referred to as **nativism**. An extreme early version of this view, **preformationism**, held that the individual's adult characteristics were present from conception, or even before.
Development Is Driven by Nurture	In contrast to nativists, extreme environmentalists believed that external forces were entirely responsible for development. Locke's notion that the infant is a "blank slate" reflects this view.
Development Is Part Nature, Part Nurture	By the middle of the twentieth century, the central question in the study of nature and nurture changed from whether nature *or* nurture drove development, to *how much* each contributed to different traits. The extent to which a trait is genetically determined is known as **heritability**.
Development Results from the Interplay of Nature and Nurture	Today, developmental scientists view development as the product of a dynamic interaction between genes and environment, a process called **epigenesis**.

characteristics of our species. Other defining human traits include handiness (opposable thumbs, the better to grasp things), language, the ability to alter our surroundings, a knack for calculations, and self-awareness.

In recent decades, scientists have learned that none of these traits, by itself, is unique to humans. Great apes demonstrate self-awareness (though monkeys don't). Birds and whales communicate through sound and even have local "dialects." Apes use tools; so do some birds. Birds build intricate nests, sometimes in "colonies," and even ants alter their environment. Moreover, raccoons as well as primates (apes, monkeys, and prosimians, such as lemurs and bush babies) have opposable thumbs; orangutans have grasping hands *and* feet. In experiments, parrots and great apes have demonstrated basic comprehension of words, grammar, and number. But no other animal develops this combination of abilities so easily or naturally.

canalization The degree to which an element of development is dictated by the common genetic program that all humans inherit.

"Like a Rolling Stone" These universal aspects of human development are under tighter genetic control than other traits, a phenomenon known as canalization. **Canalization** is the degree to which an element of development is dictated by the genetic program that all humans inherit. Think of development as a stone rolling down a hill inside a canal (Waddington, 1940). Gravity (maturation) pulls the stone down the hill, but where each stone ends up depends on the terrain, or environment. In some places the canal is deep and narrow, so every stone follows that route. For example, all normal children learn to walk, regardless of the environment in which they grow up; locomotion is highly canalized. But in other places the canal is shallow and bumpy, so the stone may roll around and even bounce out of the canal. The development of morality is less highly canalized than the development of walking—which is why the world is made up of people who are as moral as Mother Teresa; those who are mass murderers, serial killers, and others who show no concern for others; and most of the rest of us, who fall somewhere between these two extremes.

In general, early development is more highly canalized than later development. Thus there are more universals in early development (walking, talking, wondering why) than in later development (dancing, writing poetry or rap, or becoming a scientist or philosopher, a poet or criminal investigator).

The Importance of Being Cute One distinctive feature of human development is that we are born "prematurely." The great evolutionary biologist Stephen Jay Gould (1977) wrote that human babies are essentially "embryos" at birth and remain so for

their first year. Horses are able to stand, walk, run, and whinny within hours of birth. Kittens and puppies need care for their first month or two but thereafter can survive independently. Humans can't even get from one place to another by themselves until age nine or ten months, when they first begin crawling.

One reason for this is that humans have evolved to be highly social animals. A prolonged period of juvenile appearance and behavior promotes the development of social bonds by attracting caregivers to infants, and vice versa. Quite simply, babies of many species are "cute"—think kittens, puppies, and bunnies. Complete strangers go "gaga" when they see an infant and will do almost anything to get a baby to smile. (Borrow an infant and see for yourself!) This is why advertisers so often use babies to sell everything from automobile tires to paper towels. An adult smiles at a baby, the baby smiles back, the adult responds, and so on, in a natural cycle of attraction. Both the baby and the adult are "programmed" to form a bond.

From an evolutionary perspective, babies who smiled a lot (even reflexively as newborns do, usually while sleeping)

Babies of many species are cute, which draws caregivers to them, thereby increasing their chances of survival.

probably got more attention than somber babies, so the trait became common. Likewise, parents who were drawn to their babies probably reared more offspring who survived (and later had children of their own) than parents who were unresponsive, so this trait became widespread.

A second reason for the prolonged immaturity of human infants is that humans depend on learning more than other species do. Like newborn horses, most mammals are capable of getting around on their own soon after they are born; human babies aren't. Our evolutionary cousins, the great apes, also stay with their mother for a long time. Only elephants have as long a period of dependency. Our "immaturity" at birth makes us more receptive to environmental influence. At the same time, we are predisposed to learning and thus better able than most other species to change our behavior in response to environmental conditions. We are adaptable in part because much of our early development takes place in the world, not the womb.

We are not as unique as we might think, however. The Human Genome Project has shown that we share some of our genes with even the simplest organisms, such as bacteria and molds; many of our genes with all other mammals; and most of our genes with our closest evolutionary kin, the great apes. Humans' and chimpanzees' DNA is 98–99 percent identical. If blood types are matched, a human can receive a transfusion from a chimpanzee and vice versa (McGrew, 2004). Within the human species, 99.9 percent of genetic material is identical—that's right, you and the person sitting next to you in class have 99.9 percent of your genes in common. Yet we have so many genes that even the small amount we don't share with others leaves much room for variation (Plomin et al., 2001).

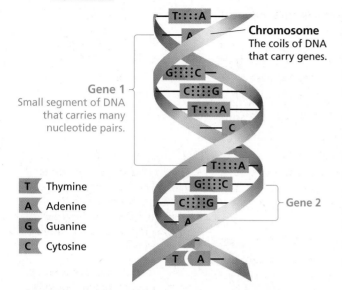

T Thymine

A Adenine

G Guanine

C Cytosine

Chromosome
The coils of DNA
that carry genes.

Gene 1
Small segment of DNA
that carries many
nucleotide pairs.

Gene 2

FIGURE 2.4

Chromosomes and Genes

Chromosomes are made up of two long strands of DNA twisted into a ladder-like structure called a *double helix*; each cell nucleus contains twenty-three identical pairs of chromosomes. The rungs of the DNA ladder are composed of pairs of chemical bases (adenine pairs with thymine, and guanine pairs with cytosine), and the chromosomes have millions of base pairs. Short segments of DNA are called *genes*, which contain about 3,000 base pairs on average but can be as long as 2 million base pairs.

chromosomes Strands of DNA that carry genes and associated proteins.

base pairs Pairs of adenine and thymine and of guanine and cytosine that make up the "rungs" of the DNA molecule.

gene A segment of DNA, occupying a specific place on a chromosome.

genotype The underlying genetic makeup of an individual organism (contrast with *phenotype*).

phenotype The observable traits and characteristics of an individual organism (contrast with *genotype*).

Human Diversity

That we are related to all living things makes diversity within our species even more remarkable. No two human beings have the exact same genes, except (as you know) identical twins. Here we will explain why—and why this is important.

The Genetic Code

The human body is made up of trillions of cells. The nucleus of almost every human cell contains twenty-three pairs of chromosomes, one set from the individual's mother, one from his or her father. (The exceptions are reproductive cells, or sperm and ova, described later.) **Chromosomes** are long strands of DNA (deoxyribonucleic acid). These chromosomes, present in every cell, contain a complete set of instructions for the development of a unique human being.

The rungs of the DNA ladder consist of pairs of four chemical bases: adenine (A), thymine (T), guanine (G), and cytosine (C). (See Figure 2.4.) Adenine always connects with thymine (as A-T or T-A), and guanine with cytosine (as C-G or G-C). The order of **base pairs** determines genetic instructions, much as the order of letters determines the meaning of a word (as in "dog" versus "God").

Chromosomes direct activities in the cell by attracting molecules of RNA (ribonucleic acid). RNA functions as a messenger, carrying genetic instructions out of the cell's nucleus into the cytoplasm, which contains the raw materials for synthesizing enzymes, hormones, and other proteins. Different proteins are created by combining different amino acids (and different numbers of amino acids) in different ways. Proteins, in turn, cause chemical reactions in the body that lead to the production and reproduction of cells.

Genes are the units of heredity that pass characteristics from one generation to the next, and the next. In biochemical terms, a **gene** is a segment of the chromosome that controls a particular aspect of the production of a specific protein; a gene is about 3,000 base pairs long (though length is highly variable). The key to heredity is DNA. DNA has the unique ability to reproduce itself, which permits a single cell, the fertilized egg, to develop into an adult human being, in all his or her complexity. Of course, the genetic code does not apply to humans only. It explains how *every living thing* comes into being, from elephants and snails to roses; from mice to men and women, including you and us, the authors of this book.

Genotypes and Phenotypes

The twenty-three pairs of chromosomes you inherit from your parents make up your **genotype**, a package of biochemical information that is yours and yours alone (unless you have an identical twin). Your genotype is contained in almost every cell in your body, throughout life. (This is why criminal investigators can identify a person from a single strand of hair or a few skin cells.) But—an extremely important qualification— your genotype does not *determine* who you become.

Your observable characteristics and behavior, or **phenotype**, depends on your environment and experiences, from the moment of conception. In other words, your genotype is not a tiny edition of you, a modern version of the seventeenth-century homunculus. When talking about genes, we are talking about potentials, not predetermination. What each of us becomes is only one of many possible outcomes.

To explain why (almost) everyone's genotype is unique, we look first at sexual reproduction.

Sexual Reproduction Bacteria, many plants, and some fish and reptiles reproduce asexually. The offspring are a genetically identical clone of the parent. Sexual reproduction creates more variety, and thus makes it more likely that individuals will differ in their ability to survive, thereby allowing the species to evolve through survival of the fittest.

Mitosis and meiosis As we said, the nucleus of every human cell contains twenty-three pairs of chromosomes. During ordinary cell reproduction (called **mitosis**), a cell divides and each daughter cell receives a full copy of all forty-six chromosomes. Reproductive cells (or **gametes**) are different. They are produced through a different process, called **meiosis** (see Figure 2.5).

Meiosis—the production of sperm and ova—produces cells with only half a set of chromosomes. The first phase of meiosis is known as "crossing over." Each of the twenty-three pairs of chromosomes line up, wrap around each other, and exchange bits of genetic material. For example, one chromosome may contain a gene for red hair and one for green eyes; the other a gene for brown hair and one for blue eyes. The gene for brown hair may cross over and link to the gene for green eyes, and the gene for red hair cross over and link to the gene for blue eyes. (This is somewhat simplified, to give you the general idea.) These "new" chromosomes separate and migrate to opposite sides of the cell nucleus.

In the second phase of meiosis, some of the mother's chromosomes align with the father's chromosomes and vice versa. In effect, the chromosome deck is reshuffled (Krogh, 2005). The cell then divides in two, and the "new" chromosomes produce duplicates of themselves. Last, these daughter cells divide, producing four cells with only twenty-three chromosomes each. Because of crossing over and reshuffling no two ovum or sperm are exactly alike. (If this weren't the case, every time a couple produced a child, he or she would have the exact same genotype as every other one of the couple's children.)

At fertilization, two reproductive cells merge, and the chromosomes from the mother's ovum link to the chromosomes from the father's sperm. Note that each individual has two sets of chromosomes and thus two copies of every gene, called **alleles**. The outcome of this merger depends primarily on which genes from each parent are matched with the other's genes, or gene-gene interaction.

Gene-Gene Interaction Twenty-two of our twenty-three pairs of chromosomes are "homologous"; they contain two versions of the gene for each trait (one allele from each parent). But the twenty-third pair, which determines the sex of the individual, is different. Every female has two X chromosomes; every male has one X and one Y chromosome. (There are some unusual exceptions to this that are caused by errors during fertilization, but these are very rare.) We'll say more about sex chromosomes and how they may affect development in "Conception, Prenatal Development, and Birth." Here, we focus on what takes place when the other twenty-two pairs are formed. What happens when the mother's genes link to the father's genes in a new individual? As you'll see, it all depends on the specific genes in question and the way they interact.

Additive heredity In the case of **additive heredity**, a number of the mother's and the father's genes affect a trait, and the child's phenotype, or visible traits, is a mix of the two. For example, the child of a Caucasian father and an African American mother has tan skin. Hair texture or curliness and height are also additive. If a tall man and a short woman have children, the children will probably be of medium height (assuming adequate nutrition and good physical health). Additive traits are a blend of all of both parents' genes. But because the genotype of the medium-height children includes

mitosis The process through which all cells other than gametes reproduce, in which a cell divides and each resulting cell receives a full copy of all forty-six chromosomes.

gametes Reproductive cells, sperm in males and ova (eggs) in females.

meiosis The process through which gametes (sperm and ova) are produced, in which each resulting gamete has half of the genetic material of the parent cell.

alleles Different forms of the same gene occupying the same location on each of the chromosomes that make up a chromosomal pair.

additive heredity The process of genetic transmission that results in a phenotype that is a mixture of the mother's and father's traits.

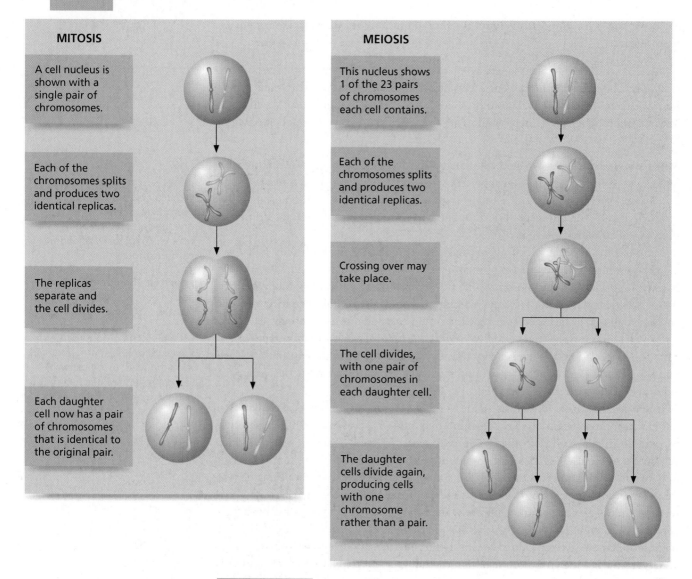

A cell nucleus is shown with a single pair of chromosomes.

Each of the chromosomes splits and produces two identical replicas.

The replicas separate and the cell divides.

Each daughter cell now has a pair of chromosomes that is identical to the original pair.

This nucleus shows 1 of the 23 pairs of chromosomes each cell contains.

Each of the chromosomes splits and produces two identical replicas.

Crossing over may take place.

The cell divides, with one pair of chromosomes in each daughter cell.

The daughter cells divide again, producing cells with one chromosome rather than a pair.

FIGURE 2.5

Mitosis and Meiosis

Mitosis is the process of cell reproduction. First, every chromosome gets duplicated and then the cell divides, resulting in two "daughter" cells that each has a full copy of all 46 chromosomes (in 23 pairs). In *meiosis,* or the production of reproductive cells (sperm and ova), the 23 pairs of chromosomes first undergo a "crossing-over" process in which some of their genetic material gets exchanged. Like in mitosis, the chromosome pairs duplicate and then divide into two daughter cells, each with 46 chromosomes. But unlike mitosis, the daughter cells divide again, resulting in four cells with only 23 chromosomes each.

genes for being short and tall, some of their own children may be taller or shorter than they are.

dominant/recessive heredity The process of genetic transmission where one version (allele) of a gene is dominant over another, resulting in the phenotypic expression of only the dominant allele.

Dominant/recessive heredity In the case of **dominant/recessive heredity**, one version of a gene is dominant over another. The gene for brown eyes, for example, is dominant over the gene for blue eyes, which is recessive. A child who inherits the gene for brown eyes from both parents will have brown eyes. So will a child who inherits the dominant gene for brown eyes from one parent and the recessive gene for blue eyes from the other. Only a child who inherits the recessive gene for blue eyes from both parents will have blue eyes. A gene may be dominant in one combination but not another. Hazel eyes result from a combination of green-eye and brown-eye genes, for example. In other words, the genotype brown-eye gene + green-eye gene produces the phenotype hazel eyes.

"Regulator" genes One of the most surprising findings from the Human Genome Project is that some genes are not tied to a particular phenotypic trait; rather, their function is to turn other genes on or off at different points in the life cycle or in response to events in the environment. In effect, they act as moderators at a convention of genes, some of which are involved in debates about whether development should take one path or another. In turning genes on or off, **regulator genes** exercise considerable power over phenotypes. For example, chimpanzees have larger jaws than humans do—not because they have different "jaw-growing" genes, because the *same* jaw-growing gene is turned on longer while the jaw is developing in a chimpanzee fetus than in a human fetus (Ridley, 2003). In other words, chimps and humans share the same jaw-growing genotype, but their phenotype is quite different.

Environmental influences The gene actions and interactions we have been describing do not take place in a vacuum. The environment is an active partner, often the most influential partner, in the translation of a genotype into a phenotype.

One example (among many identified with the help of the Human Genome Project) provides a concrete illustration of environmental influence. Researchers have identified a gene labeled 5-HTT, which influences levels of serotonin, a brain chemical known to affect depression. The alleles for this gene vary in length. Individuals with short versions of the gene are much more likely to respond to stress by becoming depressed than individuals with longer versions (Caspi et al., 2003). Note that the gene does not "cause" depression, but rather affects individual vulnerability to depression in the face of stress. In a chain reaction, stress hormones affect how the 5-HTT gene acts, which affects the proteins it instructs the body to make, which affects serotonin levels, which affects vulnerability to depression (see Figure 2.6).

Thus, the short 5-HTT gene may or may not have an impact on serotonin (and, hence, depression) depending on other aspects of the person's biology and on context. A child whose mother dies when she is young, who moves to an unfamiliar place where she has no friends at age twelve, or who faces other stressful situations might sink into depression. Another child, with the same 5-HTT gene, who grows up in a stable environment, whose family members accept (but do not fuss about) his moods, and who has supportive friends and discovers rewarding activities might never experience clinical depression. If, at age forty-five, as a husband and father of three, he is laid off and cannot find employment, the 5-HTT gene might kick in. Perhaps the best description of the translation of a genotype into a phenotype is, "It all depends. . . ."

Luck also plays a role. Occasional copying errors, or **mutations**, alter the proteins a gene or chromosome produces. The impact of mutations is usually neutral or slight, but in some cases can cause adaptive or maladaptive change.

regulator genes Genes whose function is to turn other genes on or off at different points in the life cycle or in response to events in the environment.

mutations Copying errors in the replication of DNA that alter the proteins a gene or chromosome produces.

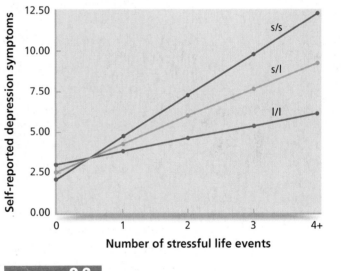

FIGURE 2.6

Environmental Influences on Gene Expression

This figure demonstrates how experience can influence the phenotypic expression of our genes. The 5-HTT gene plays a role in producing brain chemicals associated with depression, and there are three different versions of the gene whose allele pairs vary in length (short/short, short/long, and long/long). A group of researchers found that individuals who had experienced very few stressful life events all reported low levels of depressive symptoms. But among people who experienced multiple stressful life events, the level of depressive symptoms varied based on the type of 5-HTT gene they carried. Individuals with the short/short 5-HTT genotype were most affected by stressful life events and reported higher levels of depressive symptoms than individuals with the short/long or long/long genotype who were exposed to comparable levels of stress.
Source: From *Science Magazine*, July 18, 2003, Vol. 301. Reprinted with permission from AAAS.

INTERIM SUMMARY 2.2

What Are Genes, and What Do They Do?

Becoming Human	■ Humans possess a unique combination of genes that distinguish our species from others.
	■ Many universal aspects of human development are under tight genetic control, a phenomenon known as **canalization**.
	■ One distinctive aspect of human infancy is a prolonged period of immature appearance and behavior, which promotes the development of social bonds by attracting caregivers to infants, and vice versa.
	■ Even though virtually all of our genes are common to all humans, we have so many genes that even the small amount we don't share with others leaves much room for variation, which accounts for diversity in human characteristics.
Human Diversity	■ The nucleus of almost every human cell contains 23 pairs of chromosomes—one set from the individual's mother, one from his or her father. This is referred to as the individual's **genotype**.
	■ An individual's observable characteristics and behavior, or **phenotype**, depend on both the genotype and the environment.
	■ **Chromosomes** are long strands of DNA, which contain a complete set of instructions for the development of a unique human being. A **gene** is a segment of the chromosome that controls a particular aspect of the production of a specific protein.
	■ **Mitosis** is the process through which all cells, with the exception of reproductive cells, are produced, whereas **meiosis** is the process through which reproductive cells—sperm and ova—are produced.
	■ Each individual has two sets of chromosomes and thus two copies of every gene, called **alleles**. The outcome of the merger of the mother's and father's genes depends primarily on which genes from each parent are matched with the other's, referred to as gene-gene interaction.

A key point here is that genes produce proteins, not human traits, and the ultimate impact of these proteins varies as a function of many other factors. To suggest that people inherit a gene for intelligence, sociability, aggression, acrophobia (fear of heights), or any other characteristic is quite simply wrong. The reality is far more complex. (For a summary of this section, see "Interim Summary 2.2: What Are Genes, and What Do They Do?")

Likewise, to speak of the environment (singular) as "everything out there" is also wrong. As we will see, the reality is far more complex.

THE IMPORTANCE OF CONTEXT

Just as our current understanding of genetic influences is more complex than earlier views, so is our understanding of the environment, or context, and its role in development. From birth (and even before), a developing child is exposed to countless overlapping, interacting relationships and experiences that change as he or she grows older and the world itself changes (Bronfenbrenner & Morris, 2006).

The Ecological Perspective on Development

The ecological perspective (introduced in "The Study of Child Development") focuses on these external influences. Urie Bronfenbrenner, a pioneer in this field, compared the context of development to a set of Russian dolls (hollow wooden dolls of increasing size, designed to fit inside one another). As he explained, "The inner doll is the developing human being. The next doll is the immediate setting; the physical setting and the people the child is interacting with now. The next doll is the community as it influences activities and relationships; and so on" (in Scarr, Weinberg, & Levine, 1986, p. 48). Thus a child lives in a family, which lives in a neighborhood, which exists within a society, which exists within a culture at a particular point in history.

One of Bronfenbrenner's important contributions was to provide a framework to organize the way we think about contexts: the micro-, meso-, exo-, and macrosystems. His view challenged developmental scientists to think about the way that children are influenced not only by the immediate settings in which they spend time (like their home or classroom) but also by more distant contexts—their neighborhood, society, and culture. Bronfenbrenner even encouraged developmentalists to study the ways in which events in settings in which children never even set foot—like their parents' workplaces—could nonetheless influence how they developed.

Scientists who use an ecological perspective to study child development start by identifying a question and then thinking through how to look at that question at different levels of analysis. To illustrate how this might be done, let's try applying Bronfenbrenner's framework to a specific question and see where it leads us.

The question we ask is grounded in an unfortunate social fact: Hispanic American teenagers are less likely to graduate from high school than individuals from other ethnic groups (U.S. Census Bureau, 2006). Although the problem is most concentrated among foreign-born individuals who never attended high school in the United States, the dropout rate among Hispanic Americans who enrolled in U.S. high schools is about twice that for non-Hispanic white youth. This is an important social problem, because dropping out of high school often has dire consequences for the future. Individuals who don't complete high school are far more likely than graduates to live at or near the poverty level, to experience unemployment, to depend on public assistance, to become a parent while still a teenager, and to be involved in delinquent and criminal activity (Manlove, 1998). If we better understood the causes of the high dropout rate among Hispanic American youth, perhaps we could do something about it.

OK, then. Why do *you* think Hispanic American teenagers are less likely to finish high school than other adolescents? Let's see how employing an ecological perspective might help us design a research study to answer this question. We begin by looking at the immediate environment in which the child develops.

Microsystems

In Bronfenbrenner's framework, a **microsystem** is a setting in which the child interacts with others face-to-face every day. The most important microsystems in children's lives are the family, the school (or daycare setting), and—especially as children grow older—the peer group. When researchers ask questions about the way children are affected by different forms of discipline, by variations in class size, or by being popular with peers, they are asking questions about the microsystem. But keep in mind that influences within a microsystem are *bidirectional*. Not only do parents, teachers, and peers influence the child, the child influences them. Relationships within microsystems are also *multifaceted* (or many-sided). Many settings—the family living room, a cafeteria table at school—include more than two people. When a mother is dressing a toddler, for example, the presence of the father, a second child, a grandparent, or a

microsystem In Bronfenbrenner's ecological perspective on development, a setting in which the child interacts with others face-to-face, such as a family or classroom.

neighbor affect how she and the toddler act toward each other. Thus microsystems are more dynamic and complex than the term "micro" might suggest.

Is it possible that features of these microsystems in the lives of Hispanic American children might account for their lower graduation rate? Absolutely. Consider the family setting, for instance. Researchers have consistently found that the ways in which parents interact with their children influences how well they do in school. In particular, children whose parents are more involved in their education and who parent in a way that is simultaneously warm and strict—a style of parenting called "authoritative parenting" (see the chapter on socioemotional development in the "Early Childhood" part)—do better in school than children whose parents rarely attend school programs or monitor their children's schoolwork, and who are more aloof, more lenient, or both. So one thing we would surely want to study is whether Hispanic American children are raised in ways that hinder their success in American schools. For example, are their parents less likely to practice authoritative parenting? Several studies say that this may be the case (Steinberg, Dornbusch, & Brown, 1992).

The family isn't the only microsystem that influences student achievement, however. And, in fact, rarely is it the case that something as complicated as dropping out of school can be explained by looking at one microsystem alone. Perhaps there are additional factors operating in the classroom or peer group that contribute as well. We know, for example, that dropping out is less likely from schools where the environment is orderly, where academic pursuits are emphasized, and where the faculty is supportive and committed (Connell et al., 1995). So, to continue our exploration of the microsystem, we would want to ask if the quality of schools attended by Hispanic American students is lower on average than that attended by students from other ethnic groups.

The third major microsystem in children's lives is the peer group. Is it possible that something in the peer groups of Hispanic American children affects their engagement in school? One factor that has been shown to have an especially strong influence on school achievement during adolescence is the extent to which doing well in school is valued by the adolescents' friends. Although it is true that adolescents who do well in school usually choose friends who also are high achievers, research has shown that teenagers are also influenced by the peers they hang around with. A "C" student who has relatively more "B" students as friends is more likely to do well over time than a "C" student whose friends themselves aren't making high grades, either (Epstein, 1983). Another interesting microsystem question to study, then, is whether Hispanic American students are less likely than other students to have friends who are high achievers.

The Mesosystem

mesosystem In Bronfenbrenner's ecological perspective on development, the system of interconnected microsystems.

In Bronfenbrenner's model, the next level of context is the mesosystem. The **mesosystem** refers to the ways in which microsystems are connected. Although it is convenient for researchers to divide children's worlds into separate microsystems, in reality, they rarely are separate. Two types of interconnections among microsystems are important. The first is that what takes place in one setting often reverberates in others. How children are reared at home affects how they behave in preschool, how elementary school children are treated by their friends during recess affects what sort of mood they are in at the dinner table, and the values and attitudes adolescents pick up from their friends influence how they interact with their parents. One set of questions about the influence of the mesosystem on child development therefore asks how events in one microsystem affect events in another. Some questions of this sort concern simultaneous experiences in two or more settings (e.g., how experience in daycare affects children's attachments to their parents; NICHD ECCN, 1997); others concern the ways in which events in one setting affect events in another in the future (e.g., how children are raised affects their subsequent choice of peer groups; Brown et al., 1993).

A second type of interconnection among microsystems has to do with whether characteristics of one microsystem reinforce or conflict with characteristics of another. In some instances, conflict between microsystems isn't a problem—your parents expect you to be quiet and reserved around the house, but your friends expect you to be loud and boisterous, so you just shift gears when you move back and forth between these settings. But very often, experiences and expectations in different microsystems—for example, a permissive family and a disciplined classroom—conflict, which require adjustments.

© Ellen B. Senisi/The Image Works

According to the ecological perspective, the mesosystem—the interconnections among microsystems—is an important influence on development. A child whose mother and daycare provider treat her similarly may have an easier time making the transition from home to daycare each day than one whose mother and daycare provider behave differently.

How might the mesosystem in which Hispanic American children live affect their success in school? One fascinating question concerns the degrees to which cooperation and competition are valued in the home and school environments of Hispanic American children.

If you attended elementary and secondary school in the United States, you know how much emphasis is placed on individual achievement and competition. Individuals are judged by how well they perform as *individuals*. Teachers go out of their way to make sure that each student's work is his or her own—and violations of this are usually seen as cheating. Teachers may note on students' report cards how well they play with others, but in the end, it is every student for him- or herself. Unless it is explicitly encouraged by the teacher, students who help each other on tests, do homework together, or collaborate on projects are penalized—or sometimes even failed—for doing so.

In many cultures, however, and in Mexican culture especially, cooperation is valued much more than competition (Kagan & Knight, 1979). Individuals are expected to place their own needs behind those of others, and they are often judged by how well the group to which they belong performs, rather than on the basis of individual achievement. Imagine how these worlds might collide in influencing Hispanic American students' school performance. They are reared in a home environment in which cooperation, not competition, is valued, but they face a classroom setting in which just the opposite is true. One question we might ask, therefore, is how discrepant a child's home and school expectations are, and whether this contributes to academic difficulties.

When researchers look at the mesosystem, it is the connection between settings, and not any one setting considered alone, that's important. In the example we've just considered, it's not the fact that the school environment is competitive or that the home environment is cooperative that is of interest. It is the relation between them—and in this specific instance, the mismatch between them—that matters.

The Exosystem

The **exosystem** is made up of contexts outside the child's immediate, everyday experience. The exosystem includes larger settings that children know only in part, such as the neighborhood, and settings in which children themselves do not participate,

exosystem In Bronfenbrenner's ecological perspective on development, the layer of the context that includes the larger settings that children know only in part, such as the neighborhood and settings in which children themselves do not participate, such as parents' workplaces.

The ecological perspective emphasizes the importance both of immediate settings, such as the home or classroom, as well as aspects of the broader environment, such as the neighborhood, on development.

such as parents' workplaces. The exosystem influences a child indirectly, by shaping the behavior of people with whom the child does interact directly and by defining a larger context that affects what takes place inside the institutions that touch the child's life.

For example, living in an impoverished, high-crime Latino neighborhood such as South Central Los Angeles or the South Bronx puts chronic stress on the family, which may cause parents to be bad-tempered and punitive with a child (McLoyd, 1990). A working-to middle-class neighborhood in Los Angeles or New York City is a safer atmosphere, which allows parents to be more secure about their own roles and more responsive to a child. We noted earlier that children do better in school when their parents are "authoritative." And research shows that it is much easier to be this type of parent in a well-to-do neighborhood than in a disadvantaged one. As part of the child's exosystem, therefore, the neighborhood can have a profound impact on his or her performance in school through its influence on what takes place at home. One question we might want to study is whether Hispanic American children are more likely to grow up in families that live under the sorts of stressful circumstances that undermine effective parenting.

Neighborhoods influence student achievement in other ways, too, though. In some parts of the inner city, children can grow up without having contact with adults who have regular, paying jobs—where they almost never see individuals engaged in the daily routine of going to work. In contrast, they may be exposed to individuals who earn money illegally, through activities like drug dealing. As a consequence, many young people in impoverished neighborhoods may come to believe that succeeding in school in order to develop the skills and knowledge necessary to secure a good job is not an effective route toward earning a living as an adult (Little & Steinberg, 2006). Some may even believe that there are so few job opportunities in their neighborhood that even going to school—much less trying to do well there—is a waste of time. In this regard, conditions in the neighborhood—part of the child's exosystem—can affect a student's achievement without its influence operating through the family. One way to study this might be to ask whether Hispanic American children are more likely, as a group, to live in neighborhoods with unusually high unemployment rates.

The Macrosystem

macrosystem In Bronfenbrenner's ecological perspective on development, the layer of the context that includes the larger forces that define a society at a particular point in time, including culture, politics, economics, the mass media, and historical events.

The **macrosystem** is the outermost layer of the context in Bronfenbrenner's model. It includes the larger forces that define a society at a particular point in time. Among the most important of these forces are overarching cultural and religious values, the society's economic and political systems, the mass media, and major historical events that have a lasting and pervasive influence, such as wars, economic depressions, and natural disasters. It is not hard to imagine how children's development is influenced by the macrosystem. Think about what it might be like growing up in a developing country where farming is still the way of life for most people, opportunities for schooling beyond elementary school are limited, high technology has not yet defined daily life, and almost everyone shares the same cultural heritage. Now compare that with

Within the ecological perspective, the macrosystem—the cultural and historical context in which individuals grow up—is the outermost level of the environment. Major historical events such as Hurricane Katrina can transform all of the settings in which an individual develops.

the macrosystem of modern-day industrialized society—where most people work in offices, the majority of individuals need to attend college in order to be competitive in the labor force, access to the Internet has become commonplace, and individuals from an array of cultural and religious backgrounds live in close proximity to one another.

Developmentalists who focus on the macrosystem have been especially interested in whether and how child development varies between societies (e.g., comparing child development in different parts of the world), between ethnic groups (e.g., comparing child development in different ethnic groups within the same society), between socioeconomic groups (e.g., comparing child development in families living at different income levels), or across periods of time (e.g., before and after the events of 9/11).

How might the dropout rate of Hispanic American students be influenced by forces in the macrosystem? One possibility is that certain values and traditions that are widespread in Hispanic culture—part of the macrosystem in which Hispanic American children grow up—may end up making it more difficult for a Hispanic American youth to stay in school. The importance of the family—what some psychologists have called **familism** (Cuéllar, Arnold, & Gonzalez, 1995)—is especially valued in Hispanic culture, for instance, and compared with other children, Hispanic youngsters have high expectations to support and assist other family members, sacrifice their own individual needs for those of the family, and be involved in family activities (Fuligni, Tseng, & Lam, 1999). One way in which this sometimes manifests itself is that students often are expected to put family responsibilities before school. A junior high school student might be expected by her family to miss school in order to accompany an elderly, Spanish-speaking relative to the Social Security office, to serve as a translator. Another might be expected to complete household chores before attending to homework each day. Within Hispanic culture, these are perfectly reasonable expectations. But it is not hard to see how they could contribute to academic difficulties and, therefore, to the risk of dropping out of school. Indeed, some writers have suggested that one reason for the higher dropout rate of Hispanic students is that many more Hispanic than

familism Placing a high value on the interests of the family rather than the individual.

INTERIM SUMMARY **2.3**

The Importance of Context

The Ecological Perspective on Development	Bronfenbrenner was the pioneer of the ecological perspective, which provides a framework to organize the way we think about the contexts of development.
Microsystem	A **microsystem** is a setting in which the child interacts with others face-to-face, such as a home or classroom.
Mesosystem	The **mesosystem** refers to the ways in which microsystems are connected, such as the links between the home and school.
Exosystem	The **exosystem** is made up of contexts outside the child's immediate, everyday experience, such as the neighborhood, as well as settings in which the child him- or herself does not participate, such as the parents' workplace.
Macrosystem	The **macrosystem** is the outermost layer of the context in Bronfenbrenner's model and includes influences such as culture and historical time.

School

non-Hispanic students leave school to help support their family (Suárez-Orozco & Suárez-Orozco, 2001).

In reality, there is considerable disagreement among experts about the true causes of the Hispanic American dropout problem—although few people disagree that it is a problem. In addition to the factors we discussed—a less authoritative parenting style, poorer quality schools, less support for achievement in the peer group, an incompatibility between the stress placed at home on cooperation and the emphasis on competition at school, the high unemployment rate in many Hispanic neighborhoods, and the strong sense of familism in Hispanic culture—many others have been suggested, from sheer poverty to language difficulties to discriminatory practices in school. And there is evidence, although not always conclusive, to support each of these accounts. In all likelihood, something as complicated as dropping out of school is not due to any one factor, but to the cumulative effects of many different ones. The value of the ecological perspective is that it provides a framework for looking at multiple contextual influences, at different levels of analysis. (For a summary of this section, see "Interim Study 2.3: The Importance of Context.")

So far we have looked at the history of ideas about nature and nurture, at genetic influences on development (nature), and at contextual influences on development (nurture). In the last section of the chapter we look at ways to put nature and nurture together and show how they interact.

THE INTERPLAY BETWEEN GENES AND CONTEXT

There are four main types of interplay between genetic and environmental influences to consider when trying to understand children's development (Rutter, 2006). Each adds to our understanding of how genotypes (your inherited potentials and predispositions) are translated into phenotypes (how you actually turn out). These are:

1. Environmental effects on gene expression

2. Environmental effects on heritability

3. Gene-environment interactions

4. Gene-environment correlations

Environmental Effects on Gene Expression

Until recently, scientists thought that genes contained a fixed set of instructions and operated on set timetables. Now we know better. As we noted earlier in the chapter, the way that genes affect development is through the proteins they "instruct" the body to produce—what scientists refer to as **gene expression**. But, remember, the actual proteins that are produced—that is, the gene expression, rather than the gene—not only are a function of the particular set of instructions code for proteins contained in the gene, but also are dependent on factors such as temperature, light, available nutrients, and, importantly, other chemicals that are circulating in the body.

Maybe an example from the kitchen will help. The ingredients that go into a custard include milk, eggs, and some sort of flavoring (like vanilla and sugar). Most recipes have you beat the eggs and then add them to heated milk to make the base that you will eventually bake. So let's think of the eggs and milk as "genes" and the final product—the custard—as their manifestation. (Stay with us here.) But just as it would be wrong to think that genes alone can determine human traits, it is just as wrong to think that simply combining beaten eggs and hot milk will always produce a perfect custard. In fact, the environment in which you combine the milk and eggs can produce either a perfect, velvety product or a lumpy curdled mess. That's because if you heat the milk to too high a temperature before adding the beaten eggs, the eggs will cook and firm up before they have had a chance to blend with the milk. Moreover, there is no way to undo this. The environment in which the eggs and milk have "expressed" themselves makes all the difference—permanently.

gene expression The process through which genes influence the production of specific proteins, which in turn influence the phenotype.

The Nurturant Rat Manipulating the environment to see what happens to human gene expression is seldom ethical, of course. But scientists have studied this in animals, and it turns out that a change in environment can indeed affect genes. In a remarkable demonstration of this, a group of scientists examined how the biological processes that regulate rats' responses to stress could be permanently altered by changing the quality of mothering they received as newborns (Champagne et al., 2003; Meaney, 2001; Sabatini et al., 2007; Weaver et al., 2004). The scientists bred two strains of rats that differed in how the mothers treated their pups; one strain—the nurturant moms—licked and groomed their pups a great deal, and the other did not. As adults, the rats who were born to the nur-

Even if they have genes that predispose them to being fearful and anxious, rat pups raised by nurturant mothers do not show these characteristics. This is an example of how the environment can affect gene expression.

© Terry Whittaker; Frank Lane Picture Agency/Corbis

turant mothers were less fearful and anxious and showed less of a hormonal response to stress than the comparison group (the researchers were able to actually measure the biochemistry of the rats' stress response), and when they became mothers, they were more nurturant toward their own pups—no surprise, because the strain of nurturant rats had been bred with this trait in mind.

At this point, though, the researchers could not tell whether the differences between the two strains of rats in how they responded to stress were due to differences in their environments (which kind of mothering the rat received as a pup) or to differences in their genes (which mother's genes the rat inherited). So they did something very clever; they did a second experiment, in which they took rat pups born to "good moms" and transferred them to "bad moms" to be raised (a technique known as "**cross-foster-ing**"), and vice versa. Guess what? The rats raised by the bad moms turned fearful and anxious—despite their "better" genes—and the rats raised by the good moms were just the opposite. More important, the biochemical response that was usually associated with being raised by either a nurturant or non-nurturant mom changed as well. In other words, the expression of the gene regulating the stress response was altered by the way the rats were reared.

cross-fostering In animal research, the process of removing an offspring from its biological parents and having it raised by other adults, often with different attributes than the biological parents.

Environmental Effects on Heritability

Earlier we discussed the concept of "heritability," the extent to which a characteristic is influenced by genetic as opposed to environmental factors. As we explained, for decades scientists tried to attach a number—the heritability quotient—to all sorts of phenomena, from intelligence, to aggression, to self-esteem. There's a slight problem, though. No characteristic has one single heritability quotient that applies to everyone. In fact, recent studies have found that heritability varies from one group to another (e.g., from poor to middle-class families) (Bronfenbrenner & Morris, 2006). This means that it is impossible to pin down how much a trait (such as intelligence) is influenced by genes. The heritability of a trait depends on the environment.

Imagine that you have cuttings for two different strains of roses, one that has been genetically bred to produce lush blooms all summer, and one that has not. If you water and fertilize these cuttings as well as possible, the genetic differences between the plants will be clearly visible. However, if you deprive them, neither will thrive. In other words, one environment allows a genetic difference to shine through; another environment does not. If you were to compute the heritability of bloom production only looking at plants raised in the best environments, you would reach a very different conclusion (that bloom production is highly heritable) than if you were to do the same computation looking at these same plants in terrible environments (that bloom production is barely heritable).

And so it is with human potentials and predispositions. The way in which the environment changes the heritability of a trait is not always the same (Rutter, 2006). Many studies find, for example, that the heritability of intelligence is higher in more advantaged environments—presumably because under optimal contextual conditions, we can better see the result of differences in people's genetic endowment (not unlike the example of roses in the previous paragraph). Some studies also find that genetic factors matter less when the characteristic in question is already pretty much determined by the environment. If we were interested in estimating genetic influences on alcohol use, for instance, we would get an entirely different heritability quotient if we studied this question in a country in which alcohol use was illegal than we would in a country where it was easily available. In a place where using alcohol is illegal, even people with a very high genetic tendency to drink wouldn't be able to do so, so it would look as if genes had very little to do with drinking. But in a place where everyone has access to alcohol, our estimate of genetic influences would likely be much higher, because the open access allows people who don't have a genetic inclination to want to drink to avoid it, and people who have the genes for alcohol use to indulge themselves.

Gene-Environment Interaction

How a person's genotype becomes a phenotype depends on **gene-environment interaction**—that is, inherited traits lead to different characteristics in different contexts. An innately shy child might thrive in a peaceful home where her shyness is respected and she is encouraged (but not pushed) to be more outgoing and confident. The same child might become sullen and angry—a time bomb waiting to explode—in a family whose members fight, criticize and belittle one another, and constantly tease her. Likewise, a child with aggressive tendencies might become a bully in a home where he is punished physically but develop into a star athlete in a home where parents use "time-outs" and other nonconfrontational strategies to deal with his outbursts, at the same time channeling his anger into acceptable competitive outlets.

The best way to look at inherited traits is as an array of possibilities, not fixed points—what scientists call a **reaction range** (see Figure 2.7). Height is an obvious example. Individuals do not inherit a specific height (there is no gene for being 5'10"); rather, they inherit a range of possible heights (say, from 5'7" to 5'11"). Where a person falls within that range—his or her actual (phenotypic) height—is influenced by the environment (especially prenatal and postnatal health and nutrition). But the influence of the environment is not limitless. No amount of good nutrition will increase someone's height beyond the maximum of his or her reaction range for that trait.

The same is true for most other traits. Developmentalists see intellectual, personality, and behavioral traits as well as physical traits in terms of a reaction range. A child who is genotypically clumsy may learn to play basketball competently, but probably will never become a professional all-star—or even make it into the pros to begin with.

gene-environment interaction The process through which genotypes produce different phenotypes in different contexts.

reaction range An array of phenotypic possibilities that a genotype has the potential to produce as a result of the context in which the organism develops.

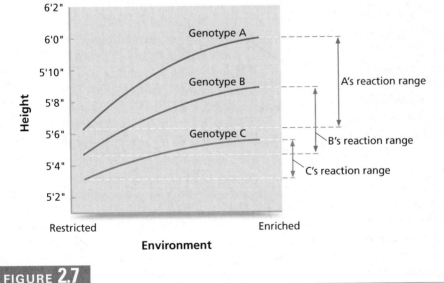

FIGURE 2.7

Reaction Range

The potential range of each person's height—the "reaction range"—is determined by his or her genotype. Person A has the potential to be anywhere from 5'6" to 6' tall, whereas person C's potential height ranges from 5'3" to 5'5". Although this reaction range is genetically determined, the environment is also very important. In an enriched environment (e.g., good prenatal care or nutrition), each person has a better chance of reaching the tallest potential height at the upper end of their reaction range.

Gene-Environment Correlation

So far we have been focusing on the effect of the environment on genes and genotypes. Sometimes overlooked is the impact of genotypes on the environment—that is, how the developing child shapes his world, just by being who he is. The idea of infants creating their environments, somehow getting the people around them to do exactly as they wish, might make a good horror movie. We're not talking about cause and effect, here, though, but rather correlations (see "The Study of Child Development"). Inherited traits and experience are not independent, unrelated influences but often go together (they are positively correlated).

passive gene-environment correlations Similarity between the results of genetic and environmental influences due to the fact that the same parents provide both genes and environments for their children.

evocative gene-environment correlations Similarity between the results of genetic and environmental influences due to the fact that genotypically different individuals elicit different responses from their environments.

Developmentalists have described three types of gene-environment correlations: *passive, evocative,* and *active* (Plomin, DeFries, & Loeblin,1977; Scarr & McCartney, 1983).

Passive gene-environment correlations result from the fact that parents provide both genes and environments for their children. (This correlation is "passive" in that the child doesn't do anything; both are part of what has been passed down, either through parents' biology or behavior.) Reading is a good illustration. Children whose parents read to them often generally do well in school. This suggests that reading enhances intellectual development. But that is only half of the story. Parents who read to their children a lot probably enjoy reading and are good at reading to others. Thus their children not only are exposed to books, but also inherit "genes" for reading. They grow up to be book lovers (and do well in school) for both genetic and environmental reasons. Passive gene-environment correlations might be called the "double whammy effect." Children who grow up in intellectually stimulating environments probably have intelligent parents—a double dose of advantage. Similarly, a child whose parents are above average in aggression inherits a genetic predisposition in this direction and is also more likely to be spanked, threatened, and ridiculed, which increase the child's aggressive tendencies (Lansford et al., 2005)—a double dose of disadvantage.

Evocative gene-environment correlations result from the fact that genotypically different individuals elicit different responses from their environments. A child who has a genetic tendency toward fearfulness may evoke overprotectiveness from his parents (because they see how anxious he is), which reinforces his apprehensiveness. A child who has a genetic predisposition to be cheerful and outgoing evokes more positive social interaction from other children than a child who is inherently shy, which then tends to make her more outgoing. A well-coordinated child will be invited to join games and teams, and so gets more athletic practice than a clumsy child does, and so on.

Active gene-environment correlations occur because children select contexts that they find stimulating and rewarding, a process called **niche-picking** (not to be confused with nitpicking, which is annoying). In other words, they choose to participate in contexts that tend to strengthen the traits that lead them to select those contexts. A child who is genetically inclined to be athletic chooses friends who enjoy the same active play she does, joins teams, practices and watches sports, chooses sports gear over other fashions, and so selects an athletic niche in her world. A child with artistic genetic tendencies chooses to play make-believe, create things from various items collected in his backyard,

© Kenna Love/Getty Images

The fact that individuals select the contexts in which they spend time makes it difficult to distinguish between genetic and environmental influence. Someone who has inherited genes for musical ability spends time making music, which further strengthens the trait.

INTERIM SUMMARY **2.4**

The Interplay Between Genes and Context

Environmental Effects on Gene Expression	The way that genes affect development is through the proteins they "instruct" the body to produce—what scientists refer to as **gene expression**. But gene expression is influenced by environmental factors.
Environmental Effects on Heritability	The heritability of a trait varies as a function of the environment. For example, some traits that appear highly heritable in advantageous environments appear less so in less advantageous ones.
Gene-Environment Interaction	Inherited traits lead to different characteristics in different contexts. The best way to view an inherited trait is as an array of possibilities—what scientists call a **reaction range**.
Gene-Environment Correlation	Genetic and environmental influences often work in the same direction, which makes it hard to separate their effects. Three types of gene-environment correlation are passive, evocative, and active.

and spend time with a grandfather who is a sculptor, and so selects his context and experiences.

The importance of these different types of gene-environment correlations changes over the course of development (Scarr & McCartney, 1983). Not surprisingly, passive gene-environment correlations are most important for infants and young children. Adults choose contexts for small children. An infant can decide what to pay attention to but cannot select where he or she goes. Active gene-environment correlations become more important with age, as children develop skills and have more opportunities to choose contexts. A toddler plays with siblings, neighbors, or whomever her mother invites to play; a six-year-old makes her own friends in school; an adolescent makes friends from other schools and neighborhoods. Evocative gene-environment correlations are important throughout the lifespan. Infants influence the way others handle them, just as the way adults act toward others affects how others act toward them. (For a summary of this section, see "Interim Study 2.4: The Interplay Between Genes and Context.")

active gene-environment correlations Similarity between the results of genetic and environmental influences due to the fact that children select contexts that they find rewarding, and that therefore tend to maintain or strengthen their genetically influenced traits.

niche-picking The process through which individuals select the environments in which they spend time.

SUMMING UP AND LOOKING AHEAD

In this chapter we described the long debate over whether nature (genes) or nurture (the environment) drives development. That debate is over. Developmentalists today know that nature works *with* nurture. Advances in our understanding of genetics (culminating in the human genome project) have shown that the interplay between genes and the environment is more complex, and gene expression more variable, than anyone suspected, even as recently as fifteen or twenty years ago. Likewise, we are more aware of the different but overlapping effects of the contexts in which children become themselves. Thus, two historically separate approaches to development have become one.

Nowhere is this more visible or significant than in prenatal development, the subject of our next chapter, "Conception, Prenatal Development, and Birth."

HERE'S WHAT YOU SHOULD KNOW

Did You Get It?

After reading this chapter, you should understand the following:

- How views of ways in which genetic and environmental forces influence development have changed over time, and how contemporary scientists think about this issue
- What genes are, and how they influence development
- The difference between mitosis and meiosis
- Why a genotype and phenotype can differ
- The various levels of context as described in the ecological perspective on development
- The different ways in which genetic and environmental influences interact to influence development

Important Terms and Concepts

active gene-environment correlations (p. 60)
additive heredity (p. 47)
adoption studies (p. 39)
alleles (p. 47)
base pairs (p. 46)
bipedalism (p. 43)
canalization (p. 44)
chromosomes (p. 46)
cross-fostering (p. 58)
dominant/recessive heredity (p. 48)
epigenesis (p. 42)
eugenics (p. 38)

evocative gene-environment correlations (p. 60)
exosystem (p. 53)
familism (p. 55)
family relatedness studies (p. 40)
fraternal twins (p. 39)
gametes (p. 47)
gene (p. 46)
gene expression (p. 57)
gene-environment interaction (p. 59)
genetic determinism (p. 38)
genotype (p. 46)

heritability (p. 39)
human genome (p. 36)
identical twins (p. 39)
macrosystem (p. 54)
meiosis (p. 47)
mesosystem (p. 52)
microsystem (p. 51)
mitosis (p. 47)
mutations (p. 49)
nativism (p. 37)
natural selection (p. 42)
niche-picking (p. 60)
nonshared environment (p. 40)

passive gene-environment correlations (p. 60)
phenotype (p. 46)
preformationism (p. 37)
reaction range (p. 59)
regulator genes (p. 49)
shared environment (p. 40)
stem cells (p. 42)
survival of the fittest (p. 42)
tabula rasa (p. 38)
theory of evolution (p. 42)
twin studies (p. 39)

Conception, Prenatal Development, and Birth

© Larry Williams/Corbis

Is it a girl or a boy?

Sex is genetically determined at the moment of conception; we are either male or female from the very beginning—or so people assume. But the reality isn't that simple. Genes do not control prenatal sex development the way a playwright determines the lines for characters in a play, creating every detail. Genes are more like the director of a play. The director creates a basic plan, but the performance depends on how the actors interpret their roles, whether the lighting engineer and backstage hands perform their jobs, what the audience and the atmosphere in the theater are like, and so on. Throughout the performance, timing is also critical.

So it is with sex differentiation. Becoming male or female is not simply the unfolding of a genetic plan, but a dynamic, interactive process. The genes a developing child inherits from his or her parents create probabilities, but the context—the world inside the mother's womb and the outside world in which she lives—plays a critical role in the outcome. Moreover, the developing child plays a leading role in this drama.

This chapter seeks to address four main questions:

- What happens during the first nine months of development?
- Will the baby be normal?
- What should parents do during pregnancy to optimize the baby's health?
- What happens during the birth process?

THE FIRST NINE MONTHS

Development begins long before birth. Some of the most rapid and dramatic developments in the human lifespan occur in the first nine months. **Gestation**—the period from conception to birth—takes about 280 days, counting from the mother's last menstrual period. During this time, a single cell, smaller than the period at the end of this sentence, develops into an approximately seven-pound, twenty-inch-long baby boy or girl, a new and unique individual.

The following sections present information on the three main stages of prenatal development: the period of the zygote (from conception to about two weeks); the period of the embryo (from about two to eight weeks); and the period of the fetus (from about eight to forty weeks).

Conception and the Zygote: The First Two Weeks

The development of a new human being starts when a male's sperm pierces the membrane of a female's ovum, or egg. (In Latin, **ovum** is the singular for egg and **ova**, the plural.) Girls are born with about 2 million immature ova, each in its own sac or follicle. After puberty, a woman experiences **ovulation** about every twenty-eight days; when a woman is ovulating, a follicle in one of her ovaries ruptures, releasing a

gestation The period from conception to birth that lasts about 280 days, counting from the mother's last menstrual period.

ovum (singular), **ova** (plural) Female sex cells (egg). Girls are born with about 2 million ova.

ovulation An event that occurs about every twenty-eight days for women, in which a follicle in one of the ovaries ruptures, releasing a mature ovum to begin its four- to five-day journey down a fallopian tube toward the uterus.

mature ovum to begin its four- to five-day journey down a fallopian tube toward the uterus, or womb. (In some cases, two or, more rarely, several ova are released.) In puberty, a boy's body begins to produce an average of 2 million sperm per day.

During sexual intercourse a man ejaculates up to 500 million sperm into the woman's body. Equipped with tails, sperm enter the vagina and attempt to swim through the cervix, into the uterus, and up the fallopian tubes. It's a difficult, upstream journey. Only a few hundred sperm will reach the fallopian tubes, and only one can fertilize the egg. After one sperm penetrates the ovum, the ovum instantaneously develops a protective coating that shuts out other sperm. This "winner-take-all" competition is a form of natural selection (see "Nature with Nurture"), in which weak or damaged sperm are eliminated. **Fertilization** is most likely if a couple has sexual intercourse on, or a few days before, ovulation. If fertilization does not occur, the sperm and ovum disintegrate and are expelled when the woman has her menstrual period.

When conception occurs, development begins almost immediately. Within hours, the sperm and egg fuse to create a new cell, called a **zygote**. As discussed in "Nature with Nurture," the twenty-three chromosomes from the mother's egg pair up with the twenty-three chromosomes from the father's sperm, creating a *genotype* (the unique genetic makeup of the individual) unlike any other, an inheritance that lasts throughout life. But development of the future child's *phenotype* (actual, observable characteristics) is only beginning.

As the zygote travels toward the uterus, the original cell divides and multiplies. By the end of the first week, *differentiation* begins—that is, the original stem cells begin to assume specialized roles. The zygote's outer cells will become a support system, including the **placenta**. The placenta—via the umbilical cord—provides food and oxygen to the developing child and carries waste products away. The zygote's inner cells will become the embryo.

During the second week, another critical event in pregnancy occurs: **implantation**. On reaching the uterus, the zygote embeds in the uterus's nutrient-rich lining (or endometrium), like roots of a growing plant into soil. But implantation is not automatic (Moore & Persaud, 2003).

When implantation is successful, a pregnancy has begun. But pregnancy eludes some couples.

Infertility and Reproductive Technology Every year, some 2 million U.S. couples seek medical help for **infertility**, the failure to conceive a child after twelve months of sexual intercourse without birth control. The risk of infertility depends on a variety of factors; three primary ones are the couple's overall health, lifestyle, and age. For example, infections—especially sexually transmitted diseases (STDs)—may interfere with conception and implantation. In addition, malnutrition at one extreme and obesity at the other reduce the chances of pregnancy. So do alcohol, smoking, and drugs (including some medications). Another major factor is age, as a woman's fertility begins to decrease around age thirty-two, and a man's declines after age thirty-five. Because many young people in developed nations postpone marriage and parenthood to pursue higher education and establish careers (see Figure 3.1), infertility is more

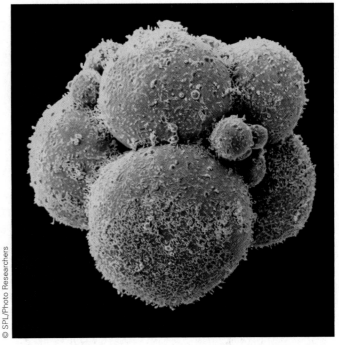

© SPL/Photo Researchers

A colored scanning electron micrograph (SEM) of a human embryo at the eight cell stage, three days after fertilization. The surface of each cell is covered in microvilli. At this stage, the embryo has not yet implanted in the uterus (womb). Magnification: x900.

fertilization Insemination of an ovum by a sperm.

zygote The new cell created when the sperm and egg fuse.

placenta The support system that—via the umbilical cord—provides food and oxygen to the developing child and carries waste products away.

implantation On reaching the uterus, the zygote embeds in the uterus's nutrient-rich lining (or endometrium), like roots of a growing plant into soil.

infertility Failure to conceive a child after 12 months of sexual intercourse without birth control.

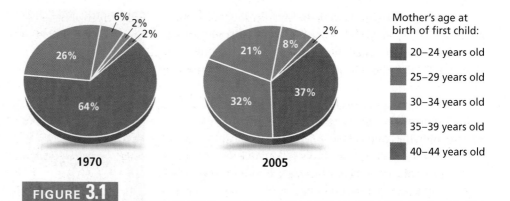

Mother's age at birth of first child:

- 20–24 years old
- 25–29 years old
- 30–34 years old
- 35–39 years old
- 40–44 years old

FIGURE 3.1

Changes Between 1970 and 2005 in the Age When Women Have Their First Child

In 1970, the majority of women (64%) were twenty to twenty-four years old when they had their first child; however, in 2005, fewer than 40 percent of women had their first child in their earlier twenties. Moreover, between 1970 and 2005, the percentage of women who had their first child at age thirty or older tripled from 10 percent to 31 percent.

fertility drugs Hormone-based agents that enhance ovarian activity.

artificial insemination The most common treatment for male infertility, which involves inserting sperm directly into the woman's uterus with a syringe.

in vitro fertilization (IVF) The best-known and most common advanced reproductive technology procedure in which the woman takes fertility drugs so that her body releases more than one egg, her ova are surgically extracted at ovulation, and then are mixed with her partner's sperm in a laboratory dish.

surrogate mother The woman who is impregnated with a male's sperm through artificial insemination or with the couple's embryo, conceived in vitro.

gametes Sex cells, the male sperm and female ova.

common today than in the past (Barber, 2001). But infertility is not sterility (permanent inability to conceive); often infertility is treatable.

The first step in treatment is to identify the cause of infertility. Perhaps the woman is not ovulating or her fallopian tubes are blocked (due to scarring caused by infections). Other causes may be that the woman has endometriosis (a buildup of tissue in the uterus over time, which interferes with implantation) or the man has a low sperm count or immobile, misshapen sperm (usually due to infections and age). In about a third of cases, no cause is found.

The simplest treatments are giving a woman hormone-based **fertility drugs** to stimulate ovulation (often of more than one egg) or performing surgery to repair a damaged part of the man or woman's reproductive system.

The most common treatment for male infertility is **artificial insemination**: inserting sperm directly into the woman's uterus with a syringe. This may be done with a concentration of the male partner's ejaculations or with sperm from an anonymous donor. Increasingly, lesbian couples and single women who want to become mothers without a male partner choose this route to pregnancy.

For couples with complex problems, more advanced reproductive technology is available. The best-known and most common procedure is **in vitro fertilization (IVF)**. First, the woman takes fertility drugs so that her body releases more than one egg. When tests show that she is at the point of ovulation, her ova are surgically extracted and mixed with her partner's sperm in a laboratory dish. (Literally, *in vitro* means "in glass.") After sperm fertilize the ova and cell duplication, or mitosis (see "Nature with Nurture"), has begun, one or more of the embryos is inserted into the woman's womb at the time in her cycle that implantation is most likely.

Several variations on IVF are available if needed, including the use of donated ova, sperm, or both. *Prenatal adoption,* as the latter is sometimes called, enables a couple to experience pregnancy and birth even though the developing child does not have their genes. If a woman cannot sustain a pregnancy, the couple may arrange for a **surrogate mother**, or "gestational carrier." The surrogate mother may be impregnated with the male partner's sperm through artificial insemination or with the couple's embryo, conceived in vitro. Technically, then, a child could have five parents: a sperm donor, an ova donor, a gestational mother, and the people the child calls Mom or Dad. But in the great majority of cases, couples use their own **gametes** (sex cells, or sperm and ova).

Reproductive technology does not increase the danger of birth defects (Shevell et al., 2005). The main "risk" is a multiple pregnancy (twins or more), which is linked to pregnancy complications, premature birth, low birth weight, and even infant death (Johnson, 2005). About 30 percent of IVF deliveries are twins, compared with only 1–2 percent of natural pregnancies.

Another risk is failure of an IVF pregnancy to succeed, and that failure is compounded by the psychological stress of repeated cycles of hope and disappointment of eventually having a child for the would-be mother and father (Kopitzke & Wilson, 2000). Less than 30 percent of IVF and related procedures result in pregnancy and birth, often only after several attempts (www.sart.org, 2006).

The good news is that 1.4 million babies conceived with IVF have been born worldwide since the first "test-tube" baby was born in England in 1978. In 2000, 25,000 U.S. women became pregnant with technological help and gave birth to more than 35,000 babies, nearly 1 percent of the babies born in the United States that year. (Note that 10,000 were multiple births.)

Reproductive technology not only has permitted many people who would have remained childless to become parents, but also has created new types of relatedness (Golombok, 2002). When donated gametes are used, either the mother or the father is not genetically related to the child. Unlike stepfamilies, however, the couple goes through pregnancy together, rears the child from birth, and introduces him or her to other people as their own. The differences between parents who used IVF and those who conceived naturally tend to be small. In general, the children appear to be well adjusted in terms of their relationships with parents and peers and their social and emotional development.

For couples who conceive without extra help, embryonic development is a given; for couples who use reproductive technologies, it is a miracle.

The Embryo: Weeks Three Through Eight

The embryonic period begins about two weeks after conception, when the zygote is firmly attached to the wall of the uterus (Hamdoun & Epel, 2007). Already the embryo's cells have formed specialized layers. The outer layer (**ectoderm**) will become skin, nerves, and sense organs; the middle layer (**mesoderm**), muscle, bones, the circulatory system, and some organs; and the inner layer (**endoderm**), the digestive system, lungs, urinary tract, and glands. The **amniotic sac**, a protective membrane filled with warm liquid that cushions the tiny embryo, takes shape.

During the next six weeks, the basic structure for a human being appears, and organs begin to function. The embryo grows about one millimeter per day, but development is not uniform. Each organ system has its own program for development, and different parts of the body develop on different days. The first visible development is the appearance of a "primitive streak," a thin line down the center of the embryo that will become the central nervous system. A portion of the ectoderm folds over to form a neural tube, the beginning of the spinal cord. At three and a half weeks, the brain begins to form at the top of the neural tube. **Neurogenesis** (the production of neurons or nerve cells) begins. Almost all of the neurons in the human brain are generated during prenatal development. This means that an average of 250,000 neurons must be generated *each minute*, although the rate is not steady over the nine months of gestation.

ectoderm The outer layer of an embryo's cells that will become fetal skin, nerves, and sense organs.

mesoderm The middle layer of an embryo's cells that will become muscle, bones, the circulatory system, and some organs.

endoderm The inner layer of an embryo's cells that will become the digestive system, lungs, urinary tract, and glands.

amniotic sac A protective membrane filled with warm liquid that cushions the embryo.

neurogenesis The production of neurons or nerve cells.

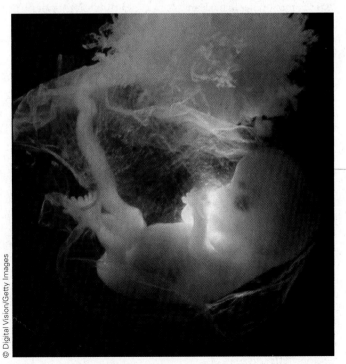

© Digital Vision/Getty Images

Even at an early stage of development, the human embryo has many anatomical features (such as eyes, hands, legs, and feet) that can be distinguished.

Two months after conception, the embryo is about one inch long (the length of the last joint of your thumb) and weighs just 0.04 ounces (one gram). Nevertheless, all of the major organs and body parts have formed. The head is rounded, and facial features are visible. Arm and leg buds are developing. The embryo's stomach produces digestive juices, its kidneys filter blood, and its heart beats. The respiratory system—designed for air, not the liquid environment of the womb—is the last to develop. The embryo's head is much larger in proportion to its body (about one-half the embryo's length) than at any other time in life.

The Fetus: Week Eight to Birth

The fetal period begins two months after conception, when major organ systems have formed. Now organs, muscles, and the nervous system become more organized and connected. Over the next seven months, the size of the fetus (length and weight) increases twentyfold. Advances in form, function, and activity are even more pronounced.

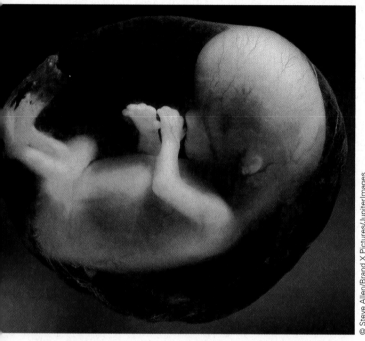

The human fetus floats in an amniotic protective sac inside the womb.

quickening The first fetal movements the mother can feel.

The embryo has almost all of its necessary parts, but they are still primitive. For example, the embryo has distinct but rudimentary arm buds. During the fetal period, arms lengthen, joints develop, fingers separate and grow nails, and a complex network of veins and muscles lays the foundation for the finely coordinated movements that develop in childhood. The fetus can make a fist and may suck its thumb, the beginning of behavior and a sign that the brain is functioning.

The Brain and Behavior Brain development accelerates in the fetal period. By the end of the sixth month of pregnancy, neurogenesis is essentially complete. Now the brain begins to organize itself: Some neurons die off as others make new connections. Brain and neurological development continue through childhood and adolescence, as we will show in later chapters. The key point here is that the central nervous system becomes active and responsive in midpregnancy.

The human fetus is not a passive voyager in the womb. Spontaneous movement begins at about four months and remains frequent up to and shortly after birth (Robertson & Bacher, 1995). The fourth month is the time of **quickening**, which refers to the first fetal movements the mother can feel.

The development of the brain and behavior is bidirectional (or two-way); that is, genetically determined brain development permits new behavior and interactions with the environment that, in turn, shape further brain development (Lecanuet et al., 1995). Prenatal behavior appears to play an important role in development. When chick embryos are immobilized, their muscles and joints do not develop normally—perhaps because their own movements would normally help to determine which neurons connect and which do not.

Although fetal behavior is at first random and infrequent, it becomes increasingly organized. At three months, the fetus swallows, urinates, kicks, curls its toes, blinks, hiccups, and occasionally yawns. These activities show that the fetus's brain is sending signals to its muscles, and the muscles are responding. At six months, fetuses have been observed "breathing" (inhaling and exhaling amniotic fluid) and even "crying" when disturbed (Gingras, Mitchell, & Grattan, 2005). Brain waves show distinct waking and sleep states. The fetus's heart rate is tied to its body movement (higher during activity, lower during inactivity), which tells us that the fetus is tuning into its environment (DiPietro et al., 2002).

At seven to eight months, the fetus is less active but more vigorous. One reason is that its quarters are cramped; another, that the brain can now inhibit as well as initiate activity. At this age the fetus responds to sounds and vibrations. For example, a mother's walking may calm her fetus; and when the mother sits or lies down, the fetus may shift into a comfortable position. Sudden movements or vibrations cause the fetus to jump, and if the mother is frightened or anxious, the fetus's heart beats faster and movement increases (DiPietro et al., 2002).

Learning As the brain develops, fetuses are capable of simple learning; they start to recognize familiar sounds and rhythms (Hopkins & Johnson, 2005). In one study (DeCasper et al., 1994), pregnant women read nursery rhymes out loud each day for several weeks to their fetuses. At age thirty-seven weeks, the fetuses' heart rate slowed (indicating heightened attention) when they heard audiotapes of their mother reading. They did not react this way when they were played tapes of another woman reading the same rhymes, before birth or after. Does this mean that if a mother listens to Mozart her child will be born with musical appreciation? No; this is modern folklore. If parents continue to play symphonies after the baby is born, he or she may develop musical appreciation, but whether the child becomes a skilled performer—much less a "genius" because of that—is highly doubtful. Research shows only that the fetuses recognize repeated, familiar sounds.

Individual differences Individual differences are already apparent in the fetal period. A series of studies explored the possibility that fetal heart rates predict later, postnatal development (Bornstein et al., 2002; DiPietro et al., 2007). Fetal heart activity was measured at 24, 30, and 36 weeks' gestation. The same children's levels of language development and symbolic play were evaluated at 27 months after birth. Children who had higher heart rate variability *in utero* (in the womb) were more advanced in both language and play. One possible explanation is that these fetuses are more reactive, which translates into more advanced cognitive skills after birth; another, that some children use oxygen more efficiently, which has a positive effect on brain growth and later cognitive development. In either case, individual prenatal variations predicted childhood differences.

In related studies, the same researchers looked at levels of fetal activity and **temperament**—a child's emotional and behavioral predispositions—at one and two years (DiPietro et al., 2002). Children who were more active as fetuses not only developed motor skills earlier, but also explored more and were more upset at being restrained at ages one and two. Temperamentally, they were more confident and independent.

Developmental scientists have long viewed temperament as inborn or genetic, but these findings go further to suggest that the development of temperament is bidirectional. When fetal connections between the brain and the muscles develop rapidly, the fetus is more active. When the fetus is more active, connections are strengthened and refined, which make the fetus more active still, and so on in a cycle. Likewise, an infant who has advanced motor skills explores more; exploration enhances motor abilities, which builds confidence; and all of this influences both brain development and temperament. These infants are upset when they can't exercise their motor skills and their curiosity. Infants who were less active in the womb are easier in the sense of being more willing to accept limits on their activity.

temperament A child's emotional and behavioral predispositions.

Boy or Girl?

Sex differentiation begins at conception. Females have two X chromosomes, so all of a woman's ova have an X chromosome. Males have an X and a Y chromosome, so their sperm may contain either an X or a Y chromosome (see "Nature with Nurture"). Which sperm fertilizes an ovum determines whether the child will have a female (XX) or male (XY) genotype. But, as we said, this is just the beginning. The child's internal reproductive organs and external genitalia—much less masculine and feminine attitudes and behaviors—are not fixed the moment X meets X (or Y).

Prenatal sexual development can be divided into four stages. The fact that an embryo has XX or XY chromosomes has little effect on stage one. For the first one and a half months after conception, the embryo is basically "unisex." All embryos have a similar *gonadal streak* and both Müllerian ducts (which may develop into female sex organs) and Wolffian ducts (which may develop into male sex organs). The only way to identify an embryo's sex is to examine its chromosomes.

In the second stage, physiological sex differences emerge. At about seven weeks, a gene on the Y chromosome sends a signal that triggers the development of testes. A week or so later, the testes begin to produce two hormones: testosterone, which stimulates the development of male reproductive organs; and Müllerian inhibiting substance (MIS), which blocks the development of female reproductive organs. If the embryo does not receive this signal, and testosterone and MIS are not produced or absorbed, the fetus develops female reproductive organs, beginning with ovaries at about ten weeks.

In the third stage (two and a half to three months), external genitals form. Testosterone stimulates the development of testicles and a penis. If not present, the fetus develops a clitoris and vulva. Finally, in stage four, testosterone inhibits the rhythmic cycles of the hypothalamus and the pituitary, which regulate female ovulation.

Note that nature's basic plan seems to be to produce a female. The development of a male requires two extra steps. The first requirement is a signal from the Y chromosome. In **Turner's syndrome**, the embryo's cells have only one (X) chromosome. In the absence of a Y chromosome, the fetus develops into a female. The second requirement is testosterone. Without testosterone, development again follows the female pattern. A genetic defect called *testicular-feminizing syndrome* prevents a male (XY) fetus from utilizing testosterone. The embryo develops testes, but because it cannot respond to male hormones, it develops female external genitalia. Both conditions are rare.

Sex differentiation can be seen as a series of hurdles or gates. Once passed, the gate cannot be reopened. Developments that took place during that stage cannot be reversed. But normal development in the next stage is not guaranteed until the next gate is closed. For example, in the 1950s and 1960s, hundreds of thousands of women were given DES (diethylstilbestrol) to prevent miscarriage. Only later did physicians learn that DES stimulated the production of the male hormone testosterone in the mother's body. When women took DES after the second month of gestation, their female (XX) fetuses were born with normal ovaries. That gate had been locked. But the next gate was still open, and many of their daughters were born with masculine-looking external genitalia. In addition, prenatal exposure to male sex hormones produces small but distinct differences in girls' behavior, such as toy preferences, engaging in rough-and-tumble play, and clothing choices (Hines & Kaufman, 1994; Lustig, 1998).

Sex differences are not limited to anatomy, of course. Males and females act, talk, and to some degree think differently. Why? One possibility is that prenatal development is confined to physiology, and the development of masculine or feminine attitudes and behaviors is largely the result of socialization. Whether a baby has male or female genitals affects how parents and others treat him or her. And socialization guides the development of a gender identity and sex-typed behavior. Another possibility is that prenatal sex development affects the brain as well as the body. Prenatal expe-

Turner's syndrome A condition in which the embryo's cells have only one (X) chromosome.

rience may program a boy's brain to respond to certain aspects of the environment, and a girl's brain to respond to other features of the environment. This does not mean that boys are naturally tough, and girls are naturally sweet, but subtle differences may exist. Or both factors may operate together. . . .

Sex differentiation is normally continuous. Thus, a child who has an XY genotype develops a male reproductive system, is reared as a boy, has a male identity, and behaves in masculine ways. As a result, it is difficult to separate the effects of prenatal, biological development from those of postnatal socialization. Most likely males and females are *predisposed* to behave in somewhat different ways, and gender socialization brings out and reinforces their predispositions.

For example, boys typically engage in more rough-and-tumble play than girls do. Let's assume

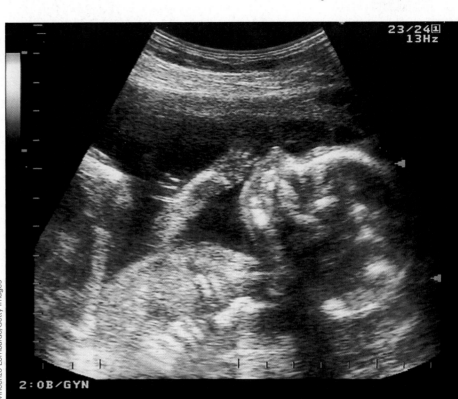

During an examination, ultrasound can be used to image the human fetus while still in utero. This one is 20 weeks old.

that males are genetically primed for physical aggression (a probability but not a certainty). Equally significant, parents are more physical with male than with female infants, strengthening this tendency. Dads tickle baby boys to excite them, but cuddle and coo to baby girls. In childhood, parents are more likely to accept and even encourage play-fighting in a son, whereas they discourage the same behavior in a daughter. Girls aren't "supposed" to fight physically, and boys aren't "supposed" to cry. Whether deliberate or unconscious, gender socialization reinforces genetic and hormonal predispositions. (See "Socioemotional Development in Early Childhood.") (For a summary of this section, see "Interim Summary 3.1: The First Nine Months.")

MONITORING PRENATAL DEVELOPMENT

Twenty-five years ago, parents didn't know the health of their child until birth. Thanks to new technology, today we can monitor prenatal development almost from the beginning. A woman's doctor can assure her and her partner that the baby is developing normally or, when necessary, help them to prepare for complications.

One technology now used to see the fetus's structure and to watch behavior directly is **ultrasound imaging**, which provides a living picture of prenatal development (including sex differentiation at about three months). In this scanning process, high-frequency sound waves are directed at the womb, and a computer transforms their reflections or echoes into an image on a monitor, called a *sonogram* (Levi & Chervenak, 1998). A noninvasive procedure with no known risk to the mother or fetus, ultrasound is used routinely to assess the growth, development, and health of the fetus (Chervenak & McCullough, 1998; Garmel & D'Alton, 1994). Ultrasound scans can be performed as early as eight weeks, but they are more accurate in later stages of pregnancy. They allow a physician to verify a baby's due date, predict multiple births, anticipate birth problems, and detect some fetal abnormalities.

ultrasound imaging A technology that provides a living picture of prenatal development (including sex differentiation).

INTERIM SUMMARY 3.1

The First Nine Months

Gestation	■ The period from conception to birth, takes about 280 days.
Infertility	■ The failure to conceive a child after 12 months of sexual intercourse without birth control.
	■ Treatments: fertility drugs, artificial insemination, in vitro fertilization (IVF)
Prenatal Development Periods	
1. Zygote (from conception to about 2 weeks)	■ Fertilization is the insemination of an ovum by a sperm.
	■ A zygote is a new cell formed when the sperm and egg fuse together.
	■ The 23 chromosomes from the mother's egg pair up with the 23 chromosomes from the father's sperm, creating a *genotype*.
2. Embryo (from about 2 to 8 weeks, beginning about 2 weeks after conception)	■ The embryo's cells form specialized layers: **ectoderm** (outer layer: skin, nerves, sense organs); **mesoderm** (middle layer: muscle, bones, the circulatory system, and some organs); **endoderm** (inner layer: digestive system, lungs, urinary tract, and glands).
	■ The **amniotic sac**—a protective membrane that cushions the tiny embryo—takes shape.
3. Fetus (from 8 to 40 weeks)	■ Organs, muscles, and the nervous system become more organized and connected.
	■ The size of the fetus (length and weight) increases twentyfold.
	■ Spontaneous movement **(quickening)** begins at about 4 months (and remains frequent up to birth).
	■ At 7 to 8 months, the fetus is less active but more vigorous.
	■ Fetuses recognize familiar sounds and rhythms.
Sex Differentiation Begins at Conception	■ Females have two X chromosomes, so all of a woman's ova have an X chromosome.
	■ Males have an X and a Y chromosome, so their sperm may contain either an X or a Y chromosome.
	■ Which sperm fertilizes an ovum determines whether the child will have a female (XX) or male (XY) genotype.
	■ The child's internal reproductive organs and external genitalia—and masculine and feminine attitudes and behaviors—are not fixed the moment X meets X (or Y).
Prenatal Sexual Development Can Be Divided Into Four Stages	1. For the first 1.5 months after conception, the embryo is basically "unisex."
	2. In the second stage, physiological sex differences emerge.
	3. In the third stage (2.5 to 3 months), external genitals form. Testosterone stimulates the development of testicles and a penis. If not present, the fetus develops a clitoris and vulva.
	4. In stage four, testosterone inhibits the rhythmic cycles of the hypothalamus and the pituitary, which regulate female ovulation.
	■ Gender socialization reinforces genetic and hormonal predispositions.

The great majority of babies (95%) are healthy and normal at birth. "Nature" (or natural selection) eliminates most malformations before birth. Estimates are that half of all conceptions are not implanted, and a quarter of implanted embryos are spontaneously aborted in the next month or two, often before the mother knows that she was pregnant. Most of these are the result of genetic abnormalities. But fetuses with certain genetic disorders survive the prenatal period.

It is still rare for scientists to be able to link particular genes to specific disorders. Many problems—from dyslexia to depression—run in families. If a grandparent, aunt or uncle, or a sibling has the disorder, the risk that a new child in the family will be affected increases. But most are **multifactoral disorders**; that is, they are the result of interactions among multiple genes and between genes and the environment. Therefore, children can inherit a predisposition for the problem, but they may or may not be affected. Next we look at abnormalities that have known causes and consequences.

multifactoral disorders
Disorders that result from interactions among multiple genes and between genes and the environment.

Chromosomal and Genetic Abnormalities

Chromosomal Malformations Some abnormalities are caused by mutations or accidents during *meiosis* (the production of sperm and ova; see "Nature with Nurture"). The most common example is *Down syndrome*, also called *trisomy 21* because the child has three instead of the normal two twenty-first chromosomes. Down syndrome is linked to many factors, especially the mother's age. About 1 in 2,000 babies born to twenty-year-old women have the disorder, a rate that climbs to 1 in 20 for forty-five-year-old women.

Children with Down syndrome are usually short and stocky with small heads, round faces, slanted eyes, and flat noses. Most have medical problems, including heart and thyroid trouble, hearing loss, and muscle weakness. These children have moderate to severe learning handicaps, especially with language. They also tend to be exceptionally cheerful, affectionate, and compliant. But no two children with Down syndrome are alike; individuals vary.

In the recent past, children with Down syndrome were frequently confined to institutions, where they received minimal attention and often died in their teens or early twenties. Today most remain with their families and attend public schools. With special attention they can develop reading, writing, and speaking skills. In adulthood they may hold jobs and live semi-independently, in group homes. With preventive health care, almost half live into their fifties and even sixties, though they may suffer from diseases of old age (such as Alzheimer's or heart disease) as early as their thirties.

Genetic abnormalities range from minor conditions like color blindness, to problems that can be corrected surgically (such as cleft palate or clubfoot), to still incurable physical and mental disabilities.

Recessive genes Most genetic disorders are carried on a recessive gene (see "Nature with Nurture"). *Sickle cell anemia* is an example. Children who inherit the sickle cell gene from both parents—homozygotes—suffer from problems ranging from chronic shortness of breath and fatigue to bouts of severe pain (from swollen joints) and frequent, sometimes fatal crises in which the heart, kidneys, and liver malfunction. But children who inherit the gene from only one parent—heterozygotes—rarely experience any symptoms. In homozygotes, all of the red blood cells are bent into a sickle shape and cannot carry adequate oxygen to the tissues and organs. In heterozygotes, only some blood cells are abnormal.

The sickle cell trait is found in populations that live, or that once lived, in tropical areas where malaria is common (Africa, the Caribbean, and Central America). Although lethal in a double dose, the sickle cell *protects* heterozygotes from malaria. About one in ten African Americans and one in twenty Hispanic Americans carry the sickle cell gene.

Some recessive gene disorders are *sex linked*. Women carry the recessive gene but, because they have two X chromosomes, almost never suffer its effects. However, there is a fifty-fifty chance that they will transmit the genetic abnormality to their sons, who have only one X chromosome. The most common example is color blindness. (Baldness is also sex linked—carried by females, expressed in males—but is not a "disorder.")

The most famous sex-linked disorder is *hemophilia*, a disease in which the victim's body does not produce blood-clotting factor. For a person with hemophilia, even minor injuries can lead to hemorrhage, and early death is common. Hemophilia can be controlled (with injections of blood-clotting factor) but not cured. England's Queen Victoria (1819–1901) carried hemophilia—of particular significance because her children married into most of the royal houses of Europe. One of her sons, three of her grandsons, and six of her great-grandsons were hemophiliac. Historians believe that the Russian Revolution of 1917 succeeded in part because the tsar and tsarina (a granddaughter of Victoria) were preoccupied with their hemophiliac son's illness.

The Founder Effect The Amish have one of the highest rates of genetic defects in the United States. The reason is the *founder effect*. Today's 150,000 Amish are all descended from a few hundred Swiss-German settlers who came to America to found religious communities in the eighteenth century. Amish traditions forbid marriage with outsiders. Hence, over many generations of intermarriage, rare genetic disorders that lie dormant or die out in the wider population have surfaced among the Amish. Although the Amish shun such "modern" inventions as television and telephones, and even electricity and cars, like all parents, the Amish want their children to be healthy. Today their horse-drawn buggies line up outside local clinics that offer genetic counseling backed by cutting-edge technology.

Genetic Counseling

genetic counseling A profession designed to help couples understand how heredity might affect their child.

Genetic counseling is a relatively new profession, designed to help couples understand how heredity might affect their child. Health practitioners who specialize in hereditary disorders, genetic counselors function as diagnosticians, educators, and therapists. They may work alone or on a team to assist patients who have already conceived or those considering pregnancy. Who should seek genetic counseling? Generally, couples who would benefit from genetic counseling include those who belong to a group known to be at risk, those who already have a child or relatives with a genetic disorder, and those who have experienced miscarriage, stillbirth, or infertility. In addition, those couples in which the woman is age thirty-five and older might seek counseling.

A genetic counselor starts by taking a couple's family histories to assess whether a genetic abnormality runs in one partner's or both partners' families. The next step would be a DNA test or **karyotype**: a picture of the man and woman's chromosomes. Karyotypes are most useful in identifying recessive genetic defects.

karyotype A picture the individual's chromosomes.

Genetic counselors help couples to understand how likely they are to have a child with a genetic disorder. For example, Tay-Sachs disease—most common among people of Eastern European Jewish heritage—is a fatal disorder characterized by steady mental and physical deterioration beginning at about six months. Homozygotes suffer seizures, muscle atrophy, and paralysis, and they rarely live beyond age four. If only one partner carries the Tay-Sachs gene, there is no risk that a child will be affected. Only homozygotes suffer from the disorder. If both the man and woman are carriers, the risk that their child will inherit this disease is the same as the "risk" that a couple who have the recessive gene for blue eyes will have a blue-eyed child: one in four (or 25%). Each partner has one dominant, healthy gene, *A,* and one recessive, Tay-Sachs gene, *a.* Their child might be *AA* (neither afflicted nor a carrier); *Aa* or *aA* (an unaffected carrier); or *aa* (afflicted). This does not mean that if a couple has four children, one will be affected and the other three healthy. Each pregnancy carries the same risk.

If both partners carry an abnormal recessive gene or the mother is thirty-five or older, they have several options. Some couples decide to adopt rather than risk bearing a child who will inevitably suffer or lead a limited life. An alternative is to conceive through IVF with donor eggs or sperm. Other couples decide to take the risk, hoping that they will conceive a healthy child. If prenatal testing reveals the fetus has a chromosomal or genetic abnormality, the couple may decide to terminate the pregnancy. Needless to say, none of these options is an easy decision. A couple may rule out abortion, for religious or emotional reasons. They may worry about the impact of these decisions on their marriage or their other children, and they may doubt their emotional (and financial) ability to rear a disabled child. Consciously or unconsciously, they may feel ashamed and guilty about being "carriers." Genetic counselors can help parents understand the underlying causes and risks associated with different choices.

If the couple conceives, the next step is prenatal testing.

Prenatal Testing

Some (but not all) genetic defects can be identified before birth. Equally important, prenatal tests can relieve prospective parents of the anxiety of not knowing whether a baby will be normal. Most women who take prenatal tests receive the good news that their fetus does *not* have the disorder for which the test was given (March of Dimes, Pregnancy & Newborn Health Education Center, 2008).

Couples using IVF may elect to have **preimplantation genetic diagnosis**. In this screening, one or two cells are removed from a three-day-old test-tube embryo; if the cell contains genes linked to fatal childhood disorders, that embryo is not used. In Britain, couples may also screen for genes linked to adult diseases, such as breast, ovarian, and colon cancer. (There are no regulations on preimplantation screening in the United States.)

The most common prenatal test is **amniocentesis**. Using ultrasound as a guide, the doctor inserts a thin needle through the woman's abdomen into the uterus and withdraws a small amount of amniotic fluid, which contains skin cells from the fetus. These cells are cultured in a laboratory for ten to twelve days and then tested for chromosomal or genetic abnormalities. Amniocentesis is usually done halfway through pregnancy, in the fourth month. Test results take three weeks. The main drawback is that the results are not known until the fifth month of pregnancy, when the fetus is relatively well along. If the results show that the fetus has a severe disorder, the parents are faced with an emotionally and morally difficult decision: whether to give birth to a handicapped baby or to abort a fetus whose movements they may have already felt.

Newer tests permit earlier results. In **chorionic villi sampling** (CVS), the doctor uses a needle to remove a small piece of the villi, extensions that attach the amniotic sac to the wall of the uterus. Cells from the villi have the same genetic and biochemical makeup as the fetus. CVS can be done in the middle of the third month of pregnancy, and it yields preliminary results in about ten days.

Both amniocentesis and CVS can be used to diagnose chromosomal, metabolic, and blood-borne conditions; screen for sickle cell anemia; and identify congenital defects (such as muscular dystrophy) (Green & Statham, 1996; Robinson & Wisner, 1993).

These tests are not risk free, however. There is a 1 in 150 chance of miscarriage following amniocentesis and a 1 in 50 chance after CVS (Green & Statham, 1996). In addition, CVS has been linked to a slight (1 in 1,000–3,000) risk of deformed limbs (Olney et al., 1995). Neither are these tests foolproof. *False positives* (test results that show a disorder is present when it is not) and *false negatives* (test results that show a disorder is not present when it is) are possible. No test can *guarantee* a normal, healthy baby. (For a summary of this section, see "Interim Summary 3.2: Monitoring Prenatal Development.")

preimplantation genetic diagnosis A screening technique that involves removing cells from a test-tube embryo to determine if the cell contains genes linked to fatal childhood disorders.

amniocentesis A prenatal test in which, using ultrasound as a guide, the doctor inserts a thin needle through the woman's abdomen into the uterus to withdraw amniotic fluid that contains skin cells from the fetus.

chorionic villi sampling A fetal test that involves removal of a small piece of the villi, extensions that attach the amniotic sac to the wall of the uterus.

INTERIM SUMMARY 3.2

Monitoring Prenatal Development

Ultrasound Imaging Provides a Living Picture of Prenatal Development	■ It is noninvasive with no known risk to the mother or the fetus. ■ It allows a physician to verify a baby's due date, predict multiple births, anticipate birth problems, and detect some fetal abnormalities.
Genetic Abnormalities	■ These can range from minor conditions like color blindness, to problems that can be corrected surgically, to incurable physical and mental disabilities. ■ Some abnormalities are caused by mutations or accidents during meiosis, the most common being Down syndrome, also called *trisomy 21,* where the child has three instead of the normal two 21st chromosomes.
Recessive Gene Disorders	■ Most genetic disorders, such as sickle cell anemia, are carried on a recessive gene. ■ Children who inherit the sickle cell gene from both parents suffer from problems ranging from chronic shortness of breath and fatigue to bouts of severe pain and frequent, sometimes fatal crises in which the heart, kidneys, and liver malfunction. ■ Children who inherit the gene from only one parent rarely experience any symptoms. ■ Some recessive gene disorders are *sex linked,* such as hemophilia, a disease in which the victim's body does not produce blood-clotting factor.
Genetic Counseling	■ Helps couples understand how heredity might affect their child and how likely they are to have a child with a genetic disorder. ■ A counselor starts by taking a couple's family histories and then by doing a DNA test or **karyotype**: a picture of the man and woman's chromosomes.
Prenatal Tests	■ **Preimplantation genetic diagnosis** (screens cells from three-day-old test-tube embryos for genes linked to fatal childhood disorders). ■ **Amniocentesis** and **chorionic villi sampling** (CVS) (used to diagnose chromosomal, metabolic, and blood-borne conditions, screen for sickle cell anemia, and identify congenital defects).

PROTECTING THE FETUS

A healthy pregnancy begins before conception (Caviness & Grant, 2006; CDC, 2008). Therefore, women who want to become pregnant need to "baby proof" their bodies. Smoking, for example, can reduce fertility (Akushevich, Kravchenko, & Manton, 2007). So can a case of mumps, if untreated. This applies to would-be fathers as well as mothers. It also applies to women who *might* become pregnant (women who are sexually active but do not use birth control). A woman who isn't planning to have a baby might not even suspect she is pregnant until ten or twelve weeks after conception—and the fetus is most vulnerable to certain disorders during the first four to ten weeks of pregnancy (CDC, 2006).

The guidelines for healthy living—eat your vegetables; don't smoke, drink, or use drugs—become imperative during pregnancy, because the main source of contact between the embryo and fetus and the outside world is the mother's bloodstream. The mother's blood does not flow directly into the fetus's veins but through the placenta to the umbilical cord. The placenta acts as a filter, protecting the fetus from some—but not all—harmful substances.

Regular visits during pregnancy to an obstetrician (a physician who specializes in pregnancy, delivery, and postnatal care) are essential. But young women, in particular, often take their health for granted . . . and take chances.

Maternal Characteristics

Aside from genetic abnormalities, the well-being of the fetus depends first on the mother.

Age For different reasons, both younger and older women are more likely to have problematic pregnancies and birth complications than are women in their twenties. Mothers under age eighteen have significantly higher rates of preterm (or premature) births and low-birth-weight babies than do mothers ages twenty to twenty-four of the same ethnicity, income level, and marital status (Bornstein & Putnick, 2007; Bornstein et al., 2006; Ekwo & Moawad, 2000). One reason is that teenage mothers typically wait longer to see a doctor when they think they might be pregnant and are less likely than older mothers to have regular prenatal checkups.

Pregnant mothers eat for two—for themselves and their developing baby—so following a healthy diet is doubly important.

Older mothers have an increased rate of birth complications. Even when medical risks and socioeconomic factors are taken into consideration, women age thirty or older are more likely than younger women to experience birth complications, to have cesarean sections (see later), and to give birth to infants who need to be admitted to newborn intensive care units. Older women also have a greater risk of miscarriage, stillbirths, high blood pressure, and even death during childbirth than do mothers under age thirty. On the positive side, the newborns of older women are as healthy as those of younger mothers, despite complicated pregnancies and delivery.

Diet and Nutrition According to an old saying, "A pregnant woman is eating for two." Like many sayings, this one contains a grain of truth. It doesn't mean that a mother-to-be should eat twice as much, but that she should eat twice as *well* (Leavitt, Tonniges, & Rogers, 2003). Nutrients are the elements of life, the fuel that propels development. Women whose diets are rich in protein have fewer complications during pregnancy, go through shorter labors, and bear healthier babies. Deficiencies in zinc and folic acid, as well as protein, have been linked to central nervous dysfunction, prematurity, and low-birth-weight births (Keen, Bendich, & Willhite, 1993).

For some pregnant women, however, eating a balanced diet isn't a matter of choice. In many regions of the developing world, malnutrition is a chronic problem (UNICEF, 2007). Moreover, this problem isn't limited to poor countries. The U.S. Special Supplemental Food Program for Women, Infants, and Children (WIC) provides food packages, nutrition education, and healthy care to low-income pregnant women, new mothers, and young children. But funding is limited, and women who apply may be put on waiting lists. More than 8 million people get WIC benefits each month (U.S. Department of Agriculture, 2006). Severe malnutrition in early pregnancy (especially

spina bifida A developmental condition in which the spinal cord does not close completely.

anencephaly A developmental condition in which part of the brain does not develop.

lack of folic acid, a B vitamin) increases the risk of neural tube defects—**spina bifida**, in which the spinal cord does not close completely, or **anencephaly**, in which part of the brain does not develop. Malnutrition later in pregnancy is associated with low birth weight. But the long-term prognosis for children chronically malnourished in utero is not entirely bleak. If children receive nutritious diets before age two, they can rebound. During World War II, western Holland endured severe food shortages. In general, children born during this famine did not suffer long-term physical or mental disabilities (Stein et al., 1975). Fetally malnourished children are most likely to recover if they eat healthy diets *and* grow up in stable, supportive environments. But if malnutrition continues and the environment is chaotic, children are at risk for cognitive, behavioral, and social problems.

Maternal malnutrition is rarely an isolated problem—it is usually compounded by continuing poverty, ongoing malnutrition, poor health, inadequate medical care, low levels of education, and high levels of stress.

Stress Pregnancy is a time of many changes—in a woman's body, in her and her partner's emotions, and in their family life. Some tension and anxiety are normal. But constant or chronic stress, or sudden acute stress, can be harmful (DiPietro et al., 2006; Davis et al., 2004; Yehuda et al., 2005). Very high stress during pregnancy is associated with premature birth. One study looked at women who had been through an earthquake (Glynn et al., 2001). The earlier in their pregnancy the earthquake happened, the earlier they delivered. On the positive side, women who were further along with pregnancy seemed better able to cope with stress.

As with malnutrition, stress is often part of a package. Stress causes—and is caused by—too little rest or too little exercise, skipping meals or overeating, and headaches and backaches; in addition, it may lead to smoking and drinking. Women who take care of themselves typically manage stress successfully.

Outside Influences

teratogen Any environmental substance that can have a negative impact on fetal development and possibly result in birth defects or even death.

A **teratogen** is any substance that can have a negative impact on fetal development and possibly result in birth defects or even death. Viruses, drugs, and environmental pollutants fall into this category (Field, 1998; Kopera-Frye & Arendt, 1999). Almost all of these hazards can be avoided or their effects can be reduced. Awareness is key. The best way for a woman to protect her fetus is to talk with her doctor and learn what is and is not safe.

rubella German measles, a disease that can be devastating for the fetus if the mother contracts it during the first three months of pregnancy.

Diseases The placenta protects the fetus from many bacteria, but not from viruses. Sexually transmitted diseases (STDs), smallpox, and measles all cross the placenta. **Rubella** (German measles) is a relatively mild disease in adults, but it can be devastating for the fetus. Women who contract rubella in the first three months of pregnancy have a 50% chance of bearing babies with cataracts, deafness, possible brain damage, and mental retardation (Moore & Persaud, 1993). During an outbreak in 1964–1965, more than 20,000 babies were born with defects, and an estimated 10,000 pregnancies ended in miscarriages and stillbirths. Since 1969 U.S. children have been routinely vaccinated against rubella, and another epidemic in the United States is unlikely. But rubella has not disappeared. Women of childbearing age can be tested and vaccinated if they are not immune.

HIV Human immunodeficiency virus that causes AIDS.

AIDS Acquired immunodeficiency syndrome.

The major threat today is **HIV** (human immunodeficiency virus), the virus that causes **AIDS** (acquired immunodeficiency syndrome). Even without treatment, a person may have HIV for as long as ten years and not develop symptoms. With AIDS, the immune system breaks down, making the individual more susceptible to infections, certain cancers, and other, often life-threatening or fatal conditions.

Through 2002, more than 9,300 American children have contracted AIDS—nearly always from their mother during pregnancy, during labor and delivery, or through breastfeeding (CDC, 2006). About one in four HIV-infected infants develops AIDS symptoms shortly after birth—these symptoms include opportunistic bacterial infections, such as pneumonia; internal organ abscesses; and meningitis, an inflammation of brain tissues. These children do not reach the developmental milestones of the first year and usually die in their fifth year. Very likely this group became infected during pregnancy, before their immune systems began to function. The remaining three in four, who probably became infected with HIV during birth, may not exhibit symptoms of AIDS until they are five years old and may survive into adolescence. But neither of these outcomes is inevitable.

A pregnant woman can protect her fetus (and herself) by getting a test for HIV, and, if she is HIV-positive, taking AZT (zidovudine) and other medications that slow or stop HIV duplication (Rutstein et al., 1998). With these new treatments, a mother can reduce the risk of transmitting HIV to her baby to 2 percent or less (Fogler, 2007). The prognosis for mothers and babies in the United States has improved dramatically, but worldwide more than 800,000 babies are infected with HIV from their mothers each year. Most are in developing countries, where appropriate medications are not widely available (World Health Organization, 2008).

Medications In the developed world, medications of all sorts are widely available and widely used. The simple rule here is: Pregnant women, beware. Whatever the mother takes, her fetus takes, too. For example, prescription and over-the-counter medications that are good for the mother can be harmful to the fetus. Even aspirin may cause blood clotting and bleeding in the fetus (Briggs, Freeman, & Sumner, 1994). A pregnant woman should not take any drugs, not even vitamins, before consulting her doctor. Even when she does, mistakes can happen.

Earlier in this chapter, we mentioned the effects of *DES* (diethylstilbestrol) on sex differentiation. It took almost thirty years for the long-term effects of DES to be recognized. Grown women who were exposed before birth have a substantially increased risk of rare cervical and vaginal cancers. Men who were similarly exposed sometimes develop cysts near the ducts where sperm are stored and may have low sperm counts as well as misshapen sperm, leading to infertility. DES daughters also have higher than average rates of infertility and problem pregnancies. Even *their* daughters are thought to be at some risk for cancers—a case in which exposure of the grandmother is visited on the granddaughters!

To protect her fetus a woman should only take medications that are necessary for her health and that of the fetus.

Drinking and Smoking Because alcoholic beverages are legal (with some restrictions) and woven into social occasions, from weddings to wakes, we don't usually think of alcohol as a "drug." And even though public opinion has turned against smoking, which many adults—though not necessarily teenagers—now see as "uncool," cigarettes are widely available, and cigars have made a comeback. Therefore, despite their acceptance as part of U.S. culture, it's important to remember that alcohol and nicotine *are* drugs: Both contain mood-changing, addictive substances that alter body chemistry.

Alcohol In 1973, Kenneth Lyons Jones and his colleagues identified a pattern of facial features and mental disabilities found in babies and children with alcoholic mothers, **fetal alcohol syndrome** (FAS). Since then a large amount of research has supported their diagnosis (Fryer et al., 2007; Jones et al., 2006; Lowe, Handmaker, & Aragon, 2006).

fetal alcohol syndrome A pattern of disabilities found in babies and children of mothers who consumed alcohol during pregnancy.

FIGURE **3.2**

Fetal Alcohol Syndrome

Fetal alcohol syndrome affects internal development (of cognition and personality) as well as external development (as shown here in the facial anatomy of these two girls).

fetal alcohol effects Fetal deformities that are the result of significant (but not chronic) prenatal exposure to alcohol.

FAS is the most common known cause of mental retardation. It is also entirely preventable. Yet every year between 1,000 and 6,000 babies in the United States are born with FAS (Bertrand, Floyd, & Weber, 2004). An estimated 40,000 are born with some alcohol-related problems (Sokol, Delaney-Black, & Deary, 2003).

Babies with FAS are small at birth and usually do not catch up with their peers as they grow older. They have small heads (microcephaly) and distinctive facial features, including small eyes, a narrow forehead, a low nasal bridge, and a thin upper lip (Astley & Claren, 1996; Roebuck, Mattson, & Riley, 1999) (see Figure 3.2). Many have brain and central nervous system abnormalities. Most have some degree of mental disability, including mental retardation, a short attention span, and emotional and behavioral disorders. Many also have low muscle tone and poor coordination. Babies with **fetal alcohol effects** (FAE), the result of significant (but not chronic) prenatal exposure to alcohol, have some but not all of these problems (Bertrand, Floyd, & Weber, 2004).

Does drinking *any* alcohol harm the fetus? This is a matter of dispute. FAS is clearly linked to alcohol *abuse* (having five or more drinks at a time, twice a week), binge drinking during a sensitive period may be harmful, but questions surround very moderate drinking at other times (Ploygenis et al., 1998). But this does not mean that moderate or "social" drinking has *no* harmful effects. Two drinks a day during pregnancy is associated with a seven-point drop in IQ; moderate drinking predicts attention deficits in children ages four to fourteen (Streissguth et al., 2004). There's a reason bottles of wine and other alcoholic beverages have clear labels with the Surgeon General's warning to pregnant women (U.S. Department of Health and Human Services, 2005).

In numerous studies, the long-term effects of fetal exposure to alcohol include not only cognitive disabilities, but also high rates of criminal and sexualized behavior, depression, suicide, and parental neglect of children (Kelly, Day, & Streissguth, 2000). Clearly, there is no one-to-one correspondence between prenatal alcohol exposure and these later difficulties. But alcohol exposure and early disruptions in cognition, attention, and social behavior, if combined with unresponsive or harsh parenting, might lead to a maladaptive lifestyle later on.

One point is clear: No one has proven that alcohol consumption is *safe* for the fetus. The best way for mothers to protect their baby is to stop drinking when they think they *might* become pregnant. Women who have a drinking problem should get help *before* they become pregnant.

Nicotine Whether the nicotine in cigarettes during pregnancy places a child at risk for delays in cognitive and social and emotional development is not clear. It *is* clear that women who smoke during pregnancy have a higher risk than nonsmokers of miscarriage, preterm deliveries, and small, low-birth-weight, and otherwise compromised babies (Schuetze & Eiden, 2005; Zaskind & Gingras, 2006). The March of Dimes (2008) estimates that if all pregnant women in the United States stopped smoking, stillbirths would be reduced by 11 percent and newborn deaths by 5 percent. Staying smoke-free after a baby is born is equally important. Newborns whose parents smoke have higher rates of respiratory illnesses (such as bronchitis and pneumonia) and ear infections, and they may be at increased risk of developing asthma (March of Dimes, 2008).

Illicit Drugs Illegal or not, heroin, cocaine, marijuana, ecstasy, and other psychoactive drugs are part of our culture. Americans of all socioeconomic levels—in suburbs, small towns, and upscale urban neighborhoods—use "street" drugs.

But in most cases, drug use is usually embedded in a web of problems. As often as not, addicted mothers use multiple drugs (including alcohol and tobacco), continue using drugs after their baby is born, neglect their health and obtain little prenatal care, live in poverty, suffer from mental illness, and are neglectful as parents (Mayes & Truman, 2002). Children of addicts may be exposed to violence, abandonment, and homelessness. As infants, they often go through frequent separations, short-term foster home placements, and/or moves. In short, it is difficult to separate the effects of prenatal exposure to a drug from other, related conditions.

Heroin Babies born to heroin-addicted mothers are themselves addicted. Within one to three days after birth, they go into withdrawal, including tremors, irritability, vomiting, diarrhea, perspiration, and sleep disturbances. Newborns also go through withdrawal when the mother is taking methadone, an oral medication used to wean adults from heroin. Many are born at low birth weights. Because heroin addicts usually inject the drug, and may share needles, these babies are also at risk for infection with HIV. Over the long term, heroin may be associated with lower IQ, attention disorders, and behavioral problems (Batshaw & Conlon, 1997). Most likely these problems also intensify with the interaction of prenatal exposure to the drug and ongoing exposure to the drug culture.

Cocaine Cocaine is of special concern (Jones, 2006). Abuse of cocaine (sometimes in the crystallized form of crack) has devastating effects on the fetus and newborn in the short term (Singer et al., 1999; Singer et al., 2005) and on the developing child in the long term (Arendt et al., 2004; Bada et al., 2007; Bendersky et al., 2003; Dennis et al., 2006). In addition, cocaine use is widespread; in inner cities, as many as 10 to 18 percent of pregnant women use this drug (Schama et al., 1998).

Cocaine is a central nervous system stimulant that interferes with the reabsorption of neurochemicals associated with pleasure and movement. The "high," or euphoria, cocaine users experience is the result of constant stimulation. And cocaine passes quickly from the mother to the fetus. Cocaine increases the risk of miscarriage, stillbirths, and premature births. Prenatal exposure to cocaine has been linked to low birth weights, small head circumference and length, irritability, hypersensitivity, and lack of muscle and mood control, as well as an increased risk of **sudden infant death syndrome** (SIDS)—an unexplained death, usually during the night, of an infant under one year old (McKenna et al., 1994).

sudden infant death syndrome
Unexplained death, usually during the night, of an infant under one year old.

The long-term effects of cocaine are not well known. Some research suggests that prenatal cocaine exposure results in small but significant problems with cognitive development and language. To clarify this picture, Linda Mayes, Marc Bornstein, and their colleagues conducted a series of developmental studies of infants exposed to cocaine in utero (Mayes et al., 1993, 2003). Compared with infants exposed to drugs (but not cocaine) as well as infants not exposed to drugs, cocaine-exposed infants scored low on tests designed to assess reflexes, motor skills, and general responsiveness at three and six months. In particular, they had problems with mood control, becoming highly distressed when presented with something new (Mayes et al., 1996).

The problems may be attributed to cocaine exposure alone, but they also may be complicated by the behavior of cocaine-using mothers. The researchers also studied face-to-face interactions between cocaine-abusing mothers and their infants at three and six months (Mayes et al., 1997). Compared with other mothers, cocaine-abusing mothers were less attentive to their infants, often looking away, distracting rather than responding to the infant, or simply withdrawing. Thus, unresponsive parenting may have a compounding effect on these children. Some good news is that discontinuing cocaine may improve child development. In another study, 40 percent of children whose mothers abused cocaine during pregnancy and continued to do so after the baby was born had IQ scores of 85 or lower; among children whose mothers stopped using cocaine after they were born, only 15 percent scored this low (Scherling, 1994).

Environmental Toxins Environmental pollutants pose health risks for everyone, but unborn babies are especially vulnerable (Talan, 2007). Of the millions of chemical mixtures found in homes and workplaces, a few are known to be teratogens: lead, mercury, DDT (an insecticide), and PCBs (polychlorinated biphenyls, once used widely in manufacturing). The fetus can be exposed when a pregnant woman inhales, consumes, or absorbs these substances through her skin. Exposure to these pollutants can lead to lower birth weights, premature birth, small head circumference, subdued reflexes, and long-term problems with memory and learning (Eskenazi et al., 2006).

Prenatal exposure to air pollution also affects cognitive development. An ongoing study has followed 200 New York City children from before birth to age three (Perera et al., 2006). The researchers focused on polycyclic aromatic hydrocarbons (PAHs), a common byproduct of combustion engines, power plants, residential heating, and smoking. At age three, children whose mothers were exposed to high levels of PAH during pregnancy were compared with children whose mothers were exposed to lower levels. The high exposed children scored lower on mental tests and were more than twice as likely to score behind their peers in psychomotor development. Airborne concentrations of PAH could be reduced by antipollution technology that is currently available, greater energy efficiency, and use of alternative energy sources. But as things stand, pollution is a regular feature of the inner city. Poor children are more likely to be affected by PAH than are better-off suburban children.

DDT, PCBs, and lead paint (the most common source of lead poisoning) have been banned in the United States since the 1970s. But residues are still found in the soil, water, air, and (especially lead) in older houses. Pregnant women can protect themselves and the fetus by having their home tested, not drinking water from wells or old lead pipes, and wearing protective gloves when cleaning.

Fish are the leading source of mercury. Mercury entering the environment as industrial pollution is deposited into the water by rain, is converted by bacteria into a more dangerous form (methylmercury), and builds up in the fatty tissue of fish. PCBs may also be found in fish caught in contaminated streams, lakes, and coastal areas. Pregnant women can learn which fish are safe and which aren't from www.epa.gov.

The Importance of Timing

The impact of outside influences—from diseases to pollutants—depends on timing and duration, on when the exposure occurs and how long it lasts. Different body parts develop according to different timetables. Damage to the fetus is most severe during the time an organ or limb is developing fastest (Bornstein, 1989). For example, in the 1950s and 1960s, European doctors prescribed the sedative thalidomide for women who were suffering from morning sickness. Women who took thalidomide during weeks six or seven of pregnancy, the period when limbs are developing, gave birth to babies with arm and leg buds rather than fully developed limbs (Newman, 1985). Taken at other times, thalidomide did not cause that damage. (Thalidomide was not approved for use in the United States.) As in this example, the effects of a teratogen depend as much or more on timing as on the nature of the teratogen itself. Two different

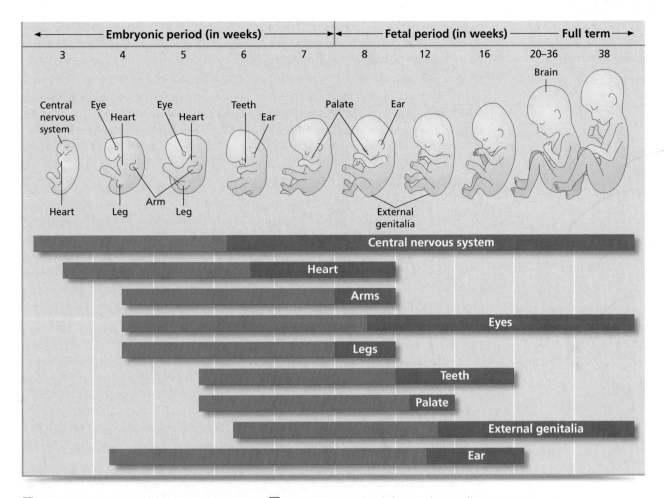

Period when major abnormality may occur   **Period when minor defect or abnormality may occur**

FIGURE **3.3**

Sensitive Periods in Prenatal Development

Exposure to teratogens during prenatal development can be detrimental and result in major defects in the structure or function of organs and systems, especially if the exposure occurs during certain "sensitive periods." The green bars indicate the period of time in which the embryo or fetus is most susceptible to outside influences; the purple bars represent the time in which teratogenic effects might be less serious. Several structures, like the central nervous system and the eyes, remain sensitive to outside influences for most of prenatal development.

Source: This figure was published in *Before we are born: Essentials of embryology and birth defects,* 5/e by K.L. Moore & T.V.N. Persaud, Copyright Elsevier 1998. Reprinted by permission of Elsevier Ltd.

toxins may have similar effects at the same phase of prenatal development, although neither affects development at other stages.

A **sensitive period** is the time during which the developing child is most vulnerable to teratogens (see Figure 3.3). During a sensitive period, outside influences—even if present for a short time—may alter anatomy or function, often irreversibly (Bailey, Bruer, Symons, & Lichtman, 2001; Bornstein, 1989). But body parts that develop earlier or later remain largely unaffected. The embryonic stage is one of high vulnerability because this is when the major organ systems develop. In general, the older fetus is less vulnerable, although oxygen supply is vital at this stage because the fetal brain has developed and is dependent on an oxygen supply.

The impact of environmental factors may be immediately apparent, as when newborns whose mothers use heroin go through withdrawal. Or it may be chronic, such

sensitive period A time in development during which the organism is especially vulnerable to experience.

sleeper effect An outcome that is displaced in time from a cause.

as the learning and behavioral problems in children with FAS. Some experiences have **sleeper effects**. For example, examinations of Dutch military recruits found that young men who were born during the great famine in World War II and experienced chronic malnutrition in utero had elevated rates of schizophrenia—suggesting that severe malnutrition caused subtle brain damage that did not emerge until later in development (Hoek, Brown, & Susser, 1999). In addition, exposure to teratogens may be ongoing. Infants whose parents smoke are at risk for bronchitis, pneumonia, and asthma.

Pregnancy and Parents-to-Be

The experience of pregnancy depends on timing, too. Chronological age is important, as is where parents stand in terms of their educational and career plans, whether they feel able to support and care for a baby, how committed they are to each other, their relationships with their own families, and, above all, whether they want to become parents at this time.

In the first trimester of pregnancy, a woman tends to concentrate on her own well-being and taking care of herself. In the second trimester, she becomes more concerned about the welfare of her developing child. In the third trimester, she begins to experience the fetus as *real* and to bond with her baby (Heinicke, 2002).

Pregnancy poses a series of social and emotional challenges for a woman (Barnard & Solchany, 2002). Learning that she is pregnant for the first time marks the beginning of a transformation, from her identity as a woman to a new identity as a mother. Often it is a period of introspection. Her relationship with her own mother can change. Her mother's advice (whether sought or imposed) can make a woman feel dependent, almost as if she were a child again. Yet, at the same time, she begins to see her mother as a peer and her-

INTERIM SUMMARY 3.3

Protecting the Fetus	
Guidelines for a Healthy Pregnancy	■ Eat well. ■ Don't smoke, drink, or use drugs. ■ See the obstetrician regularly. ■ Remember—the mother's blood flows into the fetus's veins through the placenta to the umbilical cord. The placenta acts as a filter, but it does not protect against the transmission of all harmful substances.
The Well-Being of the Fetus	Maternal characteristics play a role: ■ The mother's age ■ Diet and nutrition ■ Stress Outside influences also play a role: ■ Teratogens are substances that can have a negative impact on fetal development and possibly result in birth defects or even death. ■ They include viruses (rubella and HIV), drugs (nicotine, alcohol, and illicit drugs such as heroin and cocaine) and environmental pollutants (lead, mercury, DDT, and PCBs). ■ A **sensitive period** is the time during which the developing child is most vulnerable to teratogens. An example if the embryonic stage, a time when the major organ systems develop. ■ In general, older fetuses are less vulnerable, though oxygen supply is vital at this stage.

self as another mother. She may have feelings of loss: of her freedom and independence; her one-to-one relationship with her partner; and her youthful body and appearance. In addition, she may reexamine her feelings of competency, in light of a new and dependent person entering her life. Feeling that she made a choice can relieve these anxieties.

For couples, adaptation to pregnancy is multilayered (Heinicke, 2002). Parents-to-be cope best when they believe that a positive, sustained relationship is possible (based largely on their memories of their parents). Equally important is a positive experience of their partnership, including agreement on roles (who does what) and openness in communication. Finally, how couples feel about pregnancy and parenthood depends on how they feel about themselves and whether they feel that being a couple, soon to be a family (or larger one), enhances or interferes with their personal goals. (For a summary of this section, see "Interim Summary 3.3: Protecting the Fetus.")

BIRTH

Birth can be seen as one transition in the ongoing *process* of development. There is little change in the way the central nervous system functions or in the baby's movements after delivery, for example. Though attached to the mother's bloodstream through the umbilical cord and placenta, the baby has been developing his or her own blood chemistry throughout gestation. Like fetuses, newborns depend on others—for example, to regulate their body temperature. They lack both the insulation (subcutaneous body fat) and neural capacity to do this on their own and so rely on their caregivers. Yet birth is also an *event*. Suddenly, the baby has to breathe and obtain nourishment for him- or herself. After months of floating in the warm, dark, liquid, quiet of the womb, the baby is confronted with gravity, hunger, and totally new sights, sounds, and sensations.

© Jonathan Nourok/Getty Images

New mothers typically get to hold their newborn baby as soon as the infant is delivered.

Labor and Delivery

Birth takes place nine months after conception, give or take a week or two. (The average date is 280 days after conception, at least for first-time European American, middle-income mothers who have spontaneous, uncomplicated deliveries [Mittendorf et al., 1990].) We still do not know exactly why the birth process starts when it does, which explains why doctors cannot give a mother-to-be the exact date. What we do know is that the mother's pituitary gland releases the hormone **oxytocin**, which in turn triggers uterine contractions. The uterus is actually a muscle that expands to accommodate the growing fetus but keeps the cervix (the narrow opening between the uterus and vagina) closed during pregnancy. Labor consists of involuntary contractions—at first in widely spaced intervals, then more and more frequently—that push the baby into the world.

In the first stage of labor, the uterine muscle pulls and tugs to open the cervix to the four inches (ten to twelve centimeters) required for the baby to pass through. In the second stage, contractions push the baby's head, and then body, into the birth canal. After the head and a shoulder have emerged, the rest of the body slips through. In the third stage, contractions expel the placenta, fetal membranes, and the remainder of the umbilical cord. At first appearance, newborns are red and battered, with misshapen

oxytocin A maternal pituitary gland hormone that triggers uterine contractions.

heads as a result of being squeezed through the birth canal. These effects are temporary. For first births, a normal delivery may take sixteen to seventeen hours. But some mothers and babies need additional help.

Birth Complications and Controversies

Just as births don't occur on schedule, so they don't always go according to plan. Complications may require medical intervention.

In the week or two before birth, most fetuses shift into position for birth, with their head against the cervix. But some are positioned with their feet or buttocks first (a *breech* position) or cross-wise (the *hammock* position). These positions complicate and prolong delivery.

anoxia Cutoff of the supply of oxygen through the umbilical cord before the baby can breathe independently.

One of the most serious birth complications is **anoxia**: The supply of oxygen through the umbilical cord is cut off before the baby can breathe independently. This may happen because the baby is in an unusual position for birth, the umbilical cord is pinched or twisted, or the placenta pulls away from the wall of the uterus (*placental abruption*) or blocks the baby's exit from the womb (*placenta previa*). A brief interruption in oxygen supply is not usually a problem, but long-lasting anoxia may cause brain damage and related problems, including seizures, cerebral palsy, and mental retardation.

cesarean section (or C-section) Method of delivering a baby surgically through an incision in the mother's abdomen.

If a baby is threatened, physicians can perform a **cesarean section** (or **C-section**), delivering the baby surgically through an incision in the mother's abdomen. C-sections are also used when the baby's head is very large and/or the mother's pelvis is narrow, to prevent infection by HIV or another disease, and sometimes when the mother is having twins, triplets, or more. A cesarean section is major surgery and, like all surgery, carries risks—in this case for the baby as well as the mother. Some evidence indicates that the anesthesia given to the mother makes babies listless and prone to breathing problems. Critics hold that many cesareans are performed for the mother's or doctor's convenience, not because of medical necessity. The United States has the highest rate of cesarean sections in the world: between 20 and 25 percent of all births.

In addition, a woman may need help dealing with the pain of childbirth. The use of anesthesia during labor and delivery is controversial. Some babies whose mothers use anesthesia score below average on a range of tests and are less active and alert than other infants. However, the differences are small and noticeable only for the first few days after birth. And newer, local anesthesia—such as the epidural block, which numbs the woman's body only from the waist down—appear effective in reducing labor pain without harmful consequences for the infant (Albaladejo, Bouaziz, & Benhamou, 1998).

At the same time, natural childbirth has grown in popularity as women—and men—are seeking ways to "demedicalize" childbirth. One of the oldest approaches is the Lamaze method. The couple attends childbirth classes in which the mother learns how to relax and to concentrate on breathing and pushing the baby into the world, and the father learns how to be her coach, supporting her physically and psychologically.

Newborns at Risk

Even term babies, who enjoyed a full forty weeks' gestation, need a few days to adjust to life outside of the womb. Breathing and sucking are automatic reflexes, but newborns have frequent bouts of hiccups from doing both at once. Very small babies face more difficult challenges. Of the approximately 4 million babies born in the United States each year, about 12.5% are born too early (MacDorman et al., 2007). Babies are considered **preterm** if born before the thirty-seventh week of pregnancy, and *very* preterm if born before thirty-two weeks of gestation. Less than five and a half pounds (2,500 grams) is a **low birth weight**, and less than two and a half pounds (1,500 grams) is a *very* low birth weight. (See Figure 3.4.) Not surprisingly, premature birth and low birth weight often go together.

preterm Babies born before the thirty-seventh week of pregnancy.

low birth weight Babies born less than 5.5 pounds (2,500 grams).

Babies may be born preterm for a number of reasons. For example, the mother may be unable to carry a baby to term because of abnormalities in her uterus or cervix. In other

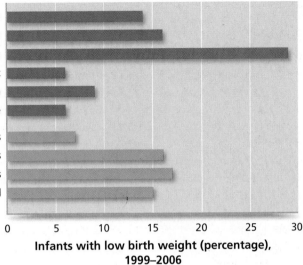

Infants with low birth weight (percentage),
1999–2006

FIGURE 3.4

Comparing Rates of Low Birth Weight Around the World

The top part of this UNICEF graph shows the percentages of infants who were born with low birth weights between 1999 and 2006 in six world regions (South Asia has the highest percentage, followed by Africa; East Asia, Latin America, and Europe have the lowest). The bottom part of the graph compares three levels of country development (not surprisingly, industrialized countries have a lower percentage than developing and least developed countries). The world rate is about 15 percent.
Source: UNICEF (2007).

cases, the mother's reproductive system may be immature: Young teens have higher rates of preterm births than other age groups (Bornstein & Putnick, 2007; Bornstein et al., 2006). Or the mother may not have had enough time to recuperate from a previous pregnancy (a birth interval of one and a half to two years is recommended). When the mother's or fetus's health is in danger, physicians may induce labor by breaking the amniotic sac and giving the mother synthetic oxytocin. Finally, disadvantaged living conditions— including poverty, malnutrition, and inadequate medical care—are linked to preterm births. So are smoking, drinking alcohol, and using drugs, which often go together.

Babies who are only slightly premature face little danger. But very small babies need help to survive. For these babies, medical complications are common. Preterm babies often suffer from **respiratory distress syndrome** (RDS) because their lungs do not produce enough *surfactin*, a soapy substance that helps to carry oxygen into, and carbon dioxide out of, the lungs. They may develop a chronic lung disease characterized by thickening and inflammation of the walls of the lungs, which reduces the amount of oxygen the baby can inhale (Vanhatalo et al., 1994). Because their immune systems are immature, preterm infants are particularly vulnerable to infection. Their nervous system may not be developed enough to perform basic functions such as sucking, so they may need to be fed intravenously or via a nasogastric tube. Very preterm, very low-birth-weight infants are in danger of brain complications, such as hemorrhages. Low-birth-weight infants are placed in an incubator or "isolette"—an antiseptic, temperature-controlled, covered crib with a high concentration of oxygen—for as long as forty-five or fifty days.

Thanks to medical and technological advances in intensive neonatal care, the prognosis for small babies has improved dramatically (Bernbaum & Batshaw, 1997). In 1960, the survival rate for *all* preterm babies was less than 50 percent. Today, more than nine in ten infants with birth weights under 5.5 pounds (2,500 grams), two-thirds of infants between

respiratory distress syndrome A condition common to preterm babies whose lungs do not produce enough surfactin that helps to carry oxygen into and carbon dioxide out of the lungs.

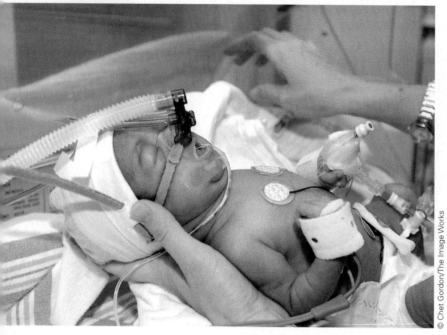

© Chet Gordon/The Image Works

Preterm newborns, like this three-day-old baby, need all the help they can get. In addition to medical paraphernalia, they get much-needed human contact in the neonatal intensive care unit (NICU).

1.65 and 2.2. pounds (750 and 1,000 grams), and one-third of infants between 1.1 and 1.65 pounds (500 and 750 grams) survive. However, their long-term prognosis is not altogether positive. Very preterm, very low-birth-weight infants are significantly more likely than term infants to have low IQs and developmental and learning disabilities later on (Skenkin, Starr, & Deary, 2004). But low birth weight is not the only reason for potential problems; gestational age at birth is a vital factor as well.

In the United States, a large proportion of very small babies are born to women who come from disadvantaged homes and return to these environments when they leave the hospital. One study of infants who weighed just over two pounds, on average, at birth, and were judged to be borderline delayed, found that most showed improvement in early childhood and scored within the normal range on intelligence tests at age eight. Children who improved the most lived in two-parent families, with mothers who had higher education, and had not suffered significant brain damage (Ment et al., 2003). Clearly, the caregiving environment made a difference.

Infant Assessment

How do parents know whether their newborn is healthy and normal? Hospital personnel give the newborn a test in the delivery room, one minute and again five minutes after birth (see Table 3.1). The **Apgar test**, named for its originator Virginia Apgar (1953), gives a baby a score of 0, 1, or 2 on each of five scales, which are easy to remember because of the acronym: **A**ppearance, **P**ulse, **G**rimace, **A**ctivity, and **R**espiration. If the score is 7 or higher, the infant is not normally in danger; if the score is below 4, he or she is in critical condition.

Apgar test   A delivery room test that assesses a newborn with a score of 0, 1, or 2 on each of five scales: **A**ppearance, **P**ulse, **G**rimace, **A**ctivity, and **R**espiration.

TABLE 3.1 The Apgar Test*

	SIGN	0	1	2
Appearance	Color of baby's body and extremities	Body is pale or blue	Body is normal color but hands and feet are blue	Body including hands and feet are nice and pink
Pulse	Baby's heart rate	No pulse	Less than 100 beats per minute	100 beats per minute or higher
Grimace	Baby's reflex response to suctioning with a bulb syringe	No response	Grimace	Active cry
Activity	Baby's muscle tone	Limp or no movement	Some movement of arms and legs	Actively moving arms and legs
Respiration	Baby's breathing	Not breathing	Slow or irregular	Breathing well/strong cry

*This test gives a baby a score of 0, 1, or 2 on each of five scales—Appearance, Pulse, Grimace, Activity, and Respiration.
Source: Apgar (1953).

INTERIM SUMMARY **3.4**

Birth

Birth Takes Place Nine Months After Conception, Give or Take a Week or Two	■ In the first stage of labor, the uterine muscle pulls and tugs to open the cervix to the four inches required for the baby to pass through. ■ In the second stage, contractions push the baby's head, and then body, into the birth canal. After the head and a shoulder have emerged from the mother, the rest of the body slips through. ■ In the third stage, contractions expel the placenta, fetal membranes, and the remainder of the umbilical cord.
Birth Complications	■ The baby may be in a breech (fetus positioned with buttocks first) or hammock position (fetus positioned crosswise). ■ The mother's pelvis may be too narrow or the baby's head too big. ■ The baby may have **anoxia**—the supply of oxygen through the umbilical cord is cut off before the baby can breathe independently.
Cesarean Sections, Anesthesia, and Natural Childbirth	■ Physicians can perform a **cesarean section** (or **C-section**) if warranted, delivering the baby surgically through an incision in the mother's abdomen. ■ The use of anesthesia is controversial, though local anesthesia such as the epidural is effective without harming the infant. ■ Natural childbirth is popular. The Lamaze method concentrates on the mother's breathing, with a partner acting as a supportive "coach."
Preterm and Low-Birth-Weight Babies	■ Babies are considered **preterm** if born before the 37th week of pregnancy, and **very** preterm if born before 32 weeks of gestation. ■ Less than 5.5 pounds is a **low birth weight**, and less than 2.5 pounds is a **very** low birth weight. ■ Preterm babies often suffer from **respiratory distress syndrome** (RDS). ■ They are particularly vulnerable to infection. ■ Their nervous system may not be developed enough to perform basic functions such as sucking, so they may need to be fed intravenously. ■ Very preterm, very low-birth-weight infants are in danger of brain complications, such as hemorrhages.
Assessing Infants—the Apgar and Neonatal Behavioral Assessment Scale (NBAS) tests	■ The Apgar test is administered 1 minute and 5 minutes after birth and gives a baby a score of 0, 1, or 2 on each of five scales—**A**ppearance, **P**ulse, **G**rimace, **A**ctivity, and **R**espiration. ■ A score of 7 or higher means the infant is not normally in danger; if the score is below 4, he or she is in critical condition. ■ The NBAS uses reflexes and social interaction to assess the newborn's overall well-being.

Neonatal Behavioral Assessment Scale A test for newborns that uses reflexes and social interaction to assess their overall well-being, including motor capabilities, state changes, attention, and central nervous system stability.

The Apgar indicates if there is a need for immediate intervention, but there are questions it cannot answer. The **Neonatal Behavioral Assessment Scale** (NBAS; Brazelton & Nugent, 1995) uses reflexes and social interaction to assess the newborn's overall well-being, including motor capabilities, state changes (irritability, excitability, and ability to calm down), attention (alertness and responsiveness), and central nervous system stability.

Although the Apgar and the NBAS have been used widely for many years, they raise questions. Which test or test session represents the baby best? Do we want to measure average behavior or best performance? Is it better to assess spontaneous or elicited behavior? Even with these questions, newborn screening is a valuable tool for identifying infants who need immediate attention (Meisels & Atkins-Burnett, 2006; Zuckerman et al., 2004). (For a summary of this section, see "Interim Summary 3.4: Birth.")

SUMMING UP AND LOOKING AHEAD

This chapter has discussed some of the most rapid and dramatic developments in the human lifespan that occur in the first nine months. The stages of prenatal development were examined, and sex differentiation and predispositions were discussed. We also explored contemporary technologies to monitor prenatal development and to protect the fetus. Finally, we discussed the delivery process and the screening tools that are used to assess newborns.

A newborn changes from moment to moment, slipping from an alert into a drowsy state (or the reverse) in a heartbeat. How does this new human being begin to adapt to his or her new environment? This is the subject of "Physical Development in Infancy."

HERE'S WHAT YOU SHOULD KNOW

Did You Get It?

After reading this chapter, you should understand the following:

- What happens during the zygote, embryo, and fetal periods of prenatal development
- What is involved in sex differentiation and the four stages of prenatal sexual development
- Genetic counseling, genetic abnormalities, and types of genetic and prenatal tests

- What/who influences the well-being of the fetus
- What happens at birth, possible birth complications, and preterm and low-weight babies
- Infant assessment tests—the APGAR test and Neonatal Behavioral Assessment Scale

Important Terms and Concepts

AIDS (p. 78)
amniocentesis (p. 75)
amniotic sac (p. 67)
anencelapathy (p. 78)
anoxia (p. 86)
Apgar test (p. 88)
artificial insemination (p. 66)
cesarean section (C-section) (p. 86)
chorionic villi sampling (p. 75)
ectoderm (p. 67)
endoderm (p. 67)

fertility drugs (p. 66)
fertilization (p. 65)
fetal alcohol effects (p. 80)
fetal alcohol syndrome (p. 79)
gametes (p. 66)
genetic counseling (p. 74)
gestation (p. 64)
HIV (p. 78)
implantation (p. 65)
infertility (p. 65)
in vitro fertilization (p. 66)
karyotype (p. 74)
low birth weight (p. 86)

mesoderm (p. 67)
multifactoral disorders (p. 73)
Neonatal Behavioral Assessment Scale (p. 90)
neurogenesis (p. 67)
ovulation (p. 64)
ovum (or ova) (p. 64)
oxytocin (p. 85)
placenta (p. 65)
preimplantation genetic diagnosis (p. 75)
preterm (p. 86)
quickening (p. 68)

respiratory distress syndrome (p. 87)
rubella (p. 78)
sensitive period (p. 83)
sleeper effect (p. 84)
spina bifida (p. 78)
sudden infant death syndrome (p. 81)
surrogate mother (p. 66)
temperament (p. 69)
teratogen (p. 78)
Turner's syndrome (p. 70)
ultrasound imaging (p. 71)
zygote (p. 65)

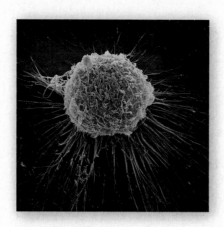

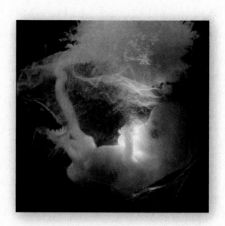

CHAPTER 1
The Study of Child Development

- Developmental research seeks to *describe* what people are like at different ages and how they change as a result of age, *explain* what causes such change, *predict* what an individual will be like based on past and present characteristics, and *intervene,* or use this knowledge to improve children's lives.

- Classical theories of development include psychoanalytic theory, learning theory, and cognitive-developmental theory.

- Contemporary theories of development include the ecological perspective, the sociocultural perspective, behavioral genetics, the evolutionary perspective and dynamic systems theory.

- The scientific method is a systematic, step-by-step procedure for testing ideas. Researchers use three main ways to gather information about people: observational research, self-reports, and standardized tests.

- Most developmental research uses one of three research designs: case studies, correlational studies, and experiments.

- The three basic strategies for studying development over time are longitudinal studies, cross-sectional studies, and accelerated longitudinal design.

CHAPTER 2
Nature with Nurture

- There are four main perspectives on nature and nurture: (1) development is driven by nature (nativism), (2) development is driven by nurture, (3) development is part nature, part nurture (heritability), and (4) development results from the interplay of nature and nurture (epigenesis).

- A **gene** is a segment of the chromosome that controls a particular aspect of the production of a specific protein. An individual's observable characteristics and behavior, or **phenotype,** depend on the genotype and environment. The outcome of the merger of the mother's and father's genes depends primarily on which genes from each parent are matched with the other's, referred to as **gene-gene interaction**.

- The environment or context plays an important role in development: Bronfenbrenner was the pioneer of the ecological perspective, which organizes the way we think about the contexts of development.

- There are four main types of interplay between genetic and environmental influences: (1) environmental effects on gene expression, (2) environmental effects on heritability, (3) gene-environment interaction, and (4).gene-environment correlation.

CHAPTER 3
Prenatal Development and Birth

- The period from conception to birth takes about 280 days. There are three prenatal periods: zygote, embryo, and fetus.

- Prenatal sexual development can be divided into four stages: (1) unisex, (2) physiological sex differences emerge, (3) external genitals form, and (4) testosterone inhibits the rhythmic cycles of the hypothalamus and the pituitary, which regulate female ovulation.

- Most genetic disorders are carried on a recessive gene. Some recessive gene disorders are sex linked. Prenatal tests screen for certain disorders. These tests include preimplantation genetic diagnosis, amniocentesis, and chorionic villi sampling.

- Maternal characteristics such as age and stress and outside influences (teratogens, viruses, and so on) play a role in the well-being of a fetus.

Infancy

Physical Development in Infancy

Did your parents keep a record of your height, either in a baby diary or as notched lines on a doorjamb? Count Philibert Guéneau de Montbeillard, who lived during the 1700s, did. In April of 1759, he began a series of measurements of his son's growth. Although these data were gathered 250 years ago, their general pattern resembles that obtained using modern scientific measurement.

Count de Montbeillard not only recorded his son's absolute height, but also plotted how much his son's height changed at each age. In this way, he showed just how rapid growth is during infancy. Look at the right panel of Figure 4.1. During the first year of life, the count's son was growing at the rate of about 8.5 inches (22 centimeters) per year. By the end of infancy, his rate of growth had slowed to about about 2.5 inches (6 centimeters) annually. Growth once again becomes rapid as children enter puberty, as we shall see in "Physical Development in Adolescence," but it is never as rapid as in infancy.

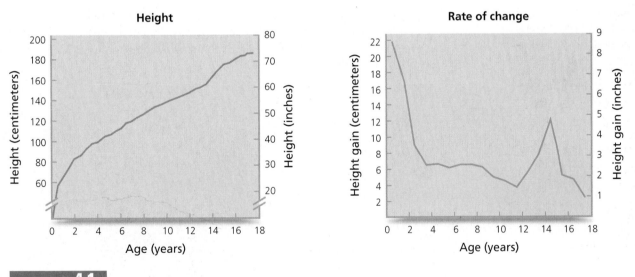

By the end of the first year of postnatal life, the average American child weighs about twenty pounds (nine kilograms) and is about thirty inches long (seventy-six centimeters)—more than double his or her height and weight at birth. (If that isn't impressive, just think about what you'd look like a year from now at twice your height and weight!) In this chapter, we look at physical growth and development during the first two years of life—not just at changes in the infant's size, but also at changes in the infant's brain, physical capabilities, and ability to perceive the world.

PHYSICAL GROWTH

Physical growth, which is easy to observe and quantify, tells us a lot about whether a child is developing normally. If a child suddenly stops growing, it is a sign for worry. That's one reason that a pediatric exam always includes an assessment of the child's height and weight. Even now, when you visit the doctor, he or she asks you to step on the scale.

Physical growth also has implications for development in many other psychological domains (Thelen & Smith, 2006). For example, when children start to walk, their parents change their own behavior in many ways, which in turn affect the child's cognitive and socioemotional development. Although this chapter separates physical development from cognitive and socioemotional development, this is just a way of organizing information. In the real world, all three domains of development are closely linked.

General Principles of Physical Growth

Studies of physical growth have revealed important general principles that apply to other realms of child development, including directionality, independence of systems, and canalization.

directionality A principle of development that refers to how body proportions change; *cephalocaudal* means advancing from head to tail, and *proximodistal* means progressing from the center of the body outward.

- *Directionality.* Development includes the principle of **directionality**, a term that refers to how body proportions change; generally, change is *cephalocaudal*—that is, development advances from "head to tail," as shown in Figure 4.2. Many other

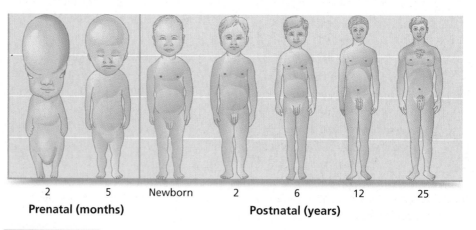

| 2 | 5 | Newborn | 2 | 6 | 12 | 25 |
Prenatal (months)   **Postnatal (years)**

FIGURE 4.2

Changes in Body Proportions from Prenatal Development Through Adulthood

The human body develops from head to tail and from the center outward. Although a fetus appears to have an abnormally large head (in fact, the head is about the same length as the rest of the body in early prenatal development), over time as the rest of the body grows, the head becomes much smaller relative to the rest of the body.

Source: Adapted from W.J. Robbins, S. Brody, A.G. Hogan, C.M. Jackson & C.W. Green (eds.), *Growth.* Copyright © 1928. Reprinted by permission of the publisher, Yale University Press.

aspects of development also proceed top-down rather than bottom-up. The eyes mature earlier than the legs, and babies can look around sooner than they begin to walk. Physical development is also *proximodistal*—it progresses from the center of the body outward. Prenatally, the heart begins to beat long before fingers can be seen, just as postnatally, the child has control over large arm movements before finer hand ones.

- *Independence of systems.* The **independence of systems** principle asserts that not all parts of the body develop along the same timetable. Figure 4.3 plots growth for three major components of the body. Some are developed at or soon after birth; others do not develop until much later. For example, by the time an infant is two years old, the nervous system has reached more than half of its mature form, whereas secondary sexual characteristics (such as pubic or underarm hair) do not appear until puberty.

- *Canalization.* Many systems in the body are genetically programmed to follow a standard and highly structured course of development, like water flowing in a canal (see "Nature with Nurture"). If something throws development off course, genetic forces make a correction as soon as a change is possible. That's **canalization**. A well-known case study illustrates this nicely. The child was growing normally during his first year, but just before his first birthday the child became sick for approximately one year. During this time the child "fell out" of his normal and expected growth pattern. Following recovery, however, he returned to his projected growth path, so that by his fourth birthday he was again well within the normal range. This *catch-up* illustrates the principle of canalization (Prader, Tanner, & von Harnack, 1963).

Catch-up also seems to occur in cognitive development. For example, Ronald Wilson (1978) studied the canalization of intelligence in relation to low birth weight. He observed identical twins who had unequal birth weights, one normal and one considerably below normal. (Babies born at a low birth weight are usually at risk for poor cognitive outcomes.) Wilson found that during development the babies' shared genotype prevailed over their different birth weights. Although one twin was born at a distinct disadvantage, by six years of age the children's IQs were almost identical.

In short, physical development isn't just growth; it is directed, multifaceted, and sometimes self-correcting. However, even if the overall blueprint for physical development may be canalized, individuals (and contexts) vary.

Norms and Individual Differences

In studying physical development, scientists consider both norms and individual differences. **Norms** represent average outcomes on some characteristic. Take physical height. Very few adults are either four or seven feet tall; many more stand between five and six feet. This norm or average tells us how height is distributed in the population and provides guidance for pediatricians to determine whether a child is developing normally. But there is a wide variation in **individual differences** within the normal range. For example, infants first walk and talk at about one year of age on average. But the range of individual differences in both achievements is considerable. Some chil-

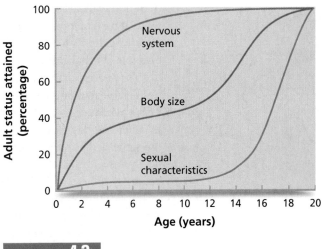

FIGURE 4.3

Differential Growth Rates in the Human Body

Not all body parts and systems develop at the same rate. The nervous system develops most rapidly in the first five years of life, while sexual characteristics remain fairly stagnant until puberty is reached in early adolescence. Body size changes quickly from birth to age three before slowing down, but rapid growth occurs again right around puberty until full adult height is reached in late adolescence.

independence of systems A principle of development that asserts that different parts of the body develop along different timetables.

canalization Development tends to follow, and return to, a normative course.

norms Average outcomes on a characteristic.

individual differences The variation among individuals on a characteristic.

dren first walk at ten months, others at eighteen months; some children say their first word at nine months, others not until twenty-nine months. Parents often worry unnecessarily about "late" developers. All normal individuals walk and talk eventually—an example of canalization. Moreover, the age at which children achieve these milestones does not necessarily predict future skills. The infant who doesn't take her first steps until eighteen months may be the first across the finish line in a race at age six.

It's also the case that development can follow many different paths to the same or to different ends. Some children may develop at different rates but eventually reach the same height. Others may develop at the same rate but stop growing at different heights. And different children may develop at different rates and reach different heights. All these paths illustrate individual differences.

Physical growth is strongly influenced by larger genetic and cultural factors. If you were born to a Pygmy family in Cameroon in Africa, you and your siblings might develop at different rates, but your genetic potential as a Pygmy would limit your ultimate height, no matter how fast you grew. (The average height of adult Pygmies is four feet.) Nutritional conditions, governed by culture, are also important. Before World War II, for example, Japanese diets were restricted to rice and small amounts of meat, fish, and vegetables. As a result, the average height of Japanese individuals at that time (including many great-grandparents still alive today) was diminutive. Since World War II the Japanese diet has changed (in terms of protein and other nutrients), altering average height among Japanese dramatically. A contemporary Japanese teenager would have seemed supersized in 1940.

At birth as well as through the first years of development, infants born in richer countries tend to be healthier, heavier, and longer than infants born in poorer countries. Furthermore, within wealthy countries (such as the United States), children born into poverty grow more slowly than those born to prosperity, and they do not reach equivalent levels of height and weight (Schroeder et al., 1995; Tanner, 1990). (For a summary of this section, see "Interim Summary 4.1: Physical Growth.")

We see the same interaction between genetic inheritance and environmental conditions in the development of the central nervous system.

INTERIM SUMMARY 4.1

Physical Growth

General Principles of Physical Growth	■ **Directionality:** How body proportions change—generally *cephalocaudal* (advances from "head to tail") though also *proximodistal* (progresses from the center of the body outward).
	■ **Independence of systems:** Different parts of the body develop along different timetables.
	■ **Canalization:** Many systems in the body follow a standard, structured course of development. If something throws development off course, a correction back on course occurs as soon as a change is possible.
Norms vs. Individual Differences	■ Norms: represent average outcomes.
	■ Individual differences—the range of variation within the normal range.

THE DEVELOPMENT OF THE CENTRAL NERVOUS SYSTEM

In just nine months, that single fertilized egg we met in "Conception, Prenatal Development, and Birth" developed into a fetus with a complex, self-regulating, and differentiated nervous system. In just nine to twelve months more, the newborn develops into a child who feels sad if you do, communicates her wants and needs, and can act in ways that make her parents marvel.

None of these many achievements would be possible without the internal wiring of the brain and nervous system. The **central nervous system (CNS),** the division of the nervous system that consists of the brain and spinal cord, processes information and directs behavior. In adapting to the complexities of life, the CNS develops at many levels at the same time, from the overall structure of the brain at one end of the spectrum to individual cells at the other. Connections between brain and behavior do not travel in only one direction, however. Genetically predetermined brain development makes possible new behaviors, and new behaviors lead to new interactions with the environment that then influence brain development. As we have stressed, development is always the product of the reciprocal interplay between biology and context, and brain development is no different.

The Brain

The CNS begins as a layer of cells on the outer surface of the embryo and is already visible just one month after conception. **Subcortical structures** that control *state*—whether we are asleep, awake, or somewhere in between—and arousal emerge first in development. Components of the **limbic system** that manage emotions develop next. The **cortex** and **association areas** of the brain concerned with awareness, attention, memory, and the integration of information emerge last.

The brain is divided into two halves or **hemispheres**, connected by the **corpus callosum**. The cortex of the brain is made up of thin layers of outer tissue that cover the brain. (*Cortex* means "bark" in Latin.) Although only about 0.12 inches (three millimeters) thick, the cortex contains 75 percent of the brain's cells (Sharpee et al., 2006). It is wrinkled and folded to fit billions of cells into a small space; otherwise, we would require giant-sized heads. The cortex of other mammals is smaller (relative to body weight) and smoother than ours is. (Nonmammals do not have a cortex.) The corpus callosum, which integrates activities of the two hemispheres by transferring information between them (Gazzaniga, Bogen, & Sperry, 1962), may not complete growth until six years of age (Thompson et al., 2000), and the cortex does not mature fully until adolescence.

Different areas of the cortex have specialized functions. The **visual cortex** regulates sight; the **auditory cortex** monitors hearing; the **sensorimotor cortex** processes touch; and the **motor cortex** controls voluntary movement. The **frontal cortex**—the brain's "command central"—is responsible for thinking, planning, initiative, impulse control, and creativity. In addition, two regions in the left cortex are dedicated to language comprehension (**Wernicke's area**) and language production or speech (**Broca's area**). See Figure 4.4.

In short, the brain is highly specialized. But it is also flexible, as we will discuss later in this chapter. First, we need a close-up view at how the brain functions at the cellular level.

Brain Cells

Your brain contains approximately 100 billion cells, a number equal to all of the stars in our galaxy (Nowakowski, 2006). **Neurons** are cells that carry information across the

central nervous system (CNS) The division of the nervous system, consisting of the brain and spinal cord, that processes information and directs behavior.

subcortical structures Brain components that control state of arousal.

limbic system The part of the nervous system that manages emotions.

cortex Thin layers of outer tissue that cover the brain.

association areas The parts of the brain concerned with awareness, attention, memory, and the integration of information.

hemispheres The two halves of the brain.

corpus callosum The connection between the two halves or hemispheres of the brain.

visual cortex The part of the brain that regulates sight.

auditory cortex The part of the cortex that monitors hearing.

sensorimotor cortex The part of the brain concerned with touch.

motor cortex The part of the brain that controls voluntary movement.

frontal cortex The brain's command central responsible for thinking, planning, initiative, impulse control, and creativity.

Wernicke's area The region on the left side of the brain dedicated to language or speech comprehension.

Broca's area The region on the left side of the brain dedicated to language or speech production.

neurons Cells that carry information across the body and brain.

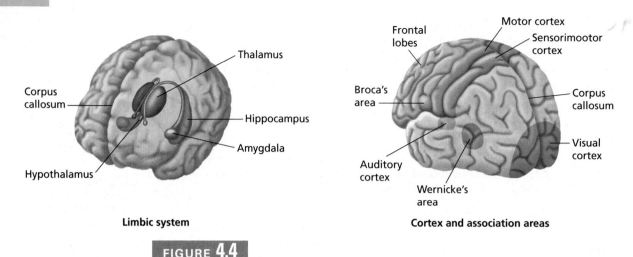

Limbic system   Cortex and association areas

FIGURE **4.4**

Areas of the Brain

Structures in the limbic system (shown on the left of the figure) are located deep within the cerebral hemispheres. Together, they oversee several important functions related to emotion, motivation, hormone secretion, and homeostasis. The cerebral cortex (show on the right of the figure) is divided into four lobes (frontal, parietal, temporal, and occipital) based on the location of fissures, or folds, in the brain tissue. Each lobe contains areas specialized for different functions. The cortex, or outer layer, of brain tissue has several association areas, including the visual cortex (sight), auditory cortex (sound), sensorimotor cortex (touch), and motor cortex (movement). Wernicke's and Broca's areas are specialized for language comprehension and language production, respectively.

Source: From Bernstein/Penner/Clarke-Stewart/Roy. *Psychology,* 8E. © 2008 Wadsworth, a part of Cengage Learning, Inc. Reproduced by permission. www.cengage.com/permissions

---

body and brain, as well as back and forth within the brain. Collectively, neurons and their connections compose the *gray matter* of the brain.

As shown in Figure 4.5, a neuron has three main parts: dendrites, a cell body, and an axon. The **dendrites** are like antennas that pick up signals from other neurons. (The word *dendrite* comes from the Greek for "little trees"; like trees, a neuron may have many branches.) The **cell body** contains the nucleus of the cell and the biochemical mechanisms to keep the cell alive and determine whether the cell will "fire" or send out signals to other cells. The **axon** carries the signals away from the cell body toward other neurons. At their tips, axons usually divide into many *axon terminals*.

The connection between one neuron's axon and another neuron's dendrite is called a **synapse**. The two neurons do not actually touch; rather, there is a minuscule gap between them, and that gap is the synapse. Neurons communicate by means of electrochemicals called **neurotransmitters**. Inside the neuron, information takes the form of an electrical charge called the **action potential**. When this charge travels along the axon and reaches the axon terminal, it stimulates the release of neurotransmitters, the electrochemicals that carry the signal across the synapse from one neuron to the next.

After neurons are born (Bhardwaj et al., 2006), they grow, they move, and they develop relations with one another to form stable interconnected pathways—many during the prenatal period (Muotri & Gage, 2006). Migrating cells move to particular locations or partner cells; that is, they seem to "know" their future addresses (Lewis, 2005). We don't know exactly why. Scientists believe that migrating cells may be drawn to those points by the neurochemicals their partners produce. Whatever the process, it is swift and sure: By about the end of the sixth month of gestation (i.e., about three months *before* birth), cell birth and migration within the brain are more or less complete (Nowakowski, 2006). At birth, the brain is about one-quarter the size of the adult brain, and virtually all of the neurons that will ever exist are in place. The dendrites,

dendrites Branched extensions of a neuron that act like antennas that pick up signals from other neurons.

cell body The part of the cell that contains the nucleus and biochemical mechanisms to keep the cell alive and determine whether the cell will fire.

axon The part of the cell that carries signals away from the cell body toward other neurons. At their tips, axons divide into many *axon terminals.*

synapse The connection between one neuron's axon and another neuron's dendrite.

neurotransmitters Electrochemicals through which neurons intercommunicate.

action potential An electrical charge inside the neuron.

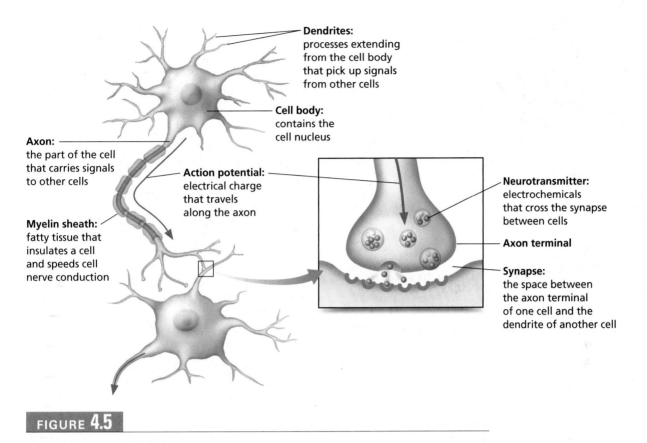

Dendrites:
processes extending
from the cell body
that pick up signals
from other cells

Cell body:
contains the
cell nucleus

Axon:
the part of the cell
that carries signals
to other cells

Action potential:
electrical charge
that travels
along the axon

Myelin sheath:
fatty tissue that
insulates a cell
and speeds cell
nerve conduction

Neurotransmitter:
electrochemicals
that cross the synapse
between cells

Axon terminal

Synapse:
the space between
the axon terminal
of one cell and the
dendrite of another cell

FIGURE 4.5

The Neuron and Synapse

Source: From Bernstein/Penner/Clarke-Stewart/Roy. *Psychology*, 8E. © 2008 Wadsworth, a part of
Cengage Learning, Inc. Reproduced by permission. www.cengage.com/permissions

axons, and synapses are still developing, however. The development parents see in
their baby—from first smiles to first steps—reflect these unseen changes.

A key process in early brain development is **synaptogenesis**, the development
of connections—synapses—between neurons through the growth of axons and dendrites. In just the first six months of life, 100,000 new synapses form every second! By
age two, a single neuron may have 10,000 connections to other neurons. No wonder
scientists call this the "exuberant" phase of synaptogenesis. The rate of synaptogenesis
peaks at about age one and slows down in early childhood, but synaptogenesis continues throughout life as children (and adults) learn new skills, acquire knowledge, build
memories, and adapt to changing circumstances. The formation of some synapses is
genetically programmed, but others depend on experience. The more a synapse is
used, the stronger its pathway.

Initially the brain produces many more connections among cells than it will use. At
one year of age, the number of synapses in the infant brain is about *twice* the number
in the adult brain (Couperus & Nelson, 2006). However, soon after birth a complementary process to synaptogenesis begins. **Synaptic pruning** eliminates unused and
unnecessary synapses. As a general rule, we tend to assume that "more is better," but
that's not the case here. Imagine hills and a meadow between two villages. Hundreds
of lightly trodden paths connect one to the other (the unpruned brain). Over time
people discover that one path is more direct than others. More people begin using
this path more often, so it becomes wider and deeper. Because the other paths are not
used anymore, the grass grows back and those paths disappear (synaptic pruning).
The complementary processes of synaptogenesis and synaptic pruning are fundamental to brain **plasticity**—the capacity of the brain to be modified by experience (Sur &
Rubenstein, 2005). (We'll discuss plasticity more later in this chapter.)

synaptogenesis The
development of connections
between neurons through
the growth of axons and
dendrites.

synaptic pruning The process
of elimination of unused and
unnecessary synapses.

plasticity The capacity of
the brain to be modified by
experience.

© Laura Dwight

A 19-month-old girl drawing with a marker. At first, her movements will be jerky, inexact, and uncontrolled, but over time they become controlled, exact, and directed.

The elimination of synapses continues through adolescence and is normal and necessary to development and functioning. Much as pruning a rose bush—cutting off weak and misshapen branches—produces a healthier bush with larger roses, so synaptic pruning enhances the brain. If synaptic pruning does not occur, the child's dendrites are too dense and too long (think of a rose garden gone wild), resulting in mental retardation and other developmental disorders (Huttenlocher, 2002). Synaptic pruning makes the brain more efficient by transforming an unwieldy network of small pathways into a better organized system of superhighways.

Another key process in brain development is *myelination.* Initially, neurons are "nude," but over development, white fatty tissue, called **myelin**, encases cell axons. Myelin, which acts a little like plastic insulation around an electrical wire, increases the speed of neural impulses and so improves information transmission between cells. Before myelination, neurotransmission along a cell axon may proceed at a rate of less than twenty feet (6.1 meters) per second; after myelination, the speed of transmission triples, to more than sixty feet (18.3 meters) per second. Myelination begins prenatally and is still ongoing during adulthood (Couperus & Nelson, 2006). Much of the brain's *white matter* is composed of myelin.

The primary sensory and motor areas of the brain, involved with vision and movement, are myelinated before areas involved with higher cognitive functions. Fibers that connect the **cerebellum** (associated with balance and control of body movements) to the cerebral cortex grow and myelinate through age four, contributing to advances in motor control. Walking, running, and jumping become more synchronized. Myelination of the prefrontal cortex, which is associated with higher cognition, continues through middle and late childhood into adolescence and young adulthood. A tragic illustration of the importance of myelin is **multiple sclerosis**, a disease in which the autoimmune system strips neurons of myelin, leading to loss of motor control, deteriorating speech and vision, and sometimes death in early adulthood.

For a number of reasons, for example the exuberance of connections among cells, the transmission of information among cells is at first *diffuse* or spread out, so that reactions to stimulation develop and end slowly, something like when the body shudders in response to the roll of thunder. In their more developed state, and after pruning, connections among cells are more orderly. The same stimulation now produces a *phasic* reaction that is locked in time with stimulation and is much more specific, like a startle. A simple illustration is the way younger versus older babies respond to a loud hand clap. Early on, a sudden sound like a clap elicits a gross response, like a whole bodily shudder. Later, clapping leads to a clear-cut and much more efficient turn of the head.

Maturation alone does not account for improved communication among cells, however; experience plays a key role. When infants look at a form—a circle, for example—they scan it with their eyes and develop a mental representation that is related to eye movements as well as to the activity of cortical neurons excited by the form. The same cortical activity is excited every time they view a circle, which in a sense makes the circle progressively easier to identify. Thus, experience smoothes connections among cells to improve perceptual pathways. One of the reasons we come to recognize a shape as a circle, and not a square, is that these shapes stimulate different patterns of neuronal activity; this gets easier with age because the pathways become better established with each use. This is how babies come to recognize their mother's face, their father's voice, and the feel of their blanket.

myelin   The white fatty tissue that encases cell axons.

cerebellum   The part of the brain associated with balance and control of body movements.

multiple sclerosis   A disease in which the autoimmune system strips neurons of myelin, leading to loss of motor control.

Cell Activity

Individual cells in the CNS typically have highly specialized functions. The 1981 Nobel laureates David Hubel and Torsten Wiesel tried to find out how individual cells in the visual cortex respond to light, in a series of experiments with cats. Hubel had developed a special technique, called **microelectrode recording**, to measure the activity of individual cells. At the beginning of their research, he and Wiesel expected to find that showing a light in front of the cat's eyes would increase or decrease the activity of single cells in the cat's brain. Instead, they found that some cells only fired when a vertical line passed in front of the cat, other cells were excited by diagonal lines, and so on. Hubel and Wiesel even found these highly specialized cells in newborn kittens that had no visual experience! Apparently the brain is prewired in ways that assist visual perception.

We cannot observe or directly measure the activity of single cells in the brains of human beings. However, it is possible to measure the electrical activity of groups of cells. **Electroencephalographic (EEG) recordings** show electrical activity at the cortex of masses of individual cells in the brain. Neuroscientists use sensors that touch the scalp to pick up the electrical signals underneath. Broadly speaking, newborns have low-level, irregular brain activity, as though they are not processing stimulation completely. By the time they are two years old, however, children have high-amplitude and regular patterns of EEG activity much more like adult brain activity (Field et al., 2004; Otero et al., 2003).

Scientists examine EEG outputs to see how long it takes the brain to respond to stimulation and how focused that response is at different ages. **Event-related potentials (ERPs)** are specific patterns of brain activity evoked by a specific stimulus. The ERP has a simple form and takes a long time to develop in infancy, but it develops quickly and has a more complex form as the child matures (Parker et al., 2005; Wiebe et al., 2006). Responses to sensory stimuli (like a light or a sound) become more rapid and more focused as children grow older.

ERPs provide valuable information about the maturation of the brain. They also help to determine how the senses are developing. Suppose a baby does not respond to a sound—for example, by turning her head. How would you learn whether she can hear? If that infant's ERP shows a similar pattern to a given repeated sound, you at least know that the infant's brain is responding, so it is likely that the neuronal pathway from the ear to the brain is all right. Interestingly, infants who have more mature auditory ERPs at birth have more mature language abilities at three years of age (Molfese & Molfese, 1994).

Brain Plasticity

Some of our description of brain development sounds as though the infant's brain is entirely *pre*programmed. Developmental scientists have discussed this in terms of **experience-expectant processes**, those the brain is wired to process. This is, of course, not the whole story. Brain development is far from fixed. Disrupting input to an area of the brain (by putting blinders over the eyes, for example) reduces the size of that area. **Experience-dependent processes** involve the active formation of new synaptic connections in response to the individual's unique experience (Greenough, Black, & Wallace, 1987; Holtmaat et al., 2006). They contribute to our individuality. Both external experiences and self-produced experiences shape brain structure and alter brain function. Individual cells change and synapses grow or are pruned to strengthen neural circuitry. For example, rats that are raised in complex environments (supplied with toys and opportunities for lots of play and exploration) develop heavier and thicker visual cortices (*cortices* is plural for *cortex*) than littermates raised in barren, standard laboratory cages; experienced rats also solve problems better (Greenough et al., 1987).

microelectrode recording
A technique used to measure the activity of individual cells.

electroencephalographic (EEG) recordings Measurements acquired with sensors at the scalp that show electrical activity of masses of individual cells.

event-related potentials (ERPs) Specific patterns of brain activity evoked by a specific stimulus.

experience-expectant processes Prewired processes in the brain.

experience-dependent processes Brain processes that involve the active formation of new synaptic connections in response to the individual's unique experience.

Of course, development is not just the result of an environment operating on a passive organism; in many respects we create our own development though our active involvement with the environment. An experiment with kittens shows this (Held & Hein, 1963). The researchers yoked two kittens together. One was allowed to walk around and explore its environment. It wore a harness that connected to a "gondola" that held another kitten with only its head sticking out. As one cat moved, the other cat moved; as one cat saw the world, the other cat saw the world. Only, for one cat, exploration and vision depended on its own movement; the other cat was passive. Kittens that were allowed to physically explore their visual environment later mastered visual tasks in more sophisticated ways than did their "yoked-control" littermates whose movement was restrained. In other words, active exploration of the environment was better for subsequent development than passive exposure to the same stimulation. (We will return to other implications of this study later.)

As all these experiments show, the brain's structure (its anatomy) and function (how it works) are *plastic*. They can be molded by experience. Our brain is programmed to respond to critical features of our environment (experience expectancy), but adapts to the environment in which we find ourselves (experience dependency). Two kinds of plasticity have been identified in the nervous system: modifiability and compensation.

modifiability A principle of development that asserts that, although cells are predestined for specific functions, they can be changed.

Modifiability means that, although cells are predestined for specific functions, they can be changed. Sometimes change must occur at critical points in development, or **sensitive periods** (Bornstein, 1989, 2003). The window of modifiability is opened early in life so that we can prepare ourselves quickly and efficiently for the particular environment in which we develop. Studies of kittens, for example, show that cells in the visual cortex that respond to visual stimuli at birth become more responsive to certain types of stimuli than to others, depending on what the kitten is exposed to during sensitive periods in visual development (Wiesel & Hubel, 1974). Indeed, the brain is so plastic early in life that some cells can be modified to serve a completely different purpose. Surgically moving a part of the brain to a different place in the brain enables the transplanted part to adapt to functions of its new location. Thus, cells from the auditory cortex moved to the visual cortex become responsive to visual stimuli (Johnson, 2001, 2005). This must take place within a specific window of time, however; if transplanted after their sensitive period, the same cells will die.

sensitive periods Times in development when the organism is especially open to environmental influence.

Compensation is a second kind of plasticity. In compensation, some cells substitute for others, permitting recovery of function after loss or damage. Cells can compensate for defects in neighboring cells. After an injury—say, limb amputation—the parts of the brain that would be stimulated by the (now missing) limb are activated by other sources of stimulation. Indeed, new connections have been observed twenty-four hours to four weeks after amputation. Congenitally blind people compensate with improved hearing, and congenitally deaf people compensate with improved sight, which assists in decoding the visual motions of American Sign Language (Neville & Lawson, 1987). The ultimate version of compensation may be embryonic **stem cells**—the newest, youngest, and least developed cells of all—that can be grafted to repair damaged parts of the CNS or replace cells that have died (Johnson, 2001, 2005). (Adult stem cells may have some of the same adaptive properties.) Brain systems are also *redundant:* We are born with multiple versions of different cell types. Up to a certain point in development, young neurons and young brains are less specialized with regard to general function and so are able to compensate more flexibly.

compensation A kind of plasticity in which cells substitute for others, permitting recovery of function after loss or damage.

stem cells The newest, youngest, and least developed cells that can be grafted to repair damaged parts of the CNS or replace cells that have died.

In summary, central nervous system development in infancy has been studied in terms of overall brain growth and structure as well as single-cell and gross electrical activity. The brain displays remarkable specificity of function, but at the same time has evolved the capacity and flexibility to adjust to the environment. An active interplay between maturation and experience transpires during the development of single cells and the brain as a whole. (For a summary of this section, see "Interim Summary 4.2: The Development of the Central Nervous System.")

INTERIM SUMMARY 4.2

The Development of the Central Nervous System

Central Nervous System (CNS)	■ The **CNS** processes information and directs behavior. ■ Brain development is always the product of reciprocal interplay between biology and experience.
The Brain	Anatomy of the brain: ■ The brain oversees several important functions related to motivation, memory, hormone secretion, and homeostasis. ■ The cerebral cortex is divided into four lobes (frontal, parietal, temporal, and occipital) based on their location. Each lobe contains areas specialized for different functions. ■ The **cortex**, or outer layer, of brain tissue has several association areas, including the visual cortex (sight), auditory cortex (sound), sensorimotor cortex (touch), and motor cortex (movement). **Wernicke's** and **Broca's areas** are specialized for language comprehension and language production, respectively.
The brain's structure and function (how it works) is plastic—cells are predestined for different functions but that changes sometimes at sensitive periods.	Two kinds of **plasticity:** 1. **Modifiability**—although cells are predestined for specific functions, they can be changed. 2. **Compensation**—cells can substitute for others, permitting recovery of function after loss or damage.
Brain development is not fixed.	We create our own development through our active involvement with the environment.
Neurons are cells that carry information across the body and brain.	Three main parts of a neuron: 1. **Dendrites:** Processes extending from the cell body that pick up signals from other cells. 2. **Cell body:** Contains the cell nucleus. 3. **Axon:** The part of the cell that carries signals to other cells.
A synapse is the connection between one neuron's axon and another neuron's dendrite.	■ **Neurotransmitters** are electrochemicals that cross the synapse between cells. ■ **Action potential** is an electrical charge that travels along the axon.

THE AUTONOMIC NERVOUS SYSTEM

Much of what very new babies do is survival oriented and may not yet be under conscious or voluntary control. The **autonomic nervous system (ANS)**, which regulates many body activities without our voluntary control (such as breathing, blood flow, or digestion), reigns early on. In considering ANS development in infancy, we focus on the *cycles* and *states*.

At first glance, a baby's activity appears random and chaotic. To a new parent, a baby seems to be constantly moving his or her mouth, eyes, hands, and feet and shifting unpredictably from alertness to sleep. Close examination tells a different story, however. Infants are much more regular than meets the eye. Many different systems **cycle** in identifiable and predictable rhythms (Rivkees, 2004).

A 4-month-old baby girl interested in a toy held out for her by her teenage mother. Even simple visual stimulation at this age promotes infant brain development, and the interaction promotes mother-infant involvement.

© Laura Dwight

Some activities repeat regularly and often, perhaps once or more every second. The heart beats, the lungs expand and contract, and when allowed, the infant sucks in rather fast rhythms. All these biological functions maintain life. Although less frequent, infant kicking and rocking also cycle quickly when they occur (Thelen & Smith, 2006). Other behaviors, like general body movements, cycle every minute or two (Groome et al., 1999). And still others, such as states of waking, quiet sleep (no rapid eye movements), and active sleep (with rapid eye movements, indicating dreaming) have cycles on the order of hours (Papoušek, 1996). Taken altogether, infant activity might appear unstructured and erratic. But actually what we see in the newborn at any one time is the simultaneous and independent cycling of several overlapping rhythms. It's as if the woodwind, percussion, and brass sections of an orchestra were all playing at the same time, but to different beats.

What purposes do these cycles serve? First, no one could keep moving all the time, so periods of activity are followed by periods of rest. Second, as we've said, development need not wait for external stimulation; sometimes babies make their own stimulation. Waving their arms or kicking their legs, for example, stimulates the development of neuronal connections—synapses—in regions of the brain responsible for these movements. Last, social activity reflects these cyclic behaviors. Rhythmic pauses in babies' sucking, and stages of the sleep-wake cycle, signal to adults when to caregive or initiate play (Bornstein & Lamb, 2008).

States of arousal in young infants are not quite as regular as some other cycles, like breathing. You can be talking or playing with a little baby and suddenly she falls fast asleep! Infants shift frequently among states of sleep, drowsiness, alertness, and activity. It sometimes takes months to establish the predictable schedule of wake and sleep states that all parents crave. Infants vary tremendously in their sleep patterns and in the age at which they begin sleeping through the night (St. James-Roberts, 2007). One of us has a research assistant whose first baby was sleeping through the night by two months; her second child was still sleeping in forty-five-minute shifts when she was a one-year-old.

The age at which infants begin to control or *regulate* their state has important implications for infant development and infant care (as well as parental well-being). State regularity provides a window on the maturity of the infant's nervous system.

autonomic nervous system (ANS) The division of the nervous system that regulates many body activities without our voluntary control, such as breathing, blood flow, or digestion.

cycle Moving in an identifiable and predictable rhythm.

INTERIM SUMMARY **4.3**

The Autonomic Nervous System

The **autonomic nervous system (ANS)** regulates many body activities without our voluntary control (such as breathing, blood flow, or digestion).

- At any one time in newborns, you can see the simultaneous and independent cycling of several overlapping rhythms.

- The age at which infants begin to regulate their state provides a window on the maturity of the nervous system.

Poor state regulation is common in preterm infants, for example. Equally important, an infant's state of arousal influences what will happen next. Adults rock and soothe distressed babies. They engage happy and alert babies in play and learning, showing them toys. Babies who are temperamentally fretful (see "Socioemotional Development in Infancy") elicit different patterns of care than do happy and content babies. In addition, state determines whether and how infants learn. In quiet alertness, infants respond to tactile and visual stimuli, and they may listen to a soothing voice that has absolutely no effect when they are engaged in out-of-control crying. During these quiet moments, infants can examine and become familiar with their parent's face or study the mobile hanging over their crib. In these ways, babies' states influence their perceptual and cognitive development.

The organization of the sleep-wake cycle reflects neurological maturation and the developing ability of babies to regulate their own states (McKenna et al., 1994; Moon, Kotch, & Aird, 2006; Scher, Epstein, & Tirosh, 2004). However, the way a baby is cared for is also influential. Experiences around birth, parental caregiving, and cultural beliefs all affect infant sleep cycles. For example, infants who receive more sensitive caregiving (from parent or nurse) spend more time in quiet sleep (Ingersoll & Thoman, 1999). Infants' sleep states are also affected by culture. Among the Kipsigis people in East Africa, infants sleep with their mothers and are permitted to nurse on demand. During the day they are strapped to their mothers' backs, accompanying them on their daily rounds of farming, household chores, and social activities. They often nap while their mothers go about their work, and so they do not begin to sleep through the night until many months later than U.S. American children. Japanese infants generally have good state regulation and few sleep problems. The reason appears to be a function of—*surprise!*—nature and nurture: A biological predisposition among Japanese infants to be less disturbed by noise during sleep *and* the custom among Japanese families of babies sleeping with their mothers (Kawasaki et al., 1994). *Co-sleeping,* which is practiced in much of the world, allows mothers to reach for and pull their infants close for feeding or comforting (McKenna et al., 1994). Western infants typically sleep in separate rooms from their parents. Although there are those who believe that co-sleeping may have advantages for the child and parent, there are also disadvantages (St. James-Roberts, 2007). (For a summary of this section, see "Interim Summary 4.3: The Autonomic Nervous System.")

REFLEXES AND MOTOR DEVELOPMENT

The development of movement during infancy is characterized by the growth of increasingly voluntary and controlled actions (Brandtstädter, 2006; von Hofsten, 2007). At birth, much infant movement is reflexive; by toddlerhood, the baby is largely in control.

Reflexes

Newborn babies look completely helpless, but they are not. They are good at a few special—if limited—behaviors, called "reflexes." **Reflexes** are simple, involuntary responses to certain stimuli. Many reflexes have *adaptive significance;* that is, they are related to survival.

Reflexes are divided into three groups. The *approach reflexes* are concerned with intake, especially breathing and rooting, sucking, and swallowing. Babies show the rooting reflex in response to stimulation around the mouth; rooting entails tracking, searching, and redirecting the head toward the source of stimulation. It typically finishes with sucking. Rooting allows infants to locate and ingest food.

The *avoidance reflexes* include coughing, sneezing, and blinking. A common characteristic of avoidance reflexes is their all-or-nothing quality; when they are elicited, they occur in full-blown form.

A third collection of reflexes (simply referred to as *other reflexes*) seems to have had more meaning once upon a time in our evolutionary history than they do now. The Palmer *grasp* and *Moro response* are two examples. The Moro reflex is the tendency for babies to swing their arms wide and bring them together again across the middle of their body—as if around the body of a caregiver. This reflex can be elicited by a loud sound or when the baby suddenly loses support. Similarly, in the Palmer grasp, babies tighten their grip if whatever they are holding is suddenly raised; this allows babies to support their own weight, if only briefly. These reflexes can still be seen in many nonhuman primate newborns, who cling to their mother's body hair.

Although these other reflexes do not seem to serve their original function any longer, they provide an important means of assessing infant development. Indeed, reflexes are a part of every major neonatal examination and screening test. Most reflexes develop before birth (we know this because infants born before term show them) and are normally present for four to eight months after birth. Then, rather suddenly, they disappear. Why? As cortical processes develop, they inhibit subcortical ones. Thus, the disappearance of some reflexes reflects the emergence of higher cortical function; their disappearance is a sign that brain development is progressing normally. As is the case with synaptic pruning, sometimes maturation is indicated by the *disappearance* of something old, rather than the *emergence* of something new.

Motor Development

The growth of motor function across infancy is as dramatic as physical growth (Adolph & Berger, 2005, 2006). Newborns can't even roll over, but toddlers are so fast at getting around that parents must monitor a two-year-old's whereabouts constantly. Now the whole house needs to be childproofed! Like other aspects of development, motor development depends on both physical maturation and the experiences infants have (von Hofsten, 2007). As motor systems develop, infants acquire the ability to move about and manipulate objects (Claxton, Keen, & McCarty, 2003; Keen et al., 2003).

Infant motor development follows a more or less predictable sequence. Until about five months, infants are horizontal unless they're being held. By six months, most babies can sit up by themselves, an accomplishment that opens new vistas. Before, babies could only look at what was put in front of them; now they can look around. By eight to ten months, most infants begin crawling, which means they can move around (unless restrained). First-time parents are often surprised at how quickly infants can scoot about. They also make active efforts to stand up and "cruise" with the support of a caregiver or piece of furniture, and they may soon begin to walk with help. On average, infants take their first, awkward, independent steps at age one, though another year passes before their walking is smooth and steady. But remember, we are talking about norms. Individuals vary in their rate of motor development. Some infants progress directly from sitting to walking at nine or ten months, without crawling; others do not even attempt to

TABLE 4.1 Norms of Motor Development

Age	Gross Motor	Nonlocomotor	Fine Motor
1 month		Supports head. Can lift head from prone lying.	Will hold on to object placed in hand.
3–4 months		Stepping reflex pattern.	Plays with hands as a first toy.
5 months	Rolls over from front to back.	Holds head and shoulders erect when sitting.	Stretches out to grasp with increased accuracy.
6–8 months	May begin to crawl.	Sits unsupported.	Begins to be able to let go.
9 months	Can stand with support.	Pulls up to stand holding furniture.	Transfers objects from one hand to the other.
10 months	Crawling established.	Can bend to pick up objects when one hand is held.	Can use two hands doing different actions at the midline of the body.
1 year	Can crawl and stand alone, and may walk unaided. Uses step-together pattern to climb stairs.	Early walking. Starts games such as peekaboo.	Can build bricks, pour water, eat finger food independently.
2 years	Can climb up and down stairs safely now using a passing-step pattern.	Problem solving—empties cupboards, dismantles toys.	Pulls on clothes. Can put on roomy garments—shoes on wrong feet. Increasing independence.

Source: Macintyre & McVitty (2004).

stand until eighteen or twenty months. All are within the normal range. Table 4.1 shows the age norms for children's acquisition of basic motor milestones.

Do rates of motor development depend on maturation? Not entirely. Cross-cultural research shows that motor development can be influenced by parental expectations and childrearing practices. Hopkins and Westra (1988, 1990) questioned mothers and observed children in European cultures, Jamaica, and the West African nation of Mali. European mothers believe that motor development is driven by maturation, without special environmental or parental input. They see crawling as an important stage, between sitting independently and walking. In contrast, Jamaican and Mali mothers believe that motor development requires training and exercise. They view crawling as primitive, undesirable behavior; only animals move on all fours. They expect their infants to sit and walk at earlier ages than do European mothers. Jamaican and Mali mothers also perform daily exercise and massage routines with their infants. In European cultures, virtually all babies went through a crawling stage. Jamaican and Mali infants sat up and started walking at earlier ages. Most surprising (to Europeans), 25 percent of Jamaican infants and 60 percent of Mali infants never crawled. Thus, parents or other caregivers can influence motor development, but only when an infant's nervous system and muscles are ready.

A toddler walking toward its mother. Development moves from unsure and unsteady to sure and steady and depends on motivation and experience.

FIGURE 4.6

Negotiating Motor Tasks in Infancy

In this laboratory paradigm, toys are placed at the bottom of a ramp in order to attract the infant. The angle of the ramp is adjusted to increase or decrease the steepness of the slope, and infants' behaviors are observed as they make their way down the ramp.

Source: Reprinted by permission of Karen Adolph.

dynamic systems theory
A theory that asserts that change in one area of development impacts others.

So, it is not simply the case that infants automatically perform more difficult motor acts as they mature. Experiences, too, are vital in shaping the course of motor development. Learning to move about and handle objects in infancy involves a complex reciprocal relation between maturation and experience (Adolph & Berger, 2005, 2006). For example, an infant's success at negotiating a challenging motor task, such as descending a sloped surface, is not automatic. Infants take into account properties of the surfaces, such as the degree of slant, as well as their own abilities and explore different methods of locomotion before settling on a specific way to descend (e.g., crawling forward or backward; see Figure 4.6). Infants who are already walking have to learn all over again how to come down the same slopes that they had mastered during crawling.

As we discussed in "The Study of Child Development," **dynamic systems theory** asserts that change in one area of development influences others. Children's motor achievements affect many other, sometimes surprising, aspects of their psychological growth (Howe & Lewis, 2005; Thelen & Smith, 2006; van Geert & Steenbeek, 2005). For example, infants have depth perception at two months (see the "Depth" subsection in the next section), but they do not show fear of height until they are able to crawl on their own, regardless of the exact age at which they begin to crawl (Bertenthal & Campos, 1990). Crawling (a motor development) allows the infant to estimate distances more accurately than before (a cognitive development), which later translates into fear (an emotional development).

Each milestone in motor development also affects parent-infant interaction. When a baby first deliberately rolls over, stands upright, or walks, it is an occasion for joy and for telephone calls to grandparents. These achievements also signal all sorts of other

INTERIM SUMMARY 4.4

Reflexes and Motor Development

Reflexes are divided into three groups and are important for providing external means of assessing development.	■ *Approach reflexes* are concerned with intake, especially breathing and rooting, sucking, and swallowing.
	■ *Avoidance reflexes* include coughing, sneezing, and blinking.
	■ *Other reflexes* such as the Palmar grasp and Moro response have more meaning in an evolutionary context.
Motor development is dependent on physical maturation and experience.	■ Until 5 months, infants are horizontal unless held.
	■ By 6 months, most babies can sit up by themselves.
	■ By 8–20 months, most babies begin to crawl.
	■ On average infants take their first step at age 1.
Dynamic Systems Theory	■ This theory asserts that one change in development impacts others. Children's motor achievements affect many other aspects of their psychological growth.

cognitive and social changes at home, as now the baby can get around and into all the cupboards. (Toddlers get a bad rap for saying no so often once they turn two, but parents start saying no to their children long before the reverse occurs, usually once children start moving around on their own.) Worse yet, the child's climbing out of his crib and making his way to the top of the stairs for the first time may cause panic . . . as well as a trip to the hardware store for a baby gate the very next morning. (For a summary of this section, see "Interim Summary 4.4: Reflexes and Motor Development.")

SENSING AND PERCEIVING

We experience the world through our five senses—seeing, hearing, touching, tasting, and smelling. These sensory systems function in utero; they do not lie dormant until they are suddenly "switched on" at birth. By the second trimester of gestation, the eye and visual system, the ear and auditory system, the skin and tactile system, the nose and olfactory (smell) system, and the tongue and gustatory (taste) system are developing structurally, but they will not function at mature levels for some time.

The different senses appear to begin their road to development and achieve maturity at slightly different times. This staggered schedule has the possible biological advantage of permitting both biology and experience to "concentrate on" reaching high levels of maturity one system at a time.

How early can the infant sense or perceive? How clear are the baby's sensations and perceptions? Do they see patterns (such as a human face) as wholes or as parts? Do they distinguish the human voice from other sounds? Do they respond to touch? Are they bombarded by sensations, or do they seek particular perceptions? Before we can begin to understand infant cognition and socioemotional development we need to know what babies perceive. The short answer is, a good deal—but that's jumping ahead of our story.

Understanding what babies see and hear or feel, taste, or smell is a challenge. After all, perception is "private": There is no way for the person sitting next to you to know what you perceive unless you tell him. But infants are mute. To study babies we must infer what infants perceive from how they behave. (Developmental scientists have engineered ways around these barriers to communication, which we will look at in some detail in "Cognitive Development in Infancy.")

Seeing

We know most about the early development of sight, so let's begin there (Aslin, 2007; Kellman & Arterberry, 2006). The visual world is made up of pattern, depth, movement, and color. To see into the infant's visual world, we review early development along each of these dimensions (Livingstone & Hubel, 1988).

Pattern, Shape, and Form Not all that long ago, people believed that newborns could *not* see—like kittens, they were thought to be blind at birth. Indeed, some people in the world today (like rural peoples in Thailand) still think this way and place their babies in folding cloth hammocks with only a slit view of the sky to look at all day long. Now we know that newborns not only see, they actively seek visual stimulation, scanning the environment to find things to look at . . . even in the dark. When they do come across a pattern, newborns focus most on its boundaries, where the greatest amount of information is found (Conde-Agudelo, Rosas-Bermúdez, & Kafury-Goeta, 2006). Think of a Mondrian painting. You could look at a red or yellow or blue field, but then that's all you would see. What makes the painting dynamic are the intersections between the colored fields. If we track eye moments, younger infants scan patterns in a limited way, whereas older babies scan more of the whole of patterns and do so systematically.

© PhotoDisc 2009

FIGURE 4.7

What the Infant Sees
Two photos of a female face that show how you, and how a baby, see another person.

Figure 4.7 provides an idea of how well newborn babies see, in comparison to the actual image. Visual acuity is relatively poor in newborns, but it improves rapidly and, by about six months of age, is almost the same as that of normal adults.

Infants are very attracted to faces, but it is not clear why. It could be that we have evolved an innate, predisposition to attend to faces (Johnson, 2005). It could be that faces contain features that infants find intrinsically interesting (three dimensions, movement, sounds, and high contrast). It could be that infants learn to look at faces because they are associated with all things good—love, nourishment, and the like. Whatever its origins, though, face preference is real, strong, and present early in life (Bornstein & Arterberry, 2003; Gallay et al., 2006; Hunnius & Geuze, 2004; Turati et al., 2006). But when a newborn looks at her mother, does she see a face *or* the parts of a face (eyes, nose, mouth, and so forth)? In other words, do infants actually perceive forms as forms, rather than as their components or pieces? If you know a baby, try this. Make a two-dimensional picture of a normal face pattern, a scrambled face pattern (i.e., with the parts of the face arranged in an unnatural way), and a blank oval, and then move each slowly in an arc-like path in front of a baby. More likely than not, even a newborn will look at and track the normal face pattern more than the scrambled face pattern (which have all the same elements as the normal face, so it's not the elements that make the face attractive, but the whole form). However, infants prefer the scrambled face pattern over the blank oval.

Infants not only see faces, they imitate facial expressions (happiness, sadness, surprise; Field et al., 1982). It is possible that newborns have a specialized brain mechanism for processing facial configurations (Johnson, 2001, 2005). This does not mean that infants' knowledge of faces is complete at birth. The ability to discriminate their mother's face from others, tell different facial expressions apart, understand that different expressions convey different emotions (see "Socioemotional Development in Infancy"), and discriminate between male versus female, or young versus old, faces are all products of everyday experience (Bornstein, Arterberry, & Mash, 2005).

Depth Parents put infants in cribs with side panels to keep them from falling out, just as they put gates at the top and bottom of stairways once babies start to crawl. Infants at the creeping and toddling stages are notoriously prone to falls from high (or even slightly elevated) places. Depth perception is crucial to determining the layout of the environment, recognizing objects, and guiding action. As their muscular coordination matures, infants begin to avoid such accidents on their own. Common sense might suggest that children learn to recognize depth through experience—that is, by falling and hurting themselves. "But is experience really the teacher? Or is the ability to perceive and avoid a brink part of the child's original endowment?" (Gibson & Walk, 1960, p. 64).

© Mark Richards/PhotoEdit

FIGURE 4.8

The Visual Cliff

The mother is gesturing for the baby to come across the "cliff"—will she go?

The story goes that two famous perceptual psychologists were on vacation with their infant daughter at the Grand Canyon when the baby began to scoot toward the edge. The mother was Jackie Gibson, and this experience gave birth to the idea of creating a "visual cliff" to investigate depth perception in infants (Gibson & Walk, 1960). The visual cliff is a Plexiglas table (with protective sides) as you can see in Figure 4.8. On half the table, there is a checkerboard surface directly below the glass; on the other ("deep") side, the checkerboard is several feet below the glass. Very few infants the researchers tested between six and fourteen months of age actually crawled across the "deep" side when their mothers called to them. These results suggested that infants as young as six months of age perceive depth.

By six months, however, children may already have had experience falling. So other researchers have studied "precrawling" babies by monitoring their heart rate when they were exposed to shallow or deep sides of the visual cliff (Bertenthal & Campos, 1990). Two-month-olds react to the deep side with a decrease in heart rate, indicating increased attention or interest. Thus, babies may perceive depth long before they themselves move about, but this does not mean they show a proper fear of heights that early. It could be that the wariness of drops shown by older infants results from the anxiety parents display when infants approach a drop, rather than from infants' own experiences. Infants often use their parents' emotional cues to help them interpret ambiguous events. (We'll say more about this *social referencing* in "Socioemotional Development in Infancy.")

More generally, when do infants see in 3D, and how do we know? Several movement or *kinetic cues* help us see depth. When an object comes directly toward us on a "hit path," its image expands, and we normally move to avoid the impending collision. Babies as young as one month consistently blink at approaching objects (Bornstein et al., 2005).

Movement Movement is important to perceiving. Things that move bring protection and nutrition, danger, and opportunities for exploration and play, so being able to perceive motion is an important survival tool. Infants will normally reach for objects in front of them even if the objects are moving. Indeed, babies as young as four and a half months will reach in a way that indicates they are good at targeting the object's next location if it moves in a predictable way (von Hofsten, 2007).

The infant's perception of motion is actually quite sophisticated (Arterberry & Bornstein, 2001). By three and a half months, infants recognize different directions of motion; by five months, they discriminate rotation (turning in a circle) from oscillation (swaying side-to-side) (Ruff, 1982, 1985).

Indeed, movement perception is important for the recognition of objects. If you show a four-month-old a stimulus such as that depicted in Figure 4.9 in common motion (i.e., the rod projecting from the top of the box, and the rod projecting from the bottom, moving together, at the same rate of speed, in the same direction, at the same time), infants mentally "connect" the two rods. Like you, they see it as a single rod that is partially blocked by the box rather than two separate rods both moving.

Other studies also show the power of movement perception. An example is the so-called point-light walker display, which shows motion typical of human beings represented by moving points of light (see Figure 4.10). Imagine seeing the dots in panel A of the figure without the lines that connect them. When adults see the stationary display, the information is essentially uninterpretable; they don't think they are looking at anything in particular. But if the same set of lights starts to move in a way that

Habituation display

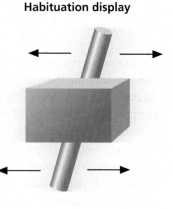

FIGURE 4.9

Infant Perception of Motion and Object Continuity

When infants as young as four months old are shown an image—like the one shown here in which a single rod appears to be moving left and right behind a box—they become surprised by (and look longer at) an image (not shown) of two separate short rods with no box in front of them. The fact that infants are surprised by the second image suggests that they mentally connected the top and bottom pieces of the rod and perceived it as one long rod (a whole object) moving behind the box, rather than as two separate shorter rods.

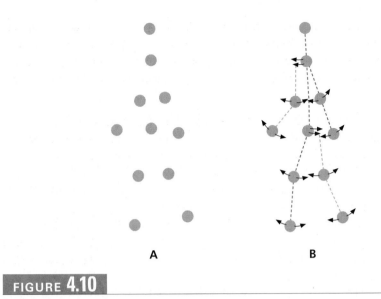

A   B

FIGURE **4.10**

Point-Light Walker Display

When infants (or adults) see points of light, such as those in panel A, they are unable to make sense of them and therefore do not perceive them as any particular object or figure. However, when the lights are set in a "walking" motion, infants as young as five months old show evidence that they perceive the moving lights to represent a human walking.

mimics someone walking, adults can identify the object as a human figure in less than two-tenths of a second. Infants, too, are sensitive to biomechanical motion of this kind by five months of age (Arterberry & Bornstein, 2001).

In sum, infants in the first year of life see elements of patterns as well as pattern wholes. They also show developing sensitivity to several dimensions of spatial information, including depth and movement. They even use movement to understand object form.

Color Patterns and objects in the environment not only vary in terms of spatial dimensions but also color. By two months, infants see colors very well. Adults do not merely see colors, however; we perceive the color spectrum like the rainbow organized as categories of hue: blue, green, yellow, and red. Although we recognize blends in between, we distinguish at least these four as qualitatively distinct hues. Four-month-old infants perceive color in the same way (Bornstein, 2006a, 2006b). Perceiving color categorically (i.e., recognizing that the color of robins' eggs, the sky, and blueberries are all in the same general color family, and that the color of a tangerine is not) combines with seeing pattern, locating in space, and tracking movement to aid very young babies in organizing and making sense of what they see.

Hearing

After vision, we know most about newborn and infant hearing. Fetuses respond to sounds beginning around the third month of gestation (Busnel, Granier-Deferre, & Lecanuet, 1992). Of course, the mother's abdominal wall and uterus lower the intensity of surrounding sounds somewhat, but they change other characteristics of the sounds surprisingly little. After birth, newborns are especially sensitive to sound frequencies that occur within the range of the human voice (Saffran, Werker, & Werner, 2006).

Obviously, newborns can hear sounds: Make a sudden loud noise, and a neonate will startle. But infants' hearing is so good that they distinguish high pitch sounds better than adults do (but not as well as dogs!) (Saffran et al., 2006). Infants can discriminate differences between melodies at six months of age (Trehub, Trainor, & Unyk, 1993). Furthermore, they show preference for music with common chords over music with uncommon chords. By four months of age reach in the direction of a sound even in the dark; by six months, their ability to locate the source of sound matches that of adults.

In other words, normal infants come equipped with good hearing. Almost immediately, infants apply their basic abilities to the much more complex tasks of perceiving, deciphering, and making sense of their world . . . especially speech. Certain characteristics of human speech attract babies. Adults (and older children) seem to know this intuitively. Remember the last time you spoke with your infant nephew or niece? We guess that you did not talk to him or her like you talk to a friend, or like your professor talks to you. Rather, you used a different speech register—one reserved for babies, and little animals, and (yes) lovers. Indeed, it is difficult not to change one's speech in addressing babies (Papoušek & Papoušek, 2002). So-called **infant-directed speech** differs from and simplifies normal adult-directed speech in all sorts of ways. We exaggerate tones and deliver them in a singsongy rhythm, use simpler words and repeat them, and abbreviate utterances and employ easier grammar (Kitamura et al., 2002; Papoušek, Papoušek, & Bornstein, 1985). Infant-directed speech is also nearly universal.

infant-directed speech
A special speech register reserved for babies that simplifies normal adult-directed speech in many ways.

Infants prefer to listen to infant-directed speech over adult-directed speech (Fernald, 2001; Henning, Striano, & Lieven, 2005). They are happier listening to "baby talk," even when the language being spoken is different from their own (Saffran et al., 2006). The exaggerated pitch, intonation, and repetitiveness of infant-directed speech may have several functions, including the following: attracting and keeping infant attention; communicating the speaker's emotion and intention; and facilitating recognition of the mother's voice.

Babies in the first year of life distinguish a great many different sounds of language (Saffran et al., 2006), even some that do not appear in the language they hear every day. However, with continuous exposure to one particular language, infants' ability to distinguish sounds outside their native language diminishes (Saffran et al., 2006). This reduced sensitivity to non-native sounds is probably not permanent, however, as adults can be trained to hear them.

So, certain auditory perceptions seem to be universal and developed at birth; they are maintained by linguistic experiences but may be (at least partially) lost if children do not hear them in their language.

Touching

We know from everyday experience that soothing pats can quiet a fussy infant, whereas a vaccination shot almost invariably causes distress. In addition to the ability to feel things, infants use the sense of touch to learn about the world (Stack, 2001). Very young babies will look at an object without reaching for it; by the middle of the first year, however, babies reach for everything in sight. They must have it—whatever it is—in their hands. Piaget (whom we met in "The Study of Child Development," and whom we will meet again as a central figure in the story of infant cognition, in "Cognitive Development in Infancy") brought the significance of touch to center stage when he proposed that seemingly simple sensorimotor behavior constitutes the foundations of knowledge (Brainerd, 1996; Lourenco, 1996).

In the same way that infant looking is guided by an active search for "where the information is," once infants have the chance to explore an object in some detail, they will change patterns of exploration to acquire more information (Ruff, 1982, 1985). Infants respond to a change in the shape of an object by rotating the object more, and to a change in texture by fingering the object more. They throw and push away or drop new objects less often than familiar ones. Furthermore, infants explore complex objects longer than simple objects, and they are less distractible when they are engaged in object exploration than when they are not (Richard et al., 2004).

Infants are highly responsive to tactile stimulation (Blossfeld et al., 2006). Touch is also vital to establishing and maintaining emotional intimacy and infant-parent attachment (Bowlby, 1969; Harlow, 1958). Regular touch promotes weight gain and growth in high-risk newborns, for example (Goldberg & DiVitto, 2002).

Harlow's (1958) studies on isolated infant monkeys showed that "contact comfort" is more a powerful motivator than food. Given a choice between a wire "mother" covered with soft cloth and one equipped with a bottle, infant monkeys clung

A baby exploring an interesting object through touching. Infants explore some objects in detail and will learn about them by looking at them, touching and manipulating them, and mouthing them.

to the first. Contact comfort is universally perceived as reassuring by infants of non-human primates and human infants alike. The first instinctive reaction of a mother to her infant's distress is to embrace, rock, or pat, and, then to sing or talk soothingly to the infant even in different cultures (Bornstein et al., 1992). The formation of a close attachment bond between infant and caregiver, which we examine in "Socioemotional Development in Infancy," is linked to touch, not just to providing of nourishment.

So touch works with vision to inform infants about key properties of the physical world. Touch also appears to be critical to the formation of infant-parent relationships.

Tasting and Smelling

Taste and smell have received less attention than have vision, hearing, and touch, but these senses play major roles in the life of the baby, including all-important decisions about what is nourishing and what is not.

Newborn babies, even those who have tasted nothing but amniotic fluid, discriminate different tastes, and they prefer certain tastes over others. Neonates display characteristic facial expressions when sweet, sour, and bitter substances are placed on their tongues. A sweet stimulus evokes an expression of satisfaction, often accompanied by a slight smile and by sucking movements. A sour stimulus evokes lip pursing, often accompanied or followed by wrinkling the nose and blinking the eyes. A bitter fluid evokes an expression of dislike and disgust or rejection, often followed by spitting or even by gagging (Steiner, 1979; Oster, 2005). Distressed preterm and term infants alike can be soothed merely by giving them a sweet (glucose) solution to taste. Sweet tastes hold a high reward value for infants; this is adaptive, because it ensures that infants will take to breast milk, which is slightly sweet.

The olfactory (smell) system is highly developed at birth as well. If you place a cotton swab with a particular odor beneath the nose of even a newborn, the baby will display facial expressions and reactions appropriate to the odors (Steiner, 1979). It's easy to tell which smells neonates like, and which they decidedly do not. Butter and banana odors elicit positive expressions; vanilla, either positive or indifferent expressions; a fishy odor, some rejection; and the odor of rotten eggs, unanimous rejection. Newborns' preferences mirror adult preferences.

INTERIM SUMMARY 4.5

Sensing and Perceiving

Sensory systems—sight, hearing, touch, taste, and smell—develop in utero.

■ Seeing—This sense involves pattern, depth, movement, and color. Newborns not only see but also actively seek visual stimulation.

■ Hearing—Normal infants come with good hearing. Infants prefer to listen to **infant-directed speech** (speech register reserved for babies) over adult-directed speech.

■ Touch—Infants use the sense of touch to learn about the world and are highly responsive to tactile stimulation. Touch is vital to establishing and maintaining emotional intimacy and infant–parent attachment.

■ Tasting and smelling—Newborn babies discriminate different tastes, and they prefer certain tastes over others. The olfactory (smell) system is also highly developed at birth.

Indeed, their sense of smell is so good that newborn babies who breastfeed are able to identify their mothers' odor (Porter et al., 1992). Only twelve to eighteen days after birth, breastfed and bottle-fed infants were exposed to pairs of gauze pads worn by an adult in the underarm area on the previous night. When the investigators gave infants the opportunity to turn their heads in one direction to smell their mother's odor or turn in the opposite direction to smell a stranger, as you probably guessed, the breast-fed babies spent more time turning toward their mother's odor. Infants did not recognize their fathers preferentially, though, and bottle-fed infants did not recognize their mothers' odor, suggesting that breastfeeding infants are exposed to and learn unique olfactory signatures. (By the way, mothers also recognize the scent of their babies after only one or two days.) The ability to recognize mothers very early in life—and vice versa—by scent alone might play an important role in the mother-infant relationship (Porter & Winberg, 1999). In sum, newborns taste and smell, and seem to be very discriminating. Just try to feed them a food they do not like! (For a summary of this section, see "Interim Summary 4.5: Sensing and Perceiving.")

MULTIMODAL AND CROSS-MODAL PERCEPTION

Although we have discussed different perceptions as though they were discrete and separate (to explain how each works), the senses do not work independently. Rather, our senses interact with one another and fuse perceptions into wholes. When we have sex, for instance, we see images that excite us, hear sounds that reinforce our passion, feel skin that scintillates, and so forth. These sensory impressions go together naturally to give rise to an integrated experience that is more intense than that from any one sensory input alone.

Objects and events in the world give rise to sights, touch, and sounds; that is, we experience **multimodal perceptions** that are often coordinated across senses. Also some information available in one modality can cross or transfer to another (Jordan & Brannon, 2006). What we learn about something through one sense (vision) is enhanced by what we experience through another (touch). For example, when we feel a ball, we also see that it is round, and we acquire the concept of what a ball is by integrating these multiple sources of information.

The American philosopher William James famously referred to the infant's world as a "blooming, buzzing confusion." But developmental science has shown that the

multimodal perceptions The perception of information about objects and events in the world that stimulates many senses at once.

INTERIM SUMMARY 4.6

Multimodal and Cross-Modal Perception

Experience and Early Perceptual Development
- The senses do not work independently. Our **multimodal perceptions** of objects are coordinated across senses.
- A baby's self-perception can come from different perceptual systems (visual, tactile, and auditory) and motor actions (sucking, rooting, and orienting).
- Babies can tell the difference between touches that come from a source external to their own bodies and self-touches.

world of the infant is not as fragmented as James believed. Information obtained by looking, listening, and touching is coordinated very early in life. For example, in one study, infants as young as twenty-nine days of age successfully identified by sight an object they had previously explored by mouth alone (i.e., a pacifier with small nubs). When researchers put the pacifier with the nubs in the infants' mouths, let them suck on it for a while, and then showed them that pacifier and one that was smooth (with no nubs), infants looked longer at the familiar one than at the new one (Meltzoff, 1993).

The study of these kinds of cross-modal perception has led to more remarkable insights about infants' developing sense of self—another illustration of how physical development and socioemotional development are linked. The earliest kind of self-knowledge might be based on the coordination of information from different perceptual systems (visual, tactile, and auditory) and motor actions (sucking, rooting, and orienting).

You know how you cannot tickle yourself? There is something about knowing that you are doing the touching that makes what otherwise would tickle you have no effect. Babies use similar knowledge as well. Normally, stroking an infant's cheek will evoke the rooting reflex. But the rooting reflex in three- to four-week-olds is stronger when their cheeks were touched by a researcher's finger or a pacifier than by the infants' own hand (Rochat, 1997). So, babies can tell the difference between (or at least they respond differently to) different kinds of touches. They can tell the difference between touches that come from a source external to their own bodies and self-touches (in which touch is felt both on their cheek and on their finger that is touching their cheek). (For a summary of this section, see "Interim Summary 4.6: Multimodal and Cross-Modal Perception.")

EXPERIENCE AND EARLY PERCEPTUAL DEVELOPMENT

Perceptual abilities are remarkably well organized at birth. However, perceptual experience is just as critical for normal psychological growth and development. One early experiment with institutionalized babies showed that simply introducing a visually interesting object into the infant's otherwise bland environment at one month nearly doubled infants' visually directed reaching and visual attentiveness (White, Castle, & Held, 1964).

The everyday perceptual experiences that infants have matter to their development. In one experiment, three-month-olds were tested in the laboratory for their sensitivity to smiling faces (Kuchuk, Vibbert, & Bornstein, 1986). A series of smiles

INTERIM SUMMARY **4.7**

Experience and Early Perceptual Development

Perceptual abilities are well organized at birth and illustrate the interplay between biology and experience.

■ The everyday perceptual experiences that infants have matter to their development.

■ At birth, the brain and central nervous system, although far from mature, are developing rapidly.

■ The basic sensory systems function at birth, and then or soon after infants perceive some even complex and sophisticated information.

■ Infants perceive some information arriving via the different senses in a coordinated way, and information acquired via one sense is available to other senses.

that graduated in intensity were shown to babies, randomly one face at a time, and the amount of time babies looked at each one was recorded. In general, babies looked more at more "smiley" faces, but babies showed individual differences. The investigators also went into the infants' homes and recorded mothers' interactions with their infants. Mothers who smiled at their babies more often themselves had infants who showed the most sensitivity to the smiling faces in the laboratory.

Perceptual development in infancy provides multiple examples of the interplay between biology and experience. At birth, the brain and central nervous system, although far from mature, are developing quite rapidly and are in place to seek out and process information about the environment. Indeed, the basic sensory systems function at birth, and then—or soon after—infants perceive even complex and sophisticated information. Moreover, infants perceive some information arriving via the different senses in a coordinated way, and information acquired via one sense is available to other senses. All these remarkable developments in an adaptive biological system interact with an experience-providing environment. (For a summary of this section, see "Interim Summary 4.7: Experience and Early Perceptual Development.")

SUMMING UP AND LOOKING AHEAD

In this chapter, we traced the remarkable physical, motor, and perceptual growth that characterizes the first two years of life. The difference between what a newborn can do and what a two-year-old is capable of is simply staggering. Part of this transformation is the result of a maturational plan encoded in our genes, but the real beauty of this plan is that it is a flexible one that is responsive to environmental stimulation. A prewired, unchangeable biological plan for maturation would be less adaptive, just as would be a totally flexible one in case experience is not forthcoming. The perfect combination of biological readiness and responsiveness to contextual input ensures that humans are able to develop in ways that are adaptive in the particular environment into which they are born. Biology assures that, in the absence of some sort of abnormality, infants are born able to hear, taste, and see, but they are also born with sensory systems that are still maturing and that are "plastic" enough to develop preferences for their mother's voice, the particular foods available in their environment, and the sights they are likely to encounter in their world.

Intellectual development during the first two years is just as amazing. That journey is the subject of "Cognitive Development in Infancy."

HERE'S WHAT YOU SHOULD KNOW

Did You Get It?

After reading this chapter, you should understand the following:

- The general principles of physical growth
- The meaning of norms versus individual differences
- How the central nervous system develops
- The anatomy of the brain
- The autonomic nervous system

- The importance of reflexes
- The sequence of motor development in infancy
- The development of an infant's sensory and perceptual systems

Important Terms and Concepts

association areas (p. 99)
auditory cortex (p. 99)
autonomic nervous system (ANS) (p. 106)
axon (p. 100)
action potential (p. 100)
Broca's area (p. 99)
canalization (p. 97)
cell body (p. 100)
central nervous system (p. 99)
corpus callosum (p. 99)
cerebellum (p. 102)
compensation (p. 104)
cortex (p. 99)

cycle (p. 106)
dendrites (p. 100)
directionality (p. 96)
dynamic systems theory (p. 110)
electroencephalographic (EEG) readings (p. 103)
event-related potentials (ERPs) (p. 103)
experience-dependent processes (p. 103)
experience-expectant processes (p. 103)
frontal cortex (p. 99)
hemispheres (p. 99)

independence of systems (p. 97)
individual differences (p. 97)
infant-directed speech (p. 116)
limbic system (p. 99)
microelectrode recording (p. 103)
modifiability (p. 104)
motor cortex (p. 99)
multimodal perceptions (p. 118)
multiple sclerosis (p. 102)
myelin (p. 102)

neurons (p. 99)
neurotransmitters (p. 100)
norms (p. 97)
plasticity (p. 101)
reflexes (p. 108)
sensitive periods (p. 104)
sensorimotor cortex (p. 99)
stem cells (p. 104)
subcortical structures (p. 99)
synapse (p. 100)
synaptic pruning (p. 101)
synaptogenesis (p. 101)
visual cortex (p. 99)
Wernicke's area (p. 99)

Cognitive Development
in Infancy

© George Doyle

The baby being carried in the infant seat across from you sees, hears, feels, tastes, and smells (with her nose, that is). But she is not a passive voyager: She must make sense of all of this "input." This is where cognitive development comes in. How does she "process" these sensations? How do we know what's going on inside her head?

In this chapter, we're going to review what developmental scientists have learned about the mind of the infant in just the last fifty years or so. (Before then, *whether* babies think, and *what* they think, was philosophical speculation.) The topics include Jean Piaget's views of cognitive development and some of the contributions of researchers who came after Piaget and questioned his views; mental representation in infancy; attempts to measure infant "intelligence"; and the development of language. We consider norms and individual differences, how learning and cognition change over infancy, and how infants' interactions with objects and people influence their mental development—especially the ability to communicate with others. Equally important, we look at how researchers know what infants think; after all, infants cannot tell us what's on their mind.

HOW SCIENTISTS KNOW WHAT BABIES KNOW

How do researchers ask babies questions about what they know, and how do babies answer them? Students of infancy have developed many different techniques and strategies to ask babies questions. Two techniques are based on the concepts of *habituation* and *novelty responsiveness* and use a similar approach. For example, a researcher shows a baby a picture once, and the baby will look at it for a while. But if the baby is shown the same picture over and over, the baby will look at it less and less. The first time, the picture was novel and attention grabbing. However, like you would, babies get "bored" with the same thing.

The baby's getting bored is perfect for the researcher, because then the researcher knows that the baby has developed some sort of *mental representation* of the picture—otherwise, why should the baby look at the picture less the tenth time it is shown than the first time? The loss of interest suggests that the baby *recognizes* the picture. Presumably, the baby is comparing each new picture presentation with a developing memory of the picture based on previous exposures. This is called **habituation**. What happens if the researcher now shows the bored (habituated) baby something new? If the baby looks more at a new picture than at the one she's been shown over and over—called **novelty responsiveness**—that tells the researcher that the baby not only recognizes the old picture but also can tell the difference between the old one and the new one (Bornstein, 1998; Sirois & Mareschal, 2002).

habituation The process in which a baby compares each new stimulus with a developing memory of the stimulus based on previous exposures, thus learning about the stimulus.

novelty responsiveness Following habituation, the process in which a baby looks more at a new stimulus than at a familiar one.

One of the ways developmental researchers test infants is by showing them stimuli and noting their reactions, like this 8-month-old baby boy looking at an image on a computer screen.

Using habituation and novelty responsiveness, researchers can ask a variety of "yes-no" questions of babies. For example, can babies tell the difference between a smiling and a frowning face? To do your own experiment, get two pictures, preferably of the same person: one happy, and another frowning. Show one to the baby until he stops looking, then show the pictures together. If the baby looks longer at the novel facial expression, then he is telling you that he can tell the difference between smiling and frowning. How good is a baby's memory? By habituating (familiarizing) infants with a picture and testing them some time afterward with the same picture, it is also possible to study memory (if the baby acts as if the picture is new, he obviously doesn't remember it).

A third approach used to tell us something about infant perception and cognition involves learning. Again, try your own experiment. Put a baby in a crib with a mobile hanging overhead. Now, take a baseline reading of how often she kicks. Then attach the mobile by a ribbon to the baby's ankle so that, when the baby kicks, the mobile jangles. Babies quickly learn that kicking moves the mobile. When attached to the mobile in this way, most babies kick at two to three times their baseline rate. Suppose now that you wait a day or two and then retest the baby. When an infant who has previously learned the association between kicking and mobile-moving re*learns* that association more rapidly than he or she did the first time, this tells us that the baby remembers (Rovee-Collier & Barr, 2001).

Finally, scientists use a fourth approach to study what babies know by showing them a sequence of events and seeing whether they imitate them. Consider this scenario. You are seated across the table from an infant. You have a spoon, a small red box, and a larger blue box. While the baby is watching, you place the spoon inside the red box, and then place the red box inside the blue one. Then, you disassemble it all

INTERIM SUMMARY 5.1

How Scientists Know What Babies Know

Four Different Approaches Used to Learn About Infant Perception and Cognition

1. **Habituation**—occurs when a baby compares each new stimulus with a developing memory of another stimulus based on previous exposures.

2. **Novelty responsiveness**—happens after habituation; if a baby looks more at a new stimulus than at the one shown repeatedly the baby not only recognizes the old stimulus but also can tell the difference between the two.

3. **Learning**—putting a baby in a crib with a mobile, taking a baseline reading of how often the baby kicks. Then conditions are changed, response noted, and the baby is retested, which tells us about infant learning and memory.

4. **Observation**—babies are shown a sequence of events and observed to see if they imitate the sequence.

and do it again. Now, you give the baby the three objects. If she does exactly what you did, in the same order, this tells us she is able to observe and remember a sequence of events (Barr & Hayne, 2000).

If you were to do some or all of these things with an infant you know, you'd rediscover what developmental scientists in the last half century have discovered. Although it might not always be apparent, infants have an active mental life. They are constantly learning, developing, and even testing—yes, *testing*—new ideas. (For a summary of this section, see "Interim Summary 5.1: How Scientists Know What Babies Know.")

PIAGET AND INFANT COGNITIVE DEVELOPMENT

Between 1925 and 1932, the Swiss biologist and philosopher Jean Piaget watched closely as his own three children—Jacqueline, Lucienne, and Laurent—grew from infancy, noting the enormous intellectual progress each made during the first two years of life. Soon afterward, Piaget (1936/1952) published the *Origins of Intelligence in Children*, a collection of his observations and informal experiments that led to a revolutionary theory of cognitive development in infancy (Brainerd, 1996; Bremner, 2001; Lourenco, 1996).

Piaget suggested that each infant constructs an understanding of the world—including space, time, causality, and substance—on the basis of his or her own motor activity and interactions in the world. At the time, other developmental scientists viewed the infant as a well-equipped, but basically passive, recipient of information from the environment. Piaget did not think that knowledge derives from sensations or perceptions, or from information provided by others. Rather, Piaget wrote that infants *actively construct* what they know. This basic notion has shaped the study of infant cognition ever since.

What does it mean to "actively construct" knowledge? Imagine that you and a friend have driven to a new restaurant in a neighboring town. A month later, you want to eat there again, so you decide to drive back. If you were the driver the first time, you'll have an easier time remembering how to go than if you had been the passenger—because you actively constructed your knowledge of how to get there by doing the driving. Recall the kitten study conducted by Richard Held and Alan Hein (1963), which was discussed in "Physical Development in Infancy." This study demonstrated the critical importance of self-produced activity for understanding the environment. The kittens who were allowed to move about on their own avoided the deep side of a visual cliff, stretched out their paws appropriately in preparation for contact with a solid surface, and blinked at approaching objects. By contrast, even after extensive transportation in the gondola, the passive cats failed to show such spatially sensitive behavior. To Piaget, an infant is the driver (not the passenger) in cognitive development; the active (not the passive) kitten.

Assimilation and Accommodation

To explain processes underlying cognitive development, Piaget invoked the idea of adaptation. **Adaptation**, in Piaget's theory, is the process whereby knowledge is altered by experience. Adaptation involves two complementary processes, **assimilation** and **accommodation**. When information can be processed according to what the infant already knows, the information is said to be *assimilated*. An infant who under-

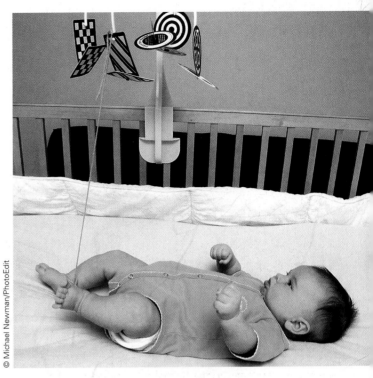

This baby is lying in a crib with a ribbon connecting his ankle to the mobile overhead so that when he kicks, the mobile jangles. In this way it is possible to study how infants react when they can control their environment.

Piagent theory & current thinking Sensory motor stages

adaptation The process whereby knowledge is altered by experience. Adaptation involves two complementary processes, assimilation and accommodation.

assimilation The process by which information can be incorporated according to what the infant already knows. Assimilation allows the infant to use existing understanding to make sense of the world.

accommodation The process by which the infant changes to reach new understanding; that is, the modification of existing understanding to make it apply to a new situation. Accommodation allows the infant to understand reality better and better.

© Laura Dwight

stands that when she drops a rattle off her high chair the toy falls downward onto the floor will easily understand that when she drops her Cheerios® they do the same thing; that is, she can assimilate this new knowledge. But at times, the infant's understanding of the world cannot successfully assimilate new information. What happens when the infant lets go of a balloon filled with helium? It goes up, not down. This violates the infant's understanding of the world (because until then, everything that was dropped followed the same pattern). When new information cannot be assimilated into the baby's existing understanding, two things can happen. One is that the infant fails to assimilate and simply moves on to another activity. Alternatively, the infant changes her understanding to permit new information to be processed. The modification of existing understanding to make it apply to a new situation is termed *accommodation*; that is, infants actively change so that they can understand the environment better. Following the experience with the helium balloon, the baby understands that some objects float rather than fall when they are released; through the process of accommodation, the baby has developed a new way of thinking. Assimilation and accommodation are not separate processes, but always co-occur so that the infant's understanding can match reality. Assimilation allows infants to use their existing understanding to make sense of the world. Accommodation allows them to modify that understanding to understand reality better and better.

To actively learn about their world, babies grasp, touch, and mouth objects just as this 9-month-old girl is doing.

sensorimotor period A developmental time, consisting of a six-stage sequence, when thinking consists of coordinating sensory information with motor activity.

object permanence The understanding that an object continues to exist, even though it cannot be sensed.

mental representation The ability to hold in the mind an image of objects (and people) that are not physically present.

Stage Theory

Perhaps the best-known feature of Piaget's theory is his principle of *stages*. Piaget held that mental development unfolds in a fixed sequence of developmental steps. As a whole, infancy encompasses the **sensorimotor period**; it is followed, in Piaget's system, by the preoperational, concrete operational, and formal operational periods of childhood, early adolescence, and late adolescence, respectively (discussed in the chapters on physical development in the early childhood, middle childhood, and adolescence parts). During the sensorimotor period, "thinking" consists of coordinating sensory information with motor activity. According to Piaget, infants learn through actions: looking, listening, touching, sucking, mouthing, and grasping. Within the sensorimotor period in infancy, Piaget sketched a six-stage sequence (see Table 5.1). The child's current stage defines the way the child views the world and processes information in it.

One of the accomplishments during the sensorimotor period is learning that certain actions produce certain results (*causality*). For example, banging a spoon on a high-chair tray produces a loud noise, attracts attention, and may bring dinner. Another major advance is **object permanence**. In early infancy, "out of sight is out of mind"—literally. The baby's world consists of what he can perceive in the here-and-now. If you give a three-month-old an interesting toy, his attention perks up. But if you cover the toy with a cloth, he doesn't look for it; rather, he behaves as if the toy no longer exists. By eight or ten months, the infant is surprised when the toy disappears, and he searches for it. He realizes that something out of sight does not go out of existence (Bogartz, Shinskey, & Schilling, 2000; Krojgaard, 2003; Mash, Arterberry, & Bornstein, 2007; Xu, 2003). Object permanence is a first step toward **mental representation**: No longer dependent on immediate sensory data, the infant has images or propositions of objects (including people) in mind that are not physically present. Piaget believed that mental representation did not develop until the end of the sensorimotor period.

Challenges to Piaget

Although Piaget's view of infant cognition has been extremely influential, many of his claims about infant development have been challenged by empirical research. In general, it seems that Piaget underestimated what infants know at different ages.

TABLE 5.1 Stages of the Sensorimotor Period of Infancy

Stage	Approximate Age	What the Baby Can and Cannot Do	Example
Stage 1	Birth to 1 Month	Infants do not accommodate, so mental development is minimal. Everything is assimilated into their existing understanding and very slowly.	They cannot recognize that stimuli belong to solid objects in the outside world—for instance, that sounds come from other things.
Stage 2	1 to 4 Months	Infants coordinate different aspects of their understanding of the world.	They coordinate hand and mouth (deliberately putting their fingers in their mouth).
Stage 3	4 to 7 Months	Infants are aware of relations between their own behavior and the environment.	When infants accidentally produce environmental events—kicking the side of the crib shakes the mobile that is attached to the railing, for instance—they may repeat them, suggesting that they want to review their effects on the environment.
Stage 4	7 to 10 Months	Infants construct relations among environmental stimuli.	They coordinate a face and a voice as being from the same source.
Stage 5	10 to 18 Months	Infants accommodate to the outside world and discover many unexpected relations among objects.	They attempt to see whether milk leaks out of a bottle at different rates depending on the angle of the bottle and the force with which it is squeezed.
Stage 6	18 to 24 Months	Infants now can form a *mental representation*; for example, imagining the whereabouts of an invisible object.	When a ball rolls under a sofa, for example, a child will move around the sofa and anticipate the reemergence of the ball.

One major criticism, for instance, is that Piaget focused on the ways that infants learn through movement (i.e., the "motor" in sensorimotor) and ignored other ways in which infants learn. For example, in one study, limbless children (whose mothers took the sedative thalidomide during the first trimester of pregnancy) developed a normal cognitive life despite the absence of normal sensorimotor experience in infancy (Décarie & Ricard, 1996). This suggests that Piaget overestimated the importance of active (mobile and tactile) exploration—and underestimated other sensory and organizational capacities of newborns and young infants. Babies make a lot of sense of the world without physically manipulating things.

Other research shows that object permanence and the capacity for mental representation of the physical world (i.e., the ability to hold an image or proposition of something in the mind) appear much earlier in development than Piaget supposed (Baillargeon, 2004). Indeed, infants can imitate some facial expressions they see soon after they are born, which says that they have some capacity to represent the external world at birth (Meltzoff & Moore, 1999).

Not only can infants imitate another person within the first months of life, as early as six months of age they can imitate a model's novel actions after a *delay*. For example, in one experiment, six- to nine-month-old infants observed an adult model lean forward and press a panel with his forehead (a highly unusual, novel behavior) (Meltzoff, 1988). One week later, the infants who had viewed this behavior, and a control group of infants who had not, returned to the laboratory and were put in front of the panel. Infants who had not seen the experimenter never pressed their foreheads to the panel, whereas two-thirds of the infants who had previously witnessed this behavior did. So not only were they able to imitate what they had seen, they were able to do so from memory!

Developmental scientists now agree that Piaget seriously underestimated infants' perceptual and cognitive capacities (Birney et al., 2005; Keil, 2006). Infants' compe-

INTERIM SUMMARY 5.2

Piaget and Infant Cognitive Development

Jean Piaget was a Swiss biologist and philosopher who laid the foundation for the study of infant cognition today.

He believed that mental development unfolds in a fixed sequence of developmental stages. The **sensorimotor period** encompasses infancy.

Developmental scientists now agree that Piaget underestimated infants' perceptual and cognitive capacities.

Piaget's theory

■ He believed infants actively construct what they know on the basis of their own motor activity and interactions in the world.

■ He believed **adaptation** is the process whereby knowledge is altered by experience.

■ It involves **assimilation** (using existing understanding) and **accommodation** (modifying understanding).

■ Advances in the sensorimotor period include causality (certain actions produce certain results) and **object permanence** (the understanding that an object continues to exist even though it cannot be sensed).

■ Object permanence paves the way toward **mental representation** (infants can hold in their mind images of objects and people that are not physically present).

tencies in understanding sequences of events, means-ends relations, space, causality, and number are all in evidence much earlier in development than Piaget predicted. Infants are more organized and sophisticated than Piaget thought. Nevertheless, his contributions—especially his belief that infants are active learners, and that infants *think*, although differently from older children and adults—laid the foundation for the study of infant cognition today. (For a summary of this section, see "Interim Summary 5.2: Piaget and Infant Cognitive Development.")

MENTAL REPRESENTATION IN INFANCY

Piaget was interested in the broad picture—in the overarching features of cognitive development from birth through adolescence. Other developmentalists concentrate on specific elements of cognitive development—on what skills infants acquire and when. Students of infant cognition are particularly interested in categorization, memory, and pretend play. Each of these developments is related to representational thinking—the ability to think about objects and people that are not present. Piaget thought that this breakthrough did not occur until eighteen to twenty-four months. Using different investigative techniques, though, contemporary researchers have found evidence of representational thinking at considerably younger ages.

Categorizing

Imagine going to a grocery store in which there is no rhyme or reason to the way that products are arranged. Chicken breasts are placed next to trash bags, which are alongside cream cheese. Chicken drumsticks are on the same shelf as toothpaste, which is right below the tangerines. What a nightmare shopping would be! Thankfully, though, grocery stores group similar objects near one another—into categories (poultry, cleaning supplies, dental products, fruits).

Categorization involves grouping separate items into a set according to some rule (Bornstein, 1984; Harnad, 1987). A Ford, a Toyota, and a Mercedes-Benz are all "cars." Oaks, elms, and pines are all "trees." Sipping, slurping, and guzzling are all "ways of consuming liquids." To better organize our experiences, we frequently treat different objects or events as similar; that is, we *categorize*. So do infants.

Categorization helps to simplify and order the infant's world in three ways (Bornstein, 1984). First, the infant comes to understand that his brown teddy bear is the same teddy bear in the light and in the dark, when it is nearby and faraway, and so on. The environment into which infants are born, and in which they develop, is constantly changing, producing an infinite variety of sensations. Moreover, infants experience the world in biological states that are frequently changing (e.g., from being asleep to being awake). Categorization structures and clarifies perception.

Second, the infant doesn't have to remember every single aspect of every single object, such as every one of his or her mother's facial expressions to recognize her face. Categorization facilitates the storage and retrieval of information. It supplies a principle of organization that allows more information to be stored in one "file" for mother, rather than multiple files.

Third, the infant's learning that her dog barks can be applied to other dogs as well. With categorization, knowledge of an attribute of one member of a category provides information about other members of the same category. And new observations (dogs also have tails) can be added to the category and automatically applied to other members of the category.

Evidence that infants categorize comes from habituation and novelty responsiveness tasks. In the habituation/novelty responsiveness paradigm, infants are first familiarized with several examples from the same category (say, several cats) and are then presented with a novel example from the same category (a new cat) and a novel example from a different category (a dog). We know infants categorize because they pay more attention to a novel out-of-category dog stimulus than to a novel in-category cat; that is, they treat one novel stimulus as "familiar" and another novel stimulus as new. To understand this concept, you can try this: Habituate a baby to pictures of a horse, a cow, and a cat. Now add either a dog or a rocking chair. The baby will look longer at the picture of the rocking chair because it is not an animal (Arterberry & Bornstein, 2001, 2002a, 2002b).

Studies of the way infants play with objects from similar and different categories also show that categorization abilities progress during the first three years. Here's how it's done: Give an infant eight small three-dimensional models (see Figure 5.1), four each belonging to two categories, say, animals (cow, dog, goose, and walrus) and vehicles (train, bus, motorbike, and all-terrain vehicle), and encourage the infant to play with them. Close analysis in such studies reveals that the infant touches objects within a category one after the other more frequently (at greater than chance levels) than objects across categories. That is, in the preceding example, the baby plays with animals or vehicles but less often with both. Categories function at different levels of *inclusiveness*, and understanding whether and how infants use them tells us whether and how infants mentally represent information (Rakison & Oakes, 2003). By one year, infants show that they have a grasp (so to speak!) of the most inclusive categories (e.g., animals vs. vehicles), but infants have to be one and a half years to recognize less inclusive categories (e.g., dogs vs. cats) and almost three to tell the least inclusive categories apart (e.g., two different kinds of cats).

Remembering

It is obviously important that infants attend to stimuli and events in their environm But it is also crucial that they be able to store, retrieve, and use that information l

categorization A process that involves grouping separate items into a set according to some rule.

© Laura Dwight

FIGURE 5.1

Categorization Abilities

To understand infants' categories of objects, researchers present them with plastic models—for example, four animals and four vehicles—and then analyze infants' patterns of holding and looking at the two groupings.

infantile amnesia The adult recollection of almost nothing of events that took place before the age of three or four.

Memory representations underlie the infant's awareness, experience, knowledge, and interpretation of the world.

For years, people believed that infants could not remember much of anything. You probably don't remember much of events that took place before you were three or four (see Bornstein, Arterberry, & Mash, 2004). Indeed, Sigmund Freud (1916/1917, 1966) coined the term **infantile amnesia** to describe this phenomenon, which he attributed to repression of memories of traumatic events. Piaget (1954) also believed that memories may not be possible during the first year because infants do not have the capacity to encode information symbolically. We now know that this view is inaccurate. Although adults may not be able to recall things from their first few years of life, infants can indeed remember previously experienced events. Whether adults accurately remember their infant experiences, and whether infants remember things from their very short past, are two different questions, with two different answers.

Infant memory has been studied using many techniques. By habituating (familiarizing) infants and testing them immediately afterward with the same stimulus, we can study *short-term memory* (i.e., see whether infants can tell the difference between something they've been shown and something new right away). Imposing a delay between habituation and a later test allows us to assess *long-term memory*. By varying the amount of delay between habituation and the subsequent test, it is possible to study the accuracy of infants' memory over different time intervals and to see if this changes with age. We can also vary how long the initial period of familiarization is to see if there are changes with age in how much an infant must be exposed to something to remember it.

Studies show that infants' ability to remember clearly improves with age. Infants habituate more quickly and more efficiently as they grow older. They also remember more information, across longer periods of time, as they get older and with helpful reminders (Hsu & Rovee-Collier, 2006; Sheffield & Hudson, 2006). **Deferred imitation**—showing babies a series of actions, then seeing whether they reproduce these actions later—is even more advanced. One team of researchers used three events—pulling a mitten off a puppet's hand, shaking the mitten, and then putting the mitten back on the puppet's hand (Barr & Hayne, 2000). They found that recall of these actions after a twenty-four-hour delay was lowest among six-month-olds (who did not perform any better than infants who never observed the modeled sequence), intermediate among twelve-month-olds, and highest among eighteen- and twenty-four-month-olds. Study time also affects infant memory. Babies do not require extremely long exposures to demonstrate short-term memory. In sum, as infants age they demonstrate an ability to hold events in memory for longer time spans, and they require fewer cues and shorter periods of familiarization to recall past events.

Playing

Play is fun and interactive, but also involves mental work—studying a doll, manipulating a busy box, building with a set of blocks, or entertaining an imaginary playmate at a make-believe tea party. Play frequently imitates life, and it is quite common to observe infants reenacting in play specific events that they observe or participate in routinely (e.g., "driving" a toy car). Such behavior indicates that infants represent events mentally well enough to reproduce them.

Piaget proposed that play increases in sophistication as children mature, and that infants progress from exploratory play to symbolic, or pretend, play. In the first year, play is predominantly characterized by sensorimotor manipulation; infants' play appears designed to extract information about objects—what objects do, what perceivable qualities they have, and what immediate effects they can produce. This is commonly referred to as **exploratory play** because children's play activities are tied to the tangible properties of objects.

In the second year, children's play actions take on a new quality: The goal of play now appears to be symbolic. In **symbolic play**, children enact activities performed by the self, others, and objects in simple make-believe scenarios, pretending to drink from empty teacups, to talk on toy telephones (as in Figure 5.2), and the like (Bornstein, 2007).

Most children pass through these two broad developmental stages of play, but children of a given age vary greatly. On average, 15 percent of one-year-olds' total play is symbolic. However, some children never exhibit symbolic play, whereas others spend as much as 50 percent of their time in symbolic play. At two years, 33 percent of toddlers' total play is symbolic on average, but for some individual children as little as 2 percent is symbolic, whereas for others 80 percent is symbolic. (More elaborate pretend play is typically not seen until early childhood, and is discussed in "Cognitive Development in Early Childhood.")

Play normally occurs in the context of social interaction. Children may initiate play, but adults influence its development by outfitting the play environment, engaging children actively, and responding to their overtures. How does adult social interaction

© Laura Dwight

FIGURE 5.2

Symbolic Play

Here's a 15-month-old girl pretending to talk on a telephone . . . just like mommy.

deferred imitation Reproducing a series of actions seen at an earlier time.

exploratory play Children's play in which activities are tied to the tangible properties of objects.

symbolic play Children's play that enacts activities performed by the self, others, and objects in pretend or make-believe scenarios.

affect play? When interacting with their mother, infants' play is more sophisticated, complex, and varied than is infants' solitary play (Bornstein, 2007). In a longitudinal study of mother-infant play interaction, researchers found that, when mothers responded to their eighteen-month-olds' object play in an "options-promoting" manner (i.e., encouraging, affirming, and/or expanding on the child's activities), the infants engaged in higher levels of symbolic play at forty months of age than did infants whose mothers responded in an "options-limiting" manner (i.e., disapproving of or obstructing the child's play) (Stilson & Harding, 1997).

In some cultures, infant play is viewed as predominantly a child's activity (e.g., in Mayan and many American Indian cultures), whereas other cultures assign an important role to parents as play partners (e.g., in middle-income U.S. culture). Differences between cultures also exist in views about the value of play (Bornstein, Venuti, & Hahn, 2002; Cote & Bornstein, 2005; Kwak, Putnick, & Bornstein, 2008; Suizzo & Bornstein, 2006; Venuti et al., 2008). Some cultures believe that play provides important development-promoting experiences; others see play primarily to amuse. Presumably, cultural beliefs about play affect the nature and frequency of infants' play with parents, siblings, and peers.

Generally speaking, Japanese infants and mothers tend to engage in more symbolic play than their American counterparts, whereas American infants and mothers tend to engage in more exploratory play (Bornstein, 2007). In line with other social features of the culture, Japanese mothers organize infant-directed pretend play in ways that incorporate a partner into play. Japanese mothers encourage interactive (other-

INTERIM SUMMARY 5.3

Mental Representation in Infancy

Specific Areas of Cognitive Development

Categorization

- Grouping separate things together according to some rule.
- It facilitates the storage and retrieval of information.
- Infants learn to apply their knowledge of attributes to other members of the same category (for example, that his/her dog's barking applies to other dogs as well).

Memory

- **Infantile amnesia** is not being able to remember much before the age of 3 or 4.
- Short-term memory has been studied by habituating/familiarizing infants and testing them afterward with the same stimulus.
- Long-term memory has been studied by imposing a delay between habituation and a later test.
- Infants' ability to remember improves with age—infants habituate more quickly and effectively as they grow older.
- **Deferred imitation** (showing babies a series of actions then seeing whether they produce these actions later) is even more advanced.

Play

- Play is fun and interactive but also involves mental work.
- Play progresses from **exploratory play** (goal of extracting information about objects) in the first year to pretend or **symbolic play** (make-believe scenarios) in the second year.
- Play normally occurs in the context of social interaction and in some cultures is predominantly a child's activity, whereas in others parents play as partners.

directed) activities ("Feed the dolly"), whereas American mothers encourage self-exploration that is more functional ("Push the bus"). For Americans, play and toys are frequently the topic or object of communication. In contrast, for Japanese, the play setting and associated toys are used to promote mother-infant communication and interaction. This difference is consistent with cultural child-rearing practices more generally, which in Japan emphasize closeness and interdependency between people, and in America encourage interest in objects, interpersonal independence, and the acquisition of information.

In summary, infants' categorization, memory, and play reflect mental representation as well as broader cultural themes and values. These abilities do not develop in isolation; indeed, they are fostered during social interactions with parents when parents are attuned to their infant's emotional cues and developmental level. (For a summary of this section, see "Interim Summary 5.3: Mental Representation in Infancy.")

INFANT "INTELLIGENCE"

Developmental scientists are also interested in how much children of a given age understand, and how much children of the same age vary in their "intelligence"—a quantitative approach to cognitive development (Siegler, 2002, 2007).

Infant Tests

Beginning in the 1920s, about the same time that Piaget began making notes on his own children's cognitive development, Nancy Bayley set out to *measure* mental and motor growth in infancy. She originally developed a scale of the performance of middle-income children tested regularly from birth through eighteen years. The Bayley Scales of Infant Development have become the most widely used assessments of infant development. Today, there are two scales: a Mental Development Index and a Psychomotor Development Index. They assess motor, sensation, perception, cognition, memory, language, and social behavior in infants and toddlers over the first years of life.

Measuring infant intelligence is problematic. When researchers want to assess the usefulness of an "IQ" measure, say, among college students, they might ask how well IQ scores correlate with student performance on another index of intelligence, like achievement in school. (In case you were wondering, the answer is "moderately well.") In other words, with adults and even older children, the degree to which a test measures what it was designed to measure—what is called the test's **validity**—can be assessed by comparing test scores with independent measures of the same or similar things. With infants, however, there is no definitive or obvious external index of achievement with which to compare intelligence test performance. One way to assess the validity of infant tests is to compare infants' performance early in life with their performance years later, as children or even as adults. Logically, if infants who perform well on infant tests do well on standardized IQ tests as children or adults, then the infant tests must be telling us something about "intelligence" in infancy. This is a particular type of validity, called **predictive validity** (validity over time). When Bayley (1949) conducted a longitudinal study, however, she found essentially no relation between test performance in the first three to four years of life and intelligence test performance of the same children at eighteen years. Only after children reached about six years of age or so did an association between childhood scores and eventual adult scores emerge—that is, adult intelligence could be predicted from tests of intelligence administered as early as six, but not from tests administered at younger ages. The Bayley is still useful in detecting developmental problems in infants; a very poor score on the Bayley may indicate serious developmental delay. But it is not predictive of later intellectual functioning (Bornstein, 1998).

validity   The degree to which a test measures what it was designed to measure.

predictive validity   When performance at one time relates meaningfully to performance at a later time.

The absence of a connection between infant intelligence and later intelligence could be due to several different things. It could reflect a genuine discontinuity in intellectual development. Maybe being a smart baby has nothing to do with being an intelligent first-grader. Or the absence of a link between infant test performance and later test performance could reflect a problem with the instrument—maybe the Bayley test is not a very good measure of the things that should predict later intelligence. The Bayley tests babies with items that tap sensory capacities, motor achievements, and responses that are influenced by the baby's emotional state, like orienting, reaching, and smiling. For an older child, very different items are used in evaluating intelligence—skills related to language, reasoning, and memory. The lack of predictive validity is therefore not surprising.

Perhaps measures of infant mental ability that are more purely cognitive and free of motor requirements or emotional components would make more appropriate tests and have more predictive validity. What might show us how well a baby is *thinking*? One way is to watch how he or she pays attention. Generally speaking, infants who process information more efficiently acquire knowledge more quickly. We can measure the efficiency of an infant's information processing with some of the tools described at the beginning of the chapter: habituation and novelty responsiveness.

Suppose you were trying to memorize in one hour all the lyrics to a hip-hop song that you've heard many times before. But because you've often been interrupted while hearing the song in the past, you've heard the first half of the song much more often than the second half. Now that you want to learn all the lyrics, which parts of the song should you pay closest attention to in the hour that you have? Obviously, the lyrics you don't know as well. As a rule, if you want to be efficient, it makes more sense to devote more time attending to things that are new than things that are familiar (Bornstein, 1998).

Just as students vary in their ability to concentrate, so infants vary in the ways they perform on tests of habituation and novelty responsiveness. Studies find that those who are more efficient (i.e., who pay more attention to novel stimuli and less to familiar ones) also tend to explore their environment more competently and play in more sophisticated ways—two other indicators of infant cognitive competence (Bornstein, 1998). Furthermore, infants who are expected to show lower intelligence later in life—those with developmental disabilities such as Down syndrome—are also poorer in attention when they are babies. Although infants' scores on the Bayley do not predict later intelligence, performance on tests of habituation and novelty responsiveness do: Infants who show efficient information processing tend to perform better on traditional assessments of cognitive competence in later childhood (Bornstein, 1998; Kavsek, 2004; Strid et al., 2006; Tasbihsazan, Nettelbeck, & Kirby, 2003; Tsao, Liu, & Kuhl, 2004).

This does not mean that intelligence is innate or fixed in early life. Certainly genetics contribute to mental development, but experience in the world is a major contributing factor (Lerner, Fisher, & Gianinno, 2006). Infant learning is assisted and guided by others. This is the *social context* of mental development in infancy (Bornstein, 1991; Bornstein & Bradley, 2003; Bronfenbrenner & Morris, 1998; Rogoff, 2003).

Infant Mental Development in Social Context

In all of their interactions, in cultural communities as farflung as Turkey, Guatemala, India, and the United States, children participate actively in culturally organized activities; in this way, they gain an understanding of the world they live in. As "apprentices" in daily living skills, infants must learn to think, act, and interact with the central characters in their culture to grow up and adapt successfully.

One way to think about how the environment influences child development is to take an *ecological perspective*, which you read about in "Nature with Nurture." As you recall, children's growth and development are influenced by some forces that are close at hand (parents, extended family, peers), other forces that are somewhat removed (their neighborhood, their parents' workplaces), and still other forces that are quite removed, although still influential (social class, culture). Closer influences are called *proximal*, and more remote influences are called *distal*. Generally speaking, distal forces influence child development through proximal forces.

We know, for example, that low socioeconomic status (a distal influence) is linked to poor intellectual development in children (McLoyd, Aikens, & Burton, 2006). Living in a poor environment per se isn't what influences the child's IQ, though. Rather, there are fewer educated parents living in poor environments (proximal influences), and poorly educated parents provide their children with less verbal stimulation (Hoff, 2006) and fewer enriching life experiences (Bradley, 2002). Children reared in more advantaged homes show superior mental development both because of genetic factors and environmental ones (Petrill et al., 2004). The influence of the family on infant cognitive development is not a one-way street, however. Infant and caregiver *jointly* contribute to developing cognitive competence—although infants learn from the experiences they have playing with their parents, the experiences that parents provide their infant are affected by infants' capabilities at that point in their development. In other words, the infant's cognitive development is always a product of the constant interplay between the infant's abilities and the environment and experiences that the caregiver provides.

Parents influence their infants' intellectual development in many ways: by structuring teaching exchanges, by being responsive to their needs, and by providing books and toys. In infancy, the vast majority of experiences stem directly from interactions within the family. Parents take principal responsibility for structuring teaching exchanges with infants: They engage infants in early games as well as in turn-taking exchanges in play. As carpenters do in constructing a building, parents sometimes use temporary aids—a process referred to as **scaffolding**—to help their child advance (Vygotsky, 1978). Later, as the edifice of intellect grows and is solidified, the scaffold may be replaced or taken down (see "Cognitive Development in Early Childhood").

Parents vary in the scaffolds they favor, and some scaffolding strategies may be more effective than others, depending on the nature and age of the child. *Joint attention*—when a mother and a child are focused on the same object, for example—appears to promote cognitive development: In infancy, joint attention has been linked to infants' communication skills (Butterworth, 2001). *Parental responsiveness* is another effective scaffolding strategy (Bornstein, 2002; Gros-Louis et al., 2006). Infants benefit when parents respond to interactions that the infant initiates. The *toys and books* that parents provide for their infants is a third effective scaffolding technique (Bradley, 2002). Toys that provide challenges and rewards (i.e., toys that infants can use with some help at first, but then by themselves) are ideal. Reading with children broadens their knowledge as well as developing prereading skills (see "Cognitive Development in Early Childhood"). The number of books and toys matters, but so does parental involvement with them.

What motivates infants' parents to behave in the ways they do? Parental belief systems, called **ethnotheories**, help to determine how parents interact with their infants.

Parents have important roles to play in their infants' learning about the world, as this dad shows in demonstrating for his 10-month-old girl how a new toy works.

scaffolding Providing learning opportunities, materials, hints, and clues when a child has difficulty with a task.

ethnotheories Parents' belief systems that motivate them to behave in the ways they do.

INTERIM SUMMARY 5.4

Infant "Intelligence"

The Bayley Scales of Infant Development are used to assess infant motor, sensation, perception, cognition, memory, language, and social behavior:

- The **validity** (the degree to which a test measures what it was designed to measure) of these tests is problematic since there's no definitive external index of achievement with which to compare infant test performance.

- **Predictive validity** (validity over time)—compares infants' performance early in life with their performance years later as children or adults.

- The Bayley is still useful in detecting developmental problems in infants but not predictive of later intellectual functioning.

- Intelligence is not fixed in early life—genetics contribute but experience in the world or social context is a major contributing factor.

- An infant's cognitive development is always a product of the infant's abilities and the environment and experiences provided by caregivers.

As a result, different approaches to scaffolding are seen around the world. For example, European American mothers tend to believe that physical development is the result of maturation but that knowledge comes from interaction with the environment. Kenyan Gisuii mothers tend to believe that physical development depends on interaction but that knowledge comes from observation. Not surprisingly, European American mothers tend to encourage infant exploration more than Gusii mothers as a way of developing their babies' cognitive skills, but Gisuii mothers deliberately encourage physical development more than their European American counterparts. (For a summary of this section, see "Interim Summary 5.4: Infant Intelligence.")

LANGUAGE DEVELOPMENT IN INFANCY

The word *infant* derives from the Latin *in + fans*, which translated literally means "nonspeaker"; the word *baby* shares a Middle English root with "babble." Beginning to speak—and understand speech—is one of most impressive, and quintessentially human, developments during infancy.

Language depends on perceptual, cognitive, and social development, and it involves many overlapping levels of production and comprehension. Sounds must be produced and perceived (**phonology**). The meaning of words (**semantics**) must be learned. The grammar (**syntax**) of language defines the ways in which words and phrases are arranged to ensure correct and meaningful communication.

Consider what the infant must do to understand his mother when she says, "Comehereloadforadrinkofjuice." The child must break up the sound stream into individual words, understand what each word means, and analyze the grammatical structure linking the words. To complicate matters further, these three types of decoding must take place simultaneously on the fly; that is, as the mother is talking.

Scholars have disagreed over the relative contributions of biology and experience to the acquisition of language. Some theoreticians have argued that language learning is based solely on the child's experiences. In the fourth century, Saint Augustine (1961) wrote that children learn language by imitating their elders; in the twentieth century, B. F. Skinner (1957) argued that children learn language through principles of learning. In contrast, other theorists have asserted that infants must come into the world with a biologically inborn ability to acquire language (Chomsky, 1965; Jakobson, 1968). The truth is somewhere between these two extremes. Language is too rich, unique, and complex a system for infants simply to "learn" passively through imitation or

phonology Sounds in language that are produced and perceived.

semantics The meaning of words and sentences, or the content of speech.

syntax The rules that define the ways in which words and phrases are arranged to ensure correct and meaningful communication. Also called *grammar*.

reinforcement, just as it is too rich, unique, and complex a system for infants simply to "know." The acquisition of language, like other developments, reflects a complex interaction between the child's developing competencies (biology) and the larger context of adult-infant social communication (experience).

Language Norms and Methods of Study

Figure 5.3 depicts some milestones of language development in infancy. As you can see, the first two years of life are a time of remarkable growth. In the first month of life, infants coo and babble; by their twenty-fourth month, toddlers generate grammatically correct sentences. In the first month, infants respond to the sound of the human voice; by their twenty-fourth month, toddlers comprehend the meaning of prepositions (e.g., *to, in, of*).

To understand how language develops in infancy, we might simply observe, record, and analyze what children themselves appear to understand and naturally say as they grow up. High-quality recordings show that the infant's early speech is more sophisticated than it sounds. For example, when children first start saying words, they often fail to make certain distinctions clear; a child might seem to pronounce the /p/ (pronounced "pa") and /b/ (pronounced "ba") at the beginnings of words in exactly the same way. This suggests that children fail to notice the distinction when they hear /p/ and /b/ words. However, analyses of recordings of children's attempts at /p/ and /b/

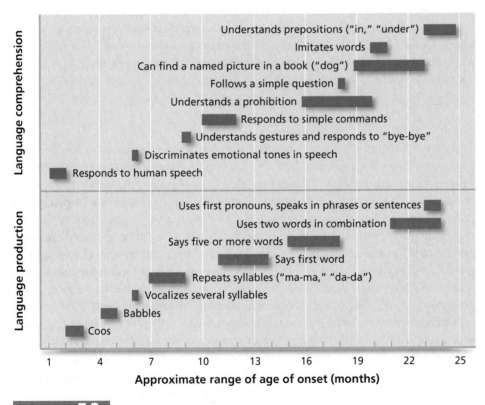

FIGURE 5.3

Milestones of Language Development in Infancy

The top half of the graph shows development of language comprehension. Across infancy, babies develop from simply responding to voices to understanding sophisticated phrases. The bottom half of the graph shows development of language production. Across infancy, babies develop from making cooing and babbling sounds to speaking in phrases and short sentences. The length of each bar represents the range of ages by which most infants achieve each ability, which is a reflection of individual differences in language development.

sounds reveal that some children actually make the sounds differently—but not differently enough for adults to hear clearly. One important implication of this finding is that children's learning certain distinctions between sounds cannot be due solely to adult reinforcement, because adults hardly hear children's initial improvements. Another implication is that our naked ears may underestimate what children know. This echoes a theme that arises again and again in the study of language development (and of cognitive development more generally): The roots of complex behaviors often exist long before those behaviors are clear and overt, and many capacities that seem to bloom overnight have in fact been developing for months.

Another strategy for studying the development of language uses parents' reports. In fact, much of the classic information about language development comes from parents' diaries of their own children (e.g., Bloom, 1976; Dromi, 1987; Leopold, 1949; Weir, 1962). As sources of information, diaries can be quite detailed, informative, and thought provoking, although they may also be biased and describe unrepresentative children (Bornstein, 2008). A variation of this method is the parent checklist, where parents note their child's use of language on preprinted lists (Fenson et al., 1993; Maital et al., 2000).

Language Comprehension and Production

comprehension Understanding language.

production Speaking the language.

When examining child language, we have to distinguish between *comprehension* and *production*. If you play with a one-year-old, you might notice that the child can follow your instructions well but cannot tell you anything about the simple game you two are playing. **Comprehension** is understanding language; **production** is speaking language. Comprehension nearly always comes before production developmentally. Infants might begin understanding words at nine months but not say any until twelve months. On average, comprehension reaches a fifty-word milestone at around thirteen months, whereas production doesn't reach this point until eighteen months (Benedict, 1979).

Individual Variation in Language Development

morphemes Units of meaning in a language.

Children of the same age vary dramatically on nearly every measure of language development (Bates & Carnevale, 1993). One researcher (Brown, 1973) traced speech development in three children—Adam, Eve, and Sarah—by indexing their verbal growth in terms of their *mean length of utterance*, measured in the number of **morphemes** (units of meaning, including spoken words, like *play*, and word parts, like the "ing" in *playing*). Figure 5.4 shows that all three children achieved common *goals* and that their growth *rates* were nearly equivalent. However, Eve began talking considerably earlier than did Adam or Sarah. For example, Eve used an average of three morphemes in an utterance at about two years of age, whereas Adam and Sarah did not do so until approximately three years of age—one-third of their lifetimes later.

At thirteen months, some toddlers comprehend ten words, others seventy-five; some produce no words, others twenty-seven (Tamis-LeMonda & Bornstein, 1990, 1991). At twenty months, individual toddlers can range from 10 to 500 words in their productive vocabularies, and this is true across cultures (Bornstein et al., 2004). Over the course of infancy, moreover, there is a fair amount of consistency within individual children: Infants who know more words at one year tend to know more words at two years.

referential A linguistic style hallmarked by vocabularies that include a high proportion of nouns and speech that provides information and refers to things in the environment.

expressive A linguistic style hallmarked by early vocabularies that have relatively more verbs and speech that uses social routines to communicate feelings and desires.

Number of words and mean length of utterance give evidence of quantitative differences among children; children also differ qualitatively. Some children are **referential**; their vocabularies include a high proportion of nouns, and their speech provides information and refers to things in the environment ("ball," "kitty," "apple"). Other children are **expressive**; their early vocabularies have relatively more verbs, and their speech uses social routines to communicate feelings and desires ("carry me," "hungry," "Mommy go"). One researcher video recorded two children at play with their mothers at home at twelve, fifteen, and eighteen months of age (Goldfield, 1985/1986). Johanna was a

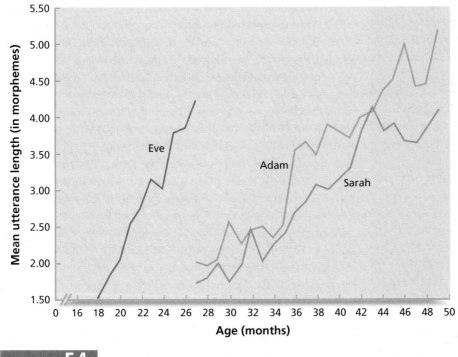

Individual Differences in Language Development

Although most children develop language abilities through a very similar sequence, there is a lot of individual variation in when the process begins and how fast the process occurs. For example, Eve was using four-morpheme utterances just after her second birthday, but Adam and Sarah did not do so until they were about three and a half years old.

Source: Reprinted by permission of the publisher from *A first language: The early stages* by Roger Brown, p. 57, Cambridge, Mass.: Harvard University Press, Copyright ©1973 by the President and Fellows of Harvard College.

referential child. Of Johanna's first fifty words, forty-nine were names for things. In play, approximately half of her attempts to engage her mother involved her giving or showing a toy, and reciprocally Johanna's mother consistently labeled toys for her. Caitlin was an expressive child. Nearly two of every three of Caitlin's first fifty words consisted of social expressions, many of them in phrases. For referential youngsters the purposes of language are to label, describe, and exchange information, whereas for expressive youngsters language is to note or confirm activity. Caitlin and Johanna are extremes, of course; most children are some of each, or their speech depends on the situation.

The Building Blocks of Language

One of the principal tasks of the first two and a half years of life is for the infant to develop into a conversational partner. Adult and infant alike are geared to this common goal, and infants come very far very fast. In learning language, the child is neither ill equipped nor alone. There are many sophisticated elements of language that infants and their caregivers bring to the process. Three are infant-directed speech, turn-taking, and gesture.

Infant-Directed Speech Think about the way you would speak to a baby: Your inflection, speed, and choice of words will no doubt vary from those you use in speaking to an adult. Although infants possess perceptual abilities that help in language learning (see "Physical Development in Infancy"), parents repackage the language directed at infants to match infant capacities. This synchrony is thought to facilitate language acquisition. Specifically, mothers, fathers, caregivers, and even

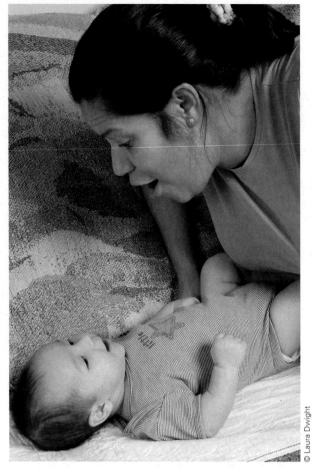

© Laura Dwight

Even the youngest babies—this boy is only 2 months old—are interested in interacting with others; this mother is using infant-directed speech (sometimes called "baby talk") to keep their interaction going.

infant-directed speech
A special speech register reserved for babies that simplifies normal adult-directed speech in many ways.

older children adopt a special dialect when addressing infants, called **infant-directed speech**. The special characteristics of infant-directed speech include: rhythm and tone (higher pitch, greater range of frequencies, more varied and exaggerated intonation); simplification (shorter utterances, slower tempo, longer pauses between phrases, fewer clauses and auxiliaries); redundancy (more repetition over shorter amounts of time); special forms of words (like *mama*); and content (restriction of topics to the child's world). Infant-directed speech may be intuitive and nonconscious (Papoušek & Papoušek, 2002), and cross-cultural developmental study attests that infant-directed speech is (essentially) universal (Papoušek, Papoušek, & Bornstein, 1985). Even two- to three-year-olds engage in such systematic language adjustments when speaking to their one-year-old siblings as opposed to their mothers (Dunn & Kendrick, 1982). And deaf mothers modify their sign language very much the way hearing mothers use infant-directed speech (Erting, Thumann-Prezioso, & Sonnenstrahl-Benedict, 2000).

Turn-Taking Turn-taking is fundamental to the structure of adult dialogue. It is impolite to interrupt; rather, we wait our turn to speak. (Setting manners aside, it is likely that turn-taking evolved because the human nervous system cannot simultaneously produce and understand speech.) Mothers and their infants engage in turn-taking to a much greater degree than speaking at the same time (Jasnow & Feldstein, 1986). After mothers and babies vocalize, they next suppress vocalization to permit their partner to join the conversation. It could be that infants understand that turn-taking signals that a conversation is taking place. When adults use conversational give-and-take patterns, infants produce more speech-like than non-speech-like sounds (Bloom, Russell, & Wassenburg, 1987). Infants participating in normal "conversation" vocalize more like they are really talking, and what adults say to three-month-olds influences what infants are likely to "reply."

Gesture Gesture is another nonverbal support to communication (Blake et al., 2003; Goldin-Meadow, 2006; Locke, 2001). By the time infants are nine months of age, parents already are labeling something while pointing or gazing at it. Mothers use their hands to attract and maintain infant attention. For example, a mother might point and at the same time ask "What is that?"

Infants are more likely to look at objects previously pointed to and labeled than at objects that were not labeled (Baldwin & Markman, 1989). That is, pointing and labeling increase infants' attention to, and memory for, objects. At about twelve months, infants themselves start to point, although the range of individual differences varies considerably: Some begin by nine months, whereas others don't start until nineteen months (Hoff, 2006). Infants whose mothers label responses to infants' pointing ("Yes, that's the *moon*") later become children with larger referential vocabularies.

Why do people use baby talk, turn-taking, and gesture with babies? These strategies elicit the baby's attention, change the baby's state of arousal (by exciting her when you want to get her attention), communicate emotion, and, of course, facilitate language comprehension. For example, infants respond more to their own mother's voice when she is using infant-directed speech than when she is not; infants also prefer to listen to infant-directed speech than to adult-directed speech even when spoken by strangers (Kitamura et al., 2002). Certain patterns in mothers' speech to a baby recur in particular situations, and they do so in a wide variety of languages, such as American English, German, and Mandarin Chinese. Mothers around the world use a rising pitch to engage infant attention, a falling pitch to soothe a distressed infant, and an up-then-down pattern to maintain infant attention (Papoušek & Papoušek, 2002; Papoušek et al., 1985). Finally, these adult modifications appear to make it easier for the baby to acquire language. For example, studies of habituation and novelty responsiveness show that, when presented with a sequence of syllables that contain some speech sounds (e.g., in English, the sound "bay" is a speech sound) and other sounds that are not a part of speech ("gwu"), infants discriminate speech sounds embedded in multisyllable sequences better in infant-directed speech than in adult-directed speech (Karzon, 1985).

© Louis Quail/Corbis

To overcome the loss of a communication channel, speech and hearing, families in the Deaf culture use visual and tactile means, like this dad signing to his infant son.

Making and Understanding Sounds

At the most basic level, language and communication involve sounds. When we speak we make sounds, and when we hear we listen to sounds. So we begin this discussion with how babies perceive and produce sounds.

Sound Perception As you read in "Physical Development in Infancy," the auditory system is well developed before birth, and so newborns hear, orient to, and distinguish

all sorts of sounds from the moment they are born. But babies seem especially primed to perceive and appreciate human speech. Consider, however, the seemingly impossible task of segmenting the speech stream—knowing where one word ends and the next begins—before knowing any words or even what a word is (if you didn't know any words, imagine figuring out that "Comeherelovelyforadrinkofjuice" is "Come here, lovely, for a drink of juice," and not "Co mehere lo velyfor adrin kof jui ce"). Moreover, infants have to do this for different speakers and in different contexts. Some competencies have evolved to address two main problems in this task, namely segmenting sounds and recognizing speech.

For example, first, infants perceive *categories* of speech sounds. Because sounds vary so much from one language to another, many have thought that meaning-

© Inspirestock/Jupiterimages

Parents use many different strategies to get and hold their infant's attention; gesturing to catch a baby's attention and pointing to direct attention are common.

ful distinctions among sounds must be shaped by experience. However, it appears that many speech sounds are not experienced as wholly different from one another or as random, but rather many sounds fit into smaller numbers of categories (and presumably more manageable categories), and infants so categorize from a very early age. The two sounds, /b/ (pronounced "ba") and /p/ (pronounced "pa"), are examples. Infants categorize different /b/s as similar and categorize different /p/s as similar, but distinguish /b/s from /p/s. Categorization of speech sounds is important to language acquisition for many reasons. For example, if infants heard each and every variant of /b/ as different, then learning "ball," "box," "bat," "bottle," and so forth would be inordinately more difficult, not to mention the challenges posed by the variations in /b/ produced by the same speaker (mother) at different times or by different speakers (mother and father).

Sound Production Infants pass through stages in early verbal development: broadly, a prelinguistic stage, a one-word stage, and a multiword stage (Bornstein, 2000; MacWhinney, 2005).

Babies' first means of vocal communication are prelinguistic—crying and babbling. But this hardly means that they are unimportant. Few adults can disregard a baby's cry; it compels us to respond (Bowlby, 1969), and the nearly universal response is to be nurturing in some way (Bornstein et al., 1992). The infant's cry is also a very revealing vocalization. Characteristics of the baby's cry are affected by many factors, including hunger and sleepiness during pregnancy, nutritional deficiency, respiratory disorder, prematurity, genetic disorders such as Down syndrome, as well as cocaine exposure during pregnancy.

If babies' cries inform parents about their unhappy state, babbling is the first significant nondistress communication. In babbling, there are frequent repetitions of the same syllable sound or syllable—ba-ba-ba-ba—and this practice makes perfect the sounds, syllables, and sequences of syllables that will later comprise full-blown speech. Babbling typically accompanies excitation and motor activity and alternates with attentive listening. Although babbling seems simple, there is more to it than first meets the ear (Dromi, 2001). Babbling is significant because it comprises infants' first "structured" vocalizations, because it sounds like fun, and because it fills the eerie void between the silence or crying so common to early infancy on the one hand, and advent of the first intelligible words of toddlerhood on the other. Even deaf infants "babble" using hand signs as well as sounds (Petitto et al., 2001), so we can conclude that having heard speech is not critical to babbling. Rather, the similarities in manual and vocal babbling indicate that babbling is an abstract language capacity of human beings related to expressive capacity.

Every child uses two sources of information when beginning to speak: the speech of others and feedback from his or her own speech. Thus, as expected, deaf infants' vocal babbles develop later than those of hearing infants (Oller, 2000). Auditory input is necessary for the normal and timely development of the range of adult-like syllables; indeed, it is crucial to developing normal vocalizations in the language where infants find themselves. Language experts and laypeople alike can identify the language of origin in samples of eight-month-olds' babbling, even though the infants will not be speaking the language for quite a while still. (In other words, babbling in Chinese sounds different from babbling in French.) Infants as young as eight months of age are influenced by the language they hear. Infants' very earliest sensitivities to sound and their earliest vocal expressions give evidence of strong biological influences. Very soon, however, both perception and production of sound are shaped by the linguistic experiences provided by parent, home, and culture.

How Infants Learn Words

Recall the "Comehere lovely for a drink of juice" problem. To understand this simple statement, even after breaking it down into separate units correctly, the child (lovely) must determine which unit refers to him- or herself, which to objects (drink, juice) in the environment, which to an action (come), and so forth. After all, connections between word sounds and word meanings are arbitrary. The decoding task is a major one. Just how semantic development occurs still remains a mystery.

Once the baby speaks his or her first word, around twelve months on average, adults can agree that the baby has a word, but the baby normally uses the word for all kinds of things. "Mickey" may stand for the cartoon character, the TV, the family pet, or a drinking cup with the mouse image on it. This use of a single word for many things is called **holophrasis**.

After the child had attained one-word speech, word learning proceeds rapidly. The

Being responsive to an infant, as this mother shows, is not only a major way of interacting, but is one way that parents show infants that infants can influence their environment.

average three-year-old possesses an estimated vocabulary of 3,000 words. Therefore, between approximately twelve and thirty-six months, the child acquires four new words per day on average (MacWhinney & Bornstein, 2003). How? Infants cry, babble, and gesture to communicate effectively. But these methods of communication are still limited. A major step in language development is for infants to start learning the connections between sounds and meanings that are characteristic of their language.

To what do children's first words refer? One would think that children's first words might be those that they hear most often. But this is not altogether true—or at least the story is not this simple. The two most frequent English words in speech to infants are *you* and *the*, which are rarely (if ever) in the list of the first fifty words a child produces. So word frequency is not the sole key to early vocabularies (although all other factors being equal, frequency matters; American children learn *cat* before *cap*). What about the grammatical class of early words? Nouns refer to concrete objects, verbs to actions, and adjectives to properties. Because notions like "dog" are easier to grasp than notions like "give" or "round," children around the world learn more nouns early on than verbs or adjectives (Bornstein et al., 2004). One way word learning occurs is through **induction**, or using a limited set of examples to draw conclusions that permit inferences about new cases. Suppose a child sees a cup referred to as "cup." For the child to recognize that the same word refers to other cups as well requires an inductive inference: going beyond the taught example to other examples. This is not as simple as it sounds, and there are several problems to solve.

First, there is what we might call the *immediate reference problem*: Mommy is holding a mug of coffee and saying the word, "cup." But what does she mean? Sometimes the speaker will be pointing to an object when labeling it, but even in these seemingly clear cases there are many logical possibilities. The word might mean "cup," but could mean "handle," "hot liquid," "drinking," "not appropriate for babies your age," or any of an infinite number of conceivable meanings. How do infants get it right?

holophrasis The use of a single word for many things.

induction The process of using a limited set of examples to draw conclusions that permit inferences about new cases.

fast mapping   A phenomenon that refers to how easily children pick up words they have heard only a few times.

whole object assumption   A concept that refers to children's belief that a novel label refers to the "whole object" and not to its parts, substance, or other properties.

mutual exclusivity   A concept that refers to an infant's assumption that any given object has only one name.

socioeconomic status (SES)   The education, occupation, and income of householders.

Second is the *extension problem*: Once the infant has guessed what is referred to, the infant should be willing to extend this word to other objects belonging to the same category—unless the word is a proper name. But what makes a cup a "cup"? Its shape? Color? Function? We cannot simply say, "things that are similar to the original cup"; without a definition of similarity, we're right back where we started. But infants manage to figure out fairly quickly how to extend the use of the word correctly if adults use the word carefully. Adults name an object a few times, and children seem to pick up the name of the object quickly (Markman, 1999). This phenomenon is called **fast mapping**.

Infants must have some rules to help them in their guesses about word meaning (Markman, 1999). An example is the **whole object assumption**. When an adult points to a novel object and labels it, the child is believed first to think the novel label refers to the "whole object" and not to its parts, substance, or other properties (although it could very well refer to these other things). Another bias is **mutual exclusivity**: The child assumes that any given object has only one name.

Children vary dramatically in their early vocabularies. In the fourth century, Emperor Constantine wrote that infants could not speak well or form words because their teeth had not yet erupted—which, if correct, should lead to earlier language development among infants with the fastest dental growth; this turns out not to be true, though. Most subsequent accounts have focused on differences in children's experience, primarily in the speech children hear from their parents. Parents who are lower in **socioeconomic status (SES)** talk substantially less than more affluent parents, and as a consequence, infants from lower SES homes speak later and less than infants from higher SES homes (Hart & Risley, 1995). But there is also a great deal of variation that SES does not account for. Even among mothers from the same SES group, some talk to their babies during as little as 3 percent of a typical home observation and others during as much as 97 percent (Bornstein & Ruddy, 1984). When both language amount (how much the parent talks) and verbal responsiveness (whether the parent's speech is responsive to the infant) are considered, verbal responsiveness is found to contribute more to children's emerging language (Bornstein, Tamis-LeMonda, & Haynes, 1999; Tamis-LeMonda & Bornstein, 2002). For example, children with verbally responsive mothers combine words into simple sentences sooner in development than do children with less verbally responsive mothers. When mothers teach infants a name for a novel toy, they tend to move the toy in synchrony with their verbal label, which also helps infants make the association (Gogate, Bahrick, & Watson, 2000). Thus, maternal stimulation style facilitates the growth of infant language skills.

Is language development biologically programmed in our genes or determined by the environment? You probably know the answer to this (or at least we hope you do): Language competence is, like everything else, the product of genetics *and* experience (Pruden et al., 2006; Waxman & Lidz, 2006). One-year-old adopted children are like their biological parents in their language abilities, indicating genetic influences on infant communicative performance, but they are like their adopted parents as well, indicating the influences of experience (Hardy-Brown & Plomin, 1985; Hardy-Brown, Plomin, & DeFries, 1981).

How Infants Learn Grammar

grammar   See *syntax*.

Grammar (or *syntax*) refers to the rules for combining words into meaningful and interpretable communications. Grammatical competence in children is a wonder to behold; particularly remarkable is their ability to detect syntactic rules and regularities even though these vary enormously across languages. In English, for example, subjects usually precede verbs, which in turn usually precede objects. Thus, when you hear "Larry, Deborah, and Marc wrote this book," you know the book was written by Larry, Deborah, and Marc. As English speakers, we are so accustomed to this word order that it seems natural, even logical. But a great many languages don't work this way. For example, in Welsh, the verb usually comes first. In Turkish and Japanese, many sentences place the verb last, but subjects and objects do not have a fixed order. Given that these rules vary across languages, one would think that they must be learned.

Here, too, both nature and nurture contribute to how children acquire the rules of language and combinations of words. Skinner (1957) argued that children learn grammatical rules by imitation and reinforcement. According to this way of thinking, children learn *transitional probabilities* among words, or which word is likely to come after which other word. "The dog ate my homework" is English, but "Homework my dog the ate" is not (and even Microsoft Word knows this, because the grammar check puts a wiggly green line underneath the words). According to this view, adults produce grammatical statements for children to model, and they also systematically reward children's grammatically correct statements.

However, Noam Chomsky (1965) argued that Skinner's account of grammatical development, with its emphasis on learned transitional probabilities, is far too simple. The grammatically correct use and meaning of an initial word in a sentence just as often depends on the end of the sentence (i.e., on an overall sentence plan) as it does on the next word. For example, "Colorless green ideas sleep furiously" is a perfectly grammatical sentence, although the transitional probabilities in the word string are nonsensically low. Thus, transitional probabilities from one word to the next cannot serve as a principle of the child's grammatical development.

Second, Skinner's notion of reinforcement requires parents to selectively reward children for producing grammatical utterances and not for ungrammatical ones. In practice, though, parents do not do this; in fact, parents are much more likely to correct young children's factual errors than their grammar. If a child who is eating an apple says, "Me eat banana," parents are more likely to say, "No, that is an apple" than "No, say 'I am eating a banana'." Thus, parents do not directly teach children grammar the way schoolteachers do. (Also, children resist explicit correction of grammar; a child saying "Me eat banana" will not generally switch to "I am eating a banana" on being corrected.)

Chomsky argued that a number of aspects of syntax are innate, built into every infant's brain in what he called **universal grammar**. Universal grammar accounts for the fact that, although children's language environments differ, children's syntactic outcomes are strikingly similar. Variation in the vocabulary size of English-learning children can be traced to environmental factors such as parents' verbal responsiveness, but variation in grammar among children learning the same language is slight; poor, middle-class, and well-to-do U.S. American children follow the subject-verb-object syntax of American English when they speak, even if the numbers of nouns, verbs, and adjectives in their vocabularies differ dramatically. Chomsky likened learning language to the growth of an organ like the heart: As long as certain very basic preconditions are met, it (whether language or the heart) will develop in all children. The claim is not that language itself is innate (if it were, why would children in Boston learn the syntax of English and children in Berlin the syntax of German?). Rather, the claim is that children have innate abilities that facilitate grammatical development.

If language is like an organ, can it be identified as a biological structure in the brain? At present it is not possible to give a complete answer to this question, but we can say that no special brain tissue is wholly dedicated to language "tools." However, certain structures in the brain are involved in particular aspects of language processing. For example, injury to **Broca's area** (in the left frontal lobe) tends to cause problems in producing fluent speech and in comprehending syntactic structure, whereas injury to **Wernicke's area** (in the left temporal lobe) tends to cause poor comprehension gen-

universal grammar
Chomsky's term for aspects of syntax that are thought to be innate and built into every infant's brain.

Broca's area The region on the left side of the brain dedicated to language or speech production.

Wernicke's area The region on the left side of the brain dedicated to language or speech comprehension.

erally, and fluent but relatively meaningless speech (Sakai, 2005). (See Figure 4.4 for reference.)

The question of whether children possess a "natural language" has been asked with surprising frequency in history—and by a surprising group of individuals, from pharaohs to phoneticians. James I of England (1566–1625), for example, posed the question and thought of how to address it. Long interested in the Bible—the King James version, of course—James sought to identify the original language of Adam and Eve. He proposed to place two infants on an otherwise uninhabited island in the care of a deafmute nurse. James reasoned that, if the two spontaneously developed speech, theirs would be the natural language of humankind. Although probably within his power, King James never (to our knowledge) conducted his study. Though imaginative, such an experiment would be wholly unethical.

Natural experiments that approximate King James's conditions suggest that children develop their own grammar and vocabulary in the absence of formal linguistic

INTERIM SUMMARY 5.5

Language Development in Infancy

Language depends on perceptual, cognitive, and social development.

The acquisition of language reflects a complex interaction between the child's developing competencies (biology) and the larger context of adult-infant social communication (experience).

Children of the same age vary dramatically on nearly every measure of language development, both quantitatively and qualitatively.

- Sounds must be produced and perceived (phonology).
- The meaning of words (semantics) must be learned.
- The grammar (syntax) of the language defines the ways in which words and phrases are arranged to ensure correct communication.
- Some children are **referential** (their vocabularies include a high proportion of nouns); some, **expressive** (their early language has more social routines).

Infant Directed Speech

- Individuals use a special dialect when addressing infants.
- Turn-taking is used in parent-child dialogue as is gesture.

Making and Understanding Sounds

- Infants perceive categories of speech sounds.
- Infants pass through prelinguistic, one-word, and multiword stages in early verbal development.
- Babies' first means of vocal communication are prelinguistic—crying and babbling.

How Infants Learn Words

- Babies tend to use single words for many things (called **holophrasis**) when they first speak (around 12 months on average).
- Between 13 and 36 months, infants acquire 4 new words a day on average.

How Infants Learn Grammar

- Noam Chomsky argued that a number of aspects of syntax are innate, built into every infant's brain in what he called **universal grammar**.
- Children have a natural inclination to develop grammatically structured communication.

experience. For example, deaf infants who are of normal intelligence but whose parents (for various reasons) have prohibited their learning sign language have essentially no experience with any formal language, but their other life experiences are normal. These children develop their own signs to refer to objects, people, and actions, and they combine signs into phrases to express relations among words in ordered ways. Their communication system is not only structured, it incorporates many properties found in hearing children's language. Clearly, in the absence of formal training and imitation, children develop syntactic rules: They sign actors before actions, and acts before objects acted on. Moreover, children (rather than their mothers) also originate such sign systems when left to their own devices.

Even under difficult circumstances, human children reveal a natural inclination to develop a grammatically structured communication. Furthermore, the timing of deaf children's invention of communication systems is roughly the same as that of hearing children learning spoken languages—their first "words" appear at around twelve months, and their first combinations of words appear several months later. (For a summary of this section, see "Interim Summary 5.5: Language Development in Infancy.")

SUMMING UP AND LOOKING AHEAD

In the not too distant past, the notion that infants "think" would have been considered laughable. Today, however, we know better, thanks largely to the work of Piaget and the decades of scientific study his work stimulated. Although Piaget's timetable for developments in this period has been challenged, his general idea still stands: Infants are active learners, who use their eyes and ears, hands and mouth to investigate and make sense of their world. Infants seem predisposed to form categories, build memories, play, and communicate with others. They are drawn to novelty and are particularly sensitive to language. Although maturation plays a central role in this process, what infants discover, and the rate at which they develop, are shaped by context. Cognitive development is in large part a social process, stimulated and shaped by the interactions the infant has with parents, siblings, and adults and children outside the family.

Naturally, there is much cognitive development that takes place after infancy and that builds especially on the foundation of language laid down during these early years. As you will read in "Cognitive Development in Early Childhood," tremendous strides in language, information processing, mathematical thinking, and social understanding take place between ages three and five. But we are getting ahead of ourselves. We still have one more broad domain of infancy to cover before we leave babyhood behind. The development of the infant as a social being—and the relationships he or she forms with others—is the subject of our next, and final, chapter on the first two years after birth.

HERE'S WHAT YOU SHOULD KNOW

Did You Get It?

After reading this chapter, you should understand the following:

- The techniques and strategies that developmental scientists use to confirm that infants have an active mental life
- Piaget's contribution to the study of infant cognition including his six stages of the sensorimotor period
- The development of infants' abilities of categorization, memory, and play
- Infant intelligence tests and their limitations
- The processes of language development in infancy

Important Terms and Concepts

accommodation (p. 125)
adaptation (p. 125)
assimilation (p. 125)
Broca's area (p. 145)
categorization (p. 129)
comprehension (p. 138)
deferred imitation (p. 131)
ethnotheories (p. 135)
exploratory play (p. 131)
expressive (p. 138)
fast mapping (p. 144)

grammar (p. 144)
habituation (p. 123)
holophrasis (p. 143)
induction (p. 143)
infant-directed speech
    (p. 140)
infantile amnesia (p. 130)
mental representation
    (p. 126)
morphemes (p. 138)

mutual exclusivity (p. 144)
novelty responsiveness
    (p. 123)
object permanence (p. 126)
phonology (p. 136)
predictive validity (p. 133)
production (p. 138)
referential (p. 138)
scaffolding (p. 135)
semantics (p. 136)

sensorimotor period (p. 126)
socioeconomic status (SES)
    (p. 144)
symbolic play (p. 131)
syntax (p. 136)
universal grammar (p. 145)
validity (p. 133)
Wernicke's Area (p. 145)
whole object assumption
    (p. 144)

6 CHAPTER

Socioemotional Development in Infancy

© rubberball/Getty

You've just had your first baby. You and your spouse are excited, but also more than a little nervous. The responsibility is enormous, and you really want to get everything right. The baby seems so tiny, helpless, and (let's be honest) demanding. A month passes, and he is crying almost every night. Is he hungry? Or wet? Is the baby afraid of the dark? Or scared because he's alone? Is this the baby's personality? Is my baby insecure? Have I done something wrong? What is it?

In your anxiety, you wouldn't be alone. Every parent wonders what his or her baby is feeling and why (Bolzani Dinehart et al., 2005). Every parent worries about what a baby's behavior might mean—whether it reflects the baby's feelings at that moment (Why is my baby angry?), his basic personality (Why is my baby so crabby?), or the way he relates to others (Why does my baby fuss so when my parents try to pick him up?).

Like parents, developmental scientists are interested in infants' emotions, temperament, and attachments. **Emotions** are feelings that provide strong and informative cues about the infant's current state. **Temperament** reflects stable, biologically based differences in behavior that impact the infant's interactions with the social and physical environment. **Attachments** are infants' specific, lasting, social relationships with others, especially parents and other caregivers. This chapter begins with questions concerning development of infants' emotional responses and sensitivity to the emotional cues of others. Next, we discuss temperament and consider how temperamental differences affect infants' behavioral functioning, as well as factors that might explain the stability of temperament over time. We conclude with attachment and the nature of parent-infant interactions.

INFANTS' EMOTIONS

Emotions—feelings as seemingly simple as happiness or sadness—pose challenging questions for infancy researchers (Bornstein, 2000; Halle, 2003; Saarni et al., 2006). Because infants cannot tell us what they are feeling, interpreting infants' emotions from their expressions is just about all researchers (and parents) have to go on. But the display of feelings is only part of the story. There are two sides to emotional behavior. One side is **emotional expression**—communicating feelings to others through facial expressions, gestures, and vocalizations. The other side is **emotional understanding**—reading the emotional expressions of others. Infancy is a time of great strides in both.

Development of Emotional Expressions

By the time their infants are only one month of age, 99 percent of mothers believe that their babies express interest; 95 percent, joy; 84 percent, anger; 75 percent, surprise; 58 percent, fear; and 34 percent, sadness (Johnson et al., 1982). Mothers base their judgments on infants' facial and vocal expressions, along with gestures and movements.

Infants display some emotions—joy, surprise, sadness, anger, fear, and shyness—reliably and in appropriate contexts (Izard & Malatesta, 1987). These are called **primary emotions** because they appear to be so deeply rooted in human biology and develop so early. Just as there is a timetable for physical and cognitive growth (infants sit before they stand, babble before they use words), so there is one for emotional growth. The primary emotions appear well before such **secondary emotions** as embarrassment, pride, guilt, shame, and envy, which do not emerge until the second and third years of life. Secondary emotions depend on higher-level mental capacities. For example, to feel guilt or shame, you have to know that you have done something wrong (Lewis, 2000).

Charles Darwin (1872/1975) observed that certain expressions are remarkably consistent across age and culture. Darwin believed in the universality of emotional expressions (Ekman, 2006). To the extent that they are culturally universal, some emotional expressions may be innate (Ekman, 1984). This suggests that they are biologically adaptive patterns that evolved early in the development of the human species to foster survival. For example, expressing distress in a way that all members of a species easily recognize makes it more likely that caregivers will attend to infants' needs. An infant's crying elicits concern; few adults can resist attempting to soothe and quiet her. Crying is programmed in babies; the response is programmed in us.

The face, which is full of muscles that can convey a broad range of expressions with subtle variations, is one of our primary means of evaluating another person's emotions. Researchers have devoted considerable effort to developing systems to measure facial expressions of emotion in infants. One example is the Maximally Discriminative Facial Movements Code, or MAX, as it is more commonly known (Izard, 1979; Izard & Dougherty, 1982). MAX allows users to identify twenty-seven distinct facial patterns that, alone or in combination, specify particular emotions—such as the way the baby's eyebrows are positioned, or how open or closed his mouth is. (If you try right now to make a "surprised" face, you will probably raise your eyebrows and open your mouth; see the photo on this page.) Another system is BabyFACS (Facial Action Coding System for Infants and Young Children) with its 92 facial components (Oster, 2005). Such systems are useful, for example, in studying the baby's emotional reactions to social events—such as the approach of an unfamiliar adult.

How well do facial expressions identify underlying emotions in infants? Because we rely on facial expressions in our everyday estimates of others' emotions, these measures carry considerable "face validity." (Yes, the pun is intended!)

Infants express different emotions vocally as well, by cooing and babbling versus by fretting and crying. Adults typically rate certain infant cries as more distressed and aversive than others: Babies who cry with a high pitch, with great intensity, and for a long time are more likely to elicit faster responses from adults than babies who cry briefly or minimally (Barr, Hopkins, & Green, 2000). Parents certainly think infants' cries are meaningful, and research suggests that parents can tell the difference among cries, say, ones that signal hunger versus ones that indicate pain (Sagi, 1981).

© Image Source/Jupiterimages

Babies wear their emotions on their faces, so it's easy to tell when they are happy, sad, or surprised, like this little girl with her father at the window.

primary emotions The feelings of joy, surprise, sadness, anger, fear, and shyness that appear to be deeply rooted in human biology and develop early in life.

secondary emotions The feelings of embarrassment, pride, guilt, shame, and envy that emerge in the second and third years of life.

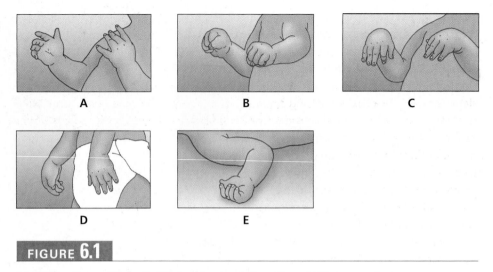

FIGURE 6.1

Identification of Infants' Behavior and Emotional States

Infants also express their emotions with gestures and movements. Figure 6.1 shows drawings used in a study of parents' and nonparents' identification of infants' emotional states (Papoušek & Papoušek, 1978). See if you can match which hand positions go with which infant states: transition to sleep, distress, sleep, alertness, and passive waking. (Correct answers appear at the bottom of page 154—no peeking!)[1]

Infants become very still when they are interested in an event, turn away from stimuli that evoke fear, show a slumped posture when sad, look intently (often with a double take) at stimuli that surprise them, and try to repeat or duplicate experiences they find joyful. Even untrained observers can identify babies' emotions, whether shown still photographs or videotapes.

Emotional expressions can be observed during the newborn period, often in response to survival-related experiences, like pain or hunger. We already discussed neonates' emotional reactions to sour, sweet, and bitter tastes (see "Physical Development in Infancy"). Newborns clearly respond to a sweet taste with what adults interpret as positive facial expressions, and to other tastes with various negative expressions of disgust or "distaste," as if wanting to eliminate the noxious substance.

Expressions of fear and anger have been observed as early as three to four months (Lemerise & Dodge, 2000). For example, when three-month-olds confront looming stimuli, they show fear. After six months, infants also begin to show fearful reactions to visual cliffs (see "Physical Development in Infancy"), approaching strangers, and sudden or unusual events. As infants grow, anger becomes increasingly typical in response to unpleasant or restricting events, like being buckled into a car seat. When two-month-olds get a painful inoculation, they show distress; by nineteen months, babies get downright angry. Put a wanted toy behind a barrier and stop an infant from playing with it by restraining the infant's arms, and you'll see anger, but have a noisy and unpredictable remote-controlled spider approach an infant, and you'll see fear. Differences among infants in the ways they behave are often accompanied by differences in emotional expressions, indicating that actions and emotions are coordinated: Infants who withdraw from fear-inducing stimuli and look to their mothers more show also more intense fear expressions; infants who resist the arm restraint more, and attempt to distract themselves more by focusing on another object, show greater intensity of anger.

Sadness has been observed in infants as young as two and a half months of age (Izard et al., 1995). When mothers play with their three-month-olds and then suddenly become unresponsive, their babies show signs of withdrawal, "wariness," and sadness in their facial expressions and posture (Bornstein, Arterberry, & Mash, 2005; Cohn & Tronick, 1983).

Although all infants show signs of sadness from time to time, some infants are sadder than others. Infants of depressed mothers are at special risk. These infants show depressed social behavior not only when interacting with their mothers (acting withdrawn, immobile, and nonresponsive), but also when interacting with a stranger who knows nothing about the baby or his family. Infants of depressed mothers might have acquired their emotions in several ways: through shared genes, through the effects of reduced opportunities for positive social interaction at home, through imitation of the mother's behavior, or through effects of the mother's depression on the baby (e.g., the baby's sense of helplessness that may have been learned through interacting with a nonresponsive mother).

Researchers have often focused on negative emotions, such as fear, anger, or sadness, but obviously, not all of an infant's emotional life is gloom and doom. Young infants readily express positive emotions (Lewis, 2000). Social interaction, such as the sound of a high-pitched human voice or the appearance of a nodding face, can elicit smiles in the first month of life. Clear expressions of joy have been observed by two and a half months, when infants are engaged in social play with their mothers and fathers; and by three to four months, infants laugh, especially during social interaction.

As infants grow older, they become capable of a broader range of emotional expressions and are responsive to a growing variety of conditions. Cognitive development contributes to emotional growth by enabling infants to evaluate situations in more sophisticated ways. Experiences that may not have elicited certain emotions earlier may now bring them out, because the infant is processing more information at a higher level—playing peekaboo won't do much for a one-month-old, but between six and twelve months, when the infant acquires object permanence (see "Cognitive Development in Infancy"), this game elicits gales of laughter. Cognitive development also affects negative emotions. Toward the end of the first year, for example, an infant's reactions to a stranger entail, not just an evaluation of the adult's unfamiliarity, but also of the context (mother's presence or absence), the setting (a comfortable and familiar home environment or an unfamiliar laboratory), and the stranger's appearance (male or female, child or adult) and behavior (approaching rapidly or slowly, looming high overhead or looking at eye level).

Infants' social experiences play a significant role in shaping their emotional expressions (Saarni, 2000). Mothers change their facial expressions an average of seven to nine times a minute, and roughly 25 percent of the time mothers respond to their infants' emotional expressions by imitating or responding to positive expressions and ignoring their negative expressions. This kind of contingent emotional responding reinforces the expression of positive emotions and mutes the expression of negative emotions. Thus, mothers who smile more have young infants who smile more (Kuchuk, Vibbert, & Bornstein, 1986). This result suggests that mothers may socialize their infants' expressive styles from the early months of life. Of course, it is also possible that these familial similarities in expressiveness reflect happy infants making their mothers happy or shared mother-infant genes.

As infants become self-aware, a variety of self-conscious secondary emotions such as embarrassment, shame, and later, guilt and pride come on line (Lewis, 2000; Lewis et al., 1989). Infants who recognize themselves (e.g., when looking in a mirror, they will touch themselves as opposed to reaching out for the person in the mirror) also look embarrassed when, for example, they are effusively praised by an adult: They smile and look away and cover their faces with their hands. Infants who do not recognize themselves do not exhibit these self-aware reactions to adult praise.

In summary, newborns and young infants express a variety of emotions that are related to specific eliciting conditions. With growth across a variety of developmental domains, infants' emotional repertoires continue to broaden, they become responsive to a greater range of stimuli and situations, and more complex emotions emerge. Emotional development includes not only these internal changes in responsiveness, but also infants' responses to the emotional expressions of others. That's our next topic.

The Development of Sensitivity to Emotional Signals

Emotional development involves reading as well as sending emotional signals. Recognizing different facial expressions is not the same as understanding their meaning: "Reading" requires important interpretive as well as perceptual skills (Barna & Legerstee, 2005). In other words, just because a baby can tell the difference between a happy face and an angry one (something researchers can determine from a habituation experiment), doesn't mean that she knows what either expression actually means.

To read an emotional signal, you first need to be able to see it, however. Visual acuity in early infancy is limited, though, making it hard for newborns to distinguish among different facial features and expressive patterns (see "Physical Development in Infancy"). At around one and a half to two months of age, infants begin to discriminate among different facial expressions of emotion (Bornstein & Arterberry, 2003) and can even distinguish variations in their intensity (Kuchuk et al., 1986). For example, show infants a series of smiles that are graded in intensity from just barely smiling to a broad toothy grin, and infants will look longer at the more intense expressions. This does not necessarily mean that infants understand the emotional meaning of the expression, but they do fuss or protest when their mothers adopt unresponsive "still-faces" (Cohn & Tronick, 1983). Apparently infants seek emotional cues from others and are upset when they don't find them.

Infants respond to adults' emotions by "resonating" or matching expressions they see some of the infants' earliest responses take the form of social "contagion," where the baby spontaneously imitates another person's emotional expressions (Saarni, Mumme, & Campos, 1998). Infants display joy when adults pose happiness or interest, and they show negative emotion when adults pose anger or fear. As we will explain in "Physical Development in Early Childhood," brain scientists have discovered that certain neurons—called **mirror neurons**—are activated both when we do something (like smile) *or* when we see someone else do the same thing (Rizzolatti et al., 1996). These neurons may play a special role in the development of empathy, allowing the infant to feel what others are feeling (Legerstee & Varghese, 2001).

mirror neurons   Cells in the brain that are activated both when we do something and when we see someone else do the same thing.

Infants also respond differently to different vocalizations of emotion (a laughing sound versus a crying sound, for instance) and coordinate their vocal and facial expressions. For example, they recognize that laughing sounds and smiling faces go together—but that laughing sounds and angry faces do not. These newfound abilities imply that infants now comprehend the meaning of emotional expressions more fully.

social referencing   The tendency to use others' emotional expressions to interpret uncertain or ambiguous events.

Starting around eight to nine months of age, infants begin to use others' emotional expressions to guide their own reactions to events, and so social referencing begins. **Social referencing** is the tendency to use others' emotional expressions to interpret uncertain or ambiguous events (Campos & Stenberg, 1981). Remember the visual cliff in "Physical Development in Infancy." When mothers beckon an infant across the "deep" side in a happy and playful way, older infants are likely to follow Mom's cues, and crawl across the glass. They will not follow, however, if Mom signals fear or fright. Similarly, infants will not play with unusual toys when their mothers show or voice disgust as opposed to pleasure. When the same toys are presented a few minutes

[1]Correct answers: D, B, E, A, C.

later, infants still avoid them, even when their mothers are silent and neutral (Hornik, Risenhoover, & Gunnar, 1987). Infants look to fathers as well as mothers for emotional cues (Dickstein & Parke, 1988; Hirshberg & Svejda, 1990), and even reference previously unfamiliar experimenters (Klinnert et al., 1986).

Facial and vocal expressions of emotion have great significance in a baby's experience of the world once they can be perceived clearly. This is hardly surprising: Emotional expressions are among the most important social signals for a baby's well-being. Thus, we should expect that babies become attuned to these signals from early in life. As they proceed through their second year, infants' increased skill at "reading" the emotions of others enhances social competence and sensitivity. Their sensitivity to others' emotions can lead to *prosocial* behavior (i.e., sharing toys). It can also lead to conflict with siblings and other family members. Toddlers are capable of teasing; that is, saying or doing something to elicit emotions, testing the limits of parental tolerance (Dunn, 2000).

In summary, from birth or shortly thereafter, infants are capable of expressing and later reading a range of different emotions in a variety of situations. Many primary emotions can be seen early in life in survival-related situations. Some links between facial and vocal expressions and underlying feelings are likely innate; others depend on social experience, nervous system maturation, and a growing emotional repertoire—or all of the

INTERIM SUMMARY 6.1

Infants' Emotions

There are two sides to emotional behavior.	**Emotional expression**—communicating feelings to others through facial expressions, gestures, and vocalizations. **Emotional understanding**—reading the emotional expressions of others.
Development of Emotional Expressions	■ **Primary emotions**—those deeply rooted in human biology (joy, anger, fear, and sadness)—develop early in infants. ■ **Secondary emotions** (embarrassment, pride, guilt, shame, and envy) develop later. ■ As infants develop cognitively, they grow emotionally, evaluating situations in more sophisticated ways, processing information at a higher level, and responding with more complex emotions.
Emotional development involves reading as well as sending emotional signals.	■ Newborns find it hard to distinguish among different facial features and expressive patterns. ■ At 1.5–2 months, infants begin to discriminate among different facial expressions of emotion. ■ Infants respond to adults' emotions by matching expressions they see. ■ Infants respond differently to different vocalizations of emotion and coordinate vocal and facial expressions. ■ At around 8–9 months, infants begin to use others' emotional expressions to guide their own reaction to events—**social referencing**.

above. Emotions organize how a baby responds to events, and how parents respond to their baby, whether they try to manage, pacify, or deflect them. Over the first two years of life, changes in an infant's emotions—for example, the first smiles or the earliest indications of stranger wariness—are seen as developmental milestones. These emotional reactions are significant also because parents view them as signs of an emerging individuality—as cues to what the child's behavioral style is like now and will be like in future years. The origins of this individuality can be found in the infant's temperament. (For a summary of this section, see "Interim Summary 6.1: Infants' Emotions.")

INFANT TEMPERAMENT

Emotions change from moment to moment, but temperament is more enduring (Bornstein, 2000). Parents and other caregivers devote considerable energy to identifying, adapting to, and channeling the temperament of their infants, just as they try to interpret, respond to, and manage their infants' emotions. Almost all infants fuss when we change their routine or when unfamiliar people come too close. When fussiness is part of the baby's persistent style, though, we view it as one of the infant's characteristics, and thus a part of the child's temperament. Moreover, we don't think of short-term fluctuations in an infant's emotional state as telling us about long-term consequences, but we view temperamental attributes as foreshadowing the child's later personality. It is difficult for parents to imagine a perpetually happy baby as growing into anything other than a perpetually happy child—and to a certain degree, they are correct.

Temperament is the biologically based source of individual differences in behavioral functioning. It emerges early in life and appears to be moderately stable over time. A child's underlying temperamental characteristics tend to show themselves and endure even though the specifics may change. Thus, a temperamentally sociable child is likely to display ease and friendliness in different ways at different ages: in smiles and reaching out as an infant; in approaching and exploring other people as a toddler; in animated conversation as a preschooler; and so forth.

Insights into the biological origins of temperament come from twin studies. Individual differences in temperamental factors such as activity level and sociability are highly heritable (Goldsmith & Lemery, 2000; Goldsmith et al., 2000). Whereas correlations between identical twins range up to .8, correlations between fraternal twins are .5 or less (remember from our discussion in "The Study of Child Development" that a correlation of .5 (or −.5) is considered moderate; and of .8 (or −.8), strong). Temperament is based in biology, but it is not fixed or unaffected by experience; rather, it is affected by the interaction between innate predispositions and experience (Rothbart & Bates, 2006). A child who starts out in life happy may continue so, but her parents' divorce when she is four may dampen her happy outlook. By the same token, a temperamentally fearful child may become less shy and cautious if reared in a comforting environment where parents help the child learn to better manage his timidity. Culture matters as well, although cross-cultural comparisons cannot by themselves tell us the extent to which temperament is biologically versus contextually influenced (Gartstein, Kinsht, & Slobodskaya, 2003). Nevertheless, cross-cultural studies have found that, on average, infants of Asian descent are less easily upset, better able to soothe themselves, and less easily aroused than their Caucasian counterparts (Kagan, 2006). Research on differences between girls and boys illustrates how difficult it is to disentangle the effects of genes and the environment on temperament. Systematic studies have not revealed many strong or consistent gender differences in temperament, although some research suggests that boys have a higher activity level than girls (Eaton & Enns, 1986). It is tempting to view such differences as genetically based (Roisman & Fraley, 2006; Rothbart, 2005). But parents and other caregivers treat male and female infants differently and in ways that are consistent with cultural stereotypes, including beliefs about the higher activity level of boys. Parents are likely to encourage rough-and-tumble play in a boy, but discourage a girl from the same behavior, regardless of the two children's individual temperaments.

Measuring Infant Temperament

How do scientists measure an infant's temperament? There are two basic ways. We can ask people who know the infant best what he or she is usually like ("How easily does your child get upset?"). Alternatively, we can observe infants ourselves and draw inferences from what we see, either during naturalistic observation (How often did we see the child get upset during play time?) or in situations designed to elicit temperamentally driven responses (How easily was the child upset when we deliberately tried to frustrate him?). Each approach has its pros and cons (Bornstein, 2008).

Parents are likely to provide highly insightful reports of their child's temperamental attributes based on their long-term and intimate experience with the child. However, parents' reports may be biased by their subjective views, their own personality dispositions, unique experiences, and other factors. A highly negative mother, for instance, or one who is under a lot of stress, may describe her child in more negative terms than would the more cheerful or stress-free mother of a temperamentally similar baby.

Children differ in their temperaments, and show how they feel quite clearly, as does this little girl clinging to her mother's skirt.

Observations by (usually unacquainted) researchers may provide less biased accounts, but they inevitably involve limited sampling (an observer can only watch an infant for a given amount of time, whereas a mother is with the infant for long periods of time, day after day), observer effects (being with a stranger can change the infant's behavior), context effects (as in the difference between laboratory and home observations), and other potential biases, such as an observer's preconceptions about gender. For instance, the same behavior that is perceived as angry when viewed in a boy may be perceived as fearful when viewed in a girl. Generally speaking, the more information we can gather about an infant's temperament (different reporters, different situations, different contexts), the more certain we can be about it. So, researchers recognize the strengths and limitations of each method and try to combine methods in the same experiment (Bornstein, Gaughran, & Segui, 1991).

Approaches to Characterizing Infant Temperament

Most approaches to characterizing temperament have focused on identifying overarching dimensions of behavior that define temperament, such as how active, how easily aroused, or how sociable an infant is. Many different formulations have been offered over the years, but two dimensions in particular that have received considerable attention are **positive affectivity** (when the infant characteristically smiles and laughs, is easily soothed, and is attentive) and **negative affectivity** (when the infant typically displays fear or is easily distressed in response to restrictions or high levels of stimulation) (Putnam, Sanson, & Rothbart, 2002; Rothbart & Bates, 2006).

Two types of children high in negative affectivity raise the anxiety levels of parents, caregivers, and teachers the most. They are **inhibited children** (who are characteristically shy, fearful, and timid) and **difficult children** (who are easily irritated and hard to soothe). Because these types of children can pose significant challenges to parents, researchers have spent a lot of time studying them.

positive affectivity A dimension of temperament that reflects the extent to which a person feels enthusiastic and alert (e.g., cheerful, outgoing, etc.).

negative affectivity A dimension of temperament that reflects the extent to which a person feels distressed (sad, angry).

inhibited children Children who are characteristically shy, fearful, and timid.

difficult children Children who are easily irritated and hard to soothe.

The Behaviorally Inhibited Child Inhibited children are fearful, wary, and shy in situations where uninhibited children are generally outgoing (Schwartz et al., 2003). Emily, the participant in a large ongoing study of temperament, is an example (Fox et al., 2001). At four months, she showed high levels of motor activity and distress in response to sounds, smells, and visual images. At fourteen and twenty-one months, she reacted fearfully to novel stimuli. By four and a half years, she showed little spontaneity and sociability with adults. By seven years, Emily suffered symptoms of anxiety. Inhibition is a stable characteristic, but it is not immutable. It can be changed through concerted efforts by parents (Kagan, 2006).

The Difficult Child Temperamental difficultness, irritability, and negativity also remain stable during the first few years of life (Rothbart & Bates, 2006). The majority (70%) of difficult infants go on to develop behavior problems in later childhood (although some 30% do not), whereas only 18 percent of "easy" infants do (Thomas, Chess, & Birch, 1970). Temperamental difficultness figures importantly in the development of emotional and behavioral problems at later ages, in part because of the ways in which a child's difficult temperament affects his or her parents' behavior. Steve is a difficult child; he reacts negatively to changes in the environment, is easily aroused, and sleeps very little. His irritability and distress often cause his parents to withdraw from him, to get angry, and to try coercive discipline techniques (Bates, Pettit, & Dodge, 1995; van den Boom, 1991). As with inhibited children, parents can make a difference in whether a difficult temperament leads to problems later in development. A temperamentally difficult child whose parents anticipate and adjust to their child's temperament by minimizing the sorts of situations that distress the child is less likely to develop problems than is a temperamentally difficult child whose parents are less sensitive and adaptive.

Does Temperament Matter?

A baby's enduring temperament can influence his or her cognitive and personality development. For example, temperamentally sociable six-month-olds do better in standardized tests than do temperamentally difficult infants (Wachs & Gandour, 1983). Furthermore, difficulty in twelve-month-olds interferes with infants' motivation to master structured laboratory tasks (Wachs, 1987). And shyness in twenty- and twenty-four-month-olds has been shown to inhibit social cognition, including role taking and self-recognition (Pipp-Siegel et al., 1997).

What accounts for these influences? On the one hand, certain temperamental attributes may promote the child's cognitive performance. Infants who are positive and persistent are likely to approach cognitive tasks more constructively than infants with more negative or distractible dispositions. On the other hand, these temperamental features may facilitate cognitive functioning indirectly, by evoking different responses from others. Parents and other caregivers may interact more positively with infants who have sociable temperaments than with those who do not, enhancing intellectual and social development. Or consider a third possible explanation. Infants with positive characteristics may receive better scores on cognitive tests because they respond better to strange examiners, adapt better to unfamiliar testing procedures, or are perceived more positively by testers.

Temperament is also an early foundation for personality. Personality is influenced by temperament, but it also is shaped by other factors. In infancy, socializing influences are only beginning, and thus the genetic and biological bases for temperamental individuality are most apparent. To the extent that we can see the person-to-be in the baby, we see the personality-to-be in the baby's temperament. Of course, temperament does not fix personality immutably, nor is temperament the only influence on personality development. Other social factors play a role, including the way a child is socialized and the experiences the child has within and outside the family. For example, parental education appears to be influential in infants' developing positive social behaviors (Putnam et al., 2002; Figure 6.2). Nevertheless, the biologically based temperament with which the child enters the world exerts a significant and enduring influence over the child's emotional and social development. An inhibited child is not necessarily destined to develop a full-blown anxiety disorder as a teenager but is very unlikely to become a gregarious extravert. By the same token, an infant who comes into the world with a strong inclination toward cheerfulness is not inoculated against feeling sad later in life, but the odds are much greater that a highly positive infant will grow into an optimistic and happy adult than into a pessimistic and perpetually cranky one.

Context Matters

Temperament is best thought of as a tendency or predisposition toward a certain personality, rather than a fixed guarantee. This is because the link between temperament and later personality is also influenced by the context in which the child develops. Temperamental inhibition or difficulty in infancy need not lead to parenting failures and child maladjustment. For example, mothers who restrict their difficult infants, but do not engage in physical discipline, have more positive results (Bates et al., 1998). That is, consistent and firm parental control, without physical coercion, is an adaptive parental response to temperamental difficulty and may foster the child's ability to self-regulate and develop internalized standards of conduct (Rothbart, Posner, & Kieras, 2006). In contrast, when parents respond to a difficult infant with hostility and anger, the infant is placed at even greater risk for later maladjustment than he is by his difficult temperament alone (Belsky, Hsieh, & Crnic, 1998).

These findings are consistent with the concept of **goodness of fit** (Chess & Thomas, 1996; Lerner, Theokas, & Bobek, 2005). Whether a child's long-term adjustment is favorable or unfavorable depends on the interaction between the child's temperament and the demands of the environment. Infant characteristics that some adults find difficult may not be difficult for others. Thus, "difficultness" in the infant, and it is also in the eye of the caregiver and in the situation. A child with a low activity level and poor adaptability "fits" well in a home or school setting that makes few demands. But such an environment is a poor fit for a highly active, distractible child. A temperamentally difficult child will not inevitably experience later problems if, say, parents understand and tolerate the child's behavioral style and can provide activities in which the child's characteristics can be channeled and valued. Conversely, even a temperamentally easy child will experience problems if parents impose excessive demands or ignore reasonable needs. As a consequence, the sensitivity and adaptability of parents to their child's temperament is an important predictor of long-term child adjustment.

In sum, a child's individual characteristics interact with environmental demands to shape and guide temperament. Contrary to views that "good" temperamental features lead to optimal development, and "bad" features invariably predict later behavioral problems, it appears that the consequences of a particular temperamental profile for a child depend in part on the demands of the environments in which the child is liv-

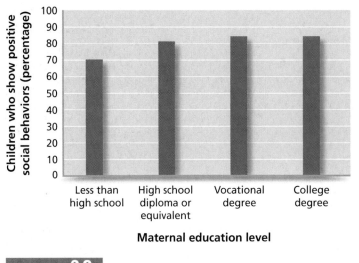

Maternal education level

Parental Education Level and Children's Social Behaviors

An infant's temperament is largely influenced by biological factors; however, external factors, like parenting, play a role in shaping temperament as well. For example, more children of parents with a high school diploma or higher show positive prosocial behaviors when they start kindergarten compared with children whose parents had not completed high school.

Source: From Early Child Development in Social Context: A Chartbook of the Commonwealth Fund, September 2004. Reprinted by permission of The Commonwealth Fund.

goodness of fit A concept that refers to a match of the child's temperament and the demands of the environment.

INTERIM SUMMARY **6.2**

Infant Temperament

Temperament is the biologically based source of individual differences in behavioral functioning.	■ A child's underlying temperamental characteristics endure even though the specifics may change.
	■ Temperament is based in biology but is influenced by the environment and experience.
Two Basic Ways to Measure Temperament	1. Ask people who know the infant best what he/she is like.
	2. Observe infants and draw inferences from what is seen, either in naturalistic observations or in situations designed to elicit temperamentally driven responses.
Two Noteworthy Ways of Characterizing Infant Temperament	1. **Positive affectivity**—when the infant characteristically smiles and laughs
	2. **Negative affectivity**—when the infant typically displays fears or is easily distressed in response to restrictions or high levels of stimulation.
	■ **Inhibited** children (characteristically show, fearful and timid) and **difficult** children (easily irritated and hard to soothe) are high in negative affectivity.
The consequences of a particular temperamental profile for a child depend on:	■ The demands of the environment in which the child is living.
	■ The sensitivity and adaptability of the child's social partners within those settings.
	■ How temperament guides the child's choice of activities and interpretation of experiences.

ing, the sensitivity and adaptability of the child's social partners within those settings, and how temperament guides the child's choice of activities and his interpretation of experiences.

Infants contribute to their interactions with people through their emotions and through their temperament. At the same time, caregivers accommodate, interpret, and channel as well as shape the child's socioemotional characteristics. When the fit is good between the two, development can be optimized. (For a summary of this section, see "Interim Summary 6.2: Infant Temperament.")

ATTACHMENT AND INFANT SOCIAL DEVELOPMENT

Developing fulfilling and dependable relationships with other people (mainly parents) is one of the most important aspects of social development in infancy. The infant's first social relationships, commonly referred to as attachments, appear to be universal (van IJzendoorn et al., 2006).There are differences in the types of attachment infants form with their parents, however, and these differences affect children's development. The quality of infant-parent attachments is influenced both by the harmony of infant-parent interaction and the infant's temperament.

The most popular explanation of the process of attachment was provided by John Bowlby, a psychoanalyst who drew on animal studies to understand interpersonal communication and the formation of social bonds. Bowlby (1969) assumed that how infants and parents behave toward one another is best considered in the context of the environment in which our species evolved. In that **environment of evolutionary adaptedness**, the survival of infants would have depended on their ability to remain close to protective adults to obtain nourishment, comfort, and security. Unlike the young of many other species, however, human infants cannot move closer or follow adults for several months after birth, and they are incapable of clinging to adults to stay in contact (human infants are not strong enough, and human parents are not hairy enough). Instead, human infants rely on different kinds of *signals* to attract adults. For these signals to be effective, adults must be predisposed to respond to them. The best example of such a signal is the infant cry, which very effectively draws adults to approach, pick up, and soothe the infant (Barr et al., 2000; Bornstein et al., 1992). As they grow older, infants develop other means of achieving closeness or contact, including independent locomotion, and they gradually come to focus on people with whom they are most familiar.

Phases of Social Development

Bowlby (1969) described four main phases in the development of infant-parent attachments.

Phase 1: Indiscriminate Social Responsiveness (One to Two Months of Age) The baby develops a repertoire of signals, like the *cry*. The common characteristic of these behaviors is that they all help to provide comfort and

Infants normally do not hide their emotions, but rather display them openly as an important means of communication, as this baby is doing. It's up to caregivers to interpret the infant's communications.

security by bringing a protective, caregiving adult close to the baby. Another potent attachment behavior in the baby's repertoire is *smiling*. Like crying, smiling is a signal that powerfully affects adult behavior. Cries encourage adults to approach the baby; smiles are effective because they encourage adults to stay near the baby.

From birth, babies are capable of affecting the social environment around them. However, in this early phase of attachment development babies are indiscriminate in the use of proximity-promoting signals: They appear to be satisfied by whoever responds to their cries, smiles, or other signals. Adults, of course, respond selectively depending on their relatedness and responsibility. Because the caregivers who are close by can be felt, smelled, heard, and seen when infants are alert, babies may come to learn a great deal about them, and rapidly learn to associate their presence with alertness and the relief of distress (Thompson & Goodvin, 2005).

Phase 2: Discriminating Sociability (Two to Seven Months of Age)
Bowlby (1969) suggested that the ability to recognize specific people marked the transition to the second phase of attachment development. (Studies we described in "Physical Development in Infancy" show that infants are able to recognize their own mothers' voice and smell within the first two weeks of life, however—much earlier than Bowlby believed.) Presumably because significant others (such as parents) have been associated with pleasurable experiences (such as feeding, cuddling, rocking, and play) and with the relief of distress, babies come to prefer to interact with familiar people. Initially, these preferences manifest themselves in fairly subtle ways: Certain people will be able to soothe the baby more easily and elicit smiles and coos more readily. They are special to the baby. Prior to this phase, the baby appeared to enjoy interacting with anyone without apparent preference.

During this second phase of social development, babies are also more coordinated behaviorally than they were earlier. Their arousal level is less variable, and they now

environment of evolutionary adaptedness The context in which our species evolved.

spend larger proportions of their time in alert states. As a result, distress is less frequent, and interactions with adults more often involve play.

Phase 3: Attachments (Seven to Twenty-four Months of Age) The beginning of Phase 3 marks the time at which the first infant-adult attachments are thought to form. By six or seven months of age, infants clearly understand and respect rules of reciprocity in their interactions and enjoy their newly acquired ability to creep around and to take responsibility for getting close to their parents, instead of waiting for others to come in response to their cries or coos. Infants increasingly initiate interaction using directed social behaviors.

Babies also now protest (by crying) when left by people to whom they are attached. According to Bowlby, **separation protest** should be viewed as a signal aimed at making attachment figures come back to the baby. Infants become increasingly sophisticated in their abilities to behave intentionally, communicate verbally, and respond appropriately. Over time, infants can begin to tolerate a growing distance from attachment figures without protesting.

separation protest A signal, characterized by crying, that is aimed at making attachment figures return.

Phase 4: Goal-Corrected Partnerships (Year Three Onward) According to Bowlby (1969), the next major transition occurs at the beginning of the third year, when children take their parents' needs into account when interacting with them. For example, they now appear to recognize that parents must sometimes give priority to other activities, and that their own needs or wants must wait.

How Do Attachments Form?

Bowlby proposed that humans have a predisposition to form attachments. But how do attachments form, and to whom do infants become attached? According to Bowlby, the consistency of the adults' presence and availability during a **sensitive period** (Bornstein, 1989, 2003)—the first six postnatal months—determines to whom the baby will become attached. If there is no consistent caregiver over this period (as might occur in institutions like hospitals), the baby would not form attachments. Bowlby and his student Mary Ainsworth believed that most babies develop a hierarchy of attachment figures and that their primary caregivers—usually their mothers, but fathers as well, so long as they engage in caregiving—become primary attachment figures before any other relationships are formed. Once infants have this foundation, Bowlby and Ainsworth argued, infants may (and often do) form relationships with others, such as daycare providers and older siblings (van den Boom, 2001).

sensitive period A time in development during which the organism is especially vulnerable to experience.

Obviously, there must be a minimal amount of exposure that these other individuals regularly interact with infants for attachments to form; unfortunately, we do not know what this minimum is, or how it varies depending on the individual. The amount of time adults spend with infants is not the only factor that determines whether infant-adult attachments will form: The *quality* of adult-infant interaction is also important. Bowlby and Ainsworth believed that an infant becomes attached to those people who have been associated over time with consistent, predictable, and appropriate responses to the baby's signals as well as to his or her needs (Ainsworth et al., 1978; Cummings & Cummings, 2002; Thompson, 2006; Thompson & Goodvin, 2005).

Mothers obviously play a central role in attachment (Cummings & Cummings, 2002), but a number of individuals (other than mothers) directly influence the child (Parke, 2002). Studies of infant-mother and infant-father attachments indicate that infants show no systematic preference for either parent on attachment behavior measures (their propensity to stay near, approach, touch, cry to, and ask to be held by specific adults), although babies show preferences for parents over relatively unfamiliar adults. When babies are distressed, they increase displays of attachment behavior and organize their behavior around the parent who is present. When both parents are present, however, distressed infants typically turn to their mothers first.

Although it may be adaptive to be cautious when first encountering strange persons, it is not adaptive for human infants to refuse all interaction with nonattachment figures. Persons other than parents have a profound impact on infants' psychosocial development, and most interactions in life involve people to whom children are not attached. Consequently, it is not surprising that **stranger wariness**, the hesitancy that infants show at around ten months when they are approached by unfamiliar people, diminishes rapidly over time, and infants eventually enter into friendly interactions with nonattachment figures (Bornstein et al., 1997; Bornstein et al., 2000).

How Is Infant Attachment Measured?

The most popular technique for studying attachment is the so-called **Strange Situation**. It can be used when infants are old enough to have formed attachments and are mobile, yet are not so old that brief separations and encounters with strangers are no longer noteworthy. As a result, the Strange Situation is appropriate for infants ranging in age from about ten to twenty-four months. The procedure has seven episodes (Table 6.1) designed to expose infants to increasing amounts of mild stress and observe how they organize their attachment behaviors around their parents when distressed. Stress is stimulated by an unfamiliar environment, the entrance of an unfamiliar adult, and two brief separations from the parent.

The Strange Situation begins with the parent and infant alone in a room (episode 1). Researchers are generally present in an adjacent room, videorecording what happens through a one-way glass. The stranger's entrance (episode 2) usually leads infants to inhibit exploration and draw a little closer to the parent, at least temporarily. The parent's departure (episode 3) usually leads infants to attempt to bring them back by crying or searching, and to reduced exploration and affiliation. Following the parent's return (episode 4), infants typically seek to reengage in interaction and, if distressed, may wish to be cuddled and comforted. The same responses should occur, with somewhat greater intensity, following the second separation and reunion (episodes 5 and 7). In fact, this is precisely how about 65% of the infants studied in the United States behave in the Strange Situation (Thompson, 2006; Thompson & Goodvin, 2005). These infants (designated *type B*) are regarded as *securely attached*. All episodes are usually three minutes long, but episodes 3, 5, and 6 can be shortened if the infant becomes too distressed, and episodes 4 and 7 are sometimes extended.

However, some infants seem unable to use their parents as secure bases from which to explore (discussed more later). Although they are distressed by their parents' absence, they behave ambivalently on reunion, seeking contact and interaction but

stranger wariness The hesitancy that infants show at around ten months when they are approached by unfamiliar people.

strange situation An experimental paradigm that reveals security of attachment.

TABLE 6.1 The Strange Situation

EPISODE	PERSONS PRESENT	CHANGE
1	Parent, infant	Parent and infant enter room
2	Parent, infant, stranger	Unfamiliar adult enters
3	Infant, stranger	Parent leaves
4	Parent, infant	Parent returns, stranger leaves
5	Infant	Parent leaves
6	Infant, stranger	Stranger returns
7	Parent, infant	Parent returns, stranger leaves

angrily rejecting it when it is offered. These infants are conventionally labeled *insecure-resistant* or *insecure-ambivalent* (*type C*). They typically account for about 10 to 15 percent of the infants in American research samples (Thompson, 2006; Thompson & Goodvin, 2005).

A third group of infants seems little concerned by their parents' absence. Instead of greeting their parents on reunion, they actively avoid interaction and ignore their parents' bids. These infants are said to exhibit *insecure-avoidant* attachments (*type A*); they typically constitute about 20 percent of the infants in American samples (Thompson, 2006; Thompson & Goodvin, 2005).

A very small fourth group of infants has also been described; their behavior is *disoriented* and/or *disorganized* (*type D*; Main & Solomon, 1990; Brisch, 2002). These infants simultaneously display contradictory behavior patterns, manifest incomplete or undirected movements, and appear confused or apprehensive about approaching their parents.

Are different types of infants consistent in their behavior? When researchers bring an infant to the laboratory to participate in the Strange Situation on different occasions, they typically find consistency. According to one researcher, forty-eight out of fifty infants—96 percent—obtained the same classification on two separate occasions (Waters, 1978). Another study reported 84 percent stability between twelve-month assessments in the Strange Situation and six-year assessments using an observational procedure appropriate for older children (Main & Cassidy, 1988).

In some cases, attachment classifications on different occasions are not related to one another, but are related in understandable ways to changes in infants' experiences. For example, a study of attachment stability in an economically disadvantaged sample of babies found that many infants changed from one classification to another between twelve and eighteen months of age, but the changes were systematic: When the families had experienced considerable social stress during the six-month period, secure (type B) attachments often changed to insecure-avoidant (type A) or insecure-ambivalent (type C), although when families experienced a low degree of stress, type A or C attachments did not necessarily become type B (Vaughn et al., 1979).

Another experience that can affect attachment security is the birth of a second child, which predicts a significant decrease in attachment security among first-born children. This decrease is not linked to changes in the mothers' sensitivity with their first-borns, mothers' psychiatric symptoms, or mothers' reports of marital harmony. Instead, the decrease in first-born attachment security seems to reflect changes in children's perceptions of their relationships with their mothers in response to the introduction of the new family members, who may be perceived as threats. These findings raise the question of the role of parent-infant interactions in the development of attachment security in the first place—at the very least, they suggest that the early experiences an infant has with a parent do not inoculate the child with an unchanging level of security or insecurity.

Parent-Child Interaction and Attachment Security

reciprocity A lesson in social interaction in which partners take turns acting and reacting to the other's behavior.

effectance A lesson in social interaction that involves learning that one's behavior can affect the behavior of others in a consistent and predictable fashion.

From repeated experiences in face-to-face play and distress-relief sequences, the baby learns several important lessons. The first lesson is **reciprocity**: Infants learn that in social interaction, partners take turns acting and reacting to the other's behavior. Two- to three-month-olds show they are learning this lesson because they respond with boredom, distress, or withdrawal when their mothers adopt unresponsive "still-faces" instead of behaving in their typical interactive fashion (Moore, Cohn, & Campbell, 2001). They seem concerned over adults' failure to follow the rules of interaction, indicating they understand these rules, find synchronized and reciprocal interactions more enjoyable, and "expect" their partners to follow the same rules. A second lesson is **effectance**: The baby learns that his or her behavior can affect the behavior of others in a consistent and predictable fashion. And the third lesson is **trust**: The infant learns that the caregiver can be counted on to respond when signaled.

Achieving reciprocity, effectance, and trust are major steps in the process of becoming social. As infants realize that their cries, smiles, and coos elicit predictable responses from others, they develop a coherent view of the social world and of themselves as individuals who significantly affect others. The degree to which babies feel confident in their predictions regarding the behavior of others—that is, the degree to which they trust or have faith in the reliability of specific people—in turn influences the security of their attachment relationships.

Individual differences in the amount of trust or perceived effectance each infant develops depend in part on individual differences in the sensitivity and responsiveness of the adults with whom the baby interacts. As we noted in "The Study of Child Development," Sigmund Freud (1949) was by far the most prominent advocate of the importance of infancy in this regard, suggesting that the ways babies are treated establish lifelong orientations and personality traits. Erik Erikson, one of Freud's students, likewise believed that early experience is extremely influential, as you also read in that chapter. From early experiences, he suggested, children develop a degree of basic trust or mistrust in their caregiver. He also believed that the harmoniousness of early interactions has implications for the way the infant negotiates the next stage of development, in which the key issue is establishing autonomy or shame.

Face-to-face and eye-to-eye contact are plain ways of connecting, as this dad and his 3-month-old baby girl show.

The Secure Base In the course of interaction with other people, babies have the opportunity to gain social competence and learn social skills. But the development of attachment relationships also facilitates the infant's physical and cognitive development. Interacting with a variety of individuals provides opportunities for infants to learn how to modulate their style of interaction in accordance with each individual's characteristic and unique interpersonal style. Infants also engage in interaction with their physical environment to develop competence and master it.

Infants count on attachment figures to protect them and to be accessible when needed, and so use them as a **secure base** from which to explore and interact with other people. Secure infants more readily explore objects in the environment, for instance. Sensitive parenting—that is, nurturant, attentive, nonrestrictive parental care—and attuned infant-mother interactions are associated with secure (type B) infant behavior in the Strange Situation, and this appears to be true in cultures outside the United States as well as in U.S.-based samples (van IJzendoorn, 1997).

Conversely, the mothers of infants who behave in either insecure-avoidant or insecure-resistant fashions manifest less socially desirable patterns of behavior. Insecure-avoidant attachments are associated with intrusive, overstimulating, rejecting parenting, whereas insecure-resistant attachments are linked to inconsistent, unresponsive parenting (De Wolff & van IJzendoorn, 1997). Although the antecedents of disorganized attachments are less well established, they are more common among abused and maltreated infants and among infants exposed to other pathological caregiving environments (Azar, 2002; Brisch, 2002). There may be consequences of parental behaviors that infants find frightening or disturbing.

Attachment Security and Infant Temperament In early face-to-face interactions, the adult assumes major responsibility for keeping the interaction going (Bornstein

trust A lesson in social interaction that involves learning that another person can be counted on to respond when signaled.

secure base The trustworthy place infants count on for protection and accessibility when needed as they explore and interact with other people.

© Laura Dwight

& Lamb, 2009), but babies are not simply passive partners. Adults respond to baby-initiated behaviors of all sorts, and so infant temperament is another important influence on the parent-infant relationship. Temperament does not have a direct effect on whether infants are classified as type A, B, or C, but infant temperament has at least an indirect effect on infant Strange Situation behavior because it likely affects the quality of infant-parent interaction, which in turn affects security of attachment. In addition, temperament may affect how infants are influenced by their parents: Distractible babies, for example, may be less affected by their parents' behavior than are attentive babies. In this sense, the security of an infant's attachment is the product of three influences: the infant's temperament, the parent's behavior, and the nature of their interaction with each other.

What Attachment Classifications Tell Us One of the reasons developmentalists have been so interested in infant attachment is that there is reason to believe that the security of the baby's early relationships influences the ways in which he or she relates to others in later periods of development (van IJzendoorn, 2005). And indeed, infants' attachment classification appears to predict aspects of the child's future behavior. Babies who have developed trust in their attachment figures tend to regard new people they encounter as trustworthy, too. Babies with secure attachments to their mothers are more cooperatively playful than insecure infants when interacting with a friendly stranger. Similarly, the quality of early attachment predicts social relationships in encounters with siblings and peers (Furman & Lanthier, 2002; Ladd & Pettit, 2002; Volling, 2003). Secure infants engage in more frequent, more prosocial, and more mature forms of interaction, sharing more and showing a greater capacity to initiate and maintain interactions, for example.

Secure infant-mother attachments at twelve or eighteen months are also associated with superior problem-solving abilities in a variety of stressful and challenging contexts in the preschool years (Sroufe, Egeland, Carlson, & Collins, 2005). Securely attached children persist longer and more enthusiastically in cognitively challenging situations than do insecurely attached children. Secure infants also seem to be more resilient when stressed or challenged and appear more socially competent and independent when they enter preschool. Insecure attachment in infancy, and in particular the disorganized/disoriented classification, predicts antisocial behavior in later childhood (van IJzendoorn & Bakermans-Kranenburg, 2006).

Cross-Cultural Research on Infant Attachment Figure 6.3 shows that most babies in most cultures are secure, but the distribution of infants across the A, B, and C categories in many countries differs from that typically found in American samples (even though researchers in different countries apply the same coding and classification criteria; True, Pisani, & Oumar, 2001; van Ijzendoorn et al., 2006). This could mean that parents in other cultures are more or less sensitive than American parents, but this ethnocentric interpretation seems incorrect. Rather, the results may point to the importance of factors other than the quality of parental behavior. For example, proportionately more Japanese, Indonesian, and Israeli babies show high degrees of stress in the Strange Situation, and their reactions may have led to increases in the proportion of infants classified as insecure-ambivalent (type C) by researchers. These infants may appear distressed either because they have much less experience with separations from their mothers than American infants typically have, or because their mothers are much more stressed by the procedures (recall the notion of social referencing, where infants look to others to help them figure out what sense to make of a situation). In either case, the Strange Situation would not be psychologically similar for these other babies and American babies. Or, possibly, for infants growing up in these places, encounters with total strangers are more unusual and thus elicit distress. In other words, even though

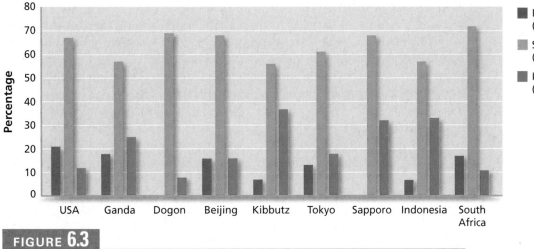

FIGURE 6.3

Attachment Styles Across Cultures

Across many cultures, secure attachments (type B) are the most common; however, in places like Israel (Kibbutz), Japan (Sapporo), and Indonesia, insecure/ambivalent attachments (type C) appear more often than in other places. This is most likely a result of cultural differences in parenting styles.

the Strange Situation procedure is *structurally* the same for Japanese, Indonesian, Israeli, and American infants, the *psychological* experiences or meaning for infants from each culture may differ (Bornstein, 1995).

In summary, infants generally form attachments around the middle of the first year of life to those adults with whom they have had the most consistent and extended interaction. The function of attachment is to ensure that infants retain access to persons

Children often enjoy other children, and the pleasure is a two-way street, as these interacting siblings show.

on whom they can rely for nurturance and protection. For the same reason that it is important for infants to ensure proximity to protective adults, it is of survival value to avoid encounters with unknown and potentially dangerous people and situations. Infants generally establish significant relationships with both of their parents, even though they tend to have more interaction with their mothers than fathers. Infants also form relationships with siblings, peers, and nonfamilial caregivers. These early relationships with mothers, fathers, brothers, sisters, and others all contribute to the rich social world of the young infant. The facts that ratings of Strange Situation behavior are consistent over time and relate to measures of earlier infant-parent interaction and later child achievement and personality suggest that the Strange Situation measures some meaningful aspect of mother-infant attachment and has important implications for understanding and predicting child development. Keep in mind, though, that the relation between Strange Situation behavior in infancy and subsequent child behavior is found only when there is stability in caregiving arrangements and family circumstances, which seem to maintain stability in patterns of parent-child interaction. (For a summary of this section, see "Interim Summary 6.3: Attachment and Infant Social Development.")

INTERIM SUMMARY 6.3

Attachment and Infant Social Development

Differences in the types of **attachments** (infants' first social relationships) infants form with their parents affect children's development.

John Bowlby, a psychoanalyst, assumed that how infants and parents behave toward one another is best considered in the context of the environment in which our species evolved (**environment of evolutionary adaptedness**). He described four main phases in the development of infant-parent attachment:

- Phase 1: Indiscriminate social responsiveness (1 to 2 months)—the baby develops a repertoire of signals that help to provide comfort and security (crying) by bringing a protective, caregiving adult close. Babies then associate the presence of adults with alertness and the relief of distress.

- Phase 2: Discriminating sociability (2 to 7 months)—babies come to prefer to interact with familiar people.

- Phase 3: Attachments (7 to 24 months)—infants understand the rules of reciprocity in their interactions and increasingly initiate interaction using directed social behaviors and protest when left by people to whom they are attached (**separation protest**).

- Phase 4: Goal-corrected partnerships (year 3 onward)—children take their parents' needs into account when interacting with them and so their needs or wants must wait.

How do attachments form?

- The consistency of the adults' presence and availability during a sensitive period—the first postnatal 6 months—determines to whom the baby will become attached, according to Bowlby and Ainsworth.

- The *quality* of adult-infant interaction is important as babies become attached to persons who have been associated over time with consistent, predictable, and appropriate responses to the baby's signals and needs.

- Mothers play a central role in attachment but other individuals such as fathers, siblings, peers, and nonfamilial caregivers directly influence the child.

(continued)

INTERIM SUMMARY **6.3** (continued)

Attachment and Infant Social Development

How is infant attachment measured?	■ The "Strange Situation" is a procedure with seven episodes that is designed to expose infants to increasing amounts of mild stress and observe how they organize their attachment behaviors around their parents when distressed.
	■ Stress is stimulated by an unfamiliar environment, the entrance of an unfamiliar adult, and two brief separations from the parent.
	■ It measures meaningful aspects of mother-infant attachment and has important implications for understanding and predicting child development.
	■ Even though the Strange Situation procedure is structurally the same for infants in different cultures, the psychological experiences or meaning for infants from each culture may differ.
Attachment Security	■ Achieving reciprocity, effectance, and trust are steps in the process of becoming social.
	■ Infants count on attachment figures to protect them and be accessible when needed and use them as a **secure base** from which to explore and interact with other people.
	■ Secure attachments are associated with sensitive and responsive parenting.
	■ Insecure-avoidant attachments are associated with intrusive, overstimulating, rejecting parenting.
	■ Insecure-resistant attachments are associated with inconsistent, unresponsive parenting.

PARENTAL BEHAVIOR AND INTERACTION WITH INFANTS

Interactions between parents and infants are like an intricate dance, not only in rhythm, but in style. Mother does one kind of step and the infant may do the same, or a different step, and it is not always clear who is in the lead. Actually, mothers and infants engage in many kinds of dances. One is *social oriented*, in which their interactions focus exclusively on each other. Contact is an important feature of this dance. Babies need **contact comfort** from adults who love them. In his experiments designed to see whether infants' attraction to their mothers was simply because mothers were a source of food, Harlow (1958) removed infant rhesus monkeys from their mothers and gave them a choice of two substitute models, one constructed of wire and the other of terry cloth (see Figure 6.4). Both models provided food. The young animals strongly preferred the cloth model, which they hugged and clutched much of the time. Contact with the material proved crucial.

Harlow's study helped pave the way for Bowlby's theory of attachment, which emphasized proximity and contact seeking rather than just feeding. It demonstrated that the parenting functions of childbearing and feeding are separate from that of protection. Furthermore, although the young monkeys thrived *physically* when they were supplied with milk in ordinary baby bottles attached to the front of the models, as the monkeys grew up and were permitted to join other monkeys, their social behavior

contact comfort The gratification derived from touch.

FIGURE **6.4**

Harlow's Monkeys

The primatologist Harry Harlow demonstrated the importance of contact comfort by showing that infant monkeys preferred terrycloth "mothers" to wire "mothers" even though both provided milk.

proved abnormal, even psychotic. They were sometimes hyperaggressive and sometimes autistic, sitting withdrawn while rocking silently back and forth. They also cried a great deal and sucked their own fingers and toes. Simply put, "mother love" (or most probably, "caregiver love"), which the monkeys lacked, is essential to normal development.

Within the first year of life, babies and their parents increasingly incorporate the outside world into their interactions (Bornstein, 2006). The *object-oriented* domain of interaction refers to interactions that turn outward from the dyad and a focus on properties, objects, and events in the environment, like playing together with a toy or taking a stroll around the neighborhood. Both social and object interactions have been observed in mothers and infants in many different countries, such as Argentina, France, Israel, Japan, and South Korea (Bornstein, 2006; Bornstein et al., 1991, 1992).

Mothers and Fathers

From the very start, mothers and fathers engage their infants in different types of interactions with different characteristics. Mothers kiss, hug, talk to, smile at, tend, or hold their infants more than fathers do. When videorecorded in face-to-face play with their one-half to six-month-old infants, for example, fathers are more rambunctious in both physical stimulation and social play, whereas mothers are nurturant, rhythmic, and containing (Barnard & Solchany, 2002; Bornstein, 2002, 2006; Parke, 2002). Indeed, parent gender has a much more powerful influence than parental role or employment status: Fathers and mothers tend to behave in their characteristic ways even in families where mothers work and fathers assume the major role in child care.

Almost anywhere in the world, mothers are likely to spend more time with infants than do fathers. Despite recent increases in the amount of time fathers spend with their infants, most fathers continue to assume little responsibility for their infants' care and rear-

© Polka Dot Images/Jupiterimages

Mothers and fathers play in different ways with infants and young children. Mothers are typically tender, soft, and nurturant, and fathers are typically more physical, playful, and vigorous.

ing. Fathers typically see themselves as helpers rather than parents with a primary responsibility for caregiving (and most mothers tend to see them that way as well). Both mothers and fathers see breadwinning as the primary responsibility of fathers. However, because most infants become attached to their father as well as their mother, we can surmise that most infants must have enough quality interaction with their fathers, despite the low quantity (Parke, 2002).

All that said, just as two heads are better than one, so are two parents better than one when it comes to rearing an infant. If we ask, other things being equal, how infants who have two (biological or adopted) parents fare relative to infants who have one biological parent and/or one stepparent or no biological parents, the results for many aspects of children's development are clear. Figure 6.5 shows differences in self-control among infants reared in different types of families. As you can see, self-control in young children suffers to the extent that children are reared in atypical families, where presumably the stresses on parents are greater. (Most psychologists believe that it is *stress*, and not the number or marital status of the parents, that is key.) Stress on parents can undermine their ability to interact with their infants in ways that promote secure attachment and healthy socioemotional development.

Nonparental Care

The majority of infants in the United States are now cared for by someone other than a parent at least some of the time (Clarke-Stewart & Allhusen, 2002; Honig, 2002). This situation may have a variety of effects on infant development. Families of all kinds need and use supplementary care for their infants, and these needs are most often driven by economic concerns and motives. Some babies are in their own home with a relative, some in their own home with a "nanny," some in the homes of family daycare providers, and some in daycare centers (see "Cognitive Development in Early Childhood").

It's impossible to generalize about the effects of nonparental child care on infant development for several reasons. First, daycare environments, like home environments, vary considerably. (Asking how infants are affected by child care is a bit like asking how children are affected by school—the answer to the first question depends on the child-

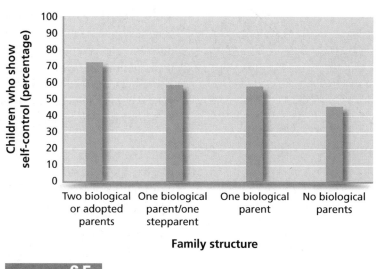

Family structure

FIGURE **6.5**

Family Structure and Children's Self-Control

Children's behavior often varies based on environmental differences, which include family structure. As this graph shows, levels of self-control were highest among children from two-parent (biological or adopted) households and lower among children with a stepparent, single biological parent, or no biological parent (e.g., foster family).

Source: From Early Child Development in Social Context: A Chartbook of the Commonwealth Fund, September 2004. Reprinted by permission of The Commonwealth Fund.

Ellen B. Senisi/The Image Works

Infant daycare is sometimes surprisingly regimented, as seen here in the assembly-line feeding method used.

care setting, just as the answer to the second depends on the school.) But it is also hard to generalize about the effects of child care because children are not randomly assigned to different care environments. The values and practices of parents who do or do not enroll their children in daycare differ, for example, and so differences in infants that might be attributed to daycare experience may really be due (at least in part) to differences in the values and behaviors of the parents and the communities in which they live.

Because so many infants and young children have been placed in nonparental care, extensive efforts have been made to conceptualize and measure the quality of infant care. The National Center for Infants, Toddlers, and Families identified eight criteria that need to be achieved to ensure high-quality infant care (Fenichel, Lurie-Hurvitz, & Griffin, 1999). These include

1. health and safety,

2. maintaining small groups (no more than three to four infants per caregiver),

3. assigning each infant to a primary caregiver,

4. ensuring continuity in care,

5. providing responsive caregiving,

6. meeting individual needs in the context of the larger group,

7. ensuring cultural and linguistic continuity, and

8. providing a stimulating physical environment.

Infants are often distressed when they begin receiving care outside their homes. In fact, one study found that Italian infants enrolled full-time in high-quality centers remained unhappy (demonstrating negative affect, immobilization, and self-comforting) six months after enrollment (Fein, 1996; Fein, Gariboldi, & Boni, 1993). Similarly, German infants who were enrolled in child care between twelve and eighteen months of age (late entry) were more irritable and negative than those enrolled before twelve months (early entry) (Rauh et al., 2000). To help children adjust, many European child-care centers have implemented adaptation programs in which mothers accompany their children during the transitional period of enrollment. When mothers familiarize their children to child care in a leisurely manner and accompany their children in the center, adjustment is easier (Rauh et al., 2000), especially when children are securely attached to their mothers (Ahnert et al., 2004).

Despite commonly held fears that daycare will disrupt the attachment relationship, the most comprehensive U.S. American study of early child care, the NICHD Study of Early Child Care and Youth Development (2005, 2006) indicates no differences in the proportion of secure attachments whether or not infants had experienced nonmaternal care. However, greater maternal sensitivity increased the probability that children would be classified as securely attached to their mothers, whereas children whose mothers were less sensitive were more likely to be insecurely attached, especially when the children spent long hours in care and the child care was of poor quality. Evidently, parenting continues to shape the quality of child-parent relationships even when children experience child care.

Maternal sensitivity and levels of positive child engagement decline when infants spend many hours in child-care facilities (NICHD Early Child Care Research Network, 2005, 2006), though, and this circumstance may result in declines in the quality of mother-child relationships (Sagi et al., 2002). In other words, any impact of early child care on attachment security is indirect and depends on the way in which the mother-child relationship is affected by the child's daycare experience. To foster secure child-parent relationships and promote children's emotional equilibrium, families need to adjust children's experiences at home. It is important, for example, that parents who use a lot of nonparental care make sure that their interactions with their infant remain high-quality when they are home.

Children's relationships with their nonparental caregivers can also have effects on their socioemotional development. For example, Israeli infants who behaved securely with care providers in the Strange Situation were more empathic, dominant, purposive, achievement oriented, and independent four years later than those whose relationships were insecure-resistant (Oppenheim, Sagi, & Lamb, 1988). Schoolchildren's perceptions of their relationships with teachers are also predicted by the quality of their first attachment to care providers, underscoring the long-lasting impact of these early relationships (Howes, Hamilton, & Phillipsen, 1998). Although it is reassuring to know that infant attachment is not affected by nonparental care, one cause for concern that has surfaced in recent years involves the impact of extensive child-care experience on children's subsequent social behavior. The NICHD Early Child Care Research Network (2005, 2006) and Marc Bornstein and his colleagues (Bornstein et al., 2006; Bornstein & Hahn, 2007) showed that the amount time spent in nonmaternal care in the first four and a half years of life predicted children's level of problem behavior (including assertiveness, disobedience, and aggression) displayed at home or in kindergarten. The elevated risk of behavior problems on the part of children with extensive child-care histories was evident in reports by mothers, care providers, and teachers, and the effects remained significant even when the effects of maternal sensitivity, family background, as well as the type, quality, and stability of child care were taken into account. However, the magnitude of the difference between the behavior of children who have been enrolled in early child care versus those who have not is very small, and few children who have had nonparental care early in life develop significant behavioral problems.

It is important to remember that the arrangements that parents make to care for their infants are greatly influenced by the broader ecology in which families live, including the availability of various alternatives. In most contemporary industrialized societies, the "problem" of how to care for an infant while the parents must work is solved by using some sort of nonparental care. But in other cultures, parents bring their infants to work with them. For example, infants among the Aka foragers in the Central African Republic are held by their parents while the parents hunt, butcher, and share game (Hewlett, 1992). Quechua infants high in the Andes spend their early months wrapped in a layers of woolen cloth strapped to their mothers' backs that forms a manchua pouch to survive the exceedingly cold, thin, dry air surrounding them. Ache infants living in the rain forests of eastern Paraguay spend 80–100 percent of their time in physical contact with their parents and are almost never more than three feet away because this hunter-gatherer group does not make permanent camps in the forest, but only clears a space that has stumps and roots remaining that are hazardous for the children (Kaplan & Dove, 1987). "Take Your Child to Work" day is a once-a-year occurrence in modern-day America, but it is the norm, not the exception, in many nonindustrialized cultures.

Gender and Infant Socioemotional Development

Male and female infants are treated differently from birth. Newborn nurseries in maternity wards use color codes (blue for boy and pink for girl) to differentiate the sexes, and early presents given to infants by friends and family members use similarly sex-typed color codes. In addition, from birth onward, fathers appear to interact preferentially with sons and mothers with daughters (Parke, 2002). In a study of mothers' and fathers' behavior with male infants while shopping at a mall, fathers were more likely than were mothers to accompany their infants to toy stores than to clothing stores (Parke, 2002), lending support to the premise that fathers are more likely to pursue play activities with their male infants than are mothers (Parke, 2002). Fathers play more boisterous games with sons than with daughters, whereas mothers' interactions with both boys and girls tend to be nurturing. Mother-daughter interactions are characterized by greater levels of closeness and intimacy than are mother-son interactions.

Many children—from a surprisingly early age—choose to play with same-sex-typed toys (often in spite of their parents' attempts at gender equality).

Whatever their origins, sex-typed differences in play are evident by the end of the first year and do not change much thereafter (Ruble, Martin, & Berenbaum, 2006).

The sex typing of infant-parent play is always fascinating because girls and boys gravitate in such different directions, regardless of parents' professed beliefs. Children, and especially boys, begin to show preferences for male-typed toys (e.g., toy trucks) as early as the second year of life. Furthermore, parents choose sex-typed toys for infants (Leaper, 2002). To determine the age at which toddlers begin to exhibit consistent sex-stereotype toy choices and investigate the association between parents' expectations and the children's own knowledge of gender-typed toys, two researchers observed the development of sex-typed play behavior in toddlers beginning at eighteen months of age (O'Brien & Huston, 1985a, 1985b). Children were observed in a daycare center with a set of masculine, feminine, and neutral toys. In addition, the homes of some of the boys and girls were visited, and the toys available to them were counted and classified. Parents were also asked to predict their children's liking for the toys used at the daycare center. Both boys and girls played significantly more often with same-sex-typed toys. Both boys and girls had more same-sex-typed than cross-sex-typed toys in their homes, and parents predicted that their children would choose to play with same-sex-typed toys. Mothers' and fathers' behaviors toward the toy play of their infant sons and daughters even earlier were observed in the laboratory where sex-typed toys and neutral toys were provided. Sex differences were found in infant toy choice starting at ten months for dolls; for example, girls were more likely to play with dolls and to give them to their parents.

Sex-typed preferences seem to be promoted by the child's social environment from early in life. And parents certainly contribute to them: Mothers of eleven-month-old male infants overestimate how well their babies would crawl down a sloped pathway, whereas mothers of eleven-month-old female infants underestimate how well their babies would do (Mondschein, Adolph, & Tamis-LeMonda, 2000). Guess what? Tests of crawling ability on the sloped path revealed no sex differences whatsoever in infant crawling. (For a summary of this section, see "Interim Summary 6.4: Parental Behavior and Interaction with Infants.")

INTERIM SUMMARY **6.4**

Parental Behavior and Interaction with Infants

Harlow's monkey study paved the way for Bowlby's attachment theory and illustrated that babies need **contact comfort** from adults.	■ Harlow's study removed infant rhesus monkeys from their mothers and gave them a choice of substitutes—one model constructed of wire and the other of terry cloth.
Mothers and Fathers	■ Mothers and fathers engage their infants in different types of interactions with different characteristics.
	■ Stress on parents can undermine their ability to interact with their infants in ways that promote secure attachment and healthy socioemotional development.
Nonparental Care	■ The majority of U.S. infants are now cared for by someone other than a parent at least some of the time.
	■ It's impossible to generalize about the effects of nonparental childcare on infant development because there are many variables, including the differences in environments from one daycare situation to another.
	■ The National Center for Infants, Toddlers, and Families identified 8 criteria that need to be achieved to ensure high-quality infant care:
	1. Health and safety
	2. Maintaining small groups
	3. Assigning each infant to a primary caregiver
	4. Ensuring continuity in care
	5. Providing responsive caregiving
	6. Meeting individual needs in the context of the larger group
	7. Ensuring cultural and linguistic continuity
	8. Providing a stimulating physical environment
Gender and Socioemotional Development	■ Sex-typed preferences seem to be promoted by the child's social environment from early in life, and parents contribute to them.

SUMMING UP AND LOOKING AHEAD

Human infants enter the world primed to form relationships with others; ours is, by any standard, a very social species. As you've read, from a very early age infants are able to express and discern different emotions and are masters at behaving in ways that elicit attention and nurturance from the adults around them. These capabilities provide the basis for the formation of attachments with parents and other caregivers—bonds that form the foundation for subsequent social relationships, not just in the family or with adults, but with the peers children will encounter as their social world expands (Ladd & Pettit, 2002). Toddlers who leave infancy with a sense of security have a substantial socioemotional advantage over those whose attachments are insecure or disorganized.

The development of emotional and social competence during the first two years of life follows a predictable timetable, but there are important variations among infants in how they express their feelings and interact with others. There are two sides to emotional behavior: Emotional expressions communicate feelings to others through facial expressions, gestures, and vocalizations, and emotional understanding is reading the emotional expressions of others.

Primary emotions are deeply rooted in human biology (joy, anger, fear, sadness) and develop early in infants; secondary emotions (embarrassment, pride, guilt, shame and envy) develop during toddlerhood. One important contributor to this variability is temperament, a biologically based source of individual differences in behavior that is evident very early in life. In combination with experience, an infant's temperament shapes the development of what will eventually become the individual's personality. Temperament is not destiny, of course, but a large measure of who we are as individuals—how shy or gregarious, how positive or negative, how energetic or calm—peeks through at a surprisingly early age.

Socioemotional development is rapid during the early years, but there is a tremendous amount of growth to come in early childhood and beyond. Infants develop their first social relationships (attachments) with their parents, but differ in the security of their attachments. These differences affect children's later development. Among the highlights we will be looking at when we turn our attention to early childhood socioemotional development, in "Socioemotional Development in Early Childhood," are the emergence of a more sophisticated sense of self (Harter, 2006), increases in the child's ability to understand and regulate his or her emotional states, the first signs of behavior that is deliberately helpful to others as well as behavior that is deliberately hurtful, and the development of more complex relationships with others, especially with peers.

Our look at the first two years of life is now complete. It is time to make the transition to a whole new period of life—early childhood. We begin with physical development.

HERE'S WHAT YOU SHOULD KNOW

Did You Get It?

After reading this chapter, you should understand the following:

- The two sides of infant emotional behavior—*emotional expression* and *emotional understanding*
- How emotional expression develops from *primary* to *secondary emotions*
- What temperament is and how it is measured
- John Bowlby's theory of attachment
- How parents and children interact and its implications

Important Terms and Concepts

attachments (p. 150)
contact comfort (p. 169)
difficult children
    (p. 157)
effectance (p. 164)
emotional expression
    (p. 150)

emotional understanding
    (p. 150)
emotions (p. 150)
environment of evolutionary
    adaptedness (p. 161)
goodness of fit (p. 159)
inhibited children (p. 157)

mirror neurons (p. 154)
negative affectivity (p. 157)
positive affectivity (p. 157)
primary emotions (p. 151)
reciprocity (p. 164)
secondary emotions (p. 151)
secure base (p. 165)

sensitive period (p. 162)
separation protest (p. 162)
social referencing (p. 154)
strange situation (p.163)
stranger wariness (p. 163)
temperament (p. 150)
trust (p. 165)

CHAPTER 4
Physical Development in Infancy

- The general principles of physical growth are *directionality, independence of systems*, and *canalization*.

- The **central nervous system** processes information and directs behavior. Brain development is the product of reciprocal interplay between biology and experience.

- The brain's structure and function is **plastic**—cells are predestined for different functions but that changes at sensitive periods. There are two kinds of plasticity: (1) **modifiability** and (2) **compensation.**

- The **autonomic nervous system** regulates many body activities (such as breathing) without our voluntary control.

- **Reflexes** are divided into three groups: (1) *Approach reflexes* (2) *Avoidance reflexes* (3) *Other reflexes* such as the Palmar grasp and Moro response.

- Motor development is dependent on physical maturation. Dynamic systems theory asserts that one change in development impacts others.

- Sensory systems develop in utero. Our **multimodal perceptions** of objects are coordinated across senses.

CHAPTER 5
Cognitive Development in Infancy

- There are four approaches used to learn about infant perception and cognition: (1) habituation, (2) novelty responsiveness, (3) learning, and (4) showing.

- Jean Piaget believed that mental development unfolds in a fixed sequence of stages. The **sensorimotor period** encompasses infancy. Advances in the sensorimotor period include causality and **object permanence,** which paves the way toward **mental representation.**

- Developmental scientists now agree that Piaget underestimated infants' perceptual and cognitive capacities.

- There are several specific areas of mental development: (1) **categorization,** (2) memory, and (3) play.

- The Bayley Scales of Infant Development are used to assess infant motor, sensation, perception, cognition, memory, language, and social behavior. The **validity** of these tests is problematic.

- The acquisition of language reflects a complex interaction between biology and experience. Some children are **referential**; some, **expressive.**

- Noam Chomsky argues that a number of aspects of syntax are innate, built into every infant's brain in what he called **universal grammar.**

CHAPTER 6
Socioemotional Development in Infancy

- There are two sides to emotional behavior: **emotional expression** and **emotional understanding. Primary emotions** develop early in infants. Secondary emotions develop later.

- **Temperament** is the biologically based source of individual differences in behavioral functioning. There are three characterizations: (1) **positive affectivity,** (2) **negative affectivity,** and (3) **inhibited and difficult children.**

- Differences in the types of **attachments** infants form with their parents affect children's development.

- John Bowlby assumed that how infants and parents behave toward one another is best considered in the context of the environment in which our species evolved (**environment of evolutionary adaptedness**).

- Harlow's monkey study illustrated that babies need **contact comfort** from adults.

- It's impossible to generalize about the effects of nonparental childcare on development because there are many variables, including the differences in daycare environments.

- Sex-typed preferences seem to be promoted by the child's social environment from early in life.

part three

Early Childhood

© C Squared Studios/Getty Images

CHAPTER

7

Physical Development in Early Childhood

© Jose Luis Pelaez Inc./Getty Images

The time was the 1930s. The place: the Babies Center of Columbia-Presbyterian Hospital in New York. The cast of characters: twins, Johnny and Jimmy Woods, and developmental scientist Myrtle McGraw. The twins' parents had agreed for them to participate in an experiment, as part of the Normal Child Development Study (McGraw, 1935). From age twenty days to twenty-four months, the boys spent their days at the center Monday through Friday. Johnny was given daily exercise and activities to promote his physical skills, including challenges thought beyond the capabilities of an infant. Meanwhile, Jimmy interacted with caregivers who fed, changed, and talked with him, but he was not exposed to these physical activities and spent much of his day in a crib. (Today a research ethics committee might not permit this experiment; see "The Study of Child Development.")

Johnny's motor development exceeded expectations. At fifteen months he could climb steep slopes, swim fifteen to twenty feet with his head in the water, and even roller-skate—all on his own, with an adult close by for safety (McGraw, 1935). These astonishing achievements made him a media star, the wonder boy of the day (Dennis, 1995). Around 20 months, however, Jimmy became increasingly frustrated with inactivity. When he was around twenty-two months, McGraw and her team began introducing him to the challenges his twin brother had faced.

McGraw's study of Johnny and Jimmy was an early demonstration of the interplay between both nature *and* nurture (Dalton, 1996; Gottlieb, 1998). A certain level of neural and muscular maturity is needed to perform a given action. When that level is reached, however, a challenging environment can and did result in children using their bodies more effectively. Experience, in turn, stimulates neural and muscular maturation. For example, McGraw observed that her staff began pushing Johnny up and down the corridor on a tricycle on a daily basis beginning at 11 months, without any discernible effects. Eight months later, at close to twenty months, Johnny suddenly seemed to grasp that pushing the pedals made the tricycle move forward. Johnny's twin brother, Jimmy, was introduced to a tricycle when he was twenty-two months old, and in a state of neuromuscular readiness. He learned how to ride faster and more easily than his brother had.

When Johnny and Jimmy were two years old, they returned to a normal family life with their parents and siblings. How did advanced training affect Johnny's motor development in later years? We will revisit the boys at age six later in this chapter. Stay tuned.

This chapter is the first of three on early childhood, sometimes called the "play" or "preschool" years, ages two to five. Early childhood is a period of transformation for all children. At age one and a half the child tottered across the grass on wobbly legs. At six she is a whirlwind of activity. She can run, skip, jump rope, catch a ball, and even ride a bicycle. She has moved from a high chair to a place at the table with a knife and fork. She can button her own blouse, zip her own jacket, and tie her own shoes. At age two, she stacked blocks any which way. At five or six, she can put a puzzle together, cut out shapes with scissors, play video games with a joystick, draw a picture of her family, and even print her own name (Case-Smith, 2005). But for some children malnutrition or maltreatment casts a shadow over the "play years."

In this chapter we explain how the child's body and brain develop, and look at the rapid advances in mobility, coordination, and dexterity during this period, as well as health. We will consider **normative development**: the pattern of development that is typical, or average. But we know that typical development, based on what occurs on average, is only part of the story because children who are the same age vary in body size and physical skills. Understanding development requires that we look at **individual differences** or the variation among individuals on a characteristic as well as what is typical or normative.

normative development A pattern of development that is typical, or average.

individual differences The variation among individuals on a characteristic.

PHYSICAL GROWTH AND DEVELOPMENT

The rapid growth rate that characterizes infancy slows in early childhood (Mei et al., 2004). Children continue to grow, of course, but the most noticeable changes are in their proportions. The child's torso, arms, and legs grow longer; and the tummy, flatter. The head is smaller in proportion to the body than in infancy. The pudgy one-and-a-half-year-old cherub looks more like an elf at age five. A typical preschooler is leaner than both his baby brother and his teenage sister.

Patterns of Normative Growth

norms Average outcomes rather than actual or even ideal ones.

The first scientific studies of physical growth were designed to establish **norms** or standards of what is "typical" for different ages (e.g., Gesell & Thompson, 1938). Studies of normative growth often use a cross-sectional research design (introduced in "The Study of Child Development"). Other researchers use a longitudinal research design, in which the same children are studied at different ages. Researchers measure the heights and weights of a large number of children of different ages, and then average the results for two-year-olds, three-year-olds, and so on.

These studies have been used to create *growth curve tables* of normative development based on heights and weights of children of different ages. The growth curves suggest that physical development is slow and steady during early childhood. On average, children grow 2.5 inches and gain 6 pounds per year during early childhood (see Figure 7.1).

Boys are slightly taller and heavier than girls, but the sexes are similar in body proportion (National Center for Health Statistics, 2000a, 2000b).

How does growth in early childhood compare in the United States and other countries? To answer this question, the World Health Organization conducted a study of approximately 8,500 children from different ethnic backgrounds and cultural settings (Brazil, Ghana, India, Norway, Oman, and the USA). The investigators concluded that children from these diverse parts of the world had very similar average growth patterns when provided healthy growth conditions in early life (Garza & de Onis, 2007).

But averages do not tell the whole story. Studies of individual children show that growth is not smooth and continuous, but rather episodic, occurring in fits and starts (Adolph & Berger, 2006). In one set of studies, researchers measured individual children daily with precise instruments (Lampl & Emde, 1983). They found that brief periods (less than twenty-four hours) of growth were followed by periods during which no growth occurred for days or even weeks (see Figure 7.2). This stop-and-start pattern characterizes growth in height, weight, head circumference, and other measures. The resulting picture is quite different from average growth curves shown in Figure 7.1. When a grandmother exclaims to her grandchild, "Why, you've grown over night!," she might be right!

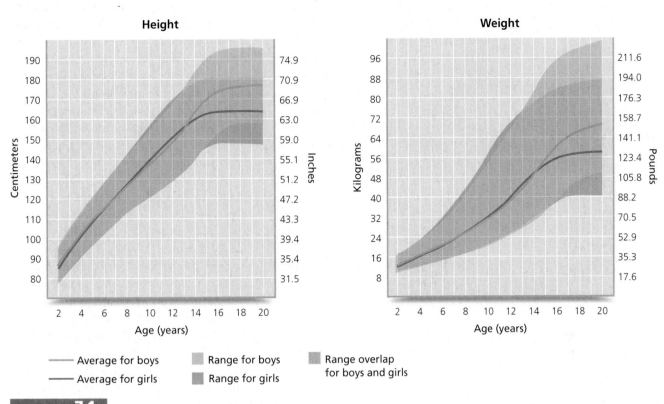

Height

Weight

—— Average for boys ▦ Range for boys ▦ Range overlap for boys and girls
—— Average for girls ▦ Range for girls

FIGURE **7.1**

Growth in Height and Weight From Age 2 to Age 20

On average, children gain about 6 pounds and grow 2.5 inches per year in early childhood. As you can see from the area shaded in green, boys and girls are fairly similar in size during this period, but differences begin to appear in early adolescence.

body mass index (BMI) BMI is calculated by dividing weight (measured in kilograms) by height (measured in meters) squared, or wt/ht².

Individual Differences

In early childhood, children begin to show a wider range of individual differences in physical development than was true during infancy. Healthy babies are fairly similar in size and shape. In early childhood, individuality blossoms. Some children stand head and shoulders above most of their peers. Some are straight and slim, even "skinny," whereas others are stocky.

An important way to measure children's health and physical development is the **body mass index (BMI)**, which helps us to judge whether a child's weight is appropriate for his or her height. The BMI is calculated by dividing weight (measured in kilograms) by height (measured in meters) squared, or wt/ht². The BMI for a four-year-old boy who weighs 36.75 pounds (16.69 kilograms) and is 40.5 inches (1.03 meters) tall is 15.8:

$$16.69/(1.03)^2 = 15.8$$

Figure 7.3 shows the variability of BMI scores in boys, ages two to ten years. An average boy at each age is in the 50th percentile, midway between 1 and 99. A boy in the 60th percentile for BMI is heavier than 60 percent, but lighter than 40 percent

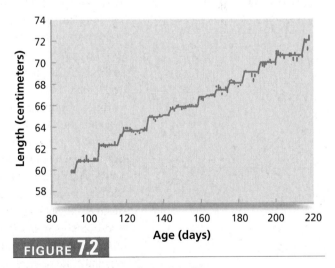

FIGURE **7.2**

One Child's Growth Over 140 Days

In contrast to the smooth growth curves found when many children's scores are averaged, an individual child's growth has a choppy stop-and-start pattern.

Source: Handbook of child psychology, Vol. 2: Cognition, perception and language, 6/e by W. Damon & R. Lerner (eds.) and D. Kuhn & R.S. Siegler (Vol. eds.). Copyright © 2006. Reproduced with permission of John Wiley & Sons, Inc.

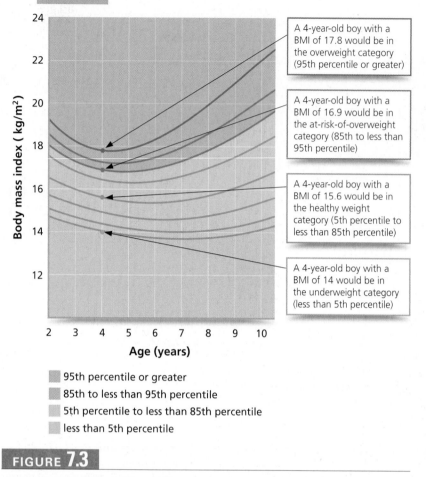

A 4-year-old boy with a BMI of 17.8 would be in the overweight category (95th percentile or greater)

A 4-year-old boy with a BMI of 16.9 would be in the at-risk-of-overweight category (85th to less than 95th percentile)

A 4-year-old boy with a BMI of 15.6 would be in the healthy weight category (5th percentile to less than 85th percentile)

A 4-year-old boy with a BMI of 14 would be in the underweight category (less than 5th percentile)

■ 95th percentile or greater
■ 85th to less than 95th percentile
■ 5th percentile to less than 85th percentile
■ less than 5th percentile

FIGURE 7.3

Body Mass Index (BMI) of Boys Who Are Overweight, Healthy Weight, and Underweight

Four-year-old boys who are considered to be in the healthy range of height-to-weight ratio have a BMI that is above 14 and below 16.9.

of children his age, sex, and height. Boys in the 85th to 94th percentiles are considered overweight, and those in the 95th percentile or higher, obese—also a cause for concern. Boys in the 5th percentile or lower are clinically underweight for their height. For medical or other reasons, they are not thriving. But 80 percent of children—in all of their variety—are within the normal range.

What is the source of these differences? Heredity is an important source. Studies that have contrasted the growth of monozygotic (MZ) or identical twins (who share 100% of their genes) and dizygotic (DZ) or fraternal twins (who share, on average, 50% of their genes) find that about two-thirds of the statistical variations in height and weight can be attributed to genetic factors (Plomin, 2007). But heredity is only part of the story. Changes in diet and physical health have resulted in increases in height and weight within families in the last hundred years in the United States, Europe, and Asia. Nutrition is a significant issue—with long-term consequences—for preschoolers and their parents.

Diet and Nutrition

Two changes in eating patterns coincide in early childhood. Because they are growing more slowly than they did as infants, children's appetites decrease. They don't need as many calories (in proportion to their size) as they did when they were babies (Kedesdy & Budd, 1998). And they aren't as hungry. At the same time, they are graduating from baby to adult food, though in smaller portions and bite-size pieces.

Some preschoolers are picky eaters. Surveys of mothers have found between 18 percent and 29 percent of young children fall into this group (Jacobi et al., 2003). They eat a limited variety of foods, accept new foods less readily, and express strong food dislikes. They are suspicious of new foods—especially vegetables. Mealtimes can become a battlefield. Parents fret, cajole, threaten, or bribe ("Eat your vegetables and you can have ice cream"). Such strategies are rarely successful; they are also unnecessary (Kedesdy & Budd, 1998). When regularly presented with a small serving of, say, broccoli, along with other food and without pressure to eat the full helping, children gradually accept the vegetable (after eight to fifteen exposures in one study; Sullivan & Birch, 1990).

What young children will eat and how much they eat will vary from meal to meal, day to day. How much a child eats at one meal doesn't matter as much as what he or she eats over the course of the day. Allowed to eat only as much as they want, children compensate for eating very little at one meal by eating more at other times. When parents insist that children clean their plates, children don't learn to pay attention to internal cues of hunger and fullness.

The danger is not that children will starve themselves, but that they will learn to overeat. Childhood **obesity** has reached epidemic levels. Estimates are that 9 million

obesity Determined by body mass index. Children in the 95th percentile or higher (for their age and sex) are considered obese. Children between the 85th and 94th percentile are classified as overweight.

U.S. children are obese and many more are at risk (overweight) (National Research Council, 2004). For many young children, being overweight is not simply a matter of having "baby fat" that they lose as they grow. One longitudinal study of more than 1,000 healthy U.S. youngsters found that 60 percent of children who were overweight at any time during the preschool years were overweight at age twelve, and none of the children who were in the 50th percentile or lower for BMI in early childhood was obese at age twelve—that's right, not one of them (Nader et al., 2006).

Obesity and overweight in early childhood is particularly troubling because serious health problems such as heart disease and diabetes—once adult illnesses—now are increasingly seen in young people. We will discuss childhood obesity in more detail in "Physical Development in Middle Childhood." The key point here is that the best way to combat obesity is to prevent weight gain in the first place.

Research (Faith et al., 2004) suggests that parents can lower the risk of overweight and obesity by doing the following:

- Providing children with a variety of healthy foods at meals and snack times, but not pressuring them to eat. When preschoolers serve themselves they eat 25 percent less than when adults fill their plates (Fisher, Rolls, & Birch, 2003).

- Not using food to bribe, punish, or entertain children. When food becomes an issue, children may learn to overeat as a way of rewarding or consoling themselves.

- Encouraging (and joining in) active play and limiting sedentary pastimes, such as watching TV. (If parents are couch potatoes, they are modeling this behavior for the child.)

- Serving as good role models, by practicing healthy eating habits and exercising themselves, and by planning active family time (raking leaves, bicycle rides, and the like).

© Marcy Maloy/Getty Images

Providing children with a variety of healthy foods at meals and snack times, but *not* pressuring them to eat, reduces the risk of future obesity.

In early childhood, then, growth rates slow and children become more adult-like in their proportions. Individual differences in body build, measured as BMI, increase. Appetites typically decline. Yet childhood obesity, which may persist to adulthood and lead to serious health problems, is a growing public health concern. We will discuss the opposite problem, malnutrition, later in this chapter. (For a summary of this section, see "Interim Summary 7.1: Physical Growth and Development.")

BRAIN DEVELOPMENT

During early childhood, the brain matures both structurally and functionally, a process that continues into adolescence and young adulthood (Nelson, Thomas, & de Haan, 2006). An important aspect of brain development in early childhood is establishing and fine tuning communications within the brain and between the brain and nervous system.

To review: The brain is composed of billions of cells called **neurons** (see "Physical Development in Infancy"). These neurons have two types of specialized extensions: **dendrites**, which collect information and carry it to the body of the neuron, and **axons**, which transmit information away from the cell body (see Figure 7.4). The connection between one neuron's axons and another neuron's dendrites (called a **synapse**) enables information to pass from one neuron to another. As electrical impulses travel from the body of the neuron to the tip of its axons, they trigger the release of chemicals called neurotransmitters, which cross the gap between one neuron and the next (Couperus & Nelson, 2006).

neuron A cell that carries information across the body and brain, as well as back and forth within the brain.

dendrites Branched extensions of a neuron that pick up signals from other neurons.

axon The part of the cell that carries signals away from the cell body toward other neurons. At their tips, axons divide into many axon terminals.

synapse The connection between one neuron's axon and another neuron's dendrite.

INTERIM SUMMARY 7.1

Physical Growth and Development

Patterns of Normative Growth	■ Scientific studies have established norms of what is typical for physical growth at different ages.
	■ Rate of physical development slows in early childhood compared with infancy.
	■ Children from diverse parts of the world show similar growth patterns when provided with healthy environments.
	■ Frequent measurements of the same children over time show that physical growth occurs in fits and starts.
Individual Differences	■ **Individual differences** in physical growth are larger in early childhood than infancy.
	■ Body mass index (BMI), the ratio of weight to height, is a common index of whether a child's weight is appropriate for his or her height.
	■ Differences in BMI are influenced by heredity, diet, physical health, and exercise.
Diet and Nutrition	■ Appetite decreases in early childhood as rate of growth slows.
	■ The incidence of obesity and being overweight in early childhood is increasing.
	■ Parents can lower the risk of obesity by providing healthy foods, not using food to bribe or entertain children, encouraging active play, and serving as good role models.

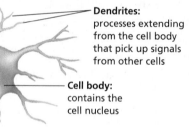
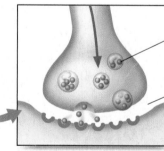

Dendrites: processes extending from the cell body that pick up signals from other cells

Cell body: contains the cell nucleus

Axon: the part of the cell that carries signals to other cells

Myelin sheath: fatty tissue that insulates a cell and speeds cell nerve conduction

Neurotransmitter: electrochemicals that cross the synapse between cells

Synapse: the space between the axon terminal of one cell and the dendrite of another cell

FIGURE 7.4

Parts of the Neuron

This diagram shows several important structures of the neuron, including the dendrites, cell body, and axons. Neurotransmitters are stored in terminals at the end of the axon and get released into the space between two neurons known as the synapse.

Source: From Bernstein/Penner/Clarke-Stewart/Roy. *Psychology,* 8E. © 2008 Wadsworth, a part of Cengage Learning, Inc. Reproduced by permission. www.cengage.com/permissions

Improvements in the Brain's Communication Network

A key process in the brain is the development of connections between neurons that occurs through the growth of axons and dendrites This process, called **synaptogenesis**, peaks at about age one year but continues into childhood, and, at lower levels, throughout life. The formation of some synapses is genetically programmed, but the formation of other synapses depends on experience (Couperus & Nelson, 2006). Conversing with young children, reading books, doing puzzles, and riding bikes are all activities that encourage the development of new synapses.

Synaptic pruning—the selective elimination of unused and unnecessary synapses—is an equally important part of brain development. The overproduction and later reduction of synapses are normal parts of brain development. Synaptic pruning begins in the first years and continues into young adulthood. From peak levels in early childhood, synaptic density is reduced by about 40 percent by adulthood (Couperus & Nelson, 2006). The "extra" synapses in a child's brain provide some "backup insurance" that supports brain plasticity (discussed later in this chapter); however, synaptic pruning also is needed. Selective elimination of some synapses while others are strengthened supports brain adaptation and plasticity by making the brain more efficient. An overabundance of synapses is too unwieldy in the long run (Couperus & Nelson, 2006).

Another process that improves connections and communication within the brain is **myelination**. **Myelin** is a fatty substance that wraps itself around the axon. Not unlike the way in which plastic insulation helps keep electricity traveling along a wire, myelin increases both the speed and efficiency at which information travels across the brain's circuits (Webb, Monk, & Nelson, 2001).

With lots of practice, throwing a soccer ball while keeping both feet firmly planted becomes more automatic. Repetition helps to strengthen connections among synapses.

© Jeff Greenberg/PhotoEdit

Myelination of different areas of the brain occurs sequentially, beginning prenatally and continuing into young adulthood (Nelson et al., 2006). The areas of the brain involved with vision and movement are myelinated first. During early childhood, the fibers that connect the cerebellum to the cerebral cortex grow and myelinate. These changes improve children's balance and control of body movements. Walking, running, and jumping become more synchronized. Myelination in the regions of the brain that govern hand-eye coordination also continues through early childhood, enabling children to be able to print their name or use a crayon to color a picture. Myelination of the frontal lobes, perhaps the most plastic area of the brain, continues into late adolescence and early adulthood.

Mirror Neurons

A particular type of brain cell, called **mirror neurons**, has been discovered. These neurons may explain why young children learn so readily by observing others (Winerman, 2005). The discovery of mirror neurons was made in Italy at the University of Parma during a study of monkeys whose brains were wired to record neuronal activity. First, the researchers observed that particular neurons in monkeys' premotor cortex fired when the monkeys did things like reach for a peanut (Rizzolatti & Arbib, 1998). Then, the researchers made an interesting discovery. They found that these same motor neurons would fire when the researchers picked up a peanut to hand to the monkey. Mirror neurons fired both when the animal *performed* an action and when the animal observed the action being performed by another. Using brain imaging, other

synaptogenesis A key process in the brain involving the development of connections between neurons through the growth of axons and dendrites.

synaptic pruning The process of elimination of unused and unnecessary synapses.

myelination The process through which cell axons become sheathed in myelin.

myelin A white fatty substance that encases cell axons. It provides insulation and improves transmission of signals.

mirror neuron A type of brain cell that fires when the individual performs an action or the action is performed by another.

Ken Seet/Corbis

Mirror neurons may enable this young girl to learn about bread making even if she doesn't actually knead the dough.

scientists have found evidence of the same phenomenon in humans—not only with actions and sensations, but also with experiencing another person's feelings and emotions (Keysers et al., 2004).

Children (and adults) don't always have to perform an action to have the experience; thanks to mirror neurons, they can share the experience vicariously. Mirror neurons may help explain why children can learn so much from watching others, as social learning theory predicts.

Brain Anatomy

Important changes in brain anatomy occur during early childhood. Using brain imaging technology to document brain activity, researchers have created time-lapse 3-D images that show changes in gray matter—the working tissue of the brain's cortex—from early childhood to adulthood (Gogtay et al., 2004). The overall size of the brain does not change very much in early childhood, but the relative size of specific structures of the brain do change. The first areas to mature are those related to the most basic functions, such as processing the senses and movement, followed by those related to spatial orientation and language (the parietal lobes), and then the areas of the brain related to reasoning and executive functioning (the prefrontal cortex) (see Figure 7.5).

The brain is composed of two halves, or hemispheres, the right and left. The nerves from the spinal cord cross over before they enter the brain. As a result, the right hemisphere controls the left side of the body and the left hemisphere, the right side of the body. Each hemisphere specializes in certain functions, a phenomenon called **lateralization**. The left side of the brain detects time and sequences, processes speech, and registers external stimuli. The right hemisphere detects patterns and images, processes body language and emotional expressions, and registers internal stimuli (Sousa, 2006). The left hemisphere is especially active from three to six years, corresponding to the changes in language development in early childhood. Activity in the right hemisphere increases from three to eleven years with a small spurt between eight and ten years, corresponding to improvements in spatial skills in middle childhood. In males, language development typically occurs in the left hemisphere. In females, the main area is in the left hemisphere, with additional processing in the right hemisphere (Cahill, 2005).

lateralization The localization of a function to one of the hemispheres of the brain.

Between ages three and six years, the **corpus callosum**—the large bundle of fibers that connects the two hemispheres—develops rapidly. Communication between the two halves of the brains facilitates quicker and smoother action, and the hemispheres can share information and learning. Incomplete or abnormal development of the corpus callosum is associated with mild to severe symptoms, including retardation, seizures, and inability to initiate or control muscle movements.

One sign of brain lateralization is *handedness*. By five years old, nearly all children prefer using one hand more than the other, and 85 percent are right-handed. In almost all right-handers (close to 95 percent), the area of the brain that processes language is located in the left hemisphere; however, in left-handers, the incidence of right-hemisphere language dominance increases linearly with the degree of left-handedness, from 15 percent in ambidextrous individuals to 27 percent in strong left-handers (Knecht et al., 2000). Handedness has a genetic component, but cultural beliefs and schooling also play a role (Annett, 2002). In the United States during the early twentieth century, left-handed children were forced to use their right hand for writing and punished for slipping into left-handedness. The bias even remains in our language today; for example, in the phrase "left-handed compliment."

The **frontal lobes** make up the area of the brain that develops most in early childhood (Gogtay et al., 2004). Sometimes called the "executive" of the brain, the frontal lobes are responsible for planning and organizing new actions, problem solving, and regulating emotions, as well as focusing attention. Rapid growth occurs in the frontal lobes between three and six years. Everyday behavior provides evidence of frontal lobe development. For example, toddlers are impulsive. Sometimes their attention span is so short they fail to follow through and complete tasks such as putting away toys when asked by parents or teachers (Rothbart, Posner, & Kieras, 2006). Other times they find it difficult to stop an activity they have begun, whether singing a jingle over and over or banging two pot lids together. By age six, however, maturation of the frontal lobes supports the development of more focused, planful, and goal-oriented behavior (Anderson et al., 2007).

A simple procedure, called the "Go/No-Go task," can be used to illustrate the difference in frontal lobe development at different ages (Nosek & Banaji, 2001). First, young children learn a way to respond to a stimulus—for example, to push a green "Go" button each time they see a picture of someone smiling on a computer screen. They are told not to push the button if the person is not smiling, the "No-Go" response. Next, they go through a series of trials in which all the photographs show someone smiling. Then, every so often the experimenters insert a picture of someone who is not smiling. The goal is to measure how often and quickly children can inhibit their first response (push the Go button). Three- and four-year-olds have a hard time inhibiting their first

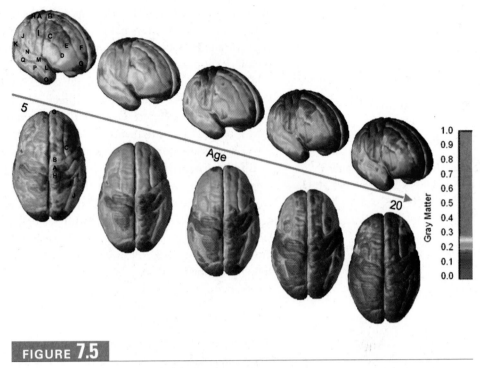

FIGURE 7.5

Right Lateral and Top Views of Gray Matter Maturation from Ages Five to Twenty

Brain scans obtained from the same children over time reveal that parts of the brain mature at different rates. Areas involved with motor and sensory functions mature first, followed by speech and language areas, and then areas related to attention and planning.

corpus callosum The connection between the two halves or hemispheres of the brain.

frontal lobes Sometimes called the "executive" of the brain, the frontal lobes are responsible for planning and organizing new actions, problem solving, and regulating emotions, as well as focusing attention.

impulse and nearly always push the Go button, even when the picture doesn't warrant it. Six-year-olds may make a few mistakes but generally get the idea. Unlike the younger children, the maturation of the prefrontal cortex enables the six-year-olds to inhibit or suppress the preferred behavior—and to think before they act.

The Go/No-Go task is similar to the game Simon Says, in which children follow the leader, but only when the leader's directions include, "Simon says." Otherwise they are out. "Simon says touch your nose" is a Go signal; the plain instruction, "Sit down," a No-Go signal. Children who sit—including most three- and four-year-olds—are out. Six-year-olds are more likely to restrain themselves.

effortful control The ability to withhold a first response and choose another.

Effortful control—the ability to withhold a first response and choose another—emerges during early childhood (Kochanska & Aksan, 2007; Rothbart et al., 2006). It requires voluntary control of attention, and it enables children to regulate their reactions. Examples of effortful control include suppressing impulses as in Go/No-Go games and Simon Says, being able to slow down movements intentionally when drawing a straight line, selective focusing (recognizing small shapes hidden in a larger shape), and lowering one's voice (as in whispering). In all cases the difference is supported by frontal lobe development.

Brain Plasticity

Brain development is more than the unfolding of a fixed genetic plan (Nelson et al., 2006). Experience plays a powerful role in sculpting the fine architecture of the brain, even as changes in the brain affect children's behavior. As we have emphasized, the interplay of biology and contexts drives development. The term **brain plasticity** refers to the degree to which the brain can be altered by experience (see "Physical Development in Infancy"). Plasticity varies over the course of brain development. As the brain passes through different stages of development, sensitivity to experience varies. The effects of experiences on brain development depend on the maturity of the brain when the experiences occur (Gunnar, Fisher, & the Early Experience, Stress, and Prevention Network, 2006). A **sensitive period** is a time in development during which the organism is especially open to environmental influence.

brain plasticity The degree to which the brain can be altered by experience.

sensitive period A time in development during which the organism is especially open to environmental influence.

Some sensitive periods in brain development are shown in Figure 7.6. We can continue learning in these areas throughout life, but after a sensitive period ends, the level of skill we achieve probably will not be as high (Couperus & Nelson, 2006).

One example of a sensitive period in the visual system is **strabismus**, a condition in which a child's eyes are not aligned properly at birth; the eyes are crossed toward the nose or veer toward the ears. This condition can be corrected by eyeglasses up to age four or five, when the number of synapses reaches adult levels. If not corrected by then, the child will not develop normal stereoscopic (three-dimensional) depth perception.

strabismus A condition in which a child's eyes are crossed toward the nose or veer toward the ears. If not corrected by eyeglasses before age five, the child will not develop normal depth perception.

Another example of a sensitive period is seen in language development. The areas of the brain associated with language remain plastic through middle childhood. Children who suffer major damage to these brain regions at birth or during infancy can develop normal language abilities, whereas adults who suffer similar damage do not recover fully (Couperus & Nelson, 2006). This is also why children find it easier than adults do to become fluent in a second language, including American Sign Language (ASL) (Petitto et al., 2000; Silverberg & Samuel, 2004).

At the same time, it is important to remember that experiences do not just happen to the brain; the brain plays a role in experience (Nelson et al., 2006). Exposed to the same environmental condition or incident, a young child and an older one do not have the same experience, because their brains process information differently. When a father reads a book to a two-year-old, she looks at the pictures and delights in recognizing the bunny or the boy. She doesn't pay attention to the printed word or associate printed with spoken words. At age four or five she follows her father's finger as he points and reads, sounding out words from the letters and the context. Thus, reading with a parent is a

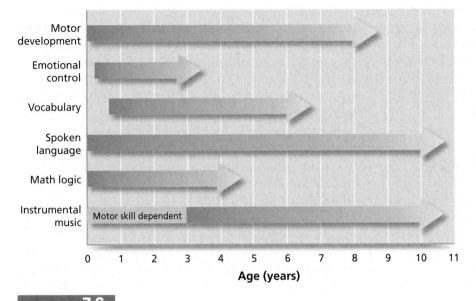

Motor development
Emotional control
Vocabulary
Spoken language
Math logic
Instrumental music

Motor skill dependent

0 1 2 3 4 5 6 7 8 9 10 11
Age (years)

FIGURE **7.6**

Windows of Opportunity

Although the brain continues to develop throughout childhood and learning can occur throughout the lifespan, there are some "windows of opportunity" during which brain development is most sensitive to experience. For example, motor skills are best learned when they occur in the first eight years of life, whereas most vocabulary learning occurs between ages one and six.
Source: How the brain learns by D.A. Sousa. Copyright 2006 by Sage Publications Inc Books. Reproduced with permission of Sage Publications Inc Books in the format Textbook via Copyright Clearance Center.

---

quite different experience for the two- and five-year-old. Brain development makes new experiences possible, and these experiences, in turn, promote brain development.

A dramatic illustration of brain plasticity is a **hemispherectomy**, surgery in which one hemisphere of the brain—half the brain—is removed (Boatman et al., 1999). This operation is performed when the patient suffers from continuous seizures that cannot be controlled with medication. Like all brain surgery, this procedure is risky and must be followed with intensive therapy. But most patients, nearly all of whom are young children, recover: The remaining hemisphere of the brain takes over for the hemisphere that has been removed. The children may experience weakness on one side of their body (the side opposite from the hemisphere that was removed; remember, nerve fibers cross over before entering the brain), yet a number are having normal high school careers and a few (the first to receive this treatment) are in college. In the words of neurosurgeon George Jallo, ". . . a lot of these people develop their seizures when they're very young, or in utero, and when you take out half of their brain in one sitting [one operation] it's as if they weren't touched" (Kenneally, 2006).

We began this section by looking at brain development at the cellular level. Synaptogenesis, synaptic pruning and myelination increase the speed and efficiency of communication within the brain and nervous system. Mirror neurons may help children to learn vicariously. We then looked at the development of the overall structure of the brain during early childhood. Development of the corpus callosum (which connects the two hemispheres of the brain) leads to better coordination; handedness illustrates lateralization (specialization in the two hemispheres). At the same time, development of the frontal lobes—one of the most plastic regions of the brain—enables children to think ahead and to organize and plan new actions. (For a summary of this section, see "Interim Summary 7.2: BrainDevelopment.")

hemispherectomy Surgery in which one hemisphere of the brain is removed.

INTERIM SUMMARY 7.2

Brain Development

Improvements in the Brain's Communication Network	■ A **synapse** is the connection between one neuron's axon and another neuron's dendrite. ■ **Synaptogenesis** is the development of connections between neurons through the growth of axons and dendrites. ■ The more a synapse is used, the stronger it becomes. Unused synapses are eliminated. ■ **Myelination**, the development of a myelin coating around axons, increases the speed and efficiency of transmitting signals between neurons.
Mirror Neurons	■ **Mirror neurons** are brain cells that fire when an action is performed by another, as if the observer did the action him- or herself. ■ Mirror neurons may explain why young children learn so readily by observing others.
Brain Anatomy	■ The brain is composed of two halves, or hemispheres, that specialize in certain functions. ■ The left hemisphere is especially active from 3 to 6 years, corresponding to the changes in language development in early childhood. ■ Between ages 3 and 6 years, the **corpus callosum** (the large bundle of fibers that connects the two hemispheres) develops rapidly. ■ Maturation of the prefrontal cortex enables 6-year-olds to inhibit or suppress the preferred actions, an ability called **effortful control**.
Brain Plasticity	■ Brain plasticity refers to the degree to which the brain can be altered by experience. ■ Plasticity varies over the course of brain development.

MOTOR DEVELOPMENT

gross motor skills Abilities required to control the large movements of the arms, legs, and feet, or the whole body, such as running, jumping, climbing, and throwing.

fine motor skills Abilities required to control smaller movements of the hand and fingers, such as picking up small objects and tying one's shoes.

Motor development in early childhood occurs on two fronts. **Gross motor skills** are the abilities required to control the large movements of the arms, legs, and feet, or the whole body—such as running, jumping, climbing, and throwing (Case-Smith, 2005). **Fine motor skills** involve smaller movements of the hand and fingers—such as picking up small objects and tying one's shoes (Case-Smith, 2005).

Both gross motor skills and fine motor skills are inseparably linked to perception and cognition (Adolph & Berger, 2006). Achieving the balance needed to run or the coordination needed to button a shirt depends on perception. Movement and perception, in turn, provide the raw material for cognitive development. To a significant degree, young children learn by and through their actions or movement.

Theories of Motor Development

What drives motor development? At the time Myrtle McGraw conducted her twin study with Johnny and Jimmy, introduced at the beginning of this chapter, there were two prevailing views that pitted nature versus nurture. Arnold Gesell, one of the leading developmental scientists in the 1930s, held that motor development was the result of **maturation** (Gesell, 1933). In his view, the emergence of new skills was determined by a genetic timetable and blueprint. Healthy children were believed to develop at

maturation Growth that proceeds by a genetic timetable.

about the same rate and in the same sequence, although with some individual variations. Gesell held that basic motor development was the result of physiological and neurological growth, not acquired through experience or learning. In other words, development follows nature's plan. According to the maturationist viewpoint, parents can relax and let development take its natural course.

Behaviorist John B. Watson (1929), a contemporary of Gesell, disagreed. Watson argued that, beyond the simple reflexes with which a baby is born, development is the result of learning. Children repeat actions for which they are reinforced or rewarded (see "The Study of Child Development"). The same basic principles apply at all ages. According to *learning theory*, all development, including motor development, is shaped by experience in a particular environment. Thus, parents and other caregivers mold their children's motor skills, just as they shape other aspects of their behavior and functioning.

Myrtle McGraw's study of Johnny and Jimmy revealed a more dynamic interplay between nature and nurture. Sidestepping both Gesell's belief that physical development is simple maturation and Watson's view that everything depends on the environment, McGraw argued that both were important—when children have the neurological and muscular maturity, they benefit from experience. Without the necessary level of biological maturity, though, environmental stimulation has little impact. As Gilbert Gottlieb (1998) observed, McGraw was an interactionist ahead of her time.

What did McGraw (1939) find when she revisited the boys at age six? Were their early differences maintained or had they faded away? Johnny's impressive motor skills had begun to fade in their home environment. In many respects, Jimmy's motor skills caught up with his brother's, and on conventional motor measures, both ranked as average. Does this mean that Gesell was correct in the longer term? That motor development depends just on maturation? Not necessarily. Johnny no longer had access to enriching physical activities, and it is not possible to know what benefit continued enrichment might have had. A few residual benefits remained. Johnny was better coordinated than Jimmy; he moved smoothly and gracefully, and he approached physical challenges more confidently.

Gross Motor Skills

Arnold Gesell and his colleagues at Yale University were the first scientists to catalog the development of gross motor skills in early childhood (Gesell & Thompson, 1938). Their normative standards for motor development (with refinements) are still in use today. The Bayley Scales of Infant Development (Black & Matula, 1999), for example, is based on norms for motor development, body control, and coordination at different ages. Like norms for height and weight, norms of motor development describe the "average child" at a given age, based on cross-sectional or longitudinal studies. Table 7.1 illustrates some of milestones in normative gross motor development.

TABLE 7.1 Some Milestones in Normative Gross Motor Development

2 years	Kicks a ball. Walks up and down stairs, two feet at a time.
2.5 years	Jumps with both feet, including off stairs. Can walk on tiptoe.
3 years	Climbs stairs using alternate feet. Can stand on one foot (briefly). Rides tricycle. Runs well.
4 years	Skips on one foot. Throws ball overhand. Jumps well from standing position.
5 years	Hops and skips. Has good balance. Can skate or ride a scooter.

Source: This table was published in J. Case-Smith, *Occupational therapy for children*, 5/e. Copyright Elsevier 2005. Used by permission of Elsevier.

© David Young-Wolff/PhotoEdit

The gross motor skills required to ride a tricycle reflect brain and muscular maturation as well as opportunity and experience.

Physicians and physical therapists use this and other scales to assess whether a child is developing normally. As discussed earlier (see "Cognitive Development in Infancy"), scores on the Bayley Scales do not predict future intellectual or physical achievements in the normal range. But, especially in the lower range, they provide warning signs that a child may have developmental problems. If a child scores significantly below the age norm, further testing is called for.

Like physical growth charts, charts of motor development imply this is a smooth curve with one milestone leading to the next and then the next. But contemporary research shows that children often straddle two stages, sometimes revert back to an earlier stage, and show wide individual differences (Adolph & Berger, 2006). Also, maturation is only part of the story.

Motor development must be studied in context. In the real world, children acquire new skills with the help of their parents and child-care providers in different places with different objects, surfaces, and opportunities. The environment in which they develop and their access to different challenges, in turn, depends on the cultural and historic context (Adolph & Berger, 2006). For example, today the Red Cross and the YMCA offer swimming classes starting at age six months. In the 1930s, when Myrtle McGraw conducted her twin study, Johnny's swimming made headlines. No one imagined that babies could swim. Children's bodies haven't changed, but ideas of what young children can do have.

Individual children vary widely in their genetic makeup, their opportunities, and their motor development. Consider golf champion Tiger Woods. Tiger's father, Earl, was an athlete. Drafted by the Kansas City Monarchs of the Negro Baseball League (professional baseball was still segregated), he chose college and a career in the military. He was forty-two when he discovered a passion for golf. Tiger was born the next year. Even before he could walk and talk, Tiger was mesmerized by golf. As an infant he spent hours in the family garage where Earl had set up a makeshift driving range, sitting in his high chair and watching his father swing. One day he tottered over to the "grass" carpet with an iron his father had cut down to his size and, after setting up, hit the ball into the net on his first try. Tiger was only ten months old. At age three he shot a 48 over nine holes at a Navy Golf Club. When he was six years old, his coach described him as a golf genius: "Mozart composed finished music in his head. I saw that in Tiger. He was composing shots in his head" (Strege, 1997, p. 17). At fifteen he became the youngest U.S. Junior Amateur Champion in golf history, one of many "firsts" to come. A born athlete, Tiger was also born into a family where golf reigned supreme. His achievements reflect the compounding of genetic and environmental influences.

Fine Motor Skills

Fine motor skills are smaller movements of the hands and fingers. To pour milk into a glass, button a sweater, draw a picture, or print one's name are some examples. These skills are complicated accomplishments that require motor control and coordination with the visual system. The development of fine motor skills during early childhood is a source of considerable pride and feelings of accomplishment. These skills are important steps toward independence that develop in early childhood.

Fine motor skills, like gross motor skills, depend in part on culture and experience. In other times and places, young children demonstrated skills that we would consider remarkable. In colonial America, for example, four-year-old girls knitted mittens and socks while their six-year-old sisters transformed raw wool into yarn on spinning wheels (Ogburn & Nimkoff, 1955). In the Mayan communities of Central America, children begin weaving rugs—an activity that requires considerable dexterity—between ages four and six (Rogoff, 2003). Table 7.2 illustrates some milestones in normative fine motor development in the United States.

Drawing—with crayons, markers, paint, or merely a stick in the dirt—is one of the fine motor skills that develops during early childhood in many cultures (Golomb, 2004). Between ages eighteen months and two years, children begin scribbling—drawing lines, curves, loops, zigzags, and the like. These marks are not random. To the child, they convey action. A series of dots is a bunny hopping; a swirl is a plane moving through the sky (Wolf & Perry, 1988). Toddlers seem to enjoy the activity of drawing as much as (or more than) what they produce.

Around age three, children make spontaneous attempts to draw recognizable objects, usually beginning with a human figure (Golomb, 2004). These early efforts look like tadpoles: a circle with eyes for the head and dangling legs. When asked to include the tummy, children do so; when asked to draw a person holding a flower, they add an arm and hand—and then go back to their tadpoles. Some children remain in the tadpole stage for months, drawing the same picture over and over. Others quickly move on to more complete figures.

By age five or six, children draw a body and head with arms and fingers, legs and feet, hair, clothes, and a smile—all in the right places. Complete scenes (with trees and flowers, houses, streets, and the members of their family or characters from a favorite cartoon or movie) begin to replace a single figure; distinct individuals appear in place of a single all-purpose human figure (Gardner, 1980; Golomb, 2004). Drawings at this age can be quite complex and detailed, as well as fanciful.

How do children learn to draw? Some developmentalists hold that drawing is a natural activity, wired into our brains. Human beings have an affinity for symbols: music and dance, as well as pictures and words (Gardner, 1980). Around the world, in varied cultures, children draw similar tadpole-like human figures at age three to four. Moreover, blind children who regain their sight and children in cultures

Do you remember learning to tie your shoes? It wasn't easy.

TABLE 7.2 Some Milestones in Normative Fine Motor Development in the United States

2 years	Builds a tower with six or seven blocks. Turns the pages of a book one at a time. Turns door knobs and untwists jar lids. Washes and dries hands. Uses spoon and fork well.
2.5 years	Builds tower with eight blocks. Holds pencil or crayon between fingers (instead of fist).
3 years	Builds tower with nine or ten blocks. Puts on shoes and socks and can button and unbutton. Carries a container without spilling or dropping (most of the time).
4 years	Except for tying, can dress him- or herself. Cuts with scissors (but not well). Washes and dries face.
5 years	Dresses without help and ties shoes. Prints simple letters.

Source: This table was published in J. Case-Smith, *Occupational therapy for children,* 5/e. Copyright Elsevier 2005. Used by permission of Elsevier.

with no tradition of representational art can draw a human figure after a few attempts (Millar, 1975).

Other developmental scientists (e.g., Kellogg, 1969) emphasize that drawing requires practice and instruction. Consciously or not, parents and others point out forms and shapes to a child; ask representation-oriented questions ("Is that the sun?"); and provide guidance ("That's a face? Here, let's draw the eyes and a smile"). Children themselves practice, observe, and experiment.

Even early drawings are influenced by culture. In Bali, children fill the page with small, repetitive designs that seem to echo a traditional Balinese dance (Gardner, 1980). Drawings by Japanese children feature simple elements spread across the page like a Haiku poem (see Figure 7.7). Drawings by U.S. children are sometimes free-form and fun, sometimes more mechanical.

In Western countries, interest in drawing and other forms of graphics tends to fade in middle childhood. Older children's drawings seem to be more conventional, with stock characters, themes, and techniques. Howard Gardner (1980) suggested several reasons why. By age eight or nine, children become increasingly concerned about "getting things right": Their clothes have to match; their games are played and judged by rules; in school there are right and wrong answers. Representational art requires skill and practice that most Westerners do not receive in school.

Writing (or printing) is another fine motor skill that develops in early childhood. Like drawing, writing begins as scribbles. Around age five, children begin to pay attention to the printed word, to distinguish writing from nonwriting, and to recognize and copy individual letters (Case-Smith, 2005). With encouragement, they begin to print their name and simple words (cat, dog), sounding out the letters as they work on their writing.

Motor norms create general guidelines, but the physical and cultural environment and individual differences in talent and experience play important roles in motor development. Whether drawing is innate or learned—and the evidence suggests both—children take to art as they do to play, at least in early childhood. (For a summary of this section, see "Interim Summary 7.3: Motor Development.")

Courtesy of Dr. Alexander Allend

Courtesy of Dr. Alexander Allend

FIGURE 7.7

Cultural Differences Are Evident in Young Children's Drawings

There is strong evidence, even in the earliest drawings, of cultural influences. In Bali, children fill the space with repetitive forms drawn separately yet snugly across the page (left). In Japan, children's drawings feature simple elements spread across the page (right).

INTERIM SUMMARY **7.3**

Motor Development

Theories of Motor Development	■ Arnold Gesell believed that motor development is the result of innate neurological and physiological growth.
	■ Others believe motor development is shaped by experience and learning.
	■ Myrtle McGraw was an interactionist who believed that both maturation and experience contribute to motor development.
Gross Motor Skills	■ Gross motor skills involve large movements of arms, legs, feet, or the whole body.
	■ The Bayley Scales of Infant Development provide norms for motor development and body control in early childhood.
	■ Gross motor skills reflect both maturation, cultural context, and opportunities.
Fine Motor Skills	■ Fine motor skills involve smaller movements of the hands and fingers.
	■ Development of particular fine motor skills depends in part on culture and experience and in part on brain development.
	■ Development of the corpus collosum sets the stage for advances in fine motor skills.

PHYSICAL HEALTH

Physical health is a prerequisite for many aspects of child development. Frequent illness or malnutrition can dull children's motivation and curiosity, as well as reduce the time they spend exploring and playing. These, in turn, slow cognitive and socioemotional development by reducing the amount of interaction children have with their environment and with other people. How healthy are today's children? How can we improve health and safety in early childhood?

Injuries and Illnesses

In the United States, unintentional injuries are the leading cause of death in early childhood (Grossman, 2000). More than 5,600 American children die from injuries each year—an average of fifteen children per day. Injuries also account for almost 14 million medical visits by U.S. children ages fourteen and under (National SAFE KIDS Campaign, 2006).

Drownings lead the list of unintended injury deaths among children ages one to four, followed by automobile accidents, fire and burns, and airway obstructions (National SAFE KIDS Campaign, 2006). Accidents may not be totally avoidable, but death and serious injury from accidents can be greatly reduced by simple precautions. Whenever small children are around water (including bathtubs), playing, or eating, they need adult supervision. Readily available safety equipment and safety measures also can prevent many of these deaths, including fences and self-locking gates around swimming pools, car safety seats and seat belts, bike helmets, and home smoke detectors. As a result of these measures and efforts, deaths from unintentional injuries in childhood dropped 40 percent between 1987 and 2000.

One reason that more U.S. children die from injuries than from illnesses is that successful immunization programs have almost eliminated some diseases such as polio and measles that previously claimed lives. The annual number of reported cases of measles in the United States, for example, has declined from 3 to 4 million cases before the introduction of a measles vaccine to fewer than a hundred cases a year (Meissner, Strebel, & Orenstein, 2004). Vaccinations prevent an estimated 10.5 million disease cases and 35,000 deaths each year (Mitka, 2004).

Medical personnel are concerned that these health advances are in danger of not being maintained because a large number of children in the United States are not fully immunized (Mitka, 2004). About 20 percent of infants and toddlers are missing one or more of the necessary set of immunizations. And, in one study, of the 80 percent who received the complete schedule in the first two years, 24 percent lacked essential immunizations as preschoolers (Chu, Barker, & Smith, 2004). There also are income disparities in who is fully immunized. Thirty-eight percent of low-income children in the United States lack essential immunizations compared with 7 percent in Great Britain and Canada (Chu et al., 2004).

One reason for the poorer immunization record in the United States is that many families lack health insurance, and their children do not have their own physicians who provide routine well-child visits. A second reason is that some parents believe that these immunizations increase the risk of conditions such as autism and multiple sclerosis (Mitka, 2004**),** Systematic review of the evidence by the National Academy of Science (National Research Council, 2004) has not found credible scientific evidence that immunizations cause these conditions. The Academy warns that children are under much greater risks of death and impairment from measles and polio if they are not properly immunized.

Minor illnesses such as colds and upset stomachs continue to be a part of growing up. For example, in the United States, young children average six to ten colds a year (National Institute of Allergy and Infectious Diseases, 2004). It is not possible to estimate the average number of gastrointestinal illnesses because they often go unreported. For well-nourished children with access to health care, these common illnesses are rarely serious.

A key factor contributing to these minor infections is coming into contact with other children. Children who attend child-care centers with other children are more likely to get sick than are children cared for at home or by a relative. A study of more than 1,100 children found that preschoolers enrolled in child-care groups with more than six children have higher rates of upper respiratory illness, diarrhea, and ear infections than do children cared for at home or in smaller groups (NICHD Early Child Care Research Network, 2003). These minor illnesses in early childhood appear to boost immunity. Three-year-olds who have just entered child care are more likely to become ill than three-year-olds who have been in care for a longer period.

A major risk is that an upper respiratory infection will lead to a middle-ear infection, called *otitis media*. Frequent ear infections can lead to social isolation because they make it difficult for a child to hear (Roberts et al., 2000). Hand-washing with soap and water, one of the simplest and most effective ways to stop the spread of the common cold, is an important practice in child-care settings as well as children's homes (National Institute of Allergy and Infectious Diseases, 2004).

Mortality and Malnutrition

Although child mortality rates are low in the United States, the picture in the poor countries of the developing world is quite different. (See Table 7.3). Globally, 9.7 million children under age five die each year, the great majority from preventable or treatable infectious diseases (especially pneumonia and diarrhea) (see Figure 7.8).

In 2000, 189 countries endorsed the United Nations Millennium Declaration, which established global goals. One of the millennium goals is to reduce child mortality to two-thirds the 1990 level by 2015 (World Bank, 2006). Public health experts (Jones et al.,

TABLE 7.3 Child Mortality Rates by Region

REGION	RATES IN 1960	RATES IN 2000
Sub-Saharan Africa	280	160
Middle East and North Africa	250	50
South Asia	240	85
Latin America and the Caribbean	155	25
East Asia and the Pacific	120	25
Central and Eastern Europe	87	25
Industrialized Countries	45	5

Note: These rates include infection, premature birth, asphyxia, and tetanus for every 1,000 children.

Source: Based on data from McNeil (2007) and Unicef (2007).

2003) believe that this goal can be achieved with a small number of well-known, cost-effective interventions, such as the following:

- Oral rehydration therapy (ORT), a solution of glucose, salt, and water that can eliminate most childhood deaths involving diarrhea
- Immunization for diseases such as measles and polio, which can be fatal for malnourished children
- The use of mosquito nets treated with insecticide to prevent malaria, which depresses the immune system and may prove fatal
- Education for mothers and other caregivers on good sanitary practices such as hand washing and proper nutrition for small children

Through systematic efforts in each of these areas, substantial progress has been made in meeting the goal (UNICEF and the World Health Organization, 2008). About 20 million children under the age of five years died in 1960. Less than half that number (9.7 million) of children died in 2007. Several countries such as Vietnam and the Dominican Republic have had big drops in child mortality. However, there are still wide disparities around the world. In the United States and Western Europe, about 6 of every 1,000 children die before the age of five years. In West and Central Africa, that number is 150 of every 1,000 children, more than twenty times as many deaths. According to UNICEF and the World Health Organization (2008), malnutrition is the underlying cause of more than half of all deaths of children under the age of five years around the world. Malnutrition increases the chances that children will catch a disease, and the effects of the disease are more severe. When children are ill, their appetites are reduced and the amount of nutrition they absorb decreases, resulting in a vicious cycle of sickness and delayed growth.

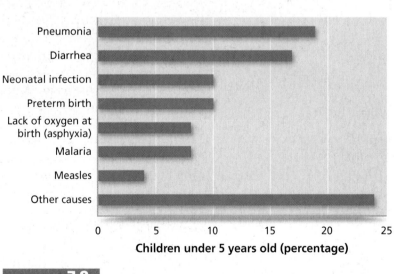

Children under 5 years old (percentage)

FIGURE 7.8

Causes of Death in Children Under Age Five Around the World

Around the world, millions of young children die each year from preventable or treatable diseases like pneumonia and diarrhea. Fortunately, due to international intervention efforts, child mortality rates are decreasing; however, large disparities still exist based on a country's available resources.

Malnutrition is more than lack of food. Children can feel "full" but still not get the amounts of protein (needed to build muscle), calories (needed for energy), iron (for proper blood cell function), and other nutrients they need to be healthy (Grigsby & Shashidhar, 2006). **Kwashiorkor** and **marasmus** are two forms of protein energy malnutrition (PEM). A child with marasmus is not receiving enough protein or enough calories, whereas a child with kwashiorkor has an adequate intake of calories but an inadequate intake of protein. In addition, malnutrition can occur when children's diets are deficient in micronutrients such as iron, iodine, zinc, and vitamin A.

In both the developed and developing countries, childhood mortality is linked to poverty. Common sense says that poverty causes malnutrition and illness; but malnutrition and illness also cause poverty—in terms of lower school achievement, fewer years of schooling, reduced wages, and loss of income due to illness.

kwashiorkor A form of malnutrition in which individuals have an adequate intake of calories, but an inadequate intake of protein.

marasmus A form of malnutrition in which individuals are not receiving enough protein or enough calories.

Sleep and Sleep Problems

Sleep patterns change in early childhood—from sleeping twelve to thirteen hours at ages two and three, to ten to eleven hours at ages four through six (Donaldson & Owens, 2006). The toddler's need for afternoon naps fades around age four or five, though rests are helpful.

Sleep problems are common in young children. Some have difficulty falling asleep and summon their parents for one, another, and another "curtain call" after lights out. They may wake during the night but are able to console themselves and fall back asleep. About half are awakened by nightmares (frightening dreams in which they or their family are threatened). Some also have night terrors (waking in a state of fright, with no memory of why) (Mindell, Owens, & Carskadon, 1999).

Sleep problems worry parents and result in sleep disruptions for the family. Occasional sleep problems are not a concern, and most children outgrow these problems in time. Chronic inability to fall asleep or frequent nightmares or night terrors, however, can be signs of daytime stress and a call for help.

Spending some quiet time with parents before lights out can help children to sleep more soundly.

© Andrew Holbrooke/Corbis

Scientists are working to understand *why* sleep is so important (Azar, 2006). A number of possible explanations are being explored, including the following:

- Sleep may help young children to "learn" about their bodies. Twitches or muscle spasms during sleep tell the brain what is "out there" in the body (Dingfelder, 2006).

- Sleep allows the brain to recharge (Azar, 2006). After a full day of stimulation and learning, with synapses constantly charging, the brain runs out of energy and space and needs time off.

- Sleep may help children to store memories by allowing new synapses to form and consolidate (Stickgold, 2005).

- Last, sleep is essential to physical development because this is when growth hormone (GH) is released (Donaldson & Owens, 2006).

Parents can adopt several practices to promote their children's sleep hygiene (Donaldson & Owens, 2006). Young children develop (and to some degree depend on) regular bedtime rituals and routines: washing or bathing, being read to by a parent, and cuddling a favorite blanket or soft toy before falling asleep. The latter, immortalized in the cartoon character Linus' blanket, are called "transitional objects." Regular bedtime routines and consistent sleep schedules, plus a quiet time before lights out, help young children to sleep more soundly.

Physiological Indicators of Stress

Stress is a normal and an inevitable part of life. Indeed, some stress is good for us; it keeps us on our toes. Coping with stress begins in the body. When we are under stress, levels of the hormone **cortisol** rise in our bloodstream (Levine, 2003). Cortisol signals our brains to be on guard and mobilizes the body for quick action in an emergency. When the threat has passed and we calm down, levels of cortisol decrease. But individuals' hormonal responses to events—their physiological coping mechanisms—vary (Gunnar, 2006).

cortisol A hormone secreted when individuals are exposed to stress.

Scientists have been studying relations between different types of stressors and cortisol during early childhood using a "spit test" that measures cortisol that leaks into saliva. Children are given an absorbent stick that has been dipped into a Kool-Aid-like mixture to suck like a lollipop. Then the children's cortisol levels are measured at different times of day and in different locations such as child care, home, and the doctor's office (Gunnar, 2006). The researchers compare the amount (and changes in the amount) of cortisol of young children as a way of understanding children's reactions to their surroundings. How do their bodies react?

Some differences in cortisol are related to children's temperament. Higher levels of cortisol and larger increases in cortisol across the day are observed in young children who have problems regulating their negative emotions and behavior (Dettling, Gunnar, & Donzella, 1999), in children who are fearful of unfamiliar situations (Watamura et al., 2003), and in children who have difficulties playing with peers (Watamura et al., 2003).

Cortisol levels also are related to children's attachment security (see "Socioemotional Development in Infancy" for more information about attachment security). In general, children who are securely attached show different patterns and levels of cortisol in the Strange Situation than do insecurely attached children. In one study, when children with secure attachments to their mothers were challenged by the Strange Situation series of separations and reunions (see "Socioemotional Development in Infancy" for a description of the procedure), their cortisol levels did not peak in the same way as did those of the insecurely attached children (Gunnar, 2000).

Lieselotte Ahnert and colleagues (2004) have measured children's cortisol when they began a new child-care arrangement. These researchers found children's reactions to the new child-care arrangement were related to their attachment security and whether their mothers were present or not. When mothers accompanied their young children to a new child-care program, children with secure attachment relationships did not show high elevations in cortisol as long as their mothers were with them. Children with insecure relationships showed elevations in cortisol even when their mothers were with them.

Finally, cortisol levels across the day are related to the quality of children's child-care settings. For children in poor-quality child care, cortisol increases across the day, whereas cortisol levels decrease across the day for children who attend high-quality child care. Increases across the day were steepest when children are in child-care settings with lots of children (Dettling et al., 2000).

We'll look more closely at how to identify high-quality and poor-quality child-care programs in "Cognitive Development in Early Childhood." Efforts are currently under

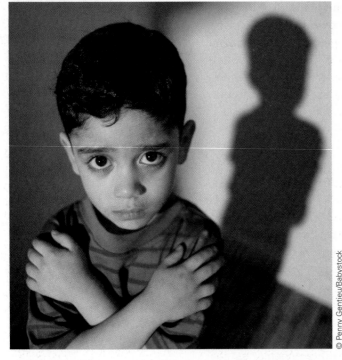

Victims of childhood abuse and neglect are at increased risk for social and cognitive problems that extend into adulthood.

way to help early childhood teachers develop effective strategies for improving program quality.

Physical Abuse and Neglect

Decades of research have provided solid evidence that maltreatment in early childhood increases the risk of later problems, ranging from poor peer relations and low academic achievement in childhood, to delinquency and substance abuse in adolescence, to depression, criminal behavior, chronic health problems, and poor parenting as adults (Cicchetti & Manly, 2001). No one doubts that child abuse is bad for children. The question is why child abuse affects so many areas of behavior so long after the abuse has stopped.

Developmental scientists are studying the impact of physical abuse and neglect as long-term and extreme stressors of young children (Gunnar, Fisher, & the Early Experience, Stress, and Prevention Network, 2006; Pollak, 2005). Studies of nonhuman animals indicate that these early patterns may become a permanent or semipermanent part of the animal's makeup—a case where experience molds biology (Levine, 2003). Evidence is accumulating that this may be true for children as well.

In a series of experiments, Seth Pollak studied how abused children process and read emotions. He found that abused children are more sensitive to cues of anger than other children are. In one study, children were asked to look at a series of computerized pictures of human faces that morphed from one emotion to another, such as happy to sad or fearful to angry (Pollak & Kistler, 2002). The abused children were much quicker to identify anger than the control, nonabused children. In another study, children were asked to look at two pictures on the screen and pick the one marked with an "X." Sometimes the abused children took longer to make a decision. Measures of brain waves showed that they paid more attention to the angry face, whether it had an "X" or not, as if they couldn't tear their eyes away from the angry person (Pollak et al., 2001).

Pollak hypothesizes that early emotional experiences, occurring when children's brains are still quite plastic, can exert a powerful and long-lasting influence. In a dangerous environment, where adults are unpredictable and abusive, being able to identify hints of anger quickly and respond by hiding or striking out is adaptive. However, when these children move to other settings, where adults are more consistently caring, oversensitivity to anger is maladaptive. These children perceive anger when it is not there or spend so much time looking for signs of anger that they ignore other, positive emotional cues. When they suspect a threat, they often become aggressive or, alternatively, withdrawn. Mild criticism by a teacher or teasing by a peer triggers an intense reaction. Whatever the setting, they experience the world as dangerous, other people as untrustworthy—and respond in kind. Whether such children can "unlearn" distorted perceptions and develop positive relationships with others is an open question. Research on different types of therapies is under way (Gunnar, Fisher, & the Early Experience, Stress, and Prevention Network, 2006).

Severely neglected children face other challenges. They are ignored and have few interactions with adults, rather than being the recipients of physical harm. These effects are being studied in a tragic "natural experiment." In the 1980s, hundreds of Romanian children were sent to orphanages where they were confined to cribs with minimal human contact beyond simple health care and feeding and where they had very little stimulation from toys or other children. The orphanages have been called "child warehouses" (Ames, 1990). After the fall of the Ceausecu government, the children's plight became known. Families from other countries, including the United States, Canada, and Great Britain adopted many of the children. Some were young infants. Others were toddlers and preschoolers.

When they joined their new families, the orphanage children had difficulty identifying *any* emotions (Wismer Fries & Pollak, 2004). For example, they could not link a facial expression to a happy, sad, fearful, or angry scenario. The longer they were institutionalized, the greater their emotional impairment. In later chapters, we will return to the development of these children who suffered extreme neglect in their early years.

Autism Spectrum Disorder

In the 1940s, Leo Kanner identified a condition he called *early infantile autism* in eleven children who were detached from other people and seemed to be "living in their own world." For some children, signs of autistic-like behaviors appear in infancy (Kanner, 1943). For others, children seem to develop normally until about age three years. Some parents report that their children change suddenly and begin to behave abnormally almost overnight. In other cases, children seem to reach a plateau and in some ways stop developing.

Today scientists recognize a range of **autism spectrum disorders** (**ASDs**), from relatively mild physical and social awkwardness (Asperger syndrome) to severe motor and mental disabilities (childhood disintegrative disorder). Children with an ASD have problems with social interaction, verbal and nonverbal communication, and repetitive behavior. They have difficulty with the everyday give-and-take of social interaction and may act indifferent to other people; resist or not respond to hugging and cuddling; and seem unable to interpret others' gestures, facial expressions, and emotions. Many cannot regulate their own emotions and at times "lose control," breaking things, attacking people, or hurting themselves.

Some children diagnosed with ASD do not talk, although they may communicate with sign language. Those who do talk use language in atypical ways. They speak in single words, parrot phrases they have heard, constantly repeat phrases, or acquire a large vocabulary but no conversational skills, delivering monologues unrelated to what other people are doing and saying. Their gestures, facial expressions, and tone of voice do not reflect their feelings. Unable to communicate their needs, they easily become angry and frustrated.

Although their physical and motor development usually is normal, children with autism may engage in odd, repetitive motions, such as flapping their arms, walking on their toes, or suddenly freezing. They develop routines and rituals, such as lining up their toys in a precise way. If someone accidentally moves a toy, they become extremely upset.

Children with ASD need—and demand—consistency in their environment. Slight changes unnerve them. One of the hallmarks of early childhood—pretend play (see "Socioemotional Development in Early Childhood")—is not evident in their play. Another hallmark of early childhood—a big advance in a *theory of mind* that recognizes that other people have different thoughts and perspectives from one's own thoughts—also is less evident in children with autism. In one study (Baron-Cohen, Leslie, & Frith, 1985), 85 percent of typically developing children and those with Down syndrome were able to pass a test that assessed skills underlying a theory of mind, whereas only 20 percent of the children with autism could do so. Theory of mind is described in more detail in "Cognitive Development in Early Childhood."

A recent survey sponsored by the Centers for Disease Control and Prevention found that 1 in 150 American children develop autism spectrum disorders by the age of eight (Centers for Disease Control, 2007)—many more than expected from prior studies.

autism spectrum disorder (ASD)   A disorder that can range from mild to severe, characterized by problems with social interaction, verbal and nonverbal communication, and repetitive behavior.

This means that ASD is more common than juvenile diabetes or Down syndrome, which have received far more attention. But does it mean that we are experiencing an "epidemic" of autism and related disorders? Maybe not. Morton Gernsbacher and colleagues argue that the increase in numbers is the result of an expanded definition of ASD that includes a wider array of symptoms. In addition, they note that the public (including parents and pediatricians) has become more aware of the syndrome, so the number of cases reported has increased (Gernsbacher, Dawson, & Goldsmith, 2005).

The widespread prevalence of autism spectrum disorders, coupled with the hardships they place on children and their families, has led scientists to search for their origins, effective interventions, and prevention. Some scientists are looking for genetic sources. Family and twin studies show that some forms of autism can be inherited. Fragile X syndrome, a family of genetic conditions caused by changes in a single gene on an X chromosome, is one of the genes that is associated with autistic-like behaviors.

INTERIM SUMMARY 7.4

Physical Health	
Injuries and Illnesses	■ Drownings, auto accidents, fires and burns, and airway obstructions are the leading causes of death of young children in the U.S. Many of these deaths are preventable.
	■ Immunizations protect children from measles, polio, and other life-threatening diseases.
	■ Hand-washing with soap and water is the most effective means of preventing the common cold.
Mortality and Malnutrition	■ Globally, 9.7 million young children die each year, many from preventable diseases.
	■ Proven, cost-effective ways to improve child health and reduce child deaths are oral rehydration therapy (ORT), childhood immunization, mosquito nets treated with insecticides, and safe hygiene and proper nutrition.
	■ Malnutrition is the underlying cause of more than half of all deaths of children under the age of 5 years.
Sleep and Sleep Problems	■ Sleep serves important functions, including giving the brain time to recuperate and to store memories.
	■ Growth hormones (GH) are released during sleep.
	■ Consistent bedtime routines help children to sleep more soundly.
Physiological Indicators of Stress	■ Amount of, and changes in, cortisol are physiological indicators of stress.
	■ Cortisol levels are related to children's temperament, sociability, attachment security, and quality of child care.
Physical Abuse and Neglect	■ Maltreatment increases the risk of social and academic problems.
	■ Abused children are quicker than nonabused children to perceive angry expressions in others.
	■ Severely neglected children have difficulties linking facial expressions to happy, sad, anger, and fear situations.
Autism Spectrum Disorder	■ First identified in the 1940s, scientists now recognize a range of **autism spectrum disorders** (ASDs), from relatively mild physical and social awkwardness to severe motor and mental disabilities.
	■ ASD is linked to more than 100 different genes, suggesting that "autism" refers to different conditions with different origins.

Fragile X also is the most common cause of inherited cognitive impairment, or mental retardation. Rett's syndrome, a severe form of autism that appears in early childhood and affects girls, also has been traced to a single gene. Other scientists (Autism Genome Project Consortium, 2007) have found that a stretch of genes on chromosome 11 to be implicated for some children. Still other children with ASD (about 10%) have numerous mutations in their genes that are not seen in other family members. For these children the disorder is genetic but not necessarily inherited. One large scale study (Sebat et al., 2007) that scanned the whole genomes of affected and unaffected family members, has reported ASD to be linked to as many as 100 different genes.

The genetic findings support the assessment by Morton Gernsbacher that the label "autism" may be used for different conditions with different origins and possibly different treatments. More research is clearly needed.

To date, there is no cure for autism. However, children with ASD often benefit from behavioral therapy. Many can be taught the social and linguistic skills that other children develop naturally without formal, specialized training. The earlier therapy begins, the more likely a child will be able to function adequately. A genetic test would aid in early diagnosis. Perhaps some day, gene therapies will be developed to "turn off" or replace the gene that causes Rett's Syndrome or Fragile X Syndrome. (For a summary of this section, see "Interim Summary 7.4: Physical Health.")

SUMMING UP AND LOOKING AHEAD

Physical growth slows in early childhood, but impressive accomplishments in motor development continue. By the end of this period the young child is running and climbing, drawing and beginning to print. In large part these advances are due to the maturation of the brain. But experience plays an important role in shaping the brain, which is still quite plastic at this age. And so it is with motor development. As Myrtle McGraw's classic study of twins demonstrated, physical skills depend on the interactions of nature and nurture, biological readiness, and practice. Each influences the other.

In this chapter we saw that individual children vary in size and shape, coordination and dexterity, eating and sleep patterns, and reactions to stress, but that most fall within the normal range for their age. Tragically, the "norm" in many poor countries is a cycle of malnutrition and illness that delays physical development and learning and can lead to early death. With global effort and simple medical precautions, progress is being made in reducing child mortality rates. Likewise, in this country available safety devices and procedures are reducing serious injury and death from childhood accidents.

A key development in early childhood is the emergence of effortful control, which has implications for both cognitive and socioemotional development, as you will see in the next two chapters. Learning to think before acting or jumping to conclusions is part of growing up. We turn now to cognitive development.

HERE'S WHAT YOU SHOULD KNOW

Did You Get It?

After reading this chapter, you should understand the following:

- The major features of physical growth and development in early childhood, and the impact of nutrition on growth and development

- The ways in which the brain matures during early childhood, structurally and functionally

- The major accomplishments during early childhood in the realms of gross and fine motor skills
- The most common physical illnesses and problems in early childhood
- The ways in which development in early childhood is affected by problems in sleep, the exposure to stress, and abuse or neglect

Important Terms and Concepts

autism spectrum disorder (ASD) (p. 203)

axon (p. 185)

body mass index (BMI) (p. 183)

brain plasticity (p. 190)

corpus callosum (p. 189)

cortisol (p. 201)

dendrites (p. 185)

effortful control (p. 190)

fine motor skills (p. 192)

frontal lobes (p. 189)

gross motor skills (p. 192)

hemispherectomy (p. 191)

individual differences (p. 182)

kwashiorkor (p. 200)

lateralization (p. 188)

marasmus (p. 200)

maturation (p. 192)

mirror neuron (p. 187)

myelin (p. 187)

myelination (p. 187)

neuron (p. 185)

normative development (p. 182)

norms (p. 182)

obesity (p. 184)

sensitive period (p. 190)

strabismus (p. 190)

synapse (p. 185)

synaptogenesis (p. 187)

synaptic pruning (p. 187)

Cognitive Development in Early Childhood

© Jamie D. Travis/Getty Images

You're at a birthday party for a four-year-old. The children have sung "Happy Birthday," the birthday boy has blown out the candles, and each child now has a piece of cake. Looking at the plate of the child next to him, one boy starts to pout. "His is bigger than mine," he complains loudly. A parent comes over, bends down, and, picking up a plastic knife, cuts his piece in two. "Look," she whispers, "now you have two pieces and he only has one." The young complainer looks up at her with a conspiratorial grin. Problem solved!

It may be difficult to believe that a child would fall for such an obvious ploy, but preschoolers do. Thinking in early childhood is a mixture of impressive accomplishments and surprising shortcomings (Gelman, 2006). Young children learn thousands of words during this period—an average of ten new words a day according to one estimate (Carey, 1978). They can count and understand basic arithmetic (Geary, 2006). They know that plants and animals grow, but that cars and clouds do not (Gelman & Kalish, 2006). Some are experts in a particular domain, such as dinosaurs or geography (Chi & Koeske, 1983). They become skilled in understanding and using symbols (DeLoache, 1995). But young children's thinking also is characterized by surprising blind spots, as shown by the cake trick.

We begin this chapter by looking at two major perspectives on cognitive development in early childhood: Piaget's stage theory, and contemporary work that challenged his ideas; and Vygotsky's sociocultural theory, and contemporary work that expanded his theory. Next, we focus in on three primary domains of cognitive development: information processing, language development, and mathematical thinking. Last, we consider the impact of early childhood programs on children's cognitive development.

PIAGET'S THEORY: THE PREOPERATIONAL PERIOD

It's obvious that young children do not think like adults do. A child may use the word *horsie* for all large animals; he may be seduced by the cake trick. Jean Piaget (1896–1980) saw such childish mistakes as a window into the child's developing mind. Piaget (1929/1955, 1970) identified the second stage of cognitive development, from about age two to age seven, as the **preoperational period**. He held that preoperational children do not just know "more" than sensorimotor children (up to age two years) or "less" than concrete operational children (roughly ages seven to twelve years). Rather, preoperational thinking is organized differently than cognition in the earlier and later stages. According to Piaget, cognitive development is more than quantitative change in how *much* children know; it also involves qualitative change in *how* children think. During this period, children acquire a mental storehouse of images and symbols, especially spoken and written words.

preoperational period The second stage in Piaget's theory of cognitive development, from about age two to age seven, during which children acquire a mental storehouse of images and symbols, especially spoken and written words.

Accomplishments of the Preoperational Period

One hallmark of the preoperational period that represents an advance from the sensorimotor period (see "Cognitive Development in Infancy") is children's ability to think about objects and events that are not present in the here and now (Piaget, 1951/1962, 1947/1973). Children are able to represent (that is, *re*-present) previous experiences to themselves mentally. These symbolic representations may take the form of internalized activities, images, or words. A year earlier the child understood the world only through direct sensory and motor contact and his actions; now he carries the world he has experienced in his head (Piaget, 1952). This is a giant step in cognitive development.

Language is one of the clearest examples of symbolic representation. Words are symbols: They stand for something else. For example, the word *bug* stands for a small creature that creeps, crawls, or flies, whereas the word *boy* represents a young male who walks, talks, and plays. Children's vocabularies expand dramatically during this period; so does their ability to combine words into original sentences. (We talk about language development and children's understanding of symbol-referent relations later in this chapter.)

Make-believe or pretend play, a favorite activity in early childhood, is another prime example of symbolic representation (Garvey, 1990; Piaget, 1951/1962). In **pretend play**, a block may stand for a telephone or a truck; a cardboard box becomes a fort or a tea table; a stick can serve as a magic wand, a broom, or a horse. Children also can assume different roles. In the housekeeping area at their preschool, they may take the role of baby one day and the role of mother the next day. They may be the horsie one day and pretend to ride the stick horsie the next day.

Piaget believed that **deferred imitation**, or reproducing actions that the child has seen produced by others, is a sign that a child is moving from action to symbols. An eighteen-month-old sitting on the floor, stirring a pot with a spoon while his mother cooks, is mimicking his mother. A three-year-old "cooking" on a play stove in her room is doing something that looks the same but is very different: She is reenacting behavior she saw at another time and in another place. She can do this because she has a mental image of her mother's behavior. For the preoperational child, out of sight is not out of mind.

Pretend play, a hallmark of the preoperational period, provides evidence of symbolic thinking. Pots and spoons are transformed into musical instruments. With a cape and a crown, identities can be transformed.

pretend play Make-believe play in which common objects are often used to symbolize other objects.

deferred imitation Reproducing a series of actions seen at an earlier time.

Gaps in Preoperational Thinking

Language and pretend play demonstrate that the preoperational child is a symbolic thinker (no small feat), but she cannot, according to Piaget, reason logically (1941/1965, 1970). Her thinking does not yet include logical operations such as **reversibility** (understanding that an item that has been changed can be returned to its original state by reversing the process—for instance, that multiplying 5 by 3 to make 15 can be reversed by dividing 15 by 3 to make 5) or **classification** (the ability to divide or sort objects into different sets and subsets, and to consider their inter-relationships—for instance, that Peyton Manning is *both* a quarterback and a member of the Indianapolis Colts, or that a poodle is both a mammal and a dog). Hence Piaget's term preoperational.

reversibility A logical operation that requires an understanding that relations can be returned to their original state by reversing operations—if nothing has been added or taken away.

classification The ability to divide or sort objects into different sets and subsets, and to consider their interrelationships.

conservation The understanding that characteristics of objects (including volume, mass, and number) do not change despite changes in form or appearance when nothing is added or taken away.

Conservation A major gap in preoperational thinking, according to Piaget (1941/1965), is the young child's inability to grasp **conservation**: the fact that some characteristics of objects (their volume, mass, and number) do not change despite changes in form or appearance. Piaget devised several tasks that test conservation.

In the *conservation of volume* task, shown in Figure 8.1, you show a child two identical beakers filled with water. Then you ask the child whether they have the same or different amounts. The child usually answers, "The same." Next, as the child watches, you pour the water from one beaker into a taller, thinner one. Again, you ask the child if they have the same or different amounts. Amazingly, the child answers that they are "different"; the taller beaker has more. With the child still watching, you pour the water back into the original beaker and repeat the question. Defying logic (which was Piaget's point), the child now asserts that they are "the same." Appearance (what the child sees and how the beakers look) trumps logic (nothing was added, nothing was taken away, so the two beakers must be holding the same amount).

Variations on this task test the *conservation of mass* (with two identical balls of clay, flattening one into a pancake shape) and *conservation of number* (with two rows of the same number of buttons, spreading one row out so that it is longer) (see Figure 8.1). Are they the same or different? Young children usually fail these tests, too.

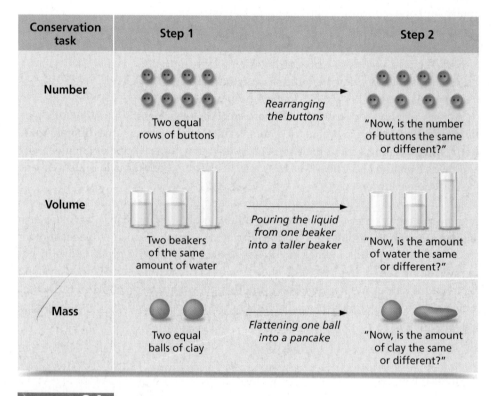

Conservation task	Step 1		Step 2
Number	Two equal rows of buttons	*Rearranging the buttons* →	"Now, is the number of buttons the same or different?"
Volume	Two beakers of the same amount of water	*Pouring the liquid from one beaker into a taller beaker* →	"Now, is the amount of water the same or different?"
Mass	Two equal balls of clay	*Flattening one ball into a pancake* →	"Now, is the amount of clay the same or different?"

FIGURE 8.1

Conservation Tasks in Preoperational Children

Conservation of number (top): When the buttons in the lower row are spread out, a preoperational child will say that the lower row contains more buttons than the upper row. *Conservation of volume* (middle): Even after a preoperational child watches the experimenter pour liquid from one beaker to the other, the child will typically say that the taller beaker contains more water than the shorter beaker. *Conservation of mass* (bottom): If one of the two balls is flattened into a pancake shape while the child is watching, a preoperational child will say that the flattened ball is bigger than the round ball.

Why can't small children grasp conservation? Piaget gave several reasons. First, preoperational children are seduced by appearances. If something *looks* different, then it must *be* different. Second, their thinking is one-dimensional. They focus on one feature (how tall the beaker is), ignoring other features (how wide the beaker is). Piaget called the focus on only one aspect *centration*. Third, a preoperational thinker does not recognize that operations are *reversible*. A child of seven or eight years (in the concrete operational stage) might laugh at the questions. "Of course it's the same." Why? "Because it came from the same glass and you could pour it back." The older child is thinking logically. She reasons that because nothing has been added or subtracted the amount must be the same. According to Piaget, the preoperational child is pre-logical.

Egocentrism Much as the preoperational child does not take into account more than one dimension at a time (e.g., focusing only on the height of the beaker not the width), so he does not consider different points of view. Piaget (1923/1955) called this **egocentrism**, which means, literally, self-centeredness. Piaget did not mean that preoperational children are "selfish" in the sense of wanting everything for themselves. Rather, preoperational children see the world from their own perspective and do not realize that other people *have* different points of view.

egocentrism In Piaget's theory of cognitive development, egocentrism refers to child's inability to see other people's viewpoints.

Children's performance on the *three mountain task* illustrates egocentrism (Piaget & Inhelder, 1967). You show the child a three-dimensional model of a mountain scene and encourage him or her to walk around the table, looking at the model from different sides. Then you ask the child to sit on one side of the table and put a doll on the other. The child's task is to decide what the doll sees from its position by selecting one of several drawings. Up to age four years, children don't understand the question. From age four to about seven years, they consistently choose the drawing that shows what *they* see no matter where the doll is located. This literal demonstration of egocentrism explains why young children may have difficulty understanding other people's motives and beliefs.

Egocentrism pops up spontaneously in children's speech. The following is a classic preoperational response.

ADULT: "Do you have a brother?"

BOY: "Yes. Jimmy is my brother."

ADULT: "Does Jimmy have a brother?"

BOY: "No."

The young child can't think about the question from his brother's point of view; he doesn't understand that the relationship of brother works in two directions. Similarly, at age four, President Kennedy's daughter Caroline was playing with her cousins. One of them announced, "Caroline, your daddy is the President." Caroline laughed, "Oh, no, he *isn't*. He's my Daddy" (*Listen!*, 1979). To her, he was Daddy, and that was all that mattered.

In conversations with each other, young children can sometimes be like ships passing in the night. Here is one of Piaget's transcripts of children in a Swiss nursery school who are sitting at a table and working on drawing.

LEV (5): "It begins with Goldylocks. I'm writing the story of the three bears. The daddy bear is dead. Only the daddy bear was too ill."

GEN (5): "I used to live at Salève. I lived in a little house and you had to take the funicular railway to go and buy things."

GEO (6): "I can't do the bear."

LI (6): "That's not Goldylocks."

LEV: "I haven't got curls."

(Piaget, 1955b, p. 77)

The children are talking about a common activity (drawing), and each understands what the others say. But each is speaking from his or her own point of view. Of course, transcripts of the dinner conversation in many families sometimes reveal similar disconnections, even when there are no young children at the table! But usually this is because people are *choosing* to ignore each other's points of view, not because they are having difficulty taking the perspective of the other person.

Animism   Piaget also observed cases in which preoperational children did not distinguish between human and nonhuman perspectives. On a rainy day, the three-year-old asks why the sky is crying. A four-year-old slips on the stairs. "The stairs are bad," he exclaims. "They *hit* me!" Such statements reflect **animism**. Young children think that inanimate objects have thoughts, wishes, motives, and feelings just as people do. On a walk with Piaget, a four-year-old girl began talking about the sun.

"Oh, the sun is moving. It's walking like us. . . . ."

"Where is it walking?"

"Why, on the sky. The sky's hard. It's made of clouds."

[Then, when she discovered the sun was following them:]

"It's doing that for fun, to play a joke on us. . . . ."

"But does it know we are here?"

"Of course it does, it can see us!"

(Piaget, 1951/1962, p. 252)

The young girl wasn't joking or trying to be poetic. To a preoperational child, the sun is alive.

animism   Belief that inanimate objects are alive and have thoughts, feelings, and motives like humans.

Can Parents and Teachers Accelerate Logical Thinking in Preschoolers?

In Piaget's view, the ways that preoperational children think are limited. Although they do use symbolic representation, their thinking is illogical, egocentric, and magical. These shortcomings raise the question, Should parents and teachers attempt to accelerate or "push" children through the preoperational period to become logical thinkers?

Piaget (1948/1972) would have answered, "No." He believed that the development of logical thinking is a natural outgrowth of everyday opportunities to observe and manipulate objects and materials. Piaget stressed the importance of independent discovery (Flavell, 1963; Piaget, 1948/1972). In his view, children develop logical thinking primarily through their own explorations and actions. He believed that efforts to teach logical operations to young children would result in empty verbalizations and rote memorization, without true understanding. A parent might try to teach a child conservation of volume, but the child wouldn't understand the underlying principle. The child would not be able to apply it to other materials or to conservation of mass or number. Because young children see adults as authorities, they might mimic what adults say without fundamentally understanding the task.

Whereas Piaget questioned whether interactions with adults can promote cognitive development, he believed that interactions with other children might serve that function. Disagreements and arguments with peers about appearances versus reality, he believed, could force a child to accommodate (i.e., to change her way of thinking in response to new information she cannot assimilate; see "Cognitive Development in Infancy"). So, in Piaget's view, peers might promote cognitive development in ways that adults (parents and teachers) cannot. (For a summary of this section, see "Interim Summary 8.1: Piaget's Theory: The Preoperational Period.")

INTERIM SUMMARY **8.1**

Piaget's Theory: The Preoperational Period

Accomplishments of the Preoperational Period	■ Language is a hallmark of the preoperational period that demonstrates an ability to think symbolically. ■ **Pretend play** is another hallmark of the period that demonstrates an ability to use symbols and representations.
Gaps in Preoperational Thinking	■ Preoperational children are **egocentric**, in that they see things from their own perspective and do not realize that other people may have different points of view. ■ Preoperational children are influenced by appearances and do not understand that characteristics such as mass, volume, and number do not change despite superficial changes in form or appearance. ■ Preoperational children are animistic and believe inanimate objects have thoughts, motives, and feelings just as people do.
Can Parents and Teachers Accelerate Logical Thinking in Preschoolers?	■ Piaget believed that adults should not try to teach conservation or other types of logical thinking. ■ Instead, he argued that development occurs through independent discovery, active manipulation of materials, and interactions with peers.

BEYOND PIAGET

Piaget revolutionized the way that we look at children by focusing on how they think, not how much they know. But like many pioneers, Piaget inspired other scientists to conduct research about his theory, which ultimately challenged many of his conclusions.

Contemporary Challenges to Piaget's Theory

In general, these scientists have found that the stages of cognitive development are not as clear-cut as Piaget believed (Gelman & Kalish, 2006; Halford & Andrews, 2006). Piaget saw functioning at each period—sensorimotor, preoperational, concrete operations, formal operations—as a unified whole, in which different domains of thinking within each stage fit together. After children experience a number of "Aha!" revelations toward the end of early childhood, he believed that the curtain would then open on the next act in cognitive development, concrete operations.

Contemporary scientists think cognitive development is better described as a series of overlapping waves than as discrete and distinctly different periods (Siegler, 1996, 2006). Some contemporary scientists also argue that using logical reasoning as an endpoint for correct reasoning is not appropriate (Halford & Andrews, 2006). Children's (and adults') responses and solutions may be based on different representations of the problem that do not involve logical deduction.

Perhaps most critical, we have learned from many careful studies that young children understand more than Piaget credited them for (Gelman, 2006). How young children perform on Piaget's tasks depends on how familiar they are with the topic, the situation in which the questions are posed, who asks the questions, and how they ask the questions. Young children may be animistic about the sun or the sea but realistic about other things. They know that people are alive and that rocks and dolls are not. They know that rocks do not have thoughts or feelings and that dolls cannot move on their own (Gelman & Kalish, 2006).

Preschoolers also aren't as consistently deceived by appearances as Piaget suggested. For example, if an experimenter pours a glass of milk and then places it behind an orange screen, they know it is still *really* milk, even though it *looks like* orange juice (Flavell, Flavell, & Green, 1983). When the experimenter asks what the glass *really* holds versus what it *looks like*, they understand the question and answer correctly. They also recognize conservation when the test involves a small number of familiar objects, such as dolls and doll beds. Small children do not apply the principle of conservation all of the time, but neither are adults logical all of the time. Much as Piaget underestimated cognition in early childhood, he may have overestimated adult cognition!

Theory of Mind

Piaget's view that preoperational children are egocentric has drawn particular attention. Are young children really locked into their own point of view? Do they really take appearances literally? A number of contemporary developmental scientists (Astington, 1993; Barr, 2006; Flavell et al., 1983; Wellman, 2002) think not. These scientists are interested in children's **theory of mind**—that is, their ability to attribute mental states—beliefs, intents, desires, knowledge—to oneself and others and to understand that others have beliefs, desires, and intentions that are different from one's own,

theory of mind The ability to attribute mental states—beliefs, intents, desires, knowledge—to oneself and others and to understand that others have beliefs, desires, and intentions that are different from one's own.

Young children aren't always egocentric. For example, when talking to a baby, three- and four-year-olds (like adults) use shorter sentences, simpler words, and a higher intonation to capture the infant's attention (Shatz & Gelman, 1973). They seem to recognize that babies do not understand speech the way older children and adults do. Three-year-olds also distinguish between real and pretend events. For example, they know the difference between a boy who is thinking about a cookie and a boy who has a cookie; they know which boy can touch, eat, or share the cookie (Astington, 1993).

Age four years is considered a watershed in the development of a theory of mind (Barr, 2006; Flavell et al., 1983). The classic demonstration is the *false-belief task*. A child is shown, say, a Band-Aids box and asked what is inside. Naturally enough, she answers "Band-Aids." But when she opens the box, she finds it contains crayons. The experimenter tells her that another child, who hasn't seen this demonstration, will be asked to guess what is in the box. What will that child think? Most three-year-olds respond that the other child will guess crayons, assuming that he knows what they know (and confirming Piaget's notion of egocentrism). However, most four-year-olds predict the other child will be fooled as they were and guess that the box contains Band-Aids. Variations of the false-belief task have been tried on children in many cultures with similar results, although sometimes a theory of mind is evident in five- and six-year-olds rather than in four-year-olds (Barr, 2006).

An understanding that other people can have false beliefs arises from the realization that what is inside a person's head may be different from what is outside; that thoughts and beliefs are mental representations, which can sometimes be wrong. Four-year-olds understand that different people can see or hear different versions of the same object or event. But not until about age six do children recognize that different people who see or hear the *same* thing may remember it differently (Pillow & Henrichon, 1996).

What causes children to begin developing a theory of mind? Researchers are learning that cognitive and language abilities play a part (Barr, 2006). But experiences with adults and older children also are important, as Judy Dunn and her colleagues observed in young children's interactions with their mothers and siblings (Dunn, 1991; Dunn et al., 1991). Dunn was particularly interested in disobedience. She found that one-and-a-half- to two-year-olds sometimes smiled or laughed as they repeated behavior that had been forbidden (dropping a toy from their high chair; spilling juice on the carpet)—as if they enjoyed their power to provoke a reaction from their mother.

At times they seemed to be testing the limits. On other occasions, they hid from their mother before engaging in a forbidden act, or they blamed a sibling for a mishap. Thus, the children showed an awareness of what their mother knew (or didn't know), what she would tolerate (or not tolerate), and how she would respond if she did know.

Dunn and her colleagues also observed young children teasing their siblings, which required a sophisticated understanding of particular actions that would be particularly distressing for their sibs. Judy Dunn has proposed that interactions between siblings may be particularly fertile ground for the development of social understanding and the theory of mind.

One of the authors of this textbook observed this type of understanding in her four-year-old daughter, Ashley. On one occasion, while Ashley was watching a favorite TV show, she quietly took the TV remote control and stuck it between the sofa cushions. A few minutes later, when her nine-year-old brother came into the room to watch his favorite show on another channel, she feigned ignorance about the location of the remote control. As Colin searched the room, she watched her show. When her show ended, the remote control reappeared.

Thus, research findings and anecdotal examples demonstrate that children begin developing a theory of mind on the border between infancy and early childhood, through repeated, everyday interactions with the people they know best. They may not know what another, hypothetical child is thinking (the false-belief test), but they have real-world understanding of what is on their mother's or a sibling's mind.

Symbol-Referent Relations

Judy DeLoache has extended and expanded Piaget's early work related to symbols and their referents (DeLoache, 1987, 1995; DeLoache, Miller, & Rosengran, 1997). DeLoache sees a **symbol** as any entity that stands for something other than itself. In a series of experiments, she and her colleagues brought children to a full-sized room where they showed them a doll named Big Terry. The researchers and the children then hid Big Terry behind a piece of furniture. Next, the researchers took the children to another location and showed them a miniature room that was an exact replica of the full-size room. They explicitly described and highlighted the similarities between the model and the original room, and then asked the children to find Little Terry. The experimenter reminded the children of the corresponding locations of the two toys: "Can you find Little Terry? Remember, he's hiding in the same place in his little room where Big Terry's hiding in his big room."

Three-year-olds could typically (i.e., more than 75% of the time) find Little Terry, whereas two-and-a-half-year-olds could rarely do so (i.e., less than 20% of the time). Virtually all of the children at both ages could go back to the big room and find Big Terry when asked to do so. What the younger children could not do was use that information to find Little Terry in the model. The younger children, according to DeLoache, do not have the representational insight that there is a relation between a symbol and the referent. This is consistent with what Piaget would have argued.

But understanding symbol-referent relations is not an all-or-none affair. DeLoache and her colleagues identified factors that assist (or undermine) young children's appreciation of the relation between symbol and referent. When object similarity is high and the model and room are similar in size, even two-and-a-half-year-olds can find Little Terry. When the experimenters do not explicitly describe and highlight the relations between the large room and the miniature, three-year-olds cannot find Little Terry. DeLoache's observations suggest that children only gradually develop an understanding that entities can stand for something other than themselves, and they do not experience the discrete qualitative shift that Piaget proposed. (For a summary of this section, see "Interim Summary 8.2: Beyond Piaget.")

symbol Any entity that stands for something other than itself.

INTERIM SUMMARY 8.2

Beyond Piaget

Contemporary Challenges to Piaget's Theory	■ Contemporary research suggests that preschoolers know more than Piaget credited them with.
Theory of Mind	■ Research on young children's theory of mind indicates that they are not as egocentric as Piaget thought.
	■ Theory of mind refers to individuals' awareness of their own and other people's thought processes and mental states.
	■ Performance on false-belief tasks indicate that age 4 is a watershed in the development of a theory of mind.
Symbol-Referent Relations	■ Young children only gradually develop an understanding of **symbols**, where an entity can stand for something other than itself.
	■ There is not a discrete qualitative shift in symbolic thinking of the sort that Piaget proposed.

VYGOTSKY'S SOCIOCULTURAL THEORY

One of Piaget's contemporaries, Russian developmental scientist Lev Vygotsky (1896–1934), also challenged his views. Although Vygotsky (1978, 1986) shared Piaget's belief that children are motivated learners who actively seek to understand their world, he disagreed with Piaget's other basic assumptions. Piaget saw the child as a solitary scientist and focused on what the child could do alone, without assistance. Vygotsky (1978) saw the child as embedded in a social context and focused on what she could do with the assistance of adults or older, more skilled children. For Vygotsky, cognitive development was the result of *collaboration* in a particular sociocultural setting. In effect, the child is an apprentice. Vygotsky also measured development in terms of the child assuming more important social roles and responsibilities, not the child's use of logic. Finally, Vygotsky saw cognitive development as continuous, not as distinct stages.

Zone of Proximal Development

zone of proximal development (ZPD) The gap between what a child can do alone and what a child can do with assistance.

scaffolding Providing learning opportunities, materials, hints, and clues when a child has difficulty with a task.

At the heart of Vygotsky's theory was an idea called the *zone of proximal development*. The **zone of proximal development (ZPD)** is the area between what a child can do alone and what a child can do with assistance. The ZPD is made up of skills, ideas, and understandings that are just beyond the child's reach, that the child is beginning to perform and can do with support or assistance from adults or more skilled peers. As you read in "Cognitive Development in Infancy," the parent or older child's role is to support the child's efforts with **scaffolding**; that is, to provide learning opportunities, materials, hints, and clues when the child gets stuck (Bruner, Jolly, & Sylva, 1976). A key feature of effective scaffolding is that the parent provides only as much support as the child needs; once skills are mastered, the parent withdraws the "scaffold" or support (because that particular support is not needed).

Take learning to ride a bicycle. When a young child is a whiz on a tricycle, parents introduce a two-wheeler with training wheels. The parent walks alongside as the child learns to apply familiar skills to a somewhat less stable vehicle. The parent will provide a push to help the child get started and may provide a hand to stabilize a wobbly rider. When he has learned to steer and pedal, it's time to take off the training wheels. The parent still walks alongside, though, providing balance when the child needs it—

until one day, the parent lets go and the child is on his own, for a short time at least. Once he has learned to ride the bike confidently, a new zone of development opens: racing and performing stunts that older and/or more skilled children show him. Parental guidance, like training wheels, bridges the gap between what is easy for the child (riding a tricycle) and what is at first impossible or unknown (riding a two-wheeled bike). And new skills lead to a new ZPD, or new competencies to be mastered with assistance.

When reading picture books, parents (ideally) adjust their prompts to the child's ZPD. With fifteen-month-olds, parents point to illustrations and ask leading questions that supply the answer: "Is that an elephant?" When the child is able to label familiar objects, parents begin to ask for information that is not visible on the page ("What do bees make?"), providing clues that lead the child to an answer ("What does Winnie-the-Pooh like to eat?" "Honey, that's right. Bees make honey. You knew."). Through these interactions in the ZPD, parents scaffold early literacy activities. Helping the child to come up with the right answer herself, providing assistance when it is needed and allowing the child to "do it herself" when she can, are part of the scaffold. Vygotsky held that children learn their culture's "intellectual tools"—language, number systems, reading and writing, religion and science, as well as ways to remember and plan—through social interaction in the ZPD (Rogoff, 2003).

Vygotsky (1967) saw pretend play as another zone of proximal development. In make-believe, children try on different roles (actual and fictional), imitating adults and experimenting with rules. As he explained, "In play a child is always above his average age, above his daily behavior; in play it is as though he were a head taller than himself" (p. 522).

A key feature of effective scaffolding is that the parent provides only as much support as the child needs. Once a particular skill is mastered, the parent withdraws the "scaffold" or support because that particular support is no longer needed.

Guided Participation

Barbara Rogoff (2003) has expanded Vygotsky's sociocultural theory and the idea of the ZPD to include **guided participation** or the varied ways children learn their society's values and practices through participation in family and community activities. Guided participation goes beyond actions intended to be instructional. It includes times when children watch adults going about their business and listen to adults talking among themselves, participate in cultural rituals and everyday activities, listen to family stories or their culture's mythology, play traditional games, and so on. When adults or older children praise, shame, or laugh about a child's behavior, they are guiding participation by providing a frame of how to behave and how *not* to behave.

For example, middle-class Euro-American families (directly and indirectly) prepare children for their future role as student. With toddlers, parents combine play with vocabulary lessons. They often ask *known-answer questions*, such as "What is this?" (holding up a toy) or "Where is your bellybutton?" Both the parent and child know the answer, so the question isn't a request for information. Rather, parents are teaching the format used for test questions in school. At the dinner table, parents ask children to talk about their day and, as in school, each child gets a turn. When a child hesitates, they prompt the child with questions such as "What did you do?" "Who was there?" "And then . . ." "And after that . . ."—providing a scaffold for the narrative format used in school (when, where, what, who, and why). Even before they learn to read, middle-class Euro-American children learn to "talk like a book" (Gauvain, 2001; Rogoff, 2003).

guided participation The varied ways children learn their society's values and practices through participation in family and community activities.

Children learn some social and cultural lessons on their own, simply by observing. In one example, a U.S. mother was working at home, spending hours every day transcribing tape-recorded conversations onto her computer for a research project, while her three-year-old daughter played nearby. One day the little girl set up her own "office."

> She had pulled her small director's chair up to her bed, which served as a desk. It held her "computer" (really a toy typewriter), as well as her small plastic tape recorder. She would play a section of *Star Wars,* and then stop the recording to bang out a message on the plastic keys of her typewriter. Back and forth she went between the recorder and her "computer," playing and typing, playing a new section and typing again, in a way more than a little reminiscent of my efforts at transcription. (Wolf & Heath, 1992, pp. 11–12)

Guided participation is seen in other cultures (Rogoff, 2003). In a Mayan village in Guatemala, for example, a young child watched her mother make tortillas each morning. One day the mother rolled a small ball of dough, flattened it a little, and gestured to her daughter to continue. After the child seemed to be doing her best, the mother began demonstrating techniques to make the play tortilla thinner and more even—an example of scaffolding. Emulating adults is one way children actively seek knowledge and skills.

Just as the content of guided participation varies, so do the rules for participation. In some cultures children are expected to learn by listening and holding their tongues. For example, in Native American communities, asking direct questions often is considered rude because it obliges the other person to reply. Silence is the appropriate response when a person does not have a reply or wish to make one. The Inuit of Arctic Quebec say, "The more intelligent [children] become, the quieter they become" (Freeman, 1978, p. 21). Euro-American teachers find these children's silence unnerving, even disrespectful. To some degree these children must *un*learn the manners they acquire at home to succeed in schools where Euro-American standards prevail and where how children talk can be as important as what they say. In classrooms, non-Inuit teachers ask children to speak up, in contrast to their parents' expectations. This clash surfaced in a parent-teacher conference:

Children learn about their society's values and practices as they participate in everyday activities.

NON-INUIT TEACHER: Your son is talking well in class. He is speaking up a lot.

INUIT PARENT: I am sorry. (Crago, 1992, p. 496)

Language and Thought

Both Piaget and Vygotsky were interested in the relationship between language and thought. Piaget (1923/1955) believed that the development of thought precedes language—that is, we think and then we communicate. In Piaget's view, children in the sensorimotor period have impressions or rudimentary ideas about objects and people before they are able to speak, and they must form mental representations before they consistently attach names to things. Thought comes first.

In contrast, Vygotsky (1986) argued that thought and language develop together. He held that the child's first attempts to speak are efforts to establish and maintain social contact. When an infant says, "Bow-wow," the mother responds, "Yes! That's a dog." Using a word elicits and maintains social interaction, which is the child's primary goal (though she may be expressing excitement, too). These interactions served to place the child in a zone of proximal development. So-called social speech is all-important at this stage.

Around age three or four, according to Vygotsky, children begin to use the language they developed for social purposes as a tool to organize their thoughts and actions. Faced with a problem, they talk out loud to themselves. Thus, language facilitates problem solving and thought. The self-directed talk helps children to recall what they know and to plan and organize what they want to do. "I want to draw a tree. I need the green pencil for the leaves. But I need a brown pencil, too, for the tree trunk," and so on. Gradually, self-directed talk becomes silent **inner speech**. The child runs through possible solutions in her mind instead of talking out loud. Vygotsky held that adult thought is an advanced version of inner talk. Of course, adults also talk to themselves out loud, usually when no one else is around. "Great! I got it. Now, what next?"

inner speech   Self-directed talk that has become internalized. It facilitates problem solving.

INTERIM SUMMARY 8.3

Vygotsky's Sociocultural Theory

The Zone of Proximal Development	■ The **zone of proximal development (ZPD)** (the area between what a child can do alone and what a child can do with assistance) is at the center of Vygotsky's theory.
	■ **Scaffolding** refers to how parents or older peers can support a child's learning by providing assistance or help when it is needed.
	■ Children learn their culture's intellectual tools, such as language, number systems, reading, and writing, through social interaction in the ZPD.
	■ Pretend play also provides a ZPD where children try on different roles, imitate adults, and experiment with rules.
Guided Participation	■ **Guided participation** refers to the varied ways children learn their society's values and practices through participation in family and community activities.
Language and Thought	■ Vygotsky believed that language and thought develop in tandem.
	■ Young children begin by using language for social purposes. Gradually, self-directed talk becomes silent **inner speech**.
	■ Piaget believed that thought precedes language. In his view, children must first form mental representations before they consistently attach names to things.

To recap: Piaget held that symbolic representation, seen in language and in play, is the most significant cognitive development during the preschool years. But he defined the preoperational period as much in terms of what young children cannot do (logical operations) as by what they can do. Others have shown that Piaget underestimated young children, especially their theory of mind. Vygotsky saw the young child as an apprentice and cognitive development as the result of the child's efforts to become a full-fledged member of his or her social and cultural community, with help from mentors and guided participation. (For a summary of this section, see "Interim Summary 8.3: Vygotsky's Sociocultural Theory.")

INFORMATION PROCESSING IN EARLY CHILDHOOD

The information-processing approach to cognitive development deals with basic questions about how people acquire, encode, store, and use information (Munakata, 2006). By analogy, the brain is similar to a computer. When you work on a computer, you encode information by typing on the keyboard. To store the information you press keys that save the information on a disk, according to your filing system. To retrieve information you open a file (or use a search and find function). You have various programs to tell stories or make written reports (word processing), edit pictures (photo processing), perform calculations (spreadsheet), communicate (e-mail), and so on.

Similarly, our brains acquire and select information (perception and attention), store and retrieve information (memory), and use information to cope with the present situation or plan for the future (problem solving) (see Figure 8.2). The question for developmental scientists is, how do these elements of information processing (perception, attention, memory, and problem solving) change over the course of development?

We discussed perception in "Cognitive Development in Infancy" when we described the development of infant cognition. Here we will look at attention and memory. Being able to focus selectively on specific information (attention) and then being able to store and retrieve that information (memory) are essential to all types of learning. The two work together: to remember something you have to pay attention to it. What do young children notice? How much do they recall?

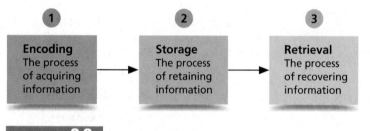

FIGURE 8.2

Information-Processing Model

Three steps involved in the information-processing model of cognitive development—encoding, storage, and retrieval—are analogous to creating a document on your computer. You begin by typing in the information (encoding) and then it is saved onto the hard drive (storage); when you need the information, you can open the saved document (retrieval).

Attention

When you finish this sentence, close your eyes for a minute and listen to everything that is going on around you. While you were reading, were you aware of the traffic beneath your window, the hum of a radiator or air conditioner, the ticking of a clock—or even what time it was? If you were concentrating on the book, the answer is probably no. This simple test demonstrates that **attention** consists of focusing on particular information while ignoring other information.

A classic measure of attention is the **Continuous Performance Task**, or CPT (Rosvold et al., 1956). In this exercise, the child is seated at a table with a TV screen and asked to push a button whenever a particular object (say, a chair) appears. The researcher flashes a series of pictures (chairs and other things) over a seven-minute period. By design, the task is fairly boring; maintaining attention requires effort. On the CPT, attention is measured by how many times the child pushes the button when

attention The process of focusing on particular information while ignoring other information.

Continuous Performance Task (CPT) A laboratory task designed to assess attentiveness and impulsivity by pushing a button when a specific object appears on the computer screen.

a chair is on the screen. **Impulsivity** is measured by how often the child (incorrectly) pushes the button when another object is on the screen.

You may recognize this procedure from the Go/No-Go task described in "Physical Development in Early Childhood." You may also recognize the problem. Think how often adults click on the "Send" key for an e-mail without adding the "Attachment."

The CPT task has been used widely. Three-year-olds and most four-year-olds perform poorly; some four- and most five-year-olds get more right than wrong answers; and six-year-olds make only a few mistakes. (See Figure 8.3.) Clearly then, attention increases and impulsivity decreases over early childhood (Ruff & Capozzoli, 2003).

Improvements in attention are linked to the maturation of the brain's prefrontal cortex and basal ganglia (Nelson, Thomas, & deHaan, 2006). But individual differences in CPT scores show that the child's environment and experience with parents are also important (NICHD Early Child Care Research Network [ECCRN], 2003). Children from stimulating homes with warm, responsive parents gain control of their attention earlier than do children from less supportive homes. Why? One reason may be that frequent conversations with parents provide young children with guided opportunities to observe and practice concentration and self-regulation.

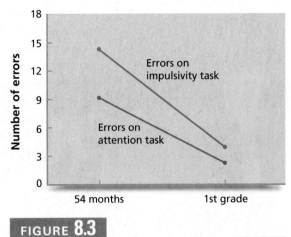

FIGURE 8.3

Errors on Impulsivity and Attention Tasks by Age

As children get older, their success on the Continuous Performance Task (CPT) improves. When four-and-a-half-year-olds were retested in first grade, the number of errors they made on tests of impulsivity (that is, clicking that the item had appeared on the screen when it had not) declined. Errors in attention (failing to click when the item appeared on the screen) also declined, indicating that older children are better at regulating these processes than younger children.

Memory

We tend to think of memory as a mental record of something we experienced, witnessed, heard, or read—much like a photograph or video recording. But there is far more to memory than pushing a save button in our minds. The information-processing model identifies three steps in memory processing: sensory memory, working memory, and long-term memory (Martinez, in press; Pressley & Hilden, 2006).

Sensory Memory and Working Memory **Sensory memory** is the entryway. It is a subconscious process of picking up sensory information from the environment (sights, sounds, smells, and touch). Sensory memory consists of fleeting impressions.

This information is either forgotten or transferred to **working memory** (sometimes referred to as "short-term memory"): conscious, short-term representations of what a person is actively thinking about at a given time. It depends on the child (or adult) paying attention and encoding the impression in some way—for example, attaching it to a known word or image. A classic test of recall is the **digit span task**, in which children are asked to repeat back a sequence of items (numbers, words) they have heard. Working memory improves substantially during early childhood from recall of two numbers at age two and a half years to five numbers at age seven, and about seven numbers in adulthood (Kail, 2003).

Part of the reason for the improvements in working memory is biological; part, social. As discussed in "Physical Development in Early Childhood," the prefrontal cortex and corpus callosum, which provide the "hardware" for short-term memory, are developing during early childhood and provide the capacity that supports an expanded working memory (Nelson et al., 2006). And, as is the case with attention, the development of working memory is accelerated by warm, stimulating interactions with parents at home and by attending preschools or child-care centers that are high quality (NICHD ECCRN, 2002).

impulsivity (As measured by CPT), how often a child incorrectly pushes a button designating that an object is on the screen.

sensory memory A subconscious process of picking up sensory information—sights, sounds, smells, touch—from the environment.

working memory Conscious, short-term representations of what a person is actively thinking about at a given time.

digit span task A research procedure in which people are asked to repeat in order a series of rapidly presented items.

Short-term or *working memory* lasts at most a few minutes. The information either fades or is stored in **long-term memory**, which has a potentially unlimited capacity and no time limitations (Martinez, in press). *Long-term memory* can store a vast amount of interconnected information, encoded in a variety of formats. Access to long-term memory may take the form of *recall* (summoning up stored information) or *recognition* (identifying something as the same as, or similar to, something encountered before). For most people (children included), recognition is easier than recall (Martinez, in press).

Some researchers (Pressley & Hilden, 2006) have used hiding and finding games to learn about young children's memory strategies. Preschoolers can be very strategic when it comes to remembering where objects have been hidden when the situations are very familiar to them—for example, finding a Big Bird doll in a living room setting (DeLoache, Cassidy, & Brown, 1985). In more difficult and less familiar tasks, such as finding a candy hidden under one of six cups on a turntable that would spin quickly, some preschoolers (but not all) are able to use directive prompts from an experimenter to develop strategies (such as marking the right cup with a gold star) that help them find the hidden candy (Ritter, 1978).

Many young children in the United States have well-developed scripts for events such as attending a birthday party (you arrive, give presents, sing "Happy Birthday," and eat cake).

long-term memory The collection of information that is mentally encoded and stored; it is believed to have potentially unlimited capacity and no time limits.

generic memory A script or general outline of how familiar activities occur based on experience.

episodic memory Recall of a particular incident that took place at a specific time and place.

autobiographical memory Recall of individual episodes that are personally meaningful, which begins at about age four and may last for decades.

Long-Term Memory Scientists distinguish among several types of long-term memory (Bauer, 2006). **Generic memory**, which begins at about age two, is a script or general outline of what happens when, based on experience (Nelson, 2006). Children have scripts for going to the grocery store (you get a cart, put in items from the shelves, go to the check-out counter, pay, and carry your groceries away in bags), going to school (you sit at a desk, do work, raise your hand to ask a question), and other familiar activities. Often children rehearse these scripts in pretend play, re-creating a trip to the doctor, a meal in a restaurant, or a visit to grandparents from memory. Scripts help children to know what to expect and how to behave in common situations.

Episodic memory is recall of a particular incident at a specific time and place (Fivush, Hudson, & Nelson, 1984). Three-year-olds may remember details of a trip to the circus for a year or more. They also recall events that particularly captured their attention—for example, a visit to the river to feed the ducks when one particularly aggressive duck kept all the others away from the bread—sometimes remembering these events years later.

Autobiographical memory, recall of individual episodes that are personally meaningful, begins at about age four and may last for decades (Nelson & Fivush, 2004). Autobiographical memories become part of the child's developing self-concept or self-image (see "Socioemotional Development in Early Childhood"). Beginning in early childhood, each of us constructs a personal history, a life story we revise and edit as we grow older to describe ourselves and explain our attitudes and behavior, to ourselves as well as to others.

Why do some early memories last while others fade? One factor is the uniqueness of the event—for example, the death of a grandparent. It may be the child's first experience of death, of the loss of someone she is close to and the emotional climate and rituals surrounding death. Another factor is personal participation, as opposed to watching. For example, riding a pony is more memorable than watching a riding class. Perhaps most important is talking to a parent or another adult about an event.

The development of memory in early childhood is partly a social process, guided by parents and others. Mary Gauvain (2001, p. 102) uses the example of Molly, age five. At a family holiday dinner, someone asked Molly about her first day at school. After some hesitation, Molly responded, "It was fun." A long silence indicated that she was finished. Then relatives began asking questions (based on their own scripts for school). "Who's your teacher? Is she nice?" "Did you have a snack? A nap?" and so on. After a lively half-hour discussion, Molly's mother thanked her for telling everyone about her day. "Yes," Molly exclaimed, "and I did it all myself!" She did, but with considerable scaffolding from her family.

Parents vary in both the frequency and style of their conversations with children about past events (Cleveland & Reese, 2005). Parents with a *highly elaborative* style introduce new information, often in the form of a leading question: "Did we see a very big, furry animal at the zoo?" They confirm their child's responses: "Yes, that's right! We saw a bear." And when the child brings in new information, they follow up with another prompt: "We did see seals. What do seals eat?" The conversation is a collaboration. Parents with a *repetitive* style tend to ask the same question over and over; tell children what happened or change the subject if the child doesn't respond; and correct the child. Here's a mother asking her child about a trip to the dentist.

MOTHER: Was it painful?

CHILD: No.

MOTHER: It wasn't painful? Why wasn't it painful?

CHILD: Because it wasn't.

MOTHER: Okay, alright, then was your mouth sore?

MOTHER: Your mouth wasn't sore?

MOTHER: Not even the next day?

CHILD: No.

MOTHER: Okay then that's good, I'm glad you don't remember that.

(Cleveland & Reese, 2005, p. 380)

In this example, the mother is asking—repeatedly—for *her* memory of the event, not engaging the child. An elaborative style elicits more detailed and better organized narratives at age three and better memories of events at ages five and six (Fivush, Haden, & Reese, 1996). Over time, children come to depend less on adult scaffolding and to provide more information, progressing from general narratives of repeated events to more detailed stories of particular events (Hoff, 2006).

The development of memory and language work hand in hand. To become verbally fluent, children need to learn (remember) many words; words, in turn, make it easier to store and recall memories. When children are able to put memories into words, they are better able to hold these memories in mind, think about them, and compare them to other people's memories (Bauer, 2006).

Long-term memories, which include recollections that may last a lifetime, begin in early childhood. These memories are part of a complex selective constructive process. Children do not remember or recall exactly what happened, but rather *construct* a memory out of what caught their attention (Bauer, 2006). (For a summary of this section, see "Interim Summary 8.4: Information Processing in Early Childhood.")

INTERIM SUMMARY 8.4

Information Processing in Early Childhood

Attention	■ **Attention** refers to how we are able to focus on some information while ignoring other information.
	■ Improvements in attention are linked to the maturation of the prefrontal cortex and basal ganglia.
	■ Children whose parents are cognitively stimulating, warm, and responsive are better at controlling their attention than children whose parents do not act in these ways.
Memory	■ **Sensory memory** is a subconscious process of picking up sensory information from the environment and lasts only a few seconds at most.
	■ **Working memory** consists of conscious, short-term representations of what a person is actively thinking about at a given time. Working memory lasts at most a few minutes. The information either fades or is stored in long-term memory.
	■ Maturation of the prefrontal cortex and corpus callosum provide the capacity that supports an expanded working memory.
	■ **Long-term memory** can store a vast amount of interconnected information, encoded in a variety of formats. Three types of long-term memory have been identified: **generic**, **episodic**, and **autobiographical**.

LANGUAGE, LITERACY, AND MATHEMATICS IN EARLY CHILDHOOD

The advances in basic cognitive processes of attention and memory and in the use of symbols and concepts are linked to other important developments in early childhood. In this section, we describe the development in three related domains that help to prepare children for success at school: language development, literacy, and mathematical thinking.

Language Development in Young Children

Language development, which begins one word at a time in infancy, takes off in early childhood (Tomasello, 2006). During this period, children progress from one- and two-word utterances ("Daddy eat") to simple sentences ("Daddy eat breakfast") to complex grammatical forms and a rich vocabulary ("Why didn't Daddy eat his cereal?"—which combines a question, a negative [did_n't], and a possessive [his]). The journey from a cooing infant to conversationalist illustrates the interplay of innate characteristics and experience (Goldin-Meadow, 2006).

Language is a distinctively human trait. Human children—and only human children, not the young of any other species—develop complex rule-governed language, and the sequence and the timetable of language development appear universal. This suggests that language is innate. Linguistic nativists argue that all human beings possess the same basic linguistic competencies in the form of a universal grammar. They emphasize the innate capacities that make language learning manageable for young children (Chomsky, 1968; Pinker, 1994). But language development also depends on experience. Usage-based linguists see language emerging from language use (Tomasello, 2006). Children who are not exposed to any language do not develop language, and children learn different languages, depending on what they hear around them. Their native language affects what sounds they can hear and produce (the reason for a "foreign accent" in other languages), what underlying rules (or grammar) they use to put words together, and the social rules they apply in communicating. (English is one of the few languages that does not have [at least] two forms for addressing another person, one familiar, one formal.) Clearly experience matters. Even so, language development is not the same as learning to ride a bicycle or to play piano. To a significant degree, language develops naturally, not because of explicit instruction or special talent (Bloom, 2000).

Developmental scientists chart language development in early childhood by looking at several different phenomena: vocabulary (the words we know and their associated knowledge), morphology and syntax (our understanding of the rules we use to put words together), semantics (our understanding of what words and sentences mean), and pragmatics (our understanding of how to use language in everyday life) (Hoff, 2006).

Vocabulary Around age two, young children's vocabularies begin to expand rapidly. Two-year-olds know about 200 words. At age three, they understand and can use 900 to 1,000 words. By age six, they have vocabularies of 8,000 to 14,000 words (Carey, 1978). This means, as we said earlier, learning an average of ten new words a day. How can children do this?

A key to vocabulary growth is **fast-mapping**, a phenomenon that refers to when children pick up a word they have heard only a few times (Carey & Bartlett, 1978). Children intuit meanings from the context, the topic of conversation, similar words, and their understanding of what kinds of words go where. For example, a child may grasp that *tomorrow* means

© Laura Dwight

The more speech children are exposed to from parents and teachers, the faster their vocabularies grow. Conversations help to fuel language development.

something like "not now" before he understands the relationship between the words *yesterday*, *today*, and *tomorrow*. A child may pick up the word *sexy* from an older sister describing her friend's outfit this way, but later learn that this is *not* a word he should use with Aunt Harriet. As children hear a word used more often and try using it themselves, their definition becomes more refined.

The more speech children are exposed to from parents and teachers, the faster the rate at which their vocabularies grow (Hart & Risley, 1995). Mothers in high-income families are likely to have higher levels of education than mothers in low-income families and so have wider vocabularies. They talk more to their children and often follow the child's interests, rather than dictating the subject. In part, this explains why poor children may be a year or more behind better-off children in vocabulary at age four (Hoff, 2006). Likewise, children who attend child-care centers with a high caregiver-to-children ratio that permits more adult/child conversations have richer vocabularies than children whose child-care center has a low caregiver-to-child ratio (NICHD Early Child Care Research Network, 2000b). Moreover, first-born children, who are exposed to more talk from parents, generally have larger vocabularies than do later-born children (Hoff-Ginsburg, 1998).

fast-mapping A phenomenon that refers to when children pick up a word they have heard only a few times.

Morphology and Syntax Children hear people talking to particular individuals about specific topics. How do they learn to produce original sentences about their own experiences? Young children are sensitive to regularities, which they use to generate rules about how words are combined to create sentences (Tomasello, 2006). Linguistic input provides opportunities to learn the language system, but it is up to the child to do the inductive work to figure out what the system is (Goldin-Meadow, 2006).

telegraphic speech Simple, meaningful two-word utterances spoken by young children.

Between about eighteen and thirty-six months, children begin putting two words together in simple utterances called **telegraphic speech** (Bloom, 1970). The young speaker provides the bare essentials, as in a telegram (or in modern technology, a text message): "Throw ball," "Mommy sock," and "Baby drink." The listener has to fill in the gaps from the context or the child's gestures and facial expressions. At age two and a half to three, children advance to longer sentences with more information: "Baby drinking bottle," "That Mommy sock," and "No eat apple."

What is revealing about the two- and three-word stage is that children are not simply repeating or imitating phrases and sentences that they've heard, but are applying some of the basic rules of their particular language (Goldin-Meadow, 2006; Tomasello, 2006). In English, the basic sentence structure is agent-verb-object (as in "I ate dinner"). "Throw ball" conforms to this structure (verb-action), as does "No eat apple" (verb-object, implying "Me" as the agent). Young children rarely violate this structure by saying "Ball throw" or "Apple no eat." Likewise, children who speak French or Chinese use the correct word order of their languages (Waxman & Lidz, 2006).

Some of the best evidence that children extract and apply rules from their language comes from the mistakes children make. Around age two and a half to three, children begin using words they never said or heard before such as "He <u>taked</u> my toy," "I <u>seed</u> a horsie," and "Mommy <u>goed</u> to work." The following scene is typical.

CHILD: My teacher holded the rabbits and we petted them.

MOTHER: Did you say your teacher held the baby rabbits?

CHILD: Yes.

MOTHER: What did you say she did?

MOTHER: Did you say she held them tightly?

CHILD: No, she holded them loosely.

(Bellugi, 1970)

overregulation When children mistakenly apply regular grammatical rules to irregular cases.

What's happening? In English, the general rule for forming the past tense is to add the suffix *–ed* to the present tense (as in jump/jump*ed* or look/look*ed*). However, for some common English verbs the past tense is irregular (as in take/*took*, go/*went*, and see/*saw*). When children discover the regular rule for the past tense, they mistakenly apply it to all verbs including irregular verbs. Young children also make mistakes with irregular plurals (e.g., calling geese *gooses* or feet *foots*). **Overregulation**, as this is called, is not a step backward but a step forward—it's a sign that children are learning the underlying structure of their language, not just mimicking what they hear (Clark, 1998). By the end of early childhood, most children learn that general rules have exceptions, though five- and six-year-olds still make mistakes.

semantics The meaning of words and sentences, or the content of speech.

Semantics **Semantics** refers to the *meaning* of words and sentences, or the content of speech (Hoff, 2006). There is more to semantics, however, than learning which word applies to which person, object, activity, or trait. In learning what words mean, children are also learning how their culture uses concepts to organize their perceptions of the world. A *concept* is a mental representation or category, a general notion that applies to many individual cases. The concept *bird*, for example, applies to all (or almost all) birds: Birds have feathers, fly, build nests, lay eggs, and so on. Some birds are better examples of the concept because they have more of these defining qualities. A robin is a typical bird. An ostrich is not because it is big and cannot fly. Concepts help a young child simplify, sort, and group the many things in the environment (Gelman, 2006).

Children do not build concepts one case at a time, but rather take their cues from the "authorities," adults and older children (Gelman & Kalish, 2006). When a father says, "That birdie is a cardinal," the child grasps that a "cardinal" is a type of bird, not a synonym for bird (Mervis, Pani, & Pani, 2003). When the child sees a new bird, she already knows something about it. She can think and talk about birds even when one isn't present, can remember birds she saw in the past, and can imagine birds she will see in the future.

Mastering concepts also requires learning how concepts relate to one another (Gelman, 2006). Concepts can be arranged in hierarchies, with specific examples at the bottom and the broadest categories at the top. Thus, robin is a subcategory of *bird*, and bird is a subcategory of *animal*. Fish are another subcategory of *animal*; so are people. As a rule, young children learn midlevel concepts (such as *flower*) but struggle with relationships between categories (flowers are *plants*, which differ from *animals*). (As we noted earlier in this chapter, a fully developed understanding of classification does not emerge until middle childhood.) Asked, "Is a robin an animal?" preschoolers typically say, "No." (To be fair, adults usually hesitate.) The answer requires two mental steps: "A robin is a bird, and birds are animals, so the answer is yes." Young children take the first step but not the second. Most regard the question "Are people animals?" as "stupid." (So, of course, do some adults.)

Current research indicates that young children's concepts are more advanced than Piaget believed. They not only have concrete concepts about things they can see or touch (birds, flowers, cars) but also have abstract concepts (Gelman, 2006). For example, they know that common objects, like spoons and scissors, were designed for a purpose (Keleman, 2004). They understand that germs can cause illness, even though you can't see them (Kalish, 1996). If they learn something new about a brontosaurus, they are more likely to apply this to a triceratops (another dinosaur, even though the two look quite different) than to a rhinoceros (which is quite similar to a brontosaurus in appearance, but not a dinosaur) (Gelman, 2006). This is the opposite of what Piaget would have predicted for a preoperational child. As you read earlier, Piaget believed that preoperational thinking was driven by the way things look. Although this is true a lot of time, it isn't true all the time, especially in situations where children have specialized knowledge about the subject matter.

Specialized knowledge accelerates the development of concepts in particular areas (Gelman, 2006). Child experts in dinosaurs, construction vehicles, or chess have richer, more defined, and hierarchical concepts for their particular field than do adult novices. Expertise (at any age) is not a reflection of general intelligence, but rather of knowledge of a specific topic or domain. Exposure is clearly important: A child cannot become an expert on birds without opportunities to bird watch, guidance from someone who is knowledgeable, and perhaps binoculars and bird books. What we do not know is whether enriched exposure leads to expertise, or whether certain children (because of curiosity and personality) seek enriched environments. It probably is a combination of the two.

Child experts have extensive knowledge in specific areas that accelerate the development of hierarchical concepts in those areas.

pragmatics The social uses and conventions of language.

Pragmatics **Pragmatics** refers to the social uses and conventions of language (Hoff, 2006). To communicate effectively children need to learn what is accepted in their culture. Knowing what to say and when to say it are as important as knowing how to put words together (Hirsh-Pasek & Golinkoff, 2003). There are rules for how to ask for something (say, "Please" and "Thank you"); when children are permitted to speak and when they are expected to be quiet; when to take a statement literally and when not ("Would you mind putting your toys away?" is not a question but an order); how to tell stories; and much more. Knowing words and grammar isn't enough; children need to learn how to communicate with other members of their cultural community.

Children begin learning the fundamentals of communication long before they speak their first words (Hirsh-Pasek & Golinkoff, 2003). By eight or nine months, infants point to call an adult's attention to an interesting object, as if to say "Look at that!" (attention-getting). Instead of grabbing for something, they reach out with an open hand, signaling "I want that" (a request). In games like peekaboo, they learn one of the basic rules of communication, taking turns.

In early childhood, parents begin teaching youngsters the finer points: "Please look at Mrs. Jones when you talk to her." For middle-class Euro-Americans, not looking someone in the eye is interpreted as disinterest or evasion. For Chicanos, however, it is considered disrespectful for a child to look directly at an adult: "Don't stare at la señora." Without half thinking about it, parents teach children how to enter a conversation—"Say hello, Adam"—and what to talk about—"Tell Mr. Robinson what we did yesterday." One lesson children need to learn is that people do not always mean exactly what they say. Here is four-year-old Jane, answering a phone call from her mother's friend Samantha.

SAMANTHA: Hi, Jane! Is your mother home?

JANE: Yes. (This is followed by a long silence as Jane, remaining on the phone, imagines that Samantha has really called to acquire just this tidbit of information.)

SAMANTHA: Jane? Are you still there? Would you get her for me?

JANE: (Puts down phone without a response and goes off to get her mom.)

(Hirsh-Pasek & Golinkoff, 2003, p. 85)

Samantha was using a polite phrase to ask Jane to put her mother on the phone, but Jane took her literally. She didn't know that you always answer a question when speaking on the phone, because the other person can't see you. Four-year-olds tend to be quite literal—though they sometimes surprise parents by producing entire phrases they have heard before. After standing silently while her mother and a friend chatted, Marissa gushes, "It was soooo lovely to see you."

Storytelling also involves pragmatics (Hirsh-Pasek & Golinkoff, 2003). The standard format is to set the scene, introduce the characters, describe how they got into a funny or scary situation, and tell how it was resolved. Young children need help—scaffolding—to put all the pieces together in the right order. Nevertheless, they enjoy the process, which is one step in emergent literacy.

Emergent Literacy

Foundations of literacy are seen during early childhood (National Research Council, 1998; NICHD ECCRN, 2005c). A typical three-year-old knows how to hold a book and turn pages; listens when read to; understands the pictures in books and names characters and features; may distinguish pictures from print; and perhaps recognizes a few letters. A typical four-year-old can recite the alphabet and recognize some letters; relates stories to "real life" (his or her own experiences); enjoys rhymes and word play; and may pretend-write in play. A typical five-year-old may track the print when being

Parents can promote literacy by reading with children, talking about the story content, pointing out letter sound correspondence, and playing language sound games.

read a simple, familiar book; spontaneously talks about the content of story and information books; can identify all, and write most, letters; recognizes and can spell some simple words (including his or her name); but mostly uses invented spellings when writing (Snow, 2006).

The last thirty years have been marked by changing expectations for these milestones. When Deborah Vandell, one of the authors of this book, was a kindergarten teacher, it was very rare for a child to begin kindergarten as an accomplished reader. Now it is common. Whether being an accomplished reader in kindergarten is beneficial (because it gives children a fast start) or detrimental (because it is done at the expense of other more developmentally appropriate activities such as pretend play) is still being studied and debated (Hirsh-Pasek & Golinkoff, 2003). But there is agreement among researchers and practitioners about the value of exposure to books and language (Snow, 2006). In a classic study, Betty Hart and Todd Risley (1995) observed the parent-child interaction of participants once a month from birth to age three years, recording everything that transpired. Some of the parents were professionals, some working class, and some on welfare. The researchers found that the gap between the poor and well-off begins early. At age three, children in professional families had a vocabulary of about 1,000 words, and children in welfare families, a vocabulary of about 500 words. The children's vocabularies correlated with their later IQ scores: an average IQ of 117 for children of professionals, compared with an average 79 for children of parents on welfare (an IQ of 100 is the overall average or mean).

Analyzing their data, the researchers concluded that parent-child communication played a crucial role in this gap. In professional families, parents directed an average of 487 "utterances"—ranging from one-word instructions to monologues—to their children per hour. In welfare families, average utterances dropped to 178 per hour. Moreover, the style of interaction varied by social class. The main differences lay in "disapprovals"—prohibitions and discouragement—versus "affirmations"—approval and praise. On average, in families on welfare, children received eleven disapprovals and five affirmations per hour. Such conversation stoppers as "No!" "Don't do that!" and "What did I say?" were common. The pattern for children from professional families was reversed: twelve affirmations and seven disapprovals per hour. Their parents were more likely to engage them in conversations about the past and the future, emotions, and what causes what, in an elaborative fashion. In a nutshell, in the professional families, children were rewarded for talking, whereas in the welfare families, children were taught to follow commands. In addition to promoting language development, conversations promote attention (and therefore aid the development of information processing), as well as introducing children to general knowledge, including mathematics.

Mathematical Thinking

Children learn math in school through formal instruction—sometimes a painstaking process. Right? Not necessarily. This assumption may apply to academic math, such as long division or adding fractions, but not to everyday mathematical knowledge, such as ideas about more and less, taking away or adding to, size, shape, and location (Ginsburg et al., 2006). Like emergent literacy, everyday mathematical knowledge and reasoning develop in ordinary environments, often without special instruction, and earlier than you might imagine. Indeed, one of the first words babies learn is "More!" (Bloom, 1970).

During early childhood, before they enter first grade, youngsters master a number basic mathematical concepts, including the following:

- *Magnitude*: Three-year-olds understand the meaning of "a lot," whether applied to a bowl of cherries or cars in a parking lot (Wagner & Walters, 1982), and recognize which of two groups of objects has "more" (Ginsburg & Baroody, 2003).

- *Numbers*: Although the first ten numbers are essentially nonsense syllables that have to be memorized, two- and three-year-olds can recite them—though not always in the right order, as in "one, three, two, seven" (Ginsburg, 1989).

- *Counting*: Two- and three-year-olds can count very small sets (up to four objects) (Ginsburg et al., 2006). Three-year-olds understand the basic rules of counting— the *one-to-one principle* (one and only one number word should be assigned to each object; i.e., a single teddy bear can't be number two *and* number three); the *stable order principle* (number words should be said in the same order all of the time); the *cardinality principle* (the last number in a counting sequence indicates the quantity of items in a set); the *abstraction principle* (anything can be counted, from sticks to trees); and the *order irrelevance principle* (counting can begin with any item in a set as long as each item is counted once and only once).

- *Addition and subtraction*: Three- and four-year-olds understand the general idea that adding increases and subtracting decreases the size of a set (Bertelli, Joanni, & Martlew, 1998). They can also perform calculations involving small numbers, such as $2 + 1$ or $3 - 1$ (Starkey & Gelman, 1982).

As adults we know these mathematical concepts so well that we might have difficulty stating the rules (and probably never learned the formal names, such as "cardinality principle"). It is all the more amazing that young children seem to pick them up before they have had any formal instruction.

What is the source of early mathematical competence? Many scientists (Gelman, 2000; Ginsburg et al., 2006) believe that there is a biological basis for mathematical concepts. Children are born with number-relevant mental structures that promote the development of counting and basic geometry (Geary, 2006; Gelman, 2000; Ginsburg et al., 2006). These scientists cite the early emergence of mathematical thinking and universality of many everyday mathematical concepts as support.

But—as is usually the case—experience also counts. Ordinary physical and social environments promote the development of mathematical thinking (Ginsburg et al., 2006). Every human environment has objects to count, shapes to recognize, locations to identify, and so forth. In addition, almost all cultures offer children counting systems (Zaslavsky, 1973), as well as games and activities that promote mathematical thinking.

At the beginning of kindergarten, children vary widely in mathematical knowledge (Klibanoff et al., 2006). As with language, children from middle-class families score much higher, on average, on tests of math achievement than do children from poor families. (Table 8.1 shows examples of questions used to test young children's mathematical comprehension [Klibanoff et al., 2006, Table 1].) However, children enrolled in full-time, high

INTERIM SUMMARY 8.5

Language, Literacy, and Mathematics in Early Childhood

Language Development	■ During early childhood, children progress from simple sentences to complex grammatical forms and a rich vocabulary.
	■ Children develop complex rule-governed language, and the sequence and the timetable of language development appear universal.
	■ At around age 2, young children's vocabularies begin to expand rapidly. A key to this growth is fast-mapping.
	■ Between 18 and 36 months, children began putting two words together in simple utterances called **telegraphic speech**.
	■ **Semantics** refers to the *meaning* of words and sentences, or the content of speech. In learning what words mean, children are also learning how their culture uses concepts to organize their perceptions of the world.
	■ A concept is a **mental representation** or category—a general notion that applies to many individual cases. Concepts help a young child simplify, sort, and group the many things in the environment.
	■ **Pragmatics** refers to the social uses and conventions of language.
Emergent Literacy	■ A typical 3-year-old knows how to hold a book and turn pages; listens when read to; understands the pictures in books; can name characters and features; and perhaps recognize a few letters.
	■ A typical 4-year-old can recite the alphabet and recognize some letters; relates stories to real life; enjoys rhymes and word play; and may pretend-write in play.
	■ A typical 5-year-old may track the print when being read a simple, familiar book; spontaneously talks about the content of story and information books; can identify all and write most letters; and recognizes and can spell some simple words but mostly uses invented spellings when writing.
	■ Adults can promote literacy by regularly reading to and reading with young children.
Mathematical Thinking	■ During early childhood, children demonstrate rudimentary understanding of fundamental mathematical concepts including magnitude, addition, and subtraction.
	■ There is a biological basis to the development of mathematical concepts, but experience also matters.

TABLE 8.1 Assessment Items

ITEM TYPE	INSTRUCTION	CHOICES
Ordinality	"Point to the one that has more."	7 dots, 5 dots
Cardinality	Written symbol: Child is shown card with the number "2" on it and is asked, "Which one of these goes with this one?" Oral number: "Point to four."	1, 2, 3, 4 dots 2, 3, 4, 5 objects
Calculation	"Johnny has one apple and his mommy gives him one more. Point to how many apples Johnny has now."	1, 2, 3, 4 apples
Shape names	"Point to the triangle."	Triangle, square, circle, rectangle
Understanding "half"	"Point to the one that shows half."	1/2, 1/4, 1/3, 2/3 of shaded circle
Recognizing conventional number symbols	"Point to the number."	B, e, 2, *

Source: From R.S. Klibanoff, S.C. Levine, J. Huttenlocher, M. Vasilyeva, & L.V. Hedges. Preschool children's mathematical knowledge: The effect of teacher "math talk." *Developmental Psychology,* 42, 2006, pp. 59–69, p. 62, Table 1, published by American Psychological Association. Reprinted with permission.

quality preschool programs show significant gains (Campbell et al., 2001). What matters most is that teachers weave "math talk" into their everyday routines (Klibanoff et al., 2006). We turn now to early education. (For a summary of this section, see "Interim Summary 8.5: Language, Literacy, and Mathematics in Early Childhood.")

CHILD CARE AND EARLY EDUCATION PROGRAMS

Clearly, parents play an important role in children's cognitive and language development, including memory, attention, conceptual development, and emerging literacy. But parents are not the only influence on their children's cognitive development. Most young children in the United States spend part of their day in other types of care.

Child Care in the United States

Families use child care for many reasons—to promote cognitive and academic skills, to promote social skills, and to provide supervision while parents are at work. As the number of women who work outside their home has increased, so has the number of children under age six who routinely spend time in nonparental care. Today almost 60 percent of small children—about 12.2 million in all—are in child care, ranging from 40 percent of infants to 80 percent of four- and five-year-olds (Mulligan, Brimhall, & West, 2005). Given the widespread use of child care, parents, educators, and social policy makers are asking about the impact of child care on children's development.

Child care comes in many shapes and sizes (Clarke-Stewart & Allhusen, 2005, Mulligan et al., 2005). See Figure 8.4. Arrangements include in-home care, child-care homes, and child-care centers and preschools. **In-home care** occurs in the child's own home. In some cases the caregiver is a relative (often a grandmother); in others she (the overwhelming majority of child-care providers are female) is a nanny or a babysitter.

in-home care Child care that occurs in the child's own home with a relative, nanny, or babysitter.

Nonparental child care	Description	Benefits	Limitations
In-home care	Child is cared for by relative or nonrelative (e.g., nanny, babysitter) in his or her own home	Familiar environment ▪	Caregivers are generally not professionally trained; fewer opportunities to interact with other children
Child-care home/ Family day care	Child is cared for in the home of an adult caregiver alone or in a small group	Home-like setting, with a "maternal" figure ▪ ▪	Caregiver may or may not have professional training
Child-care center	Children attend a program at a facility outside of the home (church, school, etc.) and are often divided into groups with same-age peers	Age-appropriate activities directed by staff who are generally trained in early childhood development ▪ ▪	In larger centers children tend to receive less individualized attention

Benefits key:

▪ Individual attention

▪ Opportunities for social interaction

▪ Professionally trained caregivers

FIGURE 8.4

Common Child-Care Arrangements in the United States

Child-care arrangements vary in the amount of individual attention and/or social interaction a child receives, and some settings are more likely to have trained professionals than others.

In-home care allows the child to remain in a familiar, safe place and the caregiver to provide individual attention to one or more siblings. It tends to provide more flexibility in terms of parents' work hours. But it does not provide professionally trained educators or frequent opportunities to interact with other children.

Child-care homes (also called *family day care*) are often chosen for infants and toddlers. The caregiver (often a neighbor) may take from one to six children into her home. Sometimes the parents and provider have a close, personal relationship. This arrangement provides the continuity of a home setting and a "mother figure," combined with the experience of interaction with other children, often of different ages. The provider may or may not have professional training in child care or plan activities around educational goals.

A third type of care, **child-care centers** and preschools, are attended by one-third of children who are five years or younger. Child-care centers are preferred by the majority of parents of children ages three to five (Clarke-Stewart & Allhusen, 2005). They may be operated by nonprofit organizations (such as a church), individual entrepreneurs, national chains, local school districts, or the federal government. Usually children are divided into classes or groups of same-age children, and activities are designed for their particular level of development. Staff members tend to have more education and special training in early childhood development than with in-home care and family day care. Centers are usually equipped with an array of blocks, books, dolls, costumes, puzzles, paints, and pets, and offer instruction as well as free play.

child-care homes Child-care settings in which a caregiver takes from one to six children into his/her home.

child-care centers Child-care settings generally run by trained staff in which children are divided into classes or groups of same-age children, and activities are designed for their particular level of development.

Child-Care Quality Matters

What is the quality of children's experiences in these different child-care settings, and do these experiences "matter" for the children's cognitive and social development? To

Well-designed centers and preschools offer age-appropriate activities and materials. Staff have specialized training in child development and education.

answer these questions, the National Institute of Child Health and Human Development (NICHD)—part of the National Institutes of Health—sponsored a detailed study of the child care of more than 1,300 children. Beginning shortly after birth and until the children entered kindergarten, mothers reported what types of child care their child attended and how much time the children spent in care each week. In addition, trained observers visited the child-care settings to evaluate the quality of the child care (NICHD ECCRN, 2000a, 2005a).

The researchers measured quality in two ways. **Structural quality** referred to characteristics of the child-care setting, such as the number of children per adult (the child/adult ratio), group size or how many children there were in the classroom or care setting, and the level of the caregivers' education and specialized training. The researchers also looked at children's experiences with caregivers, peers, and materials as indicators of **process quality** (NICHD ECCRN, 1996, 2000a; Vandell & Wolfe, 2000). High process-quality care is characterized by sensitive and warm interactions with adults, rich conversations, and a variety of stimulating materials and activities. Low process-quality care, in contrast, is characterized by disengaged, unresponsive caregivers, negative interactions with caregivers, and children wandering aimlessly.

structural quality Characteristics of child care settings such as group size, child-adult ratios, and caregiver education and training.

process quality An assessment of children's interactions and experiences in child-care settings. Higher process quality is characterized by more sensitive and caring interactions with adults, rich conversations, and stimulating materials and activities.

Structural quality and process quality are related (Lamb & Ahnert, 2006; Vandell, 2007; Vandell & Wolfe, 2000). The fewer children in a group or class, the less restrictive and more sensitive caregivers are to individual children's needs. The more education and training caregivers have, the better they organize material, the more age-appropriate the activities they offer, and the richer their language when they interact with the children.

Quality of child care is linked to children's cognitive development. Children who attend higher-quality child care—child care in which caregivers' are sensitive and stimulating—obtain higher scores on tests of memory, vocabulary, and math development. These higher scores are evident prior to kindergarten and carry over through elementary school (Belsky et al., 2007; NICHD ECCRN, 2005b). Poor quality child care is linked to poorer vocabulary, language comprehension, and memory development.

Unfortunately, as shown in Figure 8.5, high-quality child care in the United States is in short supply and mediocre and poor quality care is common (NICHD ECCRN, 1996, 2000a). According to the Study of Early Child Care (SECC), only 10 percent of the child care in the United States is excellent. Recently, the SECC investigators have developed a guide to help parents evaluate different child-care settings (NICHD ECCRN, 2001).

Effects of Different Types of Care Settings

Findings from the NICHD Study of Early Child Care indicate that experiences in different types of child care also matter. On average, children who attend child-care centers score higher on standardized tests of memory and preacademic skills at ages two three, and four and a half years than do children in in-home care and child-care homes (NICHD ECCRN, 2000b, 2002). This may be because centers include materials, conversations, and lessons related to emergent literacy and emergent mathematics.

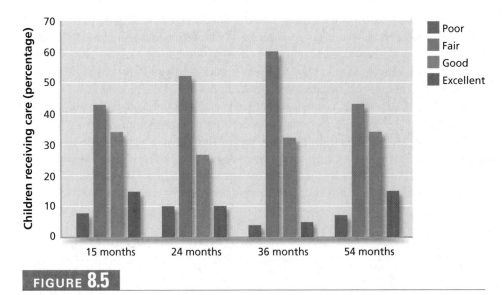

FIGURE **8.5**

Quality of Child Care in Infancy and Early Childhood

The large majority of child-care settings for children up to four and a half years old are only considered "fair" based on observations of process quality. Unfortunately, only a small percentage of child-care settings are considered to meet the criteria for being "excellent" (e.g., warm, sensitive caregivers, rich conversations, and stimulating materials).

Early Education Programs

Children of low-income families often start school with less advanced cognitive skills than children from higher-income families (Dearing, Berry, & Zaslow, 2006). According to one estimate, two-thirds of poor, urban children are not ready to learn when they enter first grade (Zigler, 1998). Can preschool programs help these economically disadvantaged children to catch up and start school on a more equal footing with their better-off peers? Several studies say that the answer is yes.

Two well-known demonstration projects—the Perry Preschool Project in Michigan (Schweinhart et al., 1993, 2005) and the Abecedarian Project in North Carolina (Campbell & Ramey, 1995; Ramey, Campbell, & Blair, 1998)—collected long-term information about the effects of high-quality preschool programs. Children entered the Perry Preschool half-day program at age three or four years. Children attended the Abecerdarian full-day program from shortly after birth to five years. Both studies used an experimental design to test the program effects. Participants from low-income families in the same neighborhoods were randomly assigned to an experimental group (who enrolled in the high-quality preschool program) or a control group (who received "care as usual" in their communities). The researchers followed these children from preschool to young adulthood.

Children in the high quality preschool programs, compared with children in the control groups, scored higher on IQ tests and on math and reading achievement tests than the control group in both elementary and high school. They were significantly less likely to be placed in special education classes or to be held back a year. They were more likely to attend a four-year college, and less likely to be arrested or to receive public assistance. At age twenty-seven, the Perry Preschool graduates had higher incomes and were more likely to own their own homes. Thus, both studies found that high-quality early education can have a *lasting* impact. However, the numbers of participants in each program were small and the interventions were mounted in only one location for each program, leaving open the possibility that they could not be "brought to scale"—that is, broadly implemented at other locations.

A third project, a study of the Chicago Parent-Child Centers, addressed these shortcomings in part (Reynolds et al., 2001). Arthur Reynolds and his colleagues have followed more than 1,500 children who lived in central Chicago. Roughly half of the children (the treatment group) attended federally funded early childhood programs; others (the control group) lived in the same neighborhoods but did not attend the programs.

The Chicago Parent-Child Centers taught basic skills in language and math; hired teachers with college degrees; and emphasized parent involvement. Children who attended the Parent-Child Centers programs achieved significantly higher scores than the control group in math and reading achievement at ages five, eight, and fourteen years. At age twenty, children in the treatment group were more likely to have completed high school. (See Figure 8.6 for comparisons of the results of the preceding projects.)

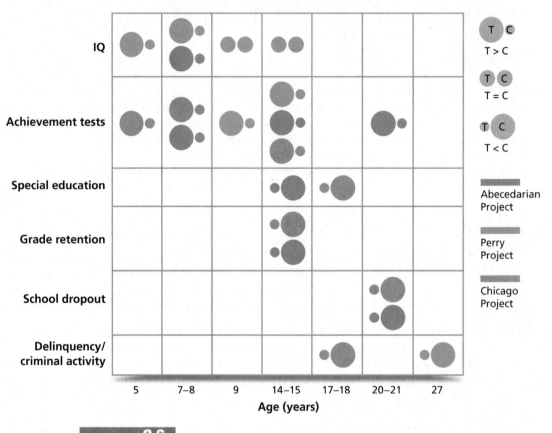

FIGURE **8.6**

The Impact of Early Intervention on Later Outcomes

This grid shows the positive results found from three early childhood intervention projects: The Abecedarian Project, Perry Preschool Project, and Chicago Parent-Child Centers. For each pair of circles, the one on the left shows the effect of attending a preschool program (e.g., the treatment group "T"), while the one on the right represents the control group ("C"), who did not attend preschool. Circles of equal size show that the outcome for both the treatment and control groups was equivalent; however, a larger circle indicates that one of the groups had higher scores in that particular category compared to the other group. On many outcomes, including IQ and achievement test scores, the preschool attendees outscored their control group peers, and these effects lasted well past childhood into early adulthood. Additionally, children who attended preschool were less likely than their peers to be in special education, drop out of high school, or become involved in delinquent activity.

Source: From W.T. Gormley, Jr., T. Gayer, D. Phillips & B. Dawson, The effects of universal Pre-K on cognitive development. *Developmental Psychology,* 41, 2005, 872–884, published by American Psychological Association. Reprinted with permission.

These three projects show that high-quality programs *can* make a difference for low-income children. The question is whether these goals can be achieved on a national scale. Project Head Start is one such national project.

Project Head Start **Head Start** was launched in 1965 as part of President Lyndon Johnson's War on Poverty. It is a comprehensive program, designed to involve low-income community members in children's education; to provide children with medical and dental care, as well as nutritious meals; and to help families and children to cope with social and emotional problems (Love et al., 2006). Head Start also seeks to foster learning (language, math readiness, and reading readiness) and good classroom behavior (paying attention, listening to teachers, taking turns, and following rules). The program serves more than 900,000 children nationwide at a cost of $6 billion each year (Love et al., 2006). To date, 21 million Americans are Head Start graduates.

The Head Start Impact Study is a large-scale experimental study of the effects of the program (Love et al., 2006). More than 2,500 three-year-olds were randomly assigned to either an experimental group who were enrolled in Head Start or the control group who received other services in the community, chosen by their parents. At the end of the year, three-year-olds who attended Head Start displayed better prereading skills in areas such as letter-word identification, letter naming, vocabulary, and color naming. The children's scores were still not up to the national average, but the achievement gap separating the children and their more affluent peers was lowered substantially. Compared with the control group, the Head Start children also had fewer behavior problems and were less hyperactive. There are plans to continue to follow these same children to see if these program effects are maintained as children go through elementary school and beyond.

Head Start is a comprehensive early intervention program that seeks to foster learning, good classroom behavior, and physical health of children who are economically disadvantaged.

Head Start A comprehensive preschool program for economically disadvantaged children.

Prekindergarten Programs In recent years, publicly funded prekindergarten (pre-K) programs have expanded to serve more young children (Gormley et al., 2005). Thirty-eight states now offer these pre-K programs, and more than 700,000 four-year-old children are enrolled nationwide. Most of the programs target economically disadvantaged children, but some states (Florida, Georgia, Massachusetts, New York, Oklahoma, and West Virginia) offer pre-K to all four-year-olds whose parents are interested (regardless of income). Pre-K programs that are open to all children (regardless of income) are called *universal programs*. Compared with day care, pre-K puts more emphasis on teaching the skills, knowledge, and behavior linked to success in elementary school.

To specifically measure the impact of prekindergarten programs, William Gormley and colleagues (2005) compared kindergartners who had completed one year of pre-K (the treatment group) to children who were just beginning their schooling (the control group). The study found pre-K programs had positive impacts on children's reading, math, and spelling skills (see Figure 8.7).

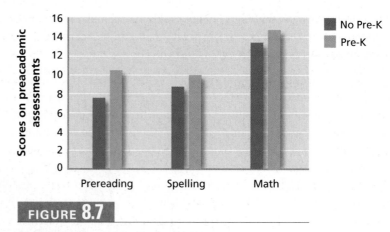

FIGURE **8.7**

Academic Benefits of Prekindergarten

Researchers found that children who attended prekindergarten programs had higher scores on reading, spelling, and math assessments when they started kindergarten compared with their peers who did not attend pre-K programs.

INTERIM SUMMARY 8.6

Child Care and Early Education Programs	
Child Care in the United States	■ Almost 60 percent of American children under 5 years are in routine nonparental child care.
	■ Arrangements include **in-home care**, **child-care homes**, and **child-care centers**.
Child Care Quality Matters	■ Quality of child care is measured with respect to structure and process.
	■ Structural quality is measured by group size, child-adult ratios, and caregiver education and training. High-quality environments have a lower child-adult ratio and better trained caregivers.
	■ Process quality is measured by assessing children's experiences in the child-care settings. Higher process-quality is characterized by more sensitive and caring interactions with adults, rich conversations, and stimulating materials and activities.
	■ Child-care quality is linked to children's vocabulary, memory, and mathematics.
Effects of Different Types of Care Settings	■ Formal child-care settings (preschools, pre-K) are linked to the cognitive and language development.
	■ On average, preschool-age children who attend high-quality child-care centers score higher on standardized tests of memory and preacademic skills.
Early Education Programs	■ Low-income children often begin elementary school with poorer preacademic skills in reading and math.
	■ Studies of **Project Head Start** and many pre-K programs suggest that these programs can also benefit the development of emergent literacy and mathematical thinking.

Hispanic, black, white, and Native American children all benefited from the pre-K program, as did children of all income groups. Further research is needed to learn exactly what goes on in pre-K classrooms, and whether these positive short-term effects have a lasting impact. (For a summary of this section, see "Interim Summary 8.6: Child Care and Early Education Programs.")

SUMMING UP AND LOOKING AHEAD

We began this chapter by looking at how young children think. Piaget saw early childhood as a transitional stage. Unlike babies, preoperational children use mental images and symbols. But unlike older children, they do not think logically. Contemporary developmental scientists have found that preschoolers are more sophisticated than Piaget believed, especially in familiar situations such as interactions with their parents and siblings. Studies of attention and memory show that cognitive development is more cumulative than stage-like.

One of the most impressive accomplishments during this period is language development. At age two children use words like signals—a juvenile Morse Code. By age six, they are fluent, chatting about past, present, future, and maybe. In between, children pick up new words, grammatical rules, and basic concepts naturally, without formal instruction. The same is true of fundamental mathematical concepts. Thus, children seem predisposed to use what culture provides.

Even so, the specific context matters. Learning language is a social process, with adults and older children providing scaffolding. Children whose parents talk *with* them—listening, prompting, and encouraging—advance faster than children whose parents talk *at* them. Today parents are not the only influence on cognitive development. Most children attend some form of preschool before age six. In addition to school readiness, high-quality day care, child centers, and pre-K promote social and emotional development, the subject to which we now turn.

HERE'S WHAT YOU SHOULD KNOW

Did You Get It?

After reading this chapter, you should understand the following:

- The characteristics of preoperational thinking, including both its strengths and limitations
- The ways in which Piaget's theory of cognitive development in early childhood has been criticized, amended, and extended
- What is meant by the "theory of mind"
- The main features of Vygotsky's sociocultural perspective on cognitive development

- The information-processing approach to cognitive development
- The ways in which memory and attention improve in early childhood
- How children progress in their language development and mathematical thinking in early childhood
- The impact of child care and early childhood education on children's development

Important Terms and Concepts

animism (p. 212)
attention (p. 220)
autobiographical memory (p. 222)

child-care centers (p. 233)
child-care homes (p. 233)
classification (p. 209)
conservation (p. 210)

continuous performance task (CPT) (p. 220)
deferred imitation (p. 209)
digit span task (p. 221)

egocentrism (p. 211)
episodic memory (p. 222)
fast-mapping (p. 225)
generic memory (p. 222)

guided participation (p. 217)
Head Start (p. 237)
impulsivity (p. 221)
in-home care (p. 232)
inner speech (p. 219)
long-term memory (p. 222)

overregulation (p. 226)
pragmatics (p. 228)
preoperational period (p. 208)
pretend play (p. 209)
process quality (p. 224)

reversibility (p. 209)
scaffolding (p. 216)
semantics (p. 226)
sensory memory (p. 221)
structural quality (p. 224)
symbol (p. 215)

telegraphic speech (p. 226)
theory of mind (p. 214)
working memory (p. 221)
zone of proximal development (ZPD) (p. 216)

Socioemotional Development in Early Childhood

At a university-based preschool, a four-year-old girl was playing in the housekeeping corner. Back and forth she went, from the play refrigerator where she selected several plastic "ingredients," to the play stove where she stirred a pot, to the cupboard where she gathered up dishes to set the dinner table. Periodically, she walked over to a cradle to cuddle a baby doll. All the while, a boy classmate sat at the table, becoming increasingly fidgety. Finally, he stood up, went to the play stove, and began to stir the pot. She rebuffed him in no uncertain terms. "Go back to the table. Mommies cook; daddies don't cook!" Looking downcast, the boy returned to the table. One might assume that the girl was re-creating her home life. She wasn't. Her mother, a medical intern, rarely cooked; her father was the family chef (Vandell, personal observation, 2006).

In early childhood, children become more themselves. They have their own ideas—including gender stereotypes that surprise their parents. Just as they are picky about their vegetables, so they have likes and dislikes for specific clothes, videos, people, and activities. Parents see two-year-olds as more capable and intentional or willful than they were as infants, and they begin expecting more obedience and cooperation. **Socialization** (Parsons & Bales, 1956)—the process of developing cultural values and rules for behavior—becomes more explicit. At the same time, as we saw in "Cognitive Development in Early Childhood," children begin spending more time with peers in preschools and other settings. Learning how to get along with other children is a central challenge. How they respond to new demands for emotional and social self-control is influenced by temperamental differences, cognitive competencies, cultural values, and ongoing social experiences with their parents, siblings, and peers.

In this chapter, we look at the major socioemotional developments of early childhood. First, we examine the child's changing sense of self, both with respect to how children evaluate and think about different aspects of who they are, and with respect to how much children like themselves. Next, we look at gender development—changes in children's beliefs and behaviors that reflect and influence their developing awareness of what it means to be a boy or a girl. Our third topic is emotional development; here we discuss how children learn about and learn to manage their feelings. Following this, we look at children's helpful and hurtful sides—their prosocial behavior and aggression. We conclude with an examination of children's experiences with parents, siblings, and peers in early childhood.

socialization The process of developing cultural values and rules for behavior.

THE DEVELOPMENT OF THE SELF

In early childhood, the child not only knows that he or she is someone, but begins to form a sense of *who* he or she is. The self is both a cognitive construction that reflects the child's level of mental development as well as a social construction that reflects the child's interactions and experiences with other people, especially parents (Harter,

2006; Thompson, 2006). The young child who has begun to form mental representations now has the tools to think about herself. She learns through social interaction what qualities and activities matter in her social world.

Self-Conceptions and Self-Esteem

Scientists study both self-conceptions and self-esteem. **Self-conceptions** are evaluative judgments about specific areas such as sports ("I am a fast runner"), physical appearance ("I am big"), and cognitive ability ("I am a good reader") (Harter, 2006), whereas **self-esteem** refers to more global assessment of self-worth—"I am special"; "I am worthless" (Coopersmith, 1967). More than a summary of self-conceptions, self-esteem sets the tone for inner experiences and outward behavior.

Young children's self-conceptions are composed primarily of concrete, observable characteristics: physical appearance (blue eyes), possessions (a kitty, a television), specific skills ("I know my ABCs"), and action ("Watch me!"). A social address (a big house and family) and preferences (for pizza) are also part of the picture. Here is one child's self-description:

> I am almost 3 years old and live in a big house with my mother and father and my brother, Jason, and my sister, Lisa. I have blue eyes and a kitty that is orange and a television in my own room. I know all of my ABCs, listen: ABC . . . XYZ. I can run real fast. I like pizza and have a nice teacher at preschool. I can count up to 100, want to hear me? I love my dog Skipper. I can climb to the top of the jungle gym, I'm not scared! I'm never scared! I am always happy. I have brown hair and I go to preschool. I'm really strong. I can lift this chair, watch me! (Harter, 2006, p. 513)

Conceptions at this age tend to be unrealistically positive. Susan Harter (2006), a scientist who studies early development of the self, sees this as normal. Young children fail Piaget's conservation test because they cannot consider two dimensions (such as the height and width of a beaker filled with water) simultaneously (see "Cognitive Development in Early Childhood"). In much the same way, they do not think of themselves as being good at some things but not at others, or as happy sometimes and sad other times. They tend to underestimate the difficulty of tasks and overestimate their own abilities, and they do not distinguish between their actual and ideal selves. All-or-none thinking ("I'm *never* scared! I'm *always* happy!") is typical. They have difficulty contrasting their own performance with others' performance, and they have difficulty differentiating between their actual performance and their desired performance (Harter, 2006). The young child's self-image is a bit disjointed, with separate bits of information pasted together. He isn't able yet to assemble the pieces in a coherent self-portrait. For example, in the preceding three-year-old's self-description, how is having brown hair related to going to preschool? Given this limitation, young children do not yet have an integrated, global representation of themselves. But the fact that they do not formulate or verbalize a sense of overall self-worth does not mean that self-esteem is unimportant in this period.

Young children's self-esteem, or feelings of global self-worth, reveals itself in behavior. According to a survey of preschool teachers, children high in self-esteem are

self-conception A cognitive construction that reflects the child's level of mental development and a social construction that reflects the child's interactions and experiences with other people.

self-esteem A global assessment of self-worth.

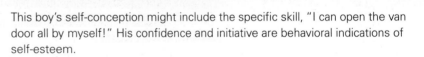
This boy's self-conception might include the specific skill, "I can open the van door all by myself!" His confidence and initiative are behavioral indications of self-esteem.

confident, curious, and independent (Harter, 2006). They trust their own ideas, take initiative and set goals independently, enjoy challenges, explore and ask questions, and eagerly try new things. They describe themselves in positive terms and take pride in their accomplishments. They also adapt well to change or stress. They adjust to transitions (e.g., from home care to preschool), persevere in the face of frustration, and are able to cope with criticism or teasing. In contrast, children low in self-esteem lack confidence, curiosity, and independence. Uncertain about their own ideas, they rarely take the initiative and rarely explore or ask questions. In the face of challenges, they withdraw, hanging back, sitting apart, and watching only. They describe themselves in negative terms and do not take pride in their accomplishments, even when praised. They have difficulty adjusting to stress or change, reverting to immature behavior during transitions and giving up in the face of frustration, criticism, or teasing.

One surprise in Harter's survey of teachers was that self-esteem is not related to actual competence at this age. Children who are high in self-esteem are not necessarily more accomplished than their peers at cognitive skills (knowing their ABCs), playground prowess (climbing to the top of the jungle gym), or in other areas. Nonetheless, they feel good about themselves. Likewise, children who are low in self-esteem are not necessarily behind their peers in specific domains (though they may be more hesitant to "show off"). This suggests that the origins of confidence in early childhood are not directly linked to abilities, but lie elsewhere.

Initiative Versus Guilt

initiative versus guilt The third stage in Erikson's theory of psychosocial development during which mastery of new skills becomes a primary goal.

Erik Erikson (1963) identified another aspect of the developing sense of self in early childhood—the development of children's feelings of **initiative versus guilt**. Mastering new skills—from learning to count to climbing up a slide—becomes a primary goal. Young children want to do things for themselves. Physical and brain maturation enable the young child to attempt activities that were beyond his or her capabilities before.

Adults react to these changes in different ways. Erikson (1963) observed that children whose parents accept and encourage their efforts, without being pushy or interfering, eagerly try new activities. These children, according to Erikson, develop a sense of themselves as capable of initiative. Children whose parents repeatedly restrict, ridicule, or criticize their efforts give up more quickly and blame themselves for failing. These children, according to Erikson, develop a sense of themselves as failures or unworthy and feel guilty.

As was noted, children do not engage in much social comparison at this age—that is, they do not judge themselves by what their peers can do. Rather, they see themselves through the looking glass of their parents' and other adults' eyes (Cooley, 1902). Young children's sense of self is rooted in their everyday interactions with adults who are important in their lives—especially their mothers and fathers, but also grandparents, other family members, and child-care providers (Thompson, 2006).

Internal Working Models

internal working model A child's evaluation of his or her worth as a person, growing out of attachment relationships.

Attachment researchers also have studied young children's sense of self, in this case, children's **internal working models** of the self (Bowlby, 1982; Bretherton & Mulholland, 1999). Similar to Erikson, these researchers see the quality of the parent-child relationship as central to the young child's developing sense of self. But attachment researchers see the internal working models as growing out of attachment relationships. When parents are sensitive, supportive, warm, and emotionally available, children are more likely to become securely attached. They also develop a working model of self as a person of value who is worthy of love. Conversely, when parents are rejecting, remote, or interfering, children are likely to develop insecure attachments. Their internal working model of self is one who is unworthy of love.

Still, these models are *working* models, according to attachment theorist John Bowlby. Based on their ongoing experiences with their parents, children's models of self can and do change. If parent-child relations worsen—due to loss of income, marital conflict, maternal depression, or other factors— children may move from a secure to an insecure attachment or to a disorganized attachment, and a more negative, disjointed and incoherent sense of self (Thompson, 2006). If the quality of parent-child interaction improves—because the family's financial situation improves, marital relations are better, or another helpful adult joins the household, for example—children can move from an insecure to a secure attachment, which also is manifested in a more positive, coherent, and articulated internal working model of the self. (See Figure 9.1.)

Abused and severely neglected children provide an extreme example of problematic internal working models. Abused children have less self-awareness and less coherent self-concepts than do other children (Toth et al., 2000). Much as young children whose parents are generally supportive tend to think of themselves as "all good," children who are maltreated may have a more fragmented and disjointed sense of self. They also may come to think of themselves as "all bad" (Harter, 2006).

Family Stories

Family narratives or stories that are told and retold also contribute to the child's developing sense of him- or herself (Fivush, 2001). At first, parents include children by telling stories about them. "When you were a baby . . . ." Gradually, children assume a more active role. The construction of autobiographical memories is a collaborative process, with adults providing the scaffolding (see "Cognitive Development in Early Childhood"). By asking questions and providing hints ("Who was there?" "What did you do?" "Was there a birthday cake?"), parents help children to develop narratives for themselves. Such memories anchor and enrich a child's self-concept. When parents ignore or dismiss children's experiences, the result can be an "impoverished self" with no grounding in the past and few hopes for the future (Harter, 1999).

In telling and listening to stories, children acquire knowledge about their culture and their place in it—what people consider worth

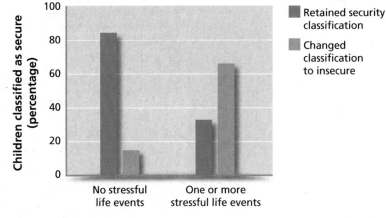

FIGURE 9.1

Stability and Change of Attachment Classifications from 12 Months to 21 Years

Experience can play a role in the stability of attachment classifications. In one study, participants' attachment security was assessed when they were twelve months old and again when they were twenty-one years old. When no stressful life experiences occurred, the majority of people who were securely attached at twelve months continued to have secure attachment relationships as young adults. However, two-thirds of those who had been classified as secure as infants but who experienced one or more stressful life events were classified as insecure in early adulthood.

Source: From Everett Waters, Susan Merrick, Dominique Treboux, Judith Crowell, and Leah Albersheim, *Child Development,* May/June 2000, Vol. 71, Number 3, pp. 684–689. Copyright © 2000 by Blackwell Publishing Ltd. Reproduced with permission of Blackwell Publishing Ltd.

By asking questions, telling family stories, and providing their own comments, parents help children to develop personal narratives as well as acquire knowledge about their culture and their place in the world.

INTERIM SUMMARY 9.1

The Development of the Self

Self-Conceptions and Self-Esteem	■ **Self-conceptions** are evaluative judgments about specific areas. Young children's self-conceptions are composed primarily of concrete, observable characteristics. They tend to be unrealistically positive.
	■ **Self-esteem** refers to a more global assessment of self-worth. In early childhood, self-esteem is manifested by behavior. Children high in self-esteem tend to be confident, curious, and independent. Children low in self-esteem are less confident, curious, and independent.
Initiative Versus Guilt	■ Erikson's third stage in which mastery of new skills is the primary challenge.
	■ Children whose parents accept and encourage their efforts without being pushy or interfering are more likely to develop initiative.
Internal Working Models	■ Attachment researchers argue that internal working models are developed in conjunction with attachment relationships.
	■ When parents are sensitive, responsive, and accepting, children are more likely to become securely attached and to develop an internal working model of self who is worthy of love.
	■ When parents are rejecting, remote, and interfering, children are likely to develop insecure attachment relationships. Their working model of self is one who is unworthy, unloved, and incompetent.
Family Stories	■ Family stories that are told and retold also play a role in children's developing sense of self. In telling and listening to stories, children acquire knowledge about their culture—what people consider worth learning and remembering, what different events mean, etc.

learning and remembering (or best forgotten), what different events mean, and how their own experiences are both personal and shared, making them both unique individuals and members of a cultural community (Gauvain, 2001). Families in all cultures talk about children's misbehavior, but the message varies (Miller et al., 1997). The Taiwanese see impolite or improper acts as bringing dishonor on the family. Irish Americans are more likely to wink: A mischievous child is considered "spunky." Parents' everyday comments to children—"You're a big girl now," "You're so smart," "Big boys don't cry"—reinforce cultural norms and values and provide a grounding for the child's self-concept within his or her particular culture (Nelson, 1993). (For a summary of this section see "Interim Summary 9.1: The Development of the Self.")

GENDER DEVELOPMENT

Being a boy or a girl has profound implications for young children everywhere (Ruble, Martin, & Berenbaum, 2006). Virtually all cultures expect males and females to differ in many ways: appearance, mannerisms, temperament, dreams, and values. Their activities at home, at school, and in their communities often differ. Expectations for the two sexes also vary from one culture to another, although most cultures follow what we consider "typical" gender roles (Maccoby, 1999).

Gender Awareness, Identity, and Constancy

How do children come to think of themselves as a boy or girl? Gender awareness develops early. Even before they can walk and talk, infants discriminate between males and females (Martin, Ruble, & Szkrybalo, 2002). Two-year-olds choose the correct picture when a researcher asks them to select a boy or girl, man or woman (Campbell, Shirley, & Candy, 2004). They also look longer at gender-inconsistent pictures, such as a man putting on makeup, as if they are puzzled (Serbin, Poulin-Dubois, & Eichstedt, 2002).

By age two-and-a-half years, if not sooner, most children can label themselves and others by sex (Fagot & Leinbach, 1989). This is the beginning of a **gender identity**: a person's sense of the self as male or female (Ruble et al., 2006). But gender is only a label at this age; only "skin deep." Young children also believe that a girl can become a boy if she dresses and acts like a boy.

Not until age six or seven do most children understand **gender constancy**: that gender is permanent and immutable, that "I am a boy and always will be a boy" (Kohlberg, 1969). Preschoolers believe that one can choose to grow up as a mommy or a daddy. The development of gender constancy parallels the development of conservation. Children come to realize that just as the amount of water remains the same when it is poured from a short, wide beaker into a tall, thin one, a woman remains a woman when she dresses in overalls and a hard hat and works in construction.

A small proportion of young children (2–5%) display gender identity disorders of childhood (GIDC). Beginning in the preschool years, these children express strong wishes to be the other sex and engage in cross-sex behavior (Zucker, 2004). For example, a boy with GIDC wants to go to preschool in a pink dress and pigtails, plays with dolls, prefers girls as playmates, and likes to be called "she." How to respond to the children is controversial (Brown, 2006). Some parents, educators, and mental health professionals advocate allowing these children to "be themselves" and follow their inclinations (to promote security and self-esteem), whereas others recommend the opposite (if only to protect them from social rejection). No one has identified the cause of GIDC. It's also rare. Still, it illustrates the degree to which children develop their own ideas about gender identity.

gender identity A person's sense of self as male or female.

gender constancy The concept that gender is permanent and immutable.

Behavioral Differences

By age three, most boys and girls are moving in different directions toward gender typical—often stereotypical—behavior. These differences are seen in their choices of toys, their play styles, and their playmates (Ruble et al., 2006). They spend most of their time playing with children of their own sex (Fabes, Hanish, & Martin, 2007; Lederberg et al., 1986) and generally have a higher opinion of their own than of the opposite sex (Ruble & Martin, 1998). Young children tend to avoid toys that are linked to the opposite sex (Emmerich & Shepard, 1982).

Boys' and girls' styles of play also differ as seen in Figure 9.2. On average, boys are more physically active, especially with groups of other boys in familiar settings (Fabes et al., 2007). They engage in more rough-and-tumble play, with more attempts to establish dominance. In observations conducted in many cultures, young boys tend to play farther away from adults and so with less supervision (Maccoby, 1999).

	Girls	Boys
Group dynamics	Cooperative	Competitive
Physical aggression	Lower	Higher
Number of playmates	Two or three	Larger groups
Role playing	Household roles, romance	Heroes, combat
Toys	Dolls, dress-up, kitchen sets	Action figures, toy vehicles
Proximity to adults	Closer	Farther away

FIGURE 9.2

Gender Comparisons in Children's Play

Gender differences are often seen in play during early childhood, including types of play activities, number of playmates, and levels of physical aggression.

Young children spend most of their time playing with same-sex peers, often engaging in gender stereotypic activities.

Boys, on average, are more physically aggressive than girls (Dodge, Coie, & Lynam, 2006)—a subject to which we will return later in this chapter.

In general, preschool boys like transportation toys, construction sets like Lego, and action figures. Their fantasy play revolves around heroes, combat, and danger (Ruble et al., 2006). In keeping with these themes, boys spend more time than girls playing video games (Huston et al., 1999).

In contrast, on average, girls tend to play in pairs or threesomes, rather than in large groups (Fabes et al., 2007). They are more likely to play indoors or close to home; to choose quieter activities, such as drawing or pretend cooking; and to seek adult approval while they play (Maccoby, 1999). Compared with boys, their play is more cooperative than competitive (Eisenberg & Fabes, 1998).

Girls play more with dolls, tea and kitchen sets, and dress up. Their fantasy play often involves household roles, glamour, and romance. Today's princess craze makes some mothers cringe (Orenstein, 2006). They want to raise their daughters to believe that they can be anything they want to be. But what many of their daughters aspire to, at ages three, four, and five, is to be princesses, with as many "girlie girl" accessories as possible. At preschool many make a beeline for the dress-up area to deck themselves out in tulle and tiaras.

Sources of Gender Differences

Where do these gender differences come from? The puzzle is that parents who don't conform to gender stereotypes themselves, and who actively try to raise their children in nonstereotyped ways, often find that their preschoolers adopt—and even insist on—stereotypes (as in the example at the beginning of this chapter). Why, then, are sex differences so pronounced in early childhood? Developmental scientists are finding multiple factors—biological differences, socialization, cognition—are playing a role.

Biological Differences Children's sex is determined at conception by a gene on one of the 23 pairs of chromosomes (see "Nature with Nurture"). Girls have two X chromosomes, and boys have one X and one Y chromosome, with gene SRY on the Y chromosome (Ruble et al., 2006). At around the sixth or seventh week of gestation, SRY initiates the development of testes in males (Grumbach, Hughes, & Conte, 2002). From this point, physical differentiation is largely dependent on hormones, particularly

androgens, which control the development of masculine characteristics (the most important androgen is the hormone, **testosterone**, secreted by testicles in males and ovaries in females). Males have larger concentrations of androgens, which cause the male external genitalia to develop seven to eight weeks prenatally.

Hormones also contribute to sexual differentiation of the brain and behavior (Wallen, 2005). Most of the research on differentiation has been conducted by manipulating hormone levels in animals at different developmental periods. But much also has been learned by "natural experiments" of children and adults whose hormone levels were atypical for their sex. These natural experiments occur as a result of genetic diseases or mothers' use of drugs during pregnancy.

One example is congenital adrenal hyperplasia (CAH)—a condition caused by fetal exposure to androgens early in pregnancy. In early childhood, girls with untreated CAH show a strong preference for traditionally male toys, male playmates, and male activities (Pasterski et al., 2005). The girls like to play with trucks, are not very interested in dolls or babies, and enjoy rough, outdoor play, whereas their unaffected sisters prefer typically female play. In one study, 50 percent of the girls with CAH chose a transportation toy to keep, whereas none of the control girls did (Berenbaum & Synder, 1995). Parents' attempts to encourage CAH girls to engage in more feminine activities are often unsuccessful. CAH overrides socialization (Pasterski et al., 2005). Clearly, hormones play a role in gender differences, but they are not the full story. Read on.

Sex differences also may lie, in part, in "his" and "her" brains. At age five, boys' brains have relatively more white matter in the cerebral cortex. There also are some differences in the hypothalamus and amygdala, areas of the brain related to emotion and emotional regulation (Ruble et al., 2006). Brain scans of preschool girls suggest greater neuronal density and a relatively larger **corpus callosum**, the brain structure that connects the brain's left and right hemispheres (Baron-Cohen, 2004). These areas of the brain are linked to physical activity, self-regulation, and effortful control, consistent with the argument that brain differences are contributing to behavioral differences. However, because the brain is changing in early childhood, it also could be that differential experiences are influencing brain development.

Gender Socialization Consciously or unconsciously, subtly and not so subtly, parents and teachers give boys and girls different messages (Gelman, Taylor, & Nguyen, 2004; Ruble et al., 2006). Mothers talk more to their daughters than to their sons, especially about emotions (Fivush et al., 2000). When girls are playing, mothers provide directions and suggestions, and they respond positively when asked for help. Parents allow—and expect—boys to be more independent. A boy who often asks for help may be seen as "whiny"; one who follows his mother around, as "clinging." With girls, parents emphasize sharing; with boys, parents are more likely to support competition (Keenan & Shaw, 1997).

Girls also are given more approval than boys are for dancing, dressing up, playing with dolls, following parents around, and asking for help, and more disapproval for jumping and manipulating objects (Lytton & Romney, 1991). Boys receive more encouragement for running, climbing, wrestling, and playing with male-typical construction and transportation toys, and more discouragement for engaging in activities considered feminine. In general, parents—especially fathers—seem to be more actively and personally concerned about appropriate sex role behavior in boys than in girls (Ruble et al., 2006). A boy playing dress up with feminine clothes is more likely to be discouraged than a girl who dresses up in the same clothes.

During everyday interaction—reading a book, going to a store, or just chatting—parents contribute to **gender socialization** by providing gender labels ("That's a girl"; "You're a big boy"), by contrasting males and females ("Is that a girl job or a

androgens Hormones that control the development of masculine characteristics, generally found in higher levels in males than females.

testosterone An androgen secreted by the testicles (in males) or ovaries (in females).

corpus callosum The connection between the two halves or hemispheres of the brain.

gender socialization Social norms conveyed to children that concern characteristics associated with being male or female.

boy job?"; "How is my little princess today?" vs. "What's happening, champ?"), and by giving approval for children's stereotyped statements ("That's right, daddies like football") (Gelman et al., 2004). Grandparents, teachers, and strangers do the same. But adults are not the only influence on the development of ideas about gender.

Carol Martin and Richard Fabes (2001) find that interactions with peers also contribute to gender socialization. In their observations of young children on the playground and in preschool classrooms, they found gender differences increased across the school year. Boys became more physically active and participated in more **rough and tumble play** (physically vigorous play such as chasing, jumping and play fighting that is accompanied by shared smiles and laughter) as the school year progresses, whereas the girls became less physically active. Additionally, as the school year progresses, the boys spent more of the time playing in larger groups with other boys. The girls spent more time playing in close proximity to the teachers. Those preschool children who spent more time playing with same-sex peers early in the school year then had greater increases in gender-typed behaviors later in the school year.

Gender Schema Children are not merely passive recipients of biological and social influences. They also are actively constructing their own ideas of what it means to be male or female (Bussey & Bandura, 1999; Martin et al., 2002). **Gender schemas** are mental networks of beliefs and expectations about males versus females. As children develop a gender identity, they begin to classify people, activities, and interests as male or female. Children first become aware of stereotypic differences in appearance, then possessions, and then behavior.

As noted earlier, knowledge of activities typically associated with gender increases rapidly between ages three and five. Once children have gender schemas they try to match their own behavior to what boys and girls in their culture are supposed to do. They also use gender schemas to organize incoming information. Focusing on external signs of gender, they try to fit everyone into one or the other category. At this stage they tend to see deviations from gender stereotypes as "bad" behavior.

Gender stereotyping peaks between ages five and six, and then becomes more flexible in middle childhood (Ruble et al., 2006). One reason for this early rigidity may be that young children have not yet grasped gender constancy. If sex depends on appearances, it makes sense to want to look and act as feminine or masculine as

rough and tumble play Physically vigorous behaviors such as chasing, jumping, and play fighting that are accompanied by shared smiles and laughter.

gender schema A mental network of beliefs and expectations about males versus females.

INTERIM SUMMARY 9.2

Gender Development	
Gender Awareness, Identity, and Constancy	■ By age 2 1/2 years, most children can label themselves and others by sex, which is the beginning of a **gender identity**.
	■ Around age 6 or 7 years, children understand **gender constancy**—that gender is permanent and immutable. This understanding parallels the development of conservation.
Behavioral Differences	■ By age 3, styles of play often differ. Boys tend to play in larger groups, be more physically active, and be more physically aggressive than girls.
	■ Preferred toys and activities also differ.
Sources of Gender Differences	■ Biology, socialization, and cognition all play a role in gender development.
	■ **Gender schemas** are mental networks of beliefs and expectations about males versus females.

possible, dressing in spangles or playing with toy sabers to reinforce one's female or male identity. Once children master gender constancy—when they understand that gender is not altered by superficial changes in appearance—they are more able to accept that males and females can *share* traits and activities. (For a summary of this section see "Interim Summary 9.2: Gender Development.")

EMOTIONAL DEVELOPMENT

Emotional development in early childhood is marked by advances in children's awareness of their own and others' emotional states and in children's ability to regulate their emotional expressions (Saarni et al., 2006). We examine these advances in turn.

Understanding Emotions

Being aware of one's own emotions and the emotions of others are a step in the direction of emotional understanding. Between ages

Self-conscious emotions such as pride develop in early childhood.

two and three, children begin to label their own and other people's subjective feelings (Bloom, 1998). Preschoolers generally are able to identify their peers' facial expressions of emotion such as sad, happy, mad, surprised, or afraid (Fabes et al., 1991). The number of emotional terms in their vocabulary increases (Ridgeway, Waters, & Kuczaj, 1985). And they begin to identify the object or target of their feeling: "I'm mad *at* you"; "I'm afraid *of* dogs"; "I'm happy *about* the party" (Harris, 2000).

Over early childhood, young children also develop a more accurate and nuanced understanding of the causes and consequences of emotion. For example, they predict that an angry child is more likely to hit, whereas a happy child will share (Lagattuta, Wellman, & Flavell, 1997). Like self-awareness, other-awareness is grounded in cognitive advances. To understand other people's feelings, children need to comprehend that other people have intentions, beliefs, and subjective experiences of their own; that certain people tend to be more positive or negative than others; and what situations commonly evoke emotions (Saarni et al., 2006).

Secondary or **self-conscious emotions**, including pride, guilt, shame, and embarrassment, develop in early childhood (Lewis, 2000). Self-conscious emotions are complex. They require an objective sense of the self as distinct from others; awareness of standards for behavior; an evaluation of one's own performance in terms of these standards; and a sense of responsibility for success or failure. In some cases an emotion is linked to specific acts: "I did a good job" (pride) or "I did a bad thing" (guilt). In other cases the emotion is more global and linked to self-esteem: "I am a bad person" (shame).

Lewis and Ramsay (2002) identified two types of embarrassment in four-year-olds. One type occurs when the child is an object of positive attention, such as when teachers or parents provide public recognition of a new accomplishment. (In one experiment, for example, these researchers induced embarrassment by having children dance and bang on a tambourine by themselves while others were watching them.) Another type of self-evaluative embarrassment occurs when a child fails a task.

self-conscious emotion An emotion that involves evaluation of oneself, such as embarrassment or pride.

Children show elevated cortisol, indicating a stress reaction, only with the second type of embarrassment.

Individual Differences in Emotional Understanding

Individual children vary in their ability to recognize and understand emotions. Some children display considerable **emotional intelligence**, defined as the ability to monitor one's own and others' feelings and to use that information to guide thinking and action (Salovey & Mayer, 1990). Children who demonstrate emotional intelligence are rated as more likable by their peers (Denham et al., 1990; Walden & Knieps, 1996). Indeed, this is a key factor in their popularity. Children who are biased toward seeing anger in ambiguous situations are rated as more hostile and are often avoided by peers (Barth & Bastiani, 1997). Socially isolated, they have fewer opportunities to observe and practice emotional self-regulation, which compounds the problem.

Some evidence indicates that young girls are better than young boys at decoding emotions (Stipek, 1995). Part of the reason may be that mothers spend more time talking with daughters than with sons about emotion states and feeling, or that girls spend more time than boys do in joint pretend play, which requires negotiation and compromise (Youngblade & Dunn, 1995). Or perhaps subtle differences in brain functioning lead girls to tune into emotions as well as actions, bring up the topic more in conversation, and choose games that allow them to "try on" other perspectives.

During early childhood, family conversations play a key role in emotional socialization (Thompson, 2006). Young children talk with family members about expectations of how they will feel and how they did feel. When parents use scaffolding, children learn the deeper meanings of emotion labels. "Why did you hit him? Were you *angry*? Why?" "How would you *feel* if someone tore up your painting?" "It was *sad* that Kendra tripped during the school play. I remember being so *embarrassed* when that happened to me once. How would you feel?" This sort of conversation draws attention not only to the child's feeling but also to others' emotions. When mothers talk about feelings and negotiate compromises (thus acknowledging the child's point of view) with their two-and-a-half-year-olds, the children are more advanced in emotional understanding (Laible, 2004). Talking with parents also introduces children to cultural expectations (a subject to which we will return).

In the absence of warm, supportive family relations, emotional understanding may be impaired. Young children who are exposed to physical abuse and family violence are hypervigilant, always on the alert for signs of danger (Pollak et al., 2005) as seen in Figure 9.3. They have difficulty understanding social cues and controlling their emotions. They interpret neutral behavior as hostile and often react aggressively. As we discussed in "Physical Development in Early Childhood," this can become a self-fulfilling prophecy. As a result of this behavior, children may be avoided by peers and singled out by teachers. Recent findings in neuroscience suggest that these social experiences can reorganize and alter brain functioning, which may explain, in part, the long-lasting effects of child abuse (Pollak et al., 2005).

emotional intelligence The ability to monitor one's own and others' feelings and to use that information to guide thinking and action.

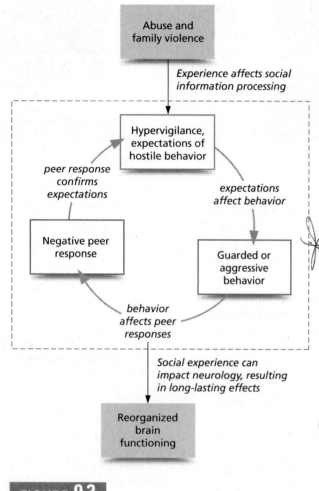

FIGURE 9.3

Links Between Experiences of Abuse in Childhood and Later Brain Functioning

Abuse and family violence during childhood can affect the way a child perceives social information. Children may become hypervigilant and perceive neutral behavior as hostile, which can affect how they react to their peers. Other children will respond accordingly, confirming the child's initial expectations for hostile behavior. Over time, this cycle of self-fulfilling prophecies can lead to the reorganization of neural pathways in the brain.

Children who have been neglected also have difficulty discriminating between different emotions (Pollak & Kistler, 2002; Pollak et al., 2001). We mentioned in an earlier chapter the Romanian children who were institutionalized in orphanages from infancy, where they had little interaction with others. Tested as preschoolers, after they had been adopted by middle-class U.S., Canadian, or British families, the Romanian orphans had problems identifying facial expressions or scenes as happy, sad, or fearful (Camras et al., 2006).

Young children whose mothers are chronically depressed have other difficulties (Zahn-Waxler & Radke-Yarrow, 1990). They may experience too much empathy and too many feelings of responsibility. Children of depressed mothers sometimes hold themselves responsible for their mothers' sadness. They express more shame and guilt and apologize more often than other children.

Regulating Emotions

Emotional regulation refers to the ability to inhibit, enhance, maintain, and modulate emotional arousal to accomplish a goal (Eisenberg, Fabes, & Spinrad, 2006). We see important gains in early childhood in children's emotional regulation. Parents and caregivers play key roles in helping infants and toddlers to regulate their emotions. In comparison, five-year-olds have more self-control. They can be frustrated without striking out; happy without going over the top; frightened but still willing to approach a new situation. When children can "down-regulate" or de-escalate internal arousal, they are better able to negotiate solutions to conflicts with parents and peers (Gottman, Katz, & Hoover, 1997). They are also more flexible in approaching situations they once feared.

Effortful control—the ability to withhold a dominant response in order to make a nondominant response, to engage in planning, and to regulate reactive tendencies—contributes to young children's ability to modulate their emotions (Kochanska, Coy, & Murray, 2001; Rothbart & Bates, 2006). With effortful control, children can inhibit some actions (such as touching an attractive, but forbidden toy) and can perform actions they would prefer *not* to do (such as putting away their toys). Effortful control enables children to think about others' feelings as well as their own without being overwhelmed by their emotional reactions. A lack of effortful control is linked to **externalizing problems** such as impulsively striking out at people or objects that the child sees as standing in his way (Eisenberg et al., 1994).

The development of effortful control in early childhood reflects children's individual predispositions or temperament, as well as their social experiences (Rothbart & Bates, 2006). Researchers have found continuity between early differences in infants' ability to focus and sustain attention and effortful control when the children are preschoolers (Vaughn, Kopp, & Krakow, 1984; Kochanska & Knaack, 2003), suggesting that effortful control is a temperamental dimension rooted in early emotional reactivity and control systems (Rothbart & Bates, 2006).

But this is only part of the story. The association between poor self-regulation and externalizing behaviors is greater when children experience hostile and intrusive parenting (Rubin et al., 2003) (see Figure 9.4), whereas positive parenting (to be discussed in more detail later in this chapter) helps to offset the negative effects of poor regulation (Bates & Pettit, 2007). So, among children who have poor self-regulation skills, those whose parents are hostile and intrusive are more likely to "act out," compared with children whose parents provide authoritative parenting that combines warmth with firm control.

Emotions in a Cultural Context

Emotional regulation occurs in a cultural context. In contemporary mainstream American culture, expressing and talking about one's emotions is encouraged. But the idea that the open expression and discussion of emotions is healthy is not universal

emotional regulation The ability to inhibit, enhance, maintain, and modulate emotional arousal to accomplish a goal.

effortful control The ability to withhold a dominant response in order to make a nondominant response, to engage in planning, and to regulate reactive tendencies.

externalizing problems Psychosocial problems that are manifested in outward symptoms, such as aggression or noncompliance.

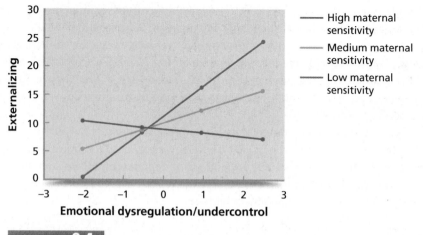

FIGURE 9.4

The Importance of Maternal Sensitivity for Children with Emotional Regulation Difficulties

Children who have trouble regulating their emotions often show higher levels of aggressive, or "externalizing," behavior than their peers. Rubin et al. (2003) find that children who score high on a measure of emotional dysregulation have lower levels of externalizing behavior if their mothers are sensitive. Children who have difficulty regulating their emotions show higher levels of externalizing behaviors if their mothers are hostile, controlling, and insensitive.

Source: From K.H. Rubin, K.B. Burgess, K.M. Dwyer & P.D. Hastings. Predicting preschoolers' externalizing behaviors from toddler temperament, conflict, and maternal negativity. *Developmental Psychology,* 39, 2003, pp. 164–176, published by American Psychological Association. Reprinted with permission.

(Trommsdorff, 2006). In some cultures, the display of emotions (especially anger) is considered rude, immature, or even deranged (Kitayama, 2001).

Much of the cross-cultural research on emotional development has focused on the differences between *individualistic* (usually Western) cultures that emphasize self-development and *collectivist* (usually Asian) cultures that emphasize social harmony (Trommsdorff, 2006). Whereas individualistic cultures value independence, collectivist cultures value *inter*dependence; the self is defined less in terms of inner, personal traits than in terms of social relations and behavior.

These different models of the self have implications for the cultural meaning of certain emotions. In individualistic cultures, for example, pride is considered a positive emotion. Pride signals individual accomplishment, validates the independent self, and is associated with feelings of well-being (Mesquita & Karasawa, 2004). In individualistic cultures, shame is seen as a negative emotion, a blow to self-esteem. In collectivist cultures, however, pride is linked to social disengagement and dishonor, and shame is considered a positive emotion. Shame signals group involvement, striving for conformity, and motivation to perform better in the future (Trommsdorff, 2006).

Culture shapes socialization (Wang, 2006; Wang & Fivush, 2005). Consider the comparison in Table 9.1 of a conversation between a European American mother and her preschooler versus a Chinese mother and her preschooler. As a rule, European American mothers encourage children to "share" their emotions, in the belief that burying emotions is harmful. Chinese mothers see emotional displays as disruptive and believe that they should be controlled (Wang, 2006). As Table 9.1 illustrates, Chinese mothers' conversations with children focus on the proper way to behave, obedience, and the consequences of misbehavior. In different ways, though, all parents become concerned with moral development during this period.

As we will see in the next section, young children's emotional understanding and self-regulation set the stage for other areas of development in early childhood: pro-social behaviors, conscience, and the control of aggression. (For a summary of this section see "Interim Summary 9.3: Emotional Development.")

TABLE 9.1 Two Cultures, Two Conversations

EURO-AMERICAN MOTHER-CHILD DYAD	CHINESE MOTHER-CHILD DYAD
M: . . . Do you remember doing some crying?	M: . . . Do you remember why Dad spanked you last time?
C: Why did I cry?	C: Chess!
M: I'm not quite sure why you cried. But do you remember where you were?	M: Why chess? What did you do with chess?
C: I cried because I had any, no any balloon.	C: Not obedient!
M: They had no balloon. But then, you were also crying because, did you not want to go home?	M: How were you not being obedient?
C: Yeah.	C: (I) threw the pieces on the floor.
M: Where were you?	M: All over the floor, right? And did you do it on purpose?
C: At Stewart Park!	C: Umm. I'll be careful next time!
M: (Laughs). You did cry a lot at Stewart Park, but, um, this was in Joe's parking lot. Do you remember Joe's Restaurant parking lot? Do you remember standing by the door and crying?	M: Right! That's why Dad spanked your bottom, right? . . . Did you cry then?
C: Yeah	C: (I) cried.
M: You do?	M: Did it hurt?
C: Yeah.	C: It hurt.
M: What were you crying about?	M: It hurt? It doesn't hurt anymore, right?
C: 'Cause I didn't wanted to leave yet; it was because I wanted to eat.	C: Right. I'll be careful next time.
M: Oh, you wanted to eat some more (laughs); is that why?	M: Umm, be careful.
C: Yeah.	. . .
M: Hmm. I remember Mommy tried to pick you up and you put up a little bit of a fight. You were crying real hard. Maybe it was 'cause the balloon and maybe it was 'cause you were hungry. But we knew that you could get another balloon, right?	
C: Yep.	
. . .	

Source: Reproduced by permission of SAGE Publications Ltd., London, Los Angeles, New Delhi, Singapore and Washington, DC, from Q. Wang, Developing emotion knowledge in cultural contexts, *International Journal of Behavioral Development,* 30(Suppl. 1), p. 9, Copyright © SAGE Publications Ltd., 2006.

INTERIM SUMMARY 9.3

Emotional Development

Understanding Emotions	■ Between ages 2 and 3 years, children begin to label their own and other people's subjective feelings.
	■ Secondary or self-conscious emotions, such as pride, guilt, and shame, develop in early childhood.
Individual Differences in Emotional Understanding	■ Individual children vary in their ability to recognize and understand emotions. Some children display considerable emotional intelligence (the ability to monitor one's own and others' feelings and to use that information to guide thinking and emotion).
	■ In the absence of warm, supportive family relations, emotional understanding may be impaired.
Regulating Emotions	■ Emotional regulation refers to the ability to inhibit, enhance, maintain, and modulate emotional arousal to accomplish a goal.
	■ Effortful control—the ability to withhold a dominant response in order to make a nondominant response—contributes to young children's ability to modulate their emotions.
	■ Lack of effortful control is linked to externalizing problems.
	■ The link between poor self-regulation and externalizing behaviors is greater when children experience hostile and intrusive parenting.
Emotions in a Cultural Context	■ Pride and shame are viewed differently in individualistic and collectivist cultures.
	■ Cultures also differ in their views about whether emotional expressiveness is a positive or negative trait.

PROSOCIAL BEHAVIORS, CONSCIENCE, AND AGGRESSION

One goal of socialization in many cultures is to encourage children's moral development—to adopt their society's conception of right and wrong and to develop the ability to behave in ways consistent with that understanding. Children's moral development has been studied using two distinct approaches. One approach considers the ways children think about moral dilemmas and changes in moral reasoning that take place as children become more cognitively advanced (Piaget, 1932; Kohlberg, 1969). In "Socioemotional Development in Middle Childhood," we will examine this approach in more detail.

In the second approach (and the topic of this section), researchers are primarily interested in children's prosocial behaviors (actions such as helping another child or comforting a person in distress) and in their ability to control aggression. As we will see in this section, children make great strides in these areas in early childhood.

Development of Conscience

prosocial behavior A voluntary action intended to benefit another person.

Prosocial behaviors are voluntary actions intended to benefit another person (Eisenberg et al., 2006). Sharing, cooperating, helping, defending, and comforting someone who is upset or in pain all fall into this category. People are prosocial for many reasons, including self-interest (to win praise, look good, make friends, and achieve mutual goals) and altruism (aid that is motivated by concern without expectation of reward or escape from punishment).

Prosocial behavior also may be motivated by **conscience**: an internalized sense of right and wrong that makes us feel good about doing the right thing and bad about doing something wrong. When values and standards are truly internalized, children feel guilt or shame for going against their conscience—even when no one is watching.

Nazan Aksan and Grazyna Kochanska (2005) devised several tasks to assess the development of conscience in early childhood. The first dealt with guilt. The researchers staged a mishap that led the preschooler to believe she had damaged a special, highly valued object. They then observed the child's response. Indications of guilt included avoiding the experimenter's gaze and various signs of tension: squirming, hunched shoulders, head down, and covering the face with hands. Afterward, the experimenter assured the child that no harm had been done by showing her the "fixed object" (an exact but intact replica of the damaged one), so that no child left the laboratory feeling guilty.

A second task dealt with **empathy**, or understanding and sharing another person's feelings. While the child was playing with toys that were placed in the observation room, a female experimenter "accidentally" dropped a large box of neatly sorted cards on her foot. Empathy was measured by whether the child looked sad, stopped playing, and showed signs of tension.

A third task, assessing children's compliance and internalization, occurred at the end of the session. The mother was instructed to have the child help pick up the toys in the playroom. Then the mother left the room and asked the child to finish the job while she was gone (a test of internalization). Here, the researchers recorded how many toys the child put away.

The researchers found evidence of the beginnings of conscience, as evident by signs of guilt, empathy, and internalization, in children as young as thirty-three months and increases in empathy and in the internalization of standards at forty-five months. Longitudinal studies indicate that children who score high on measures of conscience at an early age continue to do so in the school years (Kochanska & Aksan, 2007).

Factors Associated with the Development of Conscience

Earlier we mentioned the development of *effortful control*—the ability to willingly suppress a dominant response (e.g., grabbing a desired toy out of another child's hands) in order to engage in a nondominant one (e.g., asking to play with the desired toy). Kochanska and Askan (2007) find effortful control to be related to conscience in early childhood. Children who scored high on effortful control (measured by tasks such as waiting for candy that could be seen under a transparent cup, drawing a line slowly, lowering their voice, and recognizing small shapes hidden in a large shape) at two and a half years displayed more empathy, and expressed feelings of guilt and shame in conscience assessments at four years.

Emotional regulation also is related to prosocial behavior. Children who have less emotional control are less sympathetic and helpful (Eisenberg et al., 2006). Children who are sociable, assertive, and good at controlling their emotions are likely to help, share, and comfort peers and adults (Eisenberg & Fabes, 1998).

To some degree, prosocial behaviors also are intrinsically motivated. In a classic study (Eisenberg-Berg, 1979), preschoolers were asked why they had done something nice. Most mentioned need ("He was hungry") or said simply that they wanted to do it. Some referred to friendship, wanting approval, or mutual benefit. None cited the fear of punishment or the expectation of reward from adults.

This does not mean that experiences with their parents and other adults are unimportant. Children with secure attachments to their mothers in infancy are more sympathetic as preschoolers (Waters, Hay, & Richters, 1986) and show more concern for

conscience An internalized sense of right and wrong that invokes positive feelings about doing the right thing and negative feelings about doing something wrong.

empathy Understanding and sharing another person's feelings.

Young children are sensitive to others' emotions and will seek to comfort peers who are in distress.

others (Kestenbaum, Farber, & Sroufe, 1989). Parental warmth and acceptance serves as a pathway for early conscience for children who are temperamentally inhibited or fearful (Kochanska, 1995).

Experiences in child care also have been linked to children's prosocial behaviors. One team of researchers compared children who attended programs with small classes and a low child/adult ratio (in line with American Public Health Association Guidelines) to children who attended programs with larger classes and a higher child/adult ratio (NICHD Early Child Care Research Network, 1999). According to mothers, children who went to the first engaged in more prosocial behavior, and had fewer behavior problems, than children who went to the second. In other analyses, preschoolers whose caregivers were more emotionally supportive, stimulating, and responsive tended to be more cooperative and sociable with peers (NICHD Early Child Care Research Network, 2001).

Children's prosocial behaviors also reflect the larger culture in which they live. Prosocial behavior is more common in collectivist societies in which people live in extended families and children are assigned household tasks at an earlier age than in individualistic societies (Whiting & Whiting, 1975). An early ethnographic study found that parents in rural Mexico, a collectivist society, were more likely to punish children's use of aggression toward peers than were parents in more individualistic societies such as suburban New England (Minturn & Lambert, 1964).

Aggression

Researchers also have studied aggression in young children. **Aggression** refers to any actions that are intended to harm or injure other people. The key element in this definition is *intentionality*. Accidental injury, due to clumsiness or ignorance, doesn't count. In early childhood, aggression can take different forms, including **physical aggression** (fighting or damaging another child's possessions), **verbal aggression** (threatening someone or name calling), and **relational aggression** (attempting to lower another child's social standing or relations with others) (Dodge et al., 2006;

aggression Actions that are intended to harm or injure another person.

physical aggression Behaviors such as hitting, pushing, and biting that are intended to harm another.

verbal aggression Aggressive behavior such as threats and name calling.

relational aggression Aggressive behavior designed to lower another child's self-esteem, social standing, or both.

Tussles over toys are examples of instrumental aggression that decline as children become more skilled in negotiating toy exchanges.

© Laura Dwight

Vitaro, Brendgen, & Barker, 2006). Ignoring another child, refusing to let a child join a group, or threatening to end a friendship are examples of relational aggression (Crick, Casas, & Mosher, 1997).

All three types of aggression (physical, verbal, and relational) may occur for various reasons. **Reactive aggression** is a defensive response to provocation (e.g., hitting someone who has been hitting you). **Instrumental aggression** is designed to achieve a goal for oneself (e.g., pushing someone aside in order to get a better place in line), and **hostile aggression** intends harm as its primary goal (e.g., hitting someone because you want to hurt them). Sometimes aggression may occur for more than one reason; for example, it may be both instrumental and hostile.

Nothing infants do is true aggression. Granted, babies can pull (hard) on their mothers' dangling earrings and their grandmothers' large noses, but these actions appear motivated by curiosity and exploration, not the intent to hurt mother or grandmother. Similarly, infants will poke their finger in a peer's eye, or topple over a peer as both reach for an attractive toy, but the hurt is not intentional (Hay, Nash, & Pedersen, 1983; Mueller & Vandell, 1979). The term that researchers use for behavior that inflicts unintentional harm is **agonism**.

Like infants, toddlers are sometimes agonistic, but other times their behavior is clearly aggressive, especially when they seek possession or control of desirable toys (acts that appear to be instrumental aggression). About *half* of toddlers' interactions with peers involve behaviors that might be perceived as agonistic or aggressive—putting sand in a peer's hair, taking a toy, pushing a peer out of the way, as well as hitting (Mueller & Vandell, 1979). For toddlers, aggression and prosocial behavior are not opposite sides of the same coin. In fact, some two-year-olds are high in aggression and agonism *and* high in prosocial behavior (Brownell, 1990). The reason is simply that they are more socially active than other children. Outgoing, they make more efforts to engage with other children—which makes them friends but also gets them into fights (Vandell, Nenide, & Van Winkle, 2006).

Between ages two and four years, acts of physical aggression such as hitting and pushing typically decrease while verbal aggression increases (Dodge et al., 2006). This is not a surprise: Children's vocabularies and verbal skills are growing rapidly in this period. Words ("Give it to me!! It's my turn!") can now substitute for actions such as hitting or pushing someone in order to get something.

The reasons for conflict change from the toddler to preschool period. For toddlers, conflicts typically revolve around resources and toys. For preschoolers, conflicts also can involve differences of opinion (Laursen & Hartup, 1989; Rubin, Bukowski, & Parker, 2006). Children as young as three years also may engage in relational aggression, but this is far more common among older children and adolescents (Crick & Grotpeter, 1995; Underwood, 2003).

Toddlers have limited abilities to understand other people's intentions and motives, to control their emotional reactions, and to formulate alternative strategies to get what they want. By age four or five most have developed a broader array of strategies for resolving conflicts (such as taking turns) and voicing their feelings ("That's not fair!")—or for getting what they want through verbal threats ("I won't be your friend")—rather than grabbing toys. Some young children are better at controlling aggression than others.

Does aggression in early childhood predict later aggression? Investigators in one large study of over 1,000 children collected mothers' reports of children's aggression at multiple times from age two through age nine (NICHD Early Child Care Research Network, 2004). They identified five groups of children (see Figure 9.5) based on different developmental trajectories of aggression over the seven-year period. (A **developmental trajectory** describes the patterns of change in performance in an individual over a relatively long period [Nagin & Tremblay, 2005].) The largest group (45% of the chil-

reactive aggression Aggressive behavior that is a defensive response to provocation.

instrumental aggression Aggressive behavior designed to achieve a goal for oneself.

hostile aggression Aggressive behavior that intends harm as its primary goal, in contrast to instrumental aggression that has the primary goal of achieving some end or controlling resources.

agonism Behaviors by very young children that may unintentionally hurt or harm another person.

developmental trajectory A pattern of changes in an individual over a relatively long period.

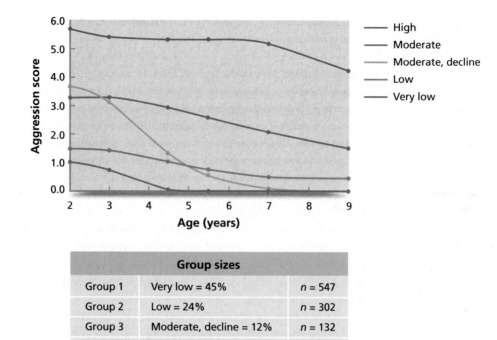

Group sizes		
Group 1	Very low = 45%	n = 547
Group 2	Low = 24%	n = 302
Group 3	Moderate, decline = 12%	n = 132
Group 4	Moderate = 15%	n = 184
Group 5	High = 3%	n = 30

FIGURE 9.5

Developmental Trajectories of Physical Aggression in Childhood

Each line in the figure represents the pattern of change in aggressive behavior for a group of children who followed a similar trajectory between ages two through nine. The majority of children showed low levels of aggression at all ages. An additional 12 percent started at a slightly higher level that declined over time. Fifteen percent of children showed moderate levels of aggression at all ages, and a small group (3%) had high levels of aggression that remained stable from toddlerhood through middle childhood. This last group also had problems in other domains, including poor peer relations and higher levels of psychological maladjustment.

internalizing problems
Psychosocial problems that are manifested in inward symptoms, such as depression and anxiety.

dren) showed very low aggression at all of the ages. Other children displayed somewhat low aggression at all ages (25%), moderate aggression that decreased sharply when they began elementary school (12%), or consistently moderate aggression (15%). A fifth group (3% of the sample) was high in aggression at all of the ages.

It was this fifth group, the children who were highly aggressive at all of the assessment ages, who were found to be at greatest risk for later problem behaviors. In elementary school, this small group had more problems with school and with peers, demonstrated more externalizing problems (acting out behavior problems such as physical aggression and rule violations) and more **internalizing problems** (behavior problems that are directed inward, such as depression and anxiety), and had fewer friends than any other group (Campbell et al., 2006). At lowest risk for later problem behaviors were the children who were consistently very low in aggression. For other children, aggression in early childhood is a phase, the result of temporary social difficulties. Children with moderate-declining aggression were better adjusted in elementary school than were children who consistently showed somewhat elevated aggression over time.

Influences on Aggression

Differences in the amount and types of aggression in early childhood reflect multiple influences, including children's temperament, gender, and social experiences.

Temperament In general, preschoolers who are low in effortful control and emotional regulation display more reactive aggression than other children (Dodge et al., 2006; Eisenberg et al., 2001). If they feel threatened, they react, without stopping to calm themselves or to think about alternatives.

Gender Boys engage in far more physical aggression than girls. In the large-scale study reported above, three out of four of the children who were consistently high in aggression were boys (NICHD Early Child Care Research Network, 2004). Preschool girls, in contrast, are more likely to use relational aggression (Crick et al., 1997).

Socialization An old saying declares, "Spare the rod, spoil the child." Research paints a different picture. Coercive, punitive, and harsh parental discipline in early childhood is associated with high levels of both physical and verbal aggression in early childhood and beyond (Gershoff, 2002).

Child Care The amount of time children spend in child care as well as the type of care setting also has been linked to aggressive behaviors in early childhood. In one study, children in child care for 45 hours a week or more from age three months to fifty-four months had more externalizing problems (including aggression) than children who attended fewer hours (NICHD Early Child Care Research Network, 2002). In follow-up analyses, the investigators found hours in settings with large numbers of peers, but not with smaller peer groups, was linked to parent and teacher reports of aggression (NICHD Early Child Care Research Network, in press).

Scientists are now studying young children's interactions with peers and caregivers in larger group settings to see *why* this might be and identify possible preventative strategies. One possibility comes from the research that measured cortisol levels in child care and at home for children of varying ages and temperament. These studies found that cortisol increased on days when children were in centers (the opposite of the typical circadian rhythm of cortisol), but not on days when the same children were at home (Watamura et al., 2003). The largest increases in cortisol were observed in children who had the most difficulty regulating negative emotions and behavior (Dettling, Gunnar, & Donzella, 1999), who were more fearful (Watamura et al., 2003), and who were less involved in peer play (Watamura et al., 2003). These findings suggest that toddlers and preschoolers, who are learning to negotiate with peers for the first time, experience large peer groups as socially demanding and stressful. Reducing group sizes in early child-care programs is one way to reduce the stress associated with early care. Explicitly working with young children to help develop ways to play cooperatively and to regulate emotional arousal are others. (For a summary of this section see "Interim Summary 9.4: Prosocial Behaviors, Conscience, and Aggression.")

SOCIAL RELATIONSHIPS IN EARLY CHILDHOOD

Socioemotional development is a transactional process. The child's own dispositions and capacities form the core. But these are tried and tested in interactions with others. Parents are a primary influence in early childhood, but siblings and peers become increasingly important.

Parents

In an influential study conducted more than forty years ago, Diana Baumrind (1967, 1971) observed middle-class, European American children at school with peers and

INTERIM SUMMARY 9.4

Prosocial Behaviors, Conscience, and Aggression

Development of Conscience	■ Prosocial behaviors are voluntary actions intended to benefit another person. ■ Conscience is an internalized sense of right and wrong. ■ Laboratory measures of guilt, empathy, and internalized standards indicate the beginnings of conscience as early as 33 months.
Factors Associated with the Development of Conscience	■ Children who display more effortful control and emotional regulation also demonstrate behavioral manifestations of conscience. ■ Children with secure attachment relationships are more sympathetic with their peers. ■ Preschoolers with emotionally supportive, stimulating, and responsive caregivers tend to be more cooperative and sociable with peers.
Aggression	■ Aggression is behavior that is *intended* to harm or injure other people. Physical aggression (fighting or damaging another child's possessions), verbal aggression (threatening someone), and relational aggression (attempting to lower another child's social standing or relations with others) are evident in early childhood. ■ Aggression can occur for various reasons: reactive aggression is a defense response to provocation; instrumental aggression is designed to achieve a goal for oneself; hostile aggression is designed to hurt or "put down" another person.
Influences on Aggression	■ Boys engage in more physical aggression than girls. ■ Preschoolers who are low in effortful control and emotional regulation display more reactive aggression than other children. ■ Coercive, punitive, and harsh parental discipline is associated with high levels of physical and verbal aggression in early childhood and beyond. ■ High hours in child care and large group sizes are associated with higher levels of aggression in early childhood.

at home with parents. Baumrind wanted to learn how parenting styles affect social competence.

Parenting Styles Baumrind identified two critical parenting dimensions—*warmth/ acceptance* and *control*—that occurred in different combinations and were exhibited in different styles of parenting (see Figure 9.6).

authoritative parenting
Parenting style characterized by high warmth and high control.

- **Authoritative parenting** is high in both warmth/acceptance and in control. Authoritative parents have high expectations, set standards, and enforce rules, but they also convey that the child is valued, loved, and accepted. Affectionate and understanding, they enjoy their child's company and take pride in his accomplishments.

authoritarian parenting
Parenting style characterized by low warmth and high control.

- **Authoritarian parenting** is high in control, but is low in warmth/acceptance. Authoritarian parents set strict standards. They rarely display affection and rarely take pride in the child's accomplishments. Their word is law, and rules are not explained or discussed.

- **Permissive parenting** is high in warmth/acceptance but low in control. Affectionate and indulgent, permissive parents often as not let the child have her way. They make few demands for responsibility or order in the home, avoid confrontations, and impose little discipline.

These different styles of parenting reflect different underlying beliefs about the nature of children and the role of parents. Authoritarian parents act as if children are "wild creatures" who need to be "tamed"—they value obedience. Permissive parents act as if children are like the seeds of beautiful flowers that only need love and care to flourish. Permissive parents value freedom and self-expression. The third group, authoritative parents, provides a balance of strong support and high expectations. Authoritative parents value responsibility.

These overarching parenting styles are related to particular parenting practices (Darling & Steinberg, 1993). Suppose three parents want their child to put away his toys before going to bed. An authoritarian parent might say, "It's bedtime. Pick up your toys, *now*!" A permissive parent might suggest, "It would be great if you put away your toys now," but is not perturbed when the child ignores the implied request and maybe even takes a few more toys out of the closet. An authoritative parent sets limits, but is also warm and accepting. The authoritative parent might say, "You'll need to put away your toys in a few minutes, so you'll want to finish up what you're doing. After you put away the toys, we'll get you ready for bed." The authoritative parent might help the young child get started with putting the toys away, turning it into a game that both enjoy. "Boy oh boy, you got those toys put away in record time!"

Eleanor Maccoby described a fourth style, **disengaged parenting**, characterized by low warmth/acceptance and low control (Maccoby & Martin, 1983). These disengaged parents focus on their own needs, not the child's, and do whatever is necessary to minimize the costs in time and effort to interact with the child. They might not set a bedtime . . . and not notice or care that the child has fallen asleep, fully dressed, on the couch.

The Influence of Parenting Styles on Social Competence Baumrind linked these parenting styles to socioemotional development. Children of authoritative parents generally are independent, self-controlled, cheerful, and cooperative. As a rule, they are popular with peers. Children of authoritarian parents tend to have high levels of both externalizing (acting out) and internalizing (withdrawing) behavior problems. Boys are often defiant while girls are often dependent and clinging. Children of permissive parents tend to be impulsive, lacking self-reliance and self-control. According to Baumrind, control without warmth/acceptance (*authoritarian parenting*) or warmth/acceptance without control (*permissive parenting*) has negative effects on development. Children thrive on a balance of the two (*authoritative parenting*).

One criticism of Baumrind's research is that she did not consider that different children may *elicit* different styles of parenting (Harris, 1998). A parent may be permissive with a child who is quiet and shy, authoritarian with a child who is aggressive and noncompliant, and authoritative with a child who is competent and reasonable. Today, most researchers conceptualize the parent-child relationship as reciprocal, with parents affecting children and children affecting parents.

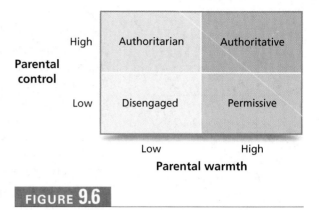

FIGURE 9.6

Parenting Style Classifications
Researchers who study parenting behaviors have identified four categories based on parental levels of warmth/responsiveness and control. Parents who are high in parental control and in parental warmth are Authoritative. Parents who are high in control and low in warmth are Authoritarian.

permissive parenting Parenting style characterized by high warmth and low control; also known as "indulgent" parenting.

disengaged parenting Parenting style characterized by low warmth and low control.

Cultural Differences Another criticism is that Baumrind's work is based on the study of only one social group—middle-class European American families. There has been much lively debate about whether her conclusions apply in other cultural contexts, such as different ethnic groups in the United States, or in other countries (Sorkhabi, 2005). Although many of Baumrind's findings have now been replicated across many different cultural contexts, a growing body of research has identified other values and beliefs that also can influence parenting.

Studies of Latino families reveal distinctive core values reflected in their parenting, including: *la familia*—maintaining strong extended family ties, feelings of loyalty to the family, and putting commitment to the family ahead of individual needs; *respeto*—maintaining harmonious interpersonal relationships through respect for the self and others; and *educación*—training in responsibility, morality, and interpersonal relationships, emphasizing good manners, warmth, and honesty (Halgunseth, Ispa, & Rudy, 2006). A study of Mexican American immigrant families found that children as young as four years old had internalized rules such as politely greeting elders, not interrupting an adult conversation, and not challenging an adult's point of view (Valdes, 1996).

China, as an ancient culture with collectivist traditions, has attracted a lot of interest from researchers. Do standards developed for an individualistic, Western society apply? Traditional Chinese parenting is based on two principles: *chia-shun* or training; and *guan*, parental involvement and investment in children (Chao & Tseng, 2002). Training emphasizes the value of hard work, self-discipline, achievement, family honor, and obedience. Parents tend to see their child's schoolwork as a parental responsibility and to take low grades or failure personally. Displays of affection primarily take the form of praise for a child's achievements, not unconditional love (a distinctively Western concept). In the Chinese context, this parenting style—*chia-shun* and *guan*—is associated with high academic achievement.

Some developmental scientists (e.g., Chao & Tseng, 2002) see this as evidence that authoritative parenting is not the best approach in all cultures; and that, in China, authoritarian parenting (high control, low warmth/acceptance) is more effective. Other developmental scientists (e.g., Chen et al., 2000) hold that Chinese parenting *is* authoritative but expressed differently. In that cultural context, children see training as just and parental involvement as an expression of love.

Siblings

Relationships with siblings represent one of our most enduring lifelong relationships. In addition to their longevity, they are among our most emotionally intense. For young children, interactions with siblings tap a wide array of emotions—laughter and shared joys but also tears and heated fights. Disagreements and reconciliations are common, everyday occurrences.

In African, Polynesian, Mexican, and Mayan cultures, children (especially girls) become caregivers and teachers for younger siblings as early as age four years. In European American families, an older sibling's role is less well defined, but still play a major role in socialization.

During the preschool period, sibling dyads play an increasingly active role in the development of communication skills and social understanding (Dunn, 2002). In their relationship with siblings, children develop patterns of interaction and social understanding that serve as models for friendship (Dunn, 2002). Interactions with siblings also provide opportunities to practice social skills learned from parents and others. They create occasions to observe their parents interacting with another child, to cope with differential treatment, and to experience such complex emotions as rivalry and jealousy. Formally or informally, older siblings act as tutors, managers, or supervisors of younger children, and sometimes as gatekeepers who can expand or limit opportunities to interact with other children and the world outside the family (Brody, 1998).

If at times "worst enemies," siblings also serve as buffers from adjustment problems for children experiencing social isolation in that outside world and perhaps as allies during conflicts or disruptions within the family (Vandell & Bailey, 1992).

Peers

Early childhood is a period in which relationships with peers blossom. Peers are age-mates who are equals in terms of skills and maturity. Peers provide a unique set of opportunities for social growth that children cannot obtain from their parents or their siblings (Hartup, 1989). With a peer, children can present their own opinions and assert themselves more freely than they do with an "all-knowing and all-powerful" adult or older child. Peers are equals who do not have the authority to order another around ("You're not the boss of me!"). Furthermore, children can choose their playmates, but not their parents and siblings. If siblings get into a bitter argument, they still remain siblings. Friends (at any age) do not have this guarantee. As a result, maintaining relationships with peers encourages developing skills in negotiation, compromise, and management.

Older siblings act as tutors and supervisors of younger children, providing opportunities for cognitive and social growth for both.

During the preschool period, interactions with peers increase in their frequency and their complexity. Interactions extend over several minutes as children converse about Halloween plans, work together to build elaborate structures out of blocks, and negotiate who is getting to wear which dress-up clothes. Children begin spending time in episodes of social pretend play of the sort described at the beginning of this chapter. Piaget (1923/1955) saw preoperational children as talking past one another in overlapping monologues. But detailed linguistic analyses reveal that most (60%) of preschoolers' utterances are directed toward another child or other children, are comprehensible, and result in an appropriate response or dialogue (Levin & Rubin, 1983; Mueller, 1972).

Pretend Play An important hallmark of early childhood is the development of social pretend play (Howes, 1984, 1992; Howes & Matheson, 1992) (see Figure 9.7). At first, young children play side by side, pretending to "eat" from a cup or "sleep" on a pillow. In this **simple pretend play**, they watch and sometimes mimic one another, but they do not collaborate in any organized way. In the next stage, **associative pretend play**, two children create a story or script with a series of actions in meaningful sequence. For example, both children are superheroes, "rescuing" damsels and others in distress. The most advanced stage is **cooperative pretend play**, in which children not only develop a script but also play reciprocal roles. Julia "feeds" Emma with a bottle, and Emma "drinks" and "cries" like a baby. Thus, how Emma plays her role depends on Julia and vice versa.

Cooperative pretend play provides unique opportunities for young children to understand and rehearse the roles of people with whom they interact in real life (such as Mommy and Daddy) as well as fantasy characters. They can practice regulating their emotions by pretending to be brave or afraid or angry; learn how to express and convince others of their ideas; and explore issues such as dependency and trust (by playing the baby, e.g.)—all in a nonthreatening context. After all, it's only pretend.

simple pretend play Fantasy play behavior in which children watch or mimic each other but do not collaborate in any organized way.

associative pretend play Social fantasy play in which children create a story or script with a series of actions in a meaningful sequence.

cooperative pretend play Social fantasy play in which children develop a script and play reciprocal roles (e.g., mother and baby).

Type	Behavior
Simple	Children play side by side without collaboration
Associative	Children create stories/scripts with sequences of actions
Cooperative	Children create scripts and play reciprocal roles

FIGURE 9.7

Developments in Social Pretend Play in Early Childhood

The development of cognitive and social skills in early childhood is reflected in how children engage in pretend play together. Young children's pretend play advances from simple, to associative, to cooperative.

homophily The tendency of individuals to associate and bond with others who are similar or "like" themselves.

Friendships During early childhood, most young children develop one or more friendships. Researchers identify friends by asking children to list their friends; if two children name one another, they're considered "friends." A study of children who attended a university preschool found that 75 percent had at least one reciprocated friendship in the fall; 85 percent did in the spring (Walden, Lemerise, & Smith, 1999). Moreover, friendships—usually between same-age, same-sex peers—were generally stable over the school year.

Children direct more social overtures, engage in more interactions, and play in more complex ways with friends than with nonfriends (Gottman, 1983; Hinde et al., 1985). Preschool friends also have more conflicts with one another than with nonfriends, but these conflicts are resolved differently: Friends are more likely to negotiate a solution, to stay together, and to continue playing (Hinde et al., 1985). Friends also provide emotional support and act as a secure base during stressful times, such as the birth of a sibling (Gottman & Parker, 1986), the transition to a new school, or the beginning of a new school year (Ladd & Kochenderfer, 1996). Kindergarten students adjust more easily to school when they have a friend in the class, and even show more cognitive improvement over the school year (Ladd & Price, 1987).

Peer Groups Even in early childhood, peer groups have an underlying structure or organization. A study of preschool classrooms found stable dominance hierarchies based on struggles over objects, threats, and conflicts (Strayer & Strayer, 1976). Children who lost an object struggle rarely initiated conflicts again with the winners. As a result, overall conflict in the classroom decreased over time.

Other researchers have found early indications of peer social status in the preschool classroom based on classmates' nominations of who they like to play with and who they do not like to play with (Ladd, Price, & Hart, 1988). These ratings, too, are relatively stable over time—suggesting that peer acceptance and peer rejection begin at a young age.

Influences on Early Peer Relations What factors influence the quality of early peer relationships? One factor that has received considerable attention is the quality of children's relationships with their parents. Children who were securely attached to their mothers as toddlers are more socially competent and popular with classmates as well as less aggressive in interactions with friends during early childhood (Schneider, Atkinson, & Tardif, 2001). In contrast, children who were insecurely attached as infants show more negative emotions, hostility, and aggression, and less assertive control with peers in early childhood (McElwain et al., 2003; Rubin et al., 2006).

Moreover, there is some evidence that "like attracts like," a process called **homophily**. Children who were securely attached as toddlers tend to form positive playgroups with one another as preschoolers, whereas insecurely attached children tend to form playgroups with other insecurely attached children (Denham et al., 2001). In a sense, children re-create with their friends the security—or insecurity—of their relations with their parents. The quality of parent-infant attachment is more highly related to children's friendships (another close relationship) than to their popularity or social status, which depend more on other social skills (Schneider et al., 2001).

So attachment alone does not explain peer relations. Parenting styles and particular behaviors can be a model for early peer relations. In his book *Friends and Enemies*, Barry Schneider (2000) describes links between the family and children's positive sociability with peers. Particularly important are a parent returning a child's affection, encouraging a child to initiate interaction, and explicit efforts to explain encounters with peers. A combination of parental explanations, nurturance, and evenhanded discipline is linked to increased peer acceptance and popularity. In contrast, punitive, coercive, and authoritarian parenting during early childhood predicts aggressive behaviors with peers and peer rejection during early childhood.

Other researchers have looked in close detail at early parent-child interactions as an opportunity to practice and hone social skills that can then be used with peers. For example, children whose interactions with their parents include balanced turn-taking are rated by teachers as being more socially competent (Lindsey, Mize, & Pettit, 1997). Cooperation and communication in the parent-child dyad is associated with more responsive communication with peers, which in turn predicts greater peer acceptance (Black & Logan, 1995).

Attachment security and opportunities to develop social competencies during well-scaffolded interactions are only two of the ways that parents influence their young children's peer relations. A third way is by providing opportunities for children to interact with peers and offering advice about play strategies. Parents who arrange "play dates" for their young children and who indirectly supervise those dates have

© Ellen B. Senisi/The Image Works

Contrary to Piaget's view, preschoolers are often skilled communicators who have extended conversations. Here, two four-year-olds are conversing at a bilingual English-Spanish preschool.

INTERIM SUMMARY 9.5

Social Relationships in Early Childhood

Parents	■ Two key parenting dimensions are warmth/acceptance and control. *Authoritative parenting* is high in both warmth and control. *Authoritarian parenting* is high in control but low in warmth/acceptance. *Permissive parenting* is high in warmth/acceptance but low in control. Disengaged parenting is low in control and low in warmth/acceptance.
	■ These parenting styles have been linked to child developmental outcomes. Children of authoritative parents generally are independent, self-controlled, cheerful, and cooperative. Children of authoritarian parents tend to have higher levels of externalizing and internalizing problems. Children of permissive parents tend to be impulsive, lacking self-reliance and self-control.
Siblings	■ Relationships with siblings are some of the most enduring and intense of all relationships.
	■ Interactions with siblings provide opportunities to develop social understanding and to hone social skills.
Peers	■ Peers are age-mates who are equals in skills and maturity.
	■ Maintaining relationships with peers encourages developing skills in negotiations, compromise, and management.
	■ Social pretend play, one of the hallmarks of early childhood, provides opportunities to coordinate complex roles in a nonthreatening context.
	■ Most young children develop one or more friendships. These friendships can provide emotional support and act as a secure base.

children who are better liked by peers, exhibit more prosocial behaviors, and have more friends (Kerns, Cole, & Andrews, 1998; Parke et al., 2002). (For a summary of this section see "Interim Summary 9.5: Social Relationships in Early Childhood.")

SUMMING UP AND LOOKING AHEAD

Brain maturation, as well as cognitive gains (especially in attention, memory, and perspective-taking), set the stage for socioemotional development in early childhood. Infants may exert a strong pull on their parents' heartstrings (and glasses, earrings, and other appendages); they are not entirely passive. But their lives are largely controlled by others. Less so with young children. Although they are still closely supervised, they are far more independent in body and mind than infants.

The emerging sense of self (though rudimentary and unrealistically positive) is the foundation for other advances. Self-conscious emotions, such as pride and embarrassment, appear. Preschoolers develop a gender identity and beliefs (often highly stereotyped) about what it means to be a boy or girl. We see the beginnings of self-control—or "effortful control"—and emotional regulation. We also see the emergence of actions deliberately intended to help—or to hurt—others. The "self" has motives.

The context in which the young child is growing up (including child care and preschool), interacting with the child's temperament and early experiences, especially at home, contribute to individual variations. Parents and others now actively attempt to shape social and emotional development, the process of socialization. Families—and cultures—have different values and different styles of parenting. And children respond in different ways. Some children are secure and develop a strong sense of initiative, whereas others feel unworthy of love and develop a sense of guilt (reflecting differences in self-esteem). Some are able to manage their emotions and actions; others respond to the slightest stress with a meltdown or tantrum (reflecting differences in self-regulation). Some find it easy to make friends or join a play group, but others are wary and hesitant, and still others are disliked (because they are pushy, overly aggressive, or do not fit in for other reasons), reflecting differences in social competence. Peer pressure does not begin in adolescence. Gender nonconformity is a particular social liability at this age.

As you will see in "Socioemotional Development in Middle Childhood," the same themes continue in middle childhood: the further development of a more realistic and integrated sense of self, more sophisticated strategies for self-control, and more advanced social skills (though some children experience rejection or victimization). The major change in middle childhood is in context. The child's social horizons—and challenges—expand: to school, where achievement counts more than getting along with peers; to peer groups that are increasingly independent of adult supervision (so that children have to negotiate rules and standards among themselves); and to a whole new set of influences, including organized afterschool and weekend programs, the neighborhood, and the mass media.

We've completed our discussion of development in early childhood and are ready to move on to the next stage of life. Our next chapter looks at children's physical development during middle childhood.

HERE'S WHAT YOU SHOULD KNOW

Did You Get It?

After reading this chapter, you should understand the following:

- What the self is and the characteristics of young children's self-conceptions

- How biology, socialization, and cognition play a role in gender development

- Major aspects of emotional development in early childhood, including the development of secondary emotions and emotional intelligence

- What prosocial behaviors are and how they indicate the development of a conscience

- How parents, siblings, and peers influence development in early childhood

- How different parenting styles are linked to children's development

Important Terms and Concepts

aggression (p. 258)
agonism (p. 259)
androgens (p. 249)
associative pretend play (p. 265)
authoritative parenting (p. 262)
authoritarian parenting (p. 262)
conscience (p. 257)
cooperative pretend play (p. 265)
corpus callosum (p. 249)
developmental trajectory (p. 259)

disengaged parenting (p. 263)
effortful control (p. 253)
emotional intelligence (p. 252)
emotional regulation (p. 253)
empathy (p. 257)
externalizing problems (p. 253)
gender identity (p. 247)
gender constancy (p. 247)
gender schema (p. 250)
gender socialization (p. 249)
homophily (p. 266)

hostile aggression (p. 259)
initiative versus guilt (p. 244)
instrumental aggression (p. 259)
internal working model (p. 244)
internalizing problems (p. 260)
permissive parenting (p. 263)
physical aggression (p. 258)
prosocial behavior (p. 256)
reactive aggression (p. 259)

relational aggression (p. 258)
rough and tumble play (p. 250)
self-conscious emotion (p. 251)
self-conception (p. 243)
self-esteem (p. 243)
simple pretend play (p. 265)
socialization (p. 242)
testosterone (p. 249)
verbal aggression (p. 258)

CHAPTER 7
Physical Development in Early Childhood

- Scientific studies have established norms of what is typical for physical growth at different ages. **Individual differences** are larger in early childhood than in infancy.

- During early childhood, the brain matures structurally and functionally. A key process is the development of connections between neurons that occurs through the growth of axons and dendrites **(synaptogenesis).**

- The left hemisphere of the brain is especially active from three to six years, during which time the **corpus callosum** develops rapidly. Maturation of the prefrontal cortex enables six-year-olds to inhibit or suppress preferred actions (called **effortful control**).

- Motor development occurs on two fronts in early childhood: (1) gross motor skills and (2) fine motor skills.

- Early childhood development is affected by injuries, illness, malnutrition, sleep problems, stress, and abuse or neglect.

- Scientists now recognize a range of **autism spectrum disorders,** from relatively mild physical and social awkwardness to severe disabilities.

CHAPTER 8
Cognitive Development in Early Childhood

- Jean Piaget identified the second stage of cognitive development, from about age two to seven years, as the **preoperational period.** According to Piaget, cognitive development is more than quantitative change; it also involves qualitative change.

- In contrast to Piaget, Lev Vygotsky argued that thought and language develop together. The **zone of proximal development (ZPD)** is at the center of his theory.

- The **information-processing approach** deals with basic questions about how people acquire, encode, store, and use information. The approach identifies three steps in memory processing: **sensory memory, working memory,** and **long-term memory.**

- During early childhood, children progress from simple sentences to complex grammatical forms. They also demonstrate rudimentary understanding of mathematical concepts.

- The quality of child care is linked to children's cognitive development. Studies like Project Head Start and many pre-K programs suggest that these programs can benefit the development of emergent literacy and mathematical thinking.

CHAPTER 9
Socioemotional Development in Early Childhood

- The **self** is a cognitive and social construction that reflects a child's level of mental development and interactions and experiences with others.

- **Self-conceptions** are evaluative judgments about specific areas such as cognitive ability. **Self-esteem** refers to a more global assessment of self-worth.

- Biology, socialization, and cognition each play a role in **gender development.** By age 2.5 years, most children can label themselves and others by sex, which is the beginning of a **gender identity.** By age 3, styles of play often differ by gender. Around age 6 or 7, children understand **gender constancy.**

- Emotional development in early childhood is marked by advances in children's awareness of their own and others' emotional states and in their ability to regulate their emotional expressions.

- Parents, siblings, and peers influence development in early childhood, Different parenting styles (authoritative, authoritarian, permissive, and disengaged) are linked to children's development.

Middle Childhood

Physical Development in Middle Childhood

© Brand X Pictures / Jupiterimages

May Chen is a lively fourth-grader whose parents left their rural Chinese village to seek a better life in New York City (Santora, 2006). At age nine, May has many new opportunities at school and in her community, but she also is vulnerable to forces that might undermine her health. Growing up, May's parents never heard of diabetes. In their home village, a standard diet consisted of two meals a day, always rice with vegetables and fish or poultry on the side, and of course, tea. Work in the fields or factories was strenuous and television rare. Overweight was not a problem. Indeed, memories of famines and food shortages during the 1950s made extra pounds a symbol of health and wealth. But May is growing up in a very different environment, and she is eager to fit in.

When May watches cartoons on her family TV, she is bombarded with ads promoting junk food as good food. At school, the lunchtime menu features pizza, chicken nuggets, hamburgers, and potato puffs, and vending machines offer drinks that are high in empty calories and sugar. If she brings American-style chips or sweets for snack time, her friends crowd round. (A child who brings Chinese-style steamed buns is ignored.) On her way home, May walks a gauntlet of fast-food restaurants that are crowded into a 100-yard strip. Meanwhile, her class has only one period of physical education per week, which provides less exercise than a child her age needs every day.

Asians are susceptible to Type 2 diabetes, a condition in which the body does not use insulin efficiently. Asian children develop the disease, which is brought on by a combination of genes, overweight, and inactivity, at younger ages and at far lower weights than people of other races (McNeeley & Boyko, 2004). At any weight, Asians are 60 percent more likely to get diabetes than Caucasians. As Chinese cities become more westernized, and more Chinese emigrate to developed nations, genetic vulnerability and abundance collide.

Culturally transplanted, Asian American children are twice as likely as their parents to be obese and therefore at risk for diabetes and other problems (Pinhas-Hamiel & Zeitler, 2005). They are not alone. All over the developed world, children are growing bigger than any generation before them. But supersize kids may face supersize health problems in the future, as we will describe.

This is the first of three chapters on middle childhood, spanning ages five to twelve and sometimes called "the school years." Children become increasingly independent during this period. They wash and dress themselves, make their own snacks, and find their way around their neighborhood. As their brains and bodies mature, children begin acquiring skills that may last a lifetime—not only in school but also in out-of-school activities such as sports and the arts. Their thinking becomes more logical as they categorize and organize material in ways that enable them to process increasing amounts of information faster and to remember more of it. Their knowledge of the world beyond their immediate experience expands, not only from school but also through media and technology. As they progress through middle childhood, they spend more time with peers and less time with their families. Friends and the peer group become an important influence on their self-esteem as well as their tastes and behavior.

In this chapter, we look at both **normative development** (typical changes in body size and shape and motor skills) and at individual differences. We also consider how social change is affecting the physical development and health of today's children. How are they different from previous generations?

PHYSICAL GROWTH AND DEVELOPMENT

With advances in health and nutrition, children are taller and heavier than children growing up 100 years ago. But today's children are facing new challenges. Almost 40 percent are overweight or at risk of overweight. Sexual maturity is occurring at younger ages.

Normative Growth

Children are growing taller and stronger (Ruff, 2003). On average, school-age children in the United States gain two to three inches and five to seven pounds per year. At age seven, the average American child (boys and girls) is 4'0" tall and weighs 50 pounds. By age eleven, the average girl is 4'9" tall and weighs 82 pounds, whereas the average boy is 4'8½" tall and weighs 78 pounds (Kuczmarski et al., 2000). (See Figure 10.1.)

This difference, although small, reflects the earlier onset of **puberty** (all the physical changes, including sexual maturation, that occur from childhood into adulthood) in girls. Their adolescent growth spurt is beginning. From here on girls have more body fat, while boys have more lean body mass per inch of height.

As in early childhood, growth occurs in spurts rather than gradually. There are brief periods (twenty-four hours) of very rapid growth followed by days or weeks when no growth occurs. Within these spurts, growth is most rapid at night while the child is

normative development A pattern of development that is typical, or average.

puberty Physical changes, including sexual maturation, that occur as children pass from childhood into adulthood.

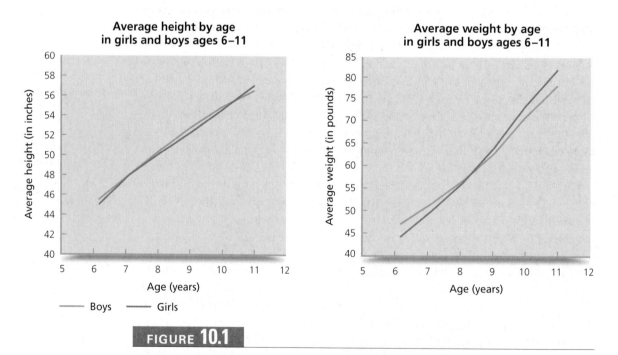

FIGURE 10.1

Increases in Height and Weight During Middle Childhood

At age seven, boys and girls are similar in height and weight, but with an earlier onset of puberty girls are heavier than boys at age eleven.
Source: Kuczmarski et al. (2000).

lying down, rather than during the day when he or she is up and active (Adolph & Berger, 2006).

Body proportions also are changing. The torso becomes slimmer, bones (especially in the arms and legs) are longer and broader, and the center of gravity shifts to the pelvic area. Because the lower half of the body grows fastest, school-age children often appear long-legged. Ligaments are not yet firmly attached to the bones, which gives children great flexibility. Back-bends and cartwheels are easy.

Children lose their primary ("baby") teeth during this period, typically beginning with the front middle teeth at age six or seven, followed by the molars at ten to twelve years (and keeping the "tooth fairy" busy). Permanent teeth come in at the rate of about four a year, so that most are in place by the end of middle childhood (Moorrees, 1959). Because the lower part of the face grows gradually, these teeth may look too big for the child's face at first.

Children's eyes are maturing in size and function. Myopia, or nearsightedness, is rarely diagnosed before first grade, but often develops between age six and adolescence (Saw et al., 2002). The reason may be that no one notices nearsightedness in the preschool years, but now a teacher notices that a child has difficulty seeing the chalkboard. Or growth (especially of the eyeball) may cause myopia. All told, more than one in five children ages six to eleven has a vision problem, a number that increases with age (Ganley & Roberts, 1983). Children in higher income families are more likely to have corrective lenses (29.9%) than children who are poor and near-poor (19%), most likely because more affluent children have better access to medical care. This difference needs to be addressed because vision problems can contribute to problems at school. Children who can't see the material on the blackboard can't read the blackboard.

Although sex organs remain physically immature in middle childhood, hormonal changes begin that eventually lead to outward signs of puberty (Susman & Rogol, 2004) (see Table 10.1). These hormonal changes start in the adrenal glands, two small organs that sit on top of either kidney. The hormones send signals to the **hypothalamus** (a small cone-like structure in the brain) and the **pituitary gland**, which in turn sends hormonal signals to the **gonads**, or primary reproductive organs (ovaries in girls, testes in boys). This system of signaling takes about two years to become fully established. The term *puberty* encompasses all the physical changes that occur in the growing girl or boy as the individual passes from childhood into adulthood.

The earliest outward sign of sexual maturation in girls is the development of breast buds (known as "the larche") between ages seven and thirteen (average age, 10.5 years). In boys, the first outward sign is testicular enlargement (average age, 11.5 years). The

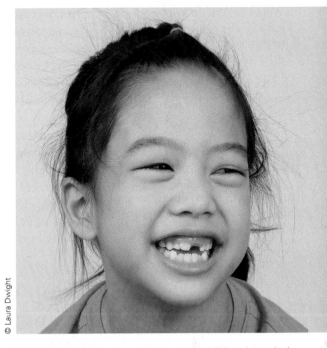

Middle childhood is the period when children lose their primary teeth.

hypothalamus   A small cone-like structure of the brain that is involved in hormonal signals that result in sexual maturation.

pituitary gland   One of the chief glands responsible for regulating levels of hormones in the body.

gonads   The primary reproductive organs (ovaries for females and testes for males).

TABLE 10.1 Signs of Puberty in Middle Childhood

Hormonal changes	Adrenal glands send hormonal signals to hypothalamus and pituitary gland.
	Hypothalamus and pituitary send hormonal signals to gonads (ovaries/testes).
Physical changes	Girls: Breast buds appear around age 10.5.
	Boys: Testicular enlargement occurs around age 11.5.

Source: Susman & Rogol (2004).

menarche The time of first menstruation, one of the important changes to occur among females during puberty.

secular trend Changes over generations.

body mass index (BMI) BMI is calculated by dividing weight (measured in kilograms) by height (measured in meters) squared, or wt/ht².

age of the onset of menstruation in girls (called **menarche**) has dropped over time—what scientists call a **secular trend** or change over generations (Tanner, 1981). In the 1840s, the average age of menarche for European women was sixteen years; in Europe and the United States today it is much younger—12.5 years on average with a normal range of nine to fifteen years. More about pubertal changes is presented in "Physical Development in Adolescence."

In many parts of the world, today's children are growing faster and bigger than earlier generations, thanks to better health and nutrition—a secular trend again. In such far-flung places as Canada, China, and Greece, children are taller and heavier, with a higher **body mass index (BMI)**, than previous generations (Hoppa & Garlie, 1998; Magkos et al., 2005; Zhen-Wang & Cheng-Ye, 2005). (As discussed in "Physical Development in Early Childhood," BMI is calculated by dividing weight [measured in kilograms] by height [measured in meters] squared, or wt/ht².) In the past, lack of food was a problem. Today, children suffer from the opposite problem, overweight.

Obesity

Childhood obesity is on the rise in the United States. In forty years, the percentage of six- to eleven-year-olds who are overweight has increased from 4 percent to 19 percent of children (National Center for Health Statistics, 2007) (see Figure 10.2). An additional 18 percent of children are now at risk for overweight (Ogden et al., 2006). All told, almost 40 percent of U.S. children—about 25 million—are either overweight or at risk for overweight.

Childhood obesity has become so commonplace that health experts believe the current generation of children could have a shorter lifespan than their parents due to obesity-related deaths in adulthood (Blom-Hoffman, George, & Franko, 2006). The epidemic of overweight can be traced to changes in lifestyle, including those discussed in the following sections.

Fast Food Families today often rely on processed convenience foods (Santora, 2006). They eat out, eat takeout food at home, and buy prepared foods at the supermarket—all of which are higher in calories than home-cooked meals. Even such healthy-sounding,

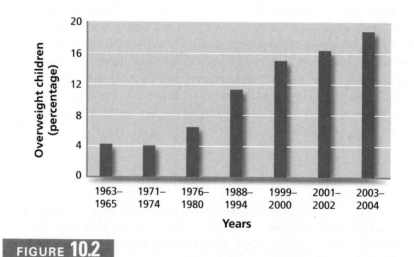

FIGURE 10.2

A Dramatic Increase in Proportion of Children Who Are Overweight: 1963 to 2004

Almost 20 percent of U.S. children are overweight in contrast to only 4 percent in 1963. *Source:* National Center for Health Statistics (2007).

store-bought items as low-fat yogurt, salad dressing, and chicken soup contain high fructose corn syrup. In low-income neighborhoods and convenience stores, the supply of fresh fruit and vegetables and low-fat dairy products is limited. Sugary drinks (not only sodas, but also juices and tea) and high-fat snacks (chips and the like) are everyday fare. Junk food has become as American as apple pie.

Advertising A recent study by the Federal Trade Commission (FTC) found that the average child in the United States sees 25,600 television commercials over the course of a single year (Holt et al., 2007). Food ads—primarily for snacks, breakfast food, and restaurant meals—account for roughly 22 percent of all ads. Children see the ads and want to try the products and—judging by advertising revenues—parents go along with their wishes. Tony the Tiger's *Frosted Flakes* cereal sells better at the breakfast table than plain corn flakes. The number of food ads children are exposed to on TV hasn't changed since 1977, before the obesity epidemic started. But families eat more convenience foods today than they did in 1977.

The FTC study also looked at other types of advertising during children's prime viewing hours. The researchers found that 43 percent of the ads during these hours are for sedentary pastimes, including: ads for other TV shows, screen and audio entertainment, and games, toys, and hobbies (Holt et al., 2007). Thus, two-thirds of ads for children feature food or passive, inactive entertainment. This *combination*, rather than ads for food or sedentary activities alone, could be a factor in childhood overweight. Child advocacy groups have called for a ban on advertising sodas, sweets, and snacks designed for children, similar to the ban on advertising cigarettes and other tobacco products on television.

School With support from the U.S. Department of Agriculture, public schools provide breakfast as well as lunch for low-income children. Schools must meet minimal federal standards for nutrition and at the same time offer food that children will eat. (If sales drop, federal subsidies are cut back.) Often the lunchroom menu is a mirror image of fast food, as at May Chen's school, described at the beginning of this chapter. Some individual school districts are experimenting with healthier menus and are having some success, but it is not easy to change eating habits (Belkin, 2006). And healthier alternatives like whole wheat bread and fresh fruit are more expensive.

In addition, many schools have vending machines with drinks and snacks that allow students to buy food not on the school menu, often including items that are high in calories and low in nutrition. Although some cities and local school districts have enacted policies to ban or replace certain foods in vending machines or to restrict access to the machines, many have not. A national survey conducted by the Centers for Disease Control and Prevention reported that 43 percent of elementary schools, 89 percent of middle/junior high schools, and 98 percent of senior high schools had either a vending machine or a school store, canteen, or snack bar where students could purchase food or beverages (American Academy of Pediatrics, 2004).

Neighborhoods and Communities Forty years ago most children walked or biked to school, had almost an hour of physical education (PE) or active recess each day, and after school played outside until suppertime. No longer. Today children are either driven to school or take a school bus, even over short distances (Nicklas et al., 2001). Outdoor play after school is limited. In cities, parents often consider their neighborhood too unsafe to allow children to go outdoors unsupervised. Since the 1960s suburban communities have been designed for cars, not pedestrians. Sidewalks (which encourage walking and biking) and playgrounds are scarce. The corner store has given way to the shopping mall, so children no longer run (literally *run*) errands for their families. The alternatives to active, outdoor play are—you guessed it—TV and video games.

Parks and other outdoor play spaces provide children with much needed opportunities to be physically active.

Children who live in neighborhoods with little or no access to parks and other outdoor recreational areas have fewer opportunities for physical activity. In one study of 128 communities in Los Angeles County, for example, the prevalence of overweight among children was lower in communities that had more green space—parks, recreation areas, wilderness areas, and beaches—per resident and higher in those communities where children had less access to green space (Los Angeles County Department of Public Health, 2007).

Physical Inactivity The link between physical inactivity and overweight is clear. In one longitudinal study, children who were less physically active between the ages of nine and twelve were more likely to become overweight by age twelve (O'Brien et al., 2007). The question is, *why* were they less active? There were two main differences between the overweight and "never overweight" children. One was the home environment. The overweight children's homes offered few opportunities for productive, engaging activity—measured in terms of the amount of books, games, and sports equipment in the home. The second difference was that overweight children spent more of their afterschool time watching TV.

These findings suggest a pattern in which children who have few toys or adult-structured activities to engage them at home fill their time by watching TV—a pattern that is a virtual recipe for gaining weight. TV encourages not only sitting, but also snacking. Sitting in front of the TV, a child might eat the caloric equivalent of a fourth meal between lunch and dinner. Microwaving a slice of pizza takes only a minute or two and can be accomplished during the commercial break.

Physical and Mental Health Consequences of Being Overweight

Extra pounds are a serious health risk. Health problems once seen only in adults are now being diagnosed in children, including Type 2 diabetes (discussed later in this chapter), high blood pressure, and high cholesterol. Overweight children are more likely to suffer from asthma and apnea (both discussed below) than normal-weight children. And children do not "outgrow" pudginess. To the contrary, overweight and risk of overweight increase with age. In the study by O'Brien and colleagues (2007) described earlier, the proportion of children who were overweight at 24 months was 15 percent; this increased to 18 percent at 36 months, 25 percent at 54 months, 26 percent at first grade, 31 percent at third grade, and 34 percent at fifth and sixth grades.

Watching TV and gaining weight go hand-in-hand because children are less physically active *and* more likely to snack.

More often than not, overweight school-age children remain so through adolescence and into adulthood. This is why experts see overweight as a "chronic" problem.

Extra pounds are a social and emotional hazard. Boys and girls who are overweight are subject to teasing and more likely to be excluded from friendship groups (O'Brien et al., 2007). The sad result may be that rejected overweight children turn to food to console themselves. Overweight children also tend to have less confidence in their athletic competency, social skills, and appearance, and they have lower opinions of their overall self-worth (Bradley et al., 2008). They score lower than normal-weight children on measures of their quality of life in physical, emotional, social, and school domains (Schwimmer, Burwinkle, & Varni, 2003). Not surprisingly, overweight children are prone to internalizing problems, such as depression and anxiety (Bradley et al., 2008). Overweight girls, in particular, are more likely to develop depressive symptoms (Erikson et al., 2000). Even as early as five years, overweight girls have more negative self-images than normal-weight peers (Davison & Birch, 2001).

Promising Interventions

Programs to help overweight children lose weight have not been very successful. But several interventions have slowed the increase in BMI typically seen in middle childhood. In one, a nurse taught a curriculum focused on reducing consumption of soft drinks to elementary school children (James et al., 2004). Over a year, the prevalence of overweight among children who took the course stayed the same, but increased 7 percent in the control group of children who did not receive instruction.

Another intervention was designed to reduce the amount of time third- and fourth-graders spend watching TV and playing video games (Robinson, 1999). Taught by classroom teachers, the program lasted most of the school year. First, the children were taught to self-monitor and record their use of TV and video games. Next, they went through a "turn off" period, in which they did not watch TV or play video games for ten days. Last, they were asked to create a seven-hour weekly budget for TV and video game time. The idea was to teach children to use these media selectively. Compared with children who were not in the program, participants had smaller increases in BMI and other measures of body size (waistline and skinfold thickness) between the beginning and end of the school year; reduced the amount of time they spent watching TV and playing video games; and ate fewer meals while watching TV.

Afterschool programs that include opportunities for outdoor free play along with structured physical activities (sports, dance, and fitness classes) appear to be another promising strategy. Joseph Mahoney and colleagues have contrasted children who attended an afterschool program with classmates who did not (Mahoney, Lord, & Carryl, 2005). In kindergarten, the two groups were similar in BMI. After two years in the afterschool program, participants had lower BMIs (see Figure 10.3) and a lower incidence of overweight than nonparticipants. Very likely, the more time they spent in the program, the less time they had for TV and video games and the fewer soft drinks they consumed, as well.

In short, the potential for obesity is woven into today's lifestyles. More than a matter of individual willpower, obesity is a social problem. These interventions show that small steps can help. But to prevent the epidemic of childhood obesity from spreading, families, schools, communities, and the media would have to take action.

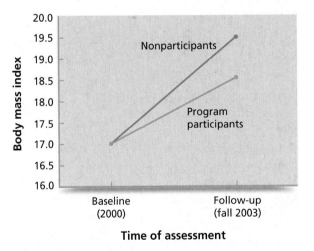

FIGURE 10.3

Changes in Body Mass Index (BMI) for Afterschool Program Participants and Nonparticipants

Although the BMI of afterschool participants and nonparticipants did not differ at baseline, program participants showed significantly lower BMI at follow-up compared to nonparticipants.
Source: Mahoney, Lord, & Carryl (2005).

INTERIM SUMMARY 10.1

Physical Growth and Development

Normative Growth	■ On average, school-age children in the United States gain 2–3 inches and 5–7 pounds per year.
	■ Growth occurs in spurts rather than gradually.
	■ In most parts of the world, children are growing faster and bigger because of improved health and nutrition.
Obesity	■ Almost 40% of U.S. children (about 25 million) are overweight or at risk for being overweight.
	■ The obesity epidemic can be traced to changes in lifestyle, including unhealthy diets and less physical activity.
Physical and Mental Consequences of Being Overweight	■ Overweight children are more likely to develop **Type 2 diabetes**, high blood pressure, high cholesterol, sleep **apnea**, and **asthma**.
	■ Overweight children are less confident in their athletic competency, social skills, and appearance, and have lower feelings of self-worth.
Promising Interventions	■ Interventions that have reduced soft drink consumption, limited television viewing, and increased physical activity have slowed the increase in **BMI**.

dendrite Branched extension of a neuron that picks up signals from other neurons.

axon An extension of the cell that carries signals away from the cell body toward other neurons.

synapse The connection between one neuron's axon and another neuron's dendrite.

myelin A white fatty substance that encases cell axons. It provides insulation and improves the transmission of signals.

competitive elimination A process that strengthens synapses that are used regularly, and prunes unused synapses to eliminate clutter. It accelerates the speed with which children can process information.

synaptic pruning The process of elimination of unused and unnecessary synapses.

lateralization The localization of function in one of the hemispheres of the brain.

corpus callosum The connection between the two halves or hemispheres of the brain.

For a summary of this section, see "Interim Summary 10.1: Physical Growth and Development."

BRAIN DEVELOPMENT

The brain has reached 90 percent of its adult size by the time the child has reached age eight, but important sculpting of the brain's circuitry continues during middle childhood (Lenroot & Giedd, 2006).

Normative Changes

Several processes of brain development described in "Physical Development in Early Childhood" continue in middle childhood. **Dendrites** and **axons** (the specialized extensions that carry information to and from the main body of the neurons) are still growing, branching, and establishing new **synapses** in response to new experiences. **Myelin** (the white fatty substance that encases cell axons that improves the speed and efficiency of transmission) also increases across middle childhood. The strengthening of synapses that are used regularly, and pruning of unused synapses to eliminate "clutter"—a process called **competitive elimination**—accelerates the speed with which children can process information (Lenroot & Giedd, 2006).

Synaptic pruning (the selective elimination of some synapses) leads to increased **lateralization** during middle childhood, with the left and right hemispheres becoming more differentiated in the brain processes for which they are responsible. At the same time, the **corpus callosum** (the band of nerve fibers connecting the two hemispheres) thickens, which improves communication between the hemispheres, so even if the "left hand" and "right hand" are doing different things, they know what each other is up to (Lenroot & Giedd, 2006). These refinements in the brain's structure, rather than an increase in sheer size or weight, are linked to the tremendous strides in cognitive development that we'll discuss in the chapter on cognitive development in middle childhood.

Brain development generally follows a cyclical process that systematically moves around the cortex (Fischer, in press). The cycle starts with the longest neural connections in the prefrontal cortex, then moves to the occipital lobe. It then gradually shifts to shorter and shorter connections in the prefrontal, parietal, and temporal areas. After completing the circuit in one hemisphere, growth moves to the other hemisphere and occurs in reverse order, from the shortest connections (solely within prefrontal) to the longest (prefrontal to occipital). And then the circuit starts all over again. Thus networks are wired and then rewired to promote new learning.

Magnetic resonance imaging (MRI) studies support this view of brain growth and development in which different parts of the brain undergo growth spurts at different times (Fischer, in press). Brain growth during early childhood is concentrated in areas at the front of the brain. Then, during middle childhood significant growth occurs farther back in the brain. Across all cortical areas, the growth of **gray matter** (neuron cell bodies responsible for information processing) follows a pattern that resembles a ∩ shape, with a proliferation of neurons and their connections increasing, reaching a peak, and then decreasing (Giedd et al., 1999; Lenroot & Giedd, 2006) (see Figure 10.4).

Although there is **apoptosis**, or programmed cell death, in the brain during the prenatal period and very early in infancy, this process does not play a role in the thinning of gray matter after two years of life. Rather, reductions in neurons during middle childhood are the result of competitive elimination.

The timetable of peaks and valleys in particular areas of the brain corresponds to developmental changes in specific cognitive abilities (Fischer, in press). Periods of development characterized by large-scale competitive elimination in specific brain regions are those that are also characterized by dramatic gains in ability to perform the functions associated with those areas. The region of the brain responsible for vision, for instance, undergoes major changes in gray matter during infancy when visual acuity is improving dramatically but not in middle childhood when eyesight doesn't change very much (Lenroot & Giedd, 2006).

gray matter Refers to nerve cell bodies (neurons, axons, and dendrites). Gray matter is contrasted to the white matter or myelinated nerve fibers in the brain.

apoptosis Programmed cell death in the brain.

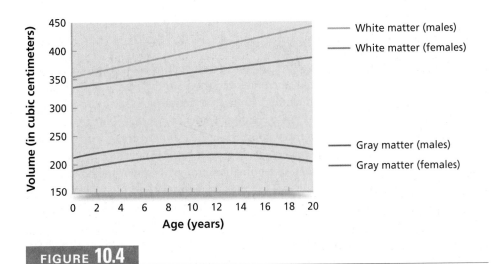

FIGURE **10.4**

Changes in White and Gray Matter

The volume of white matter increases linearly with age, increasing less in females than in males. In contrast, the volume of gray matter shows an upside-down U shape, increasing during middle childhood and then decreasing in adolescence.
Source: Giedd et al. (1999).

frontal lobe   Part of the brain located in front of the parietal lobes and above the temporal lobes that is involved in recognizing future consequences, overriding unacceptable social responses, and remembering emotional experiences

prefrontal cortex   The part of the brain involved in higher-order cognitive skills, such as decision making and planning. It is located in front of the brain, right behind the forehead.

temporal lobe   The part of the brain that is involved in speech, memory, and hearing. It is located at the side of the brain.

parietal lobe   Part of the brain associated with movement, orientation, recognition, and perception of stimuli.

white matter   Refers to myelinated nerve fibers in the brain.

The areas of change in middle childhood are those regions of the brain related to higher-level information-processing skills. The **frontal lobes**, which are responsible for critical thinking and problem solving, undergo a growth spurt between six and eight years. Gray matter in the **prefrontal cortex**, the seat of planning and emotional regulation, increases slowly until about eight years, followed by rapid growth until age fourteen (Kanemura et al., 2003). As the prefrontal cortex develops, cognitive skills such as attention, planning, and short-term (working) memory improve. Some regions of the prefrontal cortex continue to mature throughout adolescence and into the mid-twenties (Giedd et al., 1999).

There also is marked change in gray matter in the **temporal lobes** and **parietal lobes** of the brain in middle childhood (Giedd et al., 1999), areas that play important roles in memory and information processing. Within these lobes, regions where gray matter peaks relatively earlier are responsible for simpler cognitive functions; areas that show a later peak are related to more advanced functions. For example, in the temporal and parietal lobes, the latest regions to reach maturity are those responsible for the coordination and integration of different aspects of information processing (e.g., perception coordinated with attention, and memory), which requires more "brain power" than engaging in any of these processes independently (Lenroot & Giedd, 2006). This helps to explain why first-graders and teenagers can perform similarly on relatively simple tasks (e.g., recalling a list words that includes a jumbled mix of animals and vegetables) but not on relatively more complicated ones (e.g., recalling the same list of words and sorting them into categories while doing so).

The growth of **white matter**—myelin—also continues during middle childhood, but it follows a different pattern than gray matter (Giedd et al., 1999). Whereas gray matter shows the inverted-U shape we've described, white matter increases linearly during middle childhood and continues to increase well into the fourth decade of life. Because, as you know, white matter insulates brain circuits, the continued growth of white matter allows for better communication over longer distances, facilitating improved coordination between, and not just within, brain regions (Lenroot & Geidd, 2006). Many of the advances in cognitive abilities seen in middle childhood reflect not only changes that take place *within* particular regions (e.g., within the frontal lobe), but changes that improve transmission from one lobe to another (e.g., between the frontal and temporal lobes).

Differences in Brain Development

Although these patterns of change in gray and white matter characterize normative brain development for all children, there are variations in the timing and degree of change. Increases in both the number and strength of connections occur in a different order, time, and rate for boys and girls (Hanlon, Thatcher, & Cline, 1999). From birth to six years, girls experience faster development of neural networks involved in language and fine motor skills, whereas boys experience greater development in neural networks involved in spatial-visual discrimination and gross motor movement. During middle childhood, this shifts. Now, synaptic growth related to spatial-visual discrimination and gross motor movement accelerates in female brains, whereas synaptic growth related to language and fine motor skills accelerates in male brains.

There are sex differences in brain volume, with males' brains close to 10 percent larger, on average, than females' brains—a difference that is not simply due to the fact that males' bodies are larger than females' in virtually all respects (Lenroot & Giedd, 2006). But bigger is not necessarily better—in fact, children of equal cognitive ability can have brains that differ in size by as much as 50 percent.

Other brain differences are correlated with differences in intelligence, although these relations are more complicated than you might expect. What seems to be important is not the absolute size of the brain, but the pattern of change over time, especially as measured by the thickness of the **cerebral cortex**. Measuring cerebral cortex thickness is a way of tracking the proliferation and pruning of gray matter.

In a longitudinal study of more than 300 children, Shaw and colleagues (2006), charted patterns of brain development and compared those observed among children whose performance on a standard IQ test was either superior (IQ range 121–149), high (IQ range 109–120), or average (IQ range 83–108). The sample did not include any children whose IQ scores were substantially below average. Children who had IQ scores in the superior range had a thinner cortex than the high or average intelligence groups at age seven, but showed a rapid increase in gray matter during middle childhood, followed by a rapid decline during adolescence. The pruning of redundant or unused synapses (competitive elimination) results in a more orderly organization of the synapses, which in turn enhances information-processing speed. In contrast, the other groups showed no increase in cortical gray matter during middle childhood and, especially among the average children, a gradual decline in gray matter during adolescence. The difference in patterns was most pronounced in the prefrontal cortex, the brain region responsible for many of the higher-order cognitive abilities that are measured on IQ tests. In other words, superior intelligence is correlated with a pattern of brain development that suggests greater than average proliferation of gray matter during middle childhood, as well as a relatively more rapid pruning of gray matter during adolescence. It may be the rate of change (in either direction) rather than absolute degree of change that is crucial.

Traumatic Brain Injury Have you noticed how many children (and adults) wear helmets when riding a bicycle? Here are some reasons why that's a good idea. A **traumatic brain injury (TBI)** is a sudden injury to the brain, caused by either a blow to the head or a penetrating wound (Clark, 2006). Most common during auto accidents, TBIs also may be the result of falls, sports injuries, violent crimes, or child abuse. More than one million U.S. children receive brain injuries each year; more than 30,000 suffer lifelong disabilities as a result. Wearing a bike helmet is one simple way to improve the odds. Helmets can reduce bike-related head injuries by 70 percent (Grossman, 2000).

TBIs range from mild to life-threatening. Depending on the location and severity of the injury, a child may have one or more problems, including *physical disabilities* (trouble seeing or hearing, walking or talking, or reading and writing; muscle spasms or paralysis); *difficulty thinking* (trouble concentrating, poor short- or long-term memory, slow information processing and learning, or problems with comprehension, planning, and judgment); and *social, behavior, or emotional problems* (sudden mood swings, poor emotional control, and trouble relating to others).

Problems may appear immediately after the injury or develop years later. The different constellations of symptoms in combination with the delayed problems have resulted in many children with TBIs being misdiagnosed as having learning disabilities, emotional disturbance, or mental retardation (Clark, 2006). A thorough examination by a qualified professional, early and ongoing physical therapy, a thorough school evaluation, and an individualized education plan (IEP) improve the child's prognosis (Clark, 2006).

Attention Deficit Hyperactivity Disorder **Attention deficit hyperactivity disorder (ADHD)** is another condition that is linked to brain functioning and development. The American

cerebral cortex The outer layer of the brain, largely responsible for higher brain functions, including sensation, voluntary muscle movement, thought, reasoning, and memory.

traumatic brain injury (TBI) Sudden injury to the brain that can be caused by a blow to the head or a penetrating wound.

attention deficit hyperactivity disorder (ADHD) A condition in which children have difficulty getting organized, focusing on a task, or thinking before acting.

© Bill Aron / PhotoEdit

Wearing a helmet is a simple and effective way to reduce traumatic brain injuries.

Psychiatric Association (2000) identifies three subtypes of ADHD: predominantly inattentive (IA); predominantly hyperactive-impulsive (HI); and a combination of the two (C). Some children with ADHD have difficulty getting organized, focusing on a task, or thinking before acting (Whalen, 2000). Unable to sit still, they have trouble paying attention and attending to details. They do not modulate their emotions, or their energy, to fit the situation. They perform poorly in school and on tests. Other children with ADHD disorders are oppositional and noncompliant with adults, disruptive and aggressive with peers, and have difficulty making friends. They often provoke intense, negative emotions in others (parents, teachers, and peers).

About 6 percent of school-age children have been diagnosed with ADHD, with about twice as many boys as girls receiving the diagnosis (Bloom, Dey, & Freeman, 2006). Girls most often have the IA form, with low levels of hyperactivity and externalizing behavior, but high levels of cognitive disability. ADHD is most often diagnosed at ages seven to nine, the years in which children are expected to exhibit self-control, especially in school. However, symptoms may be visible in toddlers (Lehn et al., 2007). About half of children diagnosed with ADHD continue to have problems with impulsivity, concentration, and restlessness in adolescence and adulthood (Whalen, 2000).

Because ADHD is so variable, some scientist believe that is unlikely that the disorder has one, single cause. Scientists are looking for differences in the brains of children diagnosed with ADHD and those without the disorder to see if the different subtypes are actually separate and distinct disorders (Diamond, 2005). They are finding differences in the **cerebellum,** which is associated with coordination of motor movements and such other functions as timing and attention (Krain & Castellanos, 2006). Others have found evidence that abnormalities in **neurotransmitters** and brain metabolism are also involved (Whalen, 2000).

cerebellum The part of the brain associated with balance and control of body movements.

neurotransmitters Chemical substances in the brain that carry electrical impulses across synapses.

Scientists also are working to determine whether ADHD is due to delayed brain maturation or to structural deviations in the brain. In one recent study (Shaw et al., 2007), magnetic resonance imaging (MRI) was used to measure the thickness of the cortex (gray matter) at more than 40,000 points in the brain in children diagnosed with ADHD and children who were developing more typically. (Recall that growth in gray matter during middle childhood follows a ∩-shaped pattern, with gray matter increasing until it reaches a peak, and then decreasing as competitive elimination occurs.) Each child's brain was scanned two to four times; the average time between each scan was 2.8 years. The researchers calculated the age at which different areas of the brain reached peak cortical thickness (see Figure 10.5).

The ADHD and non-ADHD children followed the same overall pattern of brain development, with sensory and motor areas of the brain achieving peak cortical thickness before areas associated with higher-level skills, but there were differences in the tim-

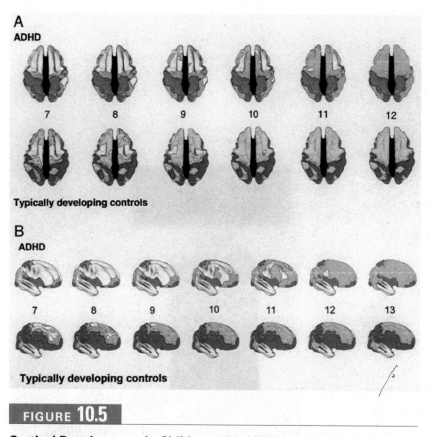

FIGURE 10.5

Cortical Development in Children with ADHD and without ADHD

Children with ADHD show a similar sequence of cortical thickening as children without ADHD, but the timing of attaining peak cortical thickness differs. ADHD children show considerable delay in attaining this marker.
Source: Shaw et al. (2007).

ing of gray matter peaks. The ADHD children reached the peak in gray matter about three years later than the non-ADHD children (10.5 years versus 7.5 years). The largest differences in the children were found in the prefrontal cortex (the area of the brain associated with attention, planning, and short-term memory), where cortical thickness peaked about five years later in the ADHD group compared with the non-ADHD group. Differences also were found for the motor cortex, where the ADHD group reached peak slightly *earlier*, at seven years, compared with 7.4 years among the typically developing children. These findings may explain why some ADHD children "age out" of the disorder and function more typically in late adolescence and adulthood.

Brain Reactions to Stress

As we learned in "Physical Development in Early Childhood," children display physiological reactions to stress. When faced with danger (imminent or imagined), a child's brain sounds an alarm, triggering a series of biochemical reactions that produce **cortisol** and other hormones (Gunnar, 2000). Cortisol has the adaptive function of stimulating the flow of energy (oxygen and glucose) to the brain and muscles. When the danger has passed, the brain sends out an "all clear" signal that stops the release of cortisol and flushes out what remains in the body. The child's brain and body return to their normal state. Ordinarily this process is extremely efficient. Moderate or occasional stress (e.g., the first day of school, a math test) primes the child to rise to a challenge, whether physical or mental. Extreme or constant danger, however, takes a toll.

With prolonged exposure, cortisol becomes toxic, injuring or even killing neurons in the **hippocampus**, which is part of the limbic region of the brain involved in memory, learning, and emotions. This is why when we are "stressed out" we sometimes go blank, forgetting what we were doing or not being able to answer a simple question. It's also why victims of a car crash often cannot remember the moments leading up to the collision.

How does prolonged, chronic, and intense stress affect children, whose brains are still growing and changing? Ordinarily we associate **posttraumatic stress disorder** (PTSD) with combat veterans who have faced life-and-death situations day in, day out and seen comrades die, for months or even years. But children can suffer from PTSD as well—when they have been physically, sexually, or emotionally abused, been neglected, witnessed violence, or experienced separation and loss (especially divorce or death of a parent) (Carion, Weems, & Reiss, 2007). The symptoms for children are much the same as for adults: intrusive thoughts and flashbacks, nightmares and sleep disorders, withdrawal, and problems with emotional control.

Carion and his colleagues (2007) studied children, ages eight to fourteen, who had been diagnosed with PTSD. Most had experienced more than one serious trauma. The researchers took readings of cortisol levels and used magnetic resonance imaging to measure the size of the children's hippocampus at the beginning of the study and twelve to eighteen months later. Children with the

cortisol   A hormone secreted when individuals are exposed to stress.

hippocampus   Part of the limbic region of the brain involved in memory, learning, and emotion.

posttraumatic stress disorder (PTSD)   A disorder caused by chronic and prolonged stress. Symptoms include intrusive thoughts and flashbacks, nightmares and sleep disorders, withdrawal, and problems with emotional control.

© Spencer Platt / Getty Images

Events such as 9/11 are more likely to lead to PTSD when they occur in combination with other severe traumas.

most severe PTSD symptoms had the highest levels of cortisol in their systems and experienced more reduction of hippocampus volume. Further research is needed before firm conclusions can be drawn, but these findings might explain the poorer memory performance of children with PTSD. Reduction of the hippocampus is common among older people suffering memory. But these are children.

One team of researchers (Davies et al., 2007) studied this question in children whose parents had highly volatile relationships and many unresolved fights. The scientists considered two possibilities (or hypotheses). The first was that children might become hypersensitive to their parents' conflict and have elevated levels of cortisol most of the time (hypercortisolism). In other words, they would react to the slightest hint of conflict. The second was that the children might become numbed (or habituated) to chronic parental conflict and have normal or low levels of cortisol (hypocortisolism)—they would tune out their parents' fights and perhaps other disturbing experiences as well.

The findings supported the second possibility: numbness (or hypocortisolism). It looked like the children's stress system was acting like a built-in thermostat that shut off cortisol when the environment became too hot. This numbing did not mean, however, that the children were untouched by the conflicts. When the researchers studied the children two years later they found that the low levels of cortisol were linked to high levels of externalizing behavior problems. Physiological numbness might have helped the children adapt to a stressful home environment in the short term, but interfered with normal social learning and adjustment in the long term. Thus, the children had difficulties in understanding the social cues from peers and adults and then responding appropriately.

Coping with Stress

All children face daily hassles—missing the school bus, losing homework assignments, being teased by a sibling, having a friend say something mean, and the like. Some children experience ongoing rejection by peers, serious conflicts at home, or chronic health conditions such as asthma or diabetes. Behavioral coping is the effortful or purposeful response to challenging situations. Adaptive coping involves three steps: first, an effort to regulate emotional arousal; second, an assessment of the situation and a realistic recognition of what the child can control—and cannot control; and third, an effort to achieve some resolution of the situation that results in a feeling of mastery and/or resilience (Saarni et al., 2006). During middle childhood, children make significant strides at each step.

The first step—emotional modulation—is central to adaptive coping (Eisenberg & Spinrad, 2004). Being able to regulate their own emotions helps children to calm down in the midst of a stressful situation, giving them time to consider the best approach. It also helps children deal with the aftermath of a stressful event—with lingering feelings of anger, betrayal, sadness, or shame—and to express those feelings in ways that are adaptive.

The second step is accurately assessing situations and determining what is controllable and what is not. Especially when children are in situations that they cannot control, it is adaptive to reinterpret situations in a more positive light, to focus on happy thoughts, and even to escape into fantasy (Marriage & Cummins, 2004).

The third step—sometimes referred to as problem-focused coping—occurs when children are able to identify what the difficulty is and then do something about it: responding to teasing with humor, asking a teacher for help with math, and so on (Lazarus, 1999). Some problem-focused strategies are social, such as seeking help and comfort from a teacher or a friend and sitting with friends on the school bus. Others are solitary, such as physical exercise and fantasy play. After a hard day at school, a young pianist pounds on the keyboard, playing only *fortissimo*. Or, after a busy week filled with tightly scheduled days, a girl retreats to the basement where she has spends time alone—outfitting her Barbie dolls and setting up elaborate play scenes.

Individual children differ in their coping strategies. Sandstrom (2004) has studied how nine- to twelve-year-old children coped with teasing and peer rejection. She found four patterns:

1. *Active coping*: problem solving, assertiveness, humor, constructive distraction, getting help/support from others

2. *Aggressive coping*: teasing, arguing, getting angry, getting others to turn against another child

3. *Denial coping*: telling oneself that it does not matter

4. *Ruminative coping*: worrying, withdrawing, wishing that it were not happening

Some of these strategies appear more adaptive than others. Active coping was associated with fewer symptoms of depression and social anxiety, whereas ruminative coping—repeatedly rehashing the experience and dwelling on social failures—was related to increased symptoms. What we do not know is whether rumination *causes* these internalizing problems, rumination *results* from them, or *both* pathways operate simultaneously, reinforcing each other. Aggressive coping also is linked to symptoms of depression and social anxiety. The effects of denial coping are mixed. Children who frequently engage in denial do not report symptoms of depression or social anxiety, but they show problems in other areas. For instance, parents and peers report that these children often ignore constructive criticism, rules, and requests.

Coping strategies are linked to children's temperamental predispositions (Mezulis, Hyde, & Abramson, 2007) and to parenting (Saarni et al., 2006). Ruminative coping is particularly likely when children are predisposed to negative emotions such as anger, sadness, and fear, *and* their parents are punitive and harsh.

For a summary of this section, see "Interim Summary 10.2: Brain Development."

MOTOR DEVELOPMENT

Muscle strength, hand-eye coordination, and stamina all improve greatly during middle childhood. For example, very few preschoolers can hit a tennis ball with a racket, dribble a basketball, or jump rope, but most ten- and eleven-year-olds can develop these skills with some practice. Few preschoolers can play chords on the piano or write in script, skills that older children can master with practice. Middle childhood is a time of great strides in both gross and fine motor skills.

Gross Motor Skills

Gross motor skills, or large motor movements, become smoother and more coordinated in middle childhood (Case-Smith, 2005). Actions the preschooler performed clumsily—running, jumping, hopping, throwing and catching a ball—become more refined. Improved flexibility, balance and coordination, agility, and strength enable children to engage in new, more complex physical activities: bike riding, skating, swimming, gymnastics, and other sports. Reaction time improves steadily (see Table 10.2).

Some children report "growing pains" during this period, characterized by pain in the thigh and calf as well as behind the knee. Contrary to common wisdom, these aches are not caused by growth itself. Rather, they are the result of increased physical activity (running, climbing, jumping) and using developing muscles in new ways (Mayo Clinic, 2006).

Historically, school-age boys have been reported to be better than girls at throwing (both distance and speed) and running, whereas girls have been reported to be more

gross motor skills Abilities required to control large movements of the arms, legs, and feet, or the whole body, such as running, jumping, climbing, and throwing.

INTERIM SUMMARY 10.2

Brain Development

Normative Changes	■ **Dendrites** and **axons** continue to grow and branch, creating **synapses**.
	■ **Competitive elimination** occurs in which synapses that are used regularly are strengthened and unused synapses are pruned to eliminate "clutter."
	■ During middle childhood, the growth of **gray matter** (neuron cell bodies) follows a pattern that resembles a ∩ shape, with neurons and their connections increasing, reaching a peak, and then decreasing.
	■ Marked changes in gray matter are seen in the **temporal** and **parietal** lobes of the brain, areas important for memory and information processing.
	■ The growth of **white matter—myelin**—increases linearly.
Differences in Brain Development	■ From birth to 6 years, girls show faster development of synapses involved in language and fine motor skills, whereas boys show greater development of synapses involved in spatial-visual discrimination and gross motor movement.
	■ During middle childhood, synapse growth shifts. Girls show faster growth in the spatial-visual discrimination and gross motor areas and boys show faster growth in the language and fine motor areas.
	■ In comparison to children with average intelligence, children with superior intelligence show a higher rate of growth of gray matter during middle childhood and more rapid pruning of gray matter during adolescence.
Brain Reactions to Stress	■ The body reacts to real or perceived dangers with a series of biochemical reactions that produce **cortisol** and other hormones.
	■ Moderate or occasional stress primes children to rise to a challenge, but extreme or constant stress can affect the development of the **hippocampus**, an area of the brain associated with memory.
Coping with Stress	■ Behavioral coping involves regulation of emotional arousal; assessment of the situation and a realistic recognition of what can be controlled—and what cannot be controlled.
	■ Children differ in their coping strategies.

flexible and to have greater balance (e.g., Thomas & French, 1985). It is unclear, however, whether these findings represent true physiological differences or whether they result from the different types of motor experiences boys and girls have. Others have linked home and family characteristics such as parental education, father's involvement in sports, and the amount of time spent watching TV with the distance that boys and girls are able to throw a ball (East & Hensley, 1985). The researchers concluded that nurture—sociocultural factors and experiences within the family—plays a significant role in the development of children's motor skills in middle childhood.

A more recent study reported no sex differences in fundamental movement skills (e.g., running, skipping, hopping, jumping) among young elementary-age children in grades K–2 (Butterfield, Lehnhard, & Coladarci, 2002). These findings may reflect the greater inclusion in recent years of young girls in sports and other activities that contrib-

TABLE 10.2 Improvement in Gross and Fine Motor Skills

	EARLY CHILDHOOD, AGES 4–5	MIDDLE CHILDHOOD, AGES 6–10
Gross motor skills	Jumps down from high step, jumps forward; hops for 4–6 steps; skips with good balance	Jumps, hops, and skips with ease
	Throws ball and hits target	Throws ball well at long distances
	Catches ball with two hands	Catches ball with accuracy
Fine motor skills	Traces letters, begins to copy letters, copies	Precision and motor planning evident in drawing simple shapes
	Completes puzzles of 10–20 pieces	Motor planning evident in completion of complex puzzles
	Strings 1/4-inch beads	Good dexterity for crafts and construction with small objects

Source: Case-Smith (2005).

ute to motor development. This broader participation may have some long-term effects on the girls' proficiencies.

Through practice and repetition, children develop "motor skills programs" that are stored in long-term memory (Martinez, in press). These programs are what allow us to ride a bike after a long period without riding. It's as if the memories were stored in our muscles (though more accurately, it is the brain's nonverbal commands to our muscles that remain accessible). To some degree, middle childhood is a sensitive period in the development of motor skills. Learning to ride a bike, swim, or skate later in life (say, age twenty-five) is possible but more difficult.

For some children, motor development problems can be significant during middle childhood. One contributor to poor gross motor skills is obesity. In a study conducted in Canada, gross motor skills that included running, galloping, hopping, leaping, horizontal jumping, skipping, and sliding were studied in

© Lori Adamski Peek / Getty Images

Physical activities like ice skating become smoother and more refined in middle childhood as a result of improved flexibility, balance, strength, and practice.

children ages five to ten (Marshall & Bouffard, 1997). The researchers found that obese children were less aerobically fit and less competent in these skills than children who were not obese.

These deficits in gross motor skills can be remediated, at least in part, by high-quality physical education at school. In the Canadian study of locomotor skills just described, the researchers compared children who attended schools that offered the Quality Daily Physical Education (QDPE) program and children who attended schools

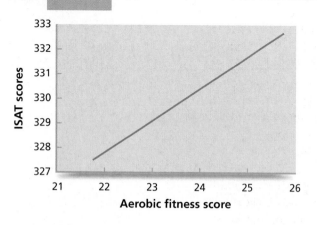

FIGURE 10.6

Relation Between Aerobic Fitness and Academic Achievement in Middle Childhood

This figure shows a linear relation between children's aerobic capacity and scores on the Illinois Standards Achievement Test (ISAT). Children who are more physically fit tend to score higher on this standardized test of reading and math.
Source: Castelli (2005).

that offered standard PE two or three times per week. The components of the QDPE program included daily PE class, maximum active participation, fitness activities in each class, adequate facilities and equipment, and qualified and competent teachers. The children who attended the QDPE schools, whether obese or not, evidenced better locomotor skills than the children who attended non-QDPE schools (Marshall & Bouffard, 1997).

Physical Activity

Physical activity is essential to growth and maturation. In addition to building strong muscles and bones, exercise increases energy and alertness, helps children to maintain a healthy weight, and can reduce stress. Health and fitness experts, pediatricians, and policymakers recommend that school-age children get a minimum of sixty minutes of vigorous physical activity every day, doing activities such as swimming, bike riding, jumping rope, running, or playing sports (Corbin & Pangrazi, 1998).

Physical activity may even stimulate brain growth and academic achievement. In a recent study, researchers compared MRIs of adults taken before and after three months of aerobic exercise (Pereria et al., 2007). Exercise increased the flow of blood (and hence the supply of oxygen) to the brain and also resulted in the creation of new neurons in the hippocampus, an area of the brain associated with learning and memory.

Exercise may have similar effects on brain development and learning in middle childhood. Indeed, researchers have found links between being more physically fit and higher scores on standardized math and reading tests (Castelli, 2005; Castelli et al., 2007) (see Figure 10.6). Of five fitness measures, aerobic capacity was most highly related to academic achievement (Castelli, 2005).

During a typical school day, children have three opportunities for physical activity: PE classes, recess, and before and after school (Beighle et al., 2006). Unfortunately, PE has been cut back in recent years. Only 8 percent of elementary schools, 6.4 percent of middle schools, and 5.8 percent of high schools provide daily PE for all students during the full school year (Burgeson et al., 2001). In one large national study (NICHD ECCRN, 2003), elementary school children had only two 33-minute PE classes each week. Of the total 66 minutes, children were engaged in moderate to vigorous activity for only 25 minutes. The remaining time (41 minutes) was devoted to instruction, class management, and waiting one's turn. All told, PE provided 6 percent of recommended weekly physical activity.

In another study, children's physical activity was measured using a pedometer (Beighle et al., 2006). The researchers found that children were quite active during recess (though recess lasted only fifteen minutes) but spent less than a quarter of their time after school in physical activity.

Put together, these studies suggest that school-age children get about half the recommended amount of exercise for their age during a typical school week. (In all three arenas and in almost all studies, boys are more active than girls.) But weekends can be different. Counteracting the social trend to ride instead of walk, and watch instead of play, are youth sports.

Youth Sports

Since the founding of Little League baseball in 1954 organized sports in the out-of-school hours have become a rite of childhood in the United States. Nine million children between ages six and eleven are in basketball leagues. Eight million play soccer;

4.6 million, baseball; and 2.9 million, volleyball. All told, some 45 million youth under age eighteen (almost 70 percent of all U.S. children) participate in one sport or another, with participation peaking around age twelve (Ewing & Seefeldt, 2002).

Conventional wisdom holds that sports are good for children. In this view, sports provide exercise and teach physical skills while building character, leadership, sportsmanship, and achievement motivation (Bandura, 1997). But sports may also expose children to anxiety and stress and build up the best players to the exclusion of average players and those who are left sitting on the bench. Much depends on the context, especially coaches and parents.

Frank Smoll and Ron Smith's research is classic. In their early work, they observed Little League coaches in over 200 games involving 500 players (Smith, Smoll, & Curtis, 1978). Then they interviewed the players and asked both players and coaches to fill out questionnaires. Children were most likely to enjoy the sport and to like the coach when the coach was positive and gave technical instruction rather than just making general comments. Not surprisingly, when the coach was punitive, children disliked the coach and the sport.

Drawing on these findings, Smoll and Smith (2002) developed a Coach Effectiveness Training (CET) program that emphasized four principles: (1) "Winning isn't everything, nor is it the only thing; (2) Failure is not the same thing as losing; (3) Success is not equivalent to winning; and (4) Success is found in striving for victory." The basic goal of the training is to teach coaches to emphasize fun and effort over winning, and to provide support in the face of failure.

The CET program has been tested by randomly assigning Little League coaches either to a control group, in which they coached as usual, or to an experimental group, in which they participated in the program (Smoll & Smith, 2002). CET-trained coaches are more consistent in praising children when they do well, handle mistakes by providing encouragement and technical instruction, and avoid punitive responses to children's behavior. The young players with CET-trained coachers like their coaches, their teammates, and the sport more in comparison to children with untrained coaches. They also show more gains in self-esteem. Studies of other sports, such as competitive swimming (Black & Weiss, 1992), have reported similar findings.

Ask coaches what is their biggest problem and many will say, "parents." When parents are supportive and enthusiastic—but not pushy—children are more likely to report enjoying the sport, looking forward to the next practice and game, and not feeling overly anxious about their own performance (Stearn, 1995). When parents were over-involved, interfering, and focused on the child winning (in an individual sport) or starring (in a team sport), children were more likely to report that they weren't having fun, felt under considerable stress, and wanted to drop out of the sport.

Fine Motor Skills

Fine motor skills involve refined use of the small muscles controlling the hand, fingers, and thumb, often coordinated with the eyes (Case-Smith, 2005). The development of these skills allows many new accomplishments in middle childhood, including: cursive handwriting; drawings with lots of details; using a joy stick and mouse; typing on a computer keyboard; sending text messages; knitting, cooking, measuring, cutting, and sewing; building models; playing piano, violin, and flute; and more. All of these contribute to a child's growing sense of competence and industry (see "Socioemotional Development in Middle Childhood").

An old saying holds that "practice makes perfect," and there is some truth to this in middle childhood. Playing an instrument, for example, provides innumerable opportunities to assess, refine, and time motor responses in relation to constant feedback (i.e., sound). One study compared a group of students who took individual piano lessons once a week and practiced three to four hours a week for two years

fine motor skills Abilities required to control small movements of the hand and fingers, such as picking up small objects and tying one's shoes.

© Richard Hutchings / PhotoEdit

Further development of fine motor skills in middle childhood enables children in this period to begin to master a musical instrument.

with a control group who got no musical training (Costa-Giomi, 2005). At the end of this time, the piano students scored higher on tests of reaction time and overall information-processing speed than the controls. Thus, brain development allows children to practice fine motor skills, such as playing an instrument, and practice in turn stimulates brain development.

Some children who have significant difficulties with both gross and fine motor skills have **Developmental Coordination Disorder** (DCD). According to the American Psychiatric Association (APA; 2000), about 6 percent of five- to eleven-year-olds have DCD. The disorder is characterized by a marked impairment in motor coordination given what would be expected for the child's chronological age and intelligence. A DCD diagnosis requires that the motor impairments (1) significantly interfere with academic achievement or daily living activities (e.g., dressing, self-care, play), and (2) are not due to a general medical condition. Children with DCD may have difficulty with, for example, catching a ball, standing on one foot, riding a bicycle, tying shoelaces, and holding a pencil. Impairments may involve gross motor skills only, fine motor skills only, or a combination of the two. The cause of DCD is unknown, and the motor problems typically last into adulthood (Skinner & Piek, 2001). Occupational and physical therapists who specialize in children have developed services to improve fine and gross motor skills.

For a summary of this section, see "Interim Summary 10.3: Motor Development."

developmental coordination disorder (DCD) A disorder characterized by a marked impairment in motor coordination given what would be expected for the child's chronological age and intelligence.

SLEEP

Sleep is essential to both physical and brain growth. During quiet sleep, blood supply to the muscles increases, tissue growth and repair take place, and important hormones for growth and development are released (Mindell & Owens, 2003). Insufficient sleep can lead to poorer attention, learning, and school performance; behavior problems (such as hyperactivity in children who do not have ADHD, and more hyperactivity in those who do); and even overweight.

Amount of Sleep That Children Need

Historically, research on sleep in childhood relied on parent reports of children's bedtimes and quality of sleep, or child reports of sleepiness during the day. About 40 percent of parents report that their child has sleep problems, including taking too long to fall asleep, waking up during the night, appearing drowsy or overtired during the day, and/or snoring (Mindell & Owens, 2003).

actigraph A motion detector that measures sleep onset and awakenings.

Recent studies have been able to assess sleep more objectively and precisely with an **actigraph**, a motion detector than measures sleep onset, morning awakening, and night awakenings. These measures, in turn, can be used to determine a child's *sleep*

INTERIM SUMMARY **10.3**

Motor Development	
Gross Motor Skills	■ Running, jumping, hopping, throwing, and catching a ball are **gross motor skills** that become more refined in middle childhood.
	■ Improved flexibility, balance and coordination, agility, and strength during this period enable children to engage in new, more complex physical activities.
	■ Sociocultural factors and experience at home, in school, and out-of-school influence the development of gross motor skills.
Physical Activity	■ Experts recommend that school-age children get at least one hour of vigorous physical activity every day.
	■ Overall, school-age children get about half the recommended amount of exercise for their age during a typical school week.
Youth Sports	■ Participation in organized sports peaks at age 12.
	■ When coaches are positive and give technical instruction rather than make general comments, children are more likely to enjoy the sport and like the coach.
	■ When parents are supportive and enthusiastic—but not pushy—children are more likely to report enjoying the sport.
Fine Motor Skills	■ **Fine motor skills** involve refined use of the small muscles controlling the hand, fingers, and thumb, often coordinated with the eyes.
	■ Practice improves these skills.

period (time between the onset of sleep and morning awakening) and *true sleep times* (sleep period minus nighttime wakings and periods of restlessness). A parent might not know how much actual sleep a child gets between going to bed and getting up in the morning; indeed, a child might not remember short nighttime awakenings in the morning. Studies with actigraphs have found that true sleep time is usually less than either parent or child estimates.

How much sleep do children need and how much sleep do they get? In a series of studies of schoolchildren, an actigraph was used to measure children's sleep periods (Sadeh, Raviv, & Gruber, 2000). The results are shown in Table 10.3. (Note that girls typically sleep more than boys, and that sleep times decrease across middle childhood.)

True sleep times were 30–44 minutes less than these sleep periods. Nearly 18 percent of the children were "poor sleepers," defined as sleeping for 90 percent or less of their time from "Lights out" to "Rise and shine" or waking three or more times per night.

A study in the United States found that the sleep period for third-graders (average age eight to nine years) was 8 hours, 23 minutes (503 minutes) but their true sleep time was 7 hours, 4 minutes (424 minutes) (El-Sheikh et al., 2006). In both studies, then, children slept an hour or more *less* than the ten to eleven hours recommended.

One sleep disruption the actigraph does not measure is **apnea**: temporary pauses in breathing lasting from a few seconds to one minute (www.sleepfoundation.org). When these pauses occur, the brain sends a signal: "Wake up! Start breathing!" And the child

apnea A sleep disruption in which there are temporary pauses in breathing, ranging from a few seconds to a minute.

TABLE 10.3 Amount of Sleep by Gender in Grades 2, 4, and 6

GRADE	AVERAGE AGE (YEARS)	GIRLS	BOYS
2	7.9	555 minutes	554 minutes
		9.25 hours	9.25 hours
4	9.7	534	514
		8.9	8.6
6	11.8	494	487
		8.2	8.1

Source: Data from Sadeh, Raviv, & Gruber (2000).

nearly always does. But even though breathing is resumed, sound sleep has been interrupted. The symptoms of apnea are loud snoring and almost-gagging sounds. Most common among middle-aged men, apnea afflicts 1–3 percent of children, often in association with asthma, allergies, and obesity.

The Sleep Context

The quality of a child's sleep is related to his or her family circumstances (El-Sheikh et al., 2006; Sadeh et al., 2000). Children of low-income families have poorer quality sleep. They sleep for shorter periods, have more waking, and their sleep is more restless than children of higher income families. Children in families that are under stress—because of death, divorce, illness, hospitalizations, relocations, or emotional turmoil within the family—get also less high-quality sleep than other children. (Of course, poverty and stress often go together.)

Children who experience this kind of stress may experience increased activity in the adrenocortical system and become hypervigilant—always on the lookout, biologically, for threats to the self or the family. In effect, the alarm is always on. A similar response may explain why abused children take longer to fall asleep, are twice as active as other children during sleep, and so are sleep deprived (Glod et al., 1997).

Because actigraphs are a relatively new invention, we don't have comparable data for children of previous generations. However, compared with earlier times, children today are living among "sleep stealers." Most sodas and teas contain caffeine; so does chocolate. The Coke or Pepsi a child drinks during the day or in the evening stays in his or her system for hours, covering up natural tiredness. Electronics are a different kind of stimulant. Children who watch TV, play video games, or instant-message friends right up to bedtime (or after, if they have their own electronics in their room) may be too "revved up" to fall asleep.

Sleep and Cognitive Functioning

Feeling rested and energetic is not the only reason children need a good night's sleep. Cognitive functioning depends on it. Information learned during the day is "hardwired" into the brain during sleep, leaving the "desktop" cleared for new learning the next day. A large body of research documents what we all know intuitively, that sleep deprivation interferes with clear thinking.

Fragmented sleep—interrupted by sleep waking—lowers performance on tests of information-processing skills, including attention, executive function (planning, reasoning, and impulse control), and processing speed and efficiency (Buckhalt, El-Sheikh, & Keller, 2007; Sadeh, Gruber, & Raviv, 2002). Sleep duration also is linked to cognitive functioning. When children get less sleep, they perform more poorly on tests of intellectual ability and processing speed. Children who extend their sleep by thirty minutes improve their performance on tests of memory and reaction time (Sadeh, Gruber, & Raviv, 2003).

Last, there is a positive association between going to sleep at the same time every night and scores on tests of verbal ability (Buckhalt et al., 2007). One problem, of course, is that most children stay up later on weekend nights, so are switching schedules every week. To complicate matters, preference for a particular **circadian rhythm**, or twenty-four-hour sleep-wake cycle, often emerges during middle childhood (Donaldson & Owens, 2006). Some children feel and perform their best early in the day, whereas other children are sluggish in the morning but more alert during the evening hours. But the "morning person" and the "night owl" have to get up at the same time for school each weekday. Moreover, by age nine or ten, children often compete with each other about how late they stayed up—staying up late being a marker of the enviable status of teenager.

Everything considered, sleep research shows that what happens at night affects children's days (and vice versa). For a summary of this section, see "Interim Summary 10.4: Sleep."

circadian rhythm A daily rhythmic activity cycle, based on 24-hour intervals.

PHYSICAL HEALTH

Physical health continues to be important in middle childhood. Injuries, chronic ailments, and acute diseases each pose threats to children's growth and development.

Unintentional Injuries

Unintentional injuries are a serious threat to health and well-being in middle childhood (see Figure 10.7). Motor vehicle accidents are the leading cause of death for children in the United States. In 2005, 1,451 children age fourteen or under died in car crashes, and approximately 203,000 were injured—an average of four deaths and 556 injuries each day (Centers for

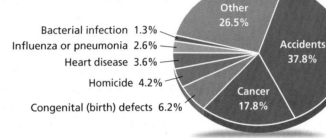

FIGURE 10.7

Leading Causes of Death in Middle Childhood

Injuries from accidents (motor vehicles and drowning) are the leading cause of death in this period. Many of these deaths are preventable. *Source:* Heron (2007).

INTERIM SUMMARY 10.4

Sleep	
Amount of Sleep That Children Need	■ Aspects of sleep (its onset, morning awakening, and night awakenings) are measured by an **actigraph**.
	■ On average, children sleep an hour or more *less* than the 10–11 hours recommended.
The Sleep Context	■ Poverty, illness, divorce, and relocations are related to poorer quality sleep (more awakenings and shorter sleep periods).
	■ Caffeine, chocolate, and electronic media are stimulants that can disrupt sleep.
Sleep and Cognitive Functioning	■ Fragmented sleep lowers performance on tests of attention, planning, reasoning, impulse control, processing speed, and processing efficiency.
	■ Children who extend their sleep by 30 minutes improve their performance on tests of memory and reaction time.

Disease Control, 2007). The tragedy is that many of these deaths and injuries could have been prevented. For children who are over 4'9", sitting in the back seat and wearing a safety belt could cut these numbers by half.

Drowning is the second most common cause of injury death in childhood (CDC, 2005). And for every child who drowns, five others require emergency room treatment for near-drownings. Again, safety procedures save lives. These include secure fences with alarms around pools, adult supervision whenever children are playing in or around water, and swimming in a lake or at a beach only when lifeguards are present.

The drowning rate for five- to fourteen-year-old African Americans is 3.2 times higher, and for American Indians and Alaskan Natives 2.6 times higher, than that for Caucasians. In these subcultures, learning to swim is not considered a routine part of growing up, so children who fall into the water cannot help themselves or count on their friends to help them get to safety (Branche et al., 2004). City parks and recreation programs, the Red Cross, and the YMCA are introducing programs in some urban neighborhoods, but many more are needed.

Illnesses

After injuries, cancer is the leading cause of death among school-age children, with approximately 8,500 new cases being diagnosed each year (Bradley-Kling, Grier, & Ax, 2006). Among different types of childhood cancer, leukemia (blood cell cancer), brain and other central nervous system (CNS) tumors, and lymphoma (originating in the lymph nodes) are most common. Caucasian children have higher rates of cancer than African American children (the opposite of the pattern in adults), with Hispanic and Asian/Pacific Islander children in between.

The overall trend in childhood cancer is a positive one. Although the overall incidence of invasive cancer in children has increased slightly over the past thirty years, mortality has declined dramatically. The combined survival rate for all childhood cancers grew from 56 percent in the 1970s to 79 percent in the 1990s as a result of improved treatments (Bradley-Kling et al., 2006).

School-age children have fewer acute, and potentially life-threatening, illnesses today for historical and developmental reasons. Fifty years ago, infectious diseases such as measles, chickenpox, mumps, influenza, and even polio were relatively common. Thanks to vaccinations, these diseases are rare today, at least in wealthy countries (see "Physical Development in Early Childhood"). In addition, the immune system develops rapidly during this period. This, plus immunities from previous exposure, also helps to protect children from gastrointestinal and respiratory illnesses.

There is no vaccination or cure for the *human immunodeficiency virus* (HIV). Without treatment, infection with HIV compromises the body's immune system, leaving the person vulnerable to "opportunistic" diseases that might not be harmful to a healthy person. The term *acquired immune deficiency syndrome* (AIDS) refers to the final stages of this disease when such illnesses take over, diminishing a victim's health and quality of life, often resulting in death. Thanks to new antiretroviral medications, the development of full-blown AIDS can be delayed and early death prevented.

It is very good news that the number of new childhood cases of HIV/AIDS has dropped dramatically, to only a few cases per year in the United States (Landau, Meyers, & Pryor, 2006). Most of these children are acquiring the virus from their mother— during pregnancy, birth, or through breastfeeding. If mothers do not know they carry the HIV virus or if they fail to seek treatment, there is a 25 percent chance that their newborns will be infected. However, if women take medications while they are pregnant, give birth by cesarean section, and do *not* breastfeed, the probability that the babies will be infected drops to 1 percent.

Without treatment, an HIV-positive baby rarely survives beyond age five. With treatment, most survive into adolescence and many to young adulthood. Tragically, treatment is not available or affordable in much of the developing world.

Can an HIV-positive child who is receiving treatment lead a normal life? The theoretical answer is, yes. They are not a danger to other children. There are no documented cases of HIV/AIDS being transmitted by casual contact at a daycare center or school (Landau et al., 2006). But HIV invades the central nervous system soon after infection. Depending on when the mother began treatment, a child may suffer cognitive and motor delays and deficits (Pulisfyer & Aylward, 2000). Isolating the impact of HIV is difficult. Many such children were also exposed to prenatal drugs, impoverished homes, a parental death, and numerous changes in living arrangements. Frequent medical treatments, hospitalizations, and school absences, as well as the social stigma attached to AIDS, complicate the picture. Thus, it is difficult to know whether developmental delays are due to the disease itself or to other issues that often accompany the disease (Landau et al., 2006).

Chronic Medical Conditions

Although acute illnesses have declined over the past fifty years, some chronic conditions have become more common, including asthma, allergies, and diabetes. But some—notably HIV/AIDS—are declining.

Asthma **Asthma** is a chronic respiratory condition that causes sudden attacks of wheezing, coughing, and shortness of breath. During an attack, the airways to the lungs contract and produce excess mucus. Severe attacks can result in difficulty speaking in complete sentences (McQuaid, Mitchell, & Esteban, 2006). Asthma attacks can be triggered by lung infections, allergic reactions to airborne substances, stress, exercise, and cold weather. It is the leading cause of school absenteeism in the United States (McQuaid et al., 2006).

asthma A chronic respiratory condition that causes sudden attacks of wheezing, coughing, and shortness of breath.

Nearly 10 percent of U.S. children ages five to eleven suffer from asthma (Bloom et al., 2006). The incidence of asthma in U.S. children in this age range increased 65 percent between 1980 and 1996 (Mannino et al., 2002). The reason or reasons for this sharp increase are difficult to pin down. Researchers have pointed to higher levels of air pollution and to the dust levels in better-insulated, airtight housing as likely suspects. Some (but not all) of the increase may be due to changes in the questions on health surveys.

Asthma is more common for boys than for girls and for African American children and Puerto Rican children than for Caucasian children. Poor children have higher rates than affluent children (Mannino et al., 2002).

Allergies Allergies also are common in middle childhood. Allergies occur when the immune system overreacts to substances in the environment, such as dust, pollen, or smoke (McQuaid et al., 2006). About 12 percent of children ages five to eleven years have respiratory (as opposed to food or skin) allergies (Bloom et al., 2006). Symptoms include a runny nose, sneezing, congestion, and a scratchy throat and eyes. Allergies have become more common, possibly due to greater exposure to indoor allergens, or to frequent antibiotic use, which reduces exposure to infection and hence the buildup of immunities (McQuaid et al., 2006). They are more frequently diagnosed in Caucasian children than in African American and Hispanic children, and in children whose parents have more education (Bloom et al., 2006). Obviously, education doesn't "cause" allergies, but educated parents may be more likely to seek medical attention for their children.

Having asthma or allergies affects a child's (and her family's) quality of life (McQuaid et al., 2006). The child may have difficulty concentrating in school as the result of active symptoms, poor sleep, or medication side effects. Asthma and allergies also can impose social limitations, such as not being able to participate in sports or go on a field trip to a zoo. Obvious symptoms and public use of medication (such as a bronchodilator) are embarrassing for some children. Moreover, acute attacks, with frightening symptoms (not being able to breathe) and visits to hospital emergency rooms, may leave a residue of anxiety. Last, controlling asthma and allergies often means following a strict medical regimen day in, day out. Colds go away; asthma and allergies don't.

Diabetes Diabetes is a third chronic condition that is common among school-age children (National Diabetes Education Program, 2006). Children who have diabetes have difficulty making and using insulin, a hormone that converts glucose into energy. As a consequence, glucose builds up in the bloodstream, causing damage to the tissues and organs. Then the glucose spills over into urine and is excreted, depriving the body of its primary source of fuel.

Type 1 diabetes A type of diabetes where the immune system destroys the beta cells in the pancreas so that pancreas produces little or no insulin.

There are two main forms of diabetes. In **Type 1 diabetes**, the immune system destroys the beta cells in the pancreas that produce insulin. Type 1 diabetes appears suddenly, most often in children, adolescents, and young adults. It is not related to being overweight. About 1 in 500–600 children under age twenty has this form of diabetes (Bradley-Kling et al., 2006). People with Type 1 diabetes need daily injections or supplements of insulin throughout their lives. Even with treatment they are at risk for long-term complications, including: damage to the cardiovascular system, which may result in heart attacks or strokes; kidney damage, which may require dialysis or transplant; poor circulation, particularly in the feet and legs, which makes people more vulnerable to infections that may lead to amputations; nerve damage; and blindness.

Type 2 diabetes A type of diabetes in which the body does not use insulin efficiently. Type 2 diabetes is brought on by a combination of genes, overweight, and inactivity.

Type 2 diabetes used to be called "adult-onset diabetes," because it occurred mainly in adults who were overweight and age forty or older. Now, with more children who are overweight and inactive, rates are rising among children. In Type 2 diabetes, the body cannot use insulin efficiently. At first the pancreas produces more, but after several years this is not enough and the person requires insulin-boosting medications and perhaps, later, insulin injections. Type 2 diabetes develops slowly and may not show symptoms for some time, so monitoring populations at risk is essential. Complications similar to those associated with Type 1 diabetes often begin ten to fifteen years after onset, but they can be delayed or even prevented through diet and exercise.

At present, about 177,000 Americans under age twenty have diabetes. Most have Type 1 diabetes, but rates of Type 2 diabetes have risen from less than 5 percent in 1994 to an estimated 30 to 50 percent of new, youthful diabetes cases today. The earlier onset of Type 2 diabetes means the earlier development of complications (when people are in their thirties and forties, not their fifties and sixties). Although no ethnic group is untouched, the disease is more common among American Indian, African American, Mexican American, and Pacific Islander youth.

Diabetes requires careful monitoring. Managing diabetes—measuring blood glucose level, taking medication and perhaps giving injections, following a strict diet, and exercising—is difficult to sustain (Kleinfield, 2006). Children with Type 1 diabetes need help and support from parents and school nurses, but many schools do not have full-time nurses. Children with Type 2 diabetes do not always follow the rules of their treatment. Many are in denial: They feel fine so insist that the doctor must be wrong, they don't have diabetes. Warned about the complications they might suffer ten or fifteen years later, when they will be in the prime of life, they shrug. They don't worry about things that might happen when they are thirty or forty, which seems like "old age" to them. Right now, following a diet and exercise program feels like punishment. Getting children (and adults) to take diabetes very seriously, as a potentially debilitating, life-shortening disease, is a major challenge.

For a summary of this section, see "Interim Summary 10.5: Physical Health."

INTERIM SUMMARY 10.5

Physical Health

Unintentional Injuries	■ Accidents are the leading cause of death for children in the United States.
	■ Motor vehicle accidents are the most common single cause of accidental death, followed by drowning.
	■ Many of these deaths are preventable.
Illnesses	■ After injuries, cancer is the leading cause of death among school-age children.
	■ Although the overall incidence of cancer has increased slightly over the past 30 years, mortality has declined dramatically.
	■ Infectious diseases such as measles, chickenpox, mumps, influenza, and polio are rare today because of vaccinations.
Chronic Medical Conditions	■ **Asthma** is a chronic respiratory condition that causes sudden attacks of wheezing, coughing, and shortness of breath.
	■ Allergies occur when the immune system overreacts to substances in the environment, such as dust, pollen, or smoke.
	■ Children who have diabetes have difficulty making and using insulin, a hormone that converts glucose into energy.

SUMMING UP AND LOOKING AHEAD

Children grow taller, stronger, and brainier in middle childhood, all of which contribute to significant advances in motor, cognitive, and social skills. With practice, a child can become adept at playing ice hockey or playing the piano at this age. Not surprisingly, out-of-school sports leagues and music lessons are quite popular.

Some school-age children are healthy and fit, but others are not. The dramatic increase in obesity illustrates how social and cultural change—the broader context— affects individual development. Fast food and soft drinks have become part of the American way of life. With today's hectic lifestyles, families take less time to prepare home-cooked meals from fresh ingredients. Schools have cut back on recess and PE classes. Many neighborhoods lack safe places for children to run and play outdoors. So too many children fill their afterschool hours with sedentary pastimes—not only TV but also video games and computers.

The overall picture of children's health is mixed. The good news is that death rates from childhood cancers and HIV/AIDS have declined. The bad news is that rates of chronic illness, such as asthma and diabetes, have increased. Moreover, formerly adult diseases—from Type 2 diabetes to posttraumatic stress disorder—are now being diagnosed in children.

Good health, a good night's sleep, and physical activity are essential not only to growth but also to cognitive development, the subject of the next chapter.

HERE'S WHAT YOU SHOULD KNOW

Did You Get It?

After reading this chapter, you should understand the following:

- The major features of physical growth and development in middle childhood, and the physical and mental impact of obesity

- How the brain develops during middle childhood and its reaction to stress

- The major accomplishments during middle childhood in the realms of gross and fine motor skills

- The importance of sleep and its relation to cognitive functioning

- The most common physical illnesses and problems in middle childhood

Important Terms and Concepts

actigraph (p. 292)
apoptosis (p. 281)
apnea (p. 293)
asthma (p. 297)
attention deficit hyperactivity disorder (ADHD) (p. 283)
axon (p. 280)
body mass index (BMI) (p. 276)
cerebellum (p. 284)
cerebral cortex (p. 283)
circadian rhythm (p. 295)

competitive elimination (p. 280)
corpus callosum (p. 280)
cortisol (p. 285)
dendrite (p. 280)
developmental coordination disorder (p. 292)
fine motor skills (p. 291)
frontal lobe (p. 282)
gonads (p. 275)
gray matter (p. 281)
gross motor skills (p. 287)

hippocampus (p. 285)
hypothalamus (p. 275)
lateralization (p. 280)
menarche (p. 275)
myelin (p. 280)
neurotransmitters (p. 284)
normative development (p. 274)
parietal lobe (p. 282)
pituitary gland (p. 275)
posttraumatic stress disorder (PTSD) (p. 285)

prefrontal cortex (p. 282)
puberty (p. 274)
secular trend (p. 276)
synapse (p. 280)
synaptic pruning (p. 280)
temporal lobe (p. 282)
traumatic brain injury (TBI) (p. 283)
Type 1 diabetes (p. 298)
Type 2 diabetes (p. 298)
white matter (p. 282)

Cognitive Development in Middle Childhood

Ashley and her brother, Colin, the daughter and son of one of this book's authors, made some impressive strides in their cognitive and academic skills during middle childhood (Vandell, 2008, personal observation). At the beginning of first grade, they knew about letters, words, and sounds, and they began to read simple sentences. They understood small numbers and quantities and could perform simple addition and subtraction problems.

By the end of third grade, they were fluent at both oral and silent reading and were able to draw inferences from cues in the text and to make interpretations beyond the text. Their grasp of mathematics displayed a similar explosion. As third-graders, they were multiplying, dividing, and understanding place values and integers to the hundreds.

By the end of fifth grade (at age eleven years), they were skilled readers of more complex works of fiction and nonfiction and used their knowledge of word meaning and literary context cues to expand their vocabulary. (Some favorite books were *Where the Red Fern Grows, A Wrinkle in Time*, and *The Giver*.) They were comfortable working with very large and very small numbers, and they were able to move beyond particular problems to more general problem solutions.

What cognitive operations and experiences support this kind of dramatic growth in academic skills in middle childhood? How do teaching strategies and school organization influence academic skills? Do experiences at home and after school contribute to these skills?

In this chapter, we start by looking at advances in children's thought as revealed by Piaget's theory, by contemporary studies of learning and strategic thinking, and by the information-processing approach. Next we consider intelligence: What is intelligence and how is it measured? We then look more closely at the growth of two academic competencies that are of particular interest in schools: reading and mathematics. We then consider schools and schooling in the United States, emphasizing efforts to improve academic achievement. We conclude by looking at ways in which technology and media are providing new settings for cognitive and academic development during middle childhood.

PIAGET AND BEYOND

How does thinking change in middle childhood? Piaget's theory emphasizes the development of more advanced reasoning. Studies of learning and strategic thinking emphasize growth in problem-solving skills. Models of information processing emphasize changes in the sequential processing of information. We will look at each of these approaches in turn.

The Concrete Operational Period

Concrete operations is the third stage of cognitive development within Piaget's theory (Piaget, 1983; Piaget & Inhelder, 1967). It is during this period (roughly between ages seven and twelve years) that children's mental activities (or *operations* in Piaget's terminology) become more logical with respect to actual (i.e., *concrete*) objects and materials.

In "Cognitive Development in Early Childhood," we described the hallmarks of children's thinking in the preoperational period, when children are strongly influenced by appearances. Preschool-age children are unable to perform **conservation** tasks involving mass and volume because they are "fooled" by how objects appear—to the preoperational child, a line of gumdrops stretched out over a larger space is preferable to one containing the same number of candies that is squished into a smaller space, because it is "more." School-age children don't fall for this. They understand that some characteristics—including volume, mass, and number—do not change despite changes in form or appearance. In the concrete operational period, according to Piaget, children's thinking is *qualitatively* different from that of the preoperational period. (Recall that qualitative differences are differences in type or kind, whereas quantitative differences are differences in amount.)

Hallmarks of Concrete Operational Thinking

The hallmarks of the concrete operational period are five interrelated competencies—classification, class inclusion, seriation, transitive inference, and reversibility—that underlie logical reasoning (see Table 11.1). The development of these competencies allows the concrete operational child to apply logic across a variety of situations—on tests of conservation in the psychologist's lab, in the classroom, at home, and with friends.

Classification is the ability to divide or sort objects into different sets and subsets and to consider their interrelationships. It includes the ability to group items along multiple dimensions (Inhelder & Piaget, 1964). Harry Potter, for instance, can be classified as a wizard, a boy, a member of Gryffindor house, and a Quidditch player, among other qualities.

Class inclusion is a logical operation that recognizes that a class (or group) can be part of a larger group. If a preoperational child is shown seven dogs and three cats and asked if there are more dogs or more animals, she will say "more dogs." She is comparing dogs to cats and not to the larger class ("animals"). The concrete operational

concrete operations The third stage of cognitive development in Piaget's theory when mental activities become more logical with respect to actual (i.e., *concrete*) objects and materials.

conservation The understanding that some characteristics of objects (including volume, mass, and number) do not change despite changes in form or appearance.

classification The ability to divide or sort objects into different sets and subsets, and to consider their interrelationships.

class inclusion A logical operation that recognizes that a class (or group) can be part of a larger group.

TABLE 11.1 Hallmarks of Cognitive Development in the Concrete Operational Period

OPERATION	DEFINITION	EXAMPLE
Classification	Dividing objects into sets and subsets and examining relationships between them	Separating objects into groups by color and shape: red triangles, blue triangles, red circles, blue circles
Class inclusion	Recognition that one class or group can be part of a larger group	Motorcycles and trucks are both recognized as "vehicles"
Seriation	Arranging items in sequence according to particular properties	Arranging sticks in order from shortest to longest
Transitive inference	Comparing two sets of relationships to each other	If stick 1 is shorter than stick 2, and stick 1 is longer than stick 3, child knows that stick 2 is longer than stick 3
Reversibility	Reversing operations in order to turn relations to their original state	A ball of clay that has been flattened out can be re-formed into a ball

Children's collections provide them with many opportunities to organize and classify objects along different dimensions.

© Laura Dwight

child, in contrast, will say "more animals." Class inclusion requires that children understand that dogs and cats can be part of a broader concept of animals.

Math classrooms in the primary grades (K–3) sometimes use what are called "attribute blocks" to provide children opportunities to develop understandings of classification and class inclusion. These small blocks vary in size (small, medium, large), shape (square, triangle, circle), and color (red, black, blue, yellow). Most second-graders (seven- to eight-year-olds) are able to sort these blocks in various ways on their own—by color, by shape, by size; and some can sort by color and shape simultaneously. Others, however, are not yet able to do this task. When asked to form a group of blocks that go together, they simply look perplexed. In a classroom observed by one of the authors when she taught young children, a student looked around as he saw others moving the blocks to create separate groups. He then proceeded to create two groups on his desk, looked up proudly, and announced, "This one's the messy group. And this one is the not so messy group"—a perceptually based response characteristic of a preoperational thinker.

School-age children enjoy classification, as seen in their intense interest in collections of all sorts—baseball cards, stamps, rocks, dolls, and action figures. When they play with their collections, they organize and reorganize them, over and over. Baseball cards can be sorted and organized by teams, player positions, years, rarity, and so forth. Rocks can be sorted by type, origin, color, size, and so on.

seriation The ability to arrange items in a sequenced order according to particular properties.

Seriation, a third operation that is acquired during middle childhood, is the ability to arrange items in a sequenced order according to particular properties (Inhelder & Piaget, 1964). Concrete operational children are able to organize items along various dimensions such as height (shortest to tallest) or color (lightest to darkest). An everyday application of seriation occurs when children organize themselves by height for their class photograph. Seriation requires that children simultaneously recognize two-way relations—Juan is taller than Jason but shorter than George. Preoperational children struggle with relational concepts, such as *taller than* or *bigger than*. They don't seem to grasp that object A can be both bigger than object B and smaller than object C. Concrete operational children "get it."

transitive inference A logical operation that builds on an understanding of seriation. It requires that two relations are combined to derive a third relation.

Transitive inference builds on an understanding of seriation. For example, we know that George is taller than Juan and Juan is taller than Jason. Is George taller than Jason? The concrete operational child can compare two relations ("George >Juan" and "Juan >Jason"), put the two together ("George >Juan >Jason"), and arrive at the answer. This ability becomes increasingly important in the development of math skills, as you can well imagine.

reversibility A logical operation that requires an understanding that relations can be returned to their original state by reversing operations—if nothing has been added or taken.

Reversibility is the fifth operation Piaget (1983) described. Reversibility is the understanding that relations can be returned to their original state by reversing operations—if nothing has been added or taken away. For example, the child understands that if 10 pennies = 1 dime this relation can be reversed: 1 dime = 10 pennies. Reversibility is one of the keys to understanding conservation, one of the crowning achievements of the concrete operational period.

The development of basic logic means that school-age children are able to think about the world using basic principles of logic, not just report what they see. But the use of logical operations during middle childhood is limited to concrete materials and tasks; not until adolescence will individuals be able to apply the same logical reasoning abilities to things that they cannot directly experience. Children in the concrete operational stage think about the real world, not abstract concepts such as *democracy*, *justice*, or *social class*. This is one of the reasons that math teachers in elementary school use "manipulatives"—materials such as an abacus or the attribute blocks described earlier—to provide hands-on experience with addition, subtraction, multiplication, division, fractions, and place value. Of course, many children discover that their fingers (and their toes) are also useful manipulatives for solving some addition and subtraction problems!

Piaget recognized that children's reasoning does not instantly shift from preoperations to concrete operations. Instead, children demonstrate conservation in some tasks before others. Inhelder and Piaget (1964) called this differential performance in logical thinking **horizontal decalage**. Children are able, typically, to successfully solve conservation of matter problems before they can successfully do conservation of number (see "Cognitive Development in Early Childhood").

horizontal decalage Differences in performance on conceptually related Piagetian tasks. For example, children typically understand conservation of mass before they understand conservation of number.

Experiences That Foster Advances in Concrete Operations

Piaget (1964) believed that concrete operational thinking is a natural outgrowth of children's opportunities to manipulate materials and objects and to "experiment" with these materials. He did not think that logical operations need to be explicitly taught. Other researchers, however, find that concrete operational thinking can be fostered by particular experiences. For example, in a study of number conservation, Robert Siegler (1995) asked five-year-old children to explain how they came up with their response to an experimenter's question about "which row has more tokens?" Simply asking children to explain their reasoning helped to prompt the development of more advanced reasoning. Reasoning based on length (a typical preoperational response) decreased over time, whereas reasoning based on counting and reversibility increased.

Formal schooling, in general, also fosters concrete operational thinking. Mathematics instruction often incorporates explicit lessons about properties of numbers such as reversibility and transitivity. Language arts and reading classes include exercises in class inclusion. "Cars are vehicles; buses are vehicles; trucks are vehicles. Can you think of any other vehicles? What are some characteristics of vehicles?" "Broccoli is a vegetable. Green beans are vegetables. Can you think of any other vegetables?"

Although schooling can foster concrete operational thinking, it is not required. Child street vendors in Brazil (who have very little formal schooling) do poorly on Piaget's classic class inclusion problems when tested by experimenters, but they demonstrate an understanding of class inclusion when the questions are worded in ways that tap knowledge they need in their businesses (e.g., that when a customer asks to buy a peach, it is better to offer a nectarine if there are no peaches left than to offer a bag of nuts, because peaches and nectarines are members of the same general class) (Ceci & Roazzi, 1994; Nunes, Schliemann, & Carraher, 1993).

Piaget's overarching goal was to describe the structure or organization of children's thinking in different developmental periods. He was less interested in determining, in detail, how and why development occurs. More recently, however, others have sought to understand *how* children process information. It is to this work that we now turn.

Learning and the Development of Strategic Thinking

Sixty years ago psychologists who studied learning were interested in seeing how rewards and punishments shaped observed behaviors (Skinner, 1953). Contemporary studies of learning have a different focus: how children are actively involved in learning and strategic thinking.

microgenetic analysis A research strategy that involves frequent, detailed observations of behavior.

The Microgenetic Approach Changes in strategic thinking within a session and across sessions are documented using a research strategy called **microgenetic analysis**. Microgenetic analysis involves close-up (*micro*) study of development (*genesis*). Robert Siegler (2006, p. 469), a respected scholar who studies learning, observed, "The only way to find out how children learn is to study them closely while they are learning." Siegler and other scientists using this approach make frequent, detailed observations of children's behavior during periods of rapid change.

Siegler and Stern (1998) provide an example of this type of study. Second-grade students were asked to solve math problems in the form of $A + B - B = ?$ An example of such a problem is, $16 + 7 - 7 = ?$ If a child solves this problem using a simple computation strategy, she adds the first two numbers together and then subtracts the third number ($16 + 7 = 23; 23 - 7 = 16$.) This strategy takes about sixteen seconds to execute. A second strategy, the shortcut strategy, takes less than four seconds. The shortcut involves reasoning that $B - B = 0$ so the answer must be A—regardless of what numbers are in the equation. Siegler and Stern documented children's progression from using the computation strategy to an unconscious use of the shortcut strategy to conscious use of the shortcut strategy over a series of sessions.

Microgenetic analyses have been applied to a wide variety of domains, including mathematical reasoning, scientific thinking, and memory. Lawler (1985) studied his daughter over a four-month period as she learned how to debug simple computer programs and solve simple arithmetic problems across a total of ninety sessions. Kuhn, Schauble, and Garcia-Mila (1992) observed ten-year-olds' learning of scientific experimentation skills over a nine-week period (eighteen different sessions), and Schagmuller & Schneider (2002) used a microgenetic approach to document changes in memory strategies over an eleven-week period. Across these and other studies, consistent patterns of learning and strategic thinking emerged, which we summarize next (Siegler, 2006).

Research Findings In contrast to the stage-like and consistent performance suggested by Piaget's theory (i.e., if a child is in the concrete operational period, he will usually demonstrate concrete operational thinking, regardless of the problem), microgenetic studies show that individual children's behavior is much more variable at any given time, with a given child using different strategies on different problems and sometimes using different strategies on the same problems. Individual variability in performance is greatest during periods of rapid learning. For most types of learning, older and more knowledgeable children learn more quickly and use more appropriate generalizations than younger children do. In general, as children learn, their strategic thinking is characterized by a greater reliance on more advanced strategies, improved choices among strategies, and improved execution of strategies over time. (For a summary of this section, see "Interim Summary 11.1: Piaget and Beyond.)

INFORMATION PROCESSING

The information-processing approach provides an additional perspective to understanding cognitive development in middle childhood. Here, researchers are studying how children come to attend to relevant information (attention), retain (or remember) the information, and then use the information to reason and solve problems

INTERIM SUMMARY 11.1

Piaget and Beyond

The Concrete Operational Period	▪ In this period (roughly ages 7 to 12 years), thought becomes more logical with respect to actual (i.e., *concrete*) objects.
	▪ The period is qualitatively different from preoperational thinking.
Hallmarks of Concrete Operations	▪ Hallmarks of the period are **classification, class inclusion, seriation, transitive inference,** and **reversibility**.
	▪ These cognitive operations enable children to perform **conservation** tasks and formal mathematics.
Experiences That Foster Advances in Concrete Operations	▪ Piaget believed that concrete operational thinking is a natural outgrowth of children's opportunities to manipulate materials and objects.
	▪ Others have studied ways to foster **concrete operations**: Asking children to explain their thinking can increase logical thinking.
	▪ Formal schooling also encourages concrete operational thinking.
Learning and the Development of Strategic Thinking	▪ **Microgenetic analysis** involves close-up (micro) study of development (genesis).
	▪ These studies show that children's behavior is more variable than Piaget suggested. A given child uses different strategies on different problems and sometimes uses different strategies on the same problems.

(Munakata, 2006). Attention, memory, and problem solving all improve in middle childhood, which makes reasoning and strategic thinking possible.

Processing Speed

One way to study how children process information is to look at their processing speed and accuracy (Kail & Ferrer, 2007). *Visual matching* and *cross out* are two procedures that researchers have used. In the visual matching procedure, a task card consists of sixty rows of six digits (e.g., 8 9 5 2 9 7). Two of the rows are identical. The child is asked to circle the identical rows. Processing speed is then measured as the number of task cards that a child can complete correctly in a set amount of time (see Figure 11.1).

In the cross-out procedure, a task card has thirty rows of geometric figures. At the left of each row is the target figure (e.g., a triangle with a circle in the middle). To the right are nineteen similar geometric figures, five of which are identical. The child is asked to cross out the five identical figures. Processing speed is measured by the number of rows the child can complete in a set period.

In a longitudinal study of children tested between five and eighteen years, Kail and Ferrer (2007) found that children's processing speed showed greater improvements in middle childhood than in adolescence. This developmental pattern

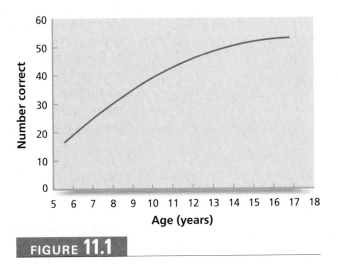

FIGURE 11.1

Processing Speed in Childhood and Adolescence

Processing speed, measured as the number of task cards completed correctly, improves more rapidly in middle childhood than in adolescence.

Source: Adapted from Kail & Ferrer (2007).

is similar to the pattern of development of gray matter in the temporal region of the brain that we discussed in "Physical Development in Middle Childhood" (Giedd et al., 1999). In general, and as we will discuss when we turn to adolescence, the development of most information-processing abilities is especially rapid during the school years, and it tends to reach a plateau in adolescence.

Faster, more efficient information processing helps to set the stage for advances in both working memory and long-term memory (Halford, 2004). It is to these advances we turn next.

Working Memory

working memory Conscious, short-term representations of what a person is actively thinking about at a given time.

When children are paying attention, they are focusing their working memory on specific information (Martinez, in press). In other words, **working memory** is conscious, short-term representations of what a person is actively thinking about at a given time. Working memory is clearly relevant for teachers and parents because it provides an upper limit to how many items children can keep in mind when being taught or when given a list of things to remember ("When you get home from school, I want you to clean up your room, walk the dog, set the table for dinner, and do your homework.").

digit span task A research procedure in which people are asked to repeat in order a series of rapidly presented items.

One way of assessing working memory is the **digit span task**, a research procedure in which people are asked to recall a series of rapidly presented items—numbers, letters, or words (Schneider, 2004). Two-year-olds have a memory span of about two items. Five-year- olds can remember about four items; seven-year-olds, about five items; and nine-year-olds, about six items. The average for adults is about seven items (Miller, 1956).

This small number of items is not as huge a limitation on how much information children can retain and use as you would think, however. Part of the reason is that children become more skilled at chunking bits of information into larger units that then serve as items (Pressley & Hilden, 2006). For example, a parent's cell phone number has ten units (e.g., 312-555-1212), which is beyond the short-term memory capacity of a seven-year-old. But these numbers can be chunked and recalled as a three units: the area code (312), the prefix (555), and the number (1212). Children (and adults) are more likely to chunk material that is familiar or has special meaning.

One of the things that distinguish experts from novices is their ability to chunk information. Expert chess players (both children and adults) are able to see common patterns of play across several turns and remember these patterns as single units of meaningful information (Chase & Simon, 1973). Child chess experts are able to outperform adult novices on chess moves, but not on the standard digit span task (Schneider et al., 1993). Similarly, at the beginning of a swim practice, coaches give complicated instructions to nine- and ten-year-old competitive swimmers who seem to have no trouble recalling a long list of commands as they swim laps back and forth in twenty-five-yard pools.

200 (yd) swim, every fourth length dolphin dives

150 (yd) kick, alternating flutter kick, dolphin kick, breaststroke kick, every 25 yds

100 (yd) pull, going down fingertip drag, coming back normal

six 50-freestyles getting faster by 3

two minutes vertical kick in the deep end

The swimmers are clearly "chunking" these instructions (as well as doing on-the-spot multiplication and division)!

Long-Term Memory

Long-term memory can span from minutes after an event to decades. It can take different forms: **declarative memory** (memories of facts, such as names of people and places, phone numbers, etc.), **procedural memory** (memories of complex skills such as riding a bicycle and typing on a keyboard), **verbatim memory** (detailed memories of specific events), and **gist memory** (a general, not specific, memory of common occurrences). Each of these types of memory improves in middle childhood.

Several factors influence whether a piece of information held in working memory becomes a long-term memory (Martinez, in press). One is the length of time that the information is actively attended to. The more time a child focuses on the thought, word, person, or sight, the more likely that it will be stored in long-term memory. Long-term memories take some recording time—roughly a minute to record a single piece of information in long-term memory (Martinez, in press).

In a classic study of more than 700 children, steady increases in memory were found between ages six and eighteen years, with, as we would expect given patterns of brain development, a somewhat sharper increase between six and eleven years than between twelve and eighteen years (Brunswik, Goldschneider, & Pilck, 1932 as cited in Schneider, 2004).

Memory Strategies Memory strategies are mental or behavioral activities that can improve recall and recognition of material. The simplest, often used by children, is rehearsal or repetition (Pressley & Hilden, 2006). Practicing spelling words and multiplication tables with flash cards are examples of this common rehearsal strategy in middle childhood. As students and parents have discovered, practice distributed over several days is more effective than one day of intensive practice.

Written notes ("to-do lists") also can improve long-term memory (Martinez, in press). It's one of the reasons that it is so helpful for teachers to write assignments on the blackboard (or, nowadays, on a website) and for students to record the assignments in their logbooks. Writing something down requires effort and is a more advanced way of rehearsing.

Explicitly relating new information to prior knowledge also increases the likelihood that the new material is remembered (Pressley & Hilden, 2006). Suppose that a child is asked to learn new facts about her state (the state bird, flower, tree, capital, largest city, etc.). She is more likely to remember the new information if she adds it to other knowledge that she has about the state. Think about it. Let's say that in March, someone asks you a question about the Super Bowl (which was played in February). If you had been following a particular football team from the beginning of the season to the championship game, over time you will have learned about the players, the team's strengths and weaknesses, the coach's play-calling, and so forth. One month after the Super Bowl you will be more likely to remember specific facts about the championship (e.g., the play that won or lost the game) than if you had ignored the regular season and had only watched the Super Bowl. (This is partly why experts recall more than novices.)

Still another memory strategy is to organize pictures or words into meaningful categories. Suppose a child is given a randomly ordered list of words to memorize: shoes, hat, cat, table, cow, pants, chair, dress, raccoon, desk. This task is easier for children in middle childhood than in early childhood because the older children can mentally sort the objects into categories: *clothes* (shoes, hat, pants, dress); *animals* (cat, cow, raccoon); and *furniture* (table, chair, desk). Organizing the items (class inclusion to use Piaget's terminology) creates chunks, and the category labels act as retrieval cues.

In middle childhood, children may not explicitly and mindfully use these sorts of strategies on their own, but they can be taught to do so, sometimes with improvements in performance (Bjorkland et al., 1997). But even after specific instructions, preschoolers do not use these deliberate strategies (Miller & Seier, 1994). Or, if they use the strat-

long-term memory Information that is mentally encoded and stored, potentially with no time limits.

declarative memory Memory of facts, such as names of people and places, and phone numbers.

procedural memory A memory of complex motor skills, such as riding a bicycle or typing on a keyboard.

verbatim memory Detailed memories of specific events.

gist memory A generalized, rather than specific, memory of common occurrences.

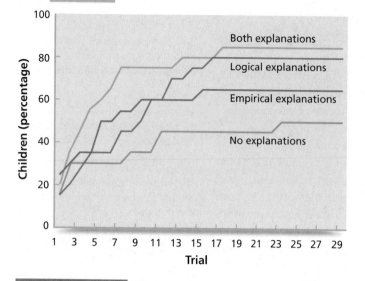

FIGURE 11.2

Cumulative Percentage of Children Who Reached Discovery Criterion at Different Trials

Children's performance jumps from near chance level to more skilled performance very quickly instead of showing a pattern of slow, steady improvement over many trials (Siegler, 2006).
Source: Siegler & Svetina (2006).

false memory   A *memory* that is a distortion of an actual experience, or a confabulation of an imagined one.

Deese-Roediger-McDermott (DRM) procedure   An experimental task that demonstrates the creation of false memories; participants often recollect or recall words that they have not heard because they make associations based on conceptual commonalities.

misinformation paradigm
Research that demonstrates that memories can be changed when misleading information is provided after the fact.

egy, they do not appear to benefit from using it—that is, their recall of material is not improved by teaching them the very same memory strategies.

Microgenetic Analyses of Memory Strategies
Recent microgenetic analyses of individual children's performance suggest that the development of strategies is not the result of slow, steady growth (Siegler, 2006). In one study, only 8 percent of the children showed gradual steady increases in their use of organizational strategies. Over 80 percent of the children jumped from chance level to near perfect performance, a pattern consistent with a qualitative shift. Eight percent were near perfect at the start, suggesting that they had already mastered these strategies. Three percent never showed use of a strategy, even when instructed to do so, a pattern similar to preschoolers (Siegler, 2006) (see Figure 11.2).

False Memories

As much as we like to believe that our memories are unerringly factual and accurate records ("I heard you say that you were putting out the trash," "I saw the man entering the house"), this is not the case. The process of constructing memories can create memory distortions and **false memories** (Brainerd et al., 2006; Brainerd & Reyna, 2004).

One way that scientists demonstrate the construction of false memories is through the use of the **Deese-Roediger-McDermott (DRM) procedure** (Deese, 1959; Roediger & McDermott, 1995). Suppose you were presented with the following list of words: bed, rest, awake, tired, dream. After taking the list away, you are asked either to recall the words or to select the words you heard off a list that includes the original words plus some new ones (a recognition task).

Adults typically recalled and recognized words that were not presented (e.g., *sleep*) about as often as words that were presented. This is because adults made associations about the conceptual or semantic commonalities among words, which then led them to include *sleep*, a word that they had not actually heard. In one study, eleven-year-olds created false memories that were similar to adults (Dewhurst & Robinson, 2004). Like adults, the eleven-year-olds "remembered" nonpresented words that were conceptually or semantically related to the words that they had heard.

Findings for younger children given the same task were different, and they tell us something about how their minds are organized. Five-year-olds tended to falsely "remember" nonpresented words based on how they *sounded*. They tended to select nonpresented words that rhymed with the presented words, making associations based on sounds (phonology) rather than on meaning (semantics). The eight-year-olds made the most errors of all because they made both phonological and semantic associations to nonpresented words!

A second procedure, called the **misinformation paradigm**, demonstrates how memories can be changed after the fact. In one early experiment, Elizabeth Loftus (1975) showed college students a brief action-filled film of a car accident. Then, the students were asked a series of questions about the accident. One group was asked, "How fast was Car A going when it ran the stop sign?" A second group was asked, "How fast was Car A going when it turned right?" Later the students were asked if there was a stoplight at the intersection. Group One was more likely to report that there was a stoplight (when in fact there was not). Simply referring to a stop *sign* in the postexposure questions increased the likelihood of students later recalling a stop-*light*. Misleading information provided after the fact can impair memory of an original event (Loftus & Hoffman, 1989).

Children's memories also can be affected by misinformation. In one study (Ceci, Ross, & Toglia, 1987), children were read a story about a girl named Loren, who went to her first day of school and had a stomachache after eating too quickly. The next day, children were asked questions about the story. The treatment group was given misinformation: "Do you remember the story about Loren who had a headache because she ate her cereal too fast?" Two days later, the children were given a test that pitted true events against misinformation.

Misinformation (that Loren had a headache) was related to false memories in all age groups (three-, five-, eight-, and ten-year-olds), although the size of the effect decreased with age. Younger children were more susceptible than older children to misinformation. So, it looks like how questions are worded can create and modify memories over time. Gist memories (which are more global and undifferentiated) are more likely to be distorted or changed following misinformation than are verbatim memories (Brainerd & Reyna, 2005).

Children's Testimony

Researchers are studying ways to improve interview techniques to decrease the likelihood of distortions and false memories (Brainerd & Reyna, 2005). This research is particularly important as children are being called upon to participate in high-stakes legal proceedings (Brainerd & Reyna, 2005).

An important question is how much and how accurately children can remember, and the extent to which their memory is influenced by misinformation, selective reinforcement, leading questions, and a desire to please the questioner.

False memories are affected by the amount of time that transpired between the event and the interview, by the number of times that the child is interviewed, and by having a highly biased interviewer who asks leading and misleading questions (Quas et al., 2007). Children (three- and five-year-olds) who are interviewed only once by a biased interviewer make the most errors. Interviewer bias appears most problematic when children's memories have weakened.

Michael Lamb and other scientists at the National Institute of Child Health and Human Development (NICHD) have devised a protocol for interviewing children that reduces memory distortions (Lamb et al., 2002). A single person specifically trained in child forensic interview techniques conducts the one-on-one conversation with the child in a child-friendly room with video and audio capability. Observers watch the interview behind one-way glass or via closed-circuit TV. The observers can pose questions to the interviewer via a small microphone in the interviewer's ear.

The structure of the questions is consistent with accurate recollections. The interviewer first seeks to have the child provide free recall narrative in his or her own words, followed by neutral prompts that are found to improve recall ("Do you remember anything more?"). If neutral prompts fail to elicit information, the interviewer moves to cued recall that names a reference point that the child has already mentioned ("Can you tell me more about what happened

© Brand X Pictures / Jupiterimages

Children's testimony can be affected by the number of times a child is interviewed and by a biased interviewer asking leading or misleading questions.

INTERIM SUMMARY 11.2

Information Processing

Processing Speed	■ Faster processing speed and more efficient information processing help to set the stage for advances in both **working memory** and **long-term memory**.
	■ Improvements in processing speed are steep during the school years and tend to reach a plateau in adolescence.
Working Memory	■ The **digit span task**, in which people are asked to recall a series of rapidly presented items, is one way to test working memory.
	■ Two-year-olds have a memory span of about two items. Five-year-olds can remember about four items; seven-year-olds about five items, and nine-year-olds about six items. The average for adults is about seven items.
	■ Limitations of working memory are not a huge problem because people become more skilled at chunking bits of information into larger units, which then serve as items.
Long-Term Memory	■ Long-term memory spans from minutes after an event to decades. Long-term memory includes **declarative, procedural, verbatim,** and **gist** memories, all of which improve in middle childhood.
	■ Factors influencing long-term memory include the length of time that the information is actively attended to, rehearsal or repetition, written notes, relating new information to prior information, and organizing information into meaningful categories.
False Memories	■ **False memories** are memory distortions.
	■ The **Deese-Roediger-McDermott (DRM)** procedure demonstrates that adults and older children create false memories around conceptually related information.
	■ The misinformation paradigm demonstrates how memories can be changed after the fact.
Children's Testimony	■ Developmental scientists have developed guidelines for interviewing children that reduce memory distortions.

in the kitchen?"). If that fails to elicit details, then the interviewer moves to paired recall ("You said that he took you to another room, can you tell me more about that?" or "You said that he took you to another room. Was it the kitchen or the living room or the bathroom?"). A key is that the interviewer does not add information that the child hasn't volunteered.

In conclusion, middle childhood is a period in which children come to process information more quickly. They also begin to develop and use strategies to organize and remember information. Like adults, their memories can be affected by misinformation after the fact as well as by the creation of false memories. Interviewers who are responsible for obtaining children's testimony in high-stakes legal cases must be particularly careful not to create false memories. (For a summary of this section, see "Interim Summary 11.2: Information Processing.")

INTELLIGENCE

Another approach to understanding children's cognitive development uses standardized tests to measure individual (and group) differences in general cognitive abilities or intelligence (Sternberg, 2004).

A Brief History of Efforts to Measure Intelligence

A cousin of Charles Darwin, Sir Francis Galton, was one of the first scientists to attempt to measure intelligence. Galton (1907), tried (unsuccessfully) to use simple cognitive tasks such as reaction times to assess intelligence. Other European scientists of the day, such as Alfred Binet and Theodore Simon (1908), argued that a broader approach was needed because intelligence involves people making complex evaluations of what has to be done and how to do it, weighing different strategies, and critiques of thoughts and actions.

Binet and Simon's ideas were brought to the United States by Louis Terman (1916), a professor at Stanford University, who created early versions of a test that became known as the Stanford-Binet Intelligence Test. Revised and updated, this test is still used today. It has separate parts that measure verbal reasoning, quantitative reasoning, abstract visual reasoning, and short-term memory. Intelligence quotients (IQ) are computed based on a relative performance within an age group. The average or mean score on the Stanford Binet is 100, with a standard deviation of 15 points. Seventeen percent of children score above 115, and 17 percent score below 85 (see Figure 11.3).

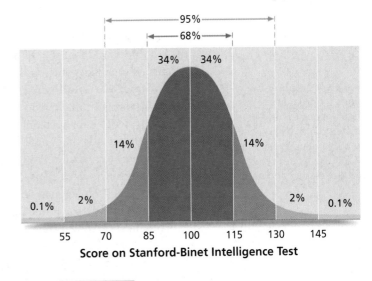

FIGURE 11.3

The Distribution of IQ Scores

The distribution of the scores on the Stanford-Binet and other commonly used IQ tests is set so the mean is 100 and the standard deviation is 15.

Another commonly used test is the Wechsler Intelligence Scale for Children (WISC-III; Wechsler, 1991), which has two main scales—a performance scale and a verbal scale. The performance scale includes tasks such as rearrangements of a scrambled set of cartoon-type pictures to tell a story and the identification of missing parts of a picture. The verbal scale includes vocabulary, similarities, and understanding of common social customs.

The adequacy of these tests is assessed by examining their **reliability** and **validity.** A reliable test is one in which individuals receive similar or consistent scores each time they are tested. Valid tests are ones that assess what the test developer claims to be measuring.

Critics of IQ tests have raised broader questions about the meaning and nature of intelligence, how it is manifested, and whether it can be modified. It is to these broader questions that we turn next.

reliability A reliable test is one in which individuals receive similar or relatively consistent scores each time they are tested.

validity The extent to which a test measures what it was designed to measure.

Are There Multiple Intelligences?

One question concerns whether intelligence is a single general trait or a number of separate, independent capabilities. Charles Spearman (1904) held that different abilities are all a manifestation of a single general factor that he called **g**, for general cognitive abilities. Louis Thurstone (1938), in contrast, argued that intelligence is composed of seven distinct factors or "primary abilities"—verbal comprehension, verbal fluency (the speed with which one can think of words starting with a particular letter), inductive reasoning (measured by analogies), number (computation and solving math problems), memory, perceptual speed, and space (measured by mental rotations).

Thurstone came up with this list using a statistical technique called *factor analysis*. Although the math is somewhat complicated, the basic principles of factor analysis are simple. If people who score high (or low) on a vocabulary test also score high (or low) on a test of reading comprehension, we can assume scores on these tests are measuring a single factor. This conclusion is strengthened if people who do well on these tests do

g A general intelligence factor believed to govern performance on cognitive tasks; proposed by Charles Spearman.

multiple intelligences Gardner's theory that proposes intelligence to have at least eight distinct forms: linguistic, logical-mathematical, spatial, musical, bodily-kinesthetic, interpersonal, intrapersonal, and naturalistic.

triarchic theory of successful intelligence Sternberg's theory that intelligence is composed of three broad components: analytical abilities, creative abilities, and practical abilities.

not necessarily do well on tests of mathematical ability or logic. Different scores on these tests suggest that they are measuring different factors.

Efforts to identify and understand the nature of intelligence continue to this day. One influential contemporary theorist is Howard Gardner (1999), who posits a theory of **multiple intelligences**. Gardner has proposed that there are at least eight distinct forms of intelligence: (a) linguistic intelligence, which is used when reading a book, writing, or speaking; (b) logical-mathematical intelligence, which is used when arguing a case and solving math problems; (c) spatial intelligence, which is used in reading maps and in doing things like loading the dishwasher efficiently; (d) musical intelligence, which is used in playing a musical instrument and singing; (e) bodily-kinesthetic intelligence, which is used in dancing, playing sports, running, and throwing; (f) interpersonal intelligence, which is used in relating to others, (g) intrapersonal intelligence, which reflects an awareness of oneself; and (h) naturalistic intelligence, which reflects an understanding of the natural world.

Gardner finds that these different intelligences are relatively independent and are associated with different portions or modules of the brain. Thus, from the perspective of the theory of multiple intelligences, professional athletes and ballet dancers possess bodily-kinesthetic intelligence, and successful salespersons are interpersonally intelligent.

Robert Sternberg (1988, 1999) is a second contemporary theorist who studies intelligence. Sternberg proposed the **triarchic theory of successful intelligence**, which identified intelligence as composed of three broad components: (a) analytical abilities that enable individuals to critique, judge, and evaluate; (b) creative abilities that enable individuals to invent, discover, and imagine; and (c) practical abilities that enable individuals to utilize and implement ideas in the real world. Sternberg finds these components are relatively independent statistically, and that children apply them to different kinds of problems. Some children are more intelligent about concrete practical problems. Others are more intelligent about abstract academic problems, and still others are better at inventing, discovering, and imagining.

An intelligent child, according to Sternberg (1999), is not necessarily one who succeeds in all aspects of intelligence. Instead, an intelligent child is one who knows his or her strengths and weaknesses and finds ways to capitalize on strengths and compensate for weaknesses. A child strong in verbal skills and weak in math skills may want to become a writer, not an engineer.

Intelligence in Different Social Contexts

Another question concerns the extent that IQ scores are an accurate measure of underlying abilities or are dependent on the social context and experience. One of the authors of this textbook observed a powerful example of how scores on the test can depend on the social context. Lisa, one of students in a second-grade classroom, would often "zone out." As long as her teacher was sitting next to her, Lisa would complete her assignments. However, as soon as the teacher moved away to another student, Lisa would sit quietly gazing out the window or staring at the floor. Sometimes she stopped working completely; other times she haphazardly completed a few items. She often failed to complete her work, and much of her work was filled with errors.

One day Lisa's class was given a group-administered IQ test. Lisa approached the task as she often did other assignments. After spending a considerable time looking out the window, she began to randomly fill in the bubbles on the score sheet. Her score of seventy on the test qualified as "mentally retarded." The score was a fair indication of her very poor performance in school. It was not, however, a good indication of her abilities under other conditions. Several weeks later, Lisa was retested in a one-on-one situation in which she was encouraged to complete each item. At the retest, she received an IQ score of 105.

In some sense, the moral here is that there is no way to measure IQ out of context. If we want to predict Lisa's intelligence in a group-based school setting, the first test is predictive; but if we want to predict her performance in other settings, it would not be.

There also are concerns that items on IQ tests favor Caucasian, middle-class children (Greenfield, Suzuki, & Rothstein-Fisch, 2006). Knowing the meaning of words such as *banister* is, no doubt, greater in multistory households in which there are banisters and opportunities to talk about them. Tests that draw on children's experiences can make a difference. As we noted earlier, Brazilian children who are street vendors can do complex math computations when selling items on the street but have difficulty on standardized tests that measure the same abilities (Nunes et al., 1993).

Are IQ Scores Malleable?

A third question concerns just how malleable (or potentially changeable) IQ scores are. Between infancy and early childhood, we see considerable movement (up and down) in individual children's test scores (McCall, Appelbaum, & Hogarty, 1973). This may be because items on the infant tests are less reliable, or it may be that young children's general cognitive abilities (intelligence) are more susceptible to environmental influences. In middle childhood and adolescence, IQ scores are more stable. Children who receive high scores at one administration tend to receive high scores at subsequent administrations of related tests. This consistency may occur because the tests are better (i.e., more reliable or consistent). It may also mean that intelligence has become more consolidated as a single trait and less susceptible to environmental influences.

Environmental Influences One way of evaluating these alternative explanations is to look at recent IQ findings reported by the English and Romanian Adoptees Study (Beckett et al., 2006). Recall this is the longitudinal study of children who spent varying amounts of time in state orphanages in Romania, under conditions of extreme deprivation, where they had little contact with caregivers or environmental stimulation, and were then adopted by families in the United Kingdom and Canada. One group of children was less than six months of age when placed with their new families. A second group was adopted between six and twenty-four months, and a third group was older than twenty-four months when adopted. A comparison group consisted of children born in the United Kingdom who were adopted by six months. In earlier chapters, we talked about the effects of this natural experiment on children's biological and social emotional development. Here, we look at the children's IQ scores.

At six years, the IQ scores of Romanian children who were adopted prior to age six months were similar to the UK children who were adopted prior to age six months (an average score of 102 versus 105). However, those adopted between six and twenty-four months had significantly lower scores (an average of 86) and those who were older than twenty-four months when adopted had the lowest scores (an average of 77). At age eleven, the IQ scores of the early adopted UK (average score = 105) and Romanian (average score = 101) children continued to differ from the children adopted when they were older (average scores of 86 for the six-month to twenty-four-month group and 82 for the after twenty-four-month group). Note that children in the after-twenty-four-month group had improved scores, but they had not caught up with the other children. These findings suggest that early severe deprivation can have long-term effects on children's general intelligence.

Others have studied the effects of high-quality, early intervention programs on children at risk for environmentally based mental retardation (Ramey & Ramey, 2004). The children who were living in deep poverty in rural North Carolina participated in the Abecedarian Project, a high-quality comprehensive early intervention project (see "Cognitive Development in Early Childhood"). When compared with children in the control group who did not participate in the program, the treatment group received higher IQ scores at age eight years.

These findings indicate that early environments (both early severe deprivation and enrichment) can exert profound effects on intelligence as measured by standard IQ tests (20 points or more), but does this mean that genetic factors are unimportant? It is to that question that we turn next.

Genetic Influences Studies of twins provide another natural "experiment" that can help us to disentangle genetic and environmental influences on intelligence. These studies follow a similar logic. As we discussed in "Nature with Nurture," identical, or **monozygotic (MZ), twins** share 100 percent of their genes, whereas fraternal, or **dizygotic (DZ), twins** share 50 percent of their genes on average. If genes are contributing to intelligence, then pairs of MZ twins should be more similar in IQ than pairs of DZ twins. If shared environments (being raised by the same parents, in the same home, and at the same time) are more important, then the size of the correlations between pairs of MZ twins and between pairs of DZ twins should be similar.

Across many studies, the average correlation of IQ scores of pairs of MZ twins is .86 (where 1.0 would mean perfect correlation) in contrast to DZ twin correlations of .60 (Plomin & Petrill, 1997). What this means is that the relative rankings of MZ twins are more similar than the relative rankings of DZ twins. It is these higher correlations between the MZ twins that suggest genes are contributing a substantial proportion to IQ (see Table 11.2). **Heritability** is the term used by behavioral geneticists to describe the similarities in relative rankings.

Thus, the research using twins and adoption designs suggests that *both* genes and environments are important influences on the development of general cognitive abilities.

monozygotic (MZ) twins Also called identical twins; refers to when a single *egg* is fertilized and then divides into two separate *embryos*, resulting in two individuals whose genetic makeup is identical.

dizygotic (DZ) twins Also called fraternal twins. Twins born when two separate eggs are fertilized, who are therefore no more alike genetically than other brothers and sisters.

heritability A term used in behavior genetics to designate the proportion of statistical variance associated with genes.

TABLE 11.2 Average Correlations Between the IQ Scores of Different Familial Relations

RELATIONSHIP	AVERAGE R	NUMBER OF PAIRS
Reared-together biological relatives		
MZ twins	.86	4,672
DZ twins	.60	5,533
Siblings	.47	26,473
Parent–offspring	.42	8,433
Half-siblings	.35	200
Cousins	.15	1,176
Reared-apart biological relatives		
MZ twins	.72	65
Siblings	.24	203
Parent–offspring	.24	720
Reared-together nonbiological relatives		
Siblings	.32	714
Parent–offspring	.24	720

Note: MZ = monozygotic; DZ = dizygotic. R was determined using sample-size-weighted average of z transformations.

Source: From J. McGue, T.J. Bouchard, Jr., W.G. Iacona, & D.T. Lykken, Behavioral genetics of cognitive ability: A life-span perspective. In R. Plomin & G.E. McClearn (eds.), *Nature, Nurture & Psychology,* pp. 59–76, published by American Psychological Association, Washington, DC, 1993. Reprinted with permission.

Very High and Very Low IQ Scores

Go back and take a look at Figure 11.3. You will see that some children are at the extremes of the distribution of IQ scores and have either very high or very low IQ scores. Let's look more closely at these children.

Gifted Children There are several definitions of **giftedness** (Sternberg, 2004). One definition, based on IQ scores, categorizes children with scores in the top 1 percent (roughly IQ scores of 135 or above) or top 2 percent (roughly 132 or above) as "gifted." Others supplement IQ scores with other measures of motivation, commitment, and achievement (Csikszentmihalyi, Rathunde, & Whalen, 1993; Renzulli, 1986; Sternberg, 1988).

Still others, such as Howe (2002), have described geniuses (perhaps the *most* talented and gifted, like Leonardo da Vinci or Albert Einstein). These individuals have several features in common: intense curiosity, dedication to their work, sustained diligence, and broad capacities that open up opportunities for new discoveries. Consistent with the broader definitions of intelligence, giftedness is indicated by extraordinary creativity or performance in music, sports, or art, as well as traditional academic subjects.

A classic longitudinal study of gifted children conducted by Louis Terman (1947) followed more than 600 children (average IQ scores of 151) into adulthood. Contrary to a stereotype that gifted children become maladjusted and unhappy adults, Terman found most of the men were successful in all types of professions and well adjusted. In a reflection of the times, most of the women had become housewives.

Both genes and enriched environments have been linked to giftedness (Geschwind & Galaburda, 1987). For example, a study of high mathematics ability in ten-year-olds found substantial genetic and moderate environmental influences (Petrill et al., in press).

Mental Retardation The Individuals with Disabilities Act is a landmark federal law that defines mental retardation as significantly below average general intellectual functioning that is accompanied by deficits in adaptive behavior and that has adverse effects on educational performance (34 *Code of Federal Regulations* §300.7[c][6]). This definition has been operationalized as an IQ score of less than 70 or 75 accompanied by deficits relative to other children of the same age in daily living skills, communication skills, and social skills.

Some forms of mental retardation, such as **Down syndrome** and **fragile X syndrome**, have genetic origins. Children with Down syndrome have all or a part of an extra chromosome 21 (Chapman, 1997). Children with fragile X have a change in a single gene on the X chromosome (Abbeduto et al., 2001). These two conditions are the most common genetic causes of intellectual disabilities, but hundreds of other rarer mutations have been identified as having effects on general intelligence (Inlow & Restifo, 2004).

Other forms of mental retardation, such as that observed in the Romanian orphans and impoverished rural communities discussed earlier, are linked to severe environmental deprivation. As noted earlier,

giftedness Indicated by extraordinary creativity or performance in music, sports, or art, as well as traditional academic subjects.

Down syndrome A condition in which children have a third copy of chromosome 21. One of the most common genetic causes of mental retardation.

fragile X syndrome A condition in which children have a change in a single gene on the X chromosome; one of the most common genetic causes of mental retardation.

© Heide Benser / zefa / Corbis

Children with Down syndrome vary in their intellectual functioning, ranging from mild to severe impairments. Early educational interventions can make a difference in their performance and achievement.

INTERIM SUMMARY 11.3

Intelligence

A Brief History of Efforts to Measure Intelligence	■ Sir Frances Galton, one of the first to attempt to measure intelligence, tried (unsuccessfully) to use reaction times to measure intelligence.
	■ Others sought to measure more complex evaluations of tasks
	■ The Stanford-Binet Intelligence Test measures verbal reasoning, quantitative reasoning, abstract visual reasoning, and short-term memory.
Are There Multiple Intelligences?	■ Gardner's theory proposes at least eight distinct forms of intelligence: linguistic, logical-mathematical, spatial, musical, bodily-kinesthetic, interpersonal, intrapersonal, and naturalistic.
	■ Sternberg's **triarchic theory** posits three separate components of intelligence: analytical, creative, and practical.
Intelligence in Different Social Contexts	■ Test performance reflects the context in which the tests are administered. Performance also reflects children's experiences and opportunities, as well as aptitudes.
Are IQ Scores Malleable?	■ There is considerable movement in individual children's test scores between early and middle childhood.
	■ IQ scores are more stable in middle childhood and adolescence.
Very High and Very Low IQ Scores	■ Genius is been defined by very high scores on IQ tests, but also by intense curiosity, sustained diligence, and broad capacities that open up opportunities for new discoveries.
	■ Mental retardation is operationalized as an IQ score of less than 70 or 75, accompanied by deficits relative to other children of the same age.
	■ Mental retardation has been linked to both genetic and environmental factors.

scientists have found that attending high-quality early education can raise IQ scores of children growing up in impoverished homes (Ramey & Ramey, 2004).

In summary, intelligence testing has a long history and some unanswered questions. Is intelligence one general capability or are there multiple intelligences? How are scores influenced by the social context? Is intelligence fixed or malleable? In the next section, we turn to children's skills in specific areas that are also often related to academic success—language, literacy, and mathematics. (For a summary of this section, see "Interim Summary 11.3: Intelligence.")

LANGUAGE, LITERACY, AND MATHEMATICS

At the beginning of this chapter, we described some of the changes that occurred in two children's academic skills during elementary school. In this section, we look at these developments in more detail.

Language Development

root words Vocabulary that must be learned, in contrast to derived and compound words that build on root words.

Beginning at about age one year, children start to add about two root words a day to their vocabularies (Biemiller & Slonim, 2001). These **root words** must be learned, whereas derived and compound words build on root words. (*Fish* is a root word; *fishy* is a derived word. *Fishhook* is a compound word.) By the time children are in sec-

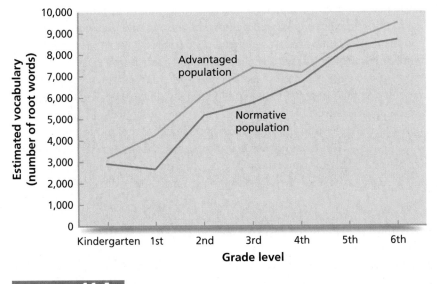

Growth of Root Word Vocabulary in Normative and Advantaged Children

Although root vocabularies increase substantially in both groups, children growing up in more advantaged homes maintain larger root vocabularies throughout middle childhood.
Source: Data from Biemiller & Slonim (2001).

code switching Changing speech to reflect the audience and situation.

ond grade (around age seven years), they have amassed root vocabularies of 5,200 words on average. Between second and fifth grade, their root vocabularies expand even more rapidly, as they add about three root words each day. By fifth grade, they have about 8,400 root words in their vocabulary. With this growth of vocabulary, their words become more precise (see Figure 11.4).

Other changes also occur in middle childhood. Sentence structures become more complex, with more use of subordinate clauses (e.g., The girl *who is a fast runner* entered two races). Stories become longer and more complex, including more details about the setting and time period. Children come to enjoy and appreciate jokes, puns, and riddles. They begin to use metaphors and similes.

Children become adept at **code switching**, changing their speech to reflect who they are talking to (Rickford & Rickford, 2000). They are more skilled in their use of formal codes of speaking at school and with unfamiliar adults. This formal code avoids colloquialisms and contractions and provides more elaboration, details, and

Children become adept at code switching, using an informal speech code with friends and family and a more formal speech code with unfamiliar adults.

background material. When speaking with friends and family in informal settings, children become adept at informal codes that presume a common body of shared history and popular expressions. African American children may use Standard English in the classroom, but Black English with friends and family (Rickford & Rickford, 2000). Children whose parents are first- and second-generation immigrants who do not speak English may serve as their parents' translators (O'Malley, 2006; Orellana et al., 2003).

Children's language reflects their experiences at home. Vocabulary is linked to variations in families' total amount of dinner table conversation, the number of different words used by parents, and the proportion of words not in the child's vocabulary. The more sophisticated words that children hear, embedded in helpful or instructive interactions, the more advanced their vocabularies in middle childhood (Weizman & Snow, 2001).

Literacy

One of the great challenges and accomplishments of middle childhood is becoming a skilled reader. Reading is a complex activity that involves two broad sets of competencies—those related to decoding and those related to comprehension (NICHD Early Child Care Research Network, 2005a; Snow, Burns, & Griffin, 1998). **Decoding** is applying knowledge of letter-sound relationships to read written words. **Comprehension** refers to understanding what you have read.

For almost fifty years, there was a debate, sometimes called "the reading wars," about the best way to teach reading (Chall, 1970). This debate is about whether a **phonics** approach or a **whole language** approach is better. The phonics approach emphasizes decoding in which readers match the printed alphabet to spoken sounds. The whole language approach emphasizes comprehension and context, and inferring what words are from context. Talking, listening, reading, and writing are seen as part of a whole language approach, in which the overarching goal is communication.

In a comprehensive review of the research evidence, the National Reading Panel (National Institute of Child Health and Human Development, 2000) concluded that both decoding and comprehension are essential components of early reading for beginning readers. Two specific elements that were identified by the panel involve decoding and two involved comprehension. They are as follows:

1. The alphabetic principle—knowing letters and that letters link to sounds

2. Phonemic awareness—being able to analyze the sound structure of spoken words

3. Oral reading fluency—being able to read aloud smoothly, accurately, and at a good speed

4. Vocabulary comprehension—understanding words and text meaning

Skills in decoding and comprehension start to develop in early childhood (see "Cognitive Development in Early Childhood") and these skills set the stage for reading performance in grade 3 (NICHD Early Child Care Research Network, 2005a). Some children enter kindergarten able to recognize and name all of the letters and to isolate beginning and ending phonemes in simple words. (Recall that a **phoneme** is the smallest contrastive sound unit. The "buh" and "puh" in *bat* and *pat* are phonemes.) Children who can sound out words in first grade are usually good readers later on. By third grade, these good readers are able to look at and process most of the letters in almost all of the words on a page. They can read chapter books independently, fluently, and with excellent comprehension (Snow & Kang, 2006).

Children learn the alphabet and letter-sound connections (the first two components identified by the National Reading Panel) relatively quickly and easily. But, although learning the alphabet and understanding letter-sound connections are necessary skills,

decoding Applying knowledge of letter-sound relationships to read written words.

comprehension Understanding what is read or said.

phonics Emphasizes decoding in which readers match the printed alphabet to spoken sounds.

whole language Emphasizes comprehension and context, and inferring what words are from context.

phoneme The smallest contrastive sound unit.

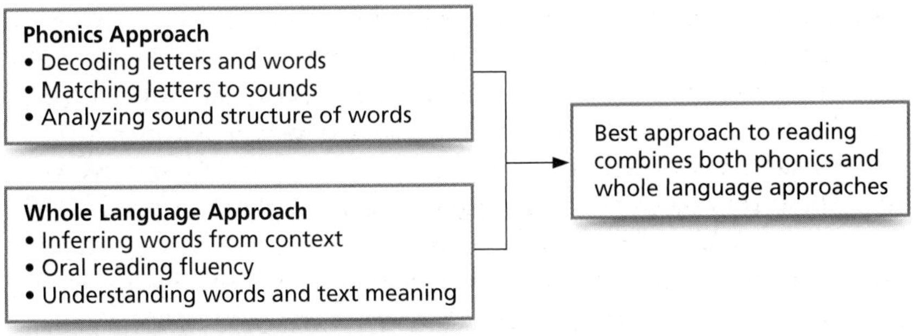

Phonics Approach
- Decoding letters and words
- Matching letters to sounds
- Analyzing sound structure of words

Whole Language Approach
- Inferring words from context
- Oral reading fluency
- Understanding words and text meaning

Best approach to reading combines both phonics and whole language approaches

FIGURE 11.5

Both Phonics and Whole Language Understanding Contribute to the Development of Skilled Readers

they are not sufficient for becoming a good reader. Vocabulary and comprehension, which take longer and require more effort, are equally important.

This means that a more structured basic skills approach in first grade is more effective for some students (those with limited decoding skills), but by third grade, more and more attention needs to be devoted to comprehension and vocabulary (Morrison & Connor, 2002). So, the reading wars have ended in a truce: Phonics and whole language understanding are both fundamental to literacy (Snow, Burns, & Griffin, 1998). Both have a place in reading instruction, depending on the developmental stage of the readers (see Figure 11.5).

Difficulties Learning to Read

Children from low-income backgrounds, whose parents have low literacy skills or learning disabilities, and whose homes have few books and reading materials are at special risk for reading problems (Snow & Kang, 2006). Individual problems, such as language delay or hearing loss, also contribute to problems learning to read.

But schools and families can make a difference. In one study of low-income children who were in the bottom 30th percentile for reading skills, 30 percent showed substantial improvement from first grade to third grade (Spira, Bracken, & Fischel, 2005). Children in first-grade classrooms where teachers spend more time on literacy and language instruction show greater gains in reading achievement and phoneme knowledge (Downer & Pianta, 2006).

Successfully addressing early problems in reading has implications for other areas of development. Poor literacy achievement in the early grades is linked not only to poor academic achievement, but also to increased aggressive behaviors in later grades (Miles & Stipek, 2006).

Dyslexia **Dyslexia** is a learning disability characterized by difficulties with word recognition and by poor spelling and decoding skills. Despite average or above-average intelligence, instruction, and environmental opportunities, most children with dyslexia have phonological difficulties (Snowling, 2004). As preschoolers, children who later are dyslexic had equal vocabulary to preschoolers who did not develop the disability, but they made more speech errors and were poorer at rhyming. Some adults with childhood dyslexia are fluent readers but still have spelling problems and difficulty decoding words they have not seen before. Today, the majority of students with dyslexia and other special needs spend most of the school day in regular classrooms (called **mainstreaming**), an increase from 45 percent in 1994–95.

dyslexia A learning disability characterized by difficulties with word recognition and by poor spelling and decoding skills.

mainstreaming Inclusion of children with special needs in regular classrooms.

English language learners (ELLs) Children for whom English is a new language.

English Language Learners The number of children in the United States who speak a language other than English in their homes more than doubled from 1979 to 2005—an increase from 3.8 million students to 10.6 million students. States vary widely in their strategies for meeting the educational needs of **English language learners (ELLs),** or those children for whom English is a new language. Ballot referenda reducing access to bilingual education have passed in some states (California, Arizona, and Massachusetts), but failed in others (e.g., Colorado).

Rosario is one of these ELL students (Snow & Kang, 2006). Rosario moved to the United States from Mexico when she was five years old. Her Spanish-speaking parents, eager for her to learn English, enrolled her in an English-only kindergarten. It was a difficult year for Rosario. Not only did she not speak English, she wasn't familiar with puzzles and other classroom materials, as her classmates were. Moreover, at home her family spoke Spanish. In first grade, she was put in the lowest-level reading group and assigned a tutor who happened to be bilingual. With the tutor's help, she began to catch up.

By fourth grade, Rosario was reading and speaking fluently in English and doing well in school, which she enjoyed. She still spoke Spanish with her parents, but she found it difficult to talk with them about events at school. She didn't have a Spanish vocabulary for math, science, or social studies. For the most part, she spoke with her younger siblings in English.

By the time she reached high school, Rosario much preferred speaking English to speaking Spanish. Although she could communicate in Spanish about routine household and family matters, she found it difficult to follow her parents' conversations about subjects such as politics in Mexico. Although proud of their daughter's success in school, her parents were puzzled that she wasn't as bright in Spanish.

What does research tell us about the development of ELLs? Findings across multiple studies are consistent (Snow & Kang, 2006). Children's first language is at some risk for loss or decline under the influence of the second language (English), as in Rosario's case. Continued development of the first language is more likely if parents are bilingual and/or highly educated. (Rosario never learned to read and write in Spanish.) Children who already know how to read in a first language have an easier time learning to read in English. Older children typically learn a second language faster than younger children, perhaps because of their better developed literacy skills. However, having an older sibling who speaks the second language and can help with homework accelerates this process. Homes that provide high-quality support for literacy development have children who become better, more skilled readers. This home support can be in either the first language or the second language. Using the first language at home does not interfere with literacy development in English as long as English is also used at home.

As the number of ELLs in the United States continues to grow, developing strategies to better support the children's literacy and academic development needs to be a priority for schools and families. We now turn to another national priority, the development of mathematical thinking.

Mathematics

Mathematical thinking, along with literacy, improves by leaps and bounds during middle childhood. Just look at Ashley's and Colin's achievements described at the beginning of this chapter.

Mathematical thinking in middle childhood involves (1) knowing math facts (e.g., that $2 + 7 = 9$ and $2 \times 7 = 14$) and procedures (e.g., how to "carry" from the ones column to the tens column), (2) using this knowledge to solve routine problems, and (3) then using reasoning and logic to solve more complex, non-routine problems.

In early elementary school, children are able to solve most simple one-step problems, such as "John has four apples and Mary has five apples. How many apples are there all together?" But mathematics is more than following a simple series of well-defined steps (Kilpatrick, Swafford, & Findell, 2001). By third grade or so, children are using more complex strategies to solve two-step problems, such as "Megan went to the store and spent $5 and had $4 left. How much money did she take to the store?" They become more adept at using strategies such as working backward from the answer, breaking the problem down into subproblems, and trying to think of a related problem.

Children also need to be able to know if their solutions are "in the ballpark" and to reflect, "Does the problem make sense? Does the solution make sense?" This kind of reflective questioning is harder to develop. For example, in one study children were presented with this story problem: "There are 26 sheep and 10 goats on a ship. How old is the captain?" A large majority provided an answer (most often, "36"), seemingly unaware that the question could not be answered. Another aspect of mathematical proficiency, which is unfortunately rare, is an inclination to see mathematics as sensible, useful, and worthwhile.

Informal Mathematics Informal experiences outside of school as well as formal experiences in math classrooms contribute to the development of mathematical thinking (Bryant & Nunes, 2004). Young musicians work with quarter notes, half notes, and whole notes (four quarter notes = a whole note; two half notes = a whole note). Young swimmers are adding, subtracting, multiplying, and dividing as they break down their swim sets. Young chefs double and halve recipes, using measuring cups and measuring spoons, to adjust proportions as they bake

© David Young-Wolff / PhotoEdit

Cooking and baking provide children with hands-on experiences in mathematics.

cookies and make soup. A central element in all of these experiences is that mathematics is embedded in activities that have meaning for the children. The most effective instruction incorporates both meaningful activities and conceptual understanding (Bryant & Nunes, 2004).

Gender Differences Researchers have studied gender differences in mathematics performance (as measured by grades) and mathematics achievement (as measured by scores on standardized tests). School-aged girls consistently receive better grades than do boys in math and science, but boys tend to score higher than girls on standardized tests in science and some areas of math (Hyde et al., 1990). What accounts for these discrepancies?

Different approaches to school work, self-efficacy, and motivation have all been identified as playing a role in gender differences in math (Halpern et al., 2007). Girls, on average, put forth more effort and refrain from disruptive behavior in the classroom (Kenney-Benson et al., 2006). Boys are less compliant to teacher requests. They talk more to classmates and annoy their teachers more. As a result, boys typically earn lower grades than girls do. But tests are a different situation, more a competition. Boys' higher performance on standardized tests has been linked to higher feelings of self-efficacy about math and science (beliefs that they are good at math and can solve math problems), and a greater focus on performance goals (how well they perform relative to others).

INTERIM SUMMARY 11.4

Language, Literacy, and Mathematics

Language Development	■ By age seven, children have amassed root vocabularies of 5,200 words on average.
	■ Root vocabularies expand rapidly in middle childhood, as children add about three root words each day between ages seven and ten.
	■ Children become adept at **code switching**, or adapting their speech to the listener.
Literacy	■ Reading is a complex activity that involves **decoding** and **comprehension**.
	■ "The reading wars" grew out of disagreements about whether a **phonics** or a **whole language** approach is better.
	■ Research shows that both sets of competencies are needed.
Difficulties Learning to Read	■ Children from low-income backgrounds, whose parents have low literacy skills, and whose homes have few reading materials are at risk for reading problems.
	■ Children whose teachers spend more time on literacy and language instruction show greater gains in reading achievement and phoneme knowledge.
	■ Dyslexia is a learning disability characterized by difficulties with word recognition and by poor spelling and decoding skills (despite average or above average intelligence).
	■ For **English language learners,** children's first language is at some risk for loss or decline under the influence of the second language. Development of the first language is more likely if parents are bilingual and/or highly educated. Children who already know how to read in a first language have an easier time learning to read in the second language. Older children typically learn a second language faster than younger children, perhaps because of their better developed literacy skills. Having an older sibling who speaks the second language and can help with homework accelerates this process.
	■ Homes that provide high-quality support for literacy development have children who become better, more skilled readers.
Mathematics	■ Mathematical competence in middle childhood involves knowing math facts and computational procedures, using this knowledge to solve routine problems, and using reasoning and logic to solve more complex, non-routine problems.
	■ Children need to be able to know if their solutions are "in the ballpark" and to reflect, "Does the problem make sense?"
	■ Informal experiences outside of school and formal experiences in math classrooms contribute to the development of mathematical thinking.

In the next section, we look at how well schools are providing instruction in math, reading, and other subjects. (For a summary of this section, see "Interim Summary 11.4: Language, Literacy, and Mathematics.")

SCHOOLS AND SCHOOLING

More than 40 million children are enrolled in public and private elementary schools across the United States, an all-time high (National Center for Education Statistics, 2008). These children and their classrooms are much more ethnically and racially diverse than in previous generations. For example, in 1970, only 21 percent of students were children of color, whereas 47 percent were students of color in 2007. The number of students who speak a language other than English at home more than doubled during this period (National Center for Education Statistics, 2007).

One demographic characteristic has not changed appreciably since the 1970s. Poverty rates have remained persistently high, with two out of every five students qualifying as either "poor" (defined as a family of four with an income of less than $20,000 a year) or "near-poor" (defined as a family of four with an income between $20,000 and $40,000 a year). How well are our schools doing in educating this large, diverse group of students?

A Typical Classroom

Until recently we had very little idea about what goes on inside a "typical" elementary school classroom in the United States. The education system in the United States is decentralized, with local school districts responsible for general policy and the day-to-day functioning of individual schools. Some school districts emphasize traditional academic skills; others have adopted a broader curriculum that incorporates the arts, computers, and problem solving on a daily basis. How common are these different approaches, and what does a typical day look like?

Recently, a large team of researchers observed approximately 2,500 first-, third-, and fifth-grade classrooms across the United States (Pianta et al., 2007) The researchers coded how many children and adults were in the classroom, how instruction was organized (whole class, small group, individual seatwork), and how much time was devoted to different content areas (literacy, mathematics, science, social studies). They also rated the quality of emotional climates (the degree of teacher support) and instructional climates (instruction in basic skills versus involvement in higher-order problem solving) across the day.

Not surprisingly, the researchers recorded considerable differences in class size, classroom organization, teacher styles, and teacher knowledge and skills. But they also saw commonalities across classrooms, suggesting what's happening in "typical" classrooms.

On average, children were spending over 90 percent of their time in whole-class instruction or individual seatwork. Very little time was spent in small-group instruction. In first grade and third grade, half of all instruction was in reading; less than 10 percent of instruction was in math. Distressingly, the ratio of time spent in basic skills versus higher-order problem solving was 10:1. Changes in instruction occurred for older students. In fifth grade, 37 percent of the time was in literacy and 25 percent in math, 11 percent in science, and 13 percent in social studies. There was five times as much instruction in basic skills as instruction in problem solving (see Figure 11.6).

In all three grades, ratings of emotional quality (e.g., how pleasant the interactions between students and teachers were) were moderately positive, whereas the quality of the instructional climate (e.g., how challenging the teaching was) was low. Teachers tended to provide generic feedback on correctness rather than encouraging more advanced thinking or discussing alternative solutions. Over a twenty-minute period,

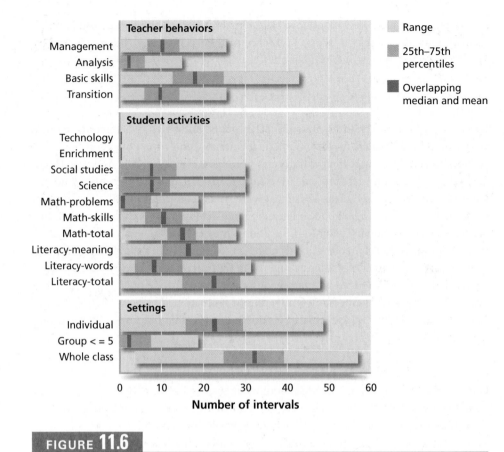

FIGURE 11.6

Learning in Fifth Grade Classrooms

Whole class instruction and basic skills instruction are predominant activities in typical fifth-grade classrooms. Little time is devoted to analysis, science, technology, or small group activities.

Source: Pianta et al. (2007).

teachers typically used a single mode of instruction (watch the teacher do math problems; or child does a vocabulary worksheet). Only 7 percent of children experienced both high-quality emotional and high-quality instructional climate.

Importantly, these differences in classrooms were linked to children's academic achievement (Pianta et al., 2008). Children in classrooms in which more time was spent in math instruction showed greater gains in mathematics from first to fifth grades. Similarly, the amount of time spent in reading instruction predicted gains in reading achievement (Downer & Pianta, 2006). These findings indicate that what happens in classrooms matters and that both quality of instruction and amount of time devoted to the subject contribute to learning.

The Nation's Report Card

Since the early 1970s the National Assessment of Educational Progress (NAEP) has been measuring student achievement in nationally representative samples of students in grades 4 (age nine), 8 (age thirteen), and 12 (age seventeen). In effect, NAEP issues a national report card indicating what America's students know and can do in reading, math, history, and science.

Overall, the NAEP findings are mixed. On the one hand, the average reading and math scores for fourth-graders are a bit higher now than they were in 1971. On the other hand, 36 percent of children scored *below* basic skills in reading, and only 31 percent were proficient or advanced in reading. There is much room for improvement.

The NAEP assessments also document significant differences in the scores of low-income, African American, and Hispanic students versus middle income, Caucasian, and Asian students. These differences, called the **achievement gap**, indicate that many African American, Hispanic, and poor students are not on track to be successful in secondary school, high school, college, and well-paying careers (see Figure 11.7).

Historically, U.S. schools have been viewed by citizens and policymakers as an institution that provides children with access and opportunities to develop the skills to achieve their dreams. The achievement gap indicates that this is not happening for many children. Later in this chapter we will describe some ways that schools, families, and communities are trying to narrow the achievement gap and to improve overall academic achievement.

International Comparisons

Today's children will be competing in a global market for jobs that increasingly require high-level skills, especially in math and science (Committee on Prospering in the Global Economy, 2007; Friedman, 2007). How do U.S. students measure up to those in other countries?

The Trends in International Mathematics and Science Study (National Center for Education Statistics, 2003) has compared students' mathematics performance in fifteen countries in grade 4. As shown in Table 11.3, U.S. students score in the middling ranks in mathematics and slightly above average in science. Fourth-grade students in the United States performed better than those in Slovenia, Cyprus, and Iran, but worse than those in England, Hong Kong, and Singapore.

A recent report of the National Academy of Science (Committee on Prospering in the Global Economy, 2007) argues that being "average" in math and science means that the United States will not be competitive in a knowledge- or technology-based

achievement gap An observed disparity on educational measures between the performance of groups of students, especially social class and ethnic disparities.

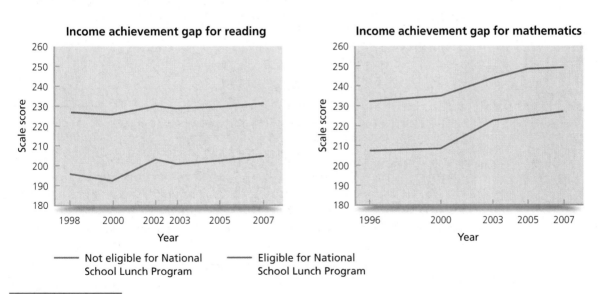

FIGURE 11.7

Average Reading Test Scores of Students by Eligibility for National School Lunch Program

On average, students who are eligible for the school lunch program have significantly lower reading test scores than students who do not qualify for the school lunch subsidy. This difference is referred to as the achievement gap.

Source: National Center for Education Statistics (2007). The Condition of Education 2007. http://nces.ed.gov/pubsearch/pubsinfo.asp?pubid=2007064. Accessed June 6, 2007.

TABLE 11.3 International Trends in Math and Science

COUNTRY	AVERAGE MATH SCORE	COUNTRY	AVERAGE SCIENCE SCORE
Singapore	594	Singapore	565
Hong Kong SAR	575	Chinese Taipei	551
Japan	565	Japan	543
Chinese Taipei	564	Hong Kong SAR	542
Belgium-Flemish	551	England	540
Netherlands	540	**United States**	**536**
Latvia	536	Latvia	532
Lithuania	534	Hungary	530
Russian Federation	532	Russian Federation	526
England	531	Netherlands	525
Hungary	529	Australia	521
United States	**518**	New Zealand	520
Cyprus	510	Belgium-Flemish	518
Moldova, Republic of	504	Italy	516
Italy	503	Lithuania	512
Australia	499	Scotland	502
New Zealand	493	Moldova, Republic of	496
Scotland	490	Slovenia	490
Slovenia	479	Cyprus	480
Armenia	456	Norway	466
Norway	451	Armenia	437
Iran, Islamic Republic of	389	Iran, Islamic Republic of	414
Philippines	358	Philippines	332
Morocco	347	Tunisia	314
Tunisia	339	Morocco	304

Note: The test for significance between the United States and the international average was adjusted to account for the U.S. contribution to the international average. Countries were required to sample students in the upper of the two grades that contained the largest number of nine-year-olds. In the United States and most countries, this corresponds to grade 4.
Source: Adapted from National Center for Education Statistics (2003).

global economy. The report predicts that companies will go to other countries for highly skilled workers who can make advances in new technologies, taking those well-paying jobs and prosperity with them if improvements in American education do not occur.

No Child Left Behind (NCLB)

No Child Left Behind (NCLB) A federal law that holds schools accountable for student performance and requires that states meet specific goals as measured by standardized achievement tests.

The persistent achievement gap, coupled with poor scores on international comparisons, has lead to widespread reform efforts at the local, state, and federal levels. Perhaps the best known is the federal law popularly known as **No Child Left Behind (NCLB)**. The law has sought to improve children's academic skills by holding schools accountable for student performance. NCLB requires that states meet specific goals as measured by standardized achievement tests. These are sometimes referred to as **high stakes tests** because failure to meet specific performance standards can result in sanctions against a school and loss of federal funds (National Center for Education Statistics, 2007).

high stakes test   A test that results in serious sanctions if performance standards are not met.

NCLB requires that children be tested in reading and math starting in third grade, with scores of English language learners reported separately (but focusing on literacy in English). All children, including members of minority groups, those who are economically disadvantaged, disabled children, and children who speak English as a second language, are tested and held to the same standards.

Some educators have questioned whether the implementation of NCLB has boosted student achievement in elementary school (Fuller et al., 2007). They note that gains in reading and math achievement, measured by NAEP scores, have tended to slow since the passage of the law in 2002. Progress in narrowing the achievement gap, they argue, also has largely disappeared since the passage of NCLB. Other criticisms of NCLB have been that the law places too much attention on test scores, forcing teachers to devote too much time to drills and other test preparation at the expense of more thought-provoking classroom activities (Nichols & Berliner, 2007). Whether these criticisms will result in substantial changes in the law remains to be seen.

Strategies to Improve Student Learning and Achievement

The achievement gap and poor performance in international comparisons indicate that "something" needs to be done. The question is, What? Emerging research has identified several promising strategies that have been successful in narrowing the achievement gap, as well as improving overall student performance and learning. Policymakers and school districts will likely need to consider multiple strategies because it is unlikely that any single strategy alone can result in the needed improvements.

Class Size   This refers to the total number of children in the class, not the pupil/teacher ratio, which includes aides, administrators, and librarians. Lower class sizes have been found to improve student achievement scores in elementary schools, with somewhat larger benefits for low-income children (Ehrenberg et al., 2001).

One of the best-known and most influential studies of the effects of class size on achievement was a large experiment conducted in 329 K–3 classrooms in 79 schools in Tennessee (Finn & Achilles, 1999). Children were randomly assigned to small (13–17 students) or regular-sized (22–26 students) classrooms. The researchers found improved teaching conditions, improved student performance, and fewer classroom disruptions in smaller-size classes. The effects were about twice as large for students of color as for Caucasian students, suggesting that lowering class size is one way to narrow the achievement gap.

An observational study of more than 651 elementary school classrooms in 200 public school districts found other differences related to class size (NICHD Early Child Care Research Network, 2004). Classrooms with fewer than twenty-two students were more child centered, spent more time on instruction, and had higher quality teacher-child interactions. As class size increased, classrooms became more structured and more teacher directed. Students in the smaller-size classes were viewed more positively (as more competent and well adjusted) by their teachers than students in large classes.

Teacher Quality   The quality of individual teachers also makes a difference (Darling-Hammond, 2008). Having an average teacher versus a very effective teacher predicts substantial differences in performance in both reading and math (Ehrenberg et

Having an effective teacher makes a difference in daily experiences at school and in how much children learn.

© Ellen B. Senisi / The Image Works

al., 2001). Effective teachers are very knowledgeable about the subjects they teach. They have strong beliefs that their students can learn. They have a large toolkit of teaching strategies and materials to draw on. When one approach does not work with students, they are able to readily adapt and use other strategies.

Efforts to increase the supply and retention of effective teachers are under way. In some universities, teacher education programs are partnering with the science and math departments to develop ways for science and math majors to simultaneously earn teacher credentials. School districts and states also are experimenting with strategies to reward high-quality teaching and gains in student performance (Wallis, 2008).

Lengthening the School Year The structure of the school calendar in the United States harkens back to a time when children were needed to help their families with farm chores (Wallis & Steptoe, 2006). Because summer was a time for planting and harvesting, the school "year" was only nine months. The school year in most industrial countries is considerably longer—seven weeks of summer vacation instead of twelve weeks.

Well-off, highly educated parents have found ways to provide enriching experiences during this time off, such as travel and summer camps. But children of less affluent families have fewer options and less access to these fee-supported activities. Many are left to their own devices for much of the summer, watching TV, playing video games, and hanging out. Although some free time is good for all of us, lots of free time is not.

Summer breaks are hard on children's mathematical computation skills. Both middle-income and low-income students lose about two months of grade-level skills in math over summer vacation (Cooper, 2004). Low-income students also lose about two months of achievement in reading, whereas middle-class students post modest gains, presumably because middle-class parents are more likely to insist that their children read over the summer.

These differences tend to accumulate over time. According to one estimate, fully two-thirds of the achievement gap separating lower income and higher income students can be explained by unequal access to summer learning opportunities (Alexander, Entwisle, & Olson, 2007). Some schools districts, communities, and organizations are testing different strategies to foster summer learning, including alternative school calendars that result in shorter break periods and tuition-free summer camps for students.

Lengthening the School Day Another holdover from our agrarian past is the length of the school (Wallis & Steptoe, 2006). Because children were needed to do chores on the farm before dark, the school day needed to end by three P.M. or so. Now many working parents are not home before dark, leaving a gap of some two to three hours between the time that school ends and parents arrive home. (In our discussion of adolescence, we'll see that having all this unstructured, unsupervised time may contribute to problem behavior, such as experimentation with drugs and alcohol.) Some states, like Massachusetts, are experimenting with lengthening the school day. What matters is what goes on during added hours. If the extra time is devoted to enriched learning, students benefit. However, using extra hours just to drill children on basic skills is stressful for teachers as well as students (Nichols & Berliner, 2007).

Participation in high-quality after-school programs has been found to predict gains in skills underlying academic performance, such as work habits and task persistence, and to academic outcomes, such as grades and standardized test scores (Mahoney, Lord, & Carryl, 2005; Pierce, Bolt, & Vandell, in press) The quality of the programs and how frequently young people attend the programs are key. High-quality programs are characterized by positive relationships between staff and students, and by high levels of student engagement in activities. The particular focus of these activities (music,

© Aristide Economopoulos / Star Ledger / Corbis

Some afterschool programs feature sports and arts; others feature science, math, and reading enrichment. The particular focus is less important than that the activities are chosen by the students, are engaging to students, and allow students to build skills over time.

sports, arts, chess, computers, academic enrichment in literacy or mathematics) is less important than that they are chosen by the students, are engaging to students, and allow students to build skills over time. Afterschool programs of this sort appear especially beneficial for low-income youth, perhaps due to a lack of other extracurricular enrichment opportunities.

Reorganizing the School Curriculum Some schools, like Explorer Elementary School in San Diego, California, are reorienting their curricula. Explorer offers writer's workshops, art, music, and Spanish as well as traditional subjects (mathematics, literature, social studies, and science). Instead of teaching these subjects as discrete and disconnected, the school encourages students to integrate what they are learning in terms of higher-level concepts such as trends over time, paradoxical thinking, universal concepts, and ethics. Teaching is project based rather than subject oriented.

In all areas of the curriculum and at every grade level, the emphasis is on higher-order thinking and the integration of knowledge. Collaboration and original research are encouraged. Children are expected to examine their work from different perspectives (e.g., from the point of view of a sociologist or political scientist) and to document evidence of their understanding. At the end of the year, Explorer holds a schoolwide exhibition in which each class presents its projects.

Early Childhood Education Another strategy for improving academic achievement is for children to come to elementary school ready to learn. Kindergarten teachers report that 10 percent of their students come to kindergarten with "serious problems," and an additional 35 percent have "some problems" in three areas: preacademic skills, attention, and relations with peers (Rimm-Kaufman, Pianta, & Cox, 2000). As we discussed in "Cognitive Development in Early Childhood," high-quality early education programs have been found to reduce these deficits and to increase the numbers of children who are ready to learn when they start kindergarten.

Family Involvement in School Family involvement in the school (defined as attending parent-teacher conferences, and performances, and volunteering in the classroom or for field trips) also has been identified as another contributor to children's academic success. In one longitudinal study that followed children from kindergarten to fifth grade, Dearing and colleagues (2006) found that increases in family involvement predicted gains in literacy. In addition, although there was an achievement gap in average literacy performance between children of more and less educated mothers when family involvement was low, this gap was nonexistent when family involvement levels were high.

These results add to other evidence on the value of family involvement in school, especially for low-income children, and suggest that efforts to support family involvement might be part of a comprehensive effort to improve student learning. The effective use of technology can be another part of this effort.

Technology and Learning

Children live in a technology-rich world, with computers, videogames, iPods®, the Internet, digital cameras, and instant-messaging. "Web2" refers to the new interactive technologies, such as YouTube and MySpace, which are creating new forms of communication, learning, and entertainment. The new media are not displacing the older media but are often being used in concert with them (Roberts & Foehr, 2008).

media multitasking   The simultaneous use of multiple forms of media.

Media multitasking—the simultaneous use of multiple forms of media—is common (Roberts & Foehr, 2008). Children watch TV while surfing the Internet, listen to an iPod® while text-messaging a friend, and play online games while sending digital images on their cell phones. To be successful in the global economy, students will need to be technology savvy and able to evaluate the information obtained from the Internet and the Web (Leu et al., in press). How has this technology-rich world influenced children's learning and what goes on in schools?

Computers at School Experimental studies have examined the effects of instructional technology on children's skills in reading, writing, and mathematics (Kulik, 2003). One example is Writing to Read programs that seek to teach children to read by giving them opportunities to write using computer software. Standardized test scores in reading are found to improve for kindergarten and first-grade students with these writing experiences, although reading results for older students are mixed. The quality of children's prose and essays also can be improved by using word processing programs (instead of writing by hand), especially when the programs include writing prompts. New, exciting work is using computer simulations to develop understanding of mathematical operations (Martinez & Kalbfleisch, in press).

To be effective, computers need to be embedded in high-quality teaching of the sort described in the previous section. Positive effects on student learning and achievement are more likely when tech-

© Michael Newman / PhotoEdit

The mere presence of computers in classrooms does not ensure their effective use. To be effective, technology must be supported by frequent interaction and feedback from teachers around the technology, systematic evaluation of learning, and active student engagement in the activity.

nology is used to support five fundamentals of learning: Students are actively engaged in the activity, students participate in groups as opposed to working alone, students have frequent interaction and feedback from teachers around technology, there are clear connections to real-world contexts, and there is systematic evaluation (Roschelle et al., 2000).

Use of Computers at Home More educated families, higher-income families, and those with parents who value or excel in math and science are more likely than others to have computers in their homes. Typically their children use computers in a variety of ways—to search for information, to communicate with peers via e-mail and instant messaging, and to participate in chatrooms. The **digital divide** refers to the gap between these children and low-income, minority, and other children who do not have computers and related materials in their homes (Warschauer, 2003).

Studies find links between having computers in the home and academic success in science and math (Jackson et al., 2006). But these data do not tell us whether the computer itself boosts academic achievement or whether other factors are involved (remember that correlation is not the same as causation). The HomeNetToo project is an experimental study that provided low-income families with a computer and Internet access (Jackson et al., 2006). The researchers then studied patterns of computer use and measured children's academic performance (grades) and achievement (test scores).

Children who participated in the project spent about thirty minutes a day on the computer, typically searching the Internet. They used the Internet less for communication purposes, such as e-mail or instant messaging probably because friends and family did not have access to the technology. The project found positive effects on Internet use and grade-point average and reading comprehension scores six months later. Contrary to what some pretechnology adults think, working on a computer is not wasting time. (For a summary of this section, see "Interim Summary 11.5: Schooling.")

digital divide The technology gap that separates children who have access to computers and those who do not have access. Low-income and ethnic minority families are less likely to have computers and related materials in their homes.

SUMMING UP AND LOOKING AHEAD

Cognitive development in middle childhood is nothing short of an "intellectual revolution." Not only do children acquire basic skills—reading, writing, and mathematics—but also the *way* they think changes. No longer seduced by appearances, they use logical operations to organize information and probe beneath the surface. They develop strategies for analyzing problems and remembering large chunks of information. Given opportunities, children this age are avid learners. At the same time, their thinking is limited to real or "concrete" objects and events. It is not until adolescence that individuals can reliably apply these logical tools to abstract concepts.

School plays a pivotal role in middle childhood. Ready or not, it's time to learn. There is much debate about what and how to teach children, from the reading wars to the length of the school year to the benefits of computers. This debate is, in part, fueled by the achievement gap between poor and better-off students within the United States, and by this country's middle ranking on international comparisons.

Of course, cognitive development is not confined to school learning. What children do when they are not in school, their family life, neighborhoods in which they live, and the media are all powerful influences, as we will see in "Socioemotional Development in Middle Childhood." Middle childhood is a time of changes in the way children see themselves, in how they relate to their parents and siblings, in how they interact with their peers, and in their experience of the wider world.

INTERIM SUMMARY **11.5**

Schools and Schooling

A Typical Classroom	■ The education system in the United States is decentralized. As a result, there are considerable differences in class size, classroom organization, teacher styles, and teacher knowledge and skills.
	■ Still, there are commonalities across many classrooms. On average, children spend over 90% of their time in whole-class instruction or individual seat work. Very little time is spent in small-group instruction.
	■ The emotional quality of the classroom tends to be moderately positive, whereas the quality of instruction (challenging lessons) tends to be low.
The Nation's Report Card	■ The National Assessment of Educational Progress (NAEP) measures student achievement in nationally representative samples in the United States. NAEP documents significant differences in the scores of low-income, African American, and Hispanic students versus middle-income, Caucasian, and Asian students. These differences have been called the **achievement gap**.
International Comparisons	■ The Trends in International Mathematics and Science Study compares mathematics performance in different countries.
	■ U.S. students score in the middling ranks in mathematics and (slightly) above average in science.
No Child Left Behind (NCLB)	■ The federal law known as **No Child Left Behind (NCLB)** has sought to improve children's academic skills by holding schools accountable for student performance on standardized achievement tests.
Strategies to Improve Student Learning and Achievement	■ Strategies that have narrowed the achievement gap include smaller class sizes, more effective teachers, a longer school year, a longer school day, afterschool programs, a reorganized curriculum, early childhood educational programs, and increased family involvement.
Technology and Learning	■ Computers and technology are more likely to support student learning when students are actively engaged in the activity, students participate in groups as opposed to working alone, students have frequent interaction and feedback from teachers around technology, there are clear connections to real-world contexts, and there is systematic evaluation.

HERE'S WHAT YOU SHOULD KNOW

Did You Get It?

After reading this chapter, you should understand the following:

■ What the concrete operational period is and the characteristics of concrete operational thinking and Piaget's beliefs about it

■ What microgenetic analysis involves and what these studies show about children's behavior

■ The development of processing speed and working and long-term memory in middle childhood

■ What false memories are and what the Deese-Roediger-McDermott (DRM) procedure demonstrates

- What guidelines developmental scientists have developed for interviewing children that reduce memory distortions
- An overview of the efforts to measure intelligence and what IQ scores mean

- The propositions of Gardner's theory of multiple intelligences and Sternberg's triarchic theory
- How children progress in their language development and mathematical thinking in middle childhood
- The impact of schools, schooling, and technology on children's development

Important Terms and Concepts

achievement gap (p. 327)
class inclusion (p. 303)
classification (p. 303)
code switching (p. 319)
comprehension (p. 320)
concrete operations (p. 303)
conservation (p. 303)
declarative memory
   (p. 309)
decoding (p. 320)
Deese-Roediger-McDermott
   (DRM) procedure
   (p. 310)
digit span task (p. 308)
digital divide (p. 333)

dizygotic (DZ) twins
   (p. 316)
Down syndrome (p. 317)
dyslexia (p. 321)
English language learners
   (ELLs) (p. 322)
false memory (p. 310)
fragile X syndrome (p. 317)
g (p. 313)
giftedness (p. 317)
gist memory (p. 309)
heritability (p. 316)
high stakes test (p. 329)
horizontal decalage
   (p. 305)

long-term memory (p. 309)
mainstreaming (p. 321)
media multitasking (p. 332)
microgenetic analysis
   (p. 306)
misinformation paradigm
   (p. 310)
monozygotic (MZ) twins
   (p. 316)
multiple intelligences
   (p. 313)
No Child Left Behind
   (NCLB) (p. 328)
phoneme (p. 320)
phonics (p. 320)

procedural memory
   (p. 309)
reliability (p. 313)
reversibility (p. 304)
root words (p. 318)
seriation (p. 304)
transitive inference (p. 304)
triarchic theory of successful
   intelligence (p. 314)
validity (p. 313)
verbatim memory (p. 309)
whole language (p. 320)
working memory (p. 308)

Socioemotional Development in Middle Childhood

For Alexander Williams, son of a lawyer and a high-level manager, weekends are jam-packed. Alexander plays soccer, basketball, and baseball; goes to Sunday school; sings in the church choir and a university choral group; takes private piano lessons; and studies guitar at school. He sometimes has five or more formal, scheduled events between Friday and Monday.

For Billy Yandell, son of a house painter and a domestic worker, weekends are leisurely. He has few scheduled activities except for attending church. He spends his weekends visiting with relatives, playing street ball, riding his bike, watching TV, playing video games, going to the store for a snack, and just hanging out with other kids in his neighborhood.

Alexander and Billy were part of sociologist Annette Lareau's (2003) ethnographic study of school-age American children. Ethnographers conduct fieldwork in which they gain access to a group and carry out intensive observations over a period of months or years. Lareau was interested in how children spend their out-of-school time and in how social class shapes the content and pace of their daily lives. She observed that the middle-class children spent much of their out-of-school time in ways that were preparing them for their roles as high-achieving students and for future careers. Their activities were organized and emphasized mastering skills and performing for an audience, whether at bat or in a music recital. At soccer practice, for example, they lined up, performed drills according to the coach's instructions, occupied the spotlight when they had the ball (much as they do at school when a teacher asks them a question), and likewise were judged by their performance. They also were "in training" for careers and family lives that demand skill in managing a crowded schedule.

The lives of the working-class children were more relaxed and informal. They were more likely to play in improvised, mixed-age groups, without adult supervision. As long as they stayed within the physical boundaries their parents set, they had autonomy and social space apart from adults. The working-class children were less dependent on their parents to chauffer them from here to there than middle-class children were. Their weekends were more kin centered, often including visits with nearby grandparents, aunts, uncles, and cousins. With few organized, structured activities, they had few performance expectations, limited opportunities "to shine," and less experience learning how to juggle competing demands. Lareau observed that these differences in out-of-school time were shaped more by social class than by race. For example, in the case of the two boys just described, Alexander Williams is African American; Billy Yandell is Irish American.

Lareau's study highlights that social and emotional development in middle childhood take place within different contexts. The immediate family is still important and provides children with widely varying opportunities, economic and social resources, and cultural expectations. In addition, peer contexts (both friendships and larger peer groups) are increasingly salient, as is the broader neighborhood context. Children's exposure to the world outside of their immediate neighborhood and community continues to expand. Television, video games, and computers open new social opportunities and new risks. We will consider the family, the peer group, organized activities, and technology in more detail later in this chapter. First, though, we look at several notable accomplishments in the socioemotional domain that occur during middle childhood.

SOCIOEMOTIONAL ACCOMPLISHMENTS

The advances in the physical domain (described in "Physical Development in Middle Childhood") and cognitive domain (described in "Cognitive Development in Middle Childhood") help set the stage for socioemotional development in middle childhood. In this section, we consider three aspects of socioemotional development that characterize this period: a more differentiated conception of self, feelings of industry versus inferiority, and gender as an important organizing framework for self and for others.

Conception of Self

In early childhood, the child's conception of self is generally positive (see "Socioemotional Development in Early Childhood"). In middle childhood, this conception has become more balanced and nuanced. One girl described herself this way:

> I'm in fourth grade this year, and I'm pretty popular, at least with my girl friends. That's because I am nice to people and helpful and can keep secrets. Mostly I am nice to my friends, although if I get in a bad mood I sometimes say something that can be a little mean. I try to control my temper, but when I don't, I'm ashamed of myself. I'm usually happy when I'm with friends, but I get sad if there is no one around to do things with. At school, I'm feeling pretty smart in certain subjects like language arts and social studies. I got A's in these subjects on my last report card and was really proud of myself. But I'm feeling pretty dumb in math and science, especially when I see how well a lot of other kids are doing. Even though I'm not doing well in these subjects, I still like myself as a person, because math and science just aren't that important to me. How I look and how popular I am are more important. I also like myself because I know my parents like me and so do other kids. That helps you like yourself. (Harter, 2006, p. 526)

Unlike a preschooler, this fourth-grader doesn't see herself as "all good" (or "all bad"), but describes her strengths and weaknesses in comparison to "other kids." Accomplishments are important, but she also sees social relationships as central to her life. Interpersonal terms have replaced the concrete descriptions of the younger child. This girl is able to recognize and reconcile conflicting traits (*smart* in some subjects, but *dumb* in others) and contradictory emotions (*happy* in some situations, but *sad* in others). More conscious of how other people see her, she begins her self-description, "I'm pretty popular. . . ." But she doesn't see herself through rose-colored glasses: sometimes she's "proud"; other times she's "ashamed."

The sense of self in middle childhood builds on cognitive advances that we described in "Cognitive Development in Middle Childhood." Children are now able to consider two different concepts or dimensions (such as *nice* and *mean*) at the same time. This means they can compare their ideal and real self (always nice vs. sometimes mean), as well as compare themselves to others. They use higher-order generalizations such as "smart" rather than mention specific skills ("I know my ABCs") and, reversing this process, analyze the components of generalizations (popularity = nice + helpful + keeping secrets).

In middle childhood, children's conception of self becomes more multifaceted, reflecting the views of their parents and peers. Children with more positive self-appraisals are more likely to have parents who are accepting, affectionate, and involved in their activities (Harter, 2006). Parents who set excessively high and unrealistic standards undermine children's sense of self, resulting in a tarnished image of self as unlovable, incompetent, and unworthy (Erikson, 1963). Children's self-appraisals also reflect their standing and reputation among classmates and teammates, as we saw in the girl's self-description. At this age, peer groups rank with parents as influences on self-concepts and self-esteem (Harris, 1995).

Societal views and standards also play a role. By middle childhood, youngsters have internalized many of their culture's values. Physical appearance is an example. Children who don't measure up to cultural ideas of physical attractiveness, in body shape or facial features, suffer from lower self-esteem and from symptoms of depression (Harter, 2006; Huesmann & Taylor, 2006). Becoming aware of others' perceptions and evaluations may provide a more realistic sense of self, but also leads to greater vulnerability.

Industry Versus Inferiority

Erik Erikson's (1963) fourth stage of psychosocial development—**industry versus inferiority**—describes another aspect of the developing sense of self in middle childhood. Children develop a view of themselves as industrious (and worthy) versus inferior when they win recognition by producing things beside and with others. Striving for recognition for their accomplishments, children develop skills and perform tasks that their society values. From these efforts, they come to appreciate (and even enjoy) persistence and hard work that leads to their success and recognition. Elementary school children are graded for their school work and often for their industry (under the label "Work Habits" or "Study Skills").

Opportunities to develop industry are not confined to school. Performing tricks on a skateboard, reaching the next level in online games like World of Warcraft, organizing a magic show, and selling Girl Scout cookies also require effort and diligence and contribute to children's growing sense of accomplishment. The danger, according to Erikson, is that parents and teachers undermine industry by failing to recognize accomplishments and by being overly critical of children's efforts, leaving the children with an abiding sense of inferiority.

The social context also affects the development of industry. Alexander Williams, one of the boys described at the beginning of this chapter, had ample opportunities to win recognition in his organized music and sports activities; Billy Yandell had fewer of these experiences. It is important to remember that, although school is probably the main context in which children develop (or fail to develop) a healthy sense of industry, it is not the only setting where this aspect of the development of the self unfolds. Many children who have difficulty achieving in school demonstrate mastery in other arenas.

Gender Development

Gender functions as an organizing principle in middle childhood. It provides a framework for children to think about themselves in relation to others; a basis for choosing interests, activities, and friends; and a guide for behavior and even emotions. Gender consciousness is not limited to middle childhood, of course, but solidifies during this period.

By eight or nine years, children's self-concepts reflect gender norms (see Table 12.1.) The differences are not large, but in self-descriptions boys emphasize skill in math and sports. Girls highlight verbal/reading ability, music, and social competence (being nice and being popular) (Eccles et al., 1993). Small differences can have long-term consequences. Girls who lack confidence in their math skills in elementary school (or lack interest, as our fourth-grader said in the earlier extract) may not put in the extra effort to master more advanced concepts in middle school. If you believe you won't be very

industry versus inferiority
Erikson's fourth stage of psychosocial development in which children develop a view of themselves as industrious (and worthy) versus inferior. Striving for recognition for their accomplishments, children develop skills and perform tasks that their society values.

TABLE 12.1 Gender Differences in Middle Childhood

DOMAIN	BOYS	GIRLS
Competencies reflected in self-descriptions	Math ability, sports	Verbal/reading ability, music, social skills
Personality traits	Instrumental; emphasis on accomplishments and action	Expressive; emphasis on communication and collaboration
Play	Rough-and-tumble play all over the playground	Social games on the sidelines
Media preferences	Science fiction, sports, comic books	Adventures, ghost stories, romances, animal themes
Self-esteem	Slightly higher than girls	Slightly lower than boys

good, why try? This leaves young women less prepared for higher-level math and physics courses in high school and college and helps to perpetuate the gender gap in science and engineering (Halpern, 2000; Hyde, Fennema, & Lamon, 1990).

Gender differences in global self-esteem appear in mid- to late childhood, with girls (on average) exhibiting lower self-esteem than boys (Kling et al., 1999). A cross-cultural study of more than 3,000 school-age children found that academic self-conceptions usually matched achievement (Stetsenko et al., 2000). However, girls who achieved top grades and test scores typically said they were "as good as boys," not crediting themselves for being better than boys, despite demonstrated superiority. In math and science classes, on the basketball court, and elsewhere, a girl might be told "You're really good" but internalize a different message, "You're good—*for a girl*" (Gelman, Taylor, & Nguyen, 2004).

Gender-linked personality traits become more apparent during this period (Ruble, Martin, & Berenbaum, 2006). **Instrumentality** is a "can do" orientation, focused on action and accomplishments. **Expressivity** is a "caring" orientation, focused on communication, collaboration, and conciliation. Parents and peers tend to encourage instrumentality in boys (Richards & Larson, 1989). The reverse is true for girls. Instrumental girls are "bossy." Girls who talk about their talents and victories are seen as "bragging." But boys who do the same are viewed as assertive. As a consequence, boys learn to make direct statements, whereas girls learn to make polite suggestions or hints (Tannen, 1994). In mixed-sex interaction, boys don't hear the hints and ignore the girls' efforts to influence activities, one possible reason that girls have lower self-esteem (Kling et al., 1999).

Different orientations are both a cause and consequence of separate lives. Gender segregation, which we first saw in early childhood, intensifies during middle childhood (Ruble et al., 2006). Visit an elementary school playground. Most likely, the boys are playing with other boys and taking up most of the space on the playground. Their play is more likely to involve **rough-and-tumble play**—physically vigorous behaviors such as chasing, jumping, and play fighting, accompanied by shared smiles and laughter. Girls are on the sidelines, most often talking and playing with other girls.

Neither sex wants much to do with the other. Each sees his or her own sex as the in-group and the other sex as the out-group (Maccoby, 2003). Put another way, what is "in" for girls is off limits for boys, and vice versa. In a typical in-group/out-group pattern, children perceive more positive traits in their own sex and negative traits in

instrumentality A gender-linked personality trait that is characterized by a focus on action and accomplishments.

expressivity A gender-linked personality trait that is marked by a "caring" orientation; a focus on communication, collaboration, and conciliation.

rough-and-tumble play Physically vigorous behaviors such as chasing, jumping, and play fighting that are accompanied by shared smiles and laughter.

the other. They exaggerate both the similarities among members of their own sex and the differences between themselves and the other sex. And so the notion of the *opposite* sex takes root.

In-group identity is echoed in gender-stereotypic preferences in reading and media (Ruble et al., 2006). Girls prefer adventure, ghost, and romance/relationship themes, animal stories, and poetry. Boys read science fiction, sports, war/spy stories, comic books, and joke books. Girls write stories about affection; boys, about aggression. Girls draw human figures, butterflies, and flowers. Boys draw mechanical objects, often cars and battle scenes. Alone and in groups, then, girls and boys create different worlds for themselves (Blatchford, Baines, & Pellegrini, 2003).

At the same time, **gender schemas**—the conceptualization of what it means to be male or female—become more complex (Ruble et al., 2006). Rigid, simplistic sex stereotypes decline after a peak at about age six years. In general, girls are more flexible about gender norms and sex roles than boys are. Both sexes are more likely to accept girls who like "masculine" activities such as playing sports than boys who like "feminine" activities, such as sewing. Actually, by the end of middle childhood, both boys *and* girls find boy-type activities (especially sports) more interesting than girl-type activities (McHale et al., 2004). This doesn't mean that they play together, though. Girls join all-girl soccer leagues and boys join all-boy leagues. Latino and Asian American children are more likely to conform to sex stereotypes, and African Americans less likely, than are European American children (Corsaro, 2006; Ruble et al., 2006).

Clearly, in the mind of the school-age child, differences between the sexes are strong and real. But how accurate are children's perceptions? Literally hundreds of studies have compared boys' and girls' performances during middle childhood (Blakemore, Berenbaum, & Liben, 2008). This means that the odds are that one or another study might have detected a statistically difference by chance. For this reason, researchers have turned to meta-analysis to weigh the evidence. **Meta-analysis** is a statistical technique that combines the findings of multiple studies, taking into account the number of children in each of the individual studies and the magnitude of the result (for instance, the size of the sex difference) reported in each one. By pooling the results of many, many studies, meta-analyses help us to be more confident that findings are robust and reliable.

For the most part, meta-analyses of research on sex differences indicate that boys are more active and more physically aggressive than girls; have better spatial abilities as reflected in their skills at mental rotations; and have better large motor skills (such as hitting a target with a ball) (Blakemore et al., 2008; Ruble et al., 2006). Girls, on the other hand, have better verbal skills, including speech, fluency, and verbal memory. Girls also are better at reading emotions.

However, as Janet Hyde (2005) has cautioned, meta-analyses also reveal a lot of overlap between boys and girls in

gender schema A conceptualization of what it means to be male or female.

meta-analysis A statistical technique that combines the findings of multiple studies, taking into account the number of children in each of the individual studies and the magnitude of the effect reported in each one.

© Tony Freeman / PhotoEdit

Girls' participation in organized sports has increased dramatically since the passage of Title IX in 1972.

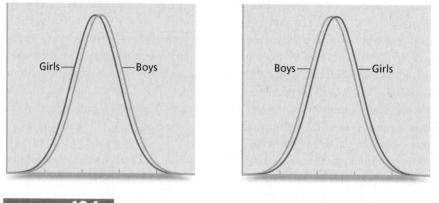

Difference in self-esteem scores   **Difference in verbal abilities**

FIGURE 12.1

The Overlap in the Performances of Boys and Girls

Boys, on average, have a slight edge in terms of self-esteem, but many girls have scores that are higher than boys. In fact, there is about an 85 percent overlap in the distributions of the scores for boys and girls.
Source: Hyde (2005).

all of these areas. Look at Figure 12.1. You see that boys, on average, have a slight edge in terms of self-esteem, but many girls have scores that are higher than boys'. In fact, there is about an 85 percent overlap in the distributions of the scores for boys and girls. In contrast, girls, on average, have a slight edge in verbal abilities. But many boys have higher verbal abilities than many girls (again, about an 85% overlap). In other areas such as physical activity, the average differences between boys and girls are larger, although there is still a lot of overlap (67%).

In summary, objective measures show that school-age boys and girls are more alike than different. But they see themselves almost as belonging to different "tribes" and act in ways that accentuate and even create gender differences. Gender structures their sense of self as well as their social lives. (For a summary of this section, see "Interim Summary 12.1: Socioemotional Development in Middle Childhood.")

MORAL REASONING, PROSOCIAL BEHAVIOR, AND AGGRESSION

Whether girl or boy, school-age children are involved in multiple groups: the family, the school class, informal friendship groups, and often teams and clubs. All of these groups have standards, rules, and sanctions (rewards for conformity and punishments for nonconformity). Understanding standards, playing by the rules, and deciding what is fair are part of group life. These social experiences, interacting with cognitive development and genetic factors, propel moral development (Pinker, 2008). They also provide contexts for behaving kindly and for behaving aggressively.

Moral Reasoning

How do children this age think about right and wrong? Lawrence Kohlberg's theory long dominated the study of moral reasoning (Kohlberg, 1976; Turiel, 2006). In this approach, researchers assess children's level of moral reasoning by examining responses to hypothetical moral dilemmas about real-world situations, such as the following:

Judy was a twelve-year-old girl. Her mother promised her that she could go to a special rock concert coming to their town if she saved up from baby-sitting and lunch

INTERIM SUMMARY **12.1**

Socioemotional Accomplishments

Conception of Self	■ Self-concepts become more balanced and nuanced in middle childhood than in early childhood.
	■ These conceptions are influenced by parents, peers, and societal standards.
Industry Versus Inferiority	■ Erikson's fourth stage of psychosocial development, industry versus inferiority, occurs in middle childhood.
	■ Children develop a view of self as industrious (and worthy) versus inferior when they obtain recognition for their accomplishments.
Gender Development	■ Gender provides an organizing framework for children to think about themselves in relation to others.
	■ Children's self-concepts reflect gender norms.
	■ Meta-analyses indicate that boys are more active, are more physically aggressive, and have better spatial abilities and better large motor skills. Girls have better verbal skills and are better at reading emotions. Most of the differences are small, and there is considerable overlap between the scores of boys and girls.

money to buy a ticket to the concert. She managed to save up the fifteen dollars the ticket cost plus another five dollars. But then her mother changed her mind and told Judy that she had to spend the money on new clothes for school. Judy was disappointed and decided to go to the concert anyway. She bought a ticket and told her mother that she had only been able to save five dollars. That Saturday she went to the performance and told her mother that she was spending the day with a friend. A week passed without her mother finding out. Judy then told her older sister, Louise, that she had gone to the performance and had lied to her mother about it. Louise wonders whether to tell their mother what Judy did.

Should Louise, the older sister, tell their mother that Judy lied or should she keep quiet?

According to Kohlberg, whether or not you think that Louise should tell her mother is less important than the reasoning behind your answer. Kohlberg theorized that individuals' reasoning about moral issues becomes more sophisticated with development. Specifically, Kohlberg held that there are three main levels of moral reasoning: **preconventional**, which is dominant during most of childhood; **conventional moral reasoning**, which is usually dominant during late childhood and early adolescence; and **postconventional** (sometimes called "principled moral reasoning"), which emerges sometime during the adolescent or young adult years (see Table 12.2).

Preconventional moral reasoning is not based on society's standards, rules, or conventions. Rather, children at this stage focus on the rewards and punishments associated with different courses of action. (Louise shouldn't tell on her sister Judy because Judy will be angry and get back at her *or* Louise should tell on her sister because Louise will get in big trouble if her mother finds out that Louise had not told what her sister had done.) In contrast, conventional thinking about moral issues focuses not so much on tangible rewards and punishments but on how an individual will be judged by others for behaving in a certain way. One behaves properly because, in so doing, one receives the approval of others and helps to maintain the social order. (Louise should tell on her sister because lying is wrong and Judy lied *or* Louise should not tell on her sister because her sister trusted her.) Individuals at this level do not question

preconventional moral reasoning In Kohlberg's theory, reasoning that focuses on the rewards and punishments associated with different courses of action, not societal standards.

conventional moral reasoning In Kohlberg's theory, reasoning that focuses on receiving the approval of others or maintaining the social order.

postconventional moral reasoning In Kohlberg's theory, reasoning guided by principles such as justice, fairness, and sanctity of life.

TABLE 12.2 Kohlberg's Theory of Moral Reasoning in Middle Childhood

LEVEL	DESCRIPTION
Preconventional	Moral decisions are based on the rewards and punishments that could be associated with an action or behavior.
Conventional	Morality is judged by whether or not the behavior conforms to social rules and whether it will be approved of by others.
Postconventional	Principles such as justice, fairness, and the sanctity of life guide decisions about moral behavior.

society's rules. They see these rules as coming from a higher authority and leading to the greater good.

At the postconventional level of reasoning, which is not seen prior to adolescence, society's rules and conventions are seen as relative, not absolute and definitive. One may have a duty to abide by society's standards for behavior—but only insofar as those standards support and serve moral ends. Occasions arise in which conventions ought to be questioned; when more important principles—such as justice, fairness, keeping one's word, or the sanctity of human life—take precedence over established social norms. (Louise shouldn't tell on her sister because their mother *promised* Judy she could go to the concert if she saved enough money but then broke her promise.)

Many studies have confirmed Kohlberg's belief that moral reasoning becomes more principled over the course of childhood and adolescence (Eisenberg & Morris, 2004). According to Kohlberg, development into higher stages of moral reasoning occurs when the child is developmentally "ready"—when his reasoning is predominantly at one stage but partially at the next higher one—and when he is exposed to the more advanced type of reasoning by other people, such as parents or peers (Eisenberg & Morris, 2004). This has led to the development of many curricula designed to stimulate the growth of advanced moral reasoning.

Kohlberg's work has been criticized because he interviewed only boys from Caucasian, middle-class backgrounds. Whether the results can be generalized to all children is questionable. Carol Gilligan (1982) argued that girls and women employ a morality of care, emphasizing nurturance and compassion, as opposed to a morality of justice, which is more evident in boys. Kohlberg's work also has been criticized because he focused on moral reasoning and not on actions or behavior. Although moral reasoning and moral behavior are related, they are not perfectly so. For instance, you know full well that it is important to have traffic laws in order to protect individuals from injuring themselves or others but there probably have been times when you have knowingly violated the law because you were in a hurry to get someplace. Others are now studying the links between moral reasoning and moral behaviors in middle childhood in different cultural contexts.

prosocial behavior Voluntary actions such as sharing, cooperating, helping, and comforting that are intended to benefit another person.

Prosocial Development

The sheer number of **prosocial behaviors**—actions such as sharing, cooperating, helping, and comforting that are intended to benefit another person—increases from the preschool period through middle childhood (Eisenberg, Fabes, & Spinrad, 2006).

These increases in prosocial behavior occur, in part, because school-aged children are better able to read emotional cues and to understand other people's emotional states and thought processes (Garner, 1996) as well as better at regulating their own emotional states so that they are less likely to be overwhelmed by their feelings (Eisenberg et al., 2006).

The increases also reflect developmental changes in children's motivations or reasons for helping (Bar-Tal, Raviv, & Leiser, 1980). When presented with hypothetical moral dilemmas (e.g., helping an injured child versus going to a party), children have been asked what they would do and why. In early childhood, children tend to use **hedonistic reasoning** that focuses on their own wishes and needs. In middle childhood, children's reasoning becomes other oriented and aimed at winning social approval and enhancing inter-

Prosocial behaviors, such as providing comfort and assistance, increase in frequency from early to middle childhood.

personal relationships. Children this age want to be seen as "good." **Altruism**—helping behaviors that are motivated by helping as an end in itself, without expectation of reward or recognition—begin to emerge in late elementary school (Bar-Tal et al., 1980).

hedonistic reasoning Moral reasoning that focuses on one's own wishes and needs.

altruism Helping behaviors that are motivated by assistance as an end in itself, without expectation of reward or recognition.

Variations Between Cultures But societies differ in the degree to which prosocial and cooperative behaviors are normative or expected (Grusec, Davidov, & Lundell, 2002). In individualistic (westernized, urban) cultures, a higher value is placed on spontaneous acts of kindness than on doing one's duty. Prosocial behaviors are thought of as an expression of personal values and individual personality. Duty is obligatory; altruism is heartfelt. Socialization emphasizes empathy (feeling *with* others) and sympathy (feeling *for* others). In collectivist (traditional Asian, African, and Latin American, rural and semiagricultural) cultures, doing one's duty is valued above spontaneous acts. Social harmony is thought to depend on individuals performing their social roles, not individual motivation. Socialization emphasizes propriety and reciprocity.

Laboratory studies in which children decide about sharing prizes with a peer highlight cultural differences. Chinese children are more willing than European American children to donate gifts or share food with classmates (Rao & Stewart, 1999; Stewart & McBride-Chang, 2000). They've been taught from an early age that food is not private property ("mine" or "yours") but communal property ("ours"). Mexican American children whose parents grew up in traditional communal villages are more generous with their peers than are European American children (Knight, Kagan & Buriel, 1981). But the difference fades in third-generation immigrants, whose behavior more closely resembles their European American peers (Knight & Kagan, 1977), a pattern that suggests that acculturation to conventional American norms may lead children to become less prosocial.

Variations Within Cultures Other developmental scientists have focused on individual variations within cultures. The likelihood that children are prosocial shows relative continuity over childhood. In one study, Chinese children who were relatively helpful (in comparison to their peers) when they entered kindergarten remained relatively helpful six years later, at the beginning of adolescence (Chen, French, & Schneider, 2006). The same was true of children who are relatively self-centered and uncooperative. This evidence is particularly significant because different teachers rated children at different ages.

This continuity may reflect biological factors (genes and brain structures) as well as cultural and family expectations. Identical twins are more similar to each other than fraternal twins, suggesting that genetic factors predispose some children toward pro-social behaviors (Knafo & Plomin, 2006).

Aggression

"I was sitting on the bus one day and a boy came up and hit me for no reason." (twelve-year-old boy)

"Three boys called me a rat and harassed me and hit me with a broom." (twelve-year-old girl)

"I started hanging out with another girl, they didn't like her, they said, 'We won't be your friend anymore if you hang with her.'" (twelve-year-old girl)

physical aggression Acts such as hitting or pushing with an intent to harm.

verbal aggression Behavior such as threats, name calling, and yelling with an angry voice.

social aggression Behavior that is directed toward damaging another's self-esteem, social status, or both.

relational aggression Any behavior that is intended to harm someone by damaging or manipulating relationships with others.

As these interviews reported by Julie Paquette and Marion Underwood (1999) illustrate, aggression in middle childhood takes different forms: **physical aggression** (hitting, pushing), **verbal aggression** (threats, name calling, yelling with an angry voice), and **social aggression** or **relational aggression** (acting in ways to undermine another's position in a group).

The amount of physical aggression declines in middle childhood (Dodge, Coie, & Lynam, 2006). In one large longitudinal study of more than 1,200 children, the most common form of early aggression (hitting others) was reported for about 70 percent of the children at age two, for about 20 percent of the children at age five, and for about 12 percent of the children at age eight years (NICHD Early Child Care Research Network, 2004b).

By the time they have entered elementary school, children have expanded their array of strategies and skills for coping with conflicts, including better reading of social cues (being able to read frustration in someone's face), being able to delay a response (holding back before hitting someone), emotional self-regulation (calming oneself down), negotiation (working out a compromise with someone), and the use of the other forms of aggression, like verbal aggression, which means they have alternatives to pushing and hitting (Rubin, Bukowski, & Parker, 2006). There are, however, a small number of children (mostly boys) who continue to pick fights (Loeber et al., 1998).

Researchers have found that highly aggressive children process social information differently (Gifford-Smith & Rabiner, 2004). They are more likely to perceive ambiguous encounters or comments as hostile. For example, they interpret an accidental bump in the hallway as a deliberate shove and provocation, and then respond in kind. Children who are highly aggressive at this age usually have a history of aggression in early childhood (Campbell et al., 2006). High levels of physical aggression in middle childhood also are associated with poverty (Bradley & Corwyn, 2002; McLoyd, 1990), coercive or harsh parenting, and parental use of physical discipline (spanking, hitting) (Dodge, Pettit, & Bates, 1994).

Whereas physical aggression becomes less common in middle childhood (for both boys and girls), social and relational aggression do not (Underwood, Beron, & Gentsch, 2007). Indeed, there are some suggestions that social aggression becomes more common in girls during the transition between middle childhood and early adolescence (Cairns, Cairns, & Neckerman, 1989). Social aggression is directed toward damaging another's self-esteem, social status, or both (Galen & Underwood, 1997). Relational aggression is an attempt to harm someone by manipulating or damaging their peer relationships (Crick & Grotpeter, 1995). These types of aggression may take the form of threatening to end a friendship unless the child does what the aggressor wants; excluding the child from play groups, social gatherings, or conversations; or spreading rumors designed to cause other peers to reject the child. As we discuss later in this chapter, peer groups and friendships become increasingly important in middle childhood and efforts to undermine children's social relations are experienced as particularly hurtful.

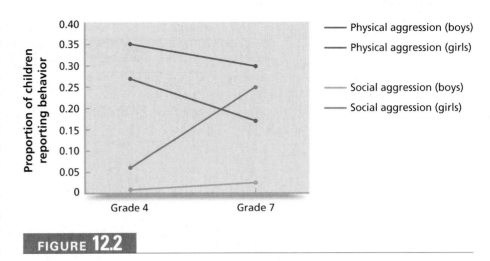

FIGURE 12.2

Differences in Social Versus Physical Aggression by Age and Gender

Physical aggression is less common in Grade 7 than in Grade 4 for both boys and girls. In contrast, social aggression is more common in girls in Grade 7 than in Grade 4. Few boys displayed social aggression at either age.

Source: Cairns, Cairns, & Neckerman (1989).

Stereotypes hold that boys are tough but girls are mean. Is social and relational aggression the female equivalent of physical aggression among boys? Yes and no. Boys do engage in more physical aggression than girls (Broidy et al., 2003), and girls do engage in more relational than physical aggression (Crick & Grotpeter, 1995). Some studies also find that girls are more likely than boys to use social aggression (see Figure 12.2). However, boys also gossip, spread rumors, and practice exclusion (Crick, Casas, & Nelson, 2002; Underwood, 2002). To the extent that girls are more concerned about social relationships than boys are, they may suffer more from relational victimization (Crick, Ostrov, & Werner, 2006).

Bullies and Victims

Bullying refers to aggression by an individual that is repeatedly directed toward particular peers (victims) (Olweus, 1993; Rubin et al., 2006). It may be physical (hitting, kicking, shoving, tripping), verbal (teasing, harassing, name-calling), or social (public humiliation or exclusion). Bullying differs from other forms of aggression in that it is characterized by specificity (bullies direct their acts to certain peers) and by an imbalance of power between the bully and the victim (Olweus, 1993; Rigby, 2002). An older child bullies a younger one; a large child picks on a small, weaker one; a verbally assertive child torments a shy, quiet child. It is not bullying when equals have an occasional fight or disagreement. Bullies are more likely to use force unemotionally and outside of the flow of an ongoing conflict (Perry, Perry, & Kennedy, 1992).

A study of bullies and victims found three broad styles of coping with victimization (Wilton, Craig, & Pepler, 2000). Some victims responded with aggression, anger, and contempt, which was not effective in stopping the bully; others, with passive capitulation or submissive avoidance, which wasn't effective, either. Very few (only 8%) responded with adaptive and constructive strategies such as getting help. Overall, the best protection against bullies is to have buddies or friends.

About one in ten children are the victims of bullying (Olweus, 1993). Research has revealed two distinct types of victims (Rubin et al., 2006). The first are children who are shy, anxious, and socially withdrawn, which makes them easy prey. Often they do not have friends to protect them. But other victims are high in aggression themselves and engage in irritating behavior that elicits aggression. Other children see them as "asking for it." Thus, bullying and victimization sometimes go hand in hand. These

bullying Aggression by an individual that is repeatedly directed toward particular peers (victims).

INTERIM SUMMARY 12.2

Moral Reasoning, Prosocial Behavior, and Aggression

Moral Reasoning	■ Kohlberg identified three main levels of moral reasoning: **preconventional**, **conventional**, and **postconventional**.
	■ Preconventional reasoning is based on rewards and punishments. Conventional thinking focuses on how an individual will be judged by others. Postconventional reasoning is guided by principles such as justice, fairness, and sanctity of life.
Prosocial Development	■ **Prosocial behaviors** (sharing, cooperating, helping, etc.) increase from early childhood through middle childhood.
	■ The increase reflects multiple factors: more skill at reading others' emotional cues and an increased ability to regulate one's own emotions.
	■ Prosocial behaviors also reflect cultural values and biological factors.
Aggression	■ Aggression can take several forms: physical aggression, verbal aggression, and social or relational aggression.
	■ **Physical aggression** (hitting, pushing, etc.) displayed by children declines in middle childhood.
	■ **Social** and **relational aggression** does not decline, and may even increase in middle childhood.
Bullies and Victims	■ **Bullying** is aggression that is repeatedly directed from an individual to particular peers (victims).
	■ Some victims are shy, anxious, and socially withdrawn, which makes them easy prey. Others are high in aggression and engage in irritating behavior that elicits aggression from others.

two types of victims have been seen in North America, South Asia, and East Asia (Schwartz et al., 2002).

Ordinarily we think of bullying as a male problem, but girls also can be bullies. With girls, bullying is more often relational; that is, the threat or actual betrayal of confidences, or shutting the victim out of social groups (Underwood, 2002). Bullying/victim relationships in middle childhood are usually between same-sex pairs, although boys may harass girls and girls may pick on boys (Rigby, 2002). (For a summary of this section, see "Interim Summary 12.2: Moral Reasoning, Prosocial Behavior, and Aggression.")

THE FAMILY CONTEXT

Although the child's social horizons are expanding (as we discuss later in this chapter), the family context is still central in middle childhood. Families have been studied by sociologists and demographers, who have focused on household structure (who lives in the home), and by psychologists, who describe transactional relations among parent-child, marital, and sibling relationships within the broader family system (how people in the home relate to one another).

postmodern family A term that describes the variation in modern-day families—two parents and single parents, married and unmarried couples, and multigenerational households.

Household Structure

Families are organized in a variety of ways: two parents and single parents, married and unmarried couples, and multigenerational households. The term **postmodern family** captures some of this variety (see Figure 12.3).

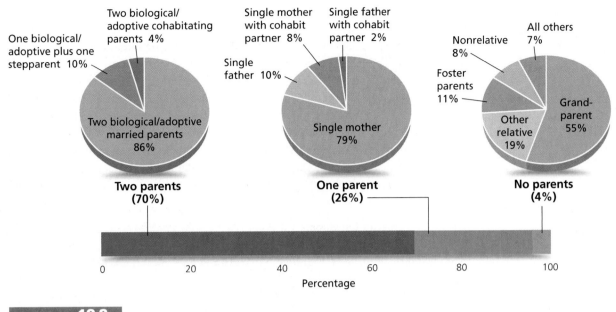

FIGURE **12.3**

Proportion of U.S. Children Who Live in Different Types of Households
Postmodern families include a diverse array of households.
Source: Federal Interagency Forum on Child and Family Statistics (2007).

The postmodern family is not only varied but also fluid. A child may live in two or more types of households in the course of growing up. For example, she may live in a nuclear family with both biological parents in a home of their own. If her parents divorce (as do about half of married couples), she may live with her single mom for a time, and then her mom may remarry (typically within three to four years).

According to the U.S. Census (see Figure 12.3), 70 percent of children live in households with two married parents—counting biological, adoptive, and stepparents. (This count excludes two parents who are not married.) About one-quarter of children live with a single parent. These single parents may be divorced, widowed, or never married; that is, any parent who is not currently living with a spouse. According to the U.S. Census Bureau, 3.3 million children (5% of all children) live in step- or blended families, although the actual number is higher because the Census Bureau does not include cohabiting couples or families in which the noncustodial parent remarries. Some 3.9 million households are multigenerational families composed of three or more generations of parents and their families. Multigenerational households are more common in immigrant families, communities where price of housing is high, and households in which single parents need assistance with child care (U.S. Census Bureau, 2004).

These differences in household structure have implications for families' economic and social resources, and they also are linked to differences in parenting and children's development.

Two-Parent Versus One-Parent Households

Two-parent families have several built-in advantages (Hay & Nash, 2002). They enjoy higher incomes than single-parent families, and levels of education backgrounds tend to be higher. Their jobs are more stable, as are their living arrangements (Bumpass & Lu, 2000). They move less often and are more likely to own their homes.

Given these advantages, it is probably not surprising that mothers in two-parent households report fewer symptoms of depression and anxiety (Hay & Nash, 2002). Their parenting practices are more likely to be authoritative, rather than authoritarian or permissive. Children in two-parent households also fare better, on average, than children in single-parent households. Their grades and test scores are higher. As a group, they have fewer internalizing and externalizing behavior problems.

This is not to say that growing up in a two-parent household is "good" and growing up in a single-parent household is "bad." There is considerable overlap in the two groups in parents' income, education, emotional well-being, and parenting styles. And there also is considerable overlap in children's academic performance, social competences, and behavior problems. Quality of parenting is a key factor in both two-parent and single-parent households.

Divorce Parents underestimate the intensity of their children's reactions to divorce (Clarke-Stewart & Brentano, 2006). Six- to eight-year-olds express grief and fear; they long for their parents to be reunited. Older school-age children react more with anger, often directed at the parent they hold responsible for the divorce. Acting out and rumination (repeatedly dwelling on the divorce) are common. One study found that a year later, 40 percent of children reported that they still thought about the divorce at least once a day (Weyer & Sandler, 1998).

Paul Amato (2001) conducted a meta-analysis of the effects of divorce on children, drawing on sixty-seven different studies conducted in the 1990s. This analysis was used to supplement an earlier one that combined analyses across ninety-two studies. (Recall that meta-analyses combine findings across studies taking into account sample sizes and effect sizes). From these analyses, Amato concluded that the children of divorced parents score lower on measures of academic achievement, conduct, psychological adjustment, self-concept, and social relations, although there was substantial overlap between the two groups. For example, between 17 percent and 25 percent of the children of divorced families display elevated behavior problems compared with 10 percent to 15 percent of children in nondivorced households (Greene et al., 2006).

It is hard to generalize about the effects of divorce on children, because much depends on the conditions surrounding the event. Children fare better when there are amicable relations between ex-spouses, when their parents use authoritative parenting, and when child support arrangements are complied with. Several factors increase the likelihood of negative effects of divorce on children's development. Understanding the factors that place some children at risk for adjustment problems can help in the design of interventions (Clarke-Stewart & Brentano, 2006). The most important risk factors include the following:

A dramatic decrease in family income. Even among couples who were relatively well off before they split up, divorce means a drop in income, averaging 13 percent to 35 percent per person (one reason is that families must maintain two households on the same amount of income) (Peterson, 1996). Children who experience a sharp decline in their family's income are twice as likely to develop behavior problems as other children of divorce.

Abandonment (or fear of abandonment). Children take their parents' presence for granted, as part of the natural order. When Dad (or less often, Mom) moves out, this security is undermined. About one-third of fathers have no contact with their children at all following a divorce. Only one-quarter see their children as often as once a week, and contact decreases with time.

Diminished parenting. In the year after a divorce, newly single parents tend to be preoccupied with their own issues, less attentive to their children, inconsistent, and irritable (Belsky & Jaffee, 2006). Often they are less concerned about household routines, such as regular family meals. They are less likely to be involved in school-related activities. Authoritative parenting often gives way to authoritarian, permissive, or detached parenting (see "Socioemotional Development in Early Childhood" for a description of these parenting styles).

Parental conflict. The conflicts that led the couple to end their marriage may spill over into postdivorce relations. Children are caught in the middle and may be pressured by both parents to choose sides.

Dislocation. Divorce typically means that the child moves to a new home—or two new homes in cases of joint custody—often in a new neighborhood and school district. At a time when he needs stability, the child is cut off from familiar, everyday sources of social making new friends, meeting new neighbors, and so on. Dislocation compounds other problems.

Longitudinal studies indicate that the negative effects of divorce generally resolve one to two years after the divorce (Hetherington, Cox, & Cox, 1982). Fear, disbelief, and the fantasy that parents will reunite fade. Behavior problems, especially aggression, decline markedly. One exception to this general rule concerns boys' academic performance, which does not rebound. Even five years later, boys whose parents split up have test scores and grades that are below the average for boys from intact families (Sun & Li, 2001, 2002).

Blended Families The composition of blended families varies. A child may have a stepfather, a stepmother, stepbrothers and stepsisters, and half-sisters and half-brothers. They may or may not live together, full- or part-time. These new relationships are uncharted territory for the child. A stepfather's role in a child's life is ambiguous; the child already has a father. Should the child call the new spouse Dad or Mom? Steve or Donna? Are Dad's new wife's parents "grandparents"? A stepparent's style and approach may differ from the biological parent's, allowing a child to play one against the other. The mother as well as the child may be torn by divided loyalties. A common problem is that the newly married couple has (unrealistic) hopes that a child will form instant bonds with the stepparent and other new family members, but this is a process that often takes considerable time and patience. Blended families require adjustments on everyone's part.

Preschoolers adapt more readily to a new family than school-age children and adolescents do, for several reasons (Clarke-Stewart & Brentano, 2006). Preschoolers don't have as long a history living with both parents. Older children are becoming more independent and peer oriented, and they don't necessarily want another adult authority in their lives. Daughters usually have more difficulty accepting remarriage than do sons (Hetherington & Clingempeel, 1992). The happier a mother and her new partner are, the more negative parent-child relationships are (the opposite of the pattern in intact families). Children do not easily or willing share their mother with someone new.

On average, children in blended families have somewhat lower grades and scores on achievement tests, and report more symptoms of depression, than do children in intact, nuclear families. But the difference is small, with substantial overlap between the groups (Clarke-Stewart & Brentano, 2006). As we saw in our earlier discussion of sex differences in personality and interests, very often the similarities among children from different groups (for instance, those from intact versus blended families) are more impressive than the differences.

Adoption More than 1 million U.S. children are adopted, and nearly that many adults are seeking to adopt. In the past three decades, the stigma for being an unwed parent has declined, and the number of healthy infants available for adoption in the United States has dropped. As a result, international adoptions (notably from China, Russia,

Like families in general, adoptive families are more diverse than ever before.

Guatemala, and South Korea) have tripled. In 2004, Americans adopted about 75,000 children—52,000 from within the United States and 23,000 from abroad (Child Welfare League of America, 2007). In addition, larger numbers of older children, children with special needs, and sibling groups are being adopted—by married couples, committed but unmarried couples, and singles (Wrobel, Hendrickson, & Grotevant, 2006).

Do adopted children differ from nonadopted children? The answer depends on what groups are being compared. To answer this question researchers have compared adopted children to their biological siblings who have remained with their biological parents and to their adoptive siblings who were born to the adopting parents. A meta-analysis of these studies found that adoptees had significantly higher scores on IQ tests, and higher grades in school, than their biological siblings (van IJzendoorn & Juffer, 2005). Their IQs are similar to those of their siblings in their adopted family and to current peers, but they lag behind them in school performance. Whereas adopted children generally fare better than their nonadopted, biological siblings, adopted children generally have more problems than their adoptive siblings (see Figure 12.4). They are twice as likely as their adoptive siblings to be referred for special education. Others report that adoptees are more likely than other children to be in counseling or psychotherapy (Miller et al., 2000; Wrobel, Hendrickson, & Gortevant, 2006).

A number of factors likely contribute to these findings, including the biological parents' genes, the children's prenatal environments, and their early postnatal environments. Temperamentally, adopted children might have problems left over from their earliest environment or be quite different from their adoptive family and be seen as a problem. The older the child is at adoption, the more likely he will have problems, particularly if the child spent extended periods of time in multiple foster homes or very deprived institutions (O'Connor et al., 2000; Gunnar, van Dulmen, & the International Adoption Project Team, 2007). Finally, adopting parents have higher than average education and incomes, and so may be more aware of child services and more willing to seek help (Stams, Juffer, & van IJzendoorn, 2002).

The problems of some adoptees and their families do not mean that adoption is "bad" for children and should be discouraged (Miller et al., 2000). Adoption clearly is good for children who might otherwise live in a series of foster homes or with families who are not able to care for them or do not want them. And a majority of young adoptees are functioning well. However, adoption policies and practices might be changed to provide long-term resources for adoptive parents, should they need them.

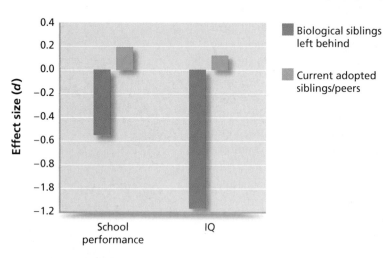

FIGURE 12.4

School Performance and IQ of Adopted Children Compared with Biological Siblings Left Behind and Current Nonbiological Siblings

The negative *d*s mean that the adopted children showed better school performance and higher IQ scores than their biological siblings left behind. The positive *d*s mean that the adopted children scored lower than their current nonbiological siblings. Larger *d*s mean larger differences.
Source: van IJzendoorn, Marinus, Juffer, & Femmie (2005)

Gay and Lesbian Parents About 5 percent of Americans are gay, lesbian, or bisexual. Many are parents. More than one-third of lesbian women have given birth, and one in six gay men has either fathered or adopted a child. An estimated 65,500 adopted children (4% of all adopted children in the United States) are living with a gay or lesbian parent, as are approximately 14,100 foster children (3% of the total) (Gates et al., 2007).

Developmental scientists have studied children of homosexual parents (mostly lesbian mothers) in relatively small community-based samples (Patterson, 2006; Wainright, Russell, & Patterson, 2004). Children of same-sex parents are similar to children of opposite-sex parents in self-concepts, preferences for same-sex playmates and activities in childhood, social competence, school grades, and quality of family relationships. However, further research of larger, nationally representative samples is needed before definitive conclusions can be made.

© GoGo Images / JupiterImages

Postmodern families include children who are growing up with same-sex parents.

The Family System

Urie Bronfenbrenner (1979) is an influential theorist whose work we discussed in "The Study of Child Development" and "Nature with Nurture." Bronfenbrenner argued that looking at static "social addresses" such as one-parent versus two-parent households is not enough. To understand development, he contended, researchers needed to study the dynamic interplay between individuals, their surroundings, and psychological processes over time (Bronfenbrenner & Morris, 1998). It is to a more dynamic systemic analysis of families that we now turn.

The family can be conceptualized as an overarching *system* composed of several subsystems (parent-child relationships, parent-parent relations, and sibling relations) that have their own features and implications for children's development, while being part of the larger system (see Figure 12.5).

Parent-Child Relationships At every age the parent-child relationship is a "two-way street" with the child influencing the parent as much as the parent influences the child. However, this reciprocity becomes more visible in middle childhood than it was earlier.

Advances in the child's cognitive and social skills (perspective taking, problem solving, and developing ideas of fairness) require parents to adjust. The content of parent-child interaction changes (Russell, Mize, & Bissaker, 2002). In early childhood, parents' main goals are to establish routines, control emotional

Family system

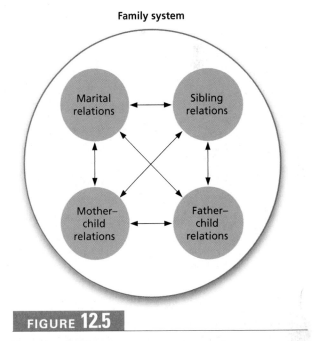

FIGURE **12.5**

The Family System

The family system is composed of subsystems (parent-child, parent-parent, and sibling relationships) that influence and are influenced by other relationships within the family.
Source: Parke & Buriel (2006).

outbursts and sibling fights, and teach children to care for themselves. In middle childhood, families shift from parental control to *co-regulation*.

Parents establish rules and supervise, but they leave many daily decisions up to the child. In return, the child is expected to keep them informed of his or her plans (and problems). Typically, direct commands decrease, and reasoning and debate increase during middle childhood. School-age children are more likely than preschoolers to argue, and when they lose, to sulk, mope, or give parents the silent treatment.

Common sources of conflict and negotiation include how much time the child watches TV and talks on the telephone, homework (when, where, and how it is done), and getting along with others (especially siblings). Ideally, parents and children begin to solve problems together and make joint decisions, achieving a balance between connectedness and closeness on the one hand, and independence and autonomy on the other (Cox & Paley, 2003).

In middle childhood, as in early childhood (see "Socioemotional Development in Early Childhood"), parental styles vary (Belsky & Jaffee, 2006). How parents establish and enforce rules, and the overall tone of parent-child interactions, are linked to both the child's adjustment and achievement. Parental warmth, emotional support, and appropriate expectations are associated with children's competence, social skills, academic achievement, positive self-image, and healthy emotion regulation (NICHD Early Child Care Research Network, 2008). In contrast, parental harshness, coercion, and punitiveness is linked to aggression and other externalizing behavior, as well as depression and other internalizing problems (Dearing, 2004; Pettit et al., 2001; Shumow, Vandell, & Posner, 1998). This pattern is observed in Western, individualistic societies such as the United States as well in as Eastern, collectivist societies such as China (Chen et al., 2001; Zhou et al., 2004).

Another change in relations between parents and children in middle childhood is in the amount of time they spend together. Children are developing lives of their own. Parents spend about half as much time supervising, entertaining, and caring for children in middle childhood as they did in early childhood, although there is lots of variability (Russell et al., 2002).

Marital Relationships The quality of the parents' relationship with each other is another aspect of the family system that has implications for children's development in middle childhood. Marital hostilities can lead to diminished parenting if parents are short-tempered, depressed, or otherwise psychologically unavailable (Cummings & Davies, 1994; Grych & Fincham, 2001). At the same time, problems in parenting can lead to marital conflict. A couple may not agree on how best to raise a child. An especially difficult child or a child who is chronically ill may put added strains on the marriage.

Marital problems have both direct and indirect effects on children. Exposure to unresolved marital conflicts and frequent, hostile confrontations between parents can depress children's moods (Katz & Gottman, 1993; Kerig, 1996) and undermine both short-term coping skills and long-term adjustment (Grych & Fincham, 2001). However, not all marital conflicts are associated with negative developmental outcomes. Family expressiveness helps children to interpret and convey emotions in constructive ways (Parke & Buriel, 2006). When parents disagree in low to moderate tones and resolve conflicts in a warm, supportive family context, children observe how to negotiate and settle disagreements without rupturing relationships (Cummings & Davies, 1994).

A longitudinal study of more than 800 two-parent families has examined how combinations of both parenting and marital quality were associated with children's functioning in middle childhood (Belsky & Fearon, 2004). The researchers identified five groups of children based on their family experiences: Consistently Supportive (good parenting, good marriage, 15% of the sample); Consistently Moderate (moderate marriage, moderate parenting, 45% of the sample); Consistently Risky (poor parenting, poor marriage, 16%); Good-Parenting/Poor-Marriage (19%), and Poor-Parenting/Good-Marriage (7%). Perhaps, not surprisingly, children in the Consistently Supportive group had higher cognitive-academic scores and fewer externalizing behavior problems than children in the Consistently Moderate Group, who outperformed those in the Consistently Poor Group, even after controlling for differences in income and other background factors that differentiated the groups. What might surprise you is the comparison of the two groups who had mixed experiences: children in the Good-Parenting/Poor-Marriage group had better language skills and cognitive-academic scores than the Poor-Parenting/Good-Marriage group, suggesting that the parent-child relationship was relatively more important for these particular outcomes (see Figure 12.6).

Sibling Relationships For families that have more than one child, sibling relationships are another component of the family system. These relationships run the gamut from close to cold (Dunn, 2002). Some sibling pairs are affectionate, cooperative, and supportive. Others are irritating, hostile, and aggressive toward one another. Some ignore one another. Many are ambivalent, vacillating between cooperative and antagonistic interchanges.

What explains differences in sibling pairs? Temperament is one factor. The closer the match between siblings, the more likely their social interactions will be affectionate, conflicted, or both (Brody, 1998; Munn & Dunn, 1989). Gender also makes a difference. From middle childhood on, sisters exhibit more warmth and intimacy than do brothers or brother-sister pairs (Brody, 1998). For brothers, "close" means doing things together; for sisters, it means sharing secrets. As you will read later, a similar difference characterizes boys' and girls' friendships outside the family.

Consistent with predictions of a family systems perspective, the quality of parent-child relationships is associated with the quality of sibling relationships. More positive parent-child relations are linked to warmer and friendlier relations between siblings (Brody, 1998). Conversely, harsh parenting is associated with aggressive, hostile sibling relations. Of course, the correlational research does not tell us the direction of cause and effect (Dunn, 2002). Siblings may model their behavior toward each other after their parents' behavior toward them or parents' behavior may be a *response* to the siblings' interactions. Or, most likely, bidirectional influences are at work.

Harmonious sibling relationships have tangible benefits for children's development. A positive relationship with a sibling can mute the impact of rejection and isolation by peers (East & Rook, 1992). During stressful experiences, such as a parental illness or relocation, siblings can provide one another with both emotional and instrumental, practical support (Dunn, 2002). Siblings with positive relationships are higher in self-regulation and the ability to set goals, plan, and persist.

Chronic sibling conflict is associated with both short- and long-term problems. In an observational study, Patterson (1986) found that siblings reinforce one another's aggression by teasing, taunting, fighting back, and otherwise escalating the conflict. This is particularly true when parents fight a lot and do not intervene in siblings' battles.

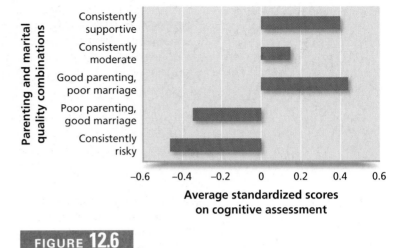

FIGURE 12.6

Patterns of Parenting and Marriage Quality Are Related to Cognitive Test Scores

Children in the Consistently Supportive group have higher cognitive-academic scores than children in the Consistently Moderate Group, who outperform those in the Consistently Poor Group. Children in the Good-Parenting/Poor-Marriage group have higher scores than the Poor-Parenting/Good-Marriage group.
Source: Data from Belsky & Fearon (2004).

Some siblings are close friends who seek one another out as playmates. Others have frequent disagreements and conflicts. And some have emotionally intense relationships that combine positive and negative emotions.

INTERIM SUMMARY 12.3

The Family Context

Household Structure	■ Refers to the types and numbers of individuals who live in a household; Examples include single-parent and two-parent households and multigenerational families.
Two-Parent Versus One-Parent Households	■ Two-parent households have higher incomes, more education, more stable jobs, and more stable living arrangements. Mothers in two-parent households report less depression and anxiety. They are more likely to use authoritative parenting.
	■ Children in two-parent households (on average) have higher grades and fewer behavior problems.
	■ Negative effects of divorce generally resolve one to two years after the divorce.
The Family System	■ The family can be conceptualized as a social system composed of interrelated subsystems (parent-child, parent-parent, and sibling relationships) that affect and are affected by other subsystems.
	■ Each subsystem also has its own features and implications for child development.

Such children are doubly handicapped. They learn to use coercion and do *not* learn techniques for de-escalation, compromise, and reconciliation.

High levels of sibling conflict in middle childhood are associated with increases in children's anxiety, depressed mood, and delinquent behavior in adolescence, over and above that explained by parental hostility or marital conflict (Stocker, Burwell, & Briggs, 2002). However, some sibling conflict—balanced with supportiveness, in an atmosphere of general goodwill—is beneficial (Brody, 1998). Conflict provides opportunities for siblings to vent their emotions and to express their feelings openly—without fear of loss, as might be the case with a classmate or friend. Reciprocal self-assertion, discussion, and compromise are lessons in anger management. Siblings can learn from each other how to express themselves and why it's important to consider another's feelings, as well as techniques for breaking tension. (For a summary of this section, see "Interim Summary 12.3: The Family Context.")

THE PEER CONTEXT

Talking and gossiping in the school cafeteria, hanging out at the mall or a playground, watching TV, playing video games, singing in a youth choir—peers are an important part of life in middle childhood. Only about 10 percent of a toddler's social interactions are with other children. In middle childhood, the figure is closer to 30 percent (Rubin et al., 2006). Peer groups are less closely supervised by adults now. And the settings are more varied. Schools, playgrounds, community centers, extracurricular activities such as sports, youth organizations such as Boys and Girls Club, shopping malls, and skating rinks are all common experiences and settings.

Time spent socializing and playing competitive games—both formal and informal—increases. Games with rules are one of the significant advances in peer play from early childhood (Piaget, 1962). To play basketball, for example, a child must be able to see the game not only from her own position as guard, but also from the other players' points of view. She needs to anticipate what the other players will do, as well as what they expect from her (an example of multiple perspective-taking). Athletic leagues organized and managed by adults provide practice in playing by the rules, as noted earlier.

The pickup games children organize on their own require different social and cognitive skills. Children have to improvise the rules and decide such issues as how to select teams so the game is fair, what to do about an odd number of participants, and what constitutes "out-of-bounds" on their own, through negotiation. No one child has authority over the others; they have to work things out together.

Friendships

Friendships play a pivotal role in children's experience of middle childhood (Rubin et al., 2006). These relationships are defined by reciprocity and mutuality. Each child particularly likes the other and counts the other as a "friend" (Hartup, 1992; Newcomb & Bagwell, 1995). They are voluntary relationships, chosen by the children, unlike the children whose parents invite for play dates in early childhood or familial relations with siblings or cousins (Hartup & Abecassis, 2002). Children expect their friends to provide more companionship and intimacy than other classmates.

Friendship expectations change over middle childhood (Rubin et al., 2006). At the beginning of this period (ages seven to eight), perceptions about friendships and selections of friends are based on rewards and costs (Bigelow, 1977). Friends are fun to be with (the reward); nonfriends are difficult or uninteresting (the costs). There also is an element of convenience in early friendship, such as living near the other child. Friendships deepen toward the end of middle childhood (ages ten to eleven), as shared values and shared social understandings become more important. Friendships among preadolescents are more exclusive, individualistic, and stable than those of younger children (Berndt, 2004).

Boys' friendships and girls' friendships differ qualitatively (Rubin et al., 2006). Girls' friendships are characterized by intimacy, self-disclosure, and validation ("I know just what you mean/how you feel"). Boys' friendships are characterized more by physical activity, which doesn't require self-disclosure, and often develop in the context of larger social networks. Because they are so close, girls' friendships are fragile (Benenson & Christakos, 2003). A violation of confidences may end the relationship.

How do children pick one another as friends? Children are drawn to children who are "like them." Researchers call this **homophily**. Friends tend to be similar not only in sex and age, but also in academic performance, interests, shyness, sociability, popularity, and ethnicity (Rubin et al., 2006). There is no evidence that opposites attract (Hartup & Abecassis, 2002). Which characteristics draw friends together depends on what interests them most (Hamm, 2000). For example, academic performance is most similar among friends who consider academic achievement important. Friends also have similar ideas about people and relationships.

Children are more likely to maintain friendships that are higher in quality (i.e., more supportive and cooperative, and less conflictual). Friendships are more likely to terminate when the children's conversations are negative and nonsupportive, although sometimes friendships cease when children simply stop interacting (Hartup & Abecassis, 2002; Rizzo, 1989).

Losing a friend can have important consequences: One study found that ten-year-olds who lost a best friend and did not replace that friend during the school year were

© David Papazian / Corbis

Children's impromptu games provide opportunities for perspective taking, problem solving, and negotiation.

homophily   The tendency of individuals to associate and bond with others who are similar or "like" themselves.

Boys' friendships are often characterized by physical activity in the context of larger peer groups.

peer group A group of children who interact frequently and who see themselves, and are seen by others, as having a common identity. Peer groups have boundaries that define who is in and who is out of the group, a structure or hierarchy, and norms about what is acceptable or unacceptable among the group members.

peer group status An indication of children's relative standing in the peer group as measured by peer nominations of acceptance and rejection.

sociometric nomination A research method used by developmental scientists to determine a peer group status. Typically children are asked to nominate or select three classmates they like and three classmates that they do not like.

at risk for victimization by classmates (Wojslawowicz et al., 2006). The friends children make, the peer groups they join, even whether they are popular among their peers depend not only on their personal qualities, but also on the broader context in which they live.

Peer Groups

A **peer group** is composed of individuals who interact frequently and who see themselves, and are seen by others, as having a common identity—for example, Mrs. Jones's third-grade class, the Strikers soccer team, or "the popular kids" (Rubin et al., 2006). Like other social groups, peer groups have boundaries defining who is inside and who is outside (other classes and grades); a structure or hierarchy (e.g., children who are leaders or followers, popular or unpopular); and their own norms or rules about what is acceptable or unacceptable behavior among the ranks.

Some writers, such as Judith Rich Harris (1995), hold that peer groups play a central role in socialization during this period. Children want to be accepted and liked by their peers, a member of a peer group. They act and dress and talk in ways that allow them to fit in. They also evaluate themselves in comparison to others in the group. Whether Harris is correct that peers are more influential than family at this age is debatable (Collins et al., 2000; Vandell, 2000), but peers are clearly significant.

Peer Group Status

In elementary school classrooms, some children are better liked by classmates than are others. Developmental scientists determine a child's **peer group status** by asking classmates questions like "Who are three children you like to play with?" and "Who are three children you do not like to play with?"—a research procedure called **sociometric nomination**. From these nominations, researchers can study peer acceptance (based on how many positive nominations a child receives) and peer rejection (based on many negative nominations a child receives). This makes it possible to divide children into five categories: popular, rejected, controversial, average, and neglected (Coie, Dodge, & Coppotelli, 1982) as seen in Table 12.3.

TABLE 12.3 Sociometric Status Differences in Peer Acceptance and Peer Rejection

		PEER ACCEPTANCE (POSITIVE NOMINATIONS)	
		HIGH	LOW
PEER REJECTION (NEGATIVE NOMINATIONS)	HIGH	Controversial	Rejected
		Average	
	LOW	Popular	Neglected

Source: Coie, Dodge, & Coppotelli (1982).

Popular children receive many positive nominations and few negative nominations. About 12 percent of children are classified as "popular" (Terry & Coie, 1991). Studies of these children conducted in a variety of settings show that they are skilled at initiating and maintaining positive interactions with their peers (Dodge, McClaskey, & Feldman, 1985). They are successful at joining groups of children on the playground because they focus on the group's activity rather than trying to call attention to themselves. They can be assertive, but usually do not interfere with the actions or goals of other children. They are good at recognizing emotions, acknowledging their own feelings, and identifying the cause of their own or another's emotions (Edwards, Manstead, & McDonald, 1984). Teachers and observers, as well as other children, see them as cooperative, friendly, and helpful (Pakaslahti, Karjalainen, & Keltikangas-Jarvinen, 2002).

There is a distinction between children who are widely *liked* or accepted by their peers (sociometric popularity) and children who are nominated as "most popular" (prestige popularity). Children who receive a lot of nominations as "most popular" can be somewhat aggressive—they like to get their own way—whereas children who are widely liked by their classmates are not pushy or antagonistic (Rubin et al., 2006).

Rejected children receive few positive nominations and many negative nominations. In sociometric studies, about 12 percent of children are classified as rejected (Terry & Coie, 1991). Studies conducted in the laboratory, classroom, and playground indicate that rejected children typically have a number of shortcomings—limited perspective-taking, poor communication skills, a tendency to perceive ambiguous social situations as hostile, and low academic achievement (Newcomb, Bukowski, & Pattee, 1993). Many rejected children are aggressive (Haselager et al., 2002). They have acquired reputations for spoiling games with disruptive behavior, negative behavior (such as verbal insults), and physical aggression. They are viewed as troublemakers. But some rejected children are the opposite: withdrawn. They ignore social overtures and keep to themselves. School-age children, who value social interaction and social competence, see them as weird.

Longer-term outcomes for rejected children are worrisome. Peer rejection predicts later problems at school, including being held back a grade, truancy, and dropping out (Hymel et al., 2002). There also is evidence that aggressive rejected children band together, forming deviant cliques that encourage delinquency (Patterson, Capaldi, & Bank, 1991). Withdrawn rejected children, in contrast, are at risk for internalizing problems, including depression and loneliness (Hymel et al., 2002). These serious consequences of peer rejection have led schools, parents, and clinicians to develop social competence coaching programs to improve skills in perspective-taking and emotional modulation (Bierman, 2004).

Controversial children receive many positive and many negative nominations. This classification is rare (6–7% of children) (Hymel et al., 2002). This group shares characteristics with both popular and rejected children. They can be aggressive and disruptive, but also helpful, cooperative, and even sensitive on others.

Neglected children are low in both positive and negative nominations. Only about 6–7 percent of children fall in this group at any one time (Terry & Coie, 1991). This classification is often temporary, with considerable movement between the average and neglected group classifications (Newcomb et al., 1993; Terry & Coie, 1991). Not surprisingly, then, neglected children tend to be similar to average children in sociability and aggression (Newcomb et al., 1993). Chronic neglect by one's peers, on the other hand, is associated with timidity, lack of social skills, and internalizing behavior problems.

Average children (58–60% of children) receive some positive and some negative peer nominations. Moderately sociable (not aggressive or withdrawn), with adequate cognitive skills, they do not stand out in the group (Newcomb et al., 1993).

Average, popular, and rejected children are more likely than neglected and controversial children to maintain their peer group status over time (Cillessen, Bukowski,

& Haselager, 2000; Hymel et al., 2002). In one study, about 41 percent of elementary students had the same status one year later. About one-quarter of the students maintained the same classification over a four-year period. Reputations in the group, as well as the children's behaviors, contribute to this stability.

Networks and Cliques

cliques Voluntary, friendship-based peer networks, generally of the same sex and age.

During elementary school, children organize themselves in clusters, or **cliques**, that are voluntary, friendship-based peer networks (Bagwell et al., 2000). The key word here is "voluntary," which distinguishes cliques from peer groups that schools or clubs create. Typically a clique is made up of three to nine children of the same sex and race. By age eleven, most children report that they are part of a clique and that most of their peer interactions take place within this clique (Rubin et al., 2006).

Both in school and out, cliques are based on similarities. Studies in many countries (Canada, Finland, the United States, and China, among others) find that clique members are similar in the levels of, and attitudes about, aggression, bullying, school motivation, and school performance (Chen, Change, & He, 2003; Rubin et al., 2006). Given self-selection, similarities, and children's desire to fit in, cliques tend to reinforce mini-cultures of their own. Some cliques reinforce academic achievement, involvement in music or sports, or particular hairstyles or clothes, all in an effort to fit in. Of concern is **deviancy training**, in which friends or clique members praise, encourage, model, and reward one another for aggression or antisocial behavior (Dishion, Poulin, & Burraston, 2001). Membership in these cliques is linked to increases in misconduct and delinquent acts. (For a summary of this section, see "Interim Summary 12.4: The Peer Context.")

deviancy training A process in which clique members praise, encourage, model, and reward one another for aggression or antisocial behavior.

INTERIM SUMMARY 12.4

The Peer Context	
Friendship	■ Friendships are defined by reciprocity in which each child counts the other as a "friend."
	■ Friendships deepen toward the end of middle childhood as shared values and shared social understandings become more important.
	■ Friends tend to be similar in sex, age, ethnicity, academic performance, interests, sociability, and popularity.
Peer Groups	■ A **peer group** is a group of children who interact frequently and who see themselves, and are seen by others, as having a common identity.
Peer Group Status	■ **Peer group status** is determined by **sociometric nominations** in which children identify classroom peers they like and do not like.
	■ Based on their positive and negative nominations, five types of peer group status have been identified: popular, rejected, controversial, neglected, and average.
Networks and Cliques	■ **Cliques** are voluntary, friendship-based peer groups.
	■ Like friends, members of cliques tend to be similar in attributes, attitudes, and behaviors.
	■ Of concern is **deviancy training**, in which clique members praise, encourage, model, and reward one another for aggression or antisocial behavior.

THE BROADER SOCIAL CONTEXT

Children's horizons expand during this period. They are going to school five days a week, spending much more time with peers, and participating in a variety of activities away from their families. Most have extensive exposure to television, computers, and video games. They know their way around the neighborhood and often the Internet. The broader social context has more direct impact on development now than in early childhood.

Out-of-School Time

To call middle childhood "the school years" would be telling only part of the story. There is more to childhood than going to school! Even on school days, children spend only about 50 percent of their waking hours in classrooms (Hofferth & Sandberg, 2001). Of course, schooling is critically important, as we discussed in the "Cognitive Development in Middle Childhood." It's just that what happens outside of school during the other 50 percent of their time also is important. What are children doing before and after school and on weekends and in the summer?

Organized Activities The majority of school-age children participate in at least one organized, out-of-school activity supervised by adults other than their parents (Vandell, Pierce, & Dadisman, 2005). These activities may be scheduled monthly, weekly, or even several times a week. Although employed parents may enroll children in activities to ensure that they are supervised while parents are at work, the primary goal of these activities is the child's enrichment and enjoyment.

Children can play in baseball leagues, belong to the 4-H and Scouts, take violin lessons or gymnastics, sing in a church choir. Some, like Alexander Williams, one of the boys described at the beginning of this chapter, participate in multiple activities. Sports is the most common organized activity but other activities are also common as shown in Figure 12.7 (National Center for Education Statistics, 2006).

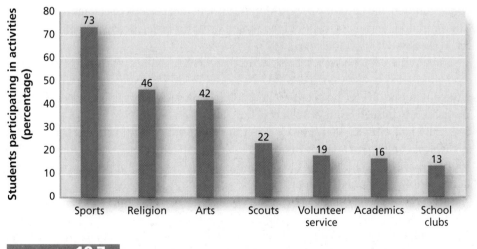

FIGURE 12.7

Percentages of Students (K–Grade 8) Who Participate in Different Types of Afterschool Activities

Organized sports, religious activities, and arts activities (music and dance lessons) are the most common afterschool activities for students (kindergarten through Grade 8).
Source: Carver & Iruka (2006).

Participation varies somewhat for boy and girls and for younger (grades K–2) and older (grades 3–5) children. Boys are more likely to participate in sports, whereas girls are more likely to participate in clubs and take lessons (Carver & Iruka, 2006). Volunteer work and academic activities are more common for older children. Participation also differs for different ethnic groups. African American children are more likely to participate in religious activities; Asian children in music activities, and Caucasian and Hispanic children in sports.

Whether children participate in organized activities depends in large part on the family's economic resources, because activities are often funded by fees paid by the family. Children whose families have higher incomes, more parental education, and two parents are more likely to participate in organized activities than children who are less well-off (Carver & Iruka, 2006). In one survey, 75 percent of children from "non-poor" families participated in sports, lessons, or clubs compared with 57 percent of "poor" families (National Center for Education Statistics, 2006).

Participation in organized activities is linked to improvements in both academic and social skills. In one longitudinal study of more than 900 children, those who consistently participated in an organized activity during kindergarten and first grade obtained higher math achievement test scores than did children who did not participate in these activities, controlling for child and family factors and children's earlier math skills (NICHD Early Child Care Research Network, 2004a). In another study, low-income urban children who participated in organized activities in grades 3–5 displayed higher test scores and better emotional adjustment in grade 5 (Posner & Vandell, 1999).

Others have found evidence that participation in organized activities outside of school improved peer acceptance scores of children who had been rejected by classmates the previous year, perhaps because the activities provided rejected children with opportunities to learn social norms and skills, and to showcase skills that were not visible in the classroom (Sandstrom & Coie, 1999).

Researchers have identified several factors that may be contributing to these positive outcomes. As we mentioned in "Cognitive Development in Middle Childhood," mathematical reasoning is embedded in many of these activities. Many require teamwork and cooperation with peers. Because the activities are voluntary and of interest to the children, they provide opportunities for extended periods of engagement, effort, concentration, and enjoyment, which are believed to foster positive youth development (Larson, 2000; Vandell et al., 2005).

Some writers have worried that children are overscheduled with activities, a phenomenon labeled "the hurried child" (Elkind, 2001). Although some children have little downtime, this is the exception, not the rule. School-aged children spend, on average, about thirteen hours a week watching television and twelve hours a week playing, fully half of their discretionary free time (Hofferth & Curtin, 2005). They spend, on average, about five hours in sports and one hour in religious activities. Low-income and working-class children spend considerably less time in organized activities and considerably more time watching TV.

Afterschool Programs Afterschool programs are a particular type of organized group activity that is held four or five days a week between the end of the school day and five to six P.M. Typically, they offer an array of activities (sports, arts and crafts, games, music, drama, and homework time). A primary goal of many programs is to provide supervision to children while their parents are at work. In the 1990s, most afterschool programs were located in child-care centers, community centers, and churches (Vandell et al., 2005). Parents paid fees or tuition for a child to attend.

Today most programs are located in schools and receive some local, state, and federal monies to support their operations. A well-known example is 21st Century

Community Learning Centers, a $40 million demonstration project started in 1998 that is now a $1 billion program serving more than 1 million students in 6,800 schools (Mahoney & Zigler, 2006). This program is free of charge (or has only a small fee), which allows larger numbers of low-income children to attend. The emphasis has shifted from recreation to hands-on extended learning opportunities and academic enrichment along with sports, music, and art.

Effects of the programs on children's developmental outcomes are related to the programs' quality and how often individual children attend. Programs are more likely to report positive effects on social competencies and academic achievement when program quality is high; that is, relationships between staff and students are emotionally supportive, activities are engaging and interesting, and children attend three to four days a week (Pierce, Bolt, & Vandell, in press).

Time Without Adult Supervision

Public support for afterschool programs and organized activities is based, in part, on concerns about the risks children face when they are without adult supervision. In this section, we consider three variations of unsupervised time. **Self-care** refers to children caring for themselves without adult supervision. Two percent of children in grades K–2 (ages five to seven years) are in self-care on a regular basis, averaging about five hours a week. Seven percent of children in grades 3–5 (ages eight to ten years) are in self-care, typically for about four hours each week (Carver & Iruka, 2006).

These numbers are worrisome because of the immediate risks to children's health and safety. In addition, self-care in middle childhood is linked to later social and academic problems. Pettit et al. (1997) have reported that children who were in self-care for four or more hours per week in first grade were less socially and academically competent in grade 6 than their classmates. More hours in self-care in middle childhood also is linked to antisocial behavior (Vandell & Ramanan, 1991), externalizing behavior (Marshall et al., 1997), and feelings of loneliness (Belle, 1999). Another form of unsupervised time is hanging out with peers away from adult supervision. It, like self-care, is linked to a variety of problems in middle childhood, including poor grades and academic achievement, misconduct, externalizing behavior, alcohol and tobacco use, and a greater likelihood of dropping out of school later on (Jordan & Nettles, 2000; McHale, Crouter, & Tucker, 2001). The direction of effects is ambiguous, however. McHale and colleagues (2001) reported that adjustment at age ten (poorer grades, poorer emotional adjustment, more behavior problems) was a better predictor of time hanging out with peers at age twelve than hanging out at age ten was of adjustment at age twelve. This suggests that poorly adjusted children may be more likely to spend their time with unsupervised peers as opposed to more developmentally positive contexts such as structured activities.

A third form of "lack of adult supervision" is care by child siblings. In traditional agricultural societies, older children (particularly girls) routinely care for younger siblings, typically with adults close by (Weisner & Gallimore, 1977; Whiting & Whiting, 1975). Older siblings also provide care for younger siblings in the United States, where almost one-quarter of children in grades K–8 are cared for by a sibling on a regular basis during the afterschool hours (National Center for Education Statistics, 2006). Sibling care is more common in Caucasian non-Hispanic families and in two-parent households in which mothers are employed. Families using sibling care also have higher incomes.

Children in grades 4 and 6 who are cared for by older siblings during the out-of-school hours report lower social acceptance and lower self-worth than children who are supervised by adults or home alone, even after controlling for child gender, family income, and race (Berman et al., 1992). Berman and colleagues speculate that this is because the older siblings have limited knowledge about child care.

self-care Refers to children caring for themselves without adult supervision.

Being cared for after school by a sibling for an extended period of time (two or more years) is also linked to participation in risky behaviors (Pettine & Rosén, 1998). Children in the care of older siblings report greater tolerance for risky behaviors compared with children in self-care at home alone. Older siblings' delinquent activities are predictive of younger siblings' delinquent activities concurrently and more strongly three years later (Slomkowski et al., 2001). The links between being cared for by an older sibling and engaging in problem behavior are particularly strong in unsafe neighborhoods (Lord & Mahoney, 2007).

Neighborhoods

Parents have long recognized that neighborhoods can be sources of risk or sources of support for their children. Those living in high-crime neighborhoods are more likely to keep their children indoors and out of harm's way and to be more restrictive in their parenting practices (Weir, Etelson, & Brand, 2006). When asked about what's important about neighborhoods, parents talk about availability of good schools, good neighbors, and safe places for their children to play (Leventhal & Brooks-Gunn, 2000).

One way that scientists study neighborhoods is by using information from the U.S. Census to measure *structural* (or demographic) *characteristics*. Disadvantaged neighborhoods are characterized by high percentages of low-income residents, female-headed households, and unemployed men, and by high rates of crime and residential instability (Nettles, Caughy, & O'Campo, 2008; Leventhal & Brooks-Gunn, 2000). In contrast, advantaged neighborhoods are characterized by high percentages of residents who are college educated, hold professional positions, and earn high incomes. Advantaged neighborhoods have more two-parent households and low crime rates.

These structural characteristics are related to developmental outcomes in middle childhood (Nettles et al., 2008). Children growing up in disadvantaged neighborhoods have more deviant peer affiliations (Brody et al., 2001), exhibit more frequent externalizing behavior problems (Leventhal & Brooks-Gunn, 2000), report more psychological distress (Shumow, Vandell, & Posner, 1999), and stronger feelings of rejection, worry, and loneliness (Homel & Burns, 1989). In a study of almost 3,000 school-age children in Chicago, concentrated neighborhood disadvantage was associated with mental health problems, even after accounting for family demographic characteristics, maternal depression, and earlier child mental health scores (Xue et al., 2005). Twenty-two percent of children in the poorest neighborhood were above the clinical threshold for internalizing behavior problems (depression, anxiety, withdrawal, and somatic problems), whereas only 12 percent of children in high SES neighborhoods were. In contrast, neighborhood affluence is positively associated with children's school achievement and cognitive abilities.

Another way to study neighborhoods is to look at residents' *perceptions* of where they live. How safe do they feel? How connected do they feel to others in their neighborhood? Do they think they could go to neighbors for material or psychological help? It turns out that mothers' perceptions of their neighborhoods are more predictive of their behaviors than are the neighborhood's actual characteristics (Christie-Mizell et al., 2003). Mothers who feel their neighborhoods are unsafe place stricter limits on their children's activities than mothers who feel secure in their neighborhood (O'Neil et al., 2001).

A challenge for scientists is how to disentangle neighborhood effects from other factors. Parental depression might be the *reason* a family lives in a disadvantaged area, not a reaction to living in a bad neighborhood. As we've said often, correlational studies do not identify cause and effect. Experiments do.

The Move to Opportunity (MTO) program, a project funded by the U.S. Department of Housing and Urban Development, provides one such experimental test. The program offered poor families a chance to move from public housing in high-poverty neighborhoods to private housing in low-poverty neighborhoods, in the hope of improving their educational and employment opportunities. All of the families had volunteered to join the MTO program. Most said the main reason they wanted to move was "gangs and drugs."

By random assignment, some families were given housing vouchers and assistance in finding new homes. This was the experimental, or treatment, group. Other families were provided some assistance but remained in housing projects in the original neighborhood (the control group). Three years after the move, boys' scores on achievement tests were comparable to girls' scores, whereas in the control group girls' scores were ten points higher than boys'. Greater school safety and more time spent on homework partially account for this gain. Moving out of a high-poverty neighborhood also had a positive impact on mothers' mental health (Leventhal & Brooks-Gunn, 2003). Further study of the MYO program is needed to determine longer-term effects. In a seven year follow-up of the Yonkers Project, for example, a study of a court-ordered desegregation in Yonkers, New York, found beneficial effects in middle childhood and early adulthood, but not adolescence (Fauth, Leventhal, & Brooks-Gunn, 2007).

Media: Television, Video Games, and Computers

The last fifty years have witnessed an explosion in the role of electronic media in children's lives (Comstock & Scharrer, 2006; Roberts & Foehr, 2008). Television, with more than 1,000 cable channels, has been joined by video consoles and games, computers and the Internet, CDs, VCRs, DVDs, and iPods®, digital cameras, and who knows what next year. The world beyond the child's neighborhood is only a click away, and most children are tuned in.

One national survey of 2,000 children and youth found that the typical American home has three TV sets, three tape players, three radios, two VCRs, two CD players, one video game console, and one computer (Roberts & Foehr, 2004). The survey also asked about direct access to media in the children's own rooms. Eighty-eight percent had a CD player; 86 percent, a radio; 65 percent, a television; 45 percent, a game console; 36 percent, a VCR; and 21 percent, a computer for their personal use.

Many adults express concern about children's use of the Internet, but TV is the single most popular form of media used by school-age children, even when they have access to other technology. Viewing starts before age two and peaks at about age twelve. On average, school-age children spend about three and one-half hours a day watching television although their total media exposure is upward of eight hours a day. Watching TV is highest in homes where there are few books and magazines, and the TV is turned on most of the time (Comstock & Scharrer, 2006).

There is a small negative relation between the amount of time that children spend watching television and academic achievement, but this relation often disappears once factors such as socioeconomic status are controlled (Schmidt & Vandewater, 2008). Much more important is the *content* of the electronic media. Educational programming, such as *Sesame Street*, is linked to long-term academic benefits programs (Anderson

Videogames have introduced new formats for play in middle childhood and beyond.

© Andersen Ross / Getty Images

et al., 2001). A recent meta-analysis found viewing prosocial programming was related to tolerance of others and altruism, with effects peaking at age seven years and then declining to age sixteen (Mares & Woodard, 2005).

Many TV shows, movies, and video games feature violence. What impact does this have on children's behavior and attitudes? In general, experiments have found that showing school-age children violent behavior on film or TV increases the likelihood that they will behave aggressively immediately afterward (Wilson, 2008). For example, in one experiment, seven- to nine-year-old boys were randomly assigned to watch either a violent or nonviolent film before playing a game of floor hockey (Josephson, 1987). In some games, the referee carried a walkie-talkie identical to one used in the violent film. The combination of the violent film and the cue from the film stimulated significantly more assaultive behavior than the other conditions.

Are there longer-term relations between consistently watching violent media and children's behavior? Studies suggest that the answer is yes. Children who watch more violent media day in and day out are more aggressive than other children (Wilson, 2008). And the relations are persistent. In a longitudinal study spanning several years, children who had a preference for violent media in middle childhood were more aggressive than their peers in adolescence (Huesmann et al., 2003).

Children may also assimilate gender stereotypes from TV. Those who watch a lot of TV (twenty-five hours or more a week) have more stereotyped ideas about men's and women's roles than children who watch a little TV (ten hours or less per week) (McGhee & Frueh, 1980). However, the number of shows a child views that depict women in nonstereotyped positions—as doctors, police officers, or farmers—can counteract this trend, opening children's minds to possibilities. The same is true for racial and ethnic stereotypes (Huesmann & Taylor, 2006).

TV influences eating patterns and body image as well. The more TV children watch, the more likely they are to be seduced by ads and to prefer junk food (Gable & Lutz, 2000). Female TV and film stars are usually exceptionally thin, which may lead to excessive dieting or excessive eating (in despair) among girls. (For a summary of this section, see "Interim Summary 12.1: The Broader Social Context.")

SUMMING UP AND LOOKING AHEAD

Themes that we saw in early childhood continue in middle childhood: the further development of a more realistic and integrated sense of self; more sophisticated strategies for self-control; and more advanced social skills. To a large degree, verbal, social, and relational aggression replaces physical, instrumental aggression. The family (whatever form it takes) plays a central role in whether children develop industry or inferiority. But children's self-images are beginning to be influenced by their friends and their standing in the peer group. We looked at why some children are popular with peers and others are rejected or victimized.

A major change in middle childhood is the expansion in social contexts. The child's social horizons—and challenges—expand: to school, where achievement counts more than getting along with peers; to peer groups that are increasingly independent of adult supervision (so that children have to negotiate rules and standards among themselves); and to a whole new set of influences, including organized afterschool and weekend programs, the neighborhood, and the mass media.

Changes in the context of socioemotional development continue unabated as the school-age child moves into adolescence. The balance of power in the family shifts often after a bumpy period. Peers take on even more importance, and romantic relationships become an important focus. School becomes more challenging, and how well or poorly students perform takes on much great importance.

These are just some of the many changes that take place during adolescence, the next stop in our journey.

INTERIM SUMMARY 12.5

The Broader Social Context

Out-of-School Time	■ Children whose families have higher incomes, more parental education, and two parents are more likely to participate in organized activities than children who are less well-off.
	■ Participation in organized activities is linked to improvements in higher test scores and better emotional adjustment.
	■ Although some children have little downtime ("the hurried child"), this is the exception, not the rule.
Time Without Adult Supervision	■ Self-care refers to children who care for themselves without adult supervision.
	■ Hanging out with unsupervised peers is linked to poor grades, misconduct, and externalizing behavior problems.
	■ Extensive and extended sibling care is linked to participation in risky behaviors.
Neighborhoods	■ Structural or demographic characteristics such as percentages of low-income residents, female-headed households, and unemployed men are one way to describe neighborhoods as disadvantaged.
	■ Neighborhood structural characteristics are related to child developmental outcomes over and above individual and family factors.
	■ Neighborhoods also can be described in relation to perceptions of safety and support.
Media: Television, Video Games, and Computers	■ The last 50 years have witnessed an explosion in the role of electronic media in children's lives.
	■ Children who watch more violent media day in and day out are more aggressive than other children.
	■ Children assimilate attitudes about gender, body image, and tolerance of others from the particular programs that they view on TV.

HERE'S WHAT YOU SHOULD KNOW

Did You Get It?

After reading this chapter, you should understand the following:

■ The characteristics of children's self-concepts in middle childhood

■ The characteristics of gender development in middle childhood

■ Kohlberg's three main levels of moral reasoning: preconventional, conventional, and postconventional

■ How the increase in prosocial behaviors reflects multiple factors

■ The forms of aggression—physical, verbal, social, and relational

■ The impact of the family system and one- and two-parent households on development

■ How friendships change in middle childhood, what peer groups are, and how networks and cliques influence behavior

■ The impact of neighborhoods, the media, and how children spend their out-of-school time on development

Important Terms and Concepts

altruism (p. 345)

bullying (p. 347)

cliques (p. 360)

conventional moral
    reasoning (p. 343)

deviancy training (p. 360)

expressivity (p. 340)

gender schema (p. 341)

hedonistic reasoning
    (p. 345)

homophily (p. 357)

industry versus inferiority
    (p. 339)

instrumentality (p. 340)

meta-analysis (p. 341)

peer group (p. 358)

peer group status (p. 358)

physical aggression
    (p. 346)

postconventional moral
    reasoning (p. 343)

postmodern family (p. 348)

preconventional moral
    reasoning (p. 343)

prosocial behavior (p. 344)

relational aggression
    (p. 346)

rough-and-tumble play
    (p. 340)

self-care (p. 363)

social aggression (p. 346)

sociometric nomination
    (p. 358)

verbal aggression (p. 346)

Part IV Review

CHAPTER 10
Physical Development in Middle Childhood

- **Normative development** refers to typical changes in physical growth and development. However, almost 40 percent of U.S. children are overweight or at risk for being overweight and more likely to develop **Type 2 diabetes,** high blood pressure, high cholesterol, sleep **apnea,** and **asthma.**

- In middle childhood, marked changes in **gray matter** occur in the brain. The growth of **white matter—myelin—** increases linearly. Synapse growth shifts and girls show faster growth in spatial-visual discrimination and **gross motor skills,** and boys show faster growth in language and **fine motor skills.**

- Extreme or constant stress can affect the development of the **hippocampus,** the area of the brain associated with memory.

- On average, children sleep an hour or more *less* than the 10 to 11 hours recommended. Fragmented sleep lowers performance on tests of attention, planning, reasoning, impulse control, and processing speed and efficiency.

- Accidents and cancer are the leading causes of death for U.S. children. Infectious diseases are rare, although asthma, allergies, and diabetes affect a number of school-aged children.

CHAPTER 11
Cognitive Development in Middle Childhood

- Hallmarks of middle childhood include **classification, class inclusion, seriation, transitive inference,** and **reversibility.** These cognitive operations enable children to perform **conservation** tasks and formal mathematics.

- Faster processing speed and more efficient information processing help set the stage for advances in **working memory** and **long-term memory.** Long-term memory includes **declarative, procedural, verbatim,** and **gist** memories, all of which improve in middle childhood.

- There have been many tests created to measure intelligence, including the Stanford-Binet Intelligence Test. There is considerable movement in children's test scores between early and middle childhood, with scores becoming more stable in middle childhood.

- Root vocabularies expand rapidly in middle childhood. Children from low-income backgrounds whose parents have low literacy skills and whose homes have few reading materials are at risk for reading problems.

- Mathematical competence in middle childhood involves knowing math facts and computational procedures, using this knowledge to solve routine problems, and using reasoning and logic to solve more complex, nonroutine problems.

CHAPTER 12
Socioemotional Development in Middle Childhood

- Erikson's fourth stage of psychosocial development, industry versus inferiority, occurs in middle childhood. Self-concepts also become more balanced, and gender provides an organizing framework for children to think about themselves in relation to others.

- Social experiences interacting with cognitive development and genetic factors propel moral development during middle childhood. **Prosocial behaviors** also increase during this time, although aggression (**physical aggression, verbal aggression, social** or **relational aggression,** and **bullying**) also takes place.

- The family context is still central in middle childhood. The family can be conceptualized as a social *system* composed of interrelated subsystems (parent-child, parent-parent, and sibling relations) that have different implications for child development.

- Friendships deepen toward the end of middle childhood, and **peer group status** and membership in **cliques** become important issues.

- The broader social context (including participation in organized activities, afterschool programs, time without adult supervision, structural or demographic characteristics, and the media) has a more direct impact on development in middle childhood than in early childhood.

© Thomas Barwick/Getty Images

Physical Development in Adolescence

Photodisc/Getty

Benjamin Franklin once remarked that "In this world, nothing is certain but death and taxes." He was only partly right. To Franklin's list we should probably add puberty—the physical changes of adolescence. Not all adolescents experience identity crises, rebel against their parents, or fall head over heels in love, but virtually all undergo the biological transition from childhood to adolescence. Along with brain development, puberty is the most important physical change of the period, with profound implications for individuals' psychological development. Some might say that without puberty, there would be no adolescence.

In this chapter, we look at the physical changes of puberty and how they affect individuals. Next, we look at one of the most obvious consequences of going through puberty—becoming sexually active. Following this, we discuss the impact of puberty on body image and eating habits—including the development of eating disorders. The fourth major section of this chapter is devoted to a hot new area of research: brain development in adolescence. Finally, we examine substance use and abuse.

PUBERTY AND ITS CONSEQUENCES

Puberty derives from the Latin word *pubertas*, which means "adult." Technically, the term refers to the period during which an individual becomes capable of sexual reproduction. More broadly speaking, however, **puberty** encompasses all the physical changes that occur in the growing girl or boy as the individual passes from childhood into adulthood.

puberty The biological changes of adolescence.

Puberty has five chief physical components (Marshall, 1978):

- A *rapid acceleration in growth,* resulting in dramatic increases in both height and weight
- The *development of primary sex characteristics,* including the further development of the gonads, or sex glands, which are the testes in males and the ovaries in females
- The *development of secondary sex characteristics,* which involve changes in the genitals and breasts, and the growth of pubic, facial, and body hair, and the further development of the sex organs
- *Changes in body composition,* specifically, in the quantity and distribution of fat and muscle
- *Changes in the circulatory and respiratory systems,* which lead to increased strength and endurance

Each of these sets of changes is the result of developments in the endocrine (hormone) and central nervous systems, many of which begin years before the external signs of puberty are evident—in fact, some occur even before birth. Puberty may appear to be rather sudden, judging from its external signs, but it is not. It is part of a gradual process that begins at conception (Susman & Dorn, in press).

373

The Endocrine System

endocrine system The system of the body that produces, circulates, and regulates hormones.

hormones Highly specialized substances secreted by one or more endocrine glands.

glands Organs that stimulate particular parts of the body to respond in specific ways to particular hormones.

gonadotropin releasing hormone neurons (GnRH neurons) Specialized brain cells that are activated by pubertal hormones.

set point A physiological level or setting (of a specific hormone, e.g.) that the body attempts to maintain through a self-regulating system.

pituitary gland One of the chief glands responsible for regulating levels of hormones in the body.

hypothalamus A part of the lower brain stem that controls the functioning of the pituitary gland.

gonads The glands that secrete sex hormones: in males, the testes; in females, the ovaries.

testes The male gonads.

ovaries The female gonads.

HPG (hypothalamic-pituitary-gonadal) axis The neuropsychological pathway that involves the hypothalamus, pituitary gland, and gonads.

androgens A class of sex hormones secreted by the gonads, found in both sexes, but in higher levels among males than among females following puberty.

estrogens A class of sex hormones secreted by the gonads, found in both sexes but in higher levels among females than among males following puberty.

adrenarche The maturation of the adrenal glands that takes place in preadolescence.

cortisol A hormone produced when we are exposed to stress.

First, a few definitions. The **endocrine system** produces, circulates, and regulates levels of hormones in the body. **Hormones** are highly specialized substances secreted by one or more endocrine glands, after which they enter the bloodstream and travel throughout the body; hormones influence the functioning of different body organs. **Glands** are organs that stimulate particular parts of the body to respond in specific ways. It's a lock and key arrangement: Specific hormones act on some glands but not others, and specific glands respond to particular hormones selectively. Many of the hormones that play important roles at puberty transmit their instructions by activating very specific types of neurons in the brain, called **gonadotropin releasing hormone (GnRH) neurons** (Sisk & Foster, 2004). (Gonadotropins are hormones that stimulate sexual maturation and regulate reproductive activity.)

The endocrine system doesn't have a mind of its own, however. It receives its instructions to increase or decrease circulating levels of particular hormones from the central nervous system, mainly through the firing of GnRH neurons in the brain. Think of a thermostat. Hormonal levels are "set" at a certain point, which may differ depending on the stage of development, just as you might set a thermostat at a certain temperature (and use different settings during different seasons or different times of the day). When you set your room's thermostat at 65°F, you are instructing your heating system to go into action when the temperature falls below this level (or your air conditioning to kick on when the temperature rises above this level). Similarly, when the level of a hormone in your body dips below the endocrine system's **set point** for that hormone, at that stage of development, secretion of the hormone increases; when the level reaches the set point, secretion temporarily stops. And, as is the case with a thermostat, the set point for a particular hormone can be adjusted up or down, depending on environmental or internal bodily conditions.

Such a *feedback loop* becomes increasingly important at the onset of puberty. Long before early adolescence—in fact, prenatally—a feedback loop develops involving the **pituitary gland** (which controls hormone levels in general), the **hypothalamus** (the part of the brain that controls the pituitary gland, and where there is a concentration of GnRH neurons), and the **gonads** (in males, the **testes**; in females, the **ovaries**), a feedback loop known as the **HPG axis** (for **h**ypothalamus, **p**ituitary, **g**onads). The gonads release the "sex" hormones—**androgens** and **estrogens** (see Figure 13.1). Androgens and estrogens, in turn, stimulate sexual maturation and other aspects of physical growth.

Puberty is not all about sexual development, though. During and just before puberty, the pituitary, instructed by the hypothalamus, also secretes hormones that act on the thyroid and on the adrenal cortex and that stimulate bodily growth more generally. The thyroid and adrenal cortex, in turn, secrete hormones that cause various bodily changes to take place at puberty.

Do you remember the first time you felt a tingle of sexual attraction to someone? Research indicates that early feelings of sexual attraction may be stimulated by maturation of the adrenal glands, called **adrenarche**. Most individuals, not only in America but around the world, report that their first sexual attraction took place at the "magical age of ten," before they went through puberty (Herdt & McClintock, 2000). Changes at puberty in the brain system that regulates the adrenal gland are especially important because this is the brain system that also controls how we respond to stress. One reason adolescence is a time for the onset of many serious mental disorders (depression, schizophrenia, substance abuse, and eating disorders are seldom seen before adolescence, for instance) is that an adverse side effect of the hormonal changes of puberty is to make us more responsive to stress (Steinberg et al., 2006; Walker, Sabuwalla, & Huot, 2004). This leads to excessive secretion of the stress hormone **cortisol**, a substance that, at high and chronic levels, can cause brain cells to die.

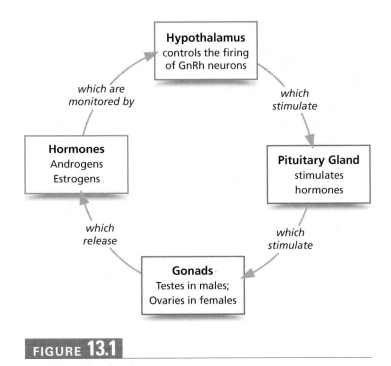

Hypothalamus
controls the firing
of GnRh neurons

*which are
monitored by*

*which
stimulate*

Hormones
Androgens
Estrogens

Pituitary Gland
stimulates
hormones

*which
release*

*which
stimulate*

Gonads
Testes in males;
Ovaries in females

FIGURE **13.1**

The Onset of Puberty
The onset of puberty is controlled by a feedback loop involving the
hypothalamus, pituitary gland, and gonads. When levels of sex
hormones drop below a certain set point, a signal is sent that
stimulates their secretion.

What Triggers Puberty?

The HPG axis is active before birth, but it is relatively quiet during much of childhood.
During middle childhood, though, something happens that reawakens the HPG axis
and signals it that the body is ready for puberty. Some of this is due to a puberty clock
whose "alarm" is genetically programmed (as we discuss later, the age at which puberty begins is largely inherited). But some of the reawakening of the HPG axis at puberty is due to environmental signals that tell the brain that it is time to start thinking
about having children. Some of these signals include whether there are sexually mature mating partners in the environment (exposure to sexually mature individuals is
one of the triggers for puberty), whether a female adolescent has sufficient nutritional
resources to support a pregnancy, and whether the individual is physically mature
and healthy enough to begin reproducing. Some evidence indicates that rising levels
of a protein produced by fat cells, **leptin**, may be the most important signal, at least in
females (Susman & Dorn, in press). This idea is consistent with observations that individuals may not go through puberty until they have accumulated a certain amount of
body fat; it is consistent as well with research showing that puberty can be delayed by
illness, nutritional deficiencies, excessive exercise, or excessive thinness (Frisch, 1983;
McClintock, 1980).

leptin   A protein produced by fat
cells that may play a role in the
onset of puberty.

Changes in Height, Weight, and Appearance

The triple whammy of growth hormones, thyroid hormones, and androgens stimulates rapid acceleration in height and weight, commonly referred to as the **adolescent
growth spurt**. Both the absolute gain of height and weight that typically occurs at this
time and the speed with which these increases take place is remarkable. Think for a

adolescent growth spurt
The dramatic increase in height
and weight that occurs during
puberty.

TABLE 13.1 The Sequence of Physical Changes at Puberty

BOYS		GIRLS	
Characteristic	*Age of First Appearance (Years)*	*Characteristic*	*Age of First Appearance (Years)*
1. Growth of testes, scrotal sac	10–13.5	1. Growth of breasts	7–13
2. Growth of pubic hair	10–15	2. Growth of pubic hair	7–14
3. Body growth	10.5–16	3. Body growth	9.5–14.5
4. Growth of penis	11–14.5	4. Menarche	10–16.5
5. Change in voice (growth of larynx)	About the same time as penis growth	5. Underarm hair	About two years after pubic hair
6. Facial and underarm hair	About two years after pubic hair appears	6. Oil- and sweat-producing glands	About the same time as underarm hair
7. Oil- and sweat-producing glands, acne	About the same time, as underarm hair		

Source: Goldstein (1976).

secondary sex characteristics
The manifestations of sexual maturation at puberty, including the development of breasts, the growth of facial and body hair, and changes in the voice.

Tanner stages A widely used system to describe the five stages of pubertal development.

moment of how quickly infants and toddlers grow, which we described in "Physical Development in Infancy." During the adolescent growth spurt, individuals grow at the same rate as a toddler. For boys, the rate averages about 4 inches (10.3 centimeters) per year; for girls, it averages about 3.5 inches (9.0 centimeters) annually. That's a lot of growing (imagine if you were to grow four inches taller over the next twelve months). On average, girls begin puberty about two years earlier than boys.

Puberty also brings with it a series of developments associated with sexual maturation. In both boys and girls, the development of the **secondary sex characteristics** (the signs of sexual maturation, such as breast development or facial hair) is typically divided into five stages, often called **Tanner stages** after the British pediatrician who devised the categorization system.

Sexual Maturation in Boys The sequence of developments in secondary sex characteristics among boys is fairly orderly (see Table 13.1). Generally, the first stages of puberty involve growth of the testes and scrotum, accompanied by the first appearance of pubic hair. Approximately one year later, the growth spurt in height begins, accompanied by growth of the penis and further development of pubic hair, which is now coarser and darker. One important point to note about male pubertal development is that boys are capable of producing semen (and fathering a pregnancy) before their physical appearance is adult-like.

The emergence of facial hair—first at the corners of the upper lip, next across the upper lip, then at the upper parts of the cheeks and in the midline below the lower lip, and finally along the sides of the face and the lower border of the chin—and body hair are relatively late developments in the pubertal process. The same is true for the deepening of the voice, which is gradual and generally does not occur until very late adolescence. During puberty, there are changes in the skin as well; the skin becomes rougher, especially around the upper arms and thighs, and there is increased development of the sweat glands, which often gives rise to acne, pimples, and oily skin. In case you were wondering, acne is not caused by masturbation—but the same hormones that contribute to acne also can increase individuals' sex drive, which may be where that myth started.

One relatively late manifestation of puberty in boys is the emergence of facial hair.

Sexual Maturation in Girls The first sign of sexual maturation in girls usually is the elevation of the breast, although in about one-third of all adolescent girls the appearance of pubic hair comes first. The development of pubic hair follows a sequence in females similar to that in males—generally, from sparse, downy, light-colored hair to more dense, curled, coarse, darker hair. **Menarche**, the beginning of menstruation, is a relatively late development that reflects the culmination of a long series of hormonal changes (Dorn et al., 1999). Generally, a girl does not ovulate regularly until about two years after menarche, and she does not become fertile until several years after her first period (Hafetz, 1976). Unlike boys, who can father a child even though they look immature, girls generally appear physically mature before they are capable of becoming pregnant.

menarche The time of first menstruation, one of the important changes to occur among females during puberty.

The Psychological and Social Impact of Puberty

Puberty can affect the adolescent's behavior and psychological functioning in a number of different ways (Brooks-Gunn, Graber, & Paikoff, 1994) (see Figure 13.2). First, the biological changes of puberty can affect behavior directly. The increase in sex drive that occurs at puberty is the direct result of hormonal changes (Halpern, Udry, & Suchindran, 1996). Second, the biological changes of puberty can cause changes in the adolescent's self-image, which in turn

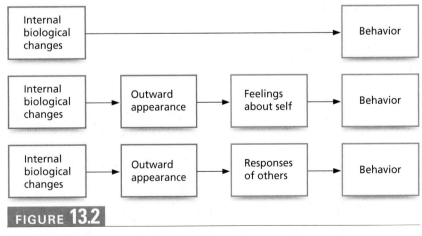

FIGURE 13.2

How Puberty Affects Adolescent Behavior

The impact of puberty on the adolescent's behavior occurs through multiple pathways. Some effects are direct, some occur through their impact on the adolescent's self-conceptions, and some occur through the reactions that the pubertal changes provoke in others.

© Laura Dwight

At least some of the psychological impact of puberty results from changes in the ways in which others respond to the adolescent's new appearance.

rite of passage A ceremony or ritual marking an individual's transition from one social status to another, especially marking the young person's transition into adulthood.

delayed phase preference A pattern of sleep characterized by later sleep and wake times, which often emerges during puberty.

may influence his or her behavior. A young teenager who looks in the mirror and sees the face of an adult may begin to demand more adult-like treatment and greater independence from his or her parents. Finally, changes in the adolescent's appearance may, in turn, elicit changes in how *others* react to the teenager. In a study that one of us conducted, a mother remarked that she wasn't sure how she could discipline her son, now that he towered over her (Steinberg & Steinberg, 1994). In some nonindustrialized societies, adolescents undergo a formal **rite of passage** when they go through puberty, a ceremony that certifies them as adult members of the community and confers new privileges and responsibilities on them. Although contemporary industrialized societies use chronological age to distinguish between adolescents and adults, in many nonindustrialized societies, a person's physical maturity is the deciding factor.

Puberty and the Adolescent's Emotions Many people believe that the "raging hormones" of puberty wreak havoc on the adolescent's emotions and mental health. But although research suggests that puberty is potentially stressful with temporary adverse psychological consequences, this is only likely when puberty occurs simultaneously with other changes that require adjustment, like changing schools (Simmons & Blyth, 1987). In this respect, the impact of puberty on adolescents' psychological functioning is to a great extent shaped by the social context in which puberty takes place (Susman, 1997). The effect of puberty on mental health varies by gender and across ethnic groups, with girls more adversely affected than boys, and with Caucasian girls, in particular, at greatest risk for developing a poor body image (Siegel et al., 1999). Given the premium placed on thinness in contemporary society, the increase in body dissatisfaction among Caucasian girls is, not surprisingly, linked to specific concerns about their changing hips, thighs, waist, and weight (Rosenblum & Lewis, 1999).

The direct connection between hormones and adolescent mood is weak (Buchanan, Eccles, & Becker, 1992; Flannery, Torquati, & Lindemeier, 1994). When studies do find a connection between hormonal changes at puberty and adolescent mood or behavior (and not many of them do), the effects are strongest early in puberty, when the system is being activated and when hormonal levels are fluctuating more than usual. For example, *rapid* increases in many of the hormones linked with puberty may be associated with increased irritability, impulsivity, aggression (in boys), and depression (in girls), especially when the increases take place very early in adolescence. There is also evidence that important changes take place around the time of puberty in regions of the brain that play major roles in the processing of emotions, social information, and rewards, although the specific ways in which hormones contribute to this is not yet fully understood (Nelson et al., 2005). Some changes in the brain coincide with puberty but are not actually caused by it (Steinberg, 2008).

Changes in Patterns of Sleep One fascinating finding on hormones and behavior in adolescence concerns adolescents' sleep preferences (Fredriksen et al., 2004). Many parents complain that their teenage children go to bed too late in the evening and sleep in too late in the morning. The emergence of this pattern—called a **delayed phase preference**—is driven by the biological changes of puberty (Carskadon et al., 1997), although as you will read, it is certainly helped along by having access 24/7 to all sorts of electronic entertainment.

Falling asleep is caused by a combination of biological and environmental factors. One of the most important influences on sleepiness is a hormone in the brain called **melatonin**. Melatonin levels change naturally over the course of the twenty-four-hour day, mainly in response to the amount of light to which we're exposed. As melatonin rises, we feel sleepier, and as it falls, we feel more awake.

The time of night at which melatonin levels begin to rise changes at puberty, becoming later and later as individuals mature physically—in fact, the nighttime increase in melatonin starts about two hours later among adolescents who have completed puberty than among those who have not yet begun (Carskadon & Acebo, 2002). As a result of this shift, individuals are able to stay up later before they start to feel sleepy. In fact, when allowed to regulate their own sleep schedules (as on weekends), most teenagers will stay up until around 1:00 A.M. and sleep until about 10:00 A.M. It's not just nighttime sleepiness that is affected, however. Because the *whole cycle* of melatonin secretion is shifted later at puberty, adolescents who have gone through puberty are sleepier early in the morning than those who are still prepubertal. (Now you know why you felt so tired during that first-period class you had in eighth grade. You probably thought it was the teacher.)

Experts agree that most American teenagers do not get enough sleep. Falling asleep in school is one symptom.

melatonin A hormone present in the brain that causes sleepiness.

Of course, if getting up early the next day was not an issue, staying up late would not be a problem. Unfortunately, most teenagers need to get up early on school days, and the combination of staying up late and getting up early leads to sleep deprivation and daytime sleepiness. Indeed, one study found that adolescents were least alert between the hours of 8:00 and 9:00 A.M. (when most schools start) and most alert after 3:00 P.M., when the school day is over (Allen & Mirabell, 1990).

Although individuals' preferred bedtime gets later as they move from childhood into adolescence, the amount of sleep they need each night remains constant, at around nine hours. Few teenagers get this much sleep, however. Scientists agree that most teenagers are not getting enough sleep, and that inadequate sleep in adolescence is associated with poorer mental health (more depression and anxiety) and lowered school performance (Fredriksen et al., 2004).

Early and Late Maturation

Puberty can begin as early as the age of seven years in girls and nine and a half in boys, or as late as thirteen in girls and thirteen and a half in boys. In girls, the interval between the first sign of puberty and complete physical maturation can be as short as a year and a half or as long as six years; in boys, from about two years to five years (Tanner, 1972). The long and short of it (pun intended) is that within a totally normal population of young adolescents, some individuals will have completed the entire sequence of pubertal changes before others have even begun. Visit a junior high school or middle school, and see for yourself!

The wide variability in the timing and tempo of puberty can create middle school classrooms in which students of the same age have very different appearances.

secular trend The tendency, over the past two centuries, for individuals to be larger in stature and to reach puberty earlier, primarily because of improvements in health and nutrition.

Genetic and Environmental Influences on Pubertal Timing
Differences in the timing and rate of puberty among individuals growing up in the same general environment result chiefly, but not exclusively, from genetic factors (Dick et al., 2001; Mustanski et al., 2004). In all likelihood, every individual inherits a predisposition to develop at a certain rate and to begin pubertal maturation at a certain time. But this predisposition is best thought of as an upper and lower age limit, not a fixed deadline. In this respect, the timing and rate of pubertal maturation are the products of an interaction between nature and nurture, between one's genetic makeup and the environmental conditions under which one has developed.

The two most important environmental influences on pubertal maturation are nutrition and health. Simply put, puberty occurs earlier among individuals who are better nourished throughout their prenatal, infant, and childhood years. Because health and nutrition have improved considerably during the past two centuries, we would expect to find a decline in the average age at menarche over time, and indeed we do. This pattern is referred to as the **secular trend**. In most European countries, where this has been most extensively tracked over time, the age of puberty has dropped by about three to four months every decade (see Figure 13.3). Scientists disagree about whether the secular trend has continued in the United States in recent years and, if so, whether the trend toward earlier puberty is greater in some ethnic groups than in others. In general, though, most scientists agree that any changes in the average age of puberty have been much less dramatic in recent decades than they were in the early twentieth century.

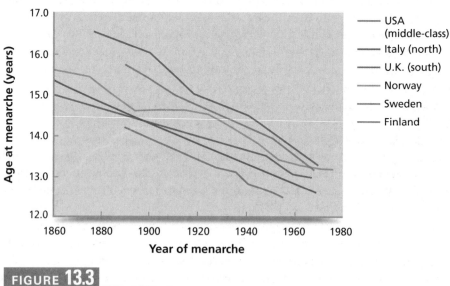

FIGURE 13.3

The Secular Trend

The average age of pubertal onset has dropped substantially in the industrialized world, due mainly to improvements in health and nutrition. This decline is referred to as the "secular trend." *Source:* Reprinted by permission of the publisher and Castlemead Publications from *Fetus Into Man: Physical Growth from Conception to Maturity* by J. M. Tanner, p. 160, Cambridge, Mass.: Harvard University Press, Copyright © 1978, 1989 by J. M. Tanner.

Within the United States, there are substantial ethnic differences in the timing of pubertal maturation that do not seem due entirely to income (which would be related to health and nutrition). (Most research comparing pubertal timing uses girls, because menarche is an indicator of puberty that is easy to measure and that individuals can recall and report accurately.) Even after controlling for group differences in socioeconomic status, studies find that African American females mature significantly earlier than Mexican American girls, who, in turn, mature earlier than Caucasian girls (Chumlea et al., 2003; Herman-Giddens et al., 1997).

How does maturing early or late affect the adolescent's psychological health and well-being? The answer depends on whether the adolescent in question is male or female.

Early Versus Late Maturation Among Boys Over the past fifty years, research on boys' pubertal timing has found that early-maturing boys feel better about themselves and are more popular than their late-maturing peers, probably because of the role that athletics plays in determining a boy's social standing (Graber, 2004). Consistent with this, boys who are more physically mature than their peers more frequently report good moods, being popular, and feeling strong (Richards & Larson, 1993).

However, early-maturing boys are more likely than their peers to get involved in antisocial or deviant activities, including truancy, minor delinquency, and problems at school (Duncan et al., 1985). They are also more likely to use drugs and alcohol and engage in other risky activities (Dick et al., 2001). The most widely accepted explanation for this is that boys who are more physically mature develop friendships with older peers and that these friendships lead them into activities that are problematic for the younger boys (Andersson & Magnusson, 1990).

Early Versus Late Maturation in Girls In contrast to the generally positive impact that early maturation has on the psychological well-being of boys, early-maturing girls have more emotional difficulties than their peers, including lowered self-image and higher rates of depression, anxiety, eating disorders, and panic attacks (Ge et al., 2003; Stice, Presnell, & Bearman, 2001). These difficulties seem to have a great deal to do with girls' feelings about their weight. In societies that view the thin, "leggy" look as the ideal of female sexiness, a late-maturing girl will look more like the model of female attractiveness than will an early-maturing girl of the same age, who will be heavier (Petersen, 1988). Early maturation in girls also may lead to heightened emotional arousal, which may leave girls more vulnerable to emotional problems (Graber, Brooks-Gunn, & Warren, 2006).

Although some early-maturing girls may have self-image difficulties, their popularity with peers is generally not jeopardized. Indeed, some studies indicate that early maturers are more popular than other girls, especially if the index of popularity includes popularity with boys (Simmons, Blyth, & McKinney, 1983). Ironically, it may be in part because the early maturer is more popular with boys that she reports more emotional upset: At a very early age, pressure to date and, perhaps, to be involved in a sexual relationship may take its toll on the adolescent girl's mental health, an issue we discuss in "Socioemotional Development in Adolescence."

Like their male counterparts, early-maturing girls are also more likely to become involved in problem behavior, including delinquency and use of drugs and alcohol; more likely to have school problems; and more likely to experience early sexual intercourse (Dick et al., 2000; Stice et al., 2001; Weisner & Ittel, 2002). As with boys, these problems appear to arise because early-maturing girls are more likely to spend time with older adolescents, especially older adolescent boys, who initiate them into activities that might otherwise be delayed (Haynie, 2003; Magnusson, Statin, & Allen, 1986). (For a summary of this section, see "Interim Summary 13.1: Puberty and Its Consequences.")

INTERIM SUMMARY 13.1

Puberty and Its Consequences

What is puberty?	Puberty refers to the set of bodily changes that takes place during the transition from childhood to adolescence. It has five chief components: 1. A rapid acceleration in growth 2. The development of primary sex characteristics 3. The development of secondary sex characteristics 4. Changes in body composition 5. Changes in the circulatory and respiratory systems
The Endocrine System	■ The endocrine system produces, circulates, and regulates levels of hormones in the body. **Hormones** are highly specialized substances secreted by one or more endocrine glands, after which they enter the bloodstream and travel throughout the body. ■ During the prenatal period, a feedback loop develops involving the **pituitary gland**, the **hypothalamus**, and the **gonads**, known as the **HPG axis**. The gonads release the "sex" hormones—**androgens** and **estrogens**. Androgens and estrogens, in turn, stimulate sexual maturation and other aspects of physical growth. ■ Other important changes at puberty involve the thyroid and the adrenal gland
What Triggers Puberty?	■ The onset of puberty is triggered by both genetic and environmental factors. There is some evidence that rising levels of a protein produced by fat cells, **leptin**, may be the most important trigger, at least in females. ■ Puberty can be delayed by illness, nutritional deficiencies, excessive exercise, or excessive thinness.
Changes in Height, Weight, and Appearance	■ Growth hormones, thyroid hormones, and androgens stimulate rapid acceleration in height and weight, commonly referred to as the **adolescent growth spurt**. ■ In both boys and girls, the development of the **secondary sex characteristics** (the signs of sexual maturation, such as breast development or facial hair) is typically divided into five stages, called **Tanner stages**. ■ The first stages of puberty in boys are the growth of the testes and scrotum, accompanied by the first appearance of pubic hair. The growth spurt in height begins approximately one year later. The emergence of facial and body hair, and the lowering of the voice, are relatively late developments. ■ The first sign of sexual maturation in girls usually is the elevation of the breast, although in about one-third of all adolescent girls the appearance of pubic hair comes first. **Menarche**, the beginning of menstruation, is a relatively late development.
The Psychological and Social Impact of Puberty	■ In some nonindustrialized societies, adolescents undergo a formal **rite of passage** when they go through puberty. ■ The direct connection between hormones and adolescent mood is weak; observed links between hormones and mood tend to be strongest early in puberty, when hormone levels are fluctuating most.

(continued)

- The biological changes of puberty lead to a **delayed phase preference** in adolescents, which is a sleep pattern of staying up late and awakening late.

- Puberty occurs earlier among individuals who are better nourished throughout their prenatal, infant, and childhood years. Because health and nutrition have improved considerably during the past two centuries, the average age of the onset of puberty has declined over time. This pattern is referred to as the **secular trend**.

- Early-maturing boys feel better about themselves and are more popular than their late-maturing peers but early maturers are more likely than their peers to get involved in antisocial or deviant activities.

- Early-maturing girls have more emotional difficulties than their peers and are more likely to become involved in problem behavior.

SEXUAL ACTIVITY DURING ADOLESCENCE

Regardless of whether it occurs early or late, one of the major consequences of puberty is its impact on sexual behavior. For most individuals, adolescence marks the onset of sexual activity. This section discusses the stages of adolescent sexual activity as well as many of the issues involved in teens' sexuality: sexual intercourse, sexual orientation, contraceptive use, sexually transmitted diseases, sex education, and teen pregnancy.

Stages of Sexual Activity

The typical adolescent's first experience with sex is alone (Katchadourian, 1990). (This isn't sad, though. As Woody Allen once said, "Don't knock masturbation—it's sex with someone I love.") The most common autoerotic activities reported by adolescents are having erotic fantasies (about three-quarters of all teenagers report having sexual fantasies, mainly about television figures or movie stars) and masturbation. Different surveys yield different estimates, depending on the age of the respondents and how the questions are worded, but about half of all adolescent boys and about one-fourth of all adolescent girls masturbate prior to age eighteen (Diamond & Savin-Williams, in press).

By the time adolescents have reached high school, most of them have made the transition to sexual activity with another person. You may be interested to know that the developmental progression of sexual behaviors, from less intimate to more intimate, has not changed very much over the past fifty years, and the sequence in which males and females engage in various sexual activities is remarkably similar. Holding hands comes first, followed by (in this order) kissing, making out, feeling breasts through clothes, feeling breasts under clothes, feeling a penis through clothes, feeling a penis under clothes or while naked, feeling a vagina through clothes, feeling a vagina under clothes or while naked, and intercourse or oral sex. Whether intercourse precedes oral sex or vice versa varies from study to study (Diamond & Savin-Williams, in press).

Most American adolescents have had experience in a sexual relationship by the time they enter high school.

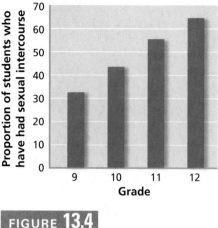

FIGURE 13.4

Sexual Intercourse in Adolescence
The proportion of American high school students having sexual intercourse rose dramatically between 1960 and 1980. It has declined only slightly since then. Today, about 40 percent of American teenagers have had sexual intercourse before the end of their sophomore year. *Source:* Steinberg, 2008.

Sexual Intercourse During Adolescence

Although there has been a slight drop since the mid-1990s in the proportion of sexually experienced teenagers, more adolescents are sexually active at an earlier age today than several decades ago (see Figure 13.4). In other words, slightly fewer adolescents are having sexual intercourse, but those who are do so at a somewhat earlier age (Santelli et al., 2000; Singh & Darroch, 1999). The best estimates we have are that, by the end of their sophomore year in high school, more than 40 percent of American adolescents have had heterosexual vaginal intercourse (these estimates, which are based on large national surveys, do not include same-sex intercourse or other types of sex, like oral or anal sex). By age eighteen, this number has risen to about two-thirds (Centers for Disease Control and Prevention, 2006).

There are substantial ethnic differences in age of sexual initiation, especially among males (Warren et al., 1998). Among African American males, the average age of first intercourse is fifteen; among Caucasian and Hispanic American males, sixteen and a half; and among Asian American males, eighteen (Upchurch et al., 1998). Ethnic differences in the age of sexual initiation are far smaller among females, although Hispanic American and Asian American females generally have their first sexual intercourse at a later age than African American and Caucasian females (Grunbaum et al., 2000). One reason for the relatively high rate of early sexual activity among African American males is the higher proportion of African American youth who grow up in single-parent homes and in poor neighborhoods, both of which are risk factors for early sexual activity (Brewster, 1994; Lauritsen, 1994). In general, Mexican American youngsters who were born in Mexico are less likely to be sexually active at an early age than Mexican Americans who are American-born, reflecting differences in norms between the two countries (Aneshensel et al., 1990). Consistent with this, Americanized Latino adolescents are more likely than their less acculturated peers to have sex at a younger age, to have multiple sex partners, and to become pregnant (Kaplan, Erickson, & Juarez-Reyes, 2002; Upchurch et al., 2001).

Many studies show that sexual activity during adolescence is decidedly *not* associated with psychological disturbance (Diamond & Savin-Williams, in press). However, *early* sexual activity (i.e., having intercourse before age sixteen) is associated with experimentation with drugs and alcohol, a low level of religious involvement, tolerance of deviant behavior, less engagement in school, and greater desires for independence (Halpern et al., 2000; Martin et al., 2005). In contrast, studies of adolescents who become sexually active at age sixteen or later do not find major differences between these youth and their virginal counterparts.

Homosexuality During Adolescence

It is not uncommon for young adolescents to engage in sex play with members of the same sex, to have sexual fantasies about people of the same sex, or to have questions about the nature of their feelings for same-sex peers (Diamond & Savin-Williams, in press). According to the national (and confidential) Add Health survey, about 8 percent of boys and 6 percent of girls reported having had strong same-sex attractions or having engaged in same-sex activity during adolescence. (Males are more likely to experiment with same-sex activity during adolescence, whereas females are more likely to experiment in young adulthood, often during college.) A smaller number of adolescents—between 3 and 4 percent—identify themselves as gay, lesbian, or bisexual, a number that increases to about 8 percent among adults (Michael et al., 1994; Diamond & Savin-Williams, in press).

Sexual orientation is shaped by a complex interaction of social and biological influences, but biology appears to play a stronger role than was once thought (Bem, 1996). First, there is evidence that gay and lesbian adults may have been exposed prenatally to certain hormones that, potentially, could affect sexual orientation through their effects on early brain organization (Meyer-Bahlburg et al., 1995; Savin-Williams, 1988). Second, there is some evidence that homosexuality has a strong genetic component, since sexual orientation is more likely to be similar among close relatives than distant relatives and between identical twins than fraternal ones (Savin-Williams, 1988). Although environmental explanations for this similarity cannot be ruled out, chances are that at least some of the predisposition to develop a homosexual orientation is inherited.

A great deal of confusion about homosexuality results because people tend to confuse **sexual orientation** (the extent to which someone is inclined toward heterosexual activity, homosexual activity, or both), **sex-role behavior** (the extent to which an individual acts in traditionally masculine or feminine ways), and **gender identity** (which gender an individual believes he or she is psychologically). There is no relation between an adolescent's sexual orientation and his or her sex-role behavior. Individuals with preferences for homosexual relationships show the same range of masculinity and femininity seen among individuals with strong heterosexual interests. In other words, exclusively gay men (like exclusively heterosexual men) may act in very masculine, very feminine, or both masculine and feminine ways. The same holds true for exclusively lesbian and exclusively heterosexual women, as it does for bisexual individuals. Along similar lines, individuals with homosexual interests are generally not confused about their gender identity—or, at least, they are no more confused than are individuals with heterosexual interests.

sexual orientation An individual's orientation toward same- or opposite-sex sexual partners.

sex-role behavior Behavior that is consistent with prevailing expectations for how individuals of a given sex are to behave.

gender identity The aspects of one's sense of self that concern one's masculinity and femininity.

Contraceptive Use

One reason adults worry about the sexual activity of adolescents is that many sexually active young people don't use contraception regularly. Nearly one-third of older adolescent males report using either no contraception or an ineffective method (i.e., pulling out before ejaculating) the first time they had sex (Manning, Longmore, & Giordano, 2000). Perhaps more important, between 20 and 30 percent of young people did not use contraception the last time they had sex, either (Coleman, 1999; Hogan, Sun, & Cornwell, 2000; Santelli et al., 2000).

Contraceptive Methods Adolescents Use Among adolescents who do use contraception, the most popular method by far is condoms, which are used by close to 60 percent of sexually active teenage couples, followed by the birth control pill, which is used by about one-fifth of couples (Everett et al., 2000). (About 20% of girls who are on the pill report that their partner uses a condom as well [Santelli et al., 1997].) Pulling out, a highly *in*effective method of preventing pregnancy, unfortunately is still used by a large number of teenagers, as is the rhythm method (calculating when a female is likely to get pregnant). The rhythm method requires more regular menstrual cycling than many teenagers have and more careful monitoring than most teenagers are willing or able to do. Studies also show that a large proportion of condom users do not use condoms correctly (e.g., putting the condom on before first entry and holding on to the condom while withdrawing) (Oakley & Bogue, 1995).

Adolescents' Reasons for Not Using Contraception There are several reasons that so few adolescents use contraception regularly and effectively. For a sizable minority of adolescents, contraceptives are not readily available. In addition, many young people are insufficiently educated about sex, contraception, and pregnancy

(Trussell, 1989). Psychological factors also play a role. More than 25 percent of nonusers of contraception report that they or their partners simply did not want to use birth control. Perhaps most important, many adolescents fail to use birth control because doing so means admitting that they are choosing to be sexually active and are planning ahead for it (Miller & Moore, 1990). Going on the pill or purchasing a condom requires an adolescent to acknowledge that he or she is having or expects to have sexual relations.

AIDS and Other Sexually Transmitted Diseases

sexually transmitted disease (STD) Any of a group of infections—including gonorrhea, herpes, chlamydia, and AIDS—passed on through sexual contact.

gonorrhea A sexually transmitted infection caused by a bacterium.

chlamydia A sexually transmitted infection caused by a bacterium.

herpes A sexually transmitted infection caused by a virus.

human papilloma virus One of several viruses that causes a sexually transmitted disease.

AIDS (acquired immune deficiency syndrome) A disease, transmitted by means of bodily fluids, that devastates the immune system.

human immunodeficiency virus (HIV) The virus associated with AIDS.

Helping youngsters understand sex, pregnancy, and contraception is an important goal of sex education programs for adolescents. Helping them avoid the risks of **sexually transmitted diseases**, or STDs, is another. Some of the most common STDs among adolescents are **gonorrhea** and **chlamydia** (both caused by a bacterium), and **herpes** and **human papilloma virus** (both caused by a virus) (Slap & Jablow, 1994). These infections pose a significant health risk to young people, because they are associated with increased rates of cancer and infertility. Several million adolescents contract an STD each year, and one in four teenagers contracts an STD before graduating from high school (Gans, 1990; Luster & Small, 1994).

AIDS, or **acquired immune deficiency syndrome**, is a disease that is transmitted through bodily fluids, especially semen, during sex, or blood when drug users share needles. **HIV**, or **human immunodeficiency virus**, is the cause of AIDS. Although the incidence of AIDS in the United States was initially concentrated among gay men and drug users who use needles, the transmission of AIDS through heterosexual activity is a clear danger within the adolescent community, particularly among inner-city minority youngsters (D'Angelo et al., 1991), homeless youth (Rotheram-Borus, Koopman, & Ehrhardt, 1991), and high school dropouts (St. Louis et al., 1991). Because there is a long period of time between HIV infection and the actual manifestation of illness, however—sometimes, as long as ten years—many more adolescents are likely to be asymptomatic carriers of the HIV virus who may develop AIDS in young adulthood and unknowingly infect others (Hein, 1988). Most experts believe that, short of abstinence, the best way for teenagers to protect themselves against contracting HIV and many other STDs is by using condoms during sex (Crosby et al., 2003).

Sex Education

Many adolescents receive some sort of classroom instruction about sex—whether through high school health classes, biology classes, classes designated exclusively for the purpose of sex education, or educational programs administered through youth or religious organizations. Evaluations of school-based sex education programs have shown them to have no effect on adolescents' sexual activity but a small impact on their use of contraceptives (Franklin et al., 1997). (That is, classroom programs don't seem to dissuade adolescents from having sex, but they do seem to get some young people to have safer sex.) Most traditional sex education programs fail because they emphasize the biological over the emotional aspects of sex (and therefore don't help adolescents make decisions about sexual involvement); they come too late in high school; and they focus primarily on changing students' knowledge rather than their behavior (Landry, Singh, & Darroch, 2000). During the mid-1980s, the emphasis in sex education shifted from encouraging "responsible" sex to encouraging sexual abstinence, an emphasis that still prevails in many school districts (Landry, Kaeser, & Richards, 1999). It was hoped that by encouraging sexual abstinence these programs would also have the effect of reducing teenage pregnancy. Unfortunately, careful evaluations of these programs have shown that they too are not successful, either in changing adolescents' sexual behavior or in reducing rates of nonmarital pregnancy (Christopher, 1995; Kirby et al., 1997; Leiberman et al., 2000).

Does anything work? One approach that makes experts cautiously optimistic involves a combination of school-based sex education and community-based health clinics through which adolescents can receive information about sex and pregnancy as well as contraception. Some evaluations indicate that this combination of sex education and clinics may diminish the rate of teen pregnancy, even within inner-city communities characterized by high rates of adolescent pregnancy and childbearing (Christopher, 1995; Frost & Forrest, 1995; Tiezzi et al., 1997).

Teenage Pregnancy and Childbearing

The high rate of sexual activity and erratic contraceptive use among today's adolescents results in many young women becoming pregnant before the end of adolescence. Each year, between 800,000 and 900,000 American adolescents become pregnant—giving the United States the highest rate of teen pregnancy in the industrialized world (Alan Guttmacher Institute, 2004). Nearly one-third of American young women become pregnant at least once by age twenty, although rates of teen pregnancy vary considerably by ethnicity: The rate is twice as high among African American youth as among Caucasian youth, and rates of teen pregnancy among Hispanic teenagers fall somewhere between (Alan Guttmacher Institute, 2004).

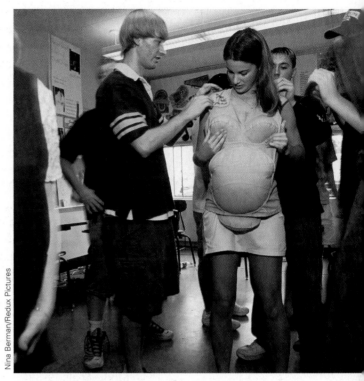

Research on school-based sex education indicates that it influences adolescents' knowledge and beliefs much more than their sexual behavior.

Not all adolescent pregnancies result in childbirth, of course. In the United States, about one-third of all teenage pregnancies are aborted, and slightly more than one-sixth end in miscarriage (Centers for Disease Control and Prevention, 2004). Among American adolescents who do not abort their pregnancy, the vast majority—over 90 percent—keep and raise the infant, whereas only one in ten chooses to have the child adopted. In other words, about 45 percent of teenage pregnancies end in abortion or miscarriage, about 50 percent result in the birth of an infant who will be raised by his or her mother (with or without the help of a partner or other family members), and about 5 percent result in the birth of an infant put up for adoption (Coley & Chase-Lansdale, 1998) (see Figure 13.5).

Because ethnic minority adolescents are more likely to grow up poor, and teenage childbearing is more common in economically disadvantaged communities, adolescent parenthood is especially high in nonwhite communities. Among Caucasian adolescents, nearly two-thirds of all births occur outside of marriage, but a large proportion of these births occur within the context of cohabitation; among African American adolescents, virtually all childbirths are out of wedlock, and relatively few of these even occur among cohabiting couples (Manning & Landale, 1996; Schellenbach et al., 1992). The rate for Hispanic teenagers falls somewhere in between; interestingly, young Mexican American women are more likely to bear their first child within marriage, whereas young Puerto Rican women are more likely to bear children out of wedlock but within the context of cohabitation (Darabi & Ortiz, 1987; East & Blaustein, 1995; Manning & Landale, 1996).

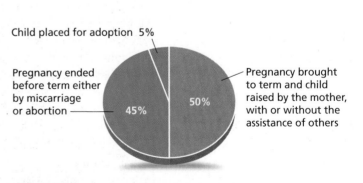

Child placed for adoption 5%

Pregnancy ended before term either by miscarriage or abortion — 45%

Pregnancy brought to term and child raised by the mother, with or without the assistance of others — 50%

FIGURE 13.5

Outcomes of Teen Pregnancies

In about half of all cases, teen pregnancy results in the birth of a child raised by the teen parent. The vast majority of the other teen pregnancies end in miscarriage or by abortion. Very few teen pregnancies result in the birth of a baby who is put up for adoption.

For the most part, children born to adolescent mothers develop similarly to children born to adults from similar social circumstances (e.g., Kalil & Kunz, 2002). In other words, infants born to middle-class adolescents differ little from their counterparts born to older middle-class mothers, and infants born to poor adolescents are similar to children born to equally poor adults. One important exception is that compared to adult mothers, adolescent mothers—even of similar socioeconomic origin—are more likely to perceive their babies as being especially difficult and may interact with their infants less often in ways that benefit the child's cognitive and social development (Coley & Chase-Lansdale, 1998). Scientists do not know the extent to which this jeopardizes the child's development, although we do know that children born to adolescent mothers are more likely to have school problems, to be involved in misbehavior and delinquent activity, and to be sexually active themselves at an early age (Coley & Chase-Lansdale, 1998; Conseur et al., 1997; Hofferth & Reid, 2002; Wakschlag et al., 2000).

The problems associated with teenage parenthood may actually be greater for the mothers than for their children (Furstenberg, Brooks-Gunn, & Morgan, 1987). Women who bear children early suffer disruptions in their educational and occupational careers (Hofferth, Reid, & Mott, 2001; Otterblad Olausson et al., 2001). Adolescent mothers are not only more likely to come from a poor background and to have had a greater history of academic difficulties, but they are also more likely to remain poor than equally disadvantaged peers who delay childbearing (Hoffman, Foster, & Furstenberg, 1993; Moore et al., 1993).

In general, young mothers who remain in, or return to, high school and delay subsequent childbearing fare a great deal better over the long run—as do their children—than their counterparts who drop out of school or have more children relatively early on (Furstenberg et al., 1987). Indeed, remaining in school and living at home with one's parents significantly diminishes the chances of a second unwanted pregnancy (Manlove, Mariner, & Papillo, 2000). Marriage, on the other hand, tends to be a high-risk strategy (Furstenberg et al., 1987). When a stable relationship is formed and economic resources are available, marriage improves the mother's and the child's chances for life success. But a hasty decision to marry in the absence of a stable relationship and economic security actually worsens many other problems (Teti & Lamb, 1989). (For a summary of this section, see "Interim Summary 13.2: Sexual Activity During Adolescence.")

INTERIM SUMMARY 13.2

Sexual Activity During Adolescence

Stages of Sexual Activity	■ Most adolescents are sexually active by the time they enter high school.
	■ The developmental progression of sexual behaviors, from less intimate to more intimate, has not changed very much over the past 50 years.
Sexual Intercourse During Adolescence	■ By the end of their sophomore year in high school, more than 40 percent of American adolescents have had intercourse. By age 18, this number has risen to about two-thirds.
	■ Slightly fewer adolescents are having sexual intercourse today than in recent years, but those who are do so at a somewhat earlier age.
	■ *Early* sexual intercourse (i.e., before age 16) is associated with a range of problem behaviors, but sexual intercourse after this age is not.

(continued)

INTERIM SUMMARY **13.2** (continued)

Sexual Activity During Adolescence

Homosexuality During Adolescence	■ About 8 percent of adolescent boys and 6 percent of adolescent girls have had strong same-sex attractions or engaged in same-sex activity during adolescence. A smaller number of adolescents—between 3 and 4 percent—identify themselves as gay, lesbian, or bisexual.
	■ Sexual orientation is shaped by a complex interaction of social and biological influences, but biology appears to play a stronger role than was once thought.
	■ It is important to distinguish among **sexual orientation**, **sex-role behavior**, and **gender identity**.
Contraceptive Use	■ The most popular contraceptive method among adolescents is condoms, followed by the birth control pill.
	■ Few adolescents use contraception regularly, however.
AIDS and Other Sexually Transmitted Diseases	■ One in four teenagers contracts a sexually transmitted disease before graduating from high school. Some of the most common STDs among adolescents are **gonorrhea**, **chlamydia**, **herpes**, and **human papilloma virus**.
	■ **AIDS**, or **acquired immune deficiency syndrome**, is a disease that is transmitted during sex through bodily fluids, especially semen, or through blood when drug users share needles. **HIV**, or **human immunodeficiency virus**, is the cause of AIDS.
	■ The transmission of AIDS through heterosexual activity is a clear danger within the adolescent community, particularly among inner-city minority youngsters, homeless youth, and high school dropouts.
Sex Education	■ Most evaluations of school-based sex education programs have shown them to have no effect on adolescents' sexual activity but a small impact on their use of contraceptives.
	■ One approach that makes experts cautiously optimistic involves a combination of school-based sex education and community-based health clinics through which adolescents can receive information about sex and pregnancy as well as contraception.
Teenage Pregnancy and Childbearing	■ Each year, between 800,000 and 900,000 American adolescents become pregnant.
	■ About 45 percent of teenage pregnancies end in abortion or miscarriage, about 50 percent result in the birth of an infant who will be raised by his or her mother, and about 5 percent result in the birth of an infant put up for adoption.
	■ In general, young mothers who remain in, or return to, high school and delay subsequent childbearing fare a great deal better over the long run than their counterparts who drop out of school or have more children relatively early on.

EATING DISORDERS

Because adolescence is a time of dramatic change in physical appearance, teenagers' overall self-image is very much tied to the way they feel about their body. Given the enormous importance that contemporary society places on being thin, particularly for females, the usual weight gain that takes place during puberty leads many adolescents, especially girls, to become very concerned about their weight. The term **disordered eating** refers to patterns of eating attitudes and behaviors that are unhealthy.

disordered eating Mild, moderate, or severe disturbance in eating habits and attitudes.

© Karen Kasmauski/Corbis

About one-third of American teenagers are obese, and another third are extremely overweight.

Obesity

Many adolescents, of course, have legitimate concerns about being overweight. According to recent surveys, 16 percent of adolescents in the United States are obese, and another 15 percent are at great risk for obesity (Institute of Medicine, 2006), a rate that has *tripled* since 1980 (see Figure 13.6). The average fifteen-year-old boy today is fifteen pounds heavier, and the average fifteen-year-old girl is ten pounds heavier than was the case in the mid-1960s—increases that cannot be explained by the fact that people have gotten a little taller since then. Today, obesity is the single most serious public health problem afflicting American teenagers. Although it is true that genetic factors contribute to how much we weigh, the dramatic increase in the prevalence of adolescent obesity over such a short time period indicates that the problem has strong environmental causes.

It is not at all difficult to understand why so many American adolescents today are overweight. As discussed in "Physical Development in Middle Childhood," too few

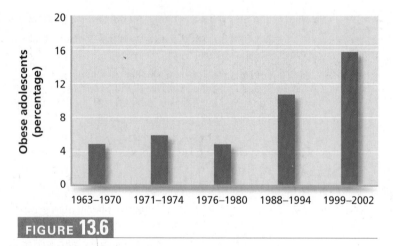

FIGURE 13.6

The Obesity Epidemic

The rate of obesity among American adolescents nearly quadrupled during the last two decades of the twentieth century.
Source: Food marketing to children and youth: Threat or opportunity?, Institute of Medicine, 2006. Reprinted with permission from the National Academies Press, Copyright 2006, National Academy of Sciences.

children and adolescents are physically active (spending far too much time watching television or at the computer); too many eat far too much high-calorie, high-fat food (drinking far too many sugary soft drinks and consuming far too much junk food); and the combination of inadequate exercise and poor nutrition is a recipe for obesity (Institute of Medicine, 2006).

Anorexia Nervosa and Bulimia

Health care professionals are concerned not only about adolescents who are obese but about adolescents of normal or even below-normal weight who have unhealthy attitudes toward eating and about their body (French et al., 1995). More than half of all adolescent girls consider themselves overweight and have attempted to diet (Fisher et al., 1995). One recent study found that 14 percent of undergraduate women were so concerned about eating that they were embarrassed to go into a store and buy a chocolate bar (Rozin, Bauer, & Catanese, 2003)!

Disordered eating among normal or below-normal weight adolescents can range from unnecessary preoccupation with weight and body image to full-blown clinical eating disorders, such as anorexia nervosa and bulimia. Disordered eating is associated with a range of psychological problems, including poor body image, depression, alcohol and tobacco use, and poor interpersonal relationships (French et al., 1995; Graber et al., 1994), although it is not clear whether these problems precede, follow from, or merely go hand in hand with disordered eating (Leon et al., 1999).

Not everyone is genetically predisposed to be as thin as fashion magazines tell people they ought to be. Some adolescent girls and young women become so worried about gaining weight that they take drastic—and dangerous—measures to become or remain thin. They might go on eating binges and then force themselves to vomit to avoid gaining weight, a pattern associated with an eating disorder called **bulimia**. In more severe cases, young women who suffer from an eating disorder called **anorexia nervosa** actually starve themselves in an effort to keep their weight down. Adolescents with these sorts of eating disorders have an extremely disturbed body image, seeing themselves as overweight when they actually are underweight. Some

bulimia An eating disorder found chiefly among young women, characterized primarily by a pattern of binge eating and self-induced vomiting.

anorexia nervosa An eating disorder found chiefly among young women, characterized by dramatic and severe self-induced weight loss.

INTERIM SUMMARY 13.3

Eating Disorders

Obesity	■ Close to one-third of American adolescents are either obese or at risk for obesity ■ The major contributors to the epidemic of obesity among contemporary adolescents are inadequate exercise and poor nutrition
Anorexia Nervosa and Bulimia	■ Disordered eating among individuals who are normal or below-normal weight range from preoccupations with weight and body image to full-blown clinical eating disorders. ■ Individuals who suffer from anorexia starve themselves to lose weight. ■ Individuals who suffer from bulimia go on eating binges and then force themselves to vomit to avoid gaining weight. ■ The incidence of genuine bulimia and anorexia is much smaller than most people think, but the rates among females are substantially higher than among males. ■ A variety of therapeutic approaches have been used successfully in the treatment of bulimia and anorexia, including individual psychotherapy and cognitive-behavior modification, group therapy, family therapy, and antidepressant medications.

youngsters with anorexia lose between 25 percent and 50 percent of their body weight. If untreated, bulimia and anorexia frequently lead to a variety of very serious physical problems; in fact, nearly 20 percent of anorectic teenagers starve themselves to death.

Although unhealthy eating and unnecessary dieting are widespread among adolescents, careful studies indicate that the incidence of genuine anorexia and genuine bulimia is much smaller than most people think (and very small when compared with rates of obesity) (Fisher et al., 1995). Fewer than one-half of 1 percent of adolescents are anorexic, and only about 3 percent are bulimic (American Psychiatric Association, 1994). Rates among females are substantially higher than among males—clinically defined anorexia and bulimia are ten times more prevalent among adolescent girls than boys (Jacobi et al., 2004). Despite widely held stereotypes that disordered eating and body dissatisfaction are concentrated among middle-class Caucasian and Asian youth, these problems have been reported among poor, as well as affluent, teenagers, and among African American and Hispanic youth as well (Jacobi et al., 2004).

A variety of therapeutic approaches have been employed successfully in the treatment of anorexia and bulimia, including individual psychotherapy and cognitive-behavior modification, group therapy, family therapy, and, more recently, the use of antidepressant medications (Agras et al., 1989; Killian, 1994). The treatment of anorexia often requires hospitalization initially to ensure that starvation does not progress to fatal or near-fatal levels (Mitchell, 1985). (For a summary of this section, see "Interim Summary 13.3: Eating Disorders.")

THE ADOLESCENT BRAIN

No area of adolescence research has generated as much attention or excitement in recent years as the study of brain development during adolescence. Scientists once believed that brain maturation was more or less complete by the end of childhood. No longer. We now know that important changes in the brain occur throughout adolescence (and even into young adulthood) (Paus, in press). More important, new research on the brain points to several aspects of brain maturation in adolescence that may be linked to behavioral, emotional, and cognitive development during this period (Steinberg, 2005).

Brain Maturation in Adolescence

prefrontal cortex The part of the brain responsible for many higher-order cognitive skills, such as decision making and planning.

First, there appears to be considerable "remodeling" of the brain through the processes of synaptic pruning and myelination, both of which you've read about in previous chapters. Although, as you now know, synaptic pruning takes place throughout infancy, childhood, and adolescence, different regions of the brain are pruned at different points in development. The part of the brain that is pruned most in adolescence is the **prefrontal cortex**, the region that is most important for various sorts of advanced thinking abilities, such as planning, thinking ahead, weighing risks and rewards, and impulse control (Casey et al., 2005). One recent study found a relation between intelligence and patterns of synaptic growth and pruning in the cortex, with relatively more intelligent adolescents showing a more dramatic and longer period of production of synapses before adolescence, and a more dramatic pruning of them after (Shaw et al., 2006). As you read in earlier chapters, synaptic pruning eliminates unused connections in the brain, reducing clutter. Myelination of the prefrontal cortex also continues throughout adolescence, improving the efficiency of communication between neurons (Paus et al., 1999; Sowell et al., 2002).

dorsolateral prefrontal cortex The outer and upper areas of the front of the brain, important for skills such as planning ahead and controlling impulses.

ventromedial prefrontal cortex The lower and central area at the front of the brain, important for gut-level decision making.

We now know that maturation of the prefrontal cortex takes place gradually over the course of adolescence and is not complete until the midtwenties (Casey et al., 2005; Hooper et al., 2004; Segalowitz & Davies, 2004). Of special importance are developments in the **dorsolateral prefrontal cortex**, the outer and upper areas of the front of the brain, which is important for skills such as planning ahead and controlling impulses (Casey et al., 2005); the **ventromedial prefrontal cortex**, the lower and central area of the front of the brain, which is important for more gut-level, intuitive decision making, and which has strong connections with the limbic system, where emotions and social information are processed (Bechara, 2005); and the **orbitofrontal cortex**, the area of the brain directly behind the eyes, which is important for evaluating risks and rewards (May et al., 2004) (see Figure 13.7).

Second, around the time of puberty, there are changes in levels of several **neurotransmitters** (the chemicals that permit the transfer of electrical charges between neurons), including dopamine and serotonin, in the parts of the brain that process rewards as well as emotional and social stimuli, most notably, areas of the **limbic system**. These changes may make individuals more emotional, more responsive to stress, and more interested in sensation seeking. Changes in the limbic system are also thought to increase individuals' vulnerability to substance abuse (because they seek higher levels of reward), depression (because of their increased vulnerability to stress), and other mental health problems

Dorsolateral prefrontal cortex: important for deliberate decision making and impulse control

Orbitofrontal cortex: important for evaluating risks and rewards

Ventromedial prefrontal cortex: important for gut-level, intuitive responding

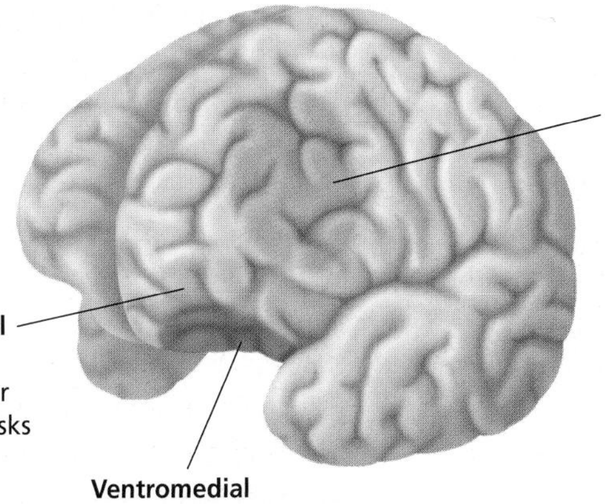

FIGURE 13.7

The Prefrontal Cortex

Important changes take place during adolescence in the dorsolateral prefrontal cortex, the orbitofrontal cortex, and the ventromedial prefrontal cortex. These regions are important for planning, thinking ahead, weighing risks and rewards, and impulse control.

(because of their easily aroused emotions, including anger and sadness) (Steinberg et al., 2006). Imaging studies have also shown that there is a significant increase in connectivity between the prefrontal cortex and other areas of the brain, including the limbic system, suggesting better "communication" between brain regions as individuals mature (Cunningham, Bhattacharyya, & Benes, 2002; Luna et al., 2001).

Changes in levels of neurotransmitters in the limbic system in early adolescence may also help explain why adolescents' concerns about what their peers think increase during this time period. The limbic system is an important region for the processing of social information (Nelson et al., 2005). Conceivably, this may make adolescents more susceptible to peer pressure, a topic we will look at in "Socioemotional Development in Adolescence." In one recent and very clever study (Nelson et al., 2008), the researchers imaged the brains of adolescents while they thought they were participating in a Facebook-style task, networking with other teenagers in different locations. Inside the fMRI equipment was a computer screen, on which the researchers could show any images of their choosing, and while they were being imaged, the adolescents were shown pictures of the other teenagers and asked to rate how interested they were in chatting with them online. The adolescents, who were told that their own photographs were "posted" online, received what they thought was feedback from the other teenagers based on reactions to the target adolescents' photos. In reality, though, there were no other teenagers connected to the network, and the feedback the adolescents received was rigged to be positive (interested in chatting) half the time, and negative (not interested in chatting) half the time. When the adolescents were told that other teenagers were interested in them, areas of their brain known to be sensitive to rewards like food and money, were activated, suggesting that social rewards may be processed during adolescence in ways similar to the ways in which we process other types of rewards.

Implications for Adolescent Behavior

The relatively late maturation of the prefrontal cortex, particularly in relation to the changes that take place in the limbic system at puberty, has been the subject of much discussion among those interested in risk taking and behavioral problems in

orbitofrontal cortex The region of the brain located directly behind the eyes, important for the evaluation of risk and reward.

neurotransmitters Chemical substances in the brain that carry electrical impulses across synapses.

limbic system An area of the brain that plays an important role in emotional experience and processing social information.

adolescence (Steinberg, 2007). It appears that the brain changes in ways that may provoke individuals to crave novelty, reward, and stimulation several years before the complete maturation of the brain systems that control judgment, decision making, and impulse control. This gap may help explain why adolescence is a period of heightened experimentation with risk. In the words of one team of writers, it's like "starting the engines with an unskilled driver" (Nelson et al., 2002, p. 515). (For a summary of this section, see "Interim Summary 13.4: The Adolescent Brain.")

INTERIM SUMMARY 13.4

The Adolescent Brain

Brain Maturation in Adolescence	■ There is considerable "remodeling" of the brain during adolescence through the processes of **synaptic pruning** and **myelination**.
	■ The part of the brain that is pruned most in adolescence is the **prefrontal cortex**, the region responsible for many advanced thinking abilities.
	■ Maturation of the prefrontal cortex takes place gradually over the course of adolescence and is not complete until the mid-20s.
	■ Developments take place in the **dorsolateral prefrontal cortex**, which is involved in skills such as planning ahead and controlling impulses, in the **ventromedial prefrontal cortex**, which is involved in more gut-level, intuitive decision making, and in **the orbitofrontal cortex**, which is important for evaluating risks and rewards.
	■ There also are important changes in the **limbic system** at puberty, which influence sensation-seeking, mood, and attentiveness to social stimuli.
Implications for Adolescent Behavior	■ The brain changes in ways during adolescence that may provoke individuals to crave novelty, reward, and stimulation several years before the complete maturation of the brain systems that control judgment, decision making, and impulse control. This gap may help explain why adolescence is a period of heightened experimentation with risk.

SUBSTANCE USE AND ABUSE IN ADOLESCENCE

The popular stereotype of contemporary young people is that they use and abuse a wide range of drugs more than their counterparts in previous generations; that the main reason adolescents use drugs is peer pressure; and that the "epidemic" level of substance use among American teenagers is behind many of the other problems associated with this age group—including academic underachievement, early pregnancy, suicide, and crime. What could be more reassuring than to identify the "real" culprit (drugs) and the "real" causes (peers) of all the maladies of young people? And what could be even more comforting than the belief that, if we simply teach young people to "say no" to their peers, these problems will all disappear?

Unfortunately, what we would like to believe about adolescent drug use is not necessarily correct. Although there are grains of truth to many of the popular claims about the causes, nature, and consequences of teenage substance use and abuse, there are many widely held misconceptions about the subject, too.

Prevalence of Substance Use and Abuse in Adolescence

Each year since 1975 a group of researchers from the University of Michigan has surveyed a nationally representative sample of about 15,000 American high school seniors on several aspects of their lifestyle and values, including their use and abuse of a variety of drugs. Beginning in 1991, comparable samples of eighth- and tenth-graders were added to the annual survey.

Although adults tend to worry a lot about adolescents' use of illegal drugs, such as marijuana, cocaine, or LSD, the Monitoring the Future surveys consistently find that the two major legal drugs—alcohol and nicotine—are by far the most commonly used and abused substances, both with regard to the percentage of teenagers who have ever used the drug and with respect to the percentage of teenagers who have used the drug within the last month. By the time they are seniors in high school, three-fourths of teenagers have tried alcohol and half have smoked cigarettes. Experimentation with marijuana is also common: 45 percent of all seniors have tried marijuana, one-third have smoked marijuana at least once within the last year, and 25 percent have done so within the past thirty days. After marijuana, however, the percentage of young people who have tried various other drugs drops significantly: Only about 10 percent of teenagers have used any illicit drug other than marijuana within the last month (Monitoring the Future, 2005).

It is one thing to have tried alcohol or marijuana, but it is something else to use either of these substances so often that one's life and behavior are markedly affected. To examine this issue, we can look at the percentage of young people who report using various substances daily or nearly daily. When we do this, it turns out that cigarettes are the only substances used daily by a substantial number of high school seniors (about one-sixth smoke daily). Of the remaining drugs, only alcohol and marijuana are used this frequently by even a modest percentage of teenagers (alcohol is used daily by about 3% of high school seniors; marijuana is used daily by about 5%). On this indicator, then, things don't look as bad as one might expect. But although daily use of alcohol is relatively infrequent, the occasional abuse of alcohol is not. Nearly 30 percent of all seniors, 20 percent of all tenth-graders, and 10 percent of all eighth-graders report having had more than five drinks in a row, referred to as **binge drinking**, at least once during the past two weeks (Monitoring the Future, 2005).

Taken together, the findings from these surveys present a mixed picture of patterns of substance use among today's teenagers (see Figure 13.8). Clearly, too many adolescents smoke cigarettes, which is certainly cause for concern given the high potential for addiction and the serious health consequences of smoking. It is also true that many adolescents who drink do so in excess—binge drinking, which can result in alcohol poisoning and unintentional injuries, is dangerous. On the other hand, only a small proportion of young people suffer from serious drug dependency (which would lead to daily use) or use hard drugs (i.e., illegal drugs other than marijuana).

binge drinking   Consuming five or more drinks in a row on one occasion, an indicator of alcohol abuse.

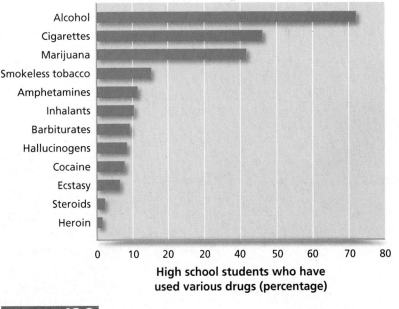

High school students who have used various drugs (percentage)

FIGURE 13.8

Substance Use in Adolescence

This figure shows percentages of American high school students who have ever used various drugs, according to data from Monitoring the Future, an annual survey of a representative sample of American teenagers.

Perhaps the most important message is that it is very unlikely that drug and alcohol use lurks behind the wide assortment of adolescent problems for which it is so frequently blamed. Instead, the overall picture indicates that most adolescents have experimented with alcohol and marijuana, that many have used one or both of these drugs regularly, that alcohol is clearly the drug of choice among teenagers (a substantial minority of whom drink to excess), and that most teenagers have not experimented with other drugs. From a health and safety standpoint, education about alcohol and cigarette use and abuse is more urgently needed and may potentially affect a larger percentage of young people than education about any other drug type.

There is no reason to be complacent about this, though. One very troublesome finding to emerge in recent surveys is that experimentation with drugs begins today at an earlier age than previously. In other words, the most pressing problem may not be the prevalence of substance use among high school seniors but early experimentation with substances by younger adolescents. Nearly 20 percent of all eighth-graders drink alcohol regularly, and nearly one in ten smokes cigarettes at least once a month (Monitoring the Future, 2005). One-sixth of eighth-graders have tried inhalants (such as paint or glue), one-sixth have tried marijuana, and 20 percent have been drunk at least once (Monitoring the Future, 2005).

Rates of substance use among eighth-graders are important to watch, because, as you will read, there is now very good evidence that the chances of becoming addicted to alcohol or nicotine is dramatically increased when substance use begins before age fourteen. Because adolescents who smoke cigarettes usually begin around seventh or eighth grade, looking at the number of eighth-graders who smoke today is a good way of predicting rates of smoking among adults tomorrow. The news isn't good: The rate of smoking among eighth-graders, which had been declining rapidly, has leveled off in recent years.

Ethnic Differences in Substance Use

In general, Caucasian adolescents are more likely to use drugs and alcohol than minority youngsters, especially African American and Asian American youth. Rates of drug use among Hispanic adolescents are comparable to those of Caucasian youngsters, and use among Native American adolescents is the highest (Chassin, Hussong, & Beltran, in press). In general, foreign-born and less Americanized minority youngsters—whether Asian or Hispanic in background—use alcohol, drugs, and tobacco at a lower rate than do American-born and more acculturated minority youth, suggesting, unfortunately, that part of becoming an "American" teenager means experimenting with drugs (Delva et al., 2005). In fact, the rate of drug use among adolescents who were born in the United States is *twice as high* as it is among adolescents from the same ethnic group who were born outside the United States. (Harris, 1999).

Drugs and the Adolescent Brain

Researchers had long hypothesized that, because the brain is still very malleable early in adolescence, experimentation with drugs was especially harmful at this point in development. Until fairly recently, this was

Alcohol and nicotine (in the forms of cigarettes and smokeless tobacco) are by far the most commonly used and abused substances by American teenagers.

© Laura Dwight

mainly speculation. But in the past several years, experimental studies, in which researchers have compared the brains of animals that have been exposed to drugs either close to the time of puberty or after reaching full maturity, has shed light on the specific neurobiological pathways that explain why the potential for addiction to both nicotine and alcohol is much greater in adolescence than adulthood (Schochet, Kelley, & Landry, 2004, 2005; Sturmhöfel & Swartzwelder, 2004; Volkow & Li, 2005). To understand what these studies say, we need to take a slight digression and revisit adolescent brain development.

As you read earlier in this chapter, changes in the limbic system take place during adolescence that affect receptors for **dopamine**, one of the brain's most important neurotransmitters, and one that plays a special role in our experience of pleasure. When we experience things that are enjoyable, like fabulous food or great sex, the reason we experience these as rewarding is because they result in higher levels of dopamine in the brain, which permit more electrical activity to flow through the synapses that connect the circuits in the brain that regulate feelings of pleasure. Keep in mind, though, that levels of dopamine are monitored and regulated so that feelings of pleasure stay within a normal range; when they get too high, dopamine levels are diminished, and when they get too low, they are increased. (Recall our discussion of the set point that plays a role in the onset of puberty—this is a similar process.)

The main reason that using drugs feels good is that they affect the same receptors that are sensitive to natural dopamine. In fact, molecules of addictive drugs are so similar to dopamine that the dopamine receptors act in the same way in their presence as they do in the presence of dopamine. As a result, when drugs enter the brain (which is where they end up whether they enter your body through your mouth, nose, or blood vessels), they are "experienced" by the brain's dopamine receptors as the real thing. On the positive side, this makes us feel good (the same way that natural dopamine does)—after all, if they didn't, people wouldn't use drugs. The problem, though, is that frequent drug use signals the brain to reduce levels of natural dopamine, in order to maintain the proper level, because the dopamine receptors can't tell the difference between the drug molecules and dopamine molecules. As a result, the more you use drugs, the less natural dopamine circulates in your brain.

This would not be a problem if it were easily reversed. But the animal studies referred to earlier have shown that experiences in early adolescence, when the limbic system is being remodeled, can *permanently* affect the way the dopamine system functions. (As you now know, various brain systems and regions change during different periods of development, and it is during periods of change that these brain systems are most easily and sometimes permanently affected by outside influences.) Repeated exposure to drugs during this period of heightened malleability in the limbic system can affect the brain in ways that make it *necessary* to use drugs in order to experience normal amounts of pleasure. That's drug addiction.

Over time, with repeated exposure, the brain's ability to produce natural dopamine is permanently hindered, and in order to experience pleasurable feelings, it is necessary to "supplement" the low levels of natural dopamine in the brain with drugs. We now know that this permanent alteration in the dopamine system is more likely to happen in early adolescence, when the limbic system is still malleable, than in adulthood, when it is less changeable. Here's a striking illustration: Compared with individuals who delay drinking until they are twenty-one, people who begin drinking in early adolescence (before age fourteen) are *seven times* more likely to binge drink as teenagers and *five times* more likely to develop a substance abuse or dependence disorder at some point in their life (Hingson, Heeren, & Winter, 2006). Similarly, individuals who begin smoking regularly before age fourteen (which, as we noted, is when most smokers begin) are at greater risk for nicotine dependence as adults than those who start in late adolescence (Orlando et al., 2004). How many exposures to a drug does it

dopamine A neurotransmitter especially important in the brain circuits that regulate the experience of pleasure.

take to permanently alter the adolescent brain's dopamine system? No one knows for sure, and the answer varies from person to person, largely because of genetic factors (this is why some people are more likely to develop addictions than others).

And it's not just that the potential for addiction is higher in adolescence. The effects of nicotine and alcohol on brain functioning actually are worse in adolescence than in adulthood—again, because the brain is more vulnerable at this point in development. One area of the adolescent brain that appears especially susceptible to the harmful effects of alcohol is the **hippocampus**, which is important for memory and, along with the prefrontal cortex, for "putting the brakes" on impulsive behavior (Sturmhöfel & Swartzwelder, 2004; Walker et al., 2004). We also know that alcohol has harmful effects on the development of regions of the brain involved in higher-order cognitive abilities, such as planning, and in the regulation of impulses (Butler, 2006).

hippocampus A structure in the brain's limbic system that is especially important for memory.

Causes and Consequences of Adolescent Substance Use and Abuse

In looking at the causes and consequences of substance use and abuse, it is especially important to keep in mind the distinction between occasional experimentation and problematic use. Psychologists distinguish between two levels of severity of pathological substance use: **substance abuse**, using drugs in a way that causes significant problems at home, school, work, or with the law, and **substance dependence**, where the individual is physically addicted. All individuals who are substance dependent by definition have substance abuse, but the reverse is not true.

substance abuse The misuse of alcohol or other drugs to a degree that causes problems in the individual's life.

substance dependence The misuse of alcohol or other drugs to a degree that causes physical addiction.

Because the majority of adolescents have experimented with alcohol and marijuana, one can speculate that occasional alcohol and marijuana use has become normative among American high school students and, consequently, that there are plenty of normal, healthy young people who have used these drugs at least once. In fact, several studies indicate that adolescents who experiment with alcohol and marijuana are as well adjusted as—if not somewhat better adjusted and more socially skilled than—their peers who abstain completely from alcohol and marijuana (Shedler & Block, 1990). These results do not mean that occasional experimentation with drugs during adolescence causes better adjustment, of course (remember, correlation does not prove causation). In fact, research shows that the psychological advantages observed among adolescents who experiment with alcohol and marijuana were evident when these individuals were younger children (Shedler & Block, 1990). Taken together, though, the studies suggest that moderate alcohol and marijuana use has become normative among adolescents in contemporary society (however troublesome some adults may find this); that these substances are typically used in social situations; and that better-adjusted and more interpersonally competent young people are likely to participate in social activities in which alcohol and other drugs are present (Shedler & Block, 1990).

Substance abuse is a different matter. Adolescents who are frequent users of alcohol, tobacco, and other drugs score lower on measures of psychological adjustment as teenagers and were more likely to be maladjusted as children (Shedler & Block, 1990). Indeed, a team of researchers who followed a sample of individuals from preschool into young adulthood reported that, at age seven, individuals who later became frequent drug users as adolescents were described as "not getting along well with other children, not showing concern for moral issues . . . not planful or likely to think ahead, not trustworthy or dependable . . . [and] not self-reliant or confident" (Shedler & Block, 1990, p. 618). As eleven-year-olds, these individuals were deviant, emotionally volatile, stubborn, and inattentive. In other words, drug and alcohol abuse during adolescence is often a symptom of prior psychological disturbance.

Substance abuse during adolescence is associated with a host of other problems. Young people who abuse alcohol, tobacco, and other drugs are more likely to experience problems at school, experience psychological distress and depression, have physical health problems, engage in unprotected sexual activity, abuse alcohol as young adults, and become involved in dangerous or deviant activities, including crime, delinquency, and truancy (Chassin et al., in press; Holmen et al., 2000; Kandel et al., 1997; Wu & Anthony, 1999). Alcohol and other drugs are often implicated in adolescent automobile crashes, the leading cause of death and disability among American teenagers (Lang, Waller, & Shope, 1996; O'Malley & Johnston, 1999), and in other fatal and nonfatal accidents, such as drownings, falls, and burns (Irwin, 1986; Wintemute et al., 1987). Adolescent substance abusers also expose themselves to the long-term health risks of excessive drug use that stem from addiction or dependency; in the case of cigarettes, alcohol, and marijuana, these risks are substantial and well documented— among them, cancer, heart disease, and kidney and liver damage. Also, it is now well established that heavy cigarette smoking during adolescence can exacerbate feelings of emotional distress and lead to depression and anxiety disorders (Goodman & Capitman, 2000).

Which adolescents are most likely to become substance abusers? Generally, four sets of **risk factors**—psychological, familial, social, and contextual—for substance abuse have been identified. The first set of risk factors is psychological. Individuals with certain personality characteristics—which typically are present before adolescence—are more likely to develop drug and alcohol problems than their peers. These characteristics include *anger, impulsivity,* and *inattentiveness* (Chassin et al., in press). Second, individuals with *distant, hostile,* or *conflicted family relationships* are more likely to develop substance abuse problems than are their peers who grow up in close, nurturing families (Dishion, Capaldi, & Yoerger, 1999; Sale et al., 2005). Third, individuals with substance abuse problems also are more likely to have *friends who use and tolerate the use of drugs,* both because they are influenced by these friends and because they have others with whom to use them (Ennett et al., 2006). Finally, adolescents who become substance abusers are more likely to live in a *social context that makes drug use easier,* such as the easy availability of drugs, community norms tolerating drug use, lax enforcement of drug laws, and positive portrayals of drug use in the mass media (Chassin et al., in press). The more risk factors that are present for an individual, the more likely he or she is to use and abuse drugs (Petraitis, Flay, & Miller, 1995).

risk factors Factors that increase individual vulnerability to harm.

Prevention and Treatment of Substance Use and Abuse

Efforts to prevent substance use and abuse among teenagers focus on one of three factors: the supply of drugs, the environment in which teenagers may be exposed to drugs, and characteristics of the potential drug user (Newcomb & Bentler, 1989). Although a good deal of government spending and media publicity has been devoted to the first of these approaches—attempts to control or limit the availability of drugs— the consensus among experts is that it is more realistic to try to change adolescents' motivation to use drugs and the environment in which they live, since it has proven virtually impossible to remove drugs totally from society. After all, the two most commonly used and abused drugs by teenagers—cigarettes and alcohol—are both legal and widely available, and as you may know from firsthand experience, laws prohibiting the sale of these substances to minors are not well enforced (Centers for Disease Control and Prevention, 2006). Research does show, however, that raising the price of alcohol and cigarettes reduces adolescents' use of them (Gruber & Zinman, 2001).

Many different types of drug abuse prevention interventions have been tried, either alone or in combination. In programs designed to change some characteristic of the adolescent, drug use is either targeted indirectly by attempting to enhance adolescents' psychological development in general or by helping adolescents to develop other activities and interests that will make drug use less likely, such as getting involved in athletics. The idea behind these sorts of efforts is that adolescents who have high self-esteem, for example, or who are involved in productive activities, will be less likely to use drugs. In other programs, the intervention is more directly aimed at preventing drug use. These programs include educating adolescents about the dangers of drugs, teaching adolescents how to turn down drugs, and some combination of informational and general psychological intervention (in which adolescents are educated about drug abuse and exposed to a program designed to enhance their self-esteem, for instance) (Newcomb & Bentler, 1989).

Generally speaking, the results of research designed to evaluate these sorts of individual-focused approaches have not been especially encouraging (Dielman, 1994; Leventhal & Keeshan, 1993). Careful evaluations of Project DARE (Drug Abuse Resistance Education), for example—the most widely implemented drug education program in the United States—show that the program is largely ineffective (Ennett et al., 1994). Experts are now fairly confident that drug education alone, whether based on rational information or scare tactics, does not prevent drug use. This is reminiscent of research on sex education, which, as we saw earlier, has shown that informational programs are not effective on their own. As a rule, educational programs may change individuals' knowledge, but they rarely affect their behavior. In addition, a recent large-scale study of drug testing in schools found that the program has no effect on adolescents' drug use (Yamaguchi, Johnston, & O'Malley, 2003).

The most encouraging results have been found in programs that do not focus just on the individual adolescent but, rather, combine some sort of social competence training (e.g., training in how to resist peer pressure) with a communitywide intervention aimed not only at adolescents but also at their peers, parents, and teachers (so that antidrug messages are consistent across these sources of information). These multifaceted efforts have been shown to be effective in reducing adolescents' use of alcohol, cigarettes, and other drugs, especially if the programs begin when youngsters are preadolescents and continue well into high school (Bruvold, 1993; Dielman, 1994; Ellickson, Bell, & McGuigan, 1993; Flynn et al., 1994; Perry et al., 1996). Overall, most experts agree that efforts designed simply to change the potential adolescent drug user without transforming the environment in which the adolescent lives are not likely to succeed. Despite their intuitive appeal, efforts to help adolescents "Just Say No" have been remarkably unsuccessful. (For a summary of this section, see "Interim Summary 13.5: Substance Use and Abuse in Adolescence.")

INTERIM SUMMARY 13.5

Substance Use and Abuse in Adolescence

Prevalence of Substance Use and Abuse	■ Alcohol and nicotine are by far the most commonly used and abused substances by teenagers, although experimentation with marijuana is also common.
	■ Although daily alcohol use is relatively infrequent, occasional abuse is not. Many adolescents engage in **binge drinking**.
	■ Recent surveys indicate that drug experimentation begins at an earlier age today than previously.
	■ Caucasian adolescents are more likely to use drugs and alcohol than minority youngsters.
Drugs and the Adolescent Brain	■ Changes in the limbic system during adolescence affect receptors for **dopamine**, a neurotransmitter that plays a special role in our experience of pleasure. The main reason that using drugs feels good is that they mimic the effects of natural dopamine.

(continued)

INTERIM SUMMARY **13.5** *(continued)*

Substance Use and Abuse in Adolescence

<table>
<tr>
<td></td>
<td>

■ With repeated exposure to drugs, the brain's ability to produce natural dopamine can be permanently affected, increasing the risk for abuse and addiction.

■ The effects of nicotine and alcohol on brain functioning are worse in adolescence than in adulthood because the brain is especially vulnerable during this stage. Individuals who are exposed to drugs early in adolescence are much more likely to develop substance abuse problems than those whose exposure is delayed until late adolescence.

■ The **hippocampus**, which is important for memory and for controlling impulsive behavior, is especially susceptible to the harmful effects of alcohol.
</td>
</tr>
<tr>
<td>

Causes and Consequences of Adolescent Substance Use and Abuse
</td>
<td>

■ Psychologists distinguish between two levels of severity of pathological substance use: **substance abuse** (using drugs in a way that causes significant problems at home, school, work, or with the law) and **substance dependence** (where the individual is physically addicted).

■ There are four sets of risk factors for substance abuse:

1. Having certain personality characteristics, including anger, impulsivity, and inattentiveness

2. Having distant, hostile, or conflicted family relationships

3. Having friends who use and tolerate the use of drugs

4. Living in a social context that makes drug use easier

■ Substance abuse is associated with other problems, such as psychological distress and depression, problems at school, physical health problems, unprotected sexual activity, dangerous or deviant activities, and the long-term health risks of excessive drug use.
</td>
</tr>
<tr>
<td>

Prevention and Treatment of Substance Use and Abuse
</td>
<td>

■ Efforts to prevent substance use and abuse focus on one of three factors: the supply of drugs, the environment in which teenagers are exposed to drugs, and characteristics of the potential drug user.

■ Most experts agree that efforts designed to simply change the potential adolescent drug user without transforming the environment in which the adolescent lives are not likely to succeed.

■ The most encouraging programs combine some sort of social competence training (how to resist peer pressure) with a community-wide intervention aimed at adolescents, their peers, parents and teachers.
</td>
</tr>
</table>

SUMMING UP AND LOOKING AHEAD

Physical development in adolescence is dramatic. Boys and girls enter adolescence looking like children, and leave looking like adults, not only taller and bigger, but with their sexual maturity in full view and their libido up and running. And, of course, there are those physical changes inside the skull that are not as easy to see (at least without an expensive machine that images the brain) but that are equally important. We are just now beginning to map out the course of brain development in adolescence and beyond, but already our view of what is happening inside the teenager's head has been radically transformed. A lot more development is taking place during adolescence than anyone had ever imagined. Scientists are just now beginning to understand the consequences of this for individuals' behavior, psychological development, and mental health.

In this chapter, we looked at several aspects of adolescent functioning that are directly linked to the physical changes of the period—sleeping, having sex, dieting, and using alcohol and other drugs. (That combination sounds like a parent's nightmare, doesn't it?) Perhaps the safest thing we can say about developments in these domains is that adolescence is a time of risk, but it is also a time of opportunity. Yes, there are teenagers who are sleep deprived, promiscuous, obese, and substance dependent. But there are plenty of young people who are well rested, sexually responsible, physically fit, and resistant to forces that lead others toward substance abuse. One of the most important things to keep in mind about physical health and well-being in adolescence is that the most significant threats to youngsters' health are self-imposed, and therefore avoidable. The challenge facing individuals who work with teenagers is to help them learn how to be, and how to stay, healthy.

To do this, we need to better understand how adolescents think. That's the subject of "Cognitive Development in Adolescence."

HERE'S WHAT YOU SHOULD KNOW

Did You Get It?

After reading this chapter, you should understand the following:

- The major physical changes in males and females at puberty, and the process that triggers the onset of puberty
- The ways in which early and later maturation affect adolescents' psychological development
- Basic facts about sexual behavior during adolescence, including patterns of sexual activity, contraceptive use, sexually transmitted disease, pregnancy, and the impact of sex education

- The most common forms of disordered eating in adolescence
- The main ways in which the brain changes during adolescence, and the impact of these changes on adolescent thinking and behavior
- Basic facts about substance use in adolescence, including patterns of use, risk factors for problems, and approaches to treatment and prevention

Important Terms and Concepts

adolescent growth spurt (p. 375)
adrenarche (p. 374)
AIDS (acquired immune deficiency syndrome) (p. 386)
androgens (p. 374)
anorexia nervosa (p. 391)
binge drinking (p. 395)
bulimia (p. 391)
chlamydia (p. 386)
cortisol (p. 374)
delayed phase preference (p. 378)
disordered eating (p. 390)
dopamine (p. 397)

dorsolateral prefrontal cortex (p. 392)
endocrine system (p. 374)
estrogens (p. 374)
gender identity (p. 385)
glands (p. 374)
gonadotropin releasing hormone neurons (GnRH neurons) (p. 374)
gonads (p. 374)
gonorrhea (p. 386)
herpes (p. 386)
hippocampus (p. 398)
hormones (p. 374)
HPG (hypothalamic-pituitary-gonadal) axis (p. 374)

human immunodeficiency virus (HIV) (p. 386)
human papilloma virus (p. 386)
hypothalamus (p. 374)
leptin (p. 375)
limbic system (p. 393)
melatonin (p. 379)
menarche (p. 377)
neurotransmitters (p. 393)
orbitofrontal cortex (p. 393)
ovaries (p. 374)
pituitary gland (p. 374)
prefrontal cortex (p. 392)
puberty (p. 373)
risk factors (p. 399)

rite of passage (p. 378)
secondary sex characteristics (p. 376)
secular trend (p. 380)
set point (p. 374)
sex-role behavior (p. 385)
sexual orientation (p. 385)
sexually transmitted disease (STD) (p. 386)
substance abuse (p. 398)
substance dependence (p. 398)
Tanner stages (p. 376)
testes (p. 374)
ventromedial prefrontal cortex (p. 392)

Cognitive Development in Adolescence

© Rubberball

Why do shows like *South Park* appeal so much to so many teenagers? Why do adolescents so often become obsessed with questions about the meaning of life? Why do teenagers argue so much with their parents? Answers to these questions, and more, in the pages that follow.

Tell a thirteen-year-old that adolescents, on average, are "smarter" than children and the response you are likely to get is, "Well, duh." (We'll explain later why the use and understanding of sarcasm increases in early adolescence.) But not only do teenagers know more than children, they actually think in different ways—in ways that are more advanced, more efficient, and more effective. As you'll read in this chapter, the changes that take place during adolescence in the way individuals think have far-reaching implications—not only for what they like to watch on television or think lofty thoughts about, but also for how they perform in school, their social relationships, and their day-to-day decision making.

Our look at cognitive development in adolescence begins with an overview of the major ways in which thinking changes during this period of development, and the two main theoretical perspectives that have been used to explain these changes. Next, we look at the ways in which changes in thinking affect adolescents' understanding of social relationships and social institutions—a domain of thinking referred to as *social cognition*. Following this, we'll take a look at adolescent risk taking, school performance and educational achievement, and adolescents' experiences in the world of work.

HOW THINKING CHANGES IN ADOLESCENCE

Five important sets of changes in thinking take place during adolescence:

- We become more able to think about what is possible, not just about what actually is.
- We become more able to think in sophisticated ways about abstract concepts, like love, democracy, and justice.
- We become better at thinking about the process of thinking.
- We improve in our ability to think about things from multiple vantage points at the same time.
- We start to see things as relative, rather than absolute.

Let's take a look at each of these changes in detail.

Thinking About Possibilities

Children's thinking is oriented to things and events that they can observe directly. But adolescents are able to consider what they observe against a backdrop of what is possible. As an example, consider how individuals think about themselves. Children do not wonder, the way adolescents often do, about the ways in which their personalities might change in the future or how they might have been different had they grown up with different parents or under different economic circumstances. For the young child, you simply are who you are. Not so for teenagers: Who you are is just one possibility of who you could be.

Adolescents' ability to reason systematically in terms of what is possible comes in handy in a variety of scientific and logical problem-solving situations they face in school. For instance, the study of mathematics in junior and senior high school (algebra, geometry, trigonometry, and calculus) often requires that you begin with an abstract or theoretical formulation—for example: "The square of a right triangle's hypotenuse is equal to the sum of the squares of the other two sides" (the Pythagorean theorem). Theorems are propositions about the possible rather than the real. It is a statement about all *possible* right triangles, not just triangles that we might actually observe.

Improvements in abstract reasoning abilities enable adolescents to learn algebra.

Deductive and Inductive Reasoning One important manifestation of the adolescent's increased facility with thinking about possibilities is the development of **deductive reasoning**. Deductive reasoning is a type of logical reasoning in which you draw logically necessary conclusions from a general set of premises, or givens. For example, consider the following problem:

deductive reasoning A type of logical reasoning in which one draws logically necessary conclusions from a general set of premises, or givens.

All soccer players wear shin guards.

Chris is a soccer player.

Does Chris wear shin guards?

Individuals who can reason deductively understand that the correct conclusion (that Chris wears shin guards) necessarily follows from the first two statements. No additional knowledge about soccer, or about Chris, or about shin guards, is necessary to reach the correct answer. By the same token, adolescents are also better able than children to recognize when a logical problem doesn't provide sufficient information and to respond by saying that the question can't be answered with any certainty. Suppose we were to change the problem to read like this:

All soccer players wear shin guards.

Chris is wearing shin guards.

Is Chris a soccer player?

If you answer this type of question quickly, without thinking it through, you might say that Chris indeed is a soccer player. But this is not necessarily the case. Whereas children are easily fooled by such problems, adolescents are more likely to say that there is no way of knowing whether Chris plays soccer or not, because we are not told that the *only* people who wear shin guards are soccer players. That's deductive reasoning.

Man (or woman) can't survive by deductive reasoning alone, however. Very often, we have to make educated guesses, even though our hunches cannot be supported by deductive reasoning. Consider the following problem:

Chris, John, Julie, Tom, Liz, and Kendra are soccer players.

Chris, John, Julie, Tom, Liz, and Kendra all wear shin guards.

Do all soccer players wear shin guards?

This problem cannot be solved using deductive reasoning, because no certain answer to the question necessarily follows from the first two statements. Instead, this problem is likely to be solved using **inductive reasoning**, in which a conclusion is drawn based on the totality of the evidence. For this problem, your answer to the question would depend on how many people were listed in the first two statements, your knowledge of soccer, your own experience playing sports, and so on. And rather than being certain of your answer, you would have different degrees of confidence in your conclusion depending on the amount of information you had.

inductive reasoning A type of reasoning in which one draws a conclusion based on the totality of evidence.

hypothetical thinking Thinking that is based on what is possible, and not just what is real; sometimes referred to as "if-then" thinking.

Inductive reasoning is used by people of all ages, even very young children (Jacobs & Portenza, 1991). Indeed, we all use inductive reasoning often in everyday situations (e.g., you are in the back of a crowd of students, all of whom are looking through a class roster posted outside your professor's door and moaning about their exam scores, so you start to worry about how you did). Unlike inductive reasoning, however, deductive reasoning is seldom seen before adolescence, because deductive reasoning requires us to think systematically about possibilities (Klaczynski & Narasimham, 1998; Morris & Sloutsky, 2001).

Hypothetical Thinking Related to the development of deductive reasoning is the emergence of **hypothetical thinking**, or "if-then" thinking, as it is sometimes called. Being able to plan ahead, to see the future consequences of an action, and to provide alternative explanations of events are all dependent on being able to hypothesize effectively.

The ability to think through hypotheses is an enormously powerful tool. For example, thinking in hypothetical terms allows us to suspend our beliefs about something in order to argue in the abstract. Prior to adolescence, individuals have difficulty in dealing with propositions that are contrary to fact, unless they are part of a larger fictional story (Markovits & Valchon, 1989). So, for example, a six-year-old would have trouble answering the question "Where would flying dogs build nests?" He might say, "Dogs don't fly," or "Dogs don't have nests," unless he had heard about flying dogs in a story that was clearly fantasy based.

Adolescents' ability to engage in hypothetical thinking may make them seem argumentative to their parents. In actuality, what adolescents may be are just better arguers.

Hypothetical thinking also has implications for the adolescent's social behavior. It helps the young person to take the perspective of others by enabling him or her to think through what someone else might be thinking or feeling, given that person's point of view. ("If someone treated me the way she was just treated, I would feel pretty angry.") Hypothetical thinking therefore helps in formulating and arguing one's viewpoint, because it allows adolescents to think a step ahead of the opposition—a cognitive tool that comes in quite handy when dealing with parents. ("If they come back with 'You have to stay home and clean out the garage,' then I'll remind them about the time they let my brother go out when *he* had chores to do.") (Many parents believe that their children become more argumentative during adolescence. There is a little of this, as you will read in "Socioemotional Development in Adolescence." What probably matters more, though, is that their children become *better arguers*.) Hypothetical thinking also plays an important role in decision making, because it permits the young person to plan ahead and to foresee the consequences of choosing one alternative over another. ("If I choose to go out for the basketball team, then I am going to have to give up my job at the mall.") Scientists now believe that the development of the ability to plan ahead and foresee the future consequences of one's actions is closely tied to the maturation of the prefrontal cortex, a development that you read about in "Physical Development in Adolescence."

Thinking About Abstract Concepts

The appearance of more systematic, abstract thinking is a second notable aspect of cognitive development during adolescence. For example, adolescents find it easier than children to comprehend the sorts of higher-order abstract logic inherent in puns, proverbs, metaphors, and analogies. The adolescent's greater facility with abstract thinking also applies to interpersonal and philosophical matters. This is clearly seen in the adolescent's increased capacity and interest in thinking about relationships, politics, religion, and morality—topics that involve such abstract concepts as friendship, democracy, faith, and honesty. As some writers have pointed out, the ability to think abstractly may prompt many adolescents to spend time thinking about the meaning of life itself (Hacker, 1994).

Thinking About Thinking

A third noteworthy gain in cognitive ability during adolescence involves thinking about thinking itself, the process sometimes referred to as **metacognition**. Metacognition often involves monitoring one's own cognitive activity during the process of thinking—when you consciously use a strategy for remembering something (such as *HOMES*, for the names of the Great Lakes—in case *you* don't remember, they are Huron, Ontario, Michigan, Erie, and Superior), or when you appraise your own comprehension of something you are reading before going on to the next paragraph. Not only do adolescents "manage" their thinking more than children, but they are also better able to explain to others the processes they are using. When asked, adolescents can explain not only *what* they know but also *why* knowing what they know enables them to think differently and solve problems more effectively (Reich, Oser, & Valentin, 1994).

One fascinating way in which thinking about thinking becomes more apparent during adolescence is in increased introspection, self-consciousness, and intellectualization. These intellectual advances may occasionally result in problems for the young adolescent, particularly before he or she adjusts to having such powerful cognitive tools. Being able to introspect, for instance, may lead to periods of extreme self-absorption—a sort of "adolescent egocentrism" (Elkind, 1967). **Adolescent egocentrism** results in two distinct problems in thinking that help to explain some of the seemingly odd beliefs and behaviors of teenagers (Goossens, Seiffge-Krenke, & Marcoen, 1992).

The first, the **imaginary audience**, involves having such a heightened sense of self-consciousness that you think your behavior is the focus of everyone else's concern and attention. For example, a teenager who is going to see the New Orleans Saints play the Philadelphia Eagles, with 68,000 other people in the stadium, may worry about dressing the right way because "everybody will notice." Given the cognitive limitations of adolescent egocentrism, it is difficult to persuade a young person that the "audience" is not all that concerned with his or her behavior or appearance. (Of course, if you were to wear a Saints jersey and the game were being played in Philadelphia, you'd be making a very big mistake.)

A second problem resulting from adolescent egocentrism is the **personal fable**. The personal fable revolves around the adolescent's egocentric (and usually erroneous) belief that his or her experiences are unique. For instance, a teenager who just broke up

metacognition The process of thinking about thinking itself.

adolescent egocentrism The tendency for adolescents to be extremely self-absorbed, thought to result from advances in thinking abilities.

imaginary audience The belief, often brought on by the heightened self-consciousness of early adolescence, that everyone is watching and evaluating one's behavior.

personal fable A person's belief that he or she is unique and therefore not subject to the rules that govern other people's behavior.

© Laura Dwight

One manifestation of adolescent egocentrism is the "imaginary audience," which leads to the belief that one is the focus of everyone else's attention.

with his girlfriend might tell his mother that she could not possibly understand what it feels like to break up with someone—even though breaking up is something that most people experienced often during their adolescent and young adult years. Adherence to a personal fable of uniqueness provides some protective benefits, in that it enhances adolescents' self-esteem and feelings of self-importance. But sometimes holding on to a personal fable can actually be quite dangerous, as in the case of a sexually active adolescent who believes that pregnancy simply won't happen to her or a reckless driver who believes that he will defy the laws of nature by taking hairpin turns on an icy road at breakneck speed. Although we associate this type of thinking with adolescence, studies show that susceptibility to the personal fable actually may appear not only in adolescence but also in adulthood (Goossens et al., 1992; Quadrel, Fischhoff, & Davis, 1993). Just ask any *adult* cigarette smoker if he or she is aware of the scientific evidence linking cigarette smoking with heart and lung disease.

Thinking in Multiple Dimensions

A fourth way in which thinking changes during adolescence involves the ability to think about things from different vantage points at the same time. Children tend to think about things one aspect at a time. Adolescents can see things through more complicated lenses, though. For instance, when a certain hitter comes up to the plate in a baseball game, a preadolescent who knows that the hitter has a good home-run record might exclaim that the batter will hit the ball out of the park. An adolescent, however, would consider the hitter's record in relation to the specific pitcher on the mound and would weigh both factors, or dimensions, before making a prediction (perhaps this player hits a lot of home runs against left-handed pitchers but strikes out often against righties).

As is the case with other gains in cognitive ability, the increasing capability of individuals to think in multiple dimensions also has consequences for their behavior and thinking in all sorts of settings. Adolescents describe themselves and others in more differentiated and complicated terms ("I'm both shy and extroverted") and find it easier to look at problems from multiple perspectives ("I know that's the way you see it, but try to look at it from her point of view"). Being able to understand that people's personalities are not one-sided, or that social situations can have different interpretations, depending on one's point of view, permits the adolescent to have far more sophisticated—and far more complicated—relationships with other people and self-conceptions, two topics we discuss in "Socioemotional Development in Adolescence."

One sign of adolescents' ability to look at things in multiple dimensions concerns their understanding of sarcasm. As an adult, you know that the meaning of a speaker's statement is communicated by a combination of what is said, how it is said, and the context in which it is said. If I turned to you during a boring lecture, rolled my eyes, and said, in an exaggeratedly serious tone, "This is the most interesting lecture I've ever heard," you would know that I actually meant just the opposite. But you only would know this if you paid attention to my inflection, my expression, and to the context, as well as the content, of my statement. Only by attending simultaneously to multiple dimensions of speech can we distinguish between the sincere and the sarcastic.

Because our ability to think in multidimensional terms improves during adolescence, improvements in our ability to understand when someone is being sarcastic take place as well (Demorest et al., 1984; Pexman & Glenwright, 2007).

Why do young adolescents laugh hysterically when characters in movies aimed at their age group say things like, "He said 'erector set'"? Adolescents' increased facility in thinking along multiple dimensions permits them to appreciate satire, metaphor, and the ways in which language can be used to convey multiple messages, as in *double-entendres*—expressions that have two meanings, one of them usually rude or crude. Teenagers' newfound ability to use and appreciate sarcasm and satire helps to explain why shows like *Beavis and Butthead*, *The Simpsons*, *South Park*, and *The Family Guy*, as well as publications like *Mad* magazine, have always had such strong appeal in this age group.

Adolescent Relativism

A final aspect of cognition that changes during adolescence concerns the way in which adolescents look at things. Children tend to see things in absolute terms—in black and white. Adolescents, in contrast, tend to see things as relative. They are more likely to question others' assertions and less likely to accept "facts" as absolute truths.

This increase in relativism can be particularly exasperating to parents, who may feel as though their adolescent children question everything just for the sake of argument. Difficulties often arise, for example, when adolescents begin seeing parents' values that they had previously considered absolutely correct ("Moral people do not have sex before they are married") as completely relative ("Welcome to the twenty-first century, Dad").

Theoretical Perspectives on Adolescent Thinking

The two theoretical viewpoints that have been especially important are Piaget's perspective and the information-processing perspective. Although these two views of adolescent thinking begin from different assumptions about the nature of cognitive development, they each provide valuable insight into why thinking changes during adolescence.

Piaget's View of Adolescent Thinking As you have read in previous chapters, Piaget theorized that intellectual development proceeds through stages, and that the stage of formal operations characterizes adolescence. Formal operational thinking is based in abstract logical principles.

The shift from concrete operational thinking, which characterizes middle childhood (see "Cognitive Development in Middle Childhood"), to formal operational thinking appears to take place in two steps. During the first step, characteristic of early adolescence, formal thinking is apparent, but it has a sort of "Now you see it, now you don't" quality to it. Young adolescents may demonstrate formal thinking at some times but at others may only be able to think in concrete terms; use formal operations on some tasks but not on others; reason formally under some but not all testing situations (Markovits et al., 1996). Virtually all adolescents go through this period of "emergent formal operations" (Kuhn et al., 1977). It is not until middle or even late adolescence that formal operational thinking becomes consolidated and integrated into the individual's general approach to reasoning (Markovits & Valchon, 1989).

Although virtually all adolescents have the potential to develop formal operational thinking, and most can and do demonstrate it from time to time, not all adolescents (or, for that matter, all adults) develop formal operational thinking or employ it regularly and across different contexts. The extent to which formal operational thinking is displayed consistently by an individual depends a great deal on the conditions under which he or she is operating (Overton, 1990). It is important, therefore, to differentiate between *competence* (i.e., what the adolescent is capable of doing) and *performance* (i.e., what the adolescent actually does). Much research, on adults as well as adolescents, indicates that gaps between individuals' logical reasoning abilities and their actual use of logical reasoning in everyday situations are very large, with everyday decision making fraught with logical errors that cannot be explained by cognitive incompetence (Klaczynski, 2000, 2001). In other words, we often think in ways that are less sophisticated than we are actually capable of.

Generally, Piaget's perspective on adolescent cognition helps to explain why adolescents are better able than children to think about possibilities, to think multidimensionally, and to think about thoughts. Where Piaget's perspective on adolescent cognitive development falls short is in its claim that cognitive development proceeds in stages and adolescents' thinking should be thought of as qualitatively different from that of children (Keating, 2004). Rather, research suggests that advanced reasoning capabilities develop gradually and continuously from childhood through adolescence and beyond, probably in more of a quantitative fashion than was proposed by Piaget (i.e., more like a ramp than like a staircase).

The Information-Processing View of Adolescent Thinking Some scientists point out that Piaget's approach has not been especially helpful in pinpointing exactly *what* it is that changes as individuals mature into and through adolescence (Keating, 2004). If we are left only with the conclusion that cognitive growth between childhood and adolescence reflects changes in "logical reasoning abilities," we have not moved a great deal closer to understanding which *specific* aspects of intellectual development during adolescence are the most important ones. Just what is it about the ways that adolescents think about things that makes them better problem solvers than children? This question has been the focus of researchers working from the information-processing perspective.

Studies of changes in specific components of information processing have focused on five areas in which improvement occurs during adolescence: attention, working memory, processing speed, organization, and metacognition. Improvements in all of these areas take place as individuals move from childhood through adolescence, mainly during the first half of the adolescent decade (Demetriou et al., 2002; Kuhn, in press).

Studies show that most basic information-processing skills, like working memory or attention, as well as logical reasoning abilities, increase throughout childhood and early adolescence and then level off around age fifteen, with only very slight improvements after that (and basically no improvements after age twenty) (see Figure 14.1) (Luciana et al., 2005). (In other words, your memory, attention, and reasoning ability are no better now than when you were a junior in high school—and they may even be a little worse.) Don't despair, though: Cognitive development continues beyond age fifteen and into young adulthood in more sophisticated skills, such as planning ahead or judging the relative costs and benefits of a risky decision. We also become better at coordinating cognition and emotion, when, for instance, one's feelings might interfere with logical reasoning (e.g., when you have to make a decision when you are angry, or in the face of peer pressure). Given what we now know about brain maturation in late adolescence, which we discussed in "Physical Development in Adolescence," it is likely that the development of these advanced abilities may not be complete until individuals reach their midtwenties. (For a summary of this section, see "Interim Summary 14.1: How Thinking Changes in Adolescence.")

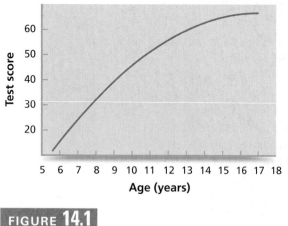

FIGURE 14.1

The Growth of Cognitive Abilities

The growth of cognitive abilities, as measured by standardized tests, is rapid between birth and age sixteen, and then levels off. Although there is little change in basic information processing after middle adolescence, there is continued development of more sophisticated thinking abilities in late adolescence. *Source:* Bayley, N. (1949). Consistency and variability in the growth of intelligence from birth to eighteen years. Journal of Genetic Psychology, 75, 165–196.

INTERIM SUMMARY 14.1

How Thinking Changes in Adolescence

Thinking About Possibilities	▪ Adolescents are more able than children to think about what is possible, not just about what actually is. Two important manifestations of this are improvements in **deductive reasoning** and in **hypothetical thinking**.
	▪ Scientists believe that the ability to plan ahead and foresee the future consequences of one's actions is closely tied to the maturation of the prefrontal cortex.
Thinking About Abstract Concepts	▪ Adolescents find it easier than children to comprehend the sorts of higher-order abstract logic inherent in puns, proverbs, metaphors, and analogies.
	▪ The adolescent's greater facility with abstract thinking also applies to interpersonal and philosophical matters, reflected in adolescent's increased capacity and interest in thinking about relationships, politics, religion, and morality.
Thinking About Thinking	▪ Improvements in **metacognition**, thinking about thinking, enable adolescents to explain what they know and use why they know what they know to solve problems more effectively.
	▪ Increased introspection, self-consciousness, and intellectualization may lead to periods of extreme self-absorption—a sort of "**adolescent egocentrism**" that contributes to the **imaginary audience** and the **personal fable**.
Thinking in Multiple Dimensions	▪ Adolescents experience improvements in the ability to think about things from different vantage points at the same time, which permits them to have far more sophisticated and far more complicated self-conceptions and relations with other people.
	▪ Adolescents' ability to understand sarcasm underscores their ability to look at things in multiple dimensions. They appreciate satire, metaphor, and double-entendres.
Adolescent Relativism	▪ Whereas children tend to see things in absolute terms, adolescents tend to see things as relative.
	▪ As a consequence, adolescents are more likely to question others' assertions and less likely to accept "facts" as absolute truths.
Theoretical Perspectives on Adolescent Thinking	▪ According to Piaget, the stage of **formal operations** characterizes adolescence. Formal thinking is apparent in early adolescence but it is not until middle or even late adolescence that formal operational thinking becomes consolidated and integrated into the individual's general approach to reasoning.
	▪ The extent to which formal operational thinking is displayed consistently by an individual depends on the conditions under which he or she is operating.
	▪ Researchers working from the information-processing perspective focus on what it is about the ways that adolescents think about things that makes them better problem solvers than children.

(continued)

INTERIM SUMMARY **14.1** *(continued)*

How Thinking Changes in Adolescence

- Improvements in attention, working memory, processing speed, organization, and metacognition all take place during early adolescence.

- Most basic information-processing skills level off around age 15, with only slight improvements after that. Cognitive development does continue beyond age 15 and into young adulthood, however, in more sophisticated skills such as planning ahead, weighing risks and rewards, and coordinating cognition and emotion.

SOCIAL COGNITION

Many of the examples of adolescent thinking that we have looked at so far have involved reasoning about scientific, mathematical, or logical problems. But the same sorts of gains in intellectual abilities that are observed in young people's thinking in these realms are apparent in their reasoning about social phenomena as well. The shift in thinking from the concrete to the abstract is apparent in the ways that adolescents think about the social world. Psychologists have paid special attention to how adolescents think about other people and about social institutions, including religion. **Social cognition** involves such cognitive activities as thinking about people, thinking about social relationships, and thinking about social institutions (Smetana, in press). Studies of social cognition during adolescence have examined *social perspective taking*, which refers to how, and how accurately, individuals make assessments about the thoughts and feelings of others; reasoning about *social conventions,* which refer to individuals' conceptions of social norms and guidelines for social interaction; and beliefs about "big" issues, including *morality and religion*. In the chapter on socioemotional development in middle childhood, we looked at the development of moral reasoning. In this chapter, we discuss changes in religious beliefs.

social cognition The aspect of cognition that concerns thinking about other people, about interpersonal relationships, and about social institutions.

Social Perspective Taking

Adolescence is a time of dramatic improvement in the ability to view events from the perspective of others, or **social perspective taking**. Not only are adolescents more capable of figuring out another person's perspective on some issue or event, they are also better able to understand that person's perspective on their own point of view ("She thinks that I think that she thinks . . .").

The development of social perspective taking progresses through a series of stages (Selman, 1980). Preadolescents can put themselves in others' shoes, but they have trouble seeing how the thoughts and feelings of one person may be related to the thoughts and feelings of another. They can take the first step, imagining what "she thinks," but not the next one "she thinks that I think." During early adolescence, with the progression into **mutual role taking**, the young adolescent can be an objective third party and see how the thoughts or actions of one person can influence those of another. In thinking about a misunderstanding that had occurred between two friends, for instance, an adolescent capable of mutual role taking would be able to see how each one's behavior affects the other's.

Later in adolescence, perspective taking develops an in-depth, societal orientation. The adolescent at this level understands that the perspectives that people have on each

social perspective taking The ability to view events from the perspective of others.

mutual role taking In Selman's theory, the stage of social perspective taking during which the young adolescent can be an objective third party and can see how the thoughts or actions of one person can influence those of another.

other are complicated, often unconscious, and influenced by forces beyond the individual's control—including each person's position in society or within a social institution. For example, your perspective on the instructor teaching your class is influenced not only by your own personality and by the instructor's, but also by the way the relationship between a teacher and student is socially defined.

Social Conventions

The realization that individuals' perspectives vary, and that their opinions may differ as a result, leads to changes in the ways that individuals think about society and social norms. During childhood, social norms are seen as absolutes emanating from such authorities as parents or teachers; judgments of what sort of behavior is correct are made according to concrete rules. During adolescence, however, such absolutes and rules are questioned, as the young person begins to see that standards for behavior are subjective and based on points of view that are subject to disagreement.

The development of individuals' understanding of **social conventions**—the social norms that guide day-to-day behavior—follows a similar course (Smetana, in press). During middle childhood, social conventions—such as waiting in line for a table at a restaurant—are seen as arbitrary and changeable, but adherence to them is not; compliance with such conventions is based on rules and on the dictates of authority. When you were seven years old, you might not have seen why people had to wait in line (especially if you were starving and cranky at the moment), but when your mother or father told you to wait in line, you waited. By early adolescence, however, conventions are seen as arbitrary and changeable in both their origins and their enforcement (recall our earlier discussion of relativistic thinking); conventions are merely social expectations. As an adolescent, you begin to realize that people wait in line because they are expected to, not because they are forced to. Indeed, young adolescents often see social conventions as *nothing but* social expectations and, consequently, as insufficient reasons for compliance. You can probably imagine youngsters in their midteens saying something like, "Why wait in line simply because other people are lined up? There isn't a *law* that forces you to wait in line, is there?"

Gradually, however, adolescents begin to see social conventions as the means by which society regulates people's behavior. Conventions may be arbitrary, but we follow them because we all share an understanding of how people are expected to behave in various situations. We wait in line to be seated not because we want to comply with any rule, but because it is something we are accustomed to doing. Ultimately, individuals come to see that social conventions serve a function in regulating the way people interact. Shared expectations create order and predictability. Social norms exist because individuals have a common perspective and agree that, in given situations, certain behaviors are more desirable than others, because such behavior helps things function more smoothly. Without the convention of waiting in line for a table in a restaurant, the pushiest people would always get seated first, and the entranceway to the restaurant would be in a state of chaos. The older adolescent can see that waiting in line not only benefits the restaurant but also preserves everyone's right to a fair chance to get a table.

Religious Beliefs During Adolescence

Religious beliefs, like beliefs in general, also become more abstract and more principled during the adolescent years (King & Roeser, in press). Adolescents are more oriented toward spiritual and ideological matters and less toward rituals, practices, and the observance of religious customs. For example, although close to 90 percent of all adolescents pray, and 95 percent believe in God, 40 percent of all young people say that organized religion does not play a very important role in their lives (Gallup & Bezilla, 1992; Holder et al., 2000; Wallace et al., 2003). Compared with children, ado-

social conventions The norms that govern everyday behavior in social situations.

lescents place more emphasis on the internal aspects of religious commitment (such as what an individual believes) and less on the external manifestations (such as whether an individual goes to church) (Elkind, 1978).

Consistent with this shift in emphasis, during adolescence there is a decline in the stated importance of religion—and especially of participation in an organized religion. Compared with older adolescents, younger ones are more likely to attend church regularly and state that religion is important to them (Wallace et al., 2003). Several studies have indicated that the decline in the importance of religion during late adolescence appears to be steeper among college than noncollege youth (Yankelovich, 1974), suggesting that college attendance may play some part in shaping (or as the case may be, in unshaping) young people's religious beliefs. (Of course, this depends on the type of college institution one attends—we would not expect to see this among students at

INTERIM SUMMARY 14.2

Social Cognition	
	■ **Social cognition** involves such cognitive abilities as thinking about other people, thinking about social relationships, and thinking about social institutions.
Social Perspective Taking	■ **Social perspective taking** involves the ability to view events from the perspective of others.
	■ **Mutual role taking** refers to the adolescent's increasing ability to be an objective third party and see how the thoughts or actions of one person can influence those of another.
Social Conventions	■ Reasoning about **social conventions** refers to individuals' conceptions of social norms and guidelines for social interactions.
	■ During middle childhood, social conventions are seen as arbitrary and changeable but adherence to them is not; compliance with such conventions is based on rules and on the dictates of authority.
	■ By early adolescence, conventions are often seen as nothing but social expectations with insufficient reasons for compliance.
	■ Gradually, adolescents begin to see social conventions as the means by which society regulates peoples' behavior.
Religious Beliefs During Adolescence	■ Religious beliefs become more abstract and more principled during the adolescent years and there is a decline in the stated importance of religion.
	■ Adolescents are more oriented toward spiritual and ideological matters and less toward rituals, practices, and the observance of religious customs.
	■ The early years of college appear to be a time when individuals reevaluate many of the beliefs and values they have grown up with.
	■ Religious adolescents are less depressed than other adolescents; and less likely to engage in premarital sexual intercourse, use drugs, or engage in delinquent behavior; and are more altruistic, more prosocial and more likely to be involved in the community.

explicitly religious institutions.) The early years of college appear to be a time when some individuals reexamine and reevaluate many of the beliefs and values they have grown up with. For many, this involves a decline in regular participation in organized religious activities, but an increase in spirituality and religious faith (Lefkowitz, 2005).

Although individuals typically become less involved in formal religion during the adolescent years, there are differences among adolescents in their degree of religiosity. Approximately 38 percent of adolescents report weekly attendance at religious services, 17 percent attend once or twice per month, and about 45 percent rarely or never attend services; regular attendance at religious services drops over the course of high school. In general, African American and Latino adolescents are more religious than youth from other ethnic backgrounds, as are adolescents who live in the South or Midwest compared with their East or West Coast counterparts (Smith et al., 2002; Wallace et al., 2003).

A growing body of research suggests that religious adolescents, especially those who affiliate with more fundamentalist denominations, are less depressed than other adolescents; less likely to engage in premarital sexual intercourse, use drugs, or engage in delinquent behavior; and more altruistic, more prosocial, and likely to be involved in the community (Holder et al., 2000; Meier, 2003; Miller, Davies, & Greenwald, 2000; Smetana & Metzger, 2005). Some of the apparent positive effects of religious involvement are due to the fact that adolescents who are involved in religion often have other positive influences in their life (e.g., supportive parents, prosocial peers, adults who care about them) (Ebstyne King & Furrow, 2004). But religiosity—in and of itself—appears to deter problem behavior and delay sexual activity (Hardy & Raffaelli, 2003; Jones, Darroch, & Singh, 2005; Steinman & Zimmerman, 2004). Religious involvement may play an especially important role in buffering inner-city African American adolescents against the harmful effects of neighborhood disorganization and exposure to violence (Pearce et al., 2003). (For a summary of this section, see "Interim Summary 14.2: Social Cognition.")

ADOLESCENT RISK TAKING

Another application of research on cognitive development in adolescence involves the study of adolescent risk taking. The Centers for Disease Control and Prevention, a government agency that monitors the health of Americans, surveys American teenagers annually and asks whether they had engaged in various behaviors during the previous thirty days (Centers for Disease Control, 2006). According to these surveys, risk taking is common among adolescents. Nearly 80 percent of boys and 60 percent of girls take unnecessary risks while skateboarding or riding bikes, close to one-third of both sexes have been passengers in cars driven by intoxicated drivers, and one-tenth have driven while drinking (Centers for Disease Control and Prevention, 2006; Ozer, McDonald, & Irwin, 2002). Risk taking is much more common among males than females, although there is some evidence that this gender gap has been narrowing over time (Byrnes, Miller, & Schafer, 1999).

Risky driving makes automobile crashes the leading cause of death among American adolescents.

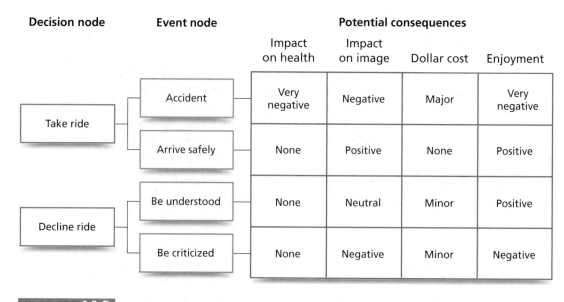

Decision node	Event node	Impact on health	Impact on image	Dollar cost	Enjoyment
Take ride	Accident	Very negative	Negative	Major	Very negative
	Arrive safely	None	Positive	None	Positive
Decline ride	Be understood	None	Neutral	Minor	Positive
	Be criticized	None	Negative	Minor	Negative

FIGURE 14.2

How Decisions Are Made

This figure shows the steps an adolescent might go through in deciding whether to accept a ride from a friend who has been drinking. Studies show that adolescents and adults engage in similar cognitive processes when making decisions. *Source: Alcohol Problems Among Adolescents: Current Directions in Prevention Research* by B. Fischott & M. Quadrel. Copyright 1995 by Taylor & Francis Group LLC – Books. Reproduced with permission of Taylor & Francis Group LLC – Books in the format Textbook via Copyright Clearance Center.

Many theories have been offered to explain why adolescents take more risks than adults (Steinberg, 2007). Two widely held beliefs are (1) that adolescents are less logical than adults, and (2) that adolescents are more likely than adults to develop personal fables. Neither has found much research support. As we have seen, adolescents, at least by the time they are fifteen or so, make decisions using the same basic cognitive processes as adults use (Beyth-Marom et al., 1993; Furbey & Beyth-Marom, 1992) (see Figure 14.2). By the same token, plenty of adults fall prey to the personal fable that they won't be harmed by engaging in risky activity.

If adolescents use the same decision-making processes as adults, and if adolescents are no more likely than adults to think of themselves as invulnerable, why do adolescents behave in ways that are excessively risky? One answer may involve the different ways in which adolescents and adults value the different potential consequences of a risky decision—in other words, differences in *what* they think, not *how* they think (Moore & Gullone, 1996). For example, an individual's decision to try cocaine at a party may involve evaluating a number of different consequences, including the legal and health risks, the pleasure the drug may induce, and the way in which one will be judged (both positively and negatively) by the other people present. Whereas an adult and an adolescent may both consider all these consequences, the adult may place relatively more weight on the health risks of trying the drug, whereas the adolescent may place relatively more weight on the social consequences of not trying.

There is also evidence, as we discussed in "Physical Development in Adolescence," that the gap between the activation of brain regions responsible for **sensation seeking** and the maturation of the brain systems that control judgment, decision making, and impulse control, may play a role in adolescent risk taking (Steinberg, 2008). Several researchers have noted that adolescents may differ from adults in important ways that are not captured by measures of logical reasoning, such as susceptibility to peer pressure, impulsivity, orientation to the immediate rather than the more distant future, or

sensation seeking The tendency of individuals to strive for novel and intense experiences.

INTERIM SUMMARY 14.3
Adolescent Risk Taking

Explanations of Adolescent Risk Taking

■ Two widely held beliefs to explain adolescent risk taking are that adolescents are less logical than adults and that adolescents are more likely than adults to develop personal fables. Neither of these theories have found much research support.

■ Instead, heightened risk taking in adolescence may involve the different ways in which adults and adolescents value the different potential consequences of a risky decision— differences in *what* they think, not *how* they think.

■ There is also evidence that links adolescent risk taking to certain changes in the brain that take place during this time. Specifically, there is an increase in **sensation seeking** in early adolescence that precedes the maturation of brain regions responsible for impulse control and thinking ahead.

■ The context in which individuals spend time matters too. A good deal of adolescents' risk taking takes place in contexts where they are unsupervised and exposed to tremendous peer pressure to engage in risky behavior.

fun seeking. Not surprisingly, individuals who are overconfident, competitive, and high in sensation seeking (i.e., they enjoy novel and intense experiences) are more likely to engage in various types of risky behaviors than their peers (Miller & Byrnes, 1997).

The context in which individuals spend time matters, too. A good deal of adolescents' risk taking takes place in contexts where they are unsupervised and exposed to tremendous peer pressure to engage in risky behavior (Byrnes, 1997). The effect of peers on adolescent risk taking is clearly evident in studies of driving accidents. Having multiple passengers in the car increases the risk of crashes dramatically among sixteen- and seventeen-year-old drivers, significantly among eighteen- and nineteen-year-old drivers, and not at all among adults. Consistent with this, in one recent experiment, adolescents, college undergraduates, and adults who were either alone or in a room with their friends played a video driving game that permitted risky driving— for instance, driving through an intersection after a traffic light had turned yellow. The researchers found that the mere presence of friends watching their performance increased risk taking among adolescents and undergraduates, but not among adults (Gardner & Steinberg, 2005). (For a summary of this section, see "Interim Summary 14.3: Adolescent Risk Taking.")

ACHIEVEMENT IN SCHOOL

One of the most important settings in which the cognitive developments of adolescence play out is school. In this section, we examine schools for adolescents, as well as why some individuals achieve more than others.

The Transition from Elementary to Secondary School

Early in this century, most school districts in the United States separated youngsters into an elementary school (which had either six or eight grades) and a secondary school (which had either four or six grades). Students changed schools once (either after sixth or eighth grade). But many educators felt that the two-school system was unable to meet the special needs of young adolescents, whose intellectual and emotional maturity was greater than that expected in elementary school, but not yet at the level necessary for high school. During the early years of compulsory secondary education, separate schools for young adolescents—**junior high schools** (which contained the seventh, eighth, and sometimes ninth grade)—were established (Hechinger, 1993). In

junior high school   An educational institution designed during the early era of public secondary education, in which young adolescents are schooled separately from older adolescents.

middle school An educational institution housing seventh- and eighth-grade students along with adolescents who are one or two years younger.

more recent years, the **middle schools**—a three- or four-year school housing the seventh and eighth grades with one or more younger grades—have gained in popularity, replacing junior high schools in many districts.

The development of separate schools for young adolescents meant that individuals would have to change schools one or more times during adolescence. To learn how changing schools affects students' achievement and behavior, researchers have compared arrangements in which students remain in elementary school until eighth grade—that is, where they have one school change—with arrangements in which they move from elementary school into middle or junior high school and, later, into high school—where they change schools twice. In general, this research suggests that school transitions, whenever they occur, can disrupt the academic performance, behavior, and self-image of adolescents. This disruption is generally temporary, however; over time, most youngsters adapt successfully to changing schools, especially when other aspects of their life—the family and peer relations, for example—remain stable and supportive and when the new school environment is well suited for adolescents (Eccles & Roeser, in press).

Not surprisingly, students who have more academic and psychosocial problems before making a school transition cope less successfully (Carlson et al., 1999; Little & Garber, 2004; Roeser, Eccles, & Freedman-Doan, 1999). Factors other than the student's prior record may also influence the adolescent's transition to middle or high school. Students who experience the transition earlier in adolescence have more difficulty with it than those who experience it later (Simmons & Blyth, 1987). And adolescents who have close friends before and during the transition usually adapt more successfully to the new school environment (Wentzel, Barry, & Caldwell, 2004). But we have to qualify this: Students who had been doing well previously benefit from staying with friends, but students who had been doing poorly adjust better if they enroll in a different school away from their friends (Schiller, 1999).

Making the transition from elementary school to middle school can be a challenge for many adolescents.

© David Barber/PhotoEdit

Some experts believe that middle and junior high schools, by and large, fail to meet the particular developmental needs of young adolescents (Eccles & Roeser, in press; Elmore, in press). They have argued that the classroom environment in the typical middle school or junior high school is quite different from that in the typical elementary school. Not only are junior high schools larger and less personal, but middle and junior high school teachers also hold different beliefs about students than do elementary school teachers—even when they teach students of the same chronological age (Midgley, Berman, & Hicks, 1995). Teachers in junior high schools are less likely to trust their students and more likely to emphasize discipline, which creates a mismatch between what students at this age desire (more independence) and what their teachers provide (more control). Teachers in junior high schools also tend to believe that students' abilities are fixed and not easily modified through instruction—a belief that interferes with their students' achievement. In addition, teachers who teach in junior high or middle schools are less likely than other teachers to feel confident about their teaching ability (Eccles & Roeser, in press). It is little surprise that students experience a drop in achievement motivation when they enter middle or junior high school. The issue, according to some, is not that adolescents have to change schools. Rather, it is the nature of the change they must make.

The Best Classroom Climate for Adolescents

According to some writers, our educational system does not encourage or stimulate the type of thinking that takes full advantage of adolescents' emerging capabilities. Rather than encouraging adolescents to think in abstract or relativistic ways, for instance, most of their classes reward the rote memorization of concrete facts and the parroting back of the teacher's "correct" answer. According to one expert, opportunities for real give-and-take in adolescents' schools account for less than 10 percent of the total time spent on instruction (Sternberg, 1994). At a time when individuals are becoming capable of seeing that most issues are too complicated to have one right answer, an educational program stifles this. Although attempts have been made to make the instruction of adolescents more compatible with our understanding of their cognitive development, these efforts have not been widespread. Yet, studies show that teaching that takes advantage of adolescents' developing reasoning abilities can result in students' more sophisticated understanding of the subject matter, especially in science classes (Linn & Songer, 1991, 1993).

Generally speaking, both adolescents and teachers are more satisfied in classes that combine a moderate degree of structure with high student involvement and high teacher support (Vieno et al., 2005; Wentzel, 2002). In these classes, teachers encourage their students' participation but do not let the class get out of control. Classes that are too task oriented—particularly when they also emphasize teacher control—tend to make students feel anxious, uninterested, and unhappy (Moos, 1978). Students do best when their teachers spend a high proportion of time on lessons (rather than on setting up equipment or dealing with discipline problems), begin and end lessons on time, provide clear feedback to students about what is expected of them and about their performance, and give ample praise to students when they perform well (Rutter, 1983). Of course, student achievement is not solely in the hands of their teachers. Adolescents' own attitudes and motivation also play a role.

Achievement Motivation and Beliefs

Individuals differ in the extent to which they strive for success, and this difference in striving—which can be measured independently of sheer ability—helps to account for differences in actual achievement. Two students may be of equal intelligence, but if one student tries much harder than the other to do well in school, their grades will probably differ.

The extent to which an individual strives for success is called his or her **need for achievement** (McClelland et al., 1953). One of the oldest findings in the study of adolescent development is that adolescents who have a strong need for achievement have parents who have set high performance standards, rewarded school success in the past, and encouraged autonomy and independence (Rosen & D'Andrade, 1959; Winterbottom, 1958). Equally important, this training for achievement and independence needs to takes place in the context of a warm parent-child relationship (Shaw & White, 1965).

Adolescents' behavior in school is also influenced by their judgments about their likelihood of succeeding or failing. Students who believe that they are good at math, for instance, will take more and more difficult math courses than their peers. But because course selection influences subsequent achievement (students who take more challenging math classes perform better on math tests), and achievement in turn influences students' beliefs about their abilities (students who do well on math examinations come to see themselves as better math students), a cycle is set in motion in

need for achievement A need that influences the extent to which an individual strives for success in evaluative situations.

Students who are intrinsically, rather than extrinsically, motivated, perform better and achieve more in school.

intrinsic motivation Motivation based on the pleasure one will experience from mastering a task.

extrinsic motivation Motivation based on the rewards one will receive for successful performance.

which students' beliefs, abilities, and actual achievement have a reciprocal influence on each other (Marsh & Yeung, 1997).

A number of studies indicate that students' beliefs about their abilities exert a particularly strong influence on their motivation and effort, which in turn influences their scholastic performance (Mac Iver, Stipek, & Daniels, 1991; Pintrich, Roeser, & De Groot, 1994). To understand this process, it is necessary to draw a distinction between **intrinsic motivation** (sometimes referred to as *mastery motivation*) and **extrinsic motivation** (sometimes referred to as *performance motivation*). Individuals who are intrinsically motivated strive to achieve because of the pleasure they get out of learning and mastering the material. Individuals who are extrinsically motivated strive to achieve because of the rewards they get for performing well and the punishments they receive for performing poorly (see Figure 14.3).

You probably know individuals who are genuinely interested in what they learn in school, and others whose main concern is really just their grade-point average. It turns out that these two approaches to achievement have very different psychological correlates and consequences. Adolescents who believe that they are competent are more likely to be intrinsically motivated and to maintain their efforts to do well in school (Pintrich et al., 1994). In contrast, adolescents who have doubts about their abilities

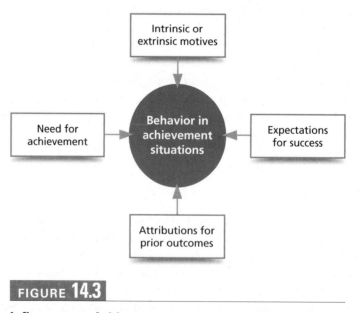

FIGURE 14.3

Influences on Achievement

Adolescents' behavior in achievement situations is influenced by their attitudes, expectations, beliefs, and motives. Students who have a strong need for achievement, expect to succeed, believe that success comes from working hard, and are intrinsically motivated are more likely to be high achievers.

are more likely to be extrinsically motivated and to be more susceptible to feelings of anxiety and hesitation in the face of challenge. Although extrinsically motivated adolescents want to do well in school, the source of their motivation puts them on shaky ground.

You read earlier that adults—parents and teachers, for instance—can affect adolescents' motivation to do well in school. It is also true that adults affect the extent to which an adolescent's achievement motives are intrinsic or extrinsic. When adults attempt to control an adolescent's achievement behavior through rewarding good grades (e.g., by giving prizes or money), punishing bad grades (e.g., by restricting privileges), or excessively supervising their performance (e.g., by constantly checking up on whether they are doing their homework), adolescents are more likely to develop an extrinsic orientation and, as a result, are less likely to do well in school. In contrast, adolescents whose parents encourage their autonomy, provide a cognitively stimulating home environment, and are supportive of school success (without rewarding it concretely) tend to perform better in the classroom (Deci & Ryan, 1985; Ginsburg & Bronstein, 1993; Gottfried, Fleming, & Gottfried, 1998).

How students interpret their successes and failures—what psychologists refer to as **achievement attribution**—is also important (Dweck & Wortman, 1980). Generally speaking, individuals attribute their performance to a combination of four factors: ability, effort, task difficulty, and luck. When individuals succeed and attribute their success to internal causes, such as their ability or effort, they are more likely to approach future tasks confidently and with self-assurance. If individuals attribute their success to external factors outside their control, however—such as luck or an easy assignment—they remain unsure of their abilities. Not surprisingly, scholastically successful individuals, who tend to be high in achievement motivation, are likely to attribute their successes to internal causes (Carr, Borkowski, & Maxwell, 1991; Randel, Stevenson, & Witruk, 2000) (see Figure 14.4).

How youngsters interpret their failures is also important. Some youngsters try harder in the face of failure, whereas others withdraw and exert less effort. When individuals attribute their failures to a lack of effort, they are more likely to try harder on future tasks (Dweck & Licht, 1980). But individuals who attribute their failure to factors that they feel cannot be changed (bad luck, lack of ability, task difficulty) are more likely to feel helpless and to exert less effort in subsequent situations. One important implication of this is that parents and teachers should encourage students to view their performance in school as primarily due to effort, rather than ability. That way, when they don't succeed (as is the case for all students from time to time), their response will be to try harder. In contrast, students who are told that they haven't done well because of a lack of ability ("You've never been good at foreign languages," "Girls just aren't as good at science as boys") see trying harder the next time as pointless.

Environmental Influences on Achievement

Ability, beliefs, and motivation may play a large role in influencing individual performance, but context also matters (Eccles & Roeser, in press). Many of the differences in achievement that are observed among adolescents result from differences in the schools and classrooms where their abilities, beliefs, and motives are expressed, and in the home and neighborhood contexts in which these factors develop.

School environments differ markedly—in physical facilities, in opportunities for pursuing academically enriched programs, and in classroom atmospheres. For example, students are more engaged and achieve more in schools that are more personal, less departmentalized, and less rigidly tracked, and in which team teaching is used more frequently (Gamoran, 1992; Lee & Smith, 1993). Unfortunately, many school districts, plagued with shrinking tax bases, are characterized by decaying school buildings, outdated equipment, and textbook and teacher shortages. In some schools,

achievement attribution The belief one holds about the causes of one's successes and failures.

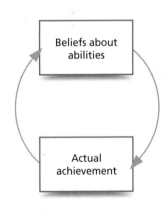

FIGURE **14.4**

The Reciprocal Relation Between Beliefs and Achievement

The links between students' beliefs about their abilities and their actual achievement work in both directions. Students' school performance affects how they view their abilities, which in turn affect their subsequent performance.

problems with crime and discipline are so overwhelming that attention to these matters takes precedence over learning and instruction. As a result, many young people who genuinely want to succeed are held back not by a lack of talent or motivation but by a school environment that makes academic success virtually impossible. Students who attend schools with a high concentration of poor, minority students are especially disadvantaged, as are students who attend schools with a high proportion of students from single-parent families (Bankston & Caldas, 1998; Pong, 1998).

The school, of course, is not the only environment that makes a difference in adolescents' achievement; indeed, few would argue that schools alone should accept full responsibility for adolescents who do not perform up to their abilities. If anything, the evidence suggests that important aspects of the home environment are better predictors of adolescents' academic achievement than are features of the school environment (Coleman et al., 1966; Steinberg, 1996). Studies have shown that adolescents' achievement is directly related to their parents' values and expectations (Jodl et al., 2001). Parents who encourage school success set higher standards for their child's school performance and homework and have higher aspirations for their child, which in turn contributes to school success (Entwisle & Hayduk, 1988; Wilson & Wilson, 1992).

Parents who encourage school success also have values that are consistent with doing well in school, and they structure the home environment to support academic pursuits. Thus, the messages children receive from their teachers are echoed at home (Jodl et al., 2001; Kurdek & Sinclair, 1988; Sui-Chu & Willms, 1996). Parents who encourage success are likely to be more involved in their child's education—more likely to attend school programs, to help in course selection, to maintain interest in school activities and assignments, and the like—all of which contribute to students' success (Hill et al., 2004; Hoover-Dempsey & Sandler, 1995; Shumow & Miller, 2001). Parental involvement seems to be an especially strong influence on the achievement of Mexican American youth, perhaps because of the strong emphasis on the importance of the family in Mexican culture (Trusty, Plata, & Salazar, 2003).

One of the most powerful influences on educational achievement is the socioeconomic status of the adolescent's family. Studies have shown over and over that middle-class adolescents score higher on basic tests of academic skills, earn higher grades in school, and complete more years of schooling than their working-class and lower-class peers (Featherman, 1980; Muller, Stage, & Kinzie, 2001; Sewell & Hauser, 1972). Although some of the socioeconomic gaps in school achievement have narrowed, disparities in achievement between the social classes remain strong, and the importance of socioeconomic status in determining educational achievement remains substantial across all ethnic groups (Kao & Tienda, 1998; Hanson, 1994; Teachman & Paasch, 1998). Of course, averages are just that—not all youngsters from affluent backgrounds have higher levels of educational achievement than adolescents from poorer families, and many youngsters from economically disadvantaged households go on to receive college and advanced degrees.

There is also evidence that friends influence adolescents' achievement. Indeed, some studies suggest that friends, not parents, are the most powerful influences on adolescents' day-to-day school behavior, such as doing homework and exerting effort in class (Steinberg, 1996). Parents are stronger influences on long-range educational plans, but what adolescents do in school on a daily basis is more affected by their friends. Indeed, one of the main reasons that adolescents growing up in poor neighborhoods achieve less is that they are often surrounded by peers who are disengaged from school (South, Baumer, & Lutz, 2003).

When most of us think about the influence of adolescents' peers on achievement, we tend immediately to think of the ways in which peers undermine academic success. But studies suggest that the impact of friends on adolescents' school performance depends on the academic orientation of the peer group. Having friends who earn high grades and aspire to further education can enhance adolescents' achievement, whereas having friends who earn low grades or mock school success may interfere with it (Natriello & McDill, 1986; Steinberg, 1996).

In the contemporary United States, the influence of the peer culture on academic achievement is more often negative than positive, though (Bishop et al., 2003; Steinberg, 1996). Perhaps because of this, adolescents with an extremely high orientation toward peers tend to perform worse in school (Fuligni & Eccles, 1993). Conversely, adolescents who are neglected by their peers often have a stronger academic orientation than more popular students (Luthar & McMahon, 1996; Wentzel & Asher, 1995). As they move into middle school, adolescents become increasingly worried about their friends' reactions to success in school. One study found, for example, that by eighth grade, students did not want their classmates to know that they worked hard in school, even though they knew that it would be helpful to convey this impression to their teachers (Juvonen & Murdock, 1995).

Ethnic Differences in Educational Achievement

Among the most controversial—and intriguing—findings in research on adolescents' achievement are those concerning ethnic differences in school success. On average, the educational achievement of African American and Hispanic American students lags behind that of Caucasian students, and all three groups achieve less in school than do Asian American students. These group differences persist even after socioeconomic factors are taken into account (Chen & Stevenson, 1995; Goyette & Xie, 1999; Hedges & Nowell, 1999; Mickelson, 1990; Steinberg, Dornbusch, & Brown, 1992). The academic superiority of Asian American students tends to emerge during the transition into junior high school—when most other students' grades typically decline—and persists through high school and into college (Fuligni, 1994; Fuligni & Witkow, 2004). What has been most puzzling to social scientists, though, is that even though African American and Hispanic American students have educational aspirations and attitudes that are similar to those of Asian American and Caucasian students, they have significantly poorer academic skills, study habits, and school-related behavior (Ainsworth-Darnell & Downey, 1998). If African American and Hispanic American students have the same long-term goals as other students, why do they not behave in similar ways?

Several explanations have been offered. Some writers have argued that even though they have high aspirations in the abstract, many African American and Hispanic youth do not genuinely believe that educational success will have substantial occupational payoff for them, because of prejudice against their ethnic group (Mickelson, 1990; Ogbu, 1974). Although intuitively appealing, this theory has not received convincing empirical support. It is true that adolescents who believe they have been victims of discrimination, or who believe that their opportunities for occupational success are unfairly limited by society, achieve less in school and report more emotional distress than do peers who do not hold these beliefs (Fisher, Wallace, & Fenton, 2000; Taylor et al., 1994). It is not true, however, that African American or Hispanic

There are significant ethnic differences in adolescent achievement. Many studies find that Asian-American students are more successful in school than their peers.

© Susie Fitzhugh

American youngsters are more likely than other adolescents to believe that their opportunities for success are blocked (Steinberg et al., 1992). Indeed, several studies indicate that African American and Hispanic American youth may actually have more optimistic beliefs and positive feelings about school than other students (e.g., Ainsworth-Darnell & Downey, 1998; Voelkl, 1997).

If anything, it may be adolescents' fear of failure, rather than their desire (or lack of desire) to succeed that matters most (Steinberg et al., 1992). Asian American youngsters not only believe in the value of school success but also are very anxious about the possible negative consequences of not doing well in school, both in terms of occupational success and in terms of their parents' disappointment (Eaton & Dembo, 1997; Steinberg et al., 1996).

An alternative account of ethnic differences in achievement stresses differences in ethnic groups' beliefs about ability. Asian cultures tend to place more emphasis on effort than on ability in explaining school success and are more likely to believe that all students have the capacity to succeed (Stevenson & Stigler, 1992). By and large, students from Asian backgrounds tend to be more invested in mastering the material than toward simply performing well—an orientation that, as we saw earlier, contributes to school success (Li, 2006). It is also important to note that Asian students—both in the United States and in Asia—spend significantly more time each week on homework and other school-related activities, and significantly less time socializing and watching television, than do other youth (Asakawa & Csikzentmihalyi, 2000; Steinberg et al., 1996).

Studies of ethnic minority youngsters also show that foreign-born adolescents as well as those who are children of immigrants tend to achieve more in school than do minority youngsters who are second- or third-generation Americans (Fuligni, 1997; Fuligni, Hughes, & Way, in press; Kao, 1999). One explanation for this has been that part of becoming acculturated to American society—at least among teenagers—may be learning to devalue academic success. There is also some evidence that the higher school achievement of immigrant youth—at least among adolescents who have immigrated from Mexico—may be due to the higher quality of the schooling they receive before coming to the United States (Padilla & Gonzalez, 2001). The exceptional achievement of immigrant youth is all the more remarkable in light of the fact that these adolescents typically have much greater family obligations—providing financial support to their parents, for instance—than their American-born peers (Fuligni & Witkow, 2004).

Dropping Out of High School

There was a time when leaving high school before graduating did not have the dire consequences that it does today. With changes in the economy, however, have come changes in the educational requirements for entry into the world of work. Today, how many years of schooling one completes is a powerful predictor of adult occupational success and earnings. Not surprisingly, high school dropouts are far more likely than graduates to live at or near the poverty level, to experience unemployment, to depend on government-subsidized income maintenance programs, to become pregnant while still a teenager, and to be involved in delinquent and criminal activity (Rumberger, 1995).

The proportion of individuals who have not completed high school has declined steadily over the past half century, to about 12 percent. There are huge variations in dropout rates from region to region, however; indeed, in some urban areas, well over 50 percent of all students leave school prematurely (Alexander, Entwisle, & Kabbani, 2001). African American youngsters drop out of high school at a rate only slightly greater than that of Caucasian youngsters (both are near the national average), but Hispanic youngsters drop out at more than twice the rate of other youth (U.S. Bureau of the Census, 2006) (see Figure 14.5). One reason for this is the large proportion of Hispanic youth who are not English-speaking; among Hispanic youth a lack of proficiency in English is a major reason for dropping out (Stanton-Salazar & Dornbusch, 1995).

Given the findings on educational achievement discussed earlier, the other correlates of dropping out come as no surprise. Adolescents who leave high school before graduating are more likely to come from lower socioeconomic levels, poor communities, large families, single-parent families, permissive or disengaged families, and households where little reading material is available (Alexander et al., 2001; Rumberger, 1995). Coupled with this disadvantage in background, adolescents who drop out of high school also are more likely to have had a history of poor school performance, low school involvement, multiple changes of schools, poor perfor-

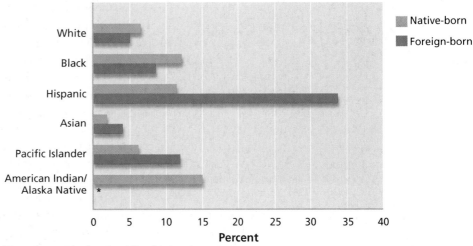

*Reporting standards not met (too few cases).

Ethnic Differences in the Rate of Dropping Out of School

There are substantial ethnic differences in dropout rates. Hispanic students are far more likely to leave school early than their African American or Caucasian peers. Although the dropout rate of Asian American students has not been tracked over as long a period, current dropout rates among Asian American students are substantially lower than in any other group.

mance on standardized tests of achievement and intelligence, negative school experiences, and a variety of behavioral problems, such as excessive aggression (Rumberger & Larson, 1998). Many high school dropouts have had to repeat one or more grades in elementary school; indeed, having been held back is one of the strongest predictors of dropping out (Janosz et al., 1997; Rumberger, 1995).

Dropping out of high school is not so much a discrete decision as the culmination of a long process (Alexander et al., 2001; Garnier, Stein, & Jacobs, 1997). Specific events may trigger a student's final decision to leave school—a suspension for misbehavior, a failed course, an unintended pregnancy, or the lure of a job. But by and large, dropping out is a process characterized by a history of repeated academic failure and increasing alienation from school (Jordan, Lara, & McPartland, 1996).

Beyond High School

Several decades ago, a discussion of school achievement in adolescence might have ended with an examination of high school. But in contemporary America, the vast majority of adolescents enroll in college.

The Transition from High School to College The enrollment of American students in colleges and universities grew dramatically between 1950 and 1970. Today, three-fourths of high school graduates enroll in college, two-thirds of them immediately after graduation (National Center for Education Statistics, 1999; Pennington, 2003). Although there were large increases in the enrollment of minority youth during the 1970s, the proportion of minority youth enrolled in higher education fell during the early 1980s, primarily because of reductions in the availability of financial aid (Baker & Velez, 1996). The proportion of African American and Hispanic high school graduates enrolled in college has increased somewhat in recent years, however (National Center for Education Statistics, 2006). Today, close to 70 percent of Caucasian high school graduates, and more than 60 percent of African American and Hispanic high school graduates, go directly into college (see Figure 14.6). Youth from immigrant families, despite the fact that their parents typically did not attend American colleges

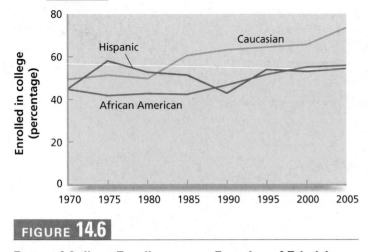

FIGURE **14.6**

Rates of College Enrollment as a Function of Ethnicity

The proportion of African American and Hispanic high school graduates enrolled in college has increased in recent years. Today, close to 70 percent of Caucasian high school graduates and more than 60 percent of African American and Hispanic high school graduates go directly into college. Changes in rates of college enrollment have not been tracked over as long a time period for Asian Americans, but current enrollment rates are higher among Asian Americans than any other group. *Source:* Data from National Center for Educational Statistics (2006).

themselves, and despite often having to support their family financially, are just as likely to enroll in and succeed in college as are American-born youth (Fuligni & Witkow, 2004).

In some respects, the transition from high school to college parallels the transition from elementary to secondary school. For many students, going to college means entering an even larger, more formidable, and more impersonal environment. For some, the transition may coincide with other life changes, such as leaving home, breaking off or beginning an important relationship, or having to manage one's own residence or finances for the first time.

As a consequence of all these factors, although many more American adolescents enroll in college today than in previous years, a very large number do not graduate (Elmore, in press). Only half of all students who enroll in a four-year college complete their degree within six years (National Center for Education Statistics, 2006). Perhaps as a consequence of increasing accessibility, poor matching, and a lack of "consumer" knowledge among college applicants, rates of college attrition are extremely high: One-third of students who enter college in the United States leave after just one year. And while it is true that many of the students who leave after one year eventually finish their degree program, it is also true that one-third of all students who enroll in college never finish. In other words, although a great deal has been done to make college entrance more likely, rates of college graduation lag far behind rates of enrollment (Pennington, 2003).

The Non-College-Bound The problems associated with moving from high school to college pale in comparison, however, with the problems associated with not going to college at all (Hamilton & Hamilton, in press). In general, college graduates earn substantially more income over their lifetime than do individuals who attend college but do not graduate, and these individuals in turn earn much more than students who do not attend college at all (Halperin, 2001; William T. Grant Foundation Commission on Work, Family, and Citizenship, 1988).

One of the unfortunate byproducts of our having made postsecondary education so accessible—and so expected—is that we have turned our backs on individuals who do not go directly to college, even though they compose *one-third* of the adolescent population. As many writers have noted, our secondary schools are geared almost exclusively toward college-bound youngsters (Krei & Rosenbaum, 2001).

Studies of high schools have found that opportunities for learning and for higher-order thinking are much greater in college-prep classes than in the general or vocational tracks. In addition to this, students who are not headed for college—some by choice, others by unavoidable circumstance—find that their high schools have not prepared them at all for the world of work. Even those who complete school and earn a diploma—who have done what they were supposed to do as adolescents—may have a hard time finding employment and a nearly impossible time finding a satisfying, well-paying job. As a consequence, many individuals who do not go to college spend their early adult years floundering between periods of part-time work, underemployment (working at a job that is less challenging than one would like), and unemployment.

One important factor contributing to the difficulties faced by adolescents who do not go to college has been the change in the world of work. As manufacturing jobs began to be replaced by minimum-wage service jobs, the chances of making a decent living without at least two years of college experience have worsened appreciably. Today, young adults without college experience often must try to make ends meet on minimum-wage jobs—jobs that offer little in the way of promotion or advancement. The economic problems faced by non-college-bound youth have been compounded by the escalating costs of such essentials as housing and health care.

Given the high dropout rate already characteristic of most colleges, the answer to the problem does not seem to be simply to encourage more individuals to continue their education past high school. Obviously, for those who want a postsecondary education, we should make every attempt to see that they can obtain and afford it. But what about those adolescents who just are not interested in a college degree? How can these individuals be helped?

Experts believe that one potential answer involves strengthening the links between the worlds of school and work during high school (Hamilton & Hamilton, in press). In most other industrialized countries, non-college-bound youth begin apprenticeships during their last two years of compulsory school, so that by the time they have completed their formal schooling, they are well trained to take on skilled jobs (Hamilton & Hamilton, in press). Instead of just dumping such adolescents into the labor force at graduation, as we do in America, schools and communities provide training, career counseling, and job placement services throughout high school. In most contemporary American high schools, counseling is geared toward helping college-bound students continue their education. Billions of dollars, in the form of financial aid and subsidized public college tuition, are given to the college-bound in America. Some critics have suggested that we should spend just as much time and money helping the other third of the adolescent population make their transition into adulthood as smooth as possible (Wald, 2005). (For

Arnold Gold/The New Haven Register

Changes in the labor force have made it almost impossible for a young adult to land more than a minimum wage job without having gone to college.

INTERIM SUMMARY 14.4

Achievement in School	
The Transition from Elementary to Secondary School	■ Making the transition from elementary school to secondary school can disrupt the academic performance, behavior, and self-image of adolescents.
	■ Students who have more academic and psychosocial problems before making this school transition cope less successfully.
The Best Classroom Climate for Adolescents	■ Rather than encouraging adolescents to think in abstract or relativistic ways, most students' classes reward the rote memorization of concrete facts. At a time when individuals are becoming capable of seeing that most issues are too complicated to have one right answer, this approach to schooling is problematic.
	■ Generally speaking, both adolescents and teachers are more satisfied in classes that combine a moderate degree of structure with high student involvement and high teacher support.
Achievement Motivation and Beliefs	■ The extent to which an individual strives for success is called the **need for achievement**. Adolescents who have a strong need for achievement have parents who set high performance standards, reward school success, and encourage autonomy and independence.

(continued)

INTERIM SUMMARY **14.4** (continued)

Achievement in School

	■ Adolescents' behavior in school is also influenced by their judgments about their likelihood of succeeding or failing, their motivation, and their attributions for success and failure.
	■ Intrinsically motivated individuals strive to achieve because of the pleasure they get out of learning and mastering the material. Extrinsically motivated individuals strive to achieve because of the rewards they get for performing well and the punishments they receive for performing poorly.
	■ When individuals attribute their failures to a lack of effort they are more likely to try harder on future tasks. Individuals who attribute their failure to factors that they feel cannot be changed are more likely to feel helpless and to exert less effort in subsequent situations.
Environmental Influences on Achievement	■ Context also influences performance—school environments differ markedly in ways that affect student success.
	■ Important aspects of the home environment are better predictors of adolescents' academic achievement than are features of the school environment.
	■ Studies have shown that adolescents' achievements are directly related to their parents' values and expectations. In addition, the socioeconomic status of the adolescents' family impacts educational achievement.
	■ Adolescents who are friends with high-achieving students do better in school, whereas those whose friends perform poorly in school do worse.
Ethnic Differences in Achievement	■ On average, the educational achievement of African American and Hispanic American students lags behind that of Caucasian students, and all three groups achieve less in school than do Asian American students.
	■ Studies have linked these differences to ethnic differences in beliefs about the causes of success and failure and to differences in beliefs about the consequences of doing poorly in school
	■ Studies of ethnic minority youngsters also show that foreign-born adolescents as well as those who are children of immigrants tend to achieve more in school than do minority youngsters who are second- or third-generation Americans.
Dropping Out of High School	■ High school dropouts are far more likely than graduates to live at or near the poverty level, to experience unemployment, to depend on government-subsidized income maintenance programs, to become pregnant while still a teenager, and to be involved in delinquent and criminal activity.
	■ Dropping out of high school is not so much a discrete decision as the culmination of a long history of repeated academic failure and increasing alienation from school.
Beyond High School	■ Today, three-fourths of high school graduates enroll in college; two-thirds immediately after graduation. However, rates of college graduation lag far behind rates of enrollment.
	■ Individuals who do not go to college are often unprepared for the world of work.
	■ Experts believe that adolescents who do not go on to college would have an easier time if the links between the worlds of school and work were strengthened.

a summary of this section, see "Interim Summary 14.4: Achievement in School.")

WORK AND OCCUPATIONAL DEVELOPMENT

Although most individuals do not enter into full-time employment until they are young adults, many teenagers, especially in the United States, hold part-time jobs while in high school (Staff, Messersmith, & Schulenberg, in press). More high school students are working today than ever before, and those who do are working for considerably more hours than adolescents have in the past (Mortimer, 2003; National Research Council, 1998) (see Figure 14.7). The average high school sophomore puts in close to fifteen hours per week at a job, and the average senior works about twenty hours per week (Mortimer, 2003).

Although in the past it was young people from less affluent families who were more likely to work, today this is no longer the case. Working during high school is just as common among middle-class teenagers as it is among poor youth (National Center for Education Statistics, 2006). Working is also more common among Caucasian than among non-Caucasian students, with employment rates being lowest among African American youth. Male and female adolescents are equally likely to be employed, although they often work in very different types of jobs (Steinberg & Cauffman, 1995).

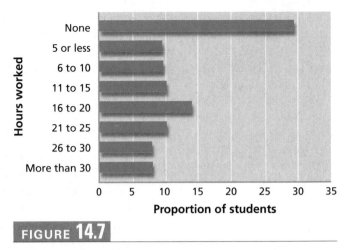

FIGURE 14.7

Working During the School Year

A dramatic increase occurred between 1940 and 1980 in the proportion of American students who work during the school year. Today, the average high school sophomore puts in close to fifteen hours per week at a job, and the average senior works about twenty hours per week.

Working and Adolescent Development

Most people believe that working builds character, teaches adolescents about the real world, and helps young people prepare for adulthood. These assumptions are not generally supported by research, however. Indeed, studies indicate that the benefits of working during adolescence have probably been overstated and, moreover, that intensive employment during the school year may even have some costs to young people's development and preparation for adult work.

Studies of contemporary youth, for example, generally do not support the view that holding a job makes adolescents become more personally responsible and "learn the value of a dollar" (Mortimer & Johnson, 1998; Wright, Cullen, & Williams, 1997). Because the average working teenager earns around $400 each month, holding a job potentially provides many opportunities for learning how to budget, save, and use money responsibly. Few teenagers exercise a great deal of control when it comes to managing their wages, however. The majority of working teenagers spend most of their wages on their own needs and activities. Few adolescents who work save a large percentage of their income for their education, and fewer still use their earnings to help their families with household expenses. Instead, wages are spent on designer clothing, expensive stereo equipment, movies, and eating out (Steinberg, Fegley, & Dornbusch, 1993). Ironically, the very experience that many adults believe builds character may, in reality, teach adolescents undesirable lessons about work and the meaning of money.

Moreover, adolescents who have jobs often express cynical attitudes toward work and endorse unethical business practices, two aspects of "character building" that few adults have in mind when they suggest that teenagers hold jobs. For example, workers are more likely than nonworkers to agree with such statements as "People who work harder at their jobs than they have to are a little crazy" and "In my opinion, it's all right for workers who are paid a low salary to take little things" (Steinberg et al., 1982). One study found high rates of misconduct among adolescent workers (e.g., stealing from employers, lying about the number of hours worked), even in the early months of their first jobs (Ruggiero, Greenberger, & Steinberg, 1982). And adolescents who work long hours (twenty-plus hours weekly) are less satisfied with their lives than are adolescents who work fewer hours (Fine, Mortimer, & Roberts, 1990). In smaller doses (less than 20 hours per week), however, working does not seem to have either a positive or negative effect on adolescents' psychological development (Staff et al., in press).

What can we make of these findings? Why would working long hours make youngsters more cynical about work and less satisfied with their lives? Perhaps the answer has something to do with the nature of the work most adolescents perform. Think for a moment about the job environment of most teenagers—or perhaps the environment you worked in as a teenager if you had a job: wrapping burgers at a fast-food restaurant, bagging groceries, staffing the cash register at a store in the mall. The work generally is dull, monotonous, and sometimes stressful (Greenberger & Steinberg, 1986). Even if you have never held such a job, you can certainly imagine that working under these conditions could make people feel cynical and protective of their own interests.

A second question that has received a fair amount of research attention concerns the impact of working on adolescents' involvement in other activities, most notably, schooling. Here studies indicate that the issue is not whether a teenager works, but how much (Staff et al., in press). Many experts now believe that working more than twenty hours a week may jeopardize adolescents' school performance and engagement (National Research Council, 1998). Youngsters who work long hours miss school more often, are less likely to participate in extracurricular activities, enjoy school less, spend less time on homework, and earn lower grades. These results occur both because youngsters who are less interested in school choose to work longer hours, and because working long hours leads to disengagement from school (Schoenhals, Tienda, & Schneider, 1998; Safron, Sy, & Schulenberg, 2003; Warren, 2002). There is no evidence that summer employment, even for long hours, affects school performance, however, suggesting that the negative impact of working on school performance may be due to the time demands of having a job while going to school (Oettinger, 1999).

Although the impact of working on students' grades and achievement test scores is small—about a third of a letter grade—several studies indicate that extensive employment during the school year may take its toll on students in ways that are not revealed by looking only at grade-point averages. Students who work a great deal, for example, report paying less attention in class, exerting less effort on their studies, and skipping class more frequently (Steinberg & Dornbusch, 1991). Additionally, when students work a great deal, they often develop strategies for protecting their grades. These strategies include taking easier courses, cutting corners on homework assignments, copying homework from friends, and cheating (Greenberger & Steinberg, 1986). Teachers express concern about the excessive involvement of students in afterschool jobs (Bills, Helms, & Ozcan, 1995), and some teachers may respond to an influx of students into the workplace by lowering classroom expectations, assigning less homework, and using class time for students to complete assignments that otherwise would be done outside of school (Bills et al., 1995). As a consequence, when large numbers of students in a school are employed, even nonworkers' schooling may be affected.

Some studies have asked if keeping teenagers busy with work will keep them out of trouble. Contrary to popular belief, employment during adolescence does not deter delinquent activity (Steinberg & Cauffman, 1995). In fact, several studies suggest that working long hours may actually be associated with *increases* in problem behavior (Gottfredson, 1985; Rich & Kim, 2002; Wright et al., 1997), although at least one study reports that the higher rate of problem behavior among working adolescents is due to the fact that delinquent youth are simply more likely to choose to work long hours than their peers (Paternoster et al., 2003). Many studies also have found that smoking, drinking, and drug use is higher among teenage workers than nonworkers, especially among students who work long hours (Mihalic & Elliott, 1997; Mortimer & Johnson, 1998; Wu, Schlenger, & Galvin, 2003). Although some writers have proposed that adolescents who are already inclined toward smoking or using drugs and alcohol are more likely to choose to work long hours (e.g., Bachman & Schulenberg, 1993), recent analyses suggest that alcohol and drug use both leads to, and follows from, intensive employment. That is, students who use alcohol and other drugs are more likely to want to work long hours, but increases in work hours lead to increases in cigarette, drug, and alcohol use (Paschall, Flewelling, & Russell, 2004; Safron et al., 2003; Steinberg et al., 1993).

Why should working lead to smoking, drinking, and drug use? The impact of extensive employment on adolescent drug and alcohol use probably reflects the fact that adolescents who work long hours have more discretionary income to spend on drugs and alcohol. In addition, drug and alcohol use are more common among adolescents who work under conditions of high job stress than among their peers who work for comparable amounts of time and money but under less stressful conditions. But the reality is that many adolescents work in stressful work settings, like fast-food restaurants (Greenberger, Steinberg, & Vaux, 1981). It may also be that working long hours disrupts adolescents' relationships with their parents, and this, in turn, leads to problem behavior (Roisman, 2002). Whatever the reason, the impact of school-year employment on drug and alcohol use persists over time. Individuals who worked long hours as teenagers drink and use drugs more in their late twenties than their peers who worked less or not at all (Mihalic & Elliott, 1997).

Influences on Occupational Choices

Although the part-time jobs most teenagers hold have little to do with the work they will do as adults, adolescence is nevertheless when individuals begin to develop ideas about their future careers. What makes one individual choose to become an attorney and another decide to be a teacher? Why do some students pursue careers in psychology while others major in computer science?

Many theorists who are interested in why people enter different occupational fields have examined the role of personality factors—traits, interests, and values—in the process of career selection. Certain occupational environments are well suited to individuals with certain personalities; others are not. From this vantage point, successful career choice requires matching a person's unique interests and personality characteristics with a vocation that allows the expression of these traits. By answering questions on a standardized personality inventory, an individual can determine which basic personality dimensions are characteristic of himself or herself and then examine directories in which occupations have been classified according to the same typology. Someone who is artistic, social, and enterprising, for example, would be better suited to a career in acting than in accounting.

A different approach to understanding vocational choice focuses on work values, which reflect the different sorts of rewards individuals seek from their work (e.g., Johnson, 2002). When you finish your education, what will you look for in a job? For example, are you most interested in making a lot of money, in having a secure job, or in having a job that permits you to have a lot of vacation time? According to most theories of work values, there are seven basic types of work rewards that define individuals' work values: *extrinsic rewards* (e.g., income), *security* (e.g., job stability), *intrinsic rewards* (e.g., being able to be creative or to learn things from work), *influence* (e.g., having authority over others or power over decision making), *altruistic rewards* (e.g., helping others), *social rewards* (e.g., working with people you like), and *leisure* (e.g., opportunity for free time or vacation). Individuals choose jobs based on the relative importance of these various work rewards to them.

One problem is that many contemporary adolescents have unrealistic and overly optimistic ideas about the rewards they will derive from their future work. The sad truth is that very large proportion of adolescents aspire to levels of work rewards that they are unlikely to ever attain (Schneider & Stevenson, 1999). One specific problem is that adolescents tend to rate almost all work rewards very highly, optimistically believing that they can find jobs that satisfy multiple rewards simultaneously. When they actually enter their first full-time adult jobs, though, they soon discover that it is difficult, if not impossible, to have a career in which one makes a lot of money, is creative, helps other people, enjoys job security, and has a lot of free time, for example. As individuals move out of adolescence and into young adulthood, they become both somewhat disillusioned and more specific and focused on what they want from a job, abandoning the unrealistic notion that one can "have it all" (Roberts, O'Donnell, & Robins, 2004). The degrees to which they value the extrinsic, altruistic, and social rewards of jobs, which are all strongly valued when individuals are seniors in high school, decline most dramatically, whereas the values they place on intrinsic rewards and job security, which are also strong at the end of high school, remain strong (Johnson, 2002) (see Figure 14.8).

There are important limitations to theories of career choice that are based solely on personality traits or reward preferences assessed in adolescence, however. First, interests and abilities are not fixed during adolescence and young adulthood (Mortimer & Lorence, 1979). They continue to develop and change during the adult years (Johnson, 2002). A second problem with theories of career choice that emphasize personality traits or work values is that they may underestimate the importance of other factors that influence and shape vocational decisions. Many career decisions are influenced more by individuals' beliefs about what sorts of jobs are accessible or "appropriate" for them rather than by their interests and preferences (Johnson, 2002). It is all well and good, for example, for an adolescent to discover that he or she is well suited for a career in medicine, but the realization is of little value if the young person's family cannot afford the cost of college or medical school. An adolescent girl may discover through taking a vocational preference inventory that she is well suited for work in the area of construction or building, but she may find that her parents, peers, teachers, and potential employers all discourage her from following this avenue of employment. Put most simply, career choices are not made solely on the basis of individual preference; they are the result of an interaction among individual preference, social influence, and important forces in the broader social environment. It is to these influences and forces that we now turn.

As is the case with school achievement, no influence on occupational choice is stronger than socioeconomic status, and as a result, adolescents' occupational ambitions and achieve-ments are highly correlated with the ambitions and achievements of those around them (Duncan, Featherman, & Duncan, 1972). Youngsters from middle-class families are more likely than their less advantaged peers to aspire to, and enter, middle-class occupations. In addition, apart from their own socioeconomic status, youngsters who have

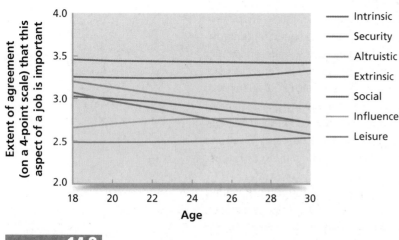

Intrinsic
Security
Altruistic
Extrinsic
Social
Influence
Leisure

FIGURE 14.8

Changes in Work Values During the Transition to Adulthood

The extent to which individuals value different aspects of work changes as they mature into adulthood. The importance individuals place on the extrinsic, altruistic, and social rewards of a job decline.

Source: Social Forces, Volume 80, no. 4, Copyright © 2002 by the University of North Carolina Press. Used by permission of the publisher. www.uncpress.unc.edu.

INTERIM SUMMARY 14.5

Work and Occupational Development

Working During High School	■ The majority of American high school students work during the school year, with the average sophomore putting in close to 15 hours per week at a job and the average senior working about 20 hours per week.
	■ Working during high school is just as common among middle-class teenagers as it is among poor youth.
Working and Adolescent Development	■ Studies indicate that the benefits of working during adolescence have probably been overstated and that intensive employment during the school year may even have some costs to young people's development.
	■ Many experts believe that working more than 20 hours a week may jeopardize adolescents' school performance and engagement and may increase delinquency and substance use.
Influences on Occupational Choices	■ Theorists have examined the role of personality factors—traits, interests, and values—in the process of career selection. A different approach focuses on individuals' work values.
	■ Career choices are the result of an interaction among individual preference, social influence, and important forces in the broader social environment.
	■ No influence on occupational choice is stronger than socioeconomic status. Not surprisingly, adolescents' occupational ambitions and achievements are highly correlated with the ambitions and achievements of those around them.

many friends from middle-class backgrounds are more likely than those who have many friends from lower socioeconomic levels to aspire to high-status occupations (Simpson, 1962). One's socioeconomic status also influences one's work values, with individuals from higher classes more likely to value intrinsic rewards and influence, and less likely to value extrinsic rewards and security. The importance of social class as a determinant of what people look for in their jobs is strong and constant throughout adolescence (Johnson, 2002).

Adolescents' occupational choices are made, of course, within a broader social context that profoundly influences the nature of their plans. At different times, different employment opportunities arise, and young people—particularly by the time they reach the end of their formal schooling, if not earlier—are often very aware of the prospects for employment in different fields. Indeed, one study of inner-city youngsters found that many had developed strong ideas about their future job prospects by the time they were in second grade (Cook et al., 1996)! Understandably, young people often tailor their plans in response to what they perceive as the needs and future demands of the labor market, and the acceptability of given occupational choices within their community. (For a summary of this section, see "Interim Summary 14.5: Work and Occupational Development.")

SUMMING UP AND LOOKING AHEAD

In this chapter we've seen how the growth of advanced thinking abilities transforms many aspects of individuals' lives as they move into, through, and out of adolescence. The child who enters adolescence focused on the immediate, who thinks concretely about right and wrong, and whose ability to see things from others' points of view is still developing grows into the adolescent who thinks about the future, questions authority, and interacts with others in a way that takes into account the fact that different people can look at the same event from different vantage points—and all be correct. By the time they are sixteen, teenagers can think just about as well as adults, at least with regard to their basic information-processing and logical reasoning abilities.

At the same time, however, adolescents' thinking is still limited in important ways, especially during the early part of the decade. They often suffer from a distinctive type of egocentrism, in which they believe that they are not only unique but also the focus of everyone else's attention. Their judgment, although better than it was during childhood, is still immature, and they often make impulsive and risky decisions. In some respects, then, there is still much cognitive development ahead.

Adolescence is also an important time for sorting people onto educational and occupational pathways. We've seen how development and behavior in school and work are affected by the psychological changes of the period, but we've also seen how much context matters. The tremendous importance of socioeconomic status makes it all too likely that the rich get richer and the poor get poorer.

The biological changes of adolescence, which we looked at in the previous chapter, and the cognitive changes of the period, which we examined in the current one, set the stage for equally profound changes in the ways in which adolescents view themselves and relate to family members and peers. That's where our examination of development in adolescence takes us next.

HERE'S WHAT YOU SHOULD KNOW

Did You Get It?

After reading this chapter, you should understand the following:

- The major ways in which thinking changes during adolescence, and the Piagetian and information-processing accounts of these changes
- The ways in which individuals' social perspective taking, reasoning about social conventions, and religious beliefs change in adolescence

- Major explanations of why adolescents engage in risk taking
- Important influences on adolescents' school achievement, as well as basic facts about patterns of educational attainment
- The impact of work experience on adolescent development, and factors that influence later career choices

Important Terms and Concepts

achievement attributions (p. 421)
adolescent egocentrism (p. 407)
deductive reasoning (p. 405)
extrinsic motivation (p. 420)

hypothetical thinking (p. 406)
imaginary audience (p. 407)
inductive reasoning (p. 406)
intrinsic motivation (p. 420)
junior high school (p. 417)

metacognition (p. 407)
middle school (p. 418)
mutual role taking (p. 412)
need for achievement (p. 419)
personal fable (p. 407)

sensation-seeking (p. 416)
social cognition (p. 412)
social conventions (p. 413)
social perspective taking (p. 412)

Socioemotional Development in Adolescence

© Spencer Grant/PhotoEdit

By virtually any indicator, adolescence is longer than it has ever been before, because young people go through puberty (one marker of the beginning of adolescence) earlier, and because they enter into adult roles of work and family (one way to define the end of adolescence) later.

In previous eras, when puberty occurred around fifteen, and when individuals left school and entered the world of work just a few years later, adolescence, at least by these markers, was only a few years long. Today, though, young people are caught between the world of childhood and the world of adulthood for an extremely long time, often longer than a decade. The lengthening of adolescence as a developmental period has had important implications for how young people see themselves, relate to others, and develop psychologically.

Here's an illustration of why this matters. If someone older tells you that people should "Wait until they're married before having sex," you might point out that this was a lot easier when they (or their parents) were growing up. A woman who was born in 1930 went through puberty when she was about fourteen and a half and probably got married when she was around twenty. So if she "waited" before losing her virginity, she waited for about five and a half years. Today, the average girl goes through puberty around twelve and will probably get married when she is in her late twenties. She'll have to wait three times as long!

In this chapter, we look at some of the main psychosocial developments of the adolescent period. We begin with what many consider to be the central psychological task of adolescence—developing an independent identity. Next, we look at two of the main contexts in which psychosocial development takes place: the family and the peer group. Following this, we turn to a discussion of two sets of problems that aren't universal during adolescence, but that affect a large number of teenagers: externalizing problems, like delinquency and aggression, and internalizing problems, like depression and suicide.

Before we begin, though, we're going to start with what may strike you as an odd question: Have there always been adolescents?

THE INVENTION OF ADOLESCENCE

Although this question seems like a simple one with an obvious answer, it actually is pretty complicated. Naturally, there have always been individuals between ten and twenty years old, who have gone through puberty, and whose prefrontal cortex was still maturing. But adolescence as we know it in contemporary society did not really exist until the middle of the nineteenth century (Fasick, 1994). Prior to that time, children were viewed as miniature adults, and the term "child" referred to anyone under the age of eighteen or even twenty-one. The main difference between "children" and "adults" was not their age or their abilities but whether they could own property

(Modell & Goodman, 1990). Thus there was little reason to label some young people as "children" and others as "adolescents." In fact, the word *adolescent* was not widely used before the nineteenth century.

With the Industrial Revolution in the late nineteenth century, however, came profound changes in work, schooling, and family life, and adolescents were among those most affected. Because the economy was moving away from the simple and predictable life known in farming societies, the connection between what individuals learned in childhood and what they would need to know in adulthood grew uncertain. Parents, especially in middle-class families, encouraged their teenagers to prepare for adulthood in school, rather than on the job. Before industrialization, adolescents spent their days working with their parents and other adults close to home. Now they were increasingly likely to spend their days in school with peers of the same age.

Industrialization also changed adolescents standing in the work force. One outcome of industrialization was a shortage of jobs, because new machines replaced many workers. Adolescents were now competing with adults for a limited supply of jobs—and adults didn't like it one bit. A convenient way of dealing with this competition was to remove adolescents from the labor force by turning them into full-time students. To accomplish this, society needed to rationalize differentiating between individuals who were "ready" for work and those who still needed to go to school. Teenagers, who earlier in the century would have been working side by side with adults, were now seen as too immature or too unskilled to carry out similar tasks—even though the adolescents themselves hadn't changed in any meaningful way (Enright et al., 1987). No one wants to admit it, but one reason we force teenagers to go to high school for as long as they must is to make sure that they don't take jobs away from adults! (Kind of puts that awful class you endured as a high school sophomore in a new light, doesn't it?)

Some adults were genuinely interested in protecting adolescents from the dangers of a changing society, of course. Families were moving from small, traditional farming communities, where everyone knew everyone else, to large, crowded, turbulent urban areas. The "evils of city life" (crime and vice) loomed large. Furthermore, factories were hazardous working environments, filled with new and unfamiliar machinery. **Child protectionists** argued that young people needed to be sheltered from the labor force for their own good (Modell & Goodman, 1990).

Whatever the reason, it was not until the late nineteenth century—a little more than 100 years ago—that adolescence became what it is today: a long period of preparation for adulthood, in which young people remain economically reliant on their parents and spend most of their time in school or in leisure activities with people of the same age. As you can imagine, the way adolescence is structured by society gives it a distinctive psychological flavor. Many of the things we take for granted as inherent features

child protectionists Individuals who argued, early in the twentieth century, that adolescents needed to be kept out of the labor force in order to protect them from the hazards of the workplace.

INTERIM SUMMARY 15.1

The Invention of Adolescence

- Adolescence, as we know it in contemporary society, did not really exist until the middle of the nineteenth century.

- As a result of the Industrial Revolution, teenagers were encouraged to prepare for adulthood in school rather than on the job, and over time, adolescents were removed from the labor force.

- Today adolescence is a long period of preparation for adulthood in which young people remain economically reliant on their parents and spend most of their time in school or in leisure activities with people of the same age.

of adolescence—peer pressure, struggles with parents over independence, having an "identity crisis"—are new phenomena. Far more than in previous times, today, one of the most important socioemotional tasks of adolescence is to develop a clearer sense of who you are and where you are headed. (For a summary of this section, see "Interim Summary 15.1: The Invention of Adolescence.")

DEVELOPING AN INDEPENDENT IDENTITY

More novels, movies, television shows, and plays have probably been written about "coming of age"—making the transition from adolescence to adulthood—than any other subject. The list is endless, and as diverse as adolescents themselves: *Hamlet*, *The Catcher in the Rye*, *I Know Why the Caged Bird Sings*, *The House on Mango Street*, *My So-Called Life*, *American Graffiti*, *Y Tu Mamá También*, *The Bluest Eye*, *The Joy Luck Club*, *Stand By Me*, *The Wonder Years*. In all of these stories, an adolescent has a series of experiences that lead to a reevaluation of who he or she is and where he or she is headed. It's not surprising that this theme is so popular—adolescence is one of the most important periods for the development of an independent identity. The dominant view in the study of adolescent identity development is that proposed by Erik Erikson. Although developing a coherent sense of identity appears to take place at a later age than Erikson thought when he first wrote about it, in the 1950s (it probably happens in the early twenties or midtwenties for most people today), his theory of the adolescent identity crisis remains extremely influential.

Erikson's Theoretical Framework

identity versus identity diffusion According to Erikson, the normative crisis characteristic of the fifth stage of psychosocial development, predominant during adolescence, during which a coherent and unique sense of self is formed.

As you read in "The Study of Child Development," Erikson viewed the developing person as moving through a series of eight psychosocial crises over the course of the lifespan. He believed that resolving the crisis of **identity versus identity diffusion** is the chief psychosocial task of adolescence. Before adolescence, the child's identity is like a jigsaw puzzle with many pieces that have not yet been connected. But after this crisis is successfully resolved, these pieces will be joined to form a coherent picture that is unique to the adolescent. According to Erikson, it is not until adolescence that individuals have the mental or emotional capacity to tackle this task. Of the many social roles available in contemporary society, which fits them? The key to resolving the identity crisis, he argued, lies in the adolescent's interactions with others. Responding to the reactions of people who matter, the adolescent selects and chooses from among the many facets that could conceivably become a part of who he or she really is. The other people with whom the young person interacts serve as a sort of mirror that reflects back information about who the adolescent is and who he or she ought to be. Through others' reactions, we learn whether we are graceful or clumsy, nice-looking or unattractive, socially competent or clueless. Perhaps more important, we learn from others what it is we do that we ought to keep doing, and what it is that we ought to stop.

Social Context and Identity Development The social context has a tremendous effect on the nature and outcome of the process of identity development. Clearly, if adolescents' identities grow out of others' responses to them, society will play an important role in determining which sorts of identities are possible alternatives, and of those identities that are genuine options, which are desirable and which are not. As a result, the course of identity development varies across cultures, among different groups within the same society, and over different historical epochs (Kroger, 1993). For example, in the past, most young women assumed that their adult identity would revolve around being a wife and mother. But many more alternative identities are open to women today, and as a result, choosing among different alternatives (What's more important to me, marriage and family or a career? Should I pursue higher education?

What occupation should I aim for? When do I want to get married? Have children?) has become much more complicated.

The rapid rate of social change in today's world has raised new sets of questions for young people (both males and females) to consider—questions not only about their occupation but also about their values, lifestyle, and relationships. Consequently, the likelihood of going through a prolonged and difficult identity crisis is probably greater today than it has ever been.

The Psychosocial Moratorium According to Erikson, the complications inherent in identity development in modern society have created the need for a **psychosocial moratorium**—a "time-out" during adolescence from responsibilities and obligations that might restrict the young person's pursuit of self-discovery. Most adolescents in contemporary America are given a moratorium of sorts by being encouraged to remain in school for a long time, where they can develop plans for the future without making decisions that are impossible to undo.

During the psychosocial moratorium, adolescents can experiment with different roles and identities in a context that permits and encourages this sort of exploration. They can try on different postures, personalities, and ways of behaving. One week, an adolescent girl will spend hours engrossed in *Vogue* or *Seventeen*; the next week she will insist to her parents that she is tired of caring so much about the way she looks. An adolescent boy will come home one day with a tattoo and pierced ear; a few weeks later he will discard this image for Abercrombie & Fitch or Polo (although he may discover that getting rid of the tattoo and piercing is not so simple).

© Andrew Holbrooke/Corbis

Adolescence is often a time for experimentation with different roles and identities.

Although many parents worry about their teenage children going through phases like these, much of this behavior is actually normal experimentation with roles and personalities.

The moratorium Erikson described is an ideal, however, perhaps even a luxury of the affluent. Many young people—possibly most—do not have the economic freedom to enjoy a long time-out before taking on adult responsibilities. For many, alternatives are not open in any realistic sense, and introspection only interferes with the more pressing task of survival. You may know people who have had to drop out of college and take a job they really did not want because of financial pressures. According to Erikson, without a chance to explore, to experiment, and to choose among options for the future, these young people may not realize all that they are capable of becoming. Some might even say that the most important part of going to college is not what you learn in class, but what you learn about yourself.

Determining an Adolescent's Identity Status

Psychologists use the term **identity status** to refer to the point in the identity development process that characterizes an adolescent at a given time (Côté, in press). Most researchers who study identity development this way use an approach developed by James Marcia (1966), which focuses on identity exploration in three areas—work, ideology (values and beliefs), and relationships. Based on responses to an interview or

psychosocial moratorium A period of time during which individuals are free from excessive obligations and responsibilities and can therefore experiment with different roles and personalities.

identity status The point in the identity development process that characterizes an adolescent at a given time.

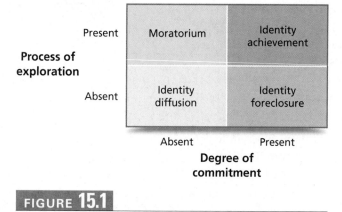

	Degree of commitment	
Process of exploration	Absent	Present
Present	Moratorium	Identity achievement
Absent	Identity diffusion	Identity foreclosure

FIGURE 15.1

Identity Status Categories, as Defined by Exploration and Commitment

Psychologists study the development of identity by interviewing adolescents about work, ideology, and relationships, and then assigning them to one of four identity status categories.

questionnaire, individuals are rated on two dimensions: (1) the degree to which they have made commitments and (2) the degree to which they engaged in a sustained search in the process. Researchers then assign individuals to one of four categories: *identity achievement* (after a period of exploration, the individual has established a coherent sense of identity); *moratorium* (the individual is in the midst of a period of crisis and experimentation); *identity foreclosure* (the individual has made commitments but without a period of crisis or experimentation); and *identity diffusion* (the individual does not have firm commitments and is not currently trying to make them). (See Figure 15.1.)

Generally speaking, research employing this approach has supported many aspects of Erikson's theory (Meeus et al., 1999). Identity achievers score highest on measures of achievement motivation, moral reasoning, intimacy with peers, reflectiveness, and career maturity. Individuals in the moratorium category score highest on measures of anxiety, show the highest levels of conflict over issues of authority, and do not have a firm set of values and beliefs. Individuals in the foreclosure group are the most authoritarian and most prejudiced, have the highest need for social approval and the lowest level of autonomy, and are especially close to their parents. Individuals in a state of identity diffusion display the most psychological and interpersonal problems, are the most socially withdrawn, and report the lowest level of intimacy with peers (Adams, Gullotta, & Montemayor, 1992).

The Development of Ethnic Identity

ethnic identity The aspect of one's sense of identity concerning ancestry or racial group membership.

For adolescents who are not part of the majority culture, integrating a sense of **ethnic identity** into their overall sense of personal identity is an important task of late adolescence, perhaps as important as establishing a coherent occupational, ideological, or interpersonal identity (Fuligni et al., in press; Newman, 2005; Phinney & Alipuria, 1987). Over the past two decades, the process through which ethnic identity develops has received a great deal of research attention, as has the link between ethnic identity and psychological adjustment. Ethnic identity has been studied in samples of African American, Hispanic American, American Indian, Asian American, and Caucasian youth (Spencer & Markstrom-Adams, 1990). In America, Caucasian youth generally have a weaker sense of ethnic identity than their non-Caucasian peers, but many Caucasian adolescents identify strongly with a particular ethnic group (e.g., German, Irish, Italian, Jewish) and derive part of their overall sense of self from this identification (Martinez & Dukes, 1997; Roberts et al., 1999).

The process of ethnic identity development follows the general process of identity development: An event or series of events makes the adolescent realize that others see him as "different," which upsets the unquestioning view he had of himself as a child (Cross, 1978; Kim, 1981, cited in Phinney & Alipuria, 1987). As a result of the crisis, the individual may become immersed in his or her own ethnic group and may turn against the majority culture. Eventually, as the value of having a strong ethnic identity becomes clear, the adolescent establishes a more coherent sense of self that includes this ethnic identity, and with growing confidence he or she attempts to help others deal with their own struggles with similar issues. Consistent with this, a recent study of ethnic identity development found that inner-city adolescents' feelings about their own ethnic group became more positive during both early and middle adolescence (when ethnic identity first becomes salient and individuals become immersed in their own culture) but that actual identity exploration did not really begin until middle adolescence (French et al., 2006).

Do members of ethnic minorities have more difficulty than Caucasian adolescents in resolving the identity crisis? The little research that has been done suggests more similarities than differences. One difference, though, appears to be quite important, if maybe unsurprising: Having a strong ethnic identity is associated with higher self-esteem, stronger feelings of self-efficacy, and better mental health among minority youngsters, whereas the link between ethnic identity and psychological functioning is weaker among Caucasian youth (DuBois et al., 2002; Martinez & Dukes, 1997).

As many writers have noted, however, developing a coherent sense of identity is much more complicated for minority adolescents than for their majority counterparts (Spencer & Dornbusch, 1990). Because identity development is so influenced by the social context in which the adolescent lives, the development of minority adolescents must be understood in relation to the specific context in which they grow up (Garcia Coll et al., 1996). All too often, this context includes racial stereotypes, discrimination, and mixed messages about the costs and benefits of identifying too closely with the majority culture.

According to psychologist Jean Phinney, an expert on this issue, minority youth have four possibilities open to them for dealing with their ethnicity: *assimilation* (i.e., adopting the majority culture's norms and standards while rejecting those of one's own group); *marginality* (i.e., living within the majority culture but feeling estranged and outcast); *separation* (i.e., associating only with members of one's own culture and rejecting the majority culture); and *biculturalism* (i.e., maintaining ties to both the majority and the minority cultures) (Phinney et al., 1994).

© Richard Cohen/Corbis

For ethnic minority youth, developing a sense of ethnic identity is an important challenge.

Advice on which of these paths is most preferable has changed considerably. In the past, minority youth were encouraged, at least by majority society, to assimilate as much as possible. Assimilation, however, has not proven to be as simple as many nonminority individuals imagine (Gil, Vega, & Dimas, 1994). First, although minority youth are told to assimilate, they may be nonetheless excluded from majority society because of their physical appearance or language (Vega et al., 1995). This leads to a situation of marginality, in which the minority youth is on the edge of majority society but is never really accepted as a full-status member.

Second, minority youth who do attempt to assimilate are often scorned by their own communities for trying to "act white." Partly in reaction to this, many minority youth in predominantly Caucasian schools adopt strategies of separation and biculturalism, especially as they get older (Hamm & Coleman, 2001). This is particularly common among African American adolescents, who are often the victims of intense discrimination and prejudice (Sellers et al., 2006; Spencer, 2005). (See Figure 15.2.)

A few studies have compared the ethnic identity orientations of Asian American, African American, Hispanic American, and Caucasian adolescents. In one such study (Rotherham-Borus, 1990), as expected, Caucasian youngsters were more likely to characterize themselves as assimilated (or "mainstream") than were minority students, who were more likely to characterize themselves as bicultural (between 40% and 50%) than as either assimilated or embedded solely within their ethnic group (separated). African American and Puerto Rican adolescents are relatively more likely to be ethnically embedded, whereas Mexican American and Asian American adolescents are more likely to be bicultural (e.g., Phinney et al., 1994). In general, positive mental health among ethnic minority adolescents is associated with having a strong and posi-

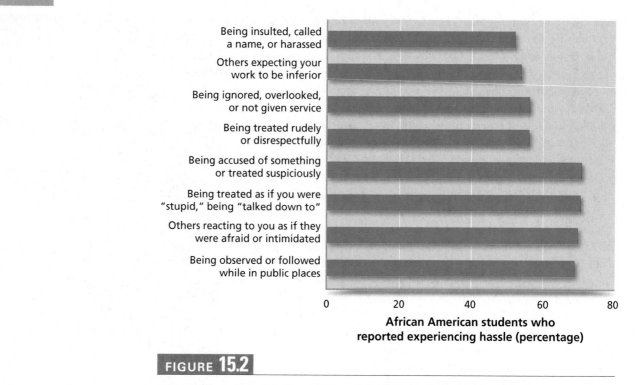

FIGURE **15.2**

African American Students' Reports of Race-Related Hassles

Many African American students report that they are the victims of discrimination. *Source:* "Racial identity matters: The relationship between racial discrimination and psychological functioning in African American adolescents" by R.M. Sellers, N. Copeland-Linder, P.P. Martin, and R.L. Lewis, *Journal of Research on Adolescence,* 16, pp. 187–216. Copyright © 2006 by Blackwell Publishing Ltd. Reproduced with permission of Blackwell Publishing Ltd.

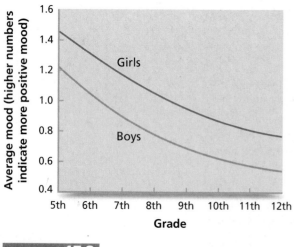

FIGURE **15.3**

Changes in Self-Evaluations in Adolescence

Early adolescence is a time of heightened self-consciousness and greater fluctuation in self-image, which may make a teenager's mood become more negative. *Source:* Larson et al., 2002.

tive ethnic identity and a healthy awareness of the potential for discrimination, but not with outright rejection of the mainstream culture (Umaña-Taylor, 2004; Yasui, Dorham, & Dishion, 2004).

Changes in Self-Esteem

Researchers interested in identity development have also studied self-esteem in adolescence, although studies have not yielded consistent findings. Some studies find that individuals' feelings about themselves decline over the course of adolescence (e.g., Jacobs et al., 2002), but others find that they increase (Cole et al., 2001). In general, however, *changes* in self-perceptions (whether positive or negative) are greater during early adolescence than during middle or late adolescence; from middle adolescence through young adulthood self-esteem either remains at about the same level or increases (Harter, 1998).

More specifically, fluctuations in adolescents' self-image are most likely to occur between the ages of twelve and fourteen. Compared with older adolescents (fifteen years and older) and with preadolescents (eight to eleven years old), early adolescents are more self-conscious and have a more unstable self-image than other youngsters (see Figure 15.3). Younger adolescents are also more prone to feel ashamed than older individuals, which may result from and contribute to their heightened self-consciousness (Reimer, 1996).

Generally speaking, the small but reliable differences between the preadolescents and the early adolescents are greater than those between the younger and the older adolescents, which indicates that the most marked fluctuations in self-image occur during the transition into adolescence, rather than over the course of adolescence itself (Simmons, Rosenberg, & Rosenberg, 1973). As you will read in the next section, early adolescence is also the time of the most dramatic changes in family relationships. (For a summary of this section, see "Interim Summary 15.2: Developing an Independent Identity.")

INTERIM SUMMARY 15.2

Developing an Independent Identity

Erikson's Theoretical Framework	■ Erikson believed that resolving the crisis of **identity versus identity diffusion** is the chief psychological task of adolescence.
	■ Erikson believed that the complications inherent in identity development in modern society have created the need for a **psychological moratorium**—a "time-out" during adolescence from responsibilities and obligations that might restrict the young person's pursuit of self-discovery.
	■ During this moratorium, adolescents can experiment with different roles and identities in a context that permits and encourages this sort of explanation.
Determining an Adolescent's Identity Status	■ The term *identity status* refers to the point in the identity development process that characterizes an adolescent at a given time.
	■ Most researchers who study development this way use an approach that focuses on identity exploration in three areas—work, ideology, and relationships.
	■ Based on responses to an interview or questionnaire, individuals are assigned to one of four categories: identity achievement, moratorium, identity foreclosure, or identity diffusion.
The Development of Ethnic Identity	■ For adolescents who are not part of the majority culture, integrating a sense of **ethnic identity** into their overall sense of personal identity is an important task of adolescence.
	■ Having a strong ethnic identity is associated with higher self-esteem, stronger feelings of self-efficacy, and better mental health among minority youngsters, whereas the link between ethnic identity and psychological functioning is weaker among Caucasian youth.
	■ According to one model, minority youth have four possibilities open to them for dealing with their ethnicity within the context of the larger society: assimilating, remaining marginal, separating, and becoming bicultural.
	■ In general, positive mental health among ethnic minority adolescents is associated with having a strong and positive ethnic identity, but not with outright rejection of the mainstream culture.
Changes in Self-Esteem	■ Some studies find that individuals' feelings about themselves become more negative over the course of adolescence, but others find that they increase.
	■ Compared with older adolescents and with preadolescents, early adolescents are more self-conscious and have a more unstable self-image.

FAMILY RELATIONSHIPS IN ADOLESCENCE

Have you ever noticed that your relationships with others sometimes alternate between periods when things are very smooth and predictable and times when they are not? The same is true in families. Not surprisingly, relationships in families change most dramatically when individual family members or the family's circumstances are changing, since that's when the family's previously established equilibrium will be upset. One period in which family relationships often become unstable is adolescence. A study of interactions between adolescent boys and their parents found that the peak time for this disequilibrium was around ages thirteen and fourteen. The researchers speculate that, because some of this transformation may be driven by puberty, in families with girls, this "disequilibrium" is more likely to occur earlier, around eleven or twelve (Granic et al., 2003).

Adolescents' Relationships with Parents

In most families, there is a shift during adolescence away from patterns of influence and interaction that are unequal to ones in which parents and their adolescent children are on more equal footing (Collins & Laursen, in press). And some evidence indicates that early adolescence—when this shift first begins—may be a time of temporary disruption in the family system. In particular, studies of family interaction suggest that in early adolescence, young people begin to try to play a more forceful role in the family but their parents may not yet acknowledge the adolescents' input. As a result, young adolescents may interrupt their parents more often but have little impact. By middle adolescence, however, teenagers act and are treated much more like adults. They have more influence over family decisions, but they do not need to assert their opinions through interruptions and similarly immature behavior (Grotevant, 1997).

Early adolescence may be a challenging time for the family, as teenagers begin to assert their influence.

To adapt to the changes triggered by the child's entrance into adolescence, family members must have some shared sense of what they are experiencing and how they are changing. Yet in many families parents and children live in "separate realities," perceiving their day-to-day experiences in very different ways (Larson & Richards, 1994). Suppose that a mother and son have a conversation about the boy's schoolwork. She may experience the conversation as a serious discussion, while he may perceive it as an argument. One interesting finding to emerge from recent research on brain maturation in adolescence is that young adolescents may be especially sensitive—perhaps even overreactive—to the emotional signals transmitted by others. A parent may speak to an adolescent in a serious voice, but the adolescent may experience it as anger (Nelson et al., 2005).

Several researchers have studied how the sorts of changes in cognitive abilities you read about in "Cognitive Development in Adolescence" may reverberate throughout the family. Early adolescence is a time of changes in youngsters' views of family relationships and in family members' expectations of one another (Lanz et al., 2001). For example, one study asked adolescents of different ages to compare their actual family with their view of an ideal one in terms of how close and dominant different family members were (Feldman & Gehring, 1988). With age, the gap between adolescents' actual and ideal portraits widened, indicating that as they became older, adolescents became more aware of their families' shortcomings.

Although adolescence is a time of transformation in family relationships for the majority of households, some families adapt more successfully than others to this challenge. In several studies, families have been asked to discuss a problem together, and their interaction is taped and later analyzed. Researchers have found that families with psychologically competent teenagers interact in ways that permit family members to express their autonomy and individuality while remaining attached, or connected, to other family members (Grotevant, 1997). In these families, verbal give-and-take is the norm, and adolescents (as well as parents) are encouraged to express their own opinions, even if this sometimes leads to disagreements. At the same time, however, the importance of maintaining close relationships in the family is emphasized, and individuals are encouraged to consider how their actions may affect other family members (Rueter & Conger, 1995a, 1995b). Indeed, adolescents who are permitted to assert their own opinions within a family context that is secure and loving develop higher self-esteem and more mature coping abilities. Adolescents whose autonomy is stifled are at risk for developing feelings of depression and low self-esteem, whereas those who do not feel connected are at risk for behavior problems (Barber, 1996). These studies remind us that it is important to distinguish between separating from one's parents in a way that nevertheless maintains emotional closeness in the relationship (which is healthy) versus breaking away from one's parents in a fashion that leads to alienation, conflict, and hostility (which is unhealthy) (Beyers et al., 2003).

Adolescents' Relationships with Siblings

Far more is known about adolescents' relations with their parents than about their relations with brothers and sisters. In general, sibling relationships during adolescence have characteristics that set them apart from other family relationships (such as those between adolescents and their parents) as well as from relationships with peers (such as those between adolescents and their close friends) (East, in press; Furman & Buhrmester, 1985; Raffaelli & Larson, 1987). Adolescents rate their sibling relationships as similar to those with their parents in companionship and importance, but as more like friendships with respect to power, assistance, and their satisfaction with the relationship.

Young adolescents often have emotionally charged relationships with siblings that are marked by conflict and rivalry, but also by nurturance and support (Lempers & Clark-Lempers 1992). Conflict between siblings increases as children mature from childhood to early adolescence (Brody, Stoneman, & McCoy, 1994), with adolescents reporting more negativity in their sibling relationships compared with their relationships with peers (Buhrmester & Furman 1990) and less effective conflict resolution than with their parents (Tucker, McHale, & Crouter, 2003). Over the course of adolescence, adolescents' relationships with siblings, and especially with younger siblings, become more egalitarian but more distant and less emotionally intense (Buhrmester & Furman, 1990; Cole & Kerns, 2001). Fortunately, sibling relationships improve as individuals leave adolescence and move into young adulthood, perhaps because they are less likely to compete with each other for resources or attention (Scharf, Shulman, & Avigad-Spitz, 2005).

There are important links among parent-child, sibling, and peer relations in adolescence. In fact, it is helpful to think of the adolescent's interpersonal world as consisting of a web of interconnected relationships rather than a set of separate ones. Having a positive parent-adolescent relationship is associated with less sibling conflict and a more positive sibling relationship (e.g., Hetherington, Henderson, & Reiss, 1999). In contrast, adolescents who experience parental rejection and negativity are more likely to fight with their siblings.

Similarly, children and adolescents learn much about social relationships from sibling interactions, and they transfer this knowledge and experience to friendships outside the family (Brody et al., 1994; Updegraff, McHale, & Crouter, 2000). In poorly functioning families, aggressive interchanges between unsupervised siblings may provide a training ground within which adolescents learn, practice, and perfect aggressive behavior (Snyder, Bank, & Burraston, 2005). The reverse is true as well—the quality of adolescents' relationships with their friends, for better or worse, influences how they interact with their siblings (Kramer & Kowal, 2005).

The quality of the sibling relationship also affects adolescents' adjustment (Stocker, Burwell, & Briggs, 2002). Positive sibling relationships contribute to school success, sociability, autonomy, and self-esteem (e.g., Hetherington et al., 1999; Yeh & Lempers, 2004). Having a close sibling relationship can partially buffer the negative effects of not having friends in school (East & Rook, 1992), and siblings can serve as sources of advice and guidance (Kramer & Kowal, 2005; Tucker, McHale, & Crouter, 2001). Of course, siblings can influence the development of problems as well (Bank, Burraston, & Snyder, 2004; Conger, Conger, & Scaramella, 1997). For example, siblings influence each other's drug use and antisocial behavior (Ardelt & Day, 2002; Bullock & Dishion, 2002; Rowe et al., 1989). And, younger sisters of childbearing adolescents are more likely to engage in early sexual activity and to become pregnant during adolescence themselves (East & Jacobson, 2001).

Although the family is certainly an important influence on adolescent development, another context—the peer group—takes on new and special significance in this stage of life. (For a summary of this section, see "Interim Summary 15.3: Family Relationships in Adolescence.")

PEER RELATIONSHIPS IN ADOLESCENCE

A visit to an elementary school playground will reveal that peer groups are an important feature of the social world of childhood. But even though peer groups exist well before adolescence, during the teenage years they change in significance and structure. Four specific developments stand out.

First, there is a sharp increase during adolescence in the sheer amount of time individuals spend with their peers and in the relative time they spend with peers versus

INTERIM SUMMARY 15.3

Family Relationships in Adolescence

Adolescents' Relationships with Parents	■ In most families, there is a shift in adolescence away from patterns of influence and interaction that are unequal to ones in which parents and their adolescent children are on more equal footing.
	■ Early adolescence is a time of changes in youngsters' views of family relationships and in family members' expectations of each other.
	■ It is important to distinguish between separating from one's parents in a way that maintains emotional closeness in the relationship, versus breaking away from in a fashion that leads to alienation, conflict, and hostility.
Adolescents' Relationships with Siblings	■ Sibling relationships in adolescence differ both from other family relationships and from relationships with friends.
	■ Young adolescents have emotionally charged relationships with siblings that are marked by conflict and rivalry but also by nurturance and support. Over the course of adolescence, adolescents' relationships with siblings become more egalitarian but more distant and less emotionally intense.
	■ Having a positive parent-adolescent relationship is associated with less sibling conflict and a more positive sibling relationship.
	■ The qualify of sibling relationships also affects adolescents' adjustment, in both positive and negative ways.

adults. If we count school as a setting in which adolescents are mainly with age-mates, well over half of the typical American adolescent's waking hours are spent with peers; only 15 percent of their time is with adults—including their parents. (A good deal of the remaining time is spent alone or with a combination of adults and age-mates.) When asked to list the people in their life who are most important to them, nearly half the people adolescents mention are people of the same age. By sixth grade, adults other than parents account for less than 25 percent of the typical adolescent's social network—the people he or she interacts with most regularly (Brown, 1990).

Second, during adolescence, peer groups function much more often without adult supervision than they do during childhood, partly because adolescents are simply more mobile than children but partly because adolescents seek, and are granted, more independence (Brown, 1990). Groups of younger children typically play where adults are present, or in activities that are organized or supervised by adults (e.g., Little League, Youth Soccer, Brownies), whereas adolescents spend more time on their own. A group of teenagers may go off to the mall or to the movies, or will choose to congregate at the home of someone whose parents are not around.

Third, adolescents have increasingly more contact with opposite-sex friends. During childhood, peer groups are highly sex segregated. This is especially true of children's peer activities in school and other settings organized by adults, although somewhat less so of their more informal activities, such as neighborhood play (Maccoby, 1990). During adolescence, however, a growing proportion of an individual's significant others are opposite-sex peers, even in public settings (Brown & Larson, in press). Part of this is due to the emergence of romantic relationships, but part is due to an increase in nonromantic friendships with other-sex peers.

Finally, whereas children's peer relationships are limited mainly to pairs of friends and relatively small groups—three or four children at a time, for example—adolescence marks the emergence of larger collectives. In junior high school cafeterias, for example, the "popular" crowd sits in one section of the room, the "brains" in another, and the "druggies" in yet a third (see Eder, 1985). These crowds typically develop their own minicultures, which dictate particular styles of dressing, talking, and behaving. It is not until early adolescence that individuals can confidently list the different crowds that characterize their schools and reliably describe the stereotypes that distinguish the different crowds from one another (Brown, Mory, & Kinney, 1994). (Movies like *The Breakfast Club* or *Heathers* illustrate this nicely.)

Cliques and Crowds

It is helpful to think of adolescents' peer groups as organized around two related, but different, structures (Brown & Larson, in press). A **clique** is a small group of between two and twelve individuals—the average is about five or six—generally of the same sex, and, of course, the same age. Cliques can be defined by common activities (e.g., the "drama" group, a group of students who study together regularly) or simply by friendship (e.g., a group of girls who have lunch together every day or a group of boys who have known one another for a long time). The clique is the social setting in which adolescents hang out, talk to each other, and form close friendships. Some cliques are more closed to outsiders than others (i.e., the members are, well, "cliquish"), but virtually all cliques are small enough so that the members feel that they know one another well and appreciate one another more than people outside the clique do (Brown & Larson, in press).

Adolescents' cliques are usually composed of individuals who are in the same grade in school, from the same social class, and of the same race, in part because cliques usually develop in schools or neighborhoods, which are often race segregated or class segregated. But what about factors beyond these? Do members of a clique also share certain interests and attitudes? Generally speaking, they do. Three factors appear to be especially important in determining adolescent clique membership and friendship

clique A small, tightly knit group of between two and twelve friends, generally of the same sex and age.

Because the clique is based on activity and friendship, it is the important setting in which the adolescent learns social skills. In contrast, because crowds are based on reputation and stereotype, and not interaction, they probably contribute more to the adolescent's self-conceptions and less to the development of social competence.

crowd A large, loosely organized group of young people, composed of several cliques and typically organized around a common shared activity.

patterns: orientation toward school, orientation toward the teen culture, and involvement in antisocial activity (Crosnoe & Needham, 2004). Adolescents who don't care much about doing well in school and who would rather spend time drinking and doing drugs usually have friends who feel the same way, whereas "nerds of a feather" usually flock together.

Cliques are quite different in structure and purpose than crowds. Membership in a **crowd** is based mainly on reputation and stereotype, rather than on actual friendship or social interaction. This is very different from membership in a clique, which, by definition, hinges on shared activity and friendship. In contemporary American high schools, typical crowds are "jocks," "brains," "nerds," "populars," "druggies," and so on. The labels for these crowds may vary from school to school ("nerds" versus "geeks," "populars" versus "preps"), but their presence is commonplace, at least in the United States and Canada. (Can you can recall the main crowds that existed in your high school?) In contrast to cliques, crowds are not settings for adolescents' intimate interactions or friendships but, instead, serve three broad purposes: to locate adolescents (to themselves and to others) within the social structure of the school, to channel adolescents into associations with some peers and away from others, and to provide contexts that reward certain lifestyles and discourage others (Brown & Larson, in press). According to recent estimates, close to half of high school students are associated with one crowd, about one-third are associated with two or more crowds, and about one-sixth do not clearly fit into any crowd (Brown & Larson, in press).

In concrete terms—and perhaps ironically—an adolescent does not have to actually have "brains" as friends, or to hang around with "brainy" students, to be one of the "brains." If he dresses like a "brain," acts like a "brain," and takes honors courses, then he is a "brain," at least as far as his crowd membership goes. The fact that crowd membership is based on reputation and stereotype can be very difficult for individual adolescents, who—if they do not change their reputation early on in high school—may find themselves stuck, at least in the eyes of their peers, with a label that they do not wish to have (or that they do not see themselves as deserving) (Brown et al., 1992).

Crowds are not simply clusters of cliques; the two different structures serve entirely different purposes. Because the clique is based on activity and friendship, it is the important setting in which the adolescent learns social skills—how to be a good friend to someone else, how to communicate with others effectively, how to be a leader, how to enjoy someone else's company, or even how to break off a friendship that is no longer satisfying. These and other social skills are important in adulthood as well as in adolescence. In contrast, because crowds are based on reputation and stereotype, and not interaction, they probably contribute more to the adolescent's sense of identity and self-conceptions—for better and for worse—than to his or her actual social development.

Because the adolescent's peer group plays such an important role as a source of identity, the nature of the crowd with which an adolescent affiliates can have an important influence on his or her behavior and activities (Prinstein & La Greca, 2002). Although most adolescents feel pressure from their friends to behave in ways that are consistent with their crowd's values and goals, the specific nature of the pressure varies from one crowd to another. Adolescents who are part of the "druggie" crowd report much more peer pressure to engage in misconduct, for example, than do adolescents from the "jock" crowd (Clasen & Brown, 1985).

Crowd membership can also affect the way adolescents feel about themselves. Adolescents' self-esteem is higher among students who are identified with peer groups that have relatively more status in their school. In one high school, in which the "jocks" and "socies" were highest in status, and the "druggies" and "toughs" were lowest, students who were identified with the higher-status groups had higher self-esteem than did those who were identified with the lower-status groups (Brown & Lohr, 1987). Another study found that over the course of adolescence, symptoms of psychological distress declined among the "populars" and "jocks," but increased among the "brains" (Prinstein & La Greca, 2002). Of course, the longer-term consequences of crowd membership during adolescence is not necessarily the same as its immediate impact. One study of the young adult outcomes of high school crowd membership found that "brains," as well as "jocks," showed the most favorable patterns of psychological adjustment over time (Barber, Eccles, & Stone, 2001). Not surprisingly, individuals who had been members of antisocial crowds fared the worst.

Responding to Peer Pressure

As adolescents come to spend more time outside the family, the opinions and advice of others—not only peers but adults as well—become more important. Adolescents are often portrayed as being extremely susceptible to the influence of peers—more so than children or young adults—and as being stubbornly resistant to the influence of their parents. Is peer pressure really more potent, and parental influence much weaker, during adolescence than during other stages?

Researchers have looked at this question by putting adolescents in situations in which they must choose either between the pressures of their parents and the pressures of their peers or between their own wishes and those of others. In a typical study of this sort, an adolescent might be told to imagine that he and his friends discover something that looks suspicious on the way home from school. His friends tell him that they should keep it a secret. But the adolescent in the imaginary scenario tells his mother about it, and she advises him to report it to the police. The adolescent study participant then would be asked by the researcher to say what he would do.

In general, studies that contrast parents' and peers' influences indicate that it is hard to generalize about who is more important. In some situations, peers' opinions are more influential, but in others situations, parents' opinions matter more. Adolescents are more likely to conform to their peers when it comes to short-term, day-to-day, and social matters—styles of dress, tastes in music, choices among leisure activities, and so on. This is particularly true during junior high school and the early years of high school. Teenagers are primarily influenced by their parents, however, when it comes to long-term questions concerning educational or occupational plans, or to questions of values, religious beliefs, or ethics (Steinberg, 2008).

Researchers also have studied how adolescents respond when placed between the pressure of their friends and their own opinions of what to do (McElhaney et al., in press). An adolescent might be asked whether she would go along with her friends' pressure to shoplift, even if she did not want to do so (Berndt, 1979). The age pattern found in these studies depends on the type of behavior under pressure. In particular, conformity to peer pressure to do something antisocial is higher during early and middle adolescence (it peaks around age fourteen) than before or after (Berndt, 1979; Steinberg & Silverberg, 1986). But when peer pressure is not specifically to do something wrong—for instance, pressure simply to change one's opinion about music or clothing—studies find that individuals' ability to stand up to the influence of their friends increases steadily during adolescence, most sharply between fourteen and eighteen (Steinberg & Monahan, 2007).

Although conformity to peer pressure is greater during early adolescence than later, it is not exactly clear just why this is so. One possibility is that adolescents are more susceptible to peer influence during this time because of their heightened orientation toward the peer group. Because they care more about what their friends think of them, they are more likely to go along with the crowd to avoid being rejected (Brown, Clasen, & Eicher, 1986). It is possible that this heightened conformity to peer pressure during early adolescence is a sign of a sort of emotional "way station" between becoming emotionally autonomous from parents and developing an independent sense of identity (Collins & Steinberg, 2006). In other words, the adolescent may become emotionally autonomous from parents before he or she is emotionally ready for this degree of independence and may turn to peers to fill this void.

Popularity and Rejection in Adolescent Peer Groups

Thus far, our discussion has focused on how and why crowds and cliques serve as the basis for adolescents' social activities and self-conceptions. But what about the internal structure of peer groups? Within a clique or a crowd, what determines which adolescents are popular and which ones are disliked?

© Elena Rostunova/Used under license from Shutterstock.com

Adolescents' susceptibility to peer pressure is an important contributor to problem behavior, like smoking.

The main determinant of a youngster's popularity during adolescence is his or her social competence. Popular adolescents act appropriately in the eyes of their peers, are skilled at perceiving and meeting the needs of others, and are confident without being conceited. Because of their social skill, popular adolescents also are good at adjusting their behavior to maintain their favored social standing when peer group norms change; if, for instance, smoking marijuana becomes something that is valued by the peer group, popular adolescents will start getting high more regularly (Allen et al., 2005). Although many determinants of popularity are common across cultures (e.g., having a good sense of humor), some differ. Shyness, for example, which is clearly a social liability in American peer groups, may be an asset in China (Chen, Rubin, & Li, 1995).

What about unpopular adolescents? Social scientists have shown that it is important to distinguish among three types of adolescents who are disliked by their peers (Bierman & Wargo, 1995; Coie et al., 1995; Parkhurst & Asher, 1992). One set is overly aggressive; they are likely to get into fights with other students, are more likely to be involved in antisocial activities, and often are involved in bullying. A second set is withdrawn; these adolescents are exceedingly shy, timid, and inhibited and, actually, are themselves more likely to be the *victims* of bullying. A third group of unpopular youngsters combine both liabilities: They are aggressive and withdrawn. Like other aggressive youngsters, aggressive-withdrawn children have problems controlling their hostility; but like other withdrawn children, they tend to be nervous about initiating friendships with other adolescents.

Sex Differences in Adolescents' Friendships

Friendships become closer and more intimate during adolescence, but there are striking sex differences in intimacy. When asked to name the people who are most important to them, adolescent girls—particularly in the middle adolescent years—list more friends than boys do, and girls are more likely to mention intimacy as a defining aspect of close friendship. In interviews, adolescent girls express greater interest in their close friendships, talk more frequently about their intimate conversations with friends, and express greater concern about their friends' faithfulness and greater anxiety over rejection. Consistent with stereotypes, sitcoms, and stand-up comedy shtick, females place greater emphasis than males do on emotional closeness in their evaluation of romantic partners (Feiring, 1999; Parker et al., 2005). Girls are more likely than boys to make distinctions in the way they treat intimate and nonintimate friends, fight more about relationship issues, and appear to prefer to keep their friendships more exclusive and be less willing to include other classmates in their cliques' activities (Berndt, 1982).

There also are interesting sex differences in the nature of conflicts between close friends. Boys' conflicts with their friends are briefer, typically over issues of power and control (e.g., whose turn it is in a game, who gets the last piece of pizza), more likely to escalate into physical aggression, and settled without any explicit effort to do so, often by just "letting

© David Young-Wolff/PhotoEdit

By most indicators, adolescent girls' friendships are more intimate than boys' friendships.

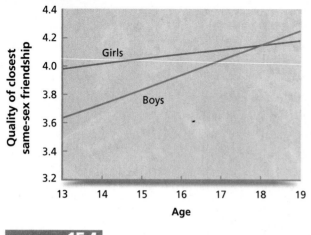

FIGURE 15.4

Males' and Females' Reports of Friendship Quality

Sex differences in friendship quality are substantial early in adolescence, but negligible by the time individuals are eighteen. There are considerable sex differences in the ways that males and females express intimacy, however. *Source: "Trajectories of perceived friendship quality during adolescence: The patterns and contextual predictors" by N. Way & M.L. Greene, Journal of Research on Adolescence, 16, pp. 293-320. Copyright © 2006 by Blackwell Publishing Ltd. Reproduced with permission of Blackwell Publishing Ltd.*

things slide." Girls' conflicts, in contrast, are longer, typically about some form of betrayal in the relationship (e.g., breaking a confidence, ignoring the other person), and only resolved when one of the friends apologizes (Raffaeli, 1997).

Although intimacy is a more conscious concern for adolescent girls than for boys, this does not mean that intimacy is absent from boys' relationships—it just is expressed differently. In general, boys' friendships are more oriented toward shared activities than toward the explicit satisfaction of emotional needs; hence, the development of intimacy between adolescent males may be a more subtle phenomenon that doesn't entail a lot of verbal expression (McNelles & Connolly, 1999). A group of adolescent boys might backpack together without much conversation but feel the same degree of closeness as a result of their trip as a group of girls who stayed up all night talking. In addition, the development of close friendships among males may start at a later age than it does among females (generally speaking, girls mature earlier emotionally, as well as physically). There are substantial sex differences in adolescents' reports of friendship quality at age thirteen, but by eighteen these sex differences are gone (Way & Greene, 2006). (See Figure 15.4.)

The importance of intimacy as a defining feature of close friendship continues to increase throughout early and middle adolescence (Berndt & Perry, 1990; McNelles & Connolly, 1999; Phillipsen, 1999). But an interesting pattern of change occurs around age fourteen. During middle adolescence (between ages thirteen and fifteen), particularly for girls, concerns about loyalty and anxieties over rejection become more pronounced (Berndt & Perry, 1990). Girls show a significant increase in jealousy over their friends' friends during early adolescence (Parker et al., 2005). Ironically, the relatively greater intimacy enjoyed by girls with their friends compared to boys is both an asset and a liability—girls get the benefits of having confidantes with whom they can easily talk about their problems, but their friendships are more fragile and easily disrupted by betrayal. As a consequence, girls' friendships on average do not last as long as boys' do (Benenson & Christakos, 2003). As we'll see in a later section, some theorists believe that this may also explain why girls are at relatively greater risk for depression than boys.

Dating and Romantic Relationships

In earlier eras, dating during adolescence was not so much a recreational activity (as it is today) but a part of the process of courtship and mate selection. Individuals would date in order to ready themselves for marriage, and unmarried individuals would play the field—under the watchful eyes of chaperones—before settling down (Montgomery, 1996). The function of adolescent dating changed, however, as individuals began to marry later and later—a trend that began in the mid-1950s and continues today (U.S. Bureau of the Census, 2006). (See Figure 15.5.) This, of course, gives adolescent dating a whole new meaning, because today it is clearly divorced from its function in mate selection. Adults continue to regulate and monitor adolescent dating in order to prevent rash or impulsive commitments to early marriage (Laursen & Jensen-Campbell, 1999), but in the minds of most young people, high school dating has little to do with marriage.

Today, the average adolescent begins dating around age thirteen or fourteen, although nearly half of all adolescents have at least one date before they turn twelve (Connolly & McIssac, in press). By the age of sixteen, more than 90 percent of adolescents of both

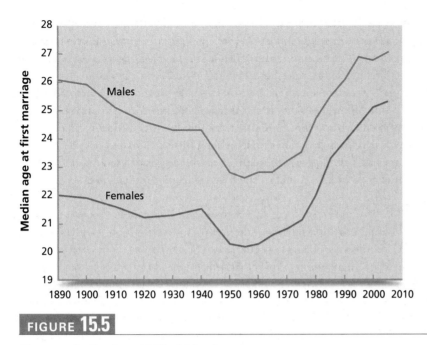

Males

Females

1890 1900 1910 1920 1930 1940 1950 1960 1970 1980 1990 2000 2010

Changes in the Age at First Marriage

The median age at first marriage for American males and females has changed over time. The fact that marriage is much later today than it was fifty years ago has changed the meaning and purpose of dating. *Source:* Date from the U.S. Bureau of the Census (2006).

sexes have had at least one date, and during the later years of high school, more than half of all students average one or more dates each week (Feiring, 1993). By age eighteen, virtually all adolescents have dated once, and three-fourths have had at least one steady boyfriend or girlfriend (Neemann, Hubbard, & Masten, 1995). Moreover, and contrary to stereotypes of adolescents' romances as being short-lived, one-fifth of adolescents fourteen or younger, one-third of fifteen- and sixteen-year-olds, and more than half of seventeen- and eighteen-year-olds who are in dating relationships have been dating the same person for nearly a year. Girls tend to become involved with boys who are slightly older, whereas boys tend to become involved with girls who are the same age or younger. Asian American adolescents are less likely than other adolescents to date, but the prevalence of dating at different ages is very similar among African American, Hispanic American, Native American, and Caucasian adolescents (Collins, 2003).

The Meaning of Dating in Adolescence

"Dating" can mean a variety of different things, of course, from group activities that bring males and females together (without much actual contact between the sexes); to group dates, in which a group of boys and girls go out jointly (and spend part of the time in couples and part of the time in large groups); to casual dating in couples; to serious involvement with a steady boyfriend or girlfriend. Generally speaking, casual socializing with opposite-sex peers and experiences in mixed-sex groups generally occur before the development of romantic relationships (Connolly & McIssac, in press).

Even for adolescents with a history of successful and intimate friendships with same- and other-sex peers, the transition into romantic relationships can be difficult. In one recent study, adolescents were asked to discuss social situations they thought were difficult. Themes having to do with communicating with the other sex were mentioned frequently. Many adolescents discussed difficulty in initiating or maintaining conversations, both face-to-face (e.g., "He will think I am an idiot," "Sometimes you don't know, if you're like sitting with a guy and you're watching a basketball game or something, you don't know if you should start talking or if you should just sit there") and on the phone ("I think it is hard to call. After it's done with, you don't know how to get off the phone"). Others mentioned problems in asking people out ("Asking a girl out on a first date—complete panic!") or in turning people down ("How about if you go on a date and you're really not interested, but he keeps calling?"). Still others noted problems in making or ending romantic commitments ("You don't know if you are going out with someone or if you are just seeing them," "It is hard to say, 'so, are we gonna make a commitment?,'" "I avoided [breaking up] for two weeks because I was trying to think of what to say") (Grover & Nangle, 2003, pp. 133–134).

The Impact of Dating on Adolescent Development Does dating have any impact on adolescents' social and emotional development? Like most influences on development, the impact of dating depends on the context in which it occurs. In this specific case, the "contextual" factor that matters most is the adolescent's age.

Early and intensive dating—for example, becoming seriously involved before age fifteen—has a somewhat stunting effect on psychosocial development (Neemann et al., 1995) and is associated with increased alcohol use, delinquency, and, not surprisingly, sexual activity (Davies & Windle, 2000). This is probably true for males and females alike, but researchers have focused primarily on girls because boys are less likely to begin serious dating quite so early. Compared with their peers, girls who begin serious dating early are less mature socially, less imaginative, less oriented toward achievement, less happy with who they are and how they look, more depressed, and more superficial—a finding that has been reported consistently for at least forty years (Neemann et al., 1995).

By the age of sixteen, more than 90 percent of adolescents of both sexes have had at least one date.

This is not to say that dating is not a valuable interpersonal experience for the adolescent, only that dating may have different effects in early adolescence than in middle and late adolescence (Neemann et al., 1995). Although early involvement in serious romance has its costs, adolescent girls who do not date at all show their own signs of delayed social development, as well as excessive dependency on their parents and feelings of insecurity (Douvan & Adelson, 1966). In contrast, adolescents who date and go to parties regularly are more popular, have a stronger self-image, and report greater acceptance by their friends (Connolly & Johnson, 1993). Stopping or cutting back on dating after having dated heavily is associated with a drop in self-esteem and an increase in depression (Davies & Windle, 2000).

All in all, experts agree that a moderate degree of dating—and delaying serious involvement until age fifteen or so—appears to be the most potentially valuable route. Perhaps adolescents need more time to develop the capacity to be intimate through same-sex friendships and less pressured group activities before they enter intensively into the more highly ritualized relationships that are encouraged through dating.

Regardless of the impact that dating does or doesn't have on the adolescent's psychosocial development, studies show that romance has a powerful impact on the adolescent's emotional state. Adolescents' real and fantasized romances trigger more of their strong emotional feelings during the course of a day (one-third of girls' strong feelings and one-fourth of boys') than do family, school, or friends. Although the majority of adolescents' feelings about their romantic relationships are positive, more than 40 percent are negative, involving feelings of anxiety, anger, jealousy, and depression (Larson, Clore, & Wood, 1999). Adolescents who have entered into a romantic relationship in the past year report more symptoms of depression than do those who have not (Joyner & Udry, 2000), perhaps because many adolescents who are involved romantically also experience breakups during the same time period (Collins, 2003). Breaking up is the single most common trigger of the first episode of major depression, which, as you will read, often occurs for the first time in adolescence (Monroe et al., 1999). (For a summary of this section, see "Interim Summary 15.4: Peer Relationships in Adolescence.")

INTERIM SUMMARY 15.4

Peer Relationships in Adolescence

Cliques and Crowds	■ Cliques are small groups of between two and twelve individuals, generally of the same sex and age, and are usually composed of individuals who are in the same grade, from the same social class, and of the same race.
	■ Orientation toward school, orientation toward teen culture, and involvement in antisocial activity are important influences on clique membership.
	■ Membership in a crowd is based mainly on reputation and stereotype rather than on actual friendship or social interaction.
	■ Crowds locate adolescents within the social structure of the school, channel adolescents into associations with some peers and away from others, and provide contexts that reward certain lifestyles and discourage others.
	■ Whereas the clique is important for learning social skills, crowds contribute more to the adolescent's sense of identity and self-conception.
Responding to Peer Pressure	■ Adolescents may be especially susceptible to peer pressure because they have a heightened orientation toward the peer group during this time.
	■ Adolescents are more likely to conform to their peers when it comes to short-term matters such as style of dress and leisure pursuits and to their parents for more long-term questions concerning education or occupational plans.
	■ Conformity to antisocial peer pressure is higher during early and middle adolescence than before or after. When peer pressure is not specifically to do something wrong, studies find that individuals' ability to stand up to the influence of their friends increases steadily during adolescence.
Popularity and Rejection in Adolescent Peer Groups	■ Popular adolescents act appropriately in the eyes of their peers, are skilled at perceiving and meeting the needs of others, and are confident without being conceited.
	■ Social scientists distinguish between three types of adolescents who are disliked by their peers: those who are overly aggressive, those who are withdrawn, and those who are both aggressive and withdrawn.

(continued)

INTERIM SUMMARY 15.4 *(continued)*

Peer Relationships in Adolescence

Sex Differences in Adolescent Friendships	■ The importance of intimacy as a defining feature of close friendship increases throughout early and middle adolescence.
	■ Intimacy is a more conscious concern for adolescent girls than for boys, but this does not mean that intimacy is absent from boys' relationships—it just is expressed differently. In general, boys' friendships are more oriented toward shared activities than toward the explicit satisfaction of emotional needs.
Dating and Romantic Relationships	■ High school dating has little to do with marriage in the minds of most young people.
	■ Generally speaking, casual socializing with opposite-sex peers and experiences in mixed-sex groups generally occur before the development of romantic relationships.
	■ Early and intensive dating has a somewhat stunting effect on psychosocial development and is associated with increased alcohol use, delinquency and sexual activity.
	■ Experts agree that a moderate degree of dating and delaying serious involvement until age 15 or so appears to be the most potentially valuable route.
	■ Adolescents' real and fantasized romances trigger more of their strong emotional feelings during the course of a day than do family, school, or friends. Breaking up is the single most common trigger of the first episode of major depression.

SOCIOEMOTIONAL PROBLEMS IN ADOLESCENCE

Although the vast majority of young people move through adolescence without experiencing major difficulty, some encounter serious psychological and behavioral problems that disrupt not only their lives but also the lives of those around them. Problems such as substance abuse, delinquency, and depression are not the norm during adolescence, but they do affect a worrisome number of teenagers. In this concluding section of the chapter, we look at some of the problems that are most often associated with adolescence.

Before we begin, though, we need to make some general observations about problems in adolescence that apply to a range of issues.

Some General Observations About Problems in Adolescence

First, let's distinguish between occasional experimentation and enduring patterns of dangerous or troublesome behavior. Although the vast majority of teenagers do something during adolescence that is against the law, very few of these young people develop criminal careers. Similarly, the majority of adolescents experiment with alcohol sometime before high school graduation, and the majority will have been drunk at least once; but relatively few teenagers will develop drinking problems or will permit alcohol to have a negative impact on their school performance or personal relationships.

Second, there's a difference between problems that have their origins and onset during adolescence and those that have their roots in earlier periods of development. Many individuals who develop depression during adolescence suffered from other types of psychological distress, such as excessive anxiety, as children. In other words, simply because a problem may be displayed during adolescence does not mean that it has adolescent origins.

Third, many of the problems experienced by adolescents are relatively transitory and resolved by the beginning of adulthood, with few long-term repercussions in most cases. The fact that some of the problems of adolescence disappear on their own with time does not make their prevalence during adolescence any less worrisome, but it should be kept in mind when rhetoric is hurled back and forth about the inevitable decline of civilization at the hands of contemporary youth.

Finally, problem behavior during adolescence is virtually never a direct consequence of going through the normative changes of adolescence itself. Popular theories about "raging hormones" causing adolescent craziness have no scientific support whatsoever, for example, nor do the widely held beliefs that problem behaviors are manifestations of an inherent need to rebel against authority, or that bizarre behavior results from having an identity crisis. When a young person exhibits a serious psychosocial problem, such as depression, the worst possible interpretation is that it is a "normal" part of growing up. It is more likely to be a sign that something is wrong (Steinberg, 2008).

Experts on the development and treatment of psychosocial problems during adolescence typically distinguish among three broad categories of problems: substance abuse (which we looked at in the chapter on adolescents' physical development), externalizing problems, and internalizing problems (Achenbach & Edelbrock, 1987). To review, an **externalizing problem** is one in which the young person's problems are turned outward and are manifested in antisocial behavior—behavior that is intended to harm others or deliberately violates society's norms. Common externalizing problems during adolescence are delinquency, antisocial aggression, and truancy. An **internalizing problem** is one in which the young person's problems are turned inward and are manifested in emotional and cognitive distress, such as depression, anxiety, or phobia.

Externalizing Problems

The most common externalizing problem, and the one that has been most researched, is **delinquency**, which refers to acts committed by juveniles that violate the law. Both violent crimes (such as assault, rape, robbery, and murder) and property crimes (such as burglary, theft, and arson) increase in frequency between the preadolescent and adolescent years, peak during the late high school years (slightly earlier for property than for violent crimes), and decline during young adulthood. The onset of serious delinquency generally begins between the ages of thirteen and sixteen (Farrington, in press). (See Figure 15.6.)

In general, the earlier an adolescent's delinquency begins—in particular, if it begins before adolescence—the more likely he or she is to become a chronic offender, to commit serious and violent crimes, and to continue committing crimes as an adult (Farrington, in press). Conversely, the older an adolescent is when the delinquent activity first appears, the less likely criminal behavior will become a lasting problem. For purposes of discussion, therefore, it is helpful to distinguish between youngsters who begin misbehaving before adolescence and those whose delinquent activity first appears during adolescence.

One of the most influential ways of characterizing these two groups of delinquents has been suggested by psychologist Terrie Moffitt (2006), who has distinguished between **life-course-persistent offenders** and **adolescence-limited offenders**. The first group demonstrates antisocial behavior before adolescence, is involved in delinquency during adolescence, and is at great risk for continuing criminal activity in adulthood. The second group engages in antisocial behavior *only* during adolescence.

externalizing problem A psychosocial problem that is manifested in a turning of the symptoms outward, as in aggression or delinquency.

internalizing problem A psychosocial problem that is manifested in a turning of the symptoms inward, as in depression or anxiety.

delinquency Juvenile offending that is processed within the juvenile justice system.

life-course-persistent offenders Individuals who begin demonstrating antisocial or aggressive behavior during childhood and continue their antisocial behavior through adolescence and into adulthood (contrast with *adolescence-limited offenders*).

adolescence-limited offenders Antisocial adolescents whose delinquent or violent behavior begins and ends during adolescence (contrast with *life-course-persistent offenders*).

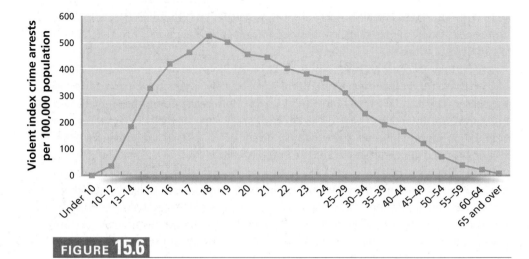

The Age-Crime Curve

Violent crime peaks around age seventeen or eighteen and then declines steadily in early adulthood. Although the vast majority of antisocial adolescents are "adolescence-limited offenders," a small minority become "life-course-persistent" offenders and continue criminal activity into adulthood.

Experts agree that the causes and the consequences of delinquent behavior that begins during childhood or preadolescence are quite different from those of delinquency that begins—and typically ends—during adolescence (e.g., McCabe et al., 2001).

Youngsters whose externalizing problems begin before adolescence are often psychologically troubled. Most of these individuals are male, many are poor, and a large number come from homes in which divorce has occurred (Farrington, in press). More important, a large and consistent body of research shows that chronic delinquents typically come from disorganized families with hostile, inept, or neglectful parents who have mistreated their children and failed to instill in them proper standards of behavior or the psychological foundations of self-control (Laub & Sampson, 1995).

In addition to family factors, there are individual characteristics that distinguish persistently delinquent youngsters from their peers at a relatively early age. First and most important, children who become delinquent—especially those who engage in violence—have histories of aggressive and antisocial behavior that were identifiable as early as age eight (Brody et al., 2003). It is important to keep in mind, though, that the majority of children who have histories of aggressive behavior problems do not grow up to be delinquent. (If this seems confusing, think about it this way: The majority of delinquents probably have eaten French fries at some point in their childhood, but the majority of children who eat French fries do not grow up to be delinquent.)

Second, studies show that many children who become persistent offenders have problems in self-regulation—they are more impulsive, less able to control their anger, and more likely than their peers to suffer from hyperactivity, or as it is technically known, **attention deficit/hyperactivity disorder (ADHD)** (Farrington, in press). Although ADHD does not directly cause antisocial behavior, it does elevate the risk for other family and academic problems, which in turn increase the likelihood of an adolescent developing externalizing problems (Nagin & Tremblay, 1999).

Third, children who become chronically delinquent are more likely to score low on standardized tests of intelligence and neuropsychological functioning and to perform poorly in school (Raine et al., 2005). Some of this is due to genetic factors, but some is also due to conditions surrounding their birth and prenatal care. A disproportionate number of persistently violent adolescents were born to poor mothers who abused

attention deficit / hyperactivity disorder (ADHD) A biologically based psychological disorder characterized by impulsivity, inattentiveness, and restlessness, often in school situations.

drugs during pregnancy and had medical complications during delivery that likely affected their baby's neuropsychological and intellectual development (Piquero & Chung, 2001).

In contrast to youngsters who show externalizing problems before adolescence (and who often continue their antisocial behavior into adulthood), those who begin after adolescence do not ordinarily show signs of psychological abnormality or severe family pathology (Moffitt, 1993). Typically, the offenses committed by these youngsters do not develop into serious criminality, and generally speaking, these individuals do not commit serious violations of the law after adolescence (Nagin, Farrington, & Moffitt, 1995).

Although adolescence-limited offenders do not show the same degree of pathology as life-course-persistent offenders, they do have more problems than youth who are not at all delinquent, both during adolescence and in early adulthood. Indeed, one long-term follow-up of individuals who had earlier been classified as life-course-persistent offenders, adolescence-limited offenders, or neither found that as young adults the adolescence-limited offenders had more mental health, substance abuse, and financial problems than individuals who had not been delinquent at all as teenagers (Moffitt et al., 2002). In other words, their delinquent behavior may be limited to adolescence, but they may have other problems that persist into early adulthood.

The two main risk factors for adolescence-limited offending are *poor parenting*, especially poor monitoring, and *affiliation with antisocial peers* (Ary et al., 1999; Lacourse, Nagin, & Tremblay, 2003). The first of these (poor parenting) usually leads to the second (hanging around with antisocial peers) (Dishion et al., 1991; Lansford et al., 2003). The role of the peer group in adolescence-limited offending is extremely important. One of the strongest predictors of delinquency and other forms of problem behavior is the amount of time the adolescent spends in unsupervised, unstructured activities with peers—activities like hanging out, driving around, and going to parties.

Internalizing Problems

In some instances, the changes and demands of adolescence may leave a teenager feeling helpless, confused, and pessimistic about the future. Although minor fluctuations in self-esteem during early adolescence are commonplace, it is not normal for adolescents (or adults, for that matter) to feel a prolonged or intense sense of hopelessness or frustration. Such young people are likely to be psychologically depressed and in need of professional help.

Depression

In its mild form, **depression** is the most common psychological disturbance during adolescence (Graber & Sontag, in press). Although we typically associate depression with feelings of sadness, there are other symptoms that are important signs of the disorder; sadness alone, without any other symptoms, may not indicate depression in the clinical sense of the term. Depression has emotional symptoms, including dejection, decreased enjoyment of pleasurable activities, and low self-esteem. It has cognitive symptoms, such as pessimism and hopelessness, and motivational symptoms, including apathy and boredom. Finally, depression usually has physical symptoms, such as a loss of appetite, difficulty in sleeping, and loss of energy. The symptoms of major depression are the same in adolescence as in adulthood and among males and females, although, as you will read, there are sex differences in the prevalence of the illness (Lewinsohn, Pettit, et al., 2003).

Many people use the term *depression* imprecisely. It is important to distinguish among depressed mood (feeling sad), depressive syndromes (having multiple symptoms of depression), and depressive disorder (having enough

depression A psychological disturbance characterized by low self-esteem, decreased motivation, sadness, and difficulty finding pleasure in formerly enjoyable activities.

At any one point in time, close to 10 percent of American teenagers report moderate or severe symptoms of depression.

symptoms to be diagnosed with the illness) (Graber & Sontag, in press). All individuals experience periods of sadness or depressed mood at one time or another; far fewer report a wider range of depressive symptoms. At any one point in time, close to 10 percent of American teenagers report moderate or severe symptoms of depression—about 5 percent have the symptoms of a depressive syndrome, and approximately 3 percent meet formal diagnostic criteria for depressive disorder (Compas, Ey, & Grant, 1993). Some studies estimate that as many as 25 percent of individuals will experience at least one bout of depressive disorder by the end of adolescence (Forbes & Dahl, 2005).

There is a dramatic increase in the prevalence of depressive feelings around the time of puberty; depression is half as common during childhood as it is during adolescence (Avenevoli & Steinberg, 2001). Symptoms of depression increase steadily throughout adolescence, and then start to decline—making late adolescence the period of greatest risk (Wight, Sepúlveda, & Aneshensel, 2004). There are ethnic differences in the prevalence of depression during adolescence, with significantly more Mexican American teenagers reporting depressive symptoms than their Caucasian, African American, or Asian American peers, especially within samples of girls (Siegel et al., 1998). At this point it is not known why this is or whether similar patterns are found when the Hispanic comparison group is drawn from other subpopulations (e.g., Puerto Rican or Dominican adolescents). Individuals who develop internalizing disorders such as depression and anxiety in adolescence are at elevated risk to suffer from these problems as adults (Lewinsohn, Rhode, et al., 2003; Pine et al., 1998).

A variety of theories have been proposed to account for the onset of depression and other types of internalizing problems during adolescence. The current consensus is that internalizing problems result from interacting environmental conditions and individual predispositions rather than either alone. Today, most experts endorse a **diathesis-stress model** of depression, which posits depression may occur when individuals who are predisposed toward internalizing problems (the term *diathesis* refers to this predisposition) are exposed to chronic or acute stressors that precipitate a depressive reaction (Hilsman & Garber, 1995; Lewinsohn, Joiner, & Rohde, 2001). Individuals without the diathesis—who are not predisposed toward depression—are able to withstand a great deal of stress, for instance, without developing any psychological problems. Other individuals, who have strong predispositions toward the disorder, may become depressed in the face of stressful circumstances that most of us would consider to be normal. Research on depression in adolescence has focused both on the diathesis and the stress. Two categories of predispositions have received the most attention. First, because depression has been found to have a strong genetic component, it is believed that at least some of the predisposition is biological and may be related to problematic patterns of neuroendocrine functioning (**neuroendocrine** refers to hormonal activity in the brain and nervous system). As you read in "Nature with Nurture," scientists have discovered that abnormalities in one gene, in particular, may make some individuals more likely to develop depression in the face of stress (Caspi et al., 2003).

Other researchers have focused more on the cognitive style of depressed individuals, suggesting that people with tendencies toward hopelessness, pessimism, and self-blame are more likely to interpret events in their lives in ways that make them depressed—to them, the proverbial glass is always half-empty (Prinstein & Aikins, 2004; Robinson, Garber, & Hilsman, 1995). These sorts of cognitive sets, which may be linked to the ways in which children think they are viewed by parents, and later by peers, develop during childhood and are thought to play a role in the onset of depression during adolescence (Cole & Jordan, 1995; Nolen-Hoeksema, Girgus, & Seligman, 1992).

Researchers who have been more concerned with the stress component of the diathesis-stress model—that is, with environmental influences on depression—have focused on three broad sets of stressors (Lewinsohn, Rhode, & Seeley, 1994). First, depression is more common among adolescents from families characterized by high

diathesis-stress model A perspective on disorder that posits that problems are the result of an interaction between a preexisting condition (the diathesis) and exposure to a stressful event or condition.

neuroendocrine Referring to hormonal activity in the brain and nervous system.

conflict and low cohesion, and it is higher among adolescents from divorced homes. Second, depression is more prevalent among adolescents who are unpopular or who have poor peer relations. Third, depressed adolescents report more chronic and acute stress than nondepressed adolescents do. There is also evidence that academic difficulties are correlated with depression, especially among adolescents from Asian and also affluent families, who place a good deal of emphasis on achievement (Chan, 1997; Greenberger et al., 2000; Luthar & Becker, 2002).

You read earlier that the prevalence of depression rises during adolescence. Can diathesis-stress models of depression account for this increase? For the most part, they can. Biological theorists can point to the hormonal changes of puberty; as you read in "Physical Development in Adolescence," one of the effects of pubertal hormones is to make individuals more sensitive to stress (Walker, Sabuwalla, & Huot, 2004). Many studies show that the increase in depression in adolescence is more closely linked to puberty than age (Graber & Sontag, in press), although it is difficult to pinpoint puberty as the cause of the problem, since many other changes typically occur around the same time (e.g., the transition out of elementary school). Cognitive theorists can point to the onset of hypothetical thinking at adolescence, which may result in new (and perhaps potentially more depressing) ways of viewing the world (Keating, 2004). And theorists who emphasize environmental factors draw attention to the new environmental demands of adolescence, such as changing schools, beginning to date, or coping with transformations in family relationships—all of which may lead to heightened stress (Graber, 2004). Thus, there are many reasons to expect that the prevalence of depression would increase as individuals pass from childhood into adolescence.

Sex Differences in Rates of Depression One of the most consistent findings to emerge in the study of adolescent depression involves the emergence of a very large sex difference in rates of depression in early adolescence. Before adolescence, boys are somewhat more likely to exhibit depressive symptoms than girls, but after puberty the sex difference in prevalence of depression reverses. From early adolescence until very late in adulthood, twice as many females as males suffer from depressive disorder, and females are somewhat more likely than males to report depressed mood (Compas et al., 1997). The increased risk for depression among girls emerges during puberty, rather than at a particular age or grade in school (Angold, Costello, & Worthman, 1998). Although sex differences in major depression persist beyond adolescence, both sexes report less depression in their midtwenties than late teens, but the decline is steeper among females, which results in a smaller sex difference (Galambos, Barker, & Krahn, 2006; Stoolmiller, Kim, & Capaldi, 2005).

Psychologists do not have a certain explanation for the emergence of sex differences in depressive disorder at adolescence. Although the association of depression with puberty suggests a biological explanation, there actually is little evidence that the sex difference in depression is directly attributable to sex differences in hormones (Rutter & Garmezy, 1983). Instead, four main explanations have received scientific support.

First, the emergence of sex differences in depression seems to have something to do with the social role that the adolescent girl may find herself in as she enters the world of boy-girl relationships (Wichstrøm, 1999). As you've read, this role may bring heightened self-consciousness over one's physical appearance and increased concern over popularity with peers. Since many of these feelings may provoke helplessness, hopelessness, and anxiety, adolescent girls may be more susceptible to depressive feelings. Consistent with this, studies show that depression in girls is significantly correlated with having a poor body image (Wichstrøm, 1999).

Second, early adolescence is generally a more stressful time for girls than boys (Rudolph & Hammen, 1999). This is because the bodily changes of puberty, especially when they occur early in adolescence, are more likely to be stressful for girls; because girls are more likely than boys to experience multiple stressors at the same time (e.g., going through puberty while making the transition into junior high school); and because girls are likely to experience more stressful life events than boys, such as sexual victimization (Graber & Sontag, in press, 2004).

Third, girls are more likely than boys to react to stress by turning their feelings inward—for instance, by ruminating about the problem and feeling helpless—whereas boys are more likely to respond either by distracting themselves or by turning their feelings outward, in aggressive behavior or in drug and alcohol abuse (Sethi & Nolen-Hoeksema, 1997). As a result, even when exposed to the same degree of stress, girls are more likely to respond to the stressors by becoming depressed (Rudolph & Hammen, 1999).

A final explanation emphasizes girls' generally greater orientation toward and sensitivity to interpersonal relations, which we noted earlier in our discussion of intimacy in adolescent friendships (Cyranowski & Frank, 2000). Females may invest more in their close relationships than males, but this may make them more distressed by interpersonal difficulties and breakups. Because adolescence is a time of many changes in relationships—in the family, with friends, and with romantic partners—the capacity of females to invest heavily in their relationships with others may be both a strength and a potential vulnerability.

Suicide According to recent national surveys, in any given year more than 10 percent of American female high school students and more than 6 percent of males attempt suicide; about one-third of these attempts are serious enough to require treatment by a physician or nurse. A much larger proportion—close to 20 percent—think about killing themselves (referred to as **suicidal ideation**), and the vast majority of these have gone so far as to make a plan (Centers for Disease Control and Prevention, 2006). Suicidal ideation increases during early adolescence, peaks around age fifteen, and then declines (Rueter & Kwon, 2005). (See Figure 15.7.) Adolescents who attempt to kill themselves usually have made appeals for help and have tried but have not found emotional support from family or friends. They report feeling trapped, lonely, worthless, and hopeless (Kidd, 2004).

suicidal ideation Thinking about ending one's life.

The most common method of suicide among adolescents is with a firearm, followed by hanging. Drug overdoses and carbon monoxide poisoning are also common (Judge & Billick, 2004). The suicide rate is highest among American Indian and Alaskan Native adolescents and lowest among African Americans; rates among Caucasian, Hispanic, and Asian adolescents fall in between these extremes (Judge & Billick, 2004). Systematic studies have identified four established sets of risk factors for attempting suicide during adolescence: having a *psychiatric problem*, especially depression or substance abuse; having a *history of suicide in the family*; being under *stress* (especially in the areas of achievement and sexuality); and experiencing *parental rejection, family disruption,* or *extensive family conflict* (Judge & Billick, 2004). Adolescents who have one of these risk factors are sig-

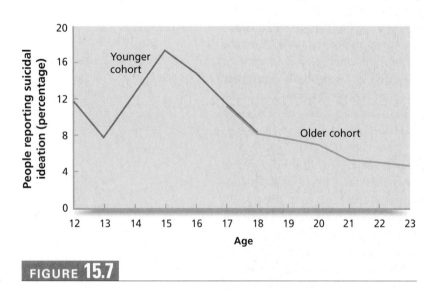

FIGURE **15.7**

Age Differences in Suicidal Ideation

Depression is the most common internalizing problem in adolescents. Middle adolescents are more likely to think about suicide than younger or older individuals. *Source:* "Developmental trends in adolescent suicidal ideation" by M. Rueter & H. Kwon, *Journal of Research on Adolescence*, 15, pp. 205–222. Copyright © 2005 by Blackwell Publishing Ltd. Reproduced with permission of Blackwell Publishing Ltd.

nificantly more likely to attempt suicide than their peers, and adolescents who have more than one risk factor are dramatically more likely to try to kill themselves. Adolescents who have attempted suicide once are at risk for attempting it again (Lewinsohn et al., 1994). Adolescents are also more likely to attempt suicide if one of their friends or someone else in their community has committed suicide (Bearman & Moody, 2004; Gould, Wallenstein, & Kleinman, 1990).

INTERIM SUMMARY **15.5**

Socioemotional Problems in Adolescence

Some General Observations	■ Problems such as substance abuse, delinquency, and depression are not the norm during adolescence, but they do affect a worrisome number of teenagers.
	■ It is important to distinguish between occasional experimentation and enduring patterns of dangerous or troublesome behavior.
	■ Many of the problems experienced by adolescents are relatively transitory and resolved by the beginning of adulthood.
	■ Problem behavior is virtually never a direct consequence of going through the normative changes of adolescence itself.
Externalizing Problems	■ Delinquency generally begins between the ages of 13 and 16 and declines during young adulthood.
	■ The earlier an adolescent's delinquency begins, the more likely he or she is to become a **life-course-persistent offender**. Conversely, the older an adolescent is when delinquency activity first appears, the more likely his or her criminal behavior will be **adolescence-limited**.
	■ Youngsters whose offending starts before adolescence often have long histories of aggressive and antisocial behavior, problems in self-regulation, and are more likely to score low on tests of intelligence and neuropsychological functioning.
	■ Adolescents whose externalizing problems begin and end in adolescence do not ordinarily show signs of psychological abnormality or severe family pathology. However, they often have been exposed to poor parenting and antisocial peers.
Internalizing Problems	■ **Depression** is the most common internalizing problem during adolescence.
	■ Depression has emotional symptoms, physical symptoms, and cognitive symptoms.
	■ It is important to distinguish between depressed mood, depressive syndromes, and depressive disorder.
	■ There is a dramatic increase in the prevalence of depressive feelings around the time of puberty. Symptoms of depression increase steadily throughout adolescence and then start to decline, making late adolescence the period of greatest risk.
	■ Most experts posit a **diathesis-stress model** of depression, which suggests that depression may occur when individuals who are biologically or cognitively predisposed toward internalizing problems are exposed to chronic or acute stressors.
	■ From early adolescence until very late in adulthood, twice as many females as males suffer from depression.
	■ In any given year, more than 10% of American female high school students and more than 6% of males attempt suicide. Suicidal ideation increases during adolescence, peaks around age 15 and then declines.

The adolescent suicide rate increased alarmingly between 1950 and 1990, fueled by the increased use of drugs and alcohol and the increased availability of firearms (Judge & Billick, 2004). The rate peaked and declined somewhat during the 1990s, as new forms of antidepressant medication became more widely prescribed to adolescents (Zito et al., 2002). Although some reports have indicated that antidepressants may actually *increase* the risk of suicide among children and adolescents, more recent studies have found that when prescriptions of antidepressants drop (after articles linking antidepressants and suicide receive a lot of attention), the number of children attempting suicide increases, suggesting that taking antidepressants off the market likely does more harm than good (Bridge et al., 2007). You may have read that suicide is a leading cause of death among young people, but this is primarily because very few young people die from other causes, such as disease. Actually, suicide is a much more common cause of death among adults than it is among young people, largely because very few suicide attempts by adolescents are successful. But hints or threats of suicide, by anyone at any age, should be taken seriously. (For a summary of this section, see "Interim Summary 15.5: Socioemotional Problems in Adolescence.")

SUMMING UP AND LOOKING AHEAD

Although the final section of this chapter ended with a discussion of socioemotional problems in adolescence, we don't want to leave you with the impression that adolescence is an inherently or inevitably difficult time. It's crucial that you keep in mind that most individuals emerge from adolescence with positive feelings about themselves and their parents; with the ability to form, maintain, and enjoy close relationships with same- and opposite-sex peers; and with the basic capabilities needed to take advantage of a range of educational, occupational, and recreational opportunities. Most adolescents settle into adulthood relatively smoothly and begin establishing their work and family careers with little serious difficulty. Although the transition into adulthood may appear forbidding to the young adolescent approaching many weighty decisions about the future, statistics tell us that, for a remarkably high proportion of youth, the transition is relatively peaceful. Yes, it is true that one in three adolescent girls gets pregnant before she is twenty-one, but it is also true that two of three do not. Although 20 percent of teenagers do not complete high school by the societally expected age, 80 percent do, and more than half of the students who drop out later receive a high school diploma or GED.

We should not gloss over the fact that many healthy adolescents at one time or another experience bouts of self-doubt, periods of family squabbling, academic setbacks, or broken hearts. But it is important to keep in mind that there is an important distinction between the normative, and usually transitory, difficulties that are encountered by many young people—and by many adults—and the serious psychosocial problems that are experienced by a relatively small minority of youth.

Adolescence is, above all, a remarkable period for the development of psychological maturity. Individuals enter with only a faint idea of who they are (and with few reasons to even question this) and leave well on the way toward developing a clear (if still changing) sense of identity. Relationships with family members are transformed, and a new equilibrium and balance of power is established—if perhaps after a temporary period of difficulty and distance. Relationships with friends change even more dramatically, with the development of closer and more intimate relationships with same and opposite-sex peers, the ascendance and decline of peer groups, and the increasing importance of romantic relationships.

Stop for a moment and recall where this expedition all started—with the joining of one sperm and one egg. In twenty or so years, that one-celled, microscopic creation develops, through the ongoing and dynamic interplay of biology and context, into a young adult, fully capable of functioning independently and interdependently—alone and in relationships with others (not to mention capable of conceiving, with the help of a partner, a child of his or her own). It is hard to think of a more amazing or wondrous journey.

HERE'S WHAT YOU SHOULD KNOW

Did You Get It?

After reading this chapter, you should understand the following:

- How adolescence as we know it today came to be "invented"
- Erikson's theory of adolescent identity development, and the ways in which scientists who study identity assess it
- Why the development of ethnic identity is important, and the different pathways associated with it
- How self-evaluations change in adolescence

- How family and sibling relationships change in adolescence
- How peer relationships change in adolescence, and the significance of cliques, crowds, and romantic relationships
- Basic facts about common externalizing and internalizing problems, including the factors that contribute to them

Important Terms and Concepts

adolescence-limited offend-
    ers (p. 457)
attention deficit/
    hyperactivity disorder
    (ADHD) (p. 458)
child protectionists (p. 437)
clique (p. 447)

crowd (p. 448)
delinquency (p. 457)
depression (p. 459)
diathesis-stress model
    (p. 460)
ethnic identity (p. 440)

externalizing problem
    (p. 457)
identity status (p. 439)
identity versus identity dif-
    fusion (p. 438)
internalizing problem
    (p. 457)

life-course-persistent of-
    fenders (p. 457)
neuroendocrine (p. 460)
psychosocial moratorium
    (p. 439)
suicidal ideation (p. 465)

CHAPTER 13
Physical Development in Adolescence

- During **puberty,** there is a rapid acceleration in growth, development of primary and secondary sex characteristics, and changes in body composition and in the circulatory and respiratory systems.

- Puberty is triggered by genetic and environmental factors. It can be delayed by illness, nutritional deficiencies, and excessive exercise or thinness.

- By age 18, about two thirds of American adolescents have had intercourse. **Sexual orientation** is shaped by a complex interaction of social and biological influences.

- **Disordered eating** refers to patterns of eating attitudes and behaviors that are unhealthy, including obesity, **anorexia nervosa,** and **bulimia.**

- Brain changes during adolescence may provoke teens to crave novelty, reward, and stimulation *before* the brain systems that control judgment, decision making, and impulse control have matured.

- Alcohol and nicotine are the most commonly used and abused substances by teenagers. Their effects on brain functioning are worse in adolescence than in adulthood because the brain is especially vulnerable.

CHAPTER 14
Cognitive Development in Adolescence

- **Deductive reasoning** and **hypothetical thinking** improve during adolescence and are tied to the maturation of the prefrontal cortex. Adolescents have an increased capacity and interest in thinking about relationships, politics, religion, and morality.

- **Social cognition** involves such cognitive abilities as thinking about other people, thinking about social relationships, and thinking about social institutions.

- By early adolescence, **social conventions** are often seen as nothing but social expectations with insufficient reasons for compliance. Gradually, adolescents begin to see these conventions as the means by which society regulates peoples' behavior.

- Adolescents who have a strong **need for achievement** have parents who set high performance standards, reward school success, and encourage autonomy and independence. The socioeconomic status of the adolescent's family impacts educational achievement.

- Today, three fourths of high school graduates enroll in college; two thirds enroll immediately after graduation. However, rates of college graduation lag far behind rates of enrollment.

CHAPTER 15
Socioemotional Development in Adolescence

- Erikson believed that resolving the crisis of **identity versus identity diffusion** is the chief psychological task of adolescence.

- The term **identity status** refers to the point in the identity development process that characterizes an adolescent at a given time. Compared with older adolescents and with preadolescents, early adolescents are more self-conscious and have a less stable self-image.

- Adolescents' relationships with siblings become increasingly more egalitarian but more distant and less emotionally intense. Having a positive parent-adolescent relationship is associated with a more positive sibling relationship.

- Adolescents may be especially susceptible to peer pressure because they have a heightened orientation toward the peer group.

- An **externalizing problem** is one in which the adolescent's problems are turned outward and are manifested in antisocial behavior that is intended to harm others or that violates society's norms. During adolescence, depression is the most common **internalizing problem**—problems that are turned inward and are manifested in emotional and cognitive distress.

References

Abbeduto, L., Pavetto, M., Kesin, E., Weissman, M. D., Kara-dottir, S., O'Brien, A., & Cawthon, S. (2001). The linguistic and cognitive profile of Down syndrome: Evidence from a comparison with fragile X syndrome. *Down Syndrome Research and Practice, 7*(1), 9–15.

Abrahamson, A., Baker, L. A., & Caspi, A. (2002). Rebellious teens? Genetic and environmental influences on the social attitudes of adolescents. *Journal of Personality and Social Psychology, 83*, 1392–1408.

Achenbach, T., & Edelbrock, C. (1987). *The manual for the Youth Self-Report and Profile.* Burlington: University of Vermont.

Adams, G., Gullotta, T., & Montemayor, R. (Eds.). (1992). *Adolescent identity formation.* Newbury Park, CA: Sage.

Adolph, K. E., & Berger, S. E. (2005). Physical and motor development. In M. H. Bornstein & M. E. Lamb (Eds.), *Developmental science: An advanced textbook* (5th ed., pp. 223–281). Mahwah, NJ: Erlbaum.

Adolph, K. E., & Berger, S. E. (2006). Motor development. In W. Damon & R. Lerner (Series Eds.) & D. Kuhn & R. S. Siegler (Vol. Eds.), *Handbook of child psychology: Vol. 2. Cognition, perception, and language* (6th ed., pp. 161–213) New York: Wiley.

Agras, W. S., Schneider, J., Arnow, B., Raeburn, S., & Telch, C. (1989). Cognitive-behavioral and response-prevention treatments for bulimia nervosa. *Journal of Consulting and Clinical Psychology, 57*, 215–221.

Ahnert, L., Gunnar, M. R., Lamb, M. E., & Barthel, M. (2004). Transition to child care: Associations with infant-mother attachment, infant negative emotion, and cortisol elevations. *Child Development, 75*, 639–650.

Ainsworth, M. S., Blehar, M. C., Waters, E., & Wall, S. (1978). *Patterns of attachment: A psychological study of the strange situation.* Oxford, England: Erlbaum.

Ainsworth-Darnell, J., & Downey, D. (1998). Assessing the oppositional culture explanation for racial/ethnic differences in school performance. *American Sociological Review, 63*, 536–553.

Aksan, N., & Kochanska, G. (2005). Conscience in childhood: Old questions, new answers. *Developmental Psychology, 41*, 506–516.

Akushevich, I., Kravchenko, J. S., & Manton, K. G. (2007, May 15). Health-based population forecasting: Effects of smoking on mortality and fertility. *Risk Analysis, 27*, 467–482. doi: 10.1111/j.1539-6924.2007.00898.x

Alan Guttmacher Institute. (2004). *U.S. teenage pregnancy statistics: Overall trends, trends by race and ethnicity and state-by-state information.* New York: Author.

Albaladejo, P., Bouaziz, H., & Benhamou, D. (1998). Epidural analgesics: How can safety and efficacy be improved? *CNS Drugs, 10*, 91–104.

Alexander, K. L., Entwisle, D. R., & Kabbani, N. S. (2001). The dropout process in life course perspective: Early risk factors at home and school. *Teachers College Record, 103*, 760–822.

Alexander, K. L., Entwisle, D. R., & Olson. L. S. (2007). Lasting consequences of the summer learning gap. *American Sociological Review, 72*(2), 167–180.

Allen, J. P., Porter, M. R., McFarland, F. C., Marsh, P., & McElhaney, K. B. (2005). The two faces of adolescents' success with peers: Adolescent popularity, social adaptation, and deviant behavior. *Child Development, 76*, 747–760.

Allen, R., & Mirabell, J. (1990, May). *Shorter subjective sleep of high school students from early compared to late starting schools.* Paper presented at the second meeting of the Society for Research on Biological Rhythms, Jacksonville, FL.

Amato, P. R. (2001). Children and divorce in the 1990s: An update of the Amato and Keith (1991) meta-analysis. *Journal of Family Psychology, 15*, 355–370.

American Academy of Pediatrics. (2004). Policy statement: Soft drinks in schools. *Pediatrics, 113*, 152–154.

American Psychiatric Association. (1994). *Diagnostic and statistical manual of the American Psychiatric Association (DSM-IV).* Washington, DC: American Psychiatric Association.

American Psychiatric Association. (2000). *Diagnostic and statistical manual of mental disorders* (4th ed., rev.). Washington, DC: Author.

American Psychological Society. (2005). In appreciation: Urie Bronfenbrenner. *APS Observer*, p. 28.

Ames, E. (1990). Spitz revised: A trip to Romanian "orphanages." *Canadian Psychological Association Developmental Psychology Section Newsletter, 9*, 8–11.

Anderson, D. R., Huston, A. C., Schmitt, K. L., Linebarger, D. L., & Wright, J. C. (2001). Early childhood television viewing and adolescent behavior. *Monographs of the Society for Research in Child Development, 66*, vii–147.

Anderson, S. W., Aksan, N., Kochanska, G., Damasio, H., Wisnowski, J., & Afifi, A. (2007). The earliest expression of focal damage to human prefrontal cortex. *Cortex, 6*, 767–816.

Andersson, T., & Magnusson, D. (1990). Biological maturation in adolescence and the development of drinking habits and alcohol abuse among young males: A prospective longitudinal study. *Journal of Youth and Adolescence, 19*, 33–42.

Aneshensel, C., Becerra, R., Fielder, E., & Schuler, R. (1990). Onset of fertility-related events during adolescence: A prospective comparison of Mexican American and non-Hispanic white females. *American Journal of Public Health, 80*, 959–963.

Angold, A., Costello, E. J., & Worthman, C. (1998). Puberty and depression: The roles of age, pubertal status, and pubertal timing. *Psychological Medicine, 28*, 51–61.

Anhert, L., Gunnar, M. R., Lamb, M., & Barthel, M. (2004). Transition to child care: Associations with infant-mother attachment, infant negative emotion, and cortisol elevations. *Child Development, 75*, 639–650.

Annett, M. (2002). *Handedness and brain asymmetry: The right shift theory.* Hove, UK: Psychology Press.

Apgar, V. (1953). A proposal for a new method of evaluation of the newborn infant. *Current Researches in Anesthesia & Analgesia, 32*, 260–267.

Ardelt, M., & Day, L. (2002). Parents, siblings, and peers: Close social relationships and adolescent deviance. *Journal of Early Adolescence, 22*, 310–349.

Arendt, R. E., Short, E. J., Singer, L. T., Minnes, S., Hewitt, J., Flynn, S., et al. (2004). Children prenatally exposed to co-caine: Developmental outcomes and environmental risks at seven years of age. *Developmental and Behavioral Pediatrics, 25*, 83–90.

Ariès, P. (1962). *Centuries of childhood.* New York: Random House.

Arterberry, M. E., & Bornstein, M. H. (2001). Three-month-old infants' categorization of animals and vehicles based on static and dynamic attributes. *Journal of Experimental Child Psychology, 80*, 333–346.

Arterberry, M. E., & Bornstein, M. H. (2002a). Infant perceptual and conceptual categorization: The roles of static and dy-namic stimulus attributes. *Cognition: International Journal of Cognitive Science, 86*, 1–24.

Arterberry, M. E., & Bornstein, M. H. (2002b). Variability and its sources in infant categorization. *Infant Behavior & Devel-opment, 25*, 515–528.

Ary, D., Duncan, T., Biglan, A., Metzler, C., Noell, J., & Smolkowski, K. (1999). Development of adolescent problem behavior. *Journal of Abnormal Child Psychology, 27*, 141–150.

Asakawa, K., & Csikszentmihalyi, M. (2000). Feelings of con-nectedness and internalization of values in Asian American adolescents. *Journal of Youth and Adolescence, 29*, 121–145.

Aslin, R. N. (2007). What's in a look? *Developmental Science, 10*, 48–53.

Astington, J. W. (1993). *The child's discovery of the mind.* Cam-bridge, MA: Harvard University Press.

Astley, S. J., & Clarren, S. K. (1996). A case definition and pho-tographic screening tool for the facial phenotype of fetal alcohol syndrome. *Journal of Pediatrics, 129*, 33–41.

Augustine, St. (1961). *Confessions.* New York: Penguin Books.

Autism Genome Project Consortium. (2007). Mapping autism risk loci using genetic linkage and chromosomal rearrange-ments. *Nature Genetics, 39*(3), 319–328.

Avenevoli, S., & Steinberg, L. (2001). The continuity of depres-sion across the adolescent transition. In H. Reese & R. Kail (Eds.), *Advances in child development and behavior* (Vol. 28, pp. 139–173). New York: Academic Press.

Azar, B. (2006). Wild findings on animal sleep. *Monitor on Psy-chology, 37*, 54–55.

Azar, S. T. (2002). Parenting and child maltreatment. In M. H. Bornstein (Ed.), *Handbook of parenting: Vol. 4. Applied parent-ing* (2nd ed., pp. 361–388). Mahwah, NJ: Erlbaum.

Bachman, J., & Schulenberg, J. (1993). How part-time work intensity relates to drug use, problem behavior, time use, and satisfaction among high school seniors: Are these con-sequences or merely correlates? *Developmental Psychology, 29*, 220–235.

Bada, H. S., Das, A., Bauer, C. R., Shankaran, S., Lester, B., La-Gasse, L., et al. (2007). Impact of prenatal cocaine exposure on child behavior problems through school age. *Pediatrics, 119*, 348–359.

Bagwell, C. L., Coie, J. D., Terry, R. A., & Lochman, J. E. (2000). Peer clique participation and social status in preadoles-cence. *Merrill-Palmer Quarterly, 46*, 280–305.

Bailey, D. B., Bruer, J. T., Symons, F. J., & Lichtman, J. W. (2001). *Critical thinking about critical periods: A series from the National Center for Early Development and Learning.* Baltimore, MD: Brookes Publishing.

Baillargeon, R. (2004). Infants' physical world. *Current Direc-tions in Psychological Science, 13*, 89–94.

Baker, T., & Velez, W. (1996). Access to and opportunity in postsecondary education in the United States: A review. *So-ciology of Education, Special Issue on Sociology and Educational Policy, 69*, 82–101.

Baldwin, D. A., & Markman, E. M. (1989). Establishing word-object relations: A first step. *Child Development, 60*, 381–398.

Baltes, P., Lindenberger, U., & Staudinger, U. (2006). Life span theory in developmental psychology. In W. Damon & R. Lerner (Series Eds.) & R. Lerner (Vol. Ed.), *Handbook of child psychology: Vol. 1. Theoretical models of human development* (6th ed., pp. 569–664). New York: Wiley.

Bandura, A. (1997). *Self-efficacy: The exercise of control.* New York: W. H. Freeman.

Bandura, A., & Walters, R. (1959). *Adolescent aggression.* New York: Ronald Press.

Bank, L., Burraston, B., & Snyder, J. (2004). Sibling conflict and ineffective parenting as predictors of adolescent boys' anti-social behavior and peer difficulties: Additive and interac-tional effects. *Journal of Research on Adolescence, 14*, 99–125.

Bankston, C. L., III, & Caldas, S. (1998). Family structure, schoolmates, and racial inequalities in school achievement. *Journal of Marriage and the Family, 60*, 715–723.

Barber, B. (1996). Parental psychological control: Revisiting a neglected construct. *Child Development, 67*, 3296–3319.

Barber, B. L., Eccles, J. S., & Stone, M. R. (2001). Whatever hap-pened to the jock, the brain, and the princess? Young adult pathways linked to adolescent activity involvement and so-cial identity. *Journal of Adolescent Research, 16*, 429–455.

Barber, J. S. (2001). Ideational influences on the transition to parenthood: Attitudes toward childbearing and competing alternatives. *Social Psychology Quarterly, 64*(2), 101–127.

Barna, J., & Legerstee, M. (2005). Nine- and twelve-month-old infants relate emotions to people's actions. *Cognition and Emotion, 19*, 53–67.

Baron-Cohen, S. (2004). *The essential difference: Male and female brains.* Basic Books.

Baron-Cohen, S., Leslie, A. M., & Frith, U. (1985). Does the au-tistic child have a "theory of mind"? *Cognition, 21*, 37–46.

Barr, R. (2006). Developing social understanding in a social context. In K. McCartney & D. Phillips (Eds.), *Blackwell handbook of early childhood development* (pp. 188–207). Mal-den, MA: Blackwell.

Barr, R. G., Hopkins, B., & Green, J. A. (2000). *Crying as a sign, a symptom, and a signal: Clinical emotional and developmental aspects of infant and toddler crying* (Vol. 152). New York: Cam-bridge University Press.

Barr, R., & Hayne, H. (2000). Age-related changes in imitation: Implications for memory development. In C. Rovee-Collier (Ed.), *Progress in infancy research* (pp. 21–67). Mahwah, NJ: Erlbaum.

Bar-Tal, D., Raviv, A., & Leiser, T. (1980). The development of altruistic behavior: Empirical evidence. *Developmental Psy-chology, 16*, 516–524.

Barth, J., & Bastiani, A. (1997). A longitudinal study of emotion regulation and preschool children's social behavior. *Merrill-Palmer Quarterly, 43*, 107–128.

Bates, E., & Carnevale, G. F. (1993). New directions in research on language development. *Developmental Review, 13,* 436–470.

Bates, J. E., & Pettit, G. S. (2007). Temperament, parenting, and socialization. In J. Grusec & P. D. Hastings (Eds.), *Handbook of socialization: Theory and research* (pp. 153–177). New York: Guilford Press.

Bates, J. E., Pettit, G. S., & Dodge, K. A. (1995). Family and child factors in stability and change in children's aggressiveness in elementary school. In J. McCord (Ed.), *Coercion and punishment in long-term perspectives* (pp. 124–138). New York: Cambridge University Press.

Bates, J. E., Pettit, G. S., Dodge, K. A., & Ridge, B. (1998). Interaction of temperamental resistance to control and restrictive parenting in the development of externalizing behavior. *Developmental Psychology, 34,* 982–995.

Batshaw, M. L., & Conlon, C. J. (1997). Substance abuse: A preventable threat to development. In M. L. Batshaw (Ed.), *Children with disabilities* (4th ed., pp. 143–162). Baltimore: Brookes.

Bauer, P. J. (2006). Event memory. In W. Damon & R. M. Lerner (Series Eds.) & D. Kuhn & R. S. Siegler (Vol. Eds.), *Handbook of child psychology: Vol. 2. Cognition, perception, and language* (6th ed., pp. 373–425). Hoboken, NJ: Wiley.

Baumrind, D. (1967). Child care practices anteceding three patterns of preschool behavior. *Genetic Psychology Monographs, 76,* 43–88.

Baumrind, D. (1971). Current patterns of parental authority. *Developmental Psychology Monographs, 4,* 1–103.

Bayley, N. (1949). Consistency and variability in the growth of intelligence from birth to eighteen years. *Journal of Genetic Psychology, 75,* 165–196.

Bearman, P. S., & Moody, J. (2004). Suicide and friendships among American adolescents. *American Journal of Public Health, 94,* 89–95.

Bechara, A. (2005). Decision making, impulse control and loss of willpower to resist drugs: A neurocognitive perspective. *Nature Neuroscience, 8,* 1458–1463.

Beckett, C., Maughan, B., Rutter, M., Castle, J., Colvert, E., Groothues, C., et al. (2006). Do the effects of early severe depriviation on cognition persist into early adolescence? Findings from the English and Romanian Adoptees Study. *Child Development, 77,* 696–711.

Beighle, A., Morgan, C. F., Le Masurier, G., & Pangrazi, R. P. (2006). Children's physical activity during recess and outside of school. *Journal of School Health, 76,* 516–520.

Belkin, L. (2006, August 20). The School-Lunch Test. *The New York Times Magazine,* 28–55.

Belle, D. (1999). *The after-school lives of children: Alone and with others while parents work.* Mahwah, NJ: Erlbaum.

Bellugi, U. (1970). Learning the language. *Psychology Today, 10,* 32–35.

Belsky, J., & Fearon, R. M. P. (2004). Exploring marriage-parenting typologies and their contextual antecedents and developmental sequelae. *Development and Psychopathology, 16,* 501–523.

Belsky, J., & Jaffee, S. (2006). The multiple determinants of parenting. In D. Cicchetti & D. Cohen (Eds.), *Developmental psychopathology: Vol. 3. Risk, disorder and adaptation* (2nd ed., pp. 38–85). Hoboken, NJ: Wiley.

Belsky, J., Hsieh, K.-H., & Crnic, K. (1998). Mothering, fathering, and infant negativity as antecedents of boys' externalizing problems and inhibition at age 3 years: Differential susceptibility to rearing experience? *Development and Psychopathology, 10,* 301–319.

Belsky, J., Vandell, D. L., Burchinal, M., Clarke-Stewart, K. A., McCartney, K., Owen, M. T., & The NICHD Early Child Care Research Network. (2007). Are there long-term effects of early child care? *Child Development, 78,* 681–701.

Bem, D. (1996). Exotic becomes erotic: A developmental theory of sexual orientation. *Psychological Review, 103,* 320–335.

Bendersky, M., Gambini, G., Lastella, A., Bennett, D. S., Lewis, M. (2003). Inhibitory motor control at five years as a function of prenatal cocaine exposure. *Developmental and Behavioral Pediatrics, 24,* 345–351.

Benedict, H. (1979). Early lexical development: Comprehension and production. *Journal of Child Language, 6,* 183–200.

Benenson, J. F., & Christakos, A. (2003). A greater fragility of female's versus male's closest same sex friendships. *Child Development, 74,* 1123–1129.

Berenbaum, S. A., & Synder, E. (1995). Early hormonal influences on childhood sex-typed activity and playmate preferences: Implications for the development of sexual orientation. *Developmental Psychology, 31,* 31–42.

Berman, B. D., Winkleby, M., Chesterman, E., & Boyce W. T. (1992). After-school child care and self-esteem in school-age children. *Pediatrics, 89,* 654–659.

Bernbaum, J. C., & Batshaw, M. L. (1997). Born too soon, born too small. In M. L. Batshaw (Ed.), *Children with disabilities* (4th ed., pp. 115–139). Baltimore: Brookes.

Berndt, T. (1979). Developmental changes in conformity to peers and parents. *Developmental Psychology, 15,* 608–616.

Berndt, T. (1982). The features and effects of friendship in early adolescence. *Child Development, 53,* 1447–1460.

Berndt, T. (2004). Children's friendships: Shifts over a half-century in perspectives on the development and their effects. *Merrill-Palmer Quarterly, 50,* 206–223.

Berndt, T., & Perry, T. (1990). Distinctive features and effects of early adolescent friendships. In R. Montemayor, G. Adams, & T. Gullota (Eds.), *Advances in adolescence research* (Vol. 2, pp. 269–287). Beverly Hills, CA: Sage.

Bertelli, R., Joanni, E., & Martlew, M. (1998). Relationship between children's counting ability and their ability to reason about number. *European Journal of Psychology of Education, 13*(3), 371–384.

Bertenthal, B. I., & Campos, J. J. (1990). A systems approach to the organizing effects of self-produced locomotion during infancy. In C. Rovee-Collier (Ed.), *Advances in infancy research* (Vol. 6, pp. 1–60). Norwood, NJ: Albex.

Bertrand, J., Floyd, R. L., & Weber, M. K. (2004). *Fetal alcohol syndrome: Guidelines for referral and diagnosis.* Atlanta, GA: U.S. Department of Health and Human Services, CDC. Retrieved August 13, 2008, from http://www.cdc.gov/ncbddd/fas/documents/FAS_guidelines_accessible.pdf

Beyers, W., Goossens, L., Vasant, I., & Moors, E. (2003). A structural model of autonomy in middle and late adolescence; Connectedness, separation, detachment, and agency. *Journal of Youth and Adolescence, 32,* 351–365.

Beyth-Marom, R., Austin, L., Fischoff, B., Palmgren, C., & Jacobs-Quadrel, M. (1993). Perceived consequences of risky behaviors: Adults and adolescents. *Developmental Psychology, 29,* 549–563.

Bhardwaj, R. D., Curtis, M. A., Spalding, K. L., Buchholz, B. A., Fink, D., Bjork-Eriksson, T. et al. (2006). Neocortical neurogenesis in humans is restricted to development. *Proceedings of the National Academy of Sciences,, 103,* 12564–12568.

Biemiller, A., & Slonim, N. (2001). Estimating root word vocabulary growth in normative and advantaged populations: Evidence for a common sequence of vocabulary acquisition. *Journal of Educational Psychology, 93,* 498–520.

Bierman, K. L. (2004). *Peer rejection: Developmental processes and intervention strategies.* New York: Guilford Press.

Bierman, K., & Wargo, J. (1995). Predicting the longitudinal course associated with aggressive- rejected, aggressivenon-rejected), and rejected nonaggressive) status. *Development and Psychopathology, 7,* 669–682.

Bigelow, B. J. (1977). Children's friendship expectations: A cognitive developmental study. *Child Development, 48,* 246–253.

Bills, D., Helms, L., & Ozcan, M. (1995). The impact of student employment on teachers' attitudes and behaviors toward working students. *Youth and Society, 27,* 169–193.

Binet, A., & Simon, T. (1908). Le développement de l'intelligence chez les enfants. *Annee Psychologique, 14*(14) 1–94.

Birney, D. P., Citron-Pousty, J. H., Lutz, D. J., & Sternberg, R. J. (2005). The development of cognitive and intellectual abilities. In M. H. Bornstein & M. E. Lamb (Eds.), *Developmental science: An advanced textbook* (pp. 327–358). Mahwah, NJ: Erlbaum.

Bishop, J., Bishop, M., Gelbwasser, L., Green, S., & Zuckerman, A. (2003). Why do we harass nerds and freaks? Towards a theory of student culture and norms. In D. Ravitch (Ed.), *Brookings papers on education policy* (pp. 141–199). Washington, DC: Brookings Institution Press.

Bjorkland, D. F., Miller, P. H., Coyle, T. R., & Slawinski, J. L. (1997). Instructing children to use memory strategies: Evidence of utilization deficiencies in memory training. *Developmental Review, 17,* 411–442.

Bjorklund, D., & Pellegrini, A. (2001). *The origins of human nature: Evolutionary developmental psychology.* Washington: American Psychological Association.

Black, B., & Logan, A. (1995). Links between communication pattern in mother-child, father-child, and child-peer interactions and children's social status. *Child Development, 66,* 255–271.

Black, M. M, & Matula, K. (1999). *Essentials of Bayley Scales of Infant Development II Assessment.* New York: John Wiley.

Black, S. J., & Weiss, M. R. (1992). The relationship among perceived coaching behaviors, perceptions of ability, and motivation in competitive age-group swimmers. *Journal of Sport and Exercise Psychology, 14,* 309–325.

Blake, J., Osborne, P., Cabral, M., & Gluck, P. (2003). The development of communicative gestures in Japanese infants. *First Language, 23,* 3–20.

Blakemore, J. E. O., Berenbaum, S. A., & Liben, L. S. (2008). *Gender development.* New York: Taylor & Francis Group, Psychology Press.

Blatchford, P., Baines, E., & Pellegrini, A. (2003). The social context of school playground games: Sex and ethnic differences and changes over time after entry to junior high. *British Journal of Developmental Psychology, 21,* 579–599.

Blom-Hoffman, J., George, J. B. E., & Franko, D. L. (2006). Childhood overweight. In G. G. Bear & K. M. Minke (Eds.), *Children's needs III: Development, prevention, and intervention* (pp. 989–1000). Bethesda, MD: National Association of School Psychologists.

Bloom, B., Dey, A. N., & Freeman, G. (2006). Summary health statistics for U.S. children: National Health Interview Survey, 2005. *Vital and Health Statistics,* Series 10, No. 231 (DHHS Publication No. 2007-1559). Hyattsville, MD: U.S. Government Printing Office.

Bloom, K., Russell, A., & Wassenberg, K. (1987). Turntaking affects the quality of infant vocalizations. *Journal of Child Language, 14,* 211–227.

Bloom, L. (1970). *Language development: Form and function in emerging grammars.* Cambridge, MA: MIT Press.

Bloom, L. (1976). An integrative perspective on language development. *Papers and Reports on Child Language Development, 12,* 1–22.

Bloom, L. (1998). Language acquisition in its developmental context. In W. Damon (Series Ed.) & D. Kuhn & R. S. Siegler (Vol. Eds.), *Handbook of child psychology: Vol. 2. Cognition, perception, and language* (5th ed., pp. 309–370). New York: Wiley.

Bloom, P. (2000). *How children learn the meanings of words.* Cambridge, MA: MIT Press.

Blossfeld, I., Collins, A., Kiely, M., & Delahunty, C. (2006). Texture preferences of 12-month-old infants and the role of early experience. *Food Quality and Preference, 18,* 396–404.

Boatman, D., Freeman, J., Vining, E., Pulsifer, M., Miglioretti, D. Minahan, R., Carson, B., Brandt, J. & McKhann, G. (1999). Language recovery after left hemispherectomy in children with late-onset seizures. *Annals of Neurology, 46,* 579–586.

Bogartz, R. S., Shinskey, J. L., & Schilling, T. H. (2000). Object permanence in five-and-a-half-month-old infants? *Infancy, 1,* 403–428

Bolzani Dinehart, L. H., Messinger, D. S., Acosta, S. I., Cassel, T., Ambadar, Z., & Cohn, J. (2005). Adult perceptions of positive and negative infant emotional expressions. *Infancy, 8,* 279–303.

Bornstein, M. H. (1984). A descriptive taxonomy of psychological categories used by infants. In C. Sophian (Ed.), *Origins of cognitive skills* (pp. 313–338). Hillsdale, NJ: Erlbaum.

Bornstein, M. H. (1989). *Maternal responsiveness: Characteristics and consequences.* San Francisco: Jossey-Bass.

Bornstein, M. H. (1989). Sensitive periods in development: Structural characteristics and causal interpretations. *Psychological Bulletin, 105,* 179–197.

Bornstein, M. H. (1991). *Cultural approaches to parenting.* Hillsdale, NJ: Erlbaum.

Bornstein, M. H. (1995). Form and function: Implications for studies of culture and human development. *Culture and Psychology, 1,* 123–137.

Bornstein, M. H. (1998). Stability in mental development from early life: Methods, measures, models, meanings and myths. In F. Simion & G. Butterworth (Eds.), *The development of sensory, motor and cognitive capacities in early infancy: From perception to cognition* (pp. 301–332). London: Psychology Press.

Bornstein, M. H. (2000a). Infancy: Emotions and temperament. In A. E. Kazdin (Ed.), *The encyclopedia of psychology* (Vol. 2, pp. 278–284). New York: American Psychological Association and Oxford University Press.

Bornstein, M. H. (2000b). Infant into conversant: Language and nonlanguage processes in developing early communication. In N. Budwig, I. C. Uzgiris, & J. V. Wertsch (Eds.), *Communication: An arena of development* (pp. 109–129). Stamford, CT: Ablex.

Bornstein, M. H. (2002). Parenting infants. In M. H. Bornstein (Ed.), *Handbook of parenting: Vol. 1. Children and parenting* (2nd ed., pp. 3–43). Mahwah, NJ: Erlbaum.

Bornstein, M. H. (2003). Sensitive periods. In J. R. Miller, R. M. Lerner, L. B. Schiamberg, & P. M. Anderson (Eds.), *Human ecology: An encyclopedia of children, families, communities, and environments* (Vol. 2, pp. 635–636). Santa Barbara, CA: ABC-CLIO.

Bornstein, M. H. (2003). Sensitive periods. In J. R. Miller, R. M. Lerner, L. B. Schiamberg, & P. M. Anderson (Eds.), *Human ecology: An encyclopedia of children, families, communities, and environments* (Vol. 2, pp. 635–636). Santa Barbara, CA: ABC-CLIO.

Bornstein, M. H. (2006). Some metatheoretical issues in culture, parenting, and developmental science. In Q. Jing, M. R. Rosenzweig, G. d'Ydewalle, H. Zhang, H. C. Chen, & K. Zhang (Eds.), *Progress in psychological science around the world: Vol. 2. Social and applied issues* (pp. 245–260). Hove, England: Psychology Press.

Bornstein, M. H. (2006a). Hue categorization and color naming: Physics to sensation to perception. In N. J. Pitchford & C. P. Biggam (Eds.), *Progress in colour studies: Volume 2. Psychological aspects* (pp. 35–68). Amsterdam/Philadelphia: John Benjamins.

Bornstein, M. H. (2006b). Hue categorization and color naming: Cognition to language to culture. In R. M. MacLaury, G. V. Paramei, & D. Dedrick (Eds.), *Anthropology of colour: Interdisciplinary multilevel modeling* (pp. 3–27). Amsterdam/Philadelphia: John Benjamins.

Bornstein, M. H. (2007). On the significance of social relationships in the development of children's earliest symbolic play: An ecological perspective. In A. Göncü & S. Gaskins (Eds.), *Play and development: Evolutionary, sociocultural, and functional perspectives* (pp. 101–129). Mahwah, NJ: Erlbaum.

Bornstein, M. H. (2008). Parents' reports about their children's lives. In A. Ben-Arieh, J. Cashmore, G. Goodman, J. Kampmann, & G. Melton (Eds.), *Handbook of Child Research.* Thousand Oaks, CA: Sage.

Bornstein, M. H., & Arterberry, M. E. (2003). Recognition, discrimination and categorization of smiling by 5-month-old infants. *Developmental Science, 6,* 585–599.

Bornstein, M. H., & Bradley, R. H. (2003). *Socioeconomic status, parenting, and child development.* Mahwah, NJ: Erlbaum.

Bornstein, M. H., & Cote, L. R., with Maital, S., Painter, K., Park, S.-Y., Pascual, L., Pêcheux, M.-G., Ruel, J., Venuti, P., & Vyt, A. (2004). Cross-linguistic analysis of vocabulary in young children: Spanish, Dutch, French, Hebrew, Italian, Korean, and American English. *Child Development, 75,* 1115–1139.

Bornstein, M. H., & Hahn, C.-S. (2007.) Infant childcare settings and the development of gender-specific adaptive behaviors. *Early Child Development and Care, 177,* 15–41.

Bornstein, M. H., & Lamb, M. E. (2008). *Development in infancy: An introduction* (5th ed.). Mahwah, NJ: Erlbaum.

Bornstein, M. H., & Putnick, D. L. (2007). Chronological age, cognitions, and practices in European American mothers: A multivariate study of parenting. *Developmental Psychology, 43,* 850–864.

Bornstein, M. H., & Ruddy, M. G. (1984). Infant attention and maternal stimulation: Prediction of cognitive and linguistic development in singletons and twins. *Attention and performance X: Control of language processes* (pp. 433–445). Hillsdale, NJ: Erlbaum.

Bornstein, M. H., Arterberry, M. E., & Mash, C. (2004). Long-term memory for an emotional interpersonal interaction occurring at 5 months of age. *Infancy, 6,* 407–416.

Bornstein, M. H., Arterberry, M. E., & Mash, C. (2005). Perceptual development. In M. H. Bornstein & M. E. Lamb (Eds.), *Developmental science: An advanced textbook* (5th ed., pp. 283–325). Mahwah, NJ: Erlbaum.

Bornstein, M. H., DiPietro, J. A., Hahn, C.-H., Painter, K. M., Haynes, O. M., & Costigan, K. A. (2002). Prenatal cardiac function and postnatal cognitive development: An exploratory study. *Infancy, 3,* 475–494.

Bornstein, M. H., Gaughran, J. M., & Segui, I. (1991). Multimethod assessment of infant temperament: Mother questionnaire and mother and observer reports evaluated and compared at five months using the Infant Temperament Measure. *International Journal of Behavioral Development, 14,* 131–151.

Bornstein, M. H., Hahn, C.-S., & Haynes, O. M. (2004). Specific and general language performance across early childhood: Stability and gender considerations. *First Language, 24,* 267–304.

Bornstein, M. H., Hahn, C.-S., Gist, N. F., & Haynes, O. M. (2006.) Long-term cumulative effects of childcare on children's mental development and socioemotional adjustment in a non-risk sample: The moderating effects of gender. *Early Child Development and Care, 176,* 129–156.

Bornstein, M. H., Haynes, O. M., Legler, J. M., O'Reilly, A. W., & Painter, K. M. (1997). Symbolic play in childhood: Interpersonal and environmental context and stability. *Infant Behavior & Development, 20,* 197–207.

Bornstein, M. H., Haynes, O. M., Painter, K. M., & Genevro, J. L. (2000.) Child language with mother and with stranger at home and in the laboratory: A methodological study. *Journal of Child Language, 27,* 407–420.

Bornstein, M. H., Putnick, D. L., Suwalsky, J. T. D., & Gini, M. (2006). Maternal chronological age, prenatal and perinatal history, social support, and parenting of infants. *Child Development, 77,* 875–892.

Bornstein, M. H., Tamis-LeMonda, C. S., & Haynes, O. M. (1999). First words in the second year: Continuity, stability, and models of concurrent and predictive correspondence in vocabulary and verbal responsiveness across age and context. *Infant Behavior and Development, 22,* 65–85.

Bornstein, M. H., Tamis-LeMonda, C. S., Pêcheux, M.-G., & Rahn, C. W. (1991). Mother and infant activity and interaction in France and in the United States: A comparative study. *International Journal of Behavioral Development, 14,* 21–43.

Bornstein, M. H., Tamis-LeMonda, C. S., Tal, J., Ludemann, P., Toda, S., Rahn, C. W., et al. (1992). Maternal responsiveness to infants in three societies: The United States, France, and Japan. *Child Development, 63,* 808–821.

Bornstein, M. H., Venuti, P., & Hahn, C.-S. (2002). Mother-child play in Italy: Regional variation, individual stability, and mutual dyadic influence. *Parenting: Science and Practice, 2,* 273–301.

Bowlby, J. (1969). *Attachment and loss.* London: Hogarth.

Bowlby, J. (1982). *Attachment and loss: Vol. 1. Attachment* (2nd ed.). New York: Basic Books. (Original work published in 1969)

Boyce, W. T. (2006). Symphonic causation and the origins of childhood psychopathology. In D. Cicchetti & D. Cohen (Eds.), *Developmental psychopathology: Vol. 2. Developmental neuroscience* (pp. 797–817). New York: Wiley.

Bradley, R. H. (2002). Environment and parenting. In M. H. Bornstein (Ed.), *Handbook of parenting: Vol. 2. Biology and ecology of parenting* (2nd ed., pp. 281–314). Mahwah, NJ: Erlbaum.

Bradley, R. H., & Corwyn, R. F. (2002). Socioeconomic status and child development. *Annual Review of Psychology, 53,* 371–399.

Bradley, R. H., Nader, P., O'Brien, M., Houts, R., Belsky, J., Crosnoe, R., and NICHD Early Child Care Research Network. (2008). Adiposity and internalizing problems: Infancy to middle childhood. In H. D. Davies & H. E. Fitzgerald (Set Eds.) & H. E. Fitzgerald & V. Mousouli (Vol. Eds.), *Obesity in childhood and adolescence: Vol. 2. Understanding development and prevention* (pp. 73–91). Westport, CT: Praeger.

Bradley-Kling, K, Grier, E, & Ax, E. (2006). Chronic illness. In G. G. Bear, & K. M. Minke (Eds.), *Children's needs III: Development, prevention, and intervention* (pp. 857–869). Washington, DC: National Association of School Psychologists.

Brainerd, C. J., & Reyna, V. F. (2004). Fuzzy-trace theory and memory development. *Developmental Review, 24,* 396–439.

Brainerd, C. J., & Reyna, V. F. (2005). *The science of false memory.* New York: Oxford University Press.

Brainerd, C. J., Forrest, T. J., Karibian, D., & Reyna, V. F. (2006). Development of the false-memory illusion. *Developmental Psychology, 42,* 962–979.

Brainerd, C.J. (1996). Piaget: A centennial celebration. *Psychological Science, 7,* 191–225.

Branche, C. M., Dellinger, A. M., Sleet, D. A., Gilchrist, J., & Olson, S. J. (2004). Unintentional injuries: The burden, risks, and preventative strategies to address diversity. In I. L. Livingston (Ed.), *Praeger handbook of Black American health: Policies and issues behind disparities in health* (2nd ed., pp. 317–327). Westport, CT: Praeger.

Brandtstädter, J. (2006). Action perspectives on human development. In W. Damon & R. Lerner (Series Eds.) & R. Lerner (Vol. Ed.), *Handbook of child psychology: Vol. 1. Theoretical models of human development* (6th ed., pp. 519–568). Hoboken, NJ: Wiley.

Brazelton, T. B., & Nugent, J. K. (1995). *Neonatal behavioral assessment scale* (3rd ed.). London: MacKeith Press.

Bremner, J. G. (2001). Cognitive development: Knowledge of the physical world. In J. G. Bremner & A. Fogel (Eds.),

Blackwell handbook of infant development (pp. 99–138). Malden, MA: Blackwell.

Bretherton, I., & Munholland, C. (1999). Internal working models in attachment relationships: A construct revisited. In J. Cassidy & P. Shaver (Eds.), *Handbook of attachment* (pp. 89–111). New York: Guilford Press.

Brewster, K. (1994). Race differences in sexual activity among adolescent women: The role of neighborhood characteristics. *American Sociological Review, 59,* 408–424.

Bridge J., Iyengar, S., Salary, C., Barbe, R., Birmaher, B., Pincus, H., et al. (2007). Clinical response and risk for reported suicidal ideation and suicide attempts in pediatric antidepressant treatment: A meta-analysis of randomized controlled trials. *JAMA, 297,* 1683–1696.

Briggs, G. G., Freeman, R. K., & Yaffe, S. J. (1994). *A reference guide to fetal and neonatal risk: Drugs in pregnancy and lactation* (4th ed.). Baltimore: Williams & Wilkins.

Brisch, K. H. (2002). *Treating attachment disorders.* New York: Guilford Press.

Brody, G. H. (1998). Sibling relationship quality: Its causes and consequences. *Annual Review of Psychology, 49,* 1–24.

Brody, G. H., Conger, R. Gibbons, F. X., Ge, X., Murry, V. M., Gerrard, M., et al. (2001). The influence of neighborhood disadvantage, collective socialization, and parenting on African American children's affiliation with deviant peers. *Child Development, 72,* 1231–1246.

Brody, G., Ge, X., Yeong, K., McBride, M., Simons, R., Gibbons, F., et al. (2003). Neighborhood disadvantage moderates associations of parenting and older sibling problem attitudes and behavior with conduct disorders in African American children. *Journal of Consulting and Clinical Psychology, 71,* 211–222.

Brody, G., Stoneman, Z., & McCoy, J. (1994). Forecasting sibling relationships in early adolescence from child temperaments and family processes in middle childhood. *Child Development, 65,* 771–784.

Broidy, L. M., Nagin, D. S., Tremblay, R. E., Brame, B. Dodge, K. A., Fergusson, D., et al. (2003). Developmental trajectories of childhood disruptive behaviors and adolescent delinquency: A six-site, cross-national study. *Developmental Psychology, 39,* 222–245.

Bronfenbrenner, U. (1979). *The ecology of human development: Experiments by nature and design.* Cambridge, MA: Harvard University Press.

Bronfenbrenner, U., & Morris, P. (1998). The ecology of developmental processes. In W. Damon & R. Lerner (Eds.), *Handbook of child psychology* (5th ed., Vol. 1, pp. 992–1028). New York: Wiley.

Bronfenbrenner, U., & Morris, P. (2006). The bioecological model of human development. In W. Damon & R. Lerner (Series Eds.) & R. Lerner (Vol. Ed.), *Handbook of child psychology: Vol. 1. Theoretical models of human development* (6th ed., pp. 793–828). New York: Wiley.

Bronfenbrenner, U., & Morris, P. A. (1998). The ecology of developmental processes. In W. Damon & R. Lerner (Series Eds.) & R. Lerner (Vol. Ed.), *Handbook of child psychology: Vol. 1. Theoretical models of human development* (pp. 993–1028). New York: Wiley.

Brooks-Gunn, J., Graber, J., & Paikoff, R. (1994). Studying links between hormones and negative affect: Models and measures. *Journal of Research on Adolescence, 4,* 469–486.

Brown, B. (1990). Peer groups. In S. Feldman & G. Elliott (Eds.), *At the threshold: The developing adolescent* (pp. 171–196). Cambridge, MA: Harvard University Press.

Brown, B. (in press). Adolescents' relationships with peers. In R. Lerner & L. Steinberg (Eds.), *Handbook of adolescent psychology* (3rd ed.). New York: Wiley.

Brown, B., & Lohr, M. J. (1987). Peer group affiliation and adolescent self-esteem: An integration of ego-identity and symbolic interaction theories. *Journal of Personality and Social Psychology, 52,* 47–55.

Brown, B., Clasen, D., & Eicher, S. (1986). Perceptions of peer pressure, peer conformity dispositions, and self-reported behavior among adolescents. *Developmental Psychology, 22,* 521–530.

Brown, B., Freeman, H., Huang, B., & Mounts, N. (1992, March). *"Crowd hopping": Incidence, correlates and consequences of change in crowd affiliation during adolescence.* Paper presented at the biennial meetings of the Society for Research on Adolescence, Washington.

Brown, B., Mory, M., & Kinney, D. (1994). Casting crowds in a relational perspective: Caricature, channel, and context. In R. Montemayor, G. Adams, & T. Gullotta (Eds.), *Advances in adolescent development: Vol. 5. Personal relationships during adolescence* (pp. 123–167). Newbury Park, CA: Sage.

Brown, B., Mounts, N., Lamborn, S., & Steinberg, L. (1993). Parenting practices and peer group affiliation in adolescence. *Child Development, 64,* 467–482.

Brown, P. L. (2006, December 2). *Supporting boys or girls when the line isn't clear.* New York Times, pp. A1, A11.

Brown, R. (1973). *A first language.* Cambridge, MA: Harvard University Press.

Brownell, C. (1990). Peer social skills in toddlers: Competencies and constraints illustrated by same age vs. mixed age interaction. *Child Development, 61,* 838–848.

Bruner, J. (1983). *Child's talk: Learning to use language.* New York: W.W. Norton.

Bruner, J., Jolly, A. & Silva, K. (1976) *Play: Its role in evolution and development.* Harmondsworth: Penguin.

Bruvold, W. (1993). A meta-analysis of adolescent smoking prevention programs. *American Journal of Public Health, 83,* 872–880.

Bryant, P., & Nunes, T. (2004). Children's understanding of mathematics. In U. Goswami (Ed.), *Blackwell handbook of cognitive development* (pp. 412–439). Malden, MA: Blackwell Publishing.

Buchanan, C., Eccles, J., & Becker, J. (1992). Are adolescents the victims of raging hormones? Evidence for activational effects of hormones on moods and behavior at adolescence. *Psychological Bulletin, 111,* 62–107.

Buckhalt, J. A., El-Sheikh, M., & Keller, P. (2007). Children's sleep and cognitive functioning: Race and socioeconomic status as moderators of effects. *Child Development, 78,* 213–231.

Bugental, D., & Grusec, J. (2006). Socialization processes. In W. Damon & R. Lerner (Series Eds.) & N. Eisenberg (Vol. Ed.), *Handbook of child psychology: Vol. 3. Social, emotional, and personality development* (6th ed., pp. 366–428). New York: Wiley.

Buhrmester, D., & Furman, W. (1990). Perceptions of sibling relationships during middle childhood and adolescence. *Child Development, 61,* 1387–1396.

Bullock, B., & Dishion, T. J. (2002). Sibling collusion and problem behavior in early adolescence: Toward a process model for family mutuality. *Journal of Abnormal Child Psychology, 30,* 143–153.

Bumpass, L., & Lu, H-H. (2000). Trends in cohabitation and implications for children's family contexts in the United States. *Population Studies, 54,* 29–41.

Burgeson, C. R., Wechsler, H., Brener, N. D., Young, J. C., & Spain, C. G. (2001). Physical education and activity: Results from the School Health Policies and Programs Study 2000. *Journal of School Health, 71,* 279–293.

Busnel, M. C., Granier-Deferre, C., & Lecanuet, J. P. (1992). Fetal audition. In G. Turkewitz (Ed.), Developmental psychobiology. *Annals of the New York Academy of Sciences* (Vol. 662, pp. 118–134). New York: The New York Academic of Sciences.

Bussey, K., & Bandura, A. (1999). Social cognitive theory of gender development and differentiation. *Psychological Review, 106,* 676–713

Butler, K. (2006, July 4). The grim neurology of teenage drinking. *The New York Times,* p. D1 and ff.

Butterfield, S. A., Lehnhard, R. A., & Coladarci, T. (2002). Age, sex, and body mass index in performance of selected locomotor and fitness tasks by children in grades K–2. *Perceptual and Motor Skills, 94*(1), 80–86.

Butterworth, G. (2001). Joint visual attention in infancy. In J. G. Bremner, & A. Fogel (Eds.), *Blackwell handbook of infant development* (pp. 213–240). Malden, MA: Blackwell.

Byrnes, J. (1997). *The nature and development of decision-making: A self-regulation model.* Hillsdale, NJ: Erlbaum.

Byrnes, J., Miller, D., & Schafer, W. (1999). Gender differences in risk taking: A meta-analysis. *Psychological Bulletin, 125,* 367–383.

Cahill, L. (2005, April 25). His brain, her brain. *Scientific American, 292,* 40–47.

Cairns, R. B., Cairns, B. D., & Neckerman, H. J. (1989). Growth and aggression: I. Childhood to early adolescence. *Developmental Psychology, 25,* 320–330.

Campbell, A., Shirley, L., & Candy, J. (2004). A longitudinal study of gender-related cognition and behavior. *Developmental Science, 7,* 1–9.

Campbell, F. A., & Ramey, C. T. (1995). Cognitive and school outcomes for high risk African-American students at middle adolescence: Positive effects of early intervention. *American Educational Research Journal, 32,* 743–772.

Campbell, F. A., Pungello, E. P., Miller-Johnson, S., Burchinal, M., & Ramey, C. T. (2001). The development of cognitive and academic abilities: Growth curves from an early childhood educational experiment. *Developmental Psychology, 37,* 231–242.

Campbell, S. B., Spieker, S., Burchinal, M., Poe, M. D., & The NICHD Early Child Care Research Network. (2006). Trajectories of aggression from toddlerhood to age 9 predict academic and social functioning through age 12. *Journal of Child Psychology and Psychiatry, 47,* 791–800.

Campos, J. J., & Stenberg, C. (1981). Perception, appraisal, and emotion: The onset of social referencing. In M. E. Lamb & L.

R. Sherrod (Eds.), *Infant social cognition: Empirical and theoretical considerations* (pp. 273–314). Hillsdale, NJ: Erlbaum.

Camras, L. A., Perlman, S. B., Wismer Fries, A. B., & Pollak, S. D. (2006). Post-institutionalized Chinese and Eastern European Children: Heterogeneity in the development of emotion understanding. *International Journal of Behavioural Development, 30,* 193–199.

Carey, S. (1978). The child as word learner. In M. Halle, J. Bresnan, & G. A. Miller (Eds.), *Linguistic theory and psychological reality* (pp. 264–293). Cambridge, MA: MIT Press.

Carey, S., & Bartlett, E. (1978). Acquiring a single new word. *Proceedings of the Stanford Child Language Conference, 15,* 17–29. (Republished in *Papers and Reports on Child Language Development, 15,* 17–29.)

Carlson, E., Sroufe, L. A., Collins, W. A., Jimerson, S., Weinfield, N., Henninghausen, K., Egeland, B., Hyson, D., Anderson, F., & Meyer, S. (1999). Early environmental support and elementary school adjustment as predictors of school adjustment in middle adolescence. *Journal of Adolescent Research, 14,* 72–94.

Carr, M., Borkowski, J., & Maxwell, S. (1991). Motivational components of underachievement. *Developmental Psychology, 27,* 108–118.

Carrion, V. G., Weems, C. F., & Reiss, A. L. (2007). Stress predicts brain changes in children: A Pilot longitudinal study on youth stress, posttraumatic stress disorder, and the hippocampus. *Pediatrics, 119,* 509–516.

Carskadon, M., & Acebo, C. (2002). Regulation of sleepiness in adolescence: Update, insights, and speculation. *Sleep, 25,* 606–616.

Carskadon, M., Acebo, C., Richardson, G., Tate, B., & Seifer, R. (1997). Long nights protocol: Access to circadian parameters in adolescents. *Journal of Biological Rhythms, 12,* 278–289.

Carver, P. R., & Iruka, I. U. (2006). *After-school programs and activities: 2005* (NCES 2006–076). Washington, DC: U.S. Department of Education, National Center for Education Statistics.

Case-Smith, J. (2005). *Occupational therapy for children* (5th ed.). St. Louis, MO: Mosby.

Casey, B. J., Tottenham, N., Liston, C., & Durston, S. (2005). Imaging the developing brain: What have we learned about cognitive development? *Trends in Cognitive Science, 9,* 104–110.

Caspi, A., Sugden, K., Moffitt, T., Taylor, A., Craig, I., Harrington, H., et al. (2003). Influence of life stress on depression: Moderation by a polymorphism in the 5-HTT gene. *Science, 301,* 386–389.

Castelli, D. (2005). Academic achievement and physical fitness in third-, fourth-, and fifth-grade students. *Research Quarterly for Exercise and Sport, 76*(1), A–15.

Castelli, D. M., Hillman, C. H., Buck, S., & Erwin, H. E. (2007). Physical fitness and academic achievement in 3rd and 5th grade students. *Journal of Sport and Exercise Psychology, 29,* 239–252.

Caviness, V. S., & Grant, P. E. (2006). Our unborn children at risk? *Proceedings for the National Academy of Sciences, 103,* 12661–12662.

Ceci, S. J., & Roazzi, A. (1994). The effects of context on cognition: Postcards from Brazil. In R. J. Sternberg & R. K. Wagnes (Eds.), *Mind in context: Interactionist perspectives on human intelligence* (pp. 74–101). New York: Cambridge University Press.

Ceci, S. J., Ross, D. F., & Toglia, M. P. (1987). Suggestibility in children's memory: Psycholegal implications. *Journal of Experimental Psychology: General, 116,* 38–49.

Centers for Disease Control. (2006a, September 12). Table 4. Estimated numbers of diagnoses of AIDS in children Centers for Disease Control. (2006b, May 12). Vaccine preventable deaths and the global immunization vision and strategy, 2006–2015. Retrieved August 11, 2008, from http://www.cdc.gov/mmwr/preview/mmwrhtml/mm5518a4.htm

Centers for Disease Control. (2006c, April 12). *Why is preconception care a public health concern?* Retrieved August 18, 2008, from http://www.cdc.gov/ncbddd/preconception/why-preconception.htm

Centers for Disease Control. (2007). Prevalence of the Autism Spectrum Disorders in multiple areas of the United States, surveillance years 2000 and 2002: A report from the Autism and Developmental Disabilities Monitoring (ADDM) Network. Retrieved July 27, 2008, from http://www.cdc.gov/ncbddd/dd/addmprevalence.htm

Centers for Disease Control. (2008, June 3). *Safe motherhood.* Retrieved August 13, 2008, from http://www.cdc.gov/reproductivehealth/

Centers for Disease Control and Prevention. (2004). *NCHS data on teenage pregnancy.* Washington: Author.

Centers for Disease Control and Prevention. (2005). Swimming and recreational water safety. In *Health information for international travel 2005–2006.* Atlanta: U.S. Department of Health and Human Services, Public Health Service.

Centers for Disease Control and Prevention. (2006).Youth risk behavior surveillance—United States, 2005. *Morbidity & Mortality Weekly Report, 55*(SS-5), 1–108.

Centers for Disease Control and Prevention. (2007). *Child passenger safety: Fact sheet.* Retrieved May 8, 2007 from http://www.cdc.gov/ncipc/factsheets/childpas.htm

Chall, J. (1970). *Learning to read: The great debate.* New York: Wiley.

Champagne F., Francis D., Mar, A., & Meaney, M. (2003). Variations in maternal care in the rat as a mediating influence for the effects of environment on development. *Physiology and Behavior, 79,* 359–371.

Chan, D. (1997). Depressive symptoms and perceived competence among Chinese secondary school students in Hong Kong. *Journal of Youth and Adolescence, 26,* 303–319.

Chao, R., & Tseng, V. (2002). Parenting of Asians. In M. H. Bornstein (Ed.), *Handbook of parenting: Vol. 4. Social conditions and applied parenting* (pp. 59–93). Mahwah, NJ: Erlbaum.

Chapman, R. S. (1997). Language development in children and adolescents with Down syndrome. *Mental Retardation and Developmental Disabilities Research Reviews, 3,* 307–312.

Chase, W. G., & Simon, H. A. (1973). Perception in chess. *Cognitive Psychology, 4,* 55–81.

Chassin, L., Hussong, A., & Beltran, I. (in press). Adolescent substance use. In R. Lerner & L. Steinberg (Eds.), *Handbook of adolescent psychology* (3rd ed.). New York: Wiley.

Chen, C., & Stevenson, H. (1995). Motivation and mathematics achievement: A comparative study of Asian-American, Caucasian-American, and East Asian high school students. *Child Development, 66,* 1215–1234.

Chen, X., Chang, L., & He, Y. (2003). The peer group as a context: Mediating and moderating effects on the relation between academic achievement and social functioning in Chinese children. *Child Development, 74*, 710–727.

Chen, X., French, D. C., & Schneider, B. H. (2006). Culture and peer relationships. In X. Chen, D. R. French, & B. H. Schneider (Eds.), *Peer relationships in cultural context* (pp. 3–20). New York: Cambridge University Press.

Chen, X., Liu, W., Li, B., Gen, G., Chen, H., & Wang, L. (2000). Maternal authoritative and authoritarian attitudes and mother-child interactions and relationships in urban China. *International Journal of Behavioral Development, 24*, 119–126.

Chen, X., Rubin, K., & Li, Z. (1995). Social functioning and adjustment in Chinese children: A longitudinal study. *Developmental Psychology, 31*, 531–539.

Chen, X., Wu, H., Chen, H., Wang, L. & Cen, G. (2001). Parenting practices and aggressive behavior in Chinese children. *Parenting, 1*, 159–184.

Chervenak, F. A., & McCullough, L. B. (1998). Ethical dimensions of ultrasound screening for fetal anomalies. *Annals of the New York Academy of Sciences, 847*, 185.

Chess, S., & Thomas, A. (1996). *Temperament: Theory and practice.* Philadelphia, PA: Brunner/Mazel.

Chi, M. T., & Koeske, R. (1983). Network representation of a child's dinosaur knowledge. *Developmental Psychology, 19*, 29–39.

Chomsky, N. (1965). *Aspects of the theory of syntax.* Oxford, England: M.I.T. Press.

Chomsky, N. (1968). *Language and mind.* New York: Harcourt Brace Jovanovich.

Christie-Mizell, C. A., Steelman, L. C., & Stewart, J. (2003). Seeing their surroundings: The effects of neighborhood setting and race on maternal distress. *Social Science Research, 32*, 402–428.

Christopher, F. (1995). Adolescent pregnancy prevention. *Family Relations, 44*, 384–391.

Chu, S. Y., Barker, L. E., & Smith, P. J. (2004). Racial/ethnic disparities in preschool immunizations: United States, 1996–2001. *American Journal of Public Health, 94*, 973–977.

Chumlea, W., Schubert, C., Roche, A., Kulin, H., Lee, P., Himes, J., et al. (2003). Age at menarche and racial comparisons in US girls. *Pediatrics, 111*, 110–113.

Cicchetti, D., & Manly, J. T. (2001). Operationalizing child maltreatment: Developmental processes and outcomes. *Developmental Psychopathology, 13*, 755–757.

Cillessen, A. H. N., Bukowski, W. M., & Haselager, G. T. (2000). Stability of dimensions and types of sociometric status. *New Directions for Child and Adolescent Development: Recent Advances in the Measurement of Acceptance and Rejection in the Peer System, 88*, 75–93.

Clark, E. (2006). Traumatic brain injuries. In G. G. Bear, & K. M. Minke (Eds.), *Children's needs III: Development, prevention, and intervention* (pp. 897–907). Washington, DC: National Association of School Psychologists.

Clark, E. V. (1998). Morphology in language acquisition. In A. Spencer & A. M. Zwicky (Eds.), *The handbook of morphology* (pp. 374–389). Oxford: Blackwell.

Clarke-Stewart, A., & Allhusen, V. D. (2005). *What we know about child care.* Cambridge, MA: Harvard University Press.

Clarke-Stewart, A., & Brentano, C. (2006). *Divorce: Causes and consequences.* New Haven, CT: Yale University Press.

Clarke-Stewart, K. A. (1998). Historical shifts and underlying themes in ideas about rearing young children in the United States: Where have we been? Where are we going? *Early Development & Parenting, 7*, 101–117.

Clarke-Stewart, K. A., & Allhusen, V. D. (2002). Nonparental caregiving. In M. H. Bornstein (Ed.), *Handbook of parenting: Vol. 3. Status and social conditions of parenting* (2nd ed., pp. 215–252). Mahwah, NJ: Erlbaum.

Clasen, D., & Brown, B. (1985). The multidimensionality of peer pressure in adolescence. *Journal of Youth and Adolescence, 14*, 451–468.

Claxton, L. J., Keen, R., & McCarty, M. E. (2003). Evidence of motor planning in infant reaching behavior. *Psychological Science, 14*, 354–356.

Cleveland, E., & Reese, E. (2005). Maternal structure and autonomy support in conversations about the past: Contributions to children's autobiographical memory. *Developmental Psychology, 41*, 376–388.

Cohen, D. A., McKenzie, T. L., Sehgal, A., Williamson, S., Golinelli, D., & Lurie, N. (2007). Contribution of public parks to physical activity. *American Journal of Public Health, 97*(3), 509–514.

Cohen, Y. (1964). *The transition from childhood to adolescence.* Chicago: Aldine.

Cohn, J. F., & Tronick, E. Z. (1983). Three-month-old infants' reaction to simulated maternal depression. *Child Development, 54*, 185–193.

Coie, J., Dodge, K. A., & Coppotelli, H. (1982). Dimensions and types of social status: A cross-age perspective. *Developmental Psychology, 18*, 557–570.

Coie, J., Terry, R., Lenox, K., Lochman, J., & Hyman, C. (1995). Childhood peer rejection and aggression as predictors of stable patterns of adolescent disorder. *Development and Psychopathology, 7*, 697–713.

Cole, A., & Kerns, K. A. (2001). Perceptions of sibling qualities and activities of early adolescents. *Journal of Early Adolescence, 21*, 204–226.

Cole, D. A., Maxwell, S. E., Martin, J. M., Peeke, L. G., Seroczynski, A. D., Tram, J. M., et al. (2001). The development of multiple domains of child and adolescent self-concept: A cohort sequential longitudinal design. *Child Development, 72*, 1723–1746.

Cole, D., & Jordan, A. (1995). Competence and memory: Integrating psychosocial and cognitive correlates of child depression. *Child Development, 66*, 459–473.

Cole, P., Zahn-Waxler, C., & Smith, D. (1994). Expressive control during a disappointment: Variations related to preschoolers' behavior problems. *Developmental Psychology, 30*, 835–846.

Coleman, J., Campbell, E., Hobson, C., McPartland, J., Mood, A., Weinfeld, F., & York, R. (1966). *Equality of educational opportunity.* Washington, DC: U.S. Government Printing Office.

Coleman, L. (1999). Comparing contraceptive use surveys of young people in the United Kingdom. *Archives of Sexual Behavior, 28*, 255–264.

Coley, R., & Chase-Lansdale, P. L. (1998). Adolescent pregnancy and parenthood: Recent evidence and future directions. *American Psychologist, 53,* 152–166.

Collins, W. A. (2003). More than a myth: The developmental significance of romantic relationships during adolescence. *Journal of Research on Adolescents, 13,* 1–24.

Collins, W. A., & Steinberg, L. (2006). Adolescent development in interpersonal context. In W. Damon & R. Lerner (Series Eds.) & N. Eisenberg (Vol. Ed.), *Handbook of child psychology: Vol. 3. Social, emotional, and personality development* (6th ed., pp. 1003–1067). New York: Wiley.

Collins, W. A., Maccoby, E. E., Steinberg, L., Hetherington, E. M., & Bornstein, M. H. (2000). Contemporary research on parenting: The case for nature and nurture. *American Psychologist, 55,* 218–232.

Committee on Prospering in the Global Economy. (2007). *Rising above the gathering storm: Energizing and employing America for a brighter economic future.* Washington, DC: National Academies Press.

Compas, B., Ey, S., & Grant, K. (1993). Taxonomy, assessment, and diagnosis of depression during adolescence. *Psychological Bulletin, 114,* 323–344.

Compas, B., Oppedisano, G., Connor, J., Gerhardt, C., Hinden, B., Achenbach, T., & Hammen, C. (1997). Gender differences in depressive symptoms in adolescence: Comparison of national samples of clinically referred and nonreferred youths. *Journal of Consulting and Clinical Psychology, 65,* 617–626.

Comstock, G., & Scharrer, E. (2006). Media and popular culture. In K. A. Renninger & I. E. Sigel (Eds.), *Handbook of child psychology: Vol. 4. Child psychology in practice* (pp. 817–863). Hoboken, NJ: Wiley.

Conde-Agudelo, A., Rosas-Bermúdez, A., & Kafury-Goeta, A. C. (2006). Birth spacing and risk of adverse perinatal outcomes a meta-analysis. *JAMA, 295,* 1809–1823.

Conger, K., Conger, R., & Scaramella, L. (1997). Parents, siblings, psychological control, and adolescent adjustment. *Journal of Adolescent Research, 12,* 113–138.

Connell, J., Halpern-Felsher, B., Clifford, E., Crichlow, W., & Usinger, P. (1995). Hanging in there: Behavioral, psychological, and contextual factors affecting whether African American adolescents stay in high school. *Journal of Adolescent Research, 10,* 41–63.

Connolly, J. (in press). Romantic relationships and intimacy in adolescence. In R. Lerner & L. Steinberg (Eds.), *Handbook of adolescent psychology.* New York: Wiley.

Connolly, J., & Johnson, A. (1993, March). *The psychosocial context of romantic relationships in adolescence.* Paper presented at the biennial meetings of the Society for Research in Child Development, New Orleans.

Conseur, A., Rivara, F., Barnoski, R., & Emanuel, I. (1997). Maternal and perinatal risk factors for later delinquency. *Pediatrics, 99,* 785–790.

Cook, T., Church, M., Ajanaku, S., Shadish, Jr., W., Kim, J., & Cohen, R. (1996). The development of occupational aspirations and expectations among inner-city boys. *Child Development, 67,* 3368–3385.

Cooley, C. H. (1902). *Human nature and the social order.* New York: Charles Scribner & Sons.

Cooper, H. (2004). Is the school calendar dated? In G. Borman & M. Boulay (Eds.), *Summer learning: Research, policies, and programs* (pp. 3–3). Mahwah, NJ: Erlbaum.

Coopersmith, S. A. (1967). *The antecedents of self-esteem.* San Francisco: Freeman.

Corbin, C. B., & Pangrazi, R. P. (1998). *Physical activity for children: A statement of guidelines.* Reston, VA: National Association for Sport and Physical Education.

Corsaro, W. A. (2006). Qualitative research on children's peer relations in cultural context. In X. Chen, D. R. French, & B. H. Schneider (Eds.), *Peer relationships in cultural context* (pp. 96–119). New York: Cambridge University Press.

Costa-Giomi, E. (2005). Does music instruction improve fine motor abilities? *Annals of the New York Academy of Science, 1060,* 262–264.

Cote, L. R., & Bornstein, M. H. (2005). Child and mother play in cultures of origin, acculturating cultures, and cultures of destination. *International Journal of Behavioral Development, 29,* 479–488.

Couperus, J. W., & Nelson, C. A. (2006). Early brain development and plasticity. In K. McCartney & D. Phillips (Eds.), *Blackwell handbook of early childhood development* (pp. 85–105). Malden, MA: Blackwell.

Cox, M. J., & Paley, B. (2003). Understanding families as systems. *Current Directions in Psychological Science, 12*(5), 193–196.

Crago, M. B. (1992). Communicative interaction and second language acquisition: An Inuit Example. *TESOL Quarterly, 26,* 487–505.

Crick, N. R., Casas, J. F., & Mosher, M. (1997). Relational and overt aggression in preschool. *Developmental Psychology, 33,* 579–588.

Crick, N. R., Casas, J. F., & Nelson, D. A. (2002). Toward a more comprehensive understanding of peer maltreatment: Studies of relational victimization. *Current Directions in Psychological Science, 11,* 98–101.

Crick, N. R., & Grotpeter, J. K. (1995). Relational aggression, gender, and social-psychological adjustment. *Child Development, 66,* 710–722.

Crick, N. R., Ostrov, J. M., & Werner, N. E. (2006). A longitudinal study of relational aggression, physical aggression, and children's social-psychological adjustment. *Journal of Abnormal Child Psychology, 34,* 131–142.

Crosby, R. A., DiClemente, R. J., Wingood, G. M., Lang, D., & Harrington, K. F. (2003). Value of consistent condom use: A study of sexually transmitted disease prevention among African American adolescent females. *American Journal of Public Health, 93,* 901–902.

Crosnoe, R., & Needham, B. (2004). Holism, contextual variability, and the study of friendships in adolescent development. *Child Development, 75,* 264–279.

Cross, W. (1978). The Thomas and Cook models of psychological nigrescence: A literature review. *Journal of Black Psychology, 4,* 13–31.

Csikszentmihalyi, M., Rathunde, K., & Whalen, S. (1993). *Talented teenagers.* New York: Cambridge University Press.

Cuéllar, I., Arnold, B., & Gonzalez, G. (1995). Cognitive referents of acculturation: Assessment of cultural constructs in Latinos. *Journal of Community Psychology, 23,* 339–356.

Cummings, E. M. & Davies, P. (1994). *Children and marital conflict: The impact of family dispute and resolution.* New York: Guilford.

Cummings, E. M., & Cummings, J. S. (2002). Parenting and attachment. In M. H. Bornstein (Ed.), *Handbook of parenting: Vol. 5. Practical parenting* (2nd ed., pp. 35–58). Mahwah, NJ: Erlbaum.

Cunningham, M., Bhattacharyya, S., & Benes, F. (2002), Amygdalo-cortical sprouting continues into early adulthood: Implications for the development of normal and abnormal function during adolescence. *Journal of Comparative Neurology, 453,* 116–30.

Cyranowski, J., & Frank, E. (2000). Adolescent onset of the gender difference in lifetime rates of major depression. *Archives of General Psychiatry, 57,* 21–27.

D'Angelo, L., Getson, P., Luban, N., & Gayle, H. (1991). Human immunodeficiency virus infection in urban adolescents: Can we predict who is at risk? *Pediatrics, 88,* 982–986.

Dalton, T. C. (1996). Was McGraw a maturationist? *American Psychologist, 51,* 551–552.

Darabi, K., & Ortiz, V. (1987). Childbearing among young Latino women in the United States. *American Journal of Public Health, 77,* 25–28.

Darling, N., & Steinberg, L. (1993). Parenting styles context: An integrative model. *Psychological Bulletin, 113,* 487–496.

Darling-Hammond, L. (2008). Creating excellent and equitable schools. *Educational Leadership, 65*(8), 14–21.

Darwin, C. (1872/1975). *The Expression of the emotions in man and animals.* Chicago: University of Chicago Press.

Darwin, C. (2003). *The origin of species.* New York: Signet Classics. (Original work published 1872)

Davies, P. T., & Windle, M. (2000). Middle adolescents' dating pathways and psychosocial adjustment. *Merrill-Palmer Quarterly, 46,* 90–118.

Davies, P.T., Sturge-Apple, M.L., Cicchetti, D., & Cummings, E.M. (2007). The role of child adrenocortical functioning in pathways between forms of interparental conflict and child maladjustment. *Developmental Psychology, 43,* 918–930.

Davis, E. P., Snidman, N., Wadhwa, P. D., Glynn, L. M., Schetter, C. D., & Sandman, C. A. (2004). Prenatal maternal anxiety and depression predict negative behavioral reactivity in infancy. *Infancy, 6,* 319–331.

Davison, K. K., & Birch, L. L. (2001). Weight status, parent reaction, and self-concept in five-year-old girls. *Pediatrics, 107,* 46–53.

De Wolff, M., & van Ijzendoorn, M. H. (1997). Sensitivity and attachment: A meta-analysis on parental antecedents of infant attachment. *Child Development, 68,* 571–591.

Dearing, E. (2004). The developmental implications of restrictive and supportive parenting across neighborhoods and ethnicities: Exceptions are the rule. *Applied Developmental Psychology, 25,* 555–575.

Dearing, E., Berry, D., & Zaslow, M. (2006). Poverty during early childhood. In K. McCartney & D. Phillips (Eds.), *Blackwell handbook of early childhood* development (pp. 399–423). Malden, MA: Blackwell.

Dearing, E., Kreider, H., Simpkins, S., & Weiss, H. B. (2006). Family involvement in school and low-income children's literacy: Longitudinal associations between and with families. *Journal of Educational Psychology, 98,* 653–664.

Deater-Deckard, K., & Plomin, R. (1999). An adoption study of etiology of teacher and parent reports of externalizing behavior problems in middle childhood. *Child Development, 70,* 144–154.

Décarie, T. G., & Ricard, M. (1996). Revisiting Piaget revisited or the vulnerability of Piaget's infancy theory in the 1990s. In G. G. Noam & K. W. Fischer (Eds.), *Development and vulnerability in close relationships* (pp. 113–132). Hillsdale, NJ: Erlbaum.

DeCasper, A. J., Lecanuet, J. P., Busnel, M. C., Granier-Deferre, C., & Maugeais, R. (1994). Fetal reactions to recurrent maternal speech. *Infant Behavior and Development, 17,* 159–164.

Deci, E., & Ryan, R. (1985). *Intrinsic motivation and self-determination in human behavior.* New York: Plenum.

Deese, J. (1959). On the prediction of certain verbal intrusions in free recall. *Journal of Experimental Psychology, 58,* 17–22.

DeLoache, J. S. (1987). Rapid change in the symbolic functioning of very young children. *Science, 238,* 1556–1557.

DeLoache, J. S. (1995). Early understanding and use of symbols: The model model. *Current Directions in Psychological Science, 4,* 109–113.

DeLoache, J. S., Cassidy, D. J., & Brown, A. L. (1985). Precursors of mnemonic strategies in very young children's memory. *Child Development, 56,* 125–137.

DeLoache, J. S., Miller, K. F., & Rosengren, K. S. (1997). The credible shrinking room: Very young children's performance with symbolic and nonsymbolic relations. *Psychological Science, 8,* 308–313.

Delva, J., Wallace, J. M., Jr., O'Malley, P. M., Bachman, J. G., Johnston, L. D. & Schulenberg, J. E. (2005). The epidemiology of alcohol, marijuana, and cocaine use among Mexican American, Puerto Rican, Cuban American, and other Latin American eighth-grade students in the United States: 1991–2002. *American Journal of Public Health, 95,* 696–702.

Demetriou, A., Christou, C., Spanoudis, G., & Platsidou, M. (2002). The development of mental processing: Efficiency, working memory, and thinking. *Monographs of the Society for Research in Child Development, 67*(1, Serial No. 268).

Demorest, A., Meyer, C., Phelps, E., Gardner, H., & Winner, E. (1984). Words speak louder than actions: Understanding deliberately false remarks. *Child Development, 55,* 1527–1534.

Denham, S., Mason, T., Caverly, S., Schmidt, M., Hackney, R., Caswell, C., & DeMulder, E. (2001). Preschoolers at play: Co-socialisers of emotional and social competence. *International Journal of Behavioral Development, 25,* 290–301.

Denham, S., McKinley, M., Couchould, E., & Holt, R. (1990). Emotional and behavioral predictors of preschool peer ratings. *Child Development, 61,* 1145–1152.

Dennis, P. (1995). Introduction: Johnny and Jimmy and the maturation controversy: Popularization, misunderstanding, and setting the record straight. In T. C. Dalton & V. W. Bergenn (Eds.), *Beyond heredity and environment: Myrtle McGraw and the maturation controversy* (pp. 67–76). Boulder, CO: Westview Press.

Dennis, T., Bendersky, M., Ramsay, D., & Lewis, M. (2006). Reactivity and regulation in children prenatally exposed to cocaine. *Developmental Psychology, 42,* 688–697.

Dettling, A. C., Gunnar, M. R., & Donzella, B. (1999). Cortisol levels of young children in full-day child care centers: Relations with age and temperament. *Psychoneuroendocrinology, 24,* 519–536.

Dettling, A. C., Parker, S. W., Lane, S. K., Sebanc, A. M., & Gunnar, M. R. (2000). Quality of care and temperament determine whether cortisol levels rise over the day for children in full-day child care. *Psychoneuroendocrinology, 25,* 819–836.

Dewhurst, S. A., & Robinson, C. A. (2004). False memories in children: Evidence for a shift from phonological to semantic associations. *Psychological Science, 15,* 782–786.

Diamond, A. (2005). Attention-deficit disorder (attention-deficit/hyperactivity disorder without hyperactivity): A neurobiologically and behaviorally distinct disorder from attention-deficit/hyperactivity disorder (with hyperactivity). *Development and Psychopathology, 17,* 807–825.

Dick, D. M., Rose, R. J., Pulkkinen, L., & Kaprio, J. (2001). Measuring puberty and understanding its impact: A longitudinal study of adolescent twins. *Journal of Youth and Adolescence, 30,* 385–400.

Dick, D. M., Rose, R. J., Viken, R. J., & Kaprio, J. (2000). Pubertal timing and substance use: Associations between and within families across late adolescence. *Developmental Psychology, 36,* 180–189.

Dickstein, S., & Parke, R. D. (1988). Social referencing in infancy: A glance at fathers and marriage. *Child Development, 59,* 506–511.

Dielman, T. (1994). School-based research on the prevention of adolescent alcohol use and misuse: Methodological issues and advances. *Journal of Research on Adolescence, 4,* 271–293.

Dingfelder, S. (2006). To sleep, perchance to twitch. *Monitor on Psychology, 37,* 51–60.

DiPietro, J. A., Bornstein, M. H., Costigan, K. A., Pressman, E. K., Hahn, C.-S., Painter, K. M. et al. (2002). What does fetal movement predict about behavior during the first two years of life? *Developmental Psychobiology, 40,* 358–371.

DiPietro, J. A., Bornstein, M. H., Hahn, C. S., Costigan, K., & Achy-Brou, A. (2007). Fetal heart rate and variability: Stability and prediction to developmental outcomes in early childhood. *Child Development, 78,* 1788–1798.

DiPietro, J. A., Novak, M. F. S. X., Costigan, K. A., Atella, L. D., & Reusing, S. P. (2006). Maternal psychological distress during pregnancy in relation to child development at age two. *Child Development, 77,* 573–587.

Dishion, T. J., Capaldi, D. M., & Yoerger, K. (1999). Middle childhood antecedents to progressions in male adolescent substance use: An ecological analysis of risk and protection. *Journal of Adolescent Research, 14,* 175–205.

Dishion, T., Patterson, G., Stoolmiller, M., & Skinner, M. (1991). Family, school, and behavioral antecedents to early adolescent involvement with antisocial peers. *Developmental Psychology, 27,* 172–180.

Dishion, T. J., Poulin, F., & Burraston, B. (2001). Peer group dynamics associated with iatrogenic effect in group interventions with high-risk young adolescents. *New Directions for Child and Adolescent Development, 91,* 79–92.

Dodge, K. A., Coie, J., & Lynam, D. (2006). Aggression and antisocial behavior in youth. In W. Damon & R. M. Lerner (Series Eds.) & N. Eisenberg (Vol. Ed.), *Handbook of child psychology: Vol. 3. Social, emotional, and personality development* (6th ed., pp. 719–788). Hoboken, NJ: Wiley.

Dodge, K. A., McClaskey, C. L., & Feldman, E. (1985). A situational approach to the assessment of social competence in children. *Journal of Consulting and Clinical Psychology, 53,* 344–353.

Dodge, K. A., Pettit, G., & Bates, J. (1994). Socialization mediators of the relation between socioeconomic status and child conduct problems. *Child Development, 65,* 649–665.

Donaldson, D. L., & Owens J. A. (2006). Sleep and sleep problems. In G. G. Bear & K. M. Minke (Eds.), *Children's needs III: Development, prevention, and intervention* (3rd ed., pp. 1025–1039). Bethesda, MD: National Association of School Psychologists.

Dorn, L. D., Nottelmann, E. D., Susman, E. J., Inoff-Germain, G., Cutler, G. B., Jr., & Chrousos, G. P. (1999). Variability in hormone concentrations and self-reported menstrual histories in young adolescents: Menarche as an integral part of a developmental process. *Journal of Youth and Adolescence, 28,* 283–304.

Douvan, E., & Adelson, J. (1966). *The adolescent experience.* New York: Wiley.

Downer, J. T., & Pianta, R. C. (2006). Academic and cognitive functioning in first grade: Associations with earlier home and child care predictors and with concurrent home and classroom experiences. *School Psychology Review, 35,* 11–30.

Dromi, E. (1987). *Early lexical development.* New York: Cambridge University Press.

Dromi, E. (2001). Babbling and early words. In N. J. Salkind & L. H. Margolis (Eds.), *Child development: Volume 1 of the Macmillan psychology reference series.* New York: Macmillan References.

DuBois, D. L., Burk-Braxton, C., Swenson, L. P., Tevendale, H. D., & Hardesty, J. L. (2002). Race and gender influences on adjustment in early adolescence: Investigation of an integrative model. *Child Development, 73,* 1573–1592.

Duncan, O., Featherman, D., & Duncan, B. (1972). *Socioeconomic background and achievement.* New York: Semmar Press.

Duncan, P., Ritter, P., Dornbusch, S., Gross, R., & Carlsmith, J. (1985). The effects of pubertal timing on body image, school behavior, and deviance. *Journal of Youth and Adolescence, 14,* 227–236.

Dunn, J. (1991). Understanding others: Evidence from naturalistic studies of children. In A. Whiten (Ed.), *Natural theories of mind: Evolution, development, and simulation of everyday mindreading* (pp. 51–61). Cambridge, MA: Blackwell.

Dunn, J. (2000). Mind-reading, emotion understanding, and relationships. *International Journal of Behavioral Development, 24,* 142–144.

Dunn, J. (2002). Sibling relationships. In P. K. Smith & C. H. Hart (Eds.), *Blackwell handbook of childhood social development* (pp. 223–237). Malden, MA: Blackwell.

Dunn, J., Brown, J., Slomkowski, C., Telsa, & Youngblade, L. (1991). Young children's understanding of other people's feelings and beliefs: Individual differences and their antecedents. *Child Development, 62,* 1352–1366.

Dunn, J., & Kendrick, C. (1982). The speech of two-and three-year-olds to infant siblings. *Journal of Child Language, 9,* 579–595.

Dweck, C., & Licht, B. (1980). Learned helplessness and intellectual achievement. In J. Garber & M. Seligman (Eds.),

Human helplessness (pp. 197–222). New York: Academic Press.

Dweck, C., & Wortman, C. (1980). Achievement, test anxiety, and learned helplessness: Adaptive and maladaptive cognitions. In H. Krohne & L. Laux (Eds.), *Achievement, stress, and anxiety* (pp. 93–125). Washington, DC: Hemisphere.

East, P. (in press). Adolescents' relationships with siblings. In R. Lerner & L. Steinberg (Eds.), *Handbook of adolescent psychology*. New York: Wiley.

East, P., & Blaustein, E. (1995, March). *Perceived timing of life-course transitions: Race differences in early adolescent girls' sexual, marriage, and childbearing expectations.* Paper presented at the biennial meetings of the Society for Research in Child Development.

East, P. L., & Jacobson, L. J. (2001). The younger siblings of teenage mothers: A follow-up of their pregnancy risk. *Developmental Psychology, 37,* 254–264.

East, P. L., & Rook, K. S. (1992). Compensatory patterns of support among children's peer relationships: Test using school friends, nonschool friends, and siblings. *Developmental Psychology, 28,* 163–172.

East, W. B., & Hensley, L. D. (1985). The effects of selected sociocultural factors upon the overhand-throwing performance of prepubescent children. In J. E. Clark & J. H. Humphrey (Eds.), *Motor development* (pp. 115–127). Princeton, NJ: Princeton Book Company.

Eaton, M. J., & Dembo, M. H. (1997). Differences in the motivational beliefs of Asian American and non-Asian students. *Journal of Educational Psychology, 89,* 433–440.

Eaton, W. O., & Enns, L. R. (1986). Sex differences in human motor activity level. *Psychological Bulletin, 100,* 19–28.

Ebstyne King, P., & Furrow, J.L. (2004). Religion as a resource for positive youth development: Religion, social capital, and moral outcomes. *Developmental Psychology, 40,* 703–713.

Eccles, J., & Roeser, R. (in press). Schools, academic motivation, and stage-environment fit. In R. Lerner & L. Steinberg (Eds.), *Handbook of adolescent psychology* (3rd ed.). New York: Wiley.

Eccles, J., Wigfield, A., Harold, R. D., & Blumenfeld, P. (1993). Age and gender differences in children's self- and task perceptions during elementary school. *Child Development, 64,* 830–847.

Eder, D. (1985). The cycle of popularity: Interpersonal relations among female adolescence. *Sociology of Education, 58,* 154–165.

Edwards, R., Manstead, A., & MacDonald, C. J. (1984). The relationship between children's sociometric status and ability to recognize facial expressions and emotion. *European Journal of Social Psychology, 14,* 235–238.

Ehrenberg, R. G., Brewer, D. J., Gamoran, A., & Willms, J. D. (2001). Class size and student achievement. *Psychological Science in the Public Interest, 2,* 1–30.

Eisenberg, N., Cumberland, A., Spinrad, T. L., Fabes, R. A., Shepard, S. A., Reiser, M., et al. (2001). The relations of regulation and emotionality to children's externalizing and internalizing problem behavior. *Development and Psychopathology, 72,* 1112–1134.

Eisenberg, N., & Fabes, R. (1998). Prosocial development. In W. Damon (Ed.) & N. Eisenberg (Vol. Ed.), *Handbook of child psychology: Vol. 3. Social, emotional, and personality development* (5th ed., pp. 701–778). New York: Wiley.

Eisenberg, N., Fabes, R., Nyman, M. Bernweig, J., & Pinuelas, A. (1994). The relations of emotionality and regulation to young children's anger-related reactions. *Child Development, 62,* 1393–1408.

Eisenberg, N., Fabes, R., & Spinrad, T. L. (2006). Prosocial development. In W. Damon & R. M. Lerner (Series Eds.) & N. Eisenberg (Vol. Ed.), *Handbook of child psychology: Vol. 3. Social, emotional, and personality development* (6th ed., pp. 646–718). Hoboken, NJ: Wiley.

Eisenberg, N., & Morris, A. S. (2004). Moral cognitions and prosocial responding. In R. M. Lerner & L. Steinberg (Eds.), *Handbook of adolescent psychology* (2nd ed., pp. 646–718). New York: Wiley.

Eisenberg, N., & Spinrad, T. (2004). Emotion-related regulation: Sharpening the definition. *Child Development, 75,* 334–339.

Eisenberg-Berg, N. (1979). The development of children's prosocial moral judgment. *Developmental Psychology, 15,* 518–534.

Ekman, P. (1984). Expression and the nature of emotion. In K. R. Scherer & P. Ekman (Eds.), *Approaches to emotion* (pp. 319–343). Hillsdale, NJ: Erlbaum.

Ekman, P. (Ed.). (2006). *Darwin and facial expression: A century of research in review.* New York: Malor Books.

Ekwo, E. E., & Moawad, A. (2000). Maternal age and preterm births in a black population. *Paediatric and Perinatal Epidemiology, 14,* 145–151.

Elder, G., Jr., & Shanahan, M. (2006_). The life course and human development. In W. Damon & R. Lerner (Series Eds.) & R. Lerner (Vol. Ed.), *Handbook of child psychology: Vol. 1. Theoretical models of human development* (6th ed., pp. 665–716). New York: Wiley.

Elkind, D. (1967). Egocentrism in adolescence. *Child Development, 38,* 1025–1034.

Elkind, D. (1978). Understanding the young adolescent. *Adolescence, 13,* 127–134.

Elkind, D. (2001). *The hurried child: Growing up too fast too soon.* Cambridge, MA: Perseus Publishing.

Elkins, I., McGue, M., & Iacono, W. (1997). Genetic and environmental influences on parent-son relationships: Evidence for increasing genetic influence during adolescence. *Developmental Psychology, 33,* 351–363.

Ellickson, P., Bell, R., & McGuigan, K. (1993). Preventing adolescent drug use: Long-term results of a junior high program. *American Journal of Public Health, 83,* 856–861.

El-Sheikh, M., Buckhalt, J. A., Mize, J., & Acebo, C. (2006). Marital conflict and disruption of children's sleep. *Child Development, 77*(1), 31–43.

Emmerich, W., & Shepard, K. (1982). Development of sex-differentiated preferences during late childhood and adolescence. *Developmental Psychology, 18,* 406–417.

Ennett, S. T., Bauman, K. E., Hussong, A., Faris, R., Foshee, V. A., Cai, L., & DuRant, R. (2006). The peer context of adolescent substance use: Findings from social network analysis. *Journal of Research on Adolescence, 16,* 159–186.

Ennett, S. T., Tobler, N. S., Ringwalt, C. L., & Flewelling, R. L. (1994). How effective is drug abuse resistance education? A meta-analysis of Project DARE outcome evaluations. *American Journal of Public Health, 84,* 1394–1401.

Enright, R., Levy, V., Harris, D., & Lapsley, D. (1987). Do economic conditions influence how theorists view adolescents? *Journal of Youth and Adolescence, 16,* 541–560.

Entwisle, D., & Hayduk, L. (1988). Lasting effects of elementary school. *Sociology of Education, 61,* 147–159.

Epstein, J. (1983). The influence of friends on achievement and affective outcomes. In J. Epstein & N. Karweit (Eds.), *Friends in school* (pp. 177–200). New York: Academic Press.

Erickson, S. J., Robinson, T., Haydel, K., & Killen, J. D. (2000). Are overweight children unhappy? Body mass index, depressive symptoms, and overweight concerns in elementary school children. *Archives of Pediatrics & Adolescent Medicine, 154,* 931–935.

Erikson, E. (1959). Identity and the life cycle. *Psychological Issues, 1,* 1–171.

Erikson, E. H. (1963). *Childhood and Society.* New York: Norton.

Erting, C., Thumann-Prezioso, C., & Sonnenstrahl-Benedict, B. (2000). Bilingualism in deaf families: Fingerspelling in early childhood. In P. E. Spencer, C. J. Erting, & M. Marschark (Eds.). *The deaf child in the family and at school* (pp. 41–54). Mahwah, NJ: Erlbaum.

Eskenazi, B., Marks, A. R., Bradman, A., Fenster, L,. Johnson, C., Barr, D. B., & Jewell, N. P. (2006). In utero exposure to dichlorodiphenyltrichloroethane (DDT) and dichlorodiphenyldichloroethylene (DDE) and neurodevelopment among young Mexican American children. *Pediatrics, 118,* 223–241.

Everett, S. A., Warren, C. W., Santelli, J. S., Kann, L., Collins, J. L., & Kolbe, L. J. (2000). Use of birth control pills, condoms, and withdrawal among U.S. high school students. *Journal of Adolescent Health, 27,* 112–118.

Ewing, M. E., & Seefeldt, V. (2002). Patterns of participation in American agency-sponsored youth sports. In F. L. Smoll & R. E. Smith (Eds.), *Children and youth in sport: A biopsychosocial perspective* (pp. 39–59). Iowa: Kendall/Hunt Publishing Company.

Fabes, R., Eisenberg, N., Nyman, M., & Michaelieu, Q. (1991). Young children's appraisals of others' spontaneous emotional reactions. *Developmental Psychology, 27,* 858–866.

Fabes, R., A., Hanish, L. D., & Martin, C. L. (2007). The next 50 years: Considering gender as a context for understanding young children's peer relationships. In G. Ladd (Ed.), *Appraising the human developmental sciences: Essays in honor of Merrill-Palmer Quarterly* (pp. 186–199). Detroit, MI: Wayne State University Press.

Fagot, B. I., & Leinbach, M. D. (1989). The young child's gender schema: Environmental input, internal organization. *Child Development, 60,* 663–672.

Faith, M. S., Scanlon, K. S., Birch, L. L., Francis, L. A., & Sherry, B. (2004). Parent-child feeding strategies and their relationships to child eating and weight status. *Obesity Research, 12,* 1711–1722.

Farrington, D. (in press). Conduct disorder, aggression, and delinquency. In R. Lerner & L. Steinberg (Eds.), *Handbook of adolescent psychology* (3rd ed.). New York: Wiley.

Fasick, F. (1994). On the "invention" of adolescence. *Journal of Early Adolescence, 14,* 6–23.

Fauth, R. C., Leventhal, T., & Brooks-Gunn, J. (2007). Welcome to the neighborhood? Long-term impacts of moving to low-poverty neighborhoods on poor children's and adolescents' outcomes. *Journal of Research on Adolescence, 17,* 249–284.

Featherman, D. (1980). Schooling and occupational careers: Constancy and change in worldly success. In O. Brim, Jr., & J. Kagan (Eds.), *Constancy and change in human development* (pp. 675–738). Cambridge, MA: Harvard University Press.

Federal Interagency Forum on Child and Family Statistics. (2007). *America's children: Key national indicators of well-being 2007.* Washington, DC: U.S. Government Printing Office.

Fein, G. G. (1996). Infants in group care: Patterns of despair and detachment. *Early Childhood Research Quarterly, 10,* 261–275.

Fein, G. G., Gariboldi, A., & Boni, R. (1993). The adjustment of infants and toddlers to group care: The first 6 months. *Early Childhood Research Quarterly, 8,* 1–14.

Feiring, C. (1993, March). *Developing concepts of romance from 15 to 18 years.* Paper presented at the biennial meetings of the Society for Research in Child Development, New Orleans.

Feiring, C. (1999). Gender identity and the development of romantic relationships in adolescence. In W. Furman, B. Brown, & C. Feiring (Eds.), *Contemporary perspectives on adolescent romantic relationships* (pp. 211–232). New York: Cambridge University Press.

Feldman, S., & Gehring, T. (1988). Changing perceptions of family cohesion and power across adolescence. *Child Development, 59,* 1034–1045.

Fenichel, E., Lurie-Hurvitz, E., & Griffin, A. (1999). Seizing the moment to build momentum for quality infant/toddler child care. *Zero to Three Bulletin, 19,* 3–17.

Fenson, L., Dale, P. S., Reznick, J. S., Thal, D., Bates, E., & Hartung, J. (1993). *User's guide and technical manual for the MacArthur Communicative Development Inventories.* San Diego, CA: Singular Press.

Field, T. (1998). Maternal depression effects on infants and early interventions. *Preventive Medicine: An International Journal Devoted to Practice and Theory, 27,* 200–203.

Field, T. M., Woodson, R., Greenberg, R., & Cohen, D. (1982). Discrimination and imitation of facial expressions by neonates. *Science, 218,* 179–181.

Field, T., Diego, M., Hernandez-Reif, M., Vera, Y., Gil, K., Schanberg, S., et al. (2004). Prenatal predictors of maternal and newborn EEG. *Infant Behavior & Development, 27,* 533–536.

Finch, C., & Kirkwood, T. (2000). *Chance, development, and aging.* New York: Oxford University Press.

Fine, G., Mortimer, J., & Roberts, D. (1990). Leisure, work, and the mass media. In S. Feldman & G. Elliott (Eds.), *At the threshold: The developing adolescent* (pp. 225–252). Cambridge, MA: Harvard University Press.

Finn, J. D., & Achilles, C. M. (1999). Tennessee's class size study: Findings, implications, and misconceptions. *Educational Evaluation and Policy Analysis, 21,* 97–109.

Fischer, K. W. (in press). Dynamic cycles of cognitive and brain development: Measuring growth in mind, brain, and education. In A. M. Battro, K. W. Fischer, & P. J. Lena (Eds.), *The educated brain.* Cambridge, UK: Cambridge University Press.

Fisher, C., Wallace, S. A., & Fenton, R. E. (2000). Discrimination distress during adolescence. *Journal of Youth and Adolescence, 29,* 679–695.

Fisher, J. O., Rolls, B. J., & Birch, L. L. (2003). Children's bite size and intake of an entrée are greater with large portions than with age-appropriate or self-selected portions. *American Journal of Clinical Nutrition, 77*, 1164–1170.

Fisher, M., Golden, N., Katzman, D., Kriepe, R., Rees, J., Schebendach, J., et al. (1995). Eating disorders in adolescents: A background paper. *Journal of Adolescent Health, 16*, 420–437.

Fivush, R. (2001). Owning experience: Developing subjective perspectives in autobiographical narratives. In C. Moore & K. Lemmon (Eds.), *The self in time* (pp. 35–52). Mahwah, NJ: Erlbaum.

Fivush, R., Brotman, M. A., Buckner, J. P., & Goodman, S. H. (2000). Gender differences in parent-child emotion narratives. *Sex Roles, 42*, 233–253.

Fivush, R., Haden, C., & Reese, E. (1996). Remembering, recounting, and reminiscing: The development of autobiographical memory in social context. In D. C. Rubin (Ed.), *Remembering our past: Studies in autobiographical memory* (pp. 341–359). Cambridge, UK: Cambridge University Press.

Fivush, R., Hudson, J. A., & Nelson, K. (1984). Children's long term memory for a novel event: An exploratory study. *Merrill-Palmer Quarterly, 30*, 303–316.

Flannery, D., Torquati, J., & Lindemeier, L. (1994). The method and meaning of emotional expression and experience during adolescence. *Journal of Adolescent Research, 9*, 8–27.

Flavell, J. (1963). *The developmental psychology of Jean Piaget.* Princeton, NJ: Van Nostrand Reinhold.

Flavell, J. H., Flavell, E. R., & Green, F. L. (1983). Development of the appearance-reality distinction. *Cognitive Psychology, 15*, 95–120.

Flynn, B., Worden, J., Secker-Walker, R., Pirie, P., Badger, G., Carpenter, J., & Geller, B. (1994). Mass media and school interventions for cogarette smoking prevention: Effects 2 years after completion. *American Journal of Public Health, 84*, 1148–1150.

Fogler, J. (2007, April 30). *Mother-to-child HIV transmission: A thing of the past?* [PowerPoint slides]. Retrieved from http://www.cdc.gov/hiv/topics/perinatal/resources/meetings/2007/pdf/Fogler_MTCT.pdf

Forbes, E. E. & Dahl, R. E. (2005). Neural systems of positive affect: Relevance to understanding child and adolescent depression? *Development and Psychopathology, 17*, 827–850.

Fox, N. A., Henderson, H. A., Rubin, K. H., Calkins, S. D., & Schmidt, L. A. (2001). Continuity and discontinuity of behavioral inhibition and exuberance: Psychophysiological and behavioral influences across the first four years of life. *Child Development, 72*, 1–21.

Franklin, C., Grant, D., Corcoran, J., Miller, P., & Bultman, L. (1997). Effectiveness of prevention programs for adolescent pregnancy: A meta-analysis. *Journal of Marriage and the Family, 59*, 551–567.

Fredriksen, K., Rhodes, J., Reddy, R., & Way. N. (2004). Sleepless in Chicago: Tracking the effects of adolescent sleep loss during the middle school years. *Child Development, 75*, 84–95.

Freeman, M. A. (1978). *Life among the Qallunaat.* Edmonton, Canada: Hurtig Publishers.

French, S. E., Seidman, E., Allen, L., & Aber, J. L. (2006). The development of ethnic identity during adolescence. *Developmental Psychology, 42*, 1–10.

French, S., Story, M., Downes, B., Resnick, M., & Blum, R. (1995). Frequent dieting among adolescents: Psychosocial and health behavior correlates. *American Journal of Public Health, 85*, 695–701.

Freud, S. (1910). The origin and development of psychoanalysis. *American Journal of Psychology, 21*, 181–218.

Freud, S. (1916/1917). *Introductory lectures on psychoanalysis.* London: Hogarth Press.

Freud, S. (1949). *An outline of psychoanalysis.* Oxford: W. W. Norton.

Freud, S. (1966). *Psychopathology of everyday life* (J. Strachey, Trans.). London: Ernest Benn. (Original work published in 1901).

Friedman, T. L. (2007). *The world is flat: A brief history of the twenty-first century (Further updated and expanded).* New York: Farrar, Straus and Giroux.

Frisch, R. (1983). Fatness, puberty, and fertility: The effects of nutrition and physical training on menarche and ovulation. In J. Brooks-Gunn & A. Petersen (Eds.), *Girls at puberty* (pp. 29–49). New York: Plenum.

Frost, J., & Forrest, J. (1995). Understanding the impact of effective teenage pregnancy prevention programs. *Family Planning Perspectives, 27*, 188–195.

Fryer, S. L., McGee, C. L., Matt, G. E., Riley, E. P., & Mattson, S. N. (2007). Evaluation of psychopathological conditions in children with heavy prenatal alcohol exposure. *Pediatrics, 119*, 733–741.

Fuligni, A. (1994, February). *Academic achievement and motivation among Asian-American and European-American early adolescents.* Paper presented at the biennial meetings of the Society for Research on Adolescence, San Diego.

Fuligni, A. (1997). The academic achievement of adolescents from immigrant families: The roles of family background, attitudes, and behavior. *Child Development, 68*, 351–363.

Fuligni, A. J., & Witkow, M. (2004). The postsecondary educational progress of youth from immigrant families. *Journal of Research on Adolescence, 14*, 159–183.

Fuligni, A., & Eccles, J. (1993). Perceived parent-child relationships and early adolescents' orientation toward peers. *Developmental Psychology, 29*, 622–632.

Fuligni, A., Tseng, V., & Lam, M. (1999). Attitudes toward family obligations among American adolescents from Asian, Latin American, and European backgrounds. *Child Development, 70*, 1030–1044.

Fuller, B., Wright, J., Gesicki, K., & Kange, E. (2007). Gauging growth: How to judge No Child Left Behind? *Educational Researcher, 36*, 268–278.

Furbey, M., & Beyth-Marom, R. (1992). Risk-taking in adolescence: A decision-making perspective. *Developmental Review, 12*, 1–44.

Furman, W., & Buhrmester, D. (1985). Children's perceptions of the personal relationships in their social networks. *Developmental Psychology, 21*, 1016–1024.

Furman, W., & Lanthier, R. (2002). Parenting siblings. In M. H. Bornstein (Ed.), *Handbook of parenting: Vol. 1. Children and parenting* (2nd ed., pp. 165–188). Mahwah, NJ: Erlbaum.

Furstenberg, F., Jr., Brooks-Gunn, J., & Morgan, S. (1987). *Adolescent mothers in later life.* New York: Cambridge University Press.

Gable, S., & Lutz, S. (2000). Household, parent, and child contributions to childhood obesity. *Family Relations, 49,* 293–300.

Galambos, N. L., Barker, E. T., & Krahn, H. J. (2006). Depression, self-esteem, and anger in emerging adulthood: Seven-year trajectories. *Developmental Psychology, 42,* 350–365.

Galen, B. R., & Underwood, M. K. (1997). A developmental investigation of social aggression among children. *Developmental Psychology, 33,* 589–600.

Gallay, M., Baudouin, J., Durand., K, Lemoine, C., & Lécuyer, R. (2006). Qualitative differences in the exploration of upright and upside-down faces in four-month-old infants: An eye-movement study. *Child Development, 77,* 984–996.

Gallup, G., & Bezilla, R. (1992). *The religion life of young Americans.* Princeton, NJ: Gallup Institute.

Galton, F. (1907). *Inquiries into human faculty and its development.* London: J. M. Dent & New York: E. R. Dutton. Retrieved September 3 , 2008, from http://www.galton.org/books/human-faculty/

Gamoran, A. (1992). The variable effects of high school tracking. *American Sociological Review, 57,* 812–828.

Ganley, J. P., & Roberts, J. (1983). Eye conditions and related need for medical care among persons 1–74 years of age, United States, 1971–72. *Vital and Health Statistics,* Series 11, No. 228 (DHHS Publication No. 83-1678). Washington, DC: U.S. Government Printing Office.

Gans, J. (1990). *America's adolescents: How healthy are they?* Chicago: American Medical Association.

Garcia Coll, C., Lamberty, G., Jenkins, R., McAdoo, H., Crnic, K., Wasik, B., & Vazquez Garcia, H. (1996). An integrative model for the study of developmental competencies in minority children. *Child Development, 67,* 1891–1914.

Gardner, H. (1980). *Artful scribbles: The significance of children's drawings.* New York: Basic Books.

Gardner, H. (1999). *Intelligence reframed: Multiple intelligences for the 21st century.* New York: Basic Books.

Gardner, M., & Steinberg, L. (2005). Peer influence on risk taking, risk preference, and risky decision making in adolescence and adulthood: An experimental study. *Developmental Psychology, 41,* 625–635.

Garmel, S. H., & D'Alton, M. E. (1994). Diagnostic ultrasound in pregnancy: an overview. *Seminars in Perinatology, 18,* 117–132. Gingras, J. L., Mitchell, E. A., & Grattan, K. E. (2005). Fetal homologue of infant crying. *Archives of Disease in Childhood—Fetal and Neonatal Edition, 90,* 415–418.

Garner, D. (1998, March 23). The Spock touch. *Salon.* Retrieved March 11, 2008, from http://www.salon.com/mwt/feature/1998/03/23feature.html

Garner, P. W. (1996). The relations of emotional role taking, affective/moral attributions, and emotional display rule knowledge to low-income school-age children's social competence. *Journal of Applied Developmental Psychology, 17,* 19–36.

Garnier, H., Stein, J., & Jacobs, J. (1997). The process of dropping out of high school: A 19-year perspective. *American Educational Research Journal, 34,* 395–419.

Gartstein, M. A., Kinsht, I. A., & Slobodskaya, H. R. (2003). Cross-cultural differences in temperament in the first year of life: United States of America (US) and Russia. *International Journal of Behavioral Development, 27,* 316–328.

Garvey, C. (1990). *Play.* Cambridge, MA: Harvard University Press.

Garza, C., & de Onis, M. (2007). New 21st century international growth standards for infants and young children. *Journal of Nutrition, 137,* 142–143.

Gates, G. J., & Badgett, M. V. L., Macomber, J. E., & Chambers, K. (2007, March). *Adoption and foster care by gay and lesbian parents in the United States.* Los Angeles: The Williams Institute, UCLA School of Law, and Washington, DC: The Urban Institute. Retrieved September 3, 2008, from http://www.law.ucla.edu/williamsinstitute/publications/FinalAdoptionReport.pdf.

Gauvain, M. (2001). *The social context of cognitive development.* New York: The Guilford Press.

Gazzaniga, M., Bogen, J., & Sperry, R. (1962). Some functional effects of sectioning the cerebral commisures in man. *Proceedings of the National Academy of Sciences, 48,* 1765–1769.

Ge, X., Kim, I. J., Brody, G. H., Conger, R. D., Simons, R. L., Gibbons, F. X., et al. (2003). It's about timing and change: Pubertal transition effects on symptoms of major depression among African American youths. *Developmental Psychology, 39,* 430–439.

Geary, D. C. (2006). Development of mathematical understanding. In W. Damon & R. M. Lerner (Series Eds.) & D. Kuhn & R. S. Siegler (Vol. Eds.), *Handbook of child psychology: Vol. 2. Cognition, perception, and language* (6th ed., pp.777–810). Hoboken, NJ: Wiley.

Gelman, R. (2000). The epigenesist of mathematical thinking. *Journal of Applied Developmental Psychology, 21,* 27–37.

Gelman, S. A. (2006). Early conceptual development. In K. McCartney & D. Phillips (Eds.), *Blackwell handbook of early childhood development* (pp. 149–166). Malden, MA: Blackwell.

Gelman, S. A., & Kalish, C. (2006). Conceptual development. In W. Damon & R. M. Lerner (Series Eds.) & D. Kuhn & R. S. Siegler (Vol. Eds.), *Handbook of child psychology: Vol. 2. Cognition, perception, and language* (6th ed., pp. 687–733). Hoboken, NJ: Wiley.

Gelman, S., Taylor, M. G., & Nguyen, S. P. (2004). Mother-child conversations about gender. *Monographs of the Society for Research in Child Development, 69,* vii–127.

Gernsbacher, M., Dawson, M., & Goldsmith, H. H. (2005). Three reasons not to believe in an autism epidemic. *Current Directions in Psychological Science, 14,* 55–58.

Gershoff, E. T. (2002). Parental corporal punishment and associated child behaviors and experiences: A meta-analytic and theoretical review. *Psychological Bulletin, 128,* 539–579.

Geschwind, N., & Galaburda, A. (1987). *Cerebral lateralization.* Cambridge, MA: MIT Press.

Gesell, A. (1933). Maturation and the patterning of behavior. In C. Murchison (Ed.), *A handbook of child psychology* (2nd ed., pp 209–235). Worcester MA: Clark University Press.

Gesell, A., & Thompson, H. (1938). *The psychology of early growth including norms of infant behavior and a method of genetic analysis.* New York: Appleton-Century Crofts.

Gibson, E. J., & Walk, R. D. (1960). The "visual cliff." *Scientific American, 202,* 64–71.

Giedd, J. N., Blumenthal, J., Jeffries, N. O., Castellanos, F. X., Liu, H., Zijdenbos, A., et al. (1999). Brain development during childhood and adolescence: A longitudinal MRI study. *Nature Neuroscience, 2,* 861–863.

Gifford-Smith, M. E., & Rabiner, D. L. (2004). Social information processing and children's social adjustment. In J. Kupersmidt & K. A. Dodge (Eds.), *Children's peer relations: From development to interventions* (pp. 69–84). Washington, DC: American Psychological Association.

Gil, A., Vega, W., & Dimas, J. (1994). Acculturative stress and personal adjustment among Hispanic adolescent boys. *Journal of Community Psychology, 22*, 43–54.

Gilligan, C. (1982). *In a different voice: Psychological theory and women's development.* Cambridge, MA: Harvard University Press.

Ginsburg, G., & Bronstein, P. (1993). Family factors related to children's intrinsic/extrinsic motivational orientation and academic performance. *Child Development, 64*, 1461–1474.

Ginsburg, H. (1989). Austin TX: Pro-Ed.

Ginsburg, H., & Baroody, A. J. (2003). The test of early mathematics ability (3rd ed.). Austin TX: Pro Ed.

Ginsburg, H. P., Cannon, J., Eisenband, J., & Pappas, S. (2006). Mathematical thinking and learning. In K. McCartney & D. Phillips (Eds.), *Blackwell handbook on early childhood development* (pp. 208–229). Malden, MA: Blackwell.

Glod, C. A., Teicher, M. H., Hartman, C. R., & Harakal, T. (1997). Increased nocturnal activity and impaired sleep maintenance in abused children. *Journal of the American Academy of Child and Adolescent Psychiatry, 36*, 1236–1243.

Glynn, L. M., Wadhwa, P. D., Dunkel-Schetter, C., Chicz-Demet, A., & Sandman, C. A. (2001). When stress happens matters: effects of earthquake timing on stress responsivity in pregnancy. *American Journal of Obstetrics and Gynecology, 184*, 637–642.

Gogate, L. J., Bahrick, L. E., & Watson, J. D. (2000). A study of multimodal motherese: The role of temporal synchrony between verbal labels and gestures. *Child Development, 71*, 878–894.

Gogtay, N., Giedd, J. N., Lusk, L., Hayashi, K., Greenstein, D., Vaituzis, C. et al. (2004, May 25). Dynamic mapping of human cortical development during childhood through early adulthood. *Proceeding of the National Academy of Sciences, 101*, 8174–8179.

Goldberg, S., & DiVitto, B. (2002). Parenting children born preterm. In M. H. Bornstein (Ed.), *Handbook of parenting* (Vol. 2, pp. 329–354). Mahwah, NJ: Erlbaum.

Goldfield, B. A. (1985/1986). Referential and expressive language: A study of two mother-child dyads. *First Language, 6*, 119–131.

Goldin-Meadow, S. (2006). How children learn language: A focus on resilience. In K. McCartney & D. Phillips (Eds.), *Blackwell handbook on early childhood development* (pp. 252–273). Malden, MA: Blackwell.

Goldin-Meadow, S. (2006). Nonverbal communication: The hand's role in talking and thinking. In W. Damon & R. Lerner (Series Eds.) & D. Kuhn & R. S. Siegler (Vol. Eds.), *Handbook of child psychology: Vol. 2. Cognition, perception, and language* (6th ed., pp. 336–369). Hoboken, NJ: Wiley.

Goldsmith, H. H., & Lemery, K. S. (2000). Linking temperamental fearfulness and anxiety symptoms: A behavior-genetic perspective. *Biological Psychiatry, 48*, 1199–1209.

Goldsmith, H. H., Lemery, K. S., Aksan, N., & Buss, K. A. (2000). Temperamental substrates of personality. In V. J. Molfese & D. L. Molfese (Eds.), *Temperament and personality development across the life span* (pp. 1–32). Mahwah, NJ: Erlbaum.

Goldstein, B. (1976). *Introduction to human sexuality.* Belmont, CA: Star.

Golomb, C. (2004). *The child's creation of a pictorial world* (2nd ed.). Mahwah, NJ: Erlbaum.

Golombok, S. (2002). Parenting and contemporary reproductive technologies. In M. H. Bornstein (Ed.), *Handbook of parenting: Vol. 3. Status and social conditions of parenting* (2nd ed., pp. 339–360). Mahwah, NJ: Erlbaum.

Goodman, E., & Capitman, J. (2000). Depressive symptoms and cigarette smoking among teens. *Pediatrics, 106*, 748–755.

Goossens, L., Seiffge-Krenke, I., & Marcoen, A. (1992, March). *The many faces of adolescent egocentrism: Two European replications.* Paper presented at the biennial meetings of the Society for Research on Adolescence, Washington, DC.

Gormley, Jr., W. T., Gayer, T., Phillips, D., & Dawson, B. (2005). The effects of universal Pre-K on cognitive development. *Developmental Psychology, 41*, 872–884.

Gottfredson, D. (1985). Youth employment, crime, and schooling: A longitudinal study of a national sample. *Developmental Psychology, 21*, 419–432.

Gottfried, A., Fleming, J., & Gottfried, A. (1998). Role of cognitively stimulating home environment in children's academic intrinsic motivation: A longitudinal study. *Child Development, 69*, 1448–1460.

Gottlieb, G. (1998). Myrtle McGraw's unrecognized conceptual contribution to developmental psychology. *Developmental Review, 18*, 437–448.

Gottlieb, G., Wahlstein, D., & Lickliter, R. (2006). The significance of biology for human development: A developmental psychobiological systems view. In W. Damon & R. Lerner (Series Eds.) & R. Lerner (Vol. Ed.), *Handbook of child psychology: Vol. 1. Theoretical models of human development* (6th ed., pp. 210–257). New York: Wiley.

Gottman, J. M. (1983). How children become friends. *Monographs of the Society for Research in Child Development, 48*(3), pp. 1–86.

Gottman, J. M., Katz, L. F., & Hoover, C. (1997). *Meta-emotion.* Hillsdale, NJ: Erlbaum.

Gottman, J. M., & Parker, J. G. (1986). *Conversations of friends: Speculations on affective development.* New York: Cambridge University Press.

Gould, M., Wallenstein, S., & Kleinman, M. (1990). Time-space clustering of teenage suicide. *American Journal of Epidemiology, 131*, 71–78.

Gould, S. (1977). *Ontogeny and phylogeny.* Cambridge, MA: Belknap Press of Harvard University Press.

Goyette, K., & Xie, Y. (1999). Educational expectations of Asian American youths: Determinants and ethnic differences. *Sociology of Education, 72*, 22–36.

Graber, J. (in press). Internalizing problems during adolescence. In R. Lerner & L. Steinberg (Eds.), *Handbook of adolescent psychology* (3rd ed.). New York: Wiley.

Graber, J. A., Brooks-Gunn, J., Paikoff, R. L., & Warren, M. P. (1994). Prediction of eating problems: An 8-year study of adolescent girls. *Developmental Psychology, 30*, 823–834.

Graber, J. A., Brooks-Gunn, J., & Warren, M. P. (2006). Pubertal effects on adjustment in girls: Moving from demonstrating effects to identifying pathways. *Journal of Youth and Adolescence, 35,* 391–401.

Granic, I., Hollenstein, T., Dishion, T. K., & Patterson, G. R. (2003). Longitudinal analysis of flexibility and reorganization in early adolescence: A dynamic systems study of family interactions. *Developmental Psychology, 39,* 606–617.

Green, J., & Statham, H. (1996). Psychosocial aspects of prenatal screening and diagnosis. In T. Marteau & M. Richards (Eds.), *The troubled helix: Social and psychological implications of the new human genetics* (pp. 140–163). New York: Cambridge University Press.

Greenberger, E., Chen, C., Tally, S., & Dong, Q. (2000). Family, peer, and individual correlates of depressive symptomatology among U.S. and Chinese adolescents. *Journal of Consulting and Clinical Psychology, 68,* 209–219.

Greenberger, E., & Steinberg, L. (1986). *When teenagers work: The psychological and social costs of adolescent employment.* New York: Basic Books.

Greenberger, E., Steinberg, L., & Vaux, A. (1981). Adolescents who work: Health and behavioral consequences of job stress. *Developmental Psychology, 17,* 691–703.

Greene, S. M., Anderson, E. R., Doyle, E. A., & Riedelbach, H. (2006). Divorce. In G. Bear & K. M. Minke (Eds.), *Children's needs: Vol. 3. Development, prevention, and intervention* (pp. 745–757). Bethesda, MD: National Association of School Psychologists.

Greenfield, P. M., Suzuki, L. K., & Rothstein-Fisch, C. (2006). Cultural pathways through human development. In W. Damon & R. Lerner (Eds.), *Handbook of child psychology: Vol. 4. Child psychology in practice* (6th ed., pp. 655–699). Hoboken, NJ: Wiley.

Greenough, W. T., Black, J. E., & Wallace, C. S. (1987). Experience and brain development. *Child Development, 58,* 539–559.

Grigsby, D. G., & Shashidhar, H. R. (2006, June 30). *Malnutrition.* Retrieved August 11, 2008, from http://www.emedicine.com/PED/topic1360.htm

Grisso, T., Steinberg, L., Woolard, J., Cauffman, E., Scott, E., Graham, S., et al. (2003). Juveniles' competence to stand trial: A comparison of adolescents' and adults' capacities as trial defendants. *Law and Human Behavior, 27,* 333–363.

Groome, L. J., Swiber, M. J., Holland, S. B., Bentz, L. S., Atterbury, J. L., & Trimm, R. F. (1999). Spontaneouls motor activity in the perinatal infant before and after birth: Stability in individual differences. *Developmental Psychobiology, 35,* 15–24.

Gros-Louis, J., West, M. J., Goldstein, M. H., & King, A. P. (2006). Mothers provide differential feedback to infants' prelinguistic sounds. *International Journal of Behavioral Development, 30,* 509–516.

Grossman, D. C. (2000). The history of injury control and the epidemiology of child and adolescent injuries. *The Future of Children: Unintentional Injuries in Childhood, 10,* 23–52.

Grotevant, H. (1997). Adolescent development in family contexts. In W. Damon & R. Lerner (Series Eds.) & N. Eisenberg (Ed.), *Handbook of child psychology: Vol. 3. Social, emotional, and personality development* (5th ed., pp. 1097–1149). New York: Wiley.

Grover, R. L., & Nangle, D. W. (2003). Adolescent perceptions of problematic heterosocial situations: A focus group study. *Journal of Youth and Adolescence, 32,* 129–139.

Gruber, J., & Zinman, J. (2001). Youth smoking in the United States. In J. Gruber (Ed.). *Risky behavior among youths: An economic analysis* (pp. 69–120). Chicago: University of Chicago Press.

Grumbach, M. M., Hughes, I. A., & Conte, F. A. (2002). Disorders of sex differentiation. In P. R. Larsen, H. M. Kronenberg, S. Melmed, & K. S. Polonsky (Eds.), *Williams textbook of endocrinology* (10th ed., pp. 842–1002). Philadelphia: Saunders.

Grunbaum, J., Lowry, R., Kann, L., & Pateman, B. (2000). Prevalence of health risk behaviors among Asian American/Pacific Islander high school students. *Journal of Adolescent Health, 27,* 322–330.

Grusec, J. E., Davidov, M., & Lundell, L. (2002). Prosocial and helping behavior. In P. K. Smith & C. H. Hart (Eds.), *Blackwell handbook of childhood social development* (pp. 457–474). Malden, MA: Blackwell.

Grych, J. H., & Fincham, F. D. (2001). *Interparental conflict and child development: Theory, Research, and applications.* Cambridge, England: Cambridge University Press.

Gunnar, M. R. (2006). Social regulation of stress in early child development. In K. McCartney & D. Phillips (Eds.), *Blackwell handbook of early childhood development* (pp. 106–105). Malden, MA: Blackwell.

Gunnar, M. R. (2000). Early adversity and the development of stress reactivity and regulation. In C. A. Nelson (Ed.), *The Minnesota Symposia on Child Psychology: Vol. 31. The effects of adversity on neurobehavioral development* (pp. 163–200). Mahwah, NJ: Erlbaum.

Gunnar, M. R., Fisher, P. A., & the Early Experience, Stress, and Prevention Network. (2006). Bringing basic research on early experience and stress neurobiology to bear on preventive interventions for neglected and maltreated children. *Development and Psychopathology, 18,* 651–677.

Gunnar, M. R., Sebanc, A., Tout, K., Donzella, B., & van Dulmen, M. M. H. (2003). Peer rejection, temperament, and cortisol activity in preschoolers. *Developmental Psychobiology, 43,* 346–358.

Gunnar, M. R., Van Dulmen, M. H. M., and the International Adoption Project Team. (2007). Behavior problems in postinstitutionalized internationally adopted children. *Development and Psychopathology, 19,* 129–148.

Hacker, D. (1994). An existential view of adolescence. *Journal of Early Adolescence, 14,* 300–327.

Hafetz, E. (1976). Parameters of sexual maturity in man. In E. Hafetz (Ed.), *Perspectives in human reproduction. Vol. 3. Sexual maturity: Physiological and clinical parameters.* Ann Arbor, MI: Ann Arbor Science Publishers.

Halford, G. S. (2004). Information-processing models of cognitive development. In U. Goswami (Ed.), *Blackwell handbook of cognitive development* (pp. 555–74). Malden, MA: Blackwell Publishing.

Halford, G. S., & Andrews, G. (2006). Reasoning and problem solving. In W. Damon & R. M. Lerner (Series Eds.) & D. Kuhn & R. S. Siegler (Vol. Eds.), *Handbook of child psychology: Vol. 2. Cognition, perception, and language* (6th ed., pp. 557–608). Hoboken, NJ: Wiley.

Halgunseth, L. C., Ispa, J. M., & Rudy, D. (2006). Parental control in Latino families: An integrated review of the literature. *Child Development, 77,* 1282–1297.

Halle, T. G. (2003). Emotional development and well-being. In M. H. Bornstein, L. Davidson, C. L. M. Keyes, & K. A. Moore (Eds.), *Well-being: Positive development across the life course* (pp. 125–138). Mahwah, NJ: Erlbaum.

Halperin, S. (Ed.). (2001). *The forgotten half revisited: American youth and young families, 1988–2008.* Washington, DC: American Youth Policy Forum.

Halpern, C., Joyner, K., Udry, J., & Suchindran, C. (2000). Smart teens don't have sex (or kiss much either). *Journal of Adolescent Health, 26,* 213–225.

Halpern, C., Udry, J., & Suchindran, C. (1996, March). *Monthly measures of salivary testosterone predict sexual activity in adolescent males.* Paper presented at the biennial meetings of the Society for Research on Adolescence, Boston.

Halpern, D. F. (2000). *Sex differences in cognitive abilities.* Mahwah, NJ: Erlbaum.

Halpern, D. F., Benbow, C. P. Geary, D. C., Gur, R. C., Hyde, J. S., & Gernsbacher, M. A. (2007). The science of sex differences in science and mathematics. *Psychological Science in the Public Interest, 8*(1), 1–51.

Hamdoun, A., & Epel, D. (2007). Embryo stability and vulnerability in an always changing world. *Proceedings for the National Academy of Sciences, 104,* 1745–1750.

Hamilton, S., & Hamilton, M. (in press). The transition to adulthood in international perspective. In R. Lerner & L. Steinberg (Eds.). *Handbook of adolescent psychology* (3rd ed). New York: Wiley.

Hamm, J. V. (2000). Do birds of a feather flock together? Individual, contextual, and relationship bases for African American, Asian American, and European American adolescents' selection of similar friends. *Developmental Psychology, 36,* 209–219.

Hamm, J. V., & Coleman, H. K. (2001). African American and White adolescents' strategies for managing cultural diversity in predominantly White high schools. *Journal of Youth and Adolescence, 30,* 281–303.

Hanlon, H. W., Thatcher, R. W., & Cline, M. J. (1999). Gender differences in the development of EEG coherence in normal children. *Developmental Neuropsychology, 16,* 479–506.

Hanson, S. (1994). Lost talent: Unrealized educational aspirations and expectations among U.S. youths. *Sociology of Education, 67,* 159–183.

Hardy, S. A., & Raffaelli, M. (2003). Adolescent religiosity and sexuality: An investigation of reciprocal influences. *Journal of Adolescence, 26,* 731–739.

Hardy-Brown, K., & Plomin, R. (1985). Infant communicative development: Evidence from adoptive and biological families for genetic and environmental influences on rate differences. *Developmental Psychology, 21,* 378–385.

Hardy-Brown, K., Plomin, R., & DeFries, J. C. (1981). Genetic and environmental influences on the rate of communicative development in the first year of life. *Developmental Psychology, 17,* 704–717.

Harlow, H. F. (1958). The nature of love. *American Psychologist, 13,* 673–685.

Harnad, S. R. (1987). *Categorical perception: The groundwork of cognition.* New York: Cambridge University Press.

Harris, J. R. (1995). Where is the child's environment? A group socialization theory of development. *Psychological Review, 102,* 458–489.

Harris, J. R. (1998). *The nurture assumption.* New York: The Free Press.

Harris, K. (1999). The health status and risk behavior of adolescents in immigrant families. In D. Hernandez (Ed.), *Children of immigrants: Health, adjustment, and public assistance* (pp. 286–347). Washington: National Academy Press.

Harris, P. L. (2000). Understanding emotion. In M. Lewis & J. Haviland (Eds.) *Handbook of emotion* (2nd ed., pp. 281–292). New York: Guilford Press.

Hart, B., & Risley, T. R. (1995). *Meaningful differences in the everyday experience of young American children.* Baltimore, MD: Brookes.

Harter, S. (1998). The development of self-representations. In W. Damon & R. Lerner (Series Eds.) & N. Eisenberg (Vol. Ed.), *Handbook of child psychology: Vol. 3. Social, emotional, and personality development* (5th ed., pp. 53–617). New York: Wiley.

Harter, S. (1999). *The construction of the self.* New York: Guilford Press.

Harter, S. (2006) The self. In W. Damon & R. M. Lerner (Series Eds.) & N. Eisenberg (Vol. Ed.). *Handbook of child psychology: Vol. 3. Social, emotional, and personality development* (pp. 505–570). Hoboken, NJ: Wiley.

Harter, S. (2006). The self. In W. Damon & R. Lerner (Series Eds.), N. Eisenberg (Vol. Ed.), *Handbook of child psychology: Vol. 3. Social, emotional, and personality development* (6th ed., pp. 505–570). Hoboken, NJ: Wiley.

Hartup, W. (1983). Peer relations. In E. M. Hetherington (Ed.), *Handbook of child psychology: Vol. 4. Socialization, personality, and social development* (pp. 103–196). New York: Wiley.

Hartup, W. W. (1989). Social relationships and their developmental significance. *American Psychologist, 44,* 120–26.

Hartup, W. W. (1992). Friendships and their developmental significance. In H McGurk (Ed.), *Childhood social development: Contemporary perspectives* (pp. 175–06). New York: Psychology Press.

Hartup, W. W., & Abecassis, M. (2002). Friends and enemies. In P. K. Smith & C. H. Hart (Eds.), *Blackwell handbook of childhood social development* (pp. 285–306). Malden, MA: Blackwell.

Haselager, G. J. T., Cillissen, H. N., van Lieshout, C. F. M., Riksen-Walraven, J. M. A., & Hartup, W. W. (2002). Heterogeneity among peer rejected boys across middle childhood: Developmental pathways of social behavior. *Child Development, 73,* 446–456.

Hay, D. F., & Nash, A. (2002). Social development in different family arrangements. In P. K. Smith & C. H. Hart (Eds.), *Blackwell handbook of childhood social development* (pp. 238–261). Malden, MA: Blackwell.

Hay, D. F., Nash, A., & Pedersen, J. (1983). Interactions between 6-month-olds. *Child Development, 54,* 105–113.

Haynie, D. L. (2003). Contexts of risk? Explaining the link between girls' pubertal development and their delinquency involvement. *Social Forces, 82,* 355–397.

Hayward, C., Gotlib, I., Schraedley, P., & Litt, I. (1999). Ethnic differences in the association between pubertal status and symptoms of depression in adolescent girls. *Journal of Adolescent Health, 25,* 143–149.

Hechinger, F. (1993). Schools for teenagers: A historic dilemma. *Teachers College Record, 94,* 522–539.

Hedges, L., & Nowell, A. (1999). Changes in the black-white gap in achievement test scores. *Sociology of Education, 72,* 111–135.

Hein, K. (1988). *AIDS in adolescence: A rationale for concern.* Washington, DC: Carnegie Council on Adolescent Development.

Heinicke, C. M. (2002). The transition to parenting. In M. H. Bornstein (Ed.), *Handbook of parenting* (2nd ed., Vol. 3, pp. 363–388). Mahwah, NJ: Erlbaum.

Held, R., & Hein, A. (1963). Movement-produced stimulation in the development of visually guided behavior. *Journal of Comparative and Physiological Psychology, 56,* 872–876.

Henning, A., Striano, T., & Lieven, E. V. M. (2005). Maternal speech to infants at 1 and 3 months of age. *Infant Behavior & Development, 28,* 519–536.

Herdt, G., & McClintock, M. (2000). The magical age of 10. *Archives of Sexual Behavior, 29,* 587–606.

Herman-Giddens, M., Slora, E., Wasserman, R., Bourdony, C., Bhapkar, M., Koch, G., & Hasemeier, C. (1997). Secondary sexual characteristics and menses in young girls seen in office practice: A study from the Pediatric Research in Office Settings Network. *Pediatrics, 88,* 505–512.

Heron, M. (2007, November 20). Deaths: Leading causes for 2004. *National Vital Statistics Reports, 56,* 5.

Hetherington, E. M., Cox, M., & Cox, R. (1982). Effects of divorce on parents and children.

In M. E. Lamb (Ed.), *Nontraditional families: Parenting and child development* (pp. 233–288). Hillsdale, NJ: Erlbaum.

Hetherington, E. M., Henderson, S., & Reiss, D. (1999). Adolescent siblings in stepfamilies: Family functioning and adolescent adjustment. *Monographs of the Society for Research in Child Development, 64,* Serial No. 259.

Hetherington, E. M., Henderson, S., & Reiss, D. (1999). Adolescent siblings in stepfamilies: Family functioning and adolescent adjustment. *Monographs of the Society for Research in Child Development, 64*(Serial No. 259).

Hetherington, M., & Clingempeel, W. G. (1992). Coping with marital transitions: A family systems perspective. *Monographs of the Society for Research in Child Development, 57*(2–3, Serial No. 227).

Hewlett, B. S. (1992). Husband-wife reciprocity and the father-infant relationship among Aka Pygmies. In B. S. Hewlett (Ed.), *Father-child relations: Cultural and biosocial contexts* (pp. 153–176). Hawthorne, NY: Aldine de Gruyter.

Hill, N. E., Castellino, D. R., Lansford, J. E., Nowlin, P., Dodge, K. A., Bates, J. E., & Pettit, G. S. (2004). Parent academic involvement as related to school behavior, achievement, and aspirations: Demographic variations across adolescence. *Child Development, 75,* 1491–1509.

Hilsman, R., & Garber, J. (1995). A test of the cognitive diathesis-stress model of depression in children: Academic stressors, attributional style, perceived competence, and control. *Journal of Personality and Social Psychology, 69,* 370–380.

Hinde, R., Titmus, G., Easton, D., & Tamplin, A. (1985). Incidence of "friendship" and behavior toward Strong Associates versus Nonassociates in preschoolers. *Child Development, 56,* 234–245.

Hines, M., & Kaufman, F. R. (1994). Androgen and the development of human sex-typical behavior: Rough-and-tumble play and sex of preferred playmates in children with con-genital adrenal hyperplasia (CAH). *Child Development, 65,* 1042–1053.

Hingson, R., Heeren, T, & Winter, M. (2006). Age at drinking onset and alcohol dependence: Age at onset, duration, and severity. *Archives of Pediatric and Adolescent Medicine, 160,* 739–746.

Hirshberg, L. M., & Svejda, M. (1990). When infants look to their parents: I. Infants' social referencing of mothers compared to fathers. *Child Development, 61,* 1175–1186

Hirsh-Pasek, K., & Golinkoff, R. M. (2003). *Einstein never used flash cards.* Emmaus, PA: Rodale.

Hoek, H. W., Brown, A. S., & Susser, E. S. (1999). The Dutch famine studies: Prenatal nutritional deficiency and schizophrenia. In E. S. Susser, A. S. Brown, & J. M. Gorman (Eds.), *Prenatal exposures in schizophrenia* (pp. 135–161). Washington, DC: American Psychiatric Association.

Hoff, E. (2006). How social contexts support and shape language development. *Developmental Review, 26,* 55–88.

Hoff, E. (2006). Language experience and language milestones during early childhood. In K. McCartney & D. Phillips (Ed.), *Blackwell handbook on early childhood development.* (pp. 233–251) Malden, MA: Blackwell.

Hofferth, S. L., & Curtin, S. C. (2005). Leisure time activities in middle childhood. In K. A. Moore & L. H. Lippman (Eds.), *What do children need to flourish?: Conceptualizing and measuring indicators of positive development* (pp. 95–110). New York: Springer.

Hofferth, S. L., & Reid, L. (2002). Early childbearing and children's achievement and behavior over time. *Perspectives on Sexual and Reproductive Health, 34,* 41–49.

Hofferth, S. L., Reid, L., & Mott, F. L. (2001). The effects of early childbearing on schooling over time. *Family Planning Perspective, 33,* 259–267.

Hofferth, S. L., & Sandberg, J. F. (2001). How American children spend their time. *Journal of Marriage and the Family, 63,* 295–308.

Hoff-Ginsburg, E. (1998). The relation of birth order and socioeconomic status to children's language experience and language development. *Applied Psycholinguistics, 19,* 603–630.

Hoffman, S., Foster, E., & Furstenberg, F., Jr. (1993). Reevaluating the costs of teenage childbearing. *Demography, 30,* 1–13.

Hogan, D., Sun, R., & Cornwell, G. (2000). Sexual and fertility behaviors of American females aged 15–19 years: 1985, 1990, and 1995. *American Journal of Public Health, 90,* 1421–1425.

Holder, D. W., DuRant, R. H., Harris, T. L., Henderson Daniel, J., Obeidallah, D., & Goodman, E. (2000). The association between adolescent spirituality and voluntary sexual activity. *Journal of Adolescent Health, 26,* 295–302.

Holloway, S. (1988). Concepts of ability and effort in Japan and the United States. *Review of Educational Research, 58,* 327–345.

Holmen, T., Barrett-Connor, E., Holmen, J., & Bjerner, L. (2000). Health problems in teenage daily smokers versus nonsmokers, Norway, 1995–1997. *American Journal of Epidemiology, 151,* 148–155.

Holt, D. J., Iappolito, P. M., Desrochers, D. M., & Kelley, C. R. (2007). *Children's exposure to TV advertising in 1977 and 2004: Information for the obesity debate.* Federal Trade Commission. Bureau of Economics Statistics_ Report. Retrieved September 2, 2008, from http://www.ftc.gov/os/2007/06/cabe-color.pdf

Holtmaat, A., Wilbrecht, L., Knott, G. W., Welker, E., & Svoboda, K. (2006). Experience-dependent and cell-type-specific spine growth in the neocortex. *Nature, 441,* 979–983.

Homel, R., & Burns, A. (1989). Environmental quality and the well-being of children. *Social Indicators Research, 21,* 133–158.

Honig, A. S. (2002). Choosing child care for young children. In M. H. Bornstein (Ed.), *Handbook of parenting: Vol. 5. Practical parenting* (2nd ed., pp. 375–405). Mahwah, NJ: Erlbaum.

Hooper, C.J., Luciana, M., Conklin, H.M., & Yarger, R.S. (2004). Adolescents' performance on the Iowa gambling task: Implications for the development of decision making and ventromedial prefrontal cortex. *Developmental Psychology, 40,* 1148–1158.

Hoover-Dempsey, K., & Sandler, H. (1995). Parental involvement in children's education: Why does it make a difference? *Teachers College Record, 97,* 310–331.

Hopkins, B., & Johnson, S. P. (Eds.). (2005). *Prenatal development of postnatal functions (Advances in infancy research).* New York: Praeger.

Hopkins, B., & Westra, T. (1988). Maternal handling and motor development: An intracultural study. *Genetic, Social, and General Psychology, 31,* 384–390.

Hopkins, B., & Westra, T. (1990). Motor development, maternal expectation, and the role of handling. *Infant Behavior and Development, 13,* 117–122.

Hoppa, R. D., & Garlie, T. N. (1998). Secular changes in the growth of Toronto children during the last century. *Annals of Human Biology, 25,* 553–561.

Hornik, R., Risenhoover, N., & Gunnar, M. (1987). The effects of maternal positive, neutral, and negative affective communications on infant responses to new toys. *Child Development, 58,* 937–944.

Howe, M. J. A. (2002). *Genius explained.* New York: Cambridge University Press.

Howe, M. L., & Lewis, M. D. (2005). The importance of dynamic systems approaches for understanding development. *Developmental Review, 25,* 247–251.

Howes, C. (1984). Sharing fantasy: Social pretend play in toddlers. *Child Development, 56,* 1253–1258.

Howes, C. (1992). *The collaborative construction of pretend.* Albany: State University of New York Press.

Howes, C., Hamilton, C. E., & Phillipsen, L. C. (1998). Stability and continuity of child-caregiver and child-peer relationships. *Child Development, 69,* 418–426.

Howes, C., & Matheson, C. C. (1992). Sequences in the development of competent play with peers: Social and social pretend play. *Developmental Psychology, 28,* 961–974.

Hsu, V. C., & Rovee-Collier, C. (2006). Memory reactivation in the second year of life. *Infant Behavior & Development, 29,* 91–107.

Hubel, D. (1981). Evolution of ideas on the primary visual cortex, 1955–1978: A biased historical account (Accessed at http://nobelprize.org/nobel_prizes/medicine/laureates/1981/hubel-lecture.html on December 17, 2007).

Huesmann, L. R., Moise-Titus, J., Podolsky, C., and Eron, L.D. (2003). Longitudinal relations between children's exposure to TV violence and their aggressive and violent behavior in young adulthood: 1977–1992. *Developmental Psychology, 39,* 201–221.

Huesmann, L. R., & Taylor, L. D. (2006). Media effects in middle childhood. In A. C. Huston & M. N. Ripke (Eds.), *Developmental contexts in middle childhood: Bridges to adolescence and adulthood* (pp. 303–326). New York: Cambridge University Press.

Hunnius, S., & Geuze, R. H. (2004). Developmental changes in visual scanning of dynamic faces and abstract stimuli in infants: A longitudinal study. *Infancy, 6,* 231–255.

Huston, A. C., Wright, J. C., Marquis, J., & Green, S. B. (1999). How young children spend their time: Television and other activities. *Developmental Psychology, 35,* 921–925.

Huttenlocher, P. R. (2002). *Neural plasticity: The effects of environment on the development of the cerebral cortex.* Cambridge, MA: Harvard University Press.

Hyde, J. S. (2005). The gender similarity hypothesis. *American Psychologist, 60,* 581–592.

Hyde, J. S., Fennema, E., & Lamon, S. J. (1990). Gender differences in mathematics performance: A meta-analysis. *Psychological Bulletin, 107,* 139–155.

Hyde, J. S., Fennema, E., Ryan, M., Frost, L. A., & Hopp, C. (1990). Gender comparisons of mathematics attitudes and affect: A meta-analysis. *Psychology of Women Quarterly, 14*(3), 299–324.

Hymel, S., Vaillancourt, T., McDougall, P., & Renshaw, P. (2002). Peer acceptance and rejection in childhood. In P. K. Smith & C. H. Hart (Eds.), *Blackwell handbook of childhood social development* (pp. 265–284). Malden, MA: Blackwell.

Ingersoll, E. W., & Thoman, E. B. (1999). Sleep/wake states of preterm infants: Stability, developmental change, diurnal variation, and relation with caregiving activity. *Child Development, 70,* 1–10.

Inhelder, B., & Piaget, J. (1964). *The early growth of logic: Classification and seriation.* London: Routledge & Kegan Paul.

Inlow, J. K., & Restifo, L. L. (2004). Molecular and comparative genetics of mental retardation. *Genetics, 166,* 835–881.

Institute of Medicine. (2006). *Food marketing to children and youth: Threat or opportunity?* Washington: National Academies Press.

International Human Genome Sequencing Consortium. (2001). Initial sequencing and analysis of the human genome. *Nature, 409,* 860–921.

Irwin, C., Jr. (1986). Biopsychosocial correlates of risk-taking behavior during adolescence: Can the physician intervene? *Journal of Adolescent Health Care, 7,* 82–96.

Izard, C. E. (1979). *The Maximally Discriminative Facial Movement Coding System (MAX).* Newark: University of Delaware, Instructional Resources Center.

Izard, C. E., & Dougherty, L. M. (1982). Two complementary systems for measuring facial expressions in infants and children. In C. E. Izard (Ed.), *Measuring emotions in infants and children* (pp. 97–126). New York: Cambridge University Press.

Izard, C. E., Fantauzzo, C. A., Castle, J. M., Haynes, O. M., Rayias, M. F., & Putnam, P. H. (1995). The ontogeny and significance of infants' facial expressions in the first 9 months of life. *Developmental Psychology, 31,* 997–1013.

Izard, C. E., & Malatesta, C. 2. (1987). Perspectives on emotional development: I. Differential emotions theory of early emotional development. In J. D. Osofsky (Ed.), *Handbook of infant development* (2nd ed., pp. 494–554). New York: Wiley-Interscience.

Jackson, L. A., von Eye, A., Biocca, F. A., Barbatsis, G., Zhao, Y., & Fitzgerald, H. (2006). Does home internet use influence the academic performance of low-income children? *Developmental Psychology, 42,* 429–435.

Jacobi, C., Agras, W. S., Bryson, S., & Hammer, L. D. (2003). Behavioral validation, precursors, and concomitants of picky eating in childhood. *Journal of the American Academy of Child & Adolescent Psychiatry, 42*(1), 76–84.

Jacobi, C., Hayward, C., de Zwaan, M., Kraemer, H. C., & Agras, W. S. (2004). Coming to terms with risk factors for eating disorders: Application of risk terminology and suggestions for a general taxonomy. *Psychological Bulletin, 130,* 19–65.

Jacobs, J. E., Lanza, S., Osgood, D., Eccles, J. S., & Wigfield, A. (2002). Changes in children's self-competence and values: Gender and domain differences across grades one through twelve. *Child Development, 73,* 509–527.

Jacobs, J., & Portenza, M. (1991). The use of judgment heuristics to make social and object decisions: A developmental perspective. *Child Development, 62,* 166–178.

Jakobson, R. (1968). *Child language, aphasia, and phonological universals.* Oxford, England: Mouton.

James, J., Thomas, P., Cavan, D., & Kerr, D. (2004). Preventing childhood obesity by reducing consumption of carbonated drinks: Cluster randomized controlled trial. *British Medical Journal, 328*(7450).

Janosz, M., LeBlanc, M., Boulerice, B., & Tremblay, R. E. (1997). Disentangling the weight of school dropout predictors: A test on two longitudinal samples. *Journal of Youth and Adolescence, 26,* 733–762.

Jarvinen, D., & Nicholls, J. (1996). Adolescents' social goals, beliefs about the causes of social success, and satisfaction in peer relations. *Developmental Psychology, 32,* 435–441.

Jasnow, M., & Feldstein, S. (1986). Adult-like temporal characteristics of mother-infant vocal interactions. *Child Development, 57,* 754–761.

Jodl, K. M., Michael, A., Malanchuk, O., Eccles, J. S., & Samer-off, A. (2001). Parents' roles in shaping early adolescents' occupational aspirations. *Child Development, 72,* 1247–1265.

Johnson, M. (2002). Social origins, adolescent experiences, and work value trajectories during the transition to adulthood. *Social Forces, 80,* 1307–1341.

Johnson, M. H. (2001). Functional brain development during infancy. In J. G. Bremner & A. Fogel (Eds.), *Blackwell handbook of infant development* (pp. 169–190). Malden, MA: Blackwell Publishers, Inc.

Johnson, M. H. (2005). Developmental neuroscience, psychophysiology, and genetics. In M. H. Bornstein & M. E. Lamb (Eds.), *Developmental science: An advanced textbook* (pp. 187–222). Mahwah, NJ: Erlbaum.

Johnson, W., Emde, R. N., Pannabecker, B., Stenberg, C., & Davis, M. (1982). Maternal perception of infant emotion from birth through 18 months. *Infant Behavior & Development, 5,* 313–322.

Jones, G., Steketee, R. W., Black, R. E., Bhutta, Z. A., Morris, S. S., & the Bellagio Child Survival Study Group. (2003, July 5). How many child deaths can we prevent this year? *Lancet, 362.*

Jones, H. E. (2006). Drug addiction during pregnancy: Advances in maternal treatment and understanding child outcomes. *Current Directions in Psychological Science, 15,* 126–130.

Jones, K. L., Robinson, L. K., Bakhireva, L. N., Marintcheva, G., Storojev, V., Strahova, A., et al. (2006). Accuracy of the diagnosis of physical features of fetal alcohol syndrome by pediatricians after specialized training. *Pediatrics, 118,* 1734–1738.

Jones, R. K., Darroch, J. E., & Singh, S. (2005). Religious differentials in the sexual and reproductive behaviors of young women in the United States. *Journal of Adolescent Health, 36,* 279–288.

Jordan, K. E., & Brannon, E. M. (2006). The multisensory representation of number in infancy. *Proceedings of the National Academy of Sciences, 103,* 3486–3489.

Jordan, W., Lara, J., & McPartland, J. (1996). Exploring the causes of early dropout among race-ethnic and gender groups. *Youth and Society, 28,* 62–94.

Jordan, W. J., & Nettles, S. M. (2000). How students invest their time outside of school: Effects on school-related outcomes. *Social Psychology of Education, 3,* 217–243.

Josephson, W. L. (1987). Television violence and children's aggression: Testing the priming, social script, and disinhibition predictions. *Journal of Personality and Social Psychology, 535,* pp. 882–890.

Joyner, K., & Udry, J. R. (2000). You don't bring me anything but down: Adolescent romance and depression. *Journal of Health and Social Behavior, 41,* 369–391.

Judge, B. & Billick, S.B. (2004). Suicidality in adolescence: Review and legal considerations. *Behavioral Sciences & the Law, 22,* 681–695.

Juvonen, J., & Murdock, T. (1995). Grade-level differences in the social value of effort: Implications for self-presentation tactics of early adolescents. *Child Development, 66,* 1694–1705.

Kagan, J. (2006). Biology, culture, and temperamental biases. In W. Damon & R. Lerner (Series Eds.) & D. Kuhn & R. S. Siegler (Vol. Eds.), *Handbook of child psychology: Vol. 2. Cognition, perception, and language* (6th ed., pp. 167–225). Hoboken, NJ: Wiley.

Kagan, S., & Knight, G. (1979). Cooperation-competition and self-esteem: A case of cultural relativism. *Journal of Cross-Cultural Psychology, 10,* 457–467.

Kail, R. (2003). Information processing and memory. In M. Bornstein, L. Davidson, C. L. M. Keyes, K. A. Moore, & the Center for Child Well-Being (Eds.), *Well-being: Positive development across the life course* (pp. 269–279). Mahwah, NJ: Erlbaum.

Kail, R. V., & Ferrer, E. (2007). Processing speed in childhood and adolescence: Longitudinal models for examining developmental change. *Child Development, 78,* 1760–1770.

Kalil, A., & Kunz, J. (2002). Teenage childbearing, marital status, and depressive symptoms in later life. *Child Development, 73,* 1748–1760.

Kalish, C. W. (1996). Preschoolers' understanding of germs as invisible mechanisms. *Cognitive Development, 11,* 83–106.

Kandel, D., Johnson, J., Bird, H., & Canino, G. (1997). Psychiatric disorders associated with substance use among children and adolescents: Findings from the Methods for the Epide-

ing: Vol. 5. Practical parenting (2nd ed., pp. 269–309). Mahwah, NJ: Erlbaum.

Ladd, G. W., & Price, J. M. (1987). Predicting children's social and school adjustment following the transition from preschool to kindergarten. *Child Development, 58,* 1168–1189.

Ladd, G. W., Price, J. M., & Hart, C. H. (1988). Predicting preschoolers' peer status from their playground behaviors. *Child Development, 59,* 986–992

Lagattuta, K., Wellman, H., & Flavell, J (1997). Preschoolers' understanding of the link between thinking and feeling: Cognitive cueing and emotional change. *Child Development, 68,* 1081–1104.

Laible, D. (2004). Mother-child discourse in two contexts: Links with child temperament, attachment security, and socioemotional competence. *Developmental Psychology, 40,* 979–992.

Lamb, M. E., & Ahnert, L. (2006). Nonparental child care: context, concepts, correlates, and consequences. In W. Damon & R. M. Lerner (Series Eds.) & K. A. Renninger & I. E. Sigel (Vol. Eds.), *Handbook of child psychology: Vol. 4. Child psychology in practice* (6th ed., pp. 950–1016). New York: Wiley.

Lamb, M. E., Sternberg, K. J., Orbach, Y., Esplin, P. W., & Mitchell, S. (2002). Is ongoing feedback necessary to maintain the quality of investigative interviews with allegedly abused children? *Applied Developmental Science, 6,* 35–41.

Lampl, M., & Emde, R. N. (1983). Episodic growth in infancy: A preliminary report on length, head circumference, and behavior. In K. W. Fischer (Ed.), *Levels and transitions in children's development* (pp. 21–36) San Francisco: Jossey–Bass.

Landau, S., Meyers, A. B., & Pryor, J. B. (2005). HIV/AIDS. In G. G. Bear & K. M. Minke (Eds.), *Children's needs III: Development, prevention, and intervention* (pp. 719–729). Washington, DC: National Association of School Psychologists.

Landry, D., Kaeser, L., & Richards, C. (1999). Abstinence promotion and the provision of information about contraception in public school district sexuality education policies. *Family Planning Perspectives, 31,* 280–286.

Landry, D., Singh, S., & Darroch, J. E. (2000). Sexuality education in fifth and sixth grades in U.S. public schools, 1999. *Family Planning Perspectives, 32,* 212–219.

Lang, S., Waller, P., & Shope, J. (1996). Adolescent driving: Characteristics associated with single-vehicle and injury crashes. *Journal of Safety Research, 27,* 241–257.

Lansford, J. E., Chang, L., Dodge, K. A., Malone, P. S., Oburu, P., Palmérus, K., et al. (2005). Physical discipline and children's adjustment: Cultural normativeness as a moderator. *Child Development, 76,* 1234–1246.

Lansford, J. E., Criss, M. M., Pettit, G. S., Dodge, K. A., & Bastes, J. E. (2003). Friendship quality, peer group affiliation, and peer antisocial behavior as moderators of the link between negative parenting and adolescent externalizing behavior. *Journal of Research on Adolescence, 13,* 161–184.

Lanz, M., Scabini, E., Vermulst, A. A., & Gerris, J. M. (2001). Congruence on child rearing in families with early adolescent and middle adolescent children. *International Journal of Behavioral Development, 25*(2), 133–139.

Lapsley, D. (1989). Continuity and discontinuity in adolescent social cognitive development. In R. Montemayor, G. Adams, & T. Gullota (Eds.), *Advances in adolescence research* (Vol. 2, pp. 183–204). Beverly Hills, CA: Sage.

Lareau, A. (2003) *Unequal childhoods: Class, race, and family life.* Berkeley, CA: University of California Press.

Larson, R. W. (2000). Toward a psychology of positive youth development. *American Psychologist, 55,* 170–183.

Larson, R., & Richards, M. (1994). *Divergent realities: The emotional lives of mothers, fathers, and adolescents.* New York: Basic Books.

Larson, R., Clore, G., & Wood, G. (1999). The emotions of romantic relationships: Do they wreak havoc on adolescents? In W. Furman, B. Brown, & C. Feiring (Eds.), *Contemporary perspectives on adolescent romantic relationships* (pp. 19–49). New York: Cambridge University Press.

Laub, J., & Sampson, R. (1995). The long-term effect of punitive discipline. In J. McCord (Ed.), *Coercion and punishment in long-term perspectives* (pp. 247–258). New York: Cambridge University Press.

Lauritsen, J. (1994). Explaining race and gender differences in adolescent sexual behavior. *Social Forces, 72,* 859–884.

Laursen, B., & Hartup, W. (1989). The dynamics of preschool children's conflicts. *Merrill-Palmer Quarterly, 35,* 281–297.

Laursen, B., & Jensen-Campbell, L. (1999). The nature and functions of social exchange in adolescent romantic relationships. In W. Furman, B. Brown, & C. Feiring (Eds.), *Contemporary perspectives on adolescent romantic relationships* (pp. 50–74). New York: Cambridge University Press.

Lawler, R. W. (1985). *Computer experience and cognitive development: A child's learning in a computer culture.* New York: Wiley.

Lazarus, R. S. (1999). *Stress and emotion: A new synthesis.* New York: Springer.

Leaper, C. (2002). Parenting girls and boys. In M. H. Bornstein (Ed.), *Handbook of parenting: Vol. 1. Children and parenting* (2nd ed., pp. 189–225). Mahwah, NJ: Erlbaum.

Leavitt, D. H., Tonniges, T. F., & Rogers, M. F. (2003). Good nutrition: The imperative for positive development. In M. H. Bornstein, L. Davidson, C. L. M. Keyes, & K. A. Moore (Eds.), *Well-being: Positive development across the life course* (pp. 35–49). Mahwah, NJ: Erlbaum.

Lecanuet, J. P., Fiferm W. P., Krasnegor, N. A., & Smotherman, W. P. (1995). *Fetal development: A psychobiological perspective.* Hillsdale, NJ: Erlbaum.

Lederberg, A. R., Chapin, S. L., Rosenblatt, V., & Vandell, D. L. (1986). Ethnic, gender, and age preferences among deaf and hearing preschool peers. *Child Development, 57,* 375–386.

Lee, V., & Smith, J. (1993). Effects of school restructuring on the achievement and engagement of middle-grade students. *Sociology of Education, 66,* 164–187.

Lefkowitz, E.S. (2005). "Things have gotten better": Developmental changes among emerging adults after the transition to university. *Journal of Adolescent Research, 20,* 40–63.

Legerstee, M., & Varghese, J. (2001). The role of maternal affect mirroring on social expectancies in three-month-old infants. *Child Development, 72,* 1301–1313.

Lehn, H., Derks, E. M., Hudziak, J. J., Heutink, P., Van Beijsterveldt, T. C. E. M., & Boomsma, D. I. (2007). Attention problems and attention-deficit/hyperactivity disorder in discordant and concordant monozygotic twins: Evidence of environmental mediators. *Journal of the American Academy of Child and Adolescent Psychiatry, 46*(1), 83–91.

Leiberman, L. D., Gray, H., Wier, M., Fiorentino, R., & Maloney, P. (2000). Long-term outcomes of an abstinence-based, small-group pregnancy prevention program in New York city schools. *Family Planning Perspectives, 32,* 237–245.

Lemerise, E. A., & Dodge, K. A. (2000). The development of anger and hostile interactions. In M. Lewis & J. M. Haviland-Jones (Eds.), *Handbook of emotions* (pp. 594–606). New York: Guilford Press.

Lempers, J., & Clark-Lempers, D. (1992). Young, middle, and late adolescents' comparisons of the functional importance of five significant relationships. *Journal of Youth and Adolescence, 21,* 53–96.

Lenroot, R. K., & Giedd, J. N. (2006). Brain development in children and adolescents: Insights from anatomical magnetic resonance imaging. *Neuroscience and Biobehavioral Reviews, 30,* 718–729.

Leon, G., Fulkerson, J. A., Perry, C. L., Keel, P. K., & Klump, K. L. (1999). Three to four year prospective evaluation of personality and behavioral risk factors for later disordered eating in adolescent girls and boys. *Journal of Youth and Adolescence, 28,* 181–196.

Leopold, W. F. (1949). *Speech development of a bilingual child.* Evanston, IL: Northwestern University Press.

Lerner, R. (2006). Developmental science, developmental systems, and contemporary theories of human development. In W. Damon & R. Lerner (Series Eds.) & R. Lerner (Vol. Ed.), *Handbook of child psychology: Vol. 1. Theoretical models of human development* (6th ed., pp. 1–17). New York: Wiley.

Lerner, R. M., Fisher, C. B., & Gianinno, L. (2006). Editorial: Constancy and change in the development of applied developmental science. *Applied Developmental Science, 10,* 172–173.

Lerner, R. M., Theokas, C., & Bobek, D. L. (2005). Concepts and theories of human development: Contemporary dimensions. In M. H. Bornstein & M. E. Lamb (Eds.), *Developmental science: An advanced textbook* (pp. 3-44). Mahwah, NJ: Erlbaum.

Leu, D. J., Zawilinski, L., Castek, J., Banerjee, M., Housand, B., Liu, Y., & O'Neil, M. (in press). What is new about the new literacies of online reading comprehension? In A. Berger, L. Rush, & J. Eakle (Eds.), *Secondary school reading and writing: What research reveals for classroom practices.* Chicago: National Council of Teachers of English/National Conference of Research on Language and Literacy.

Leventhal, H., & Keeshan, P. (1993). Promoting healthy alternatives to substance abuse. In S. Millstein, A. Petersen, & E. Nightingale (Eds.), *Promoting the health of adolescents: New directions for the twenty-first century* (pp. 260–284). New York: Oxford University Press.

Leventhal, T., & Brooks-Gunn, J. (2000). The neighborhoods they live in: The effects of neighborhood residence on child and adolescent outcomes. *Psychological Bulletin, 126,* 309–337.

Leventhal, T., & Brooks-Gunn, J. (2003). Moving to opportunity: An experimental study of neighborhood effects on mental health. *American Journal of Public Health, 93,* 1576–1582.

Leventhal, T., & Brooks-Gunn, J. (2004). A randomized study of neighborhood effects on low-iincome children's educational outcomes. *Developmental Psychology, 40,* 488–507.

Leventhal, T., & Brooks-Gunn, J. (2005). Neighborhood and gender effects on family processes: Results from the Moving to Opportunity Demonstration. *Family Relations, 54,* 633–643.

Levi, S., & Chervenak, F. A. (1998). Preface. *Annals of the New York Academy of Sciences, 847,* 1.

Levin, E., & Rubin, K. H. (1983). Getting others to do what you wanted them to do: The development of requestive strategies. In K. Nelson (Ed.), *Child language* (vol. 4, pp. 157–186). Hillsdale NJ: Erlbaum.

Levine, S. (2003). Stress: An historical perspective. In T. Steckler, N. Kalin, & J. M. M. Read (Eds.), *Handbook on stress, immunology and behavior* (pp. 3–23). Amsterdam: Elsevier.

Lewinsohn, P. M., Joiner, T. E., Jr., & Rohde, P. (2001). Evaluation of cognitive diathesis-stress models in predicting major depressive disorder in adolescents. *Journal of Abnormal Psychology, 110,* 203–215.

Lewinsohn, P. M., Pettit, J. W., Joiner, T. E., Jr., & Seeley, J. R. (2003). The symptomatic expression of major depressive disorder in adolescents and young adults. *Journal of Abnormal Psychology, 112,* 244–252.

Lewinsohn, P. M., Rohde, P., & Seeley, J. (1994). Psychosocial risk factors for future adolescent suicide attempts. *Journal of Consulting and Clinical Psychology, 62,* 297–305.

Lewinsohn, P. M., Rohde, P., Seeley, J. R., Klein, D. N., & Gotlib, I. H. (2003). Psychosocial functioning of young adults who have experienced and recovered from major depressive disorder during adolescence. *Journal of Abnormal Psychology, 112,* 353–363.

Lewis, M. (2000). Self-conscious emotions: Embarrassment, pride, shame, and guilt. In M. Lewis J. Haviland (Eds.), *Handbook of emotions* (2nd ed., pp. 623–636). New York: Guilford Press.

Lewis, M. D. (2000). Emotional self-organization at three time scales. In M. D. Lewis & I. Granic (Eds.), *Emotion, development, and self-organization: Dynamic systems approaches to emotional development* (pp. 37–69). New York: Cambridge University Press.

Lewis, M. D. (2005). Self-organizing individual differences in brain development. *Developmental Review, 25,* 252–277.

Lewis, M., & Ramsay, D. (2002). Cortisol response to embarrassment and shame. *Child Development, 73,* 1034–1045.

Lewis, M., Sullivan, M. W., Stanger, C., & Weiss, M. (1989). Self development and self-conscious emotions. *Child Development, 60,* 146–156.

Li, J. (2006). Self in learning: Chinese adolescents' goals and sense of agency. *Child Development, 77,* 482–501.

Lindsey, E. W., Mize, J., & Pettit, G. (1997). Mutuality in parent-child play: Consequences for children's competence. *Journal of Social and Personal Relationships, 14,* 523–538.

Linn, M., & Songer, N. (1991). Cognitive and conceptual change in adolescence. *American Journal of Education, 99,* 379–417.

Linn, M., & Songer, N. (1993). How do students make sense of science? *Merrill-Palmer Quarterly, 39,* 47–73.

Listen! The children speak: Anecdotes with interpretations. (1979). Washington, DC: United States National Committee, World Organization for Early Childhood Education.

Little, M., & Steinberg, L. (2006). Psychosocial predictors of adolescent drug dealing in the inner-city: Potential roles of opportunity, conventional commitments, and maturity. *Journal of Research on Crime and Delinquency, 4*, 1–30.

Little, S. A., & Garber, J. (2004). Interpersonal and achievement orientations and specific stressors predict depressive and aggressive symptoms. *Journal of Adolescent Research, 19*, 63–84.

Livingstone, M., & Hubel, D. (1988). Segregation of form, color, movement, and depth: Anatomy, physiology, and perception. *Science, 240*, 740–749.

Locke, A. (2001). Preverbal communication. In J. G. Bremner, & A. Fogel (Eds.), *Blackwell handbook of infant development* (pp. 379–403). Malden, MA: Blackwell.

Locke, J. (1690). *An essay concerning human understanding*. London: Eliz. Holt.

Loeber, R., Farrington, D. P., Stouthamer-Loeber, M., & van Kammen, W. B. (1998). *Antisocial behavior and mental health problems*. Mahwah, NJ: Erlbaum.

Loftus, E. F. (1975). Leading questions and the eyewitness report. *Cognitive Psychology, 7*, 550–572.

Loftus, E. F., & Hoffman, H. G. (1989). Misinformation and memory: The creation of new memories. *Journal of Experimental Psychology: General, 118*, 100–104.

Lord, H., & Mahoney, J. L. (2007). Neighborhood crime and self-care: Risks for aggression and lower academic performance. *Developmental Psychology, 43*, 1321–1333.

Los Angeles County Department of Public Health. (2007). *Prevention childhood obesity: The need to create healthy places*. Los Angeles: Author.

Lourenco, O. (1996). In defense of Piaget's theory: A reply to 10 common criticisms. *Psychological Review, 103*, 143–164.

Love, J. M., Tarullo, L. B., Raikes, H., & Chazan-Cohen, R. (2006). Head Start: What do we know about its effectiveness? What do we need to know? In K. McCartney & D. Phillips (Eds.), *Blackwell handbook of early childhood development* (pp. 550–576). Malden, MA: Blackwell.

Lowe, J., Handmaker, N., & Aragon, C. (2006). Impact of mother interactive style on infant affect among babies exposed to alcohol in utero. *Infant Mental Health Journal, 27*, 371–382.

Luciana, M., Conklin, H. M., Hooper, C. J. & Yarger, R. S. (2005). The development of nonverbal working memory and executive control processes in adolescents. *Child Development, 76*, 697.

Luna, B., Thulborn, K. R., Munoz, D. P., Merriam, E. P., Garver, K. E., Minshew, N. J., et al. (2001). Maturation of widely distributed brain function subserves cognitive development. *Neuroimage, 13*, 786–793.

Luster, T., & Small, S. (1994). Factors associated with sexual risk-taking behaviors among adolescents. *Journal of Marriage and the Family, 56*, 622–632.

Lustig, R. H. (1998). Sex hormonal modulation of neural development in vitro: Implications for brain sex differentiation. In L. Ellis & L. Ebertz (Eds.), *Males, females, and behavior: Toward biological understanding* (pp. 13–25). Westport, CT: Praeger Publishers/Greenwood Publishing Group.

Luthar, S. S., & Becker, B. E. (2002). Privileged but pressured? A study of affluent youth. *Child Development, 73*, 1593–1610.

Luthar, S., & McMahon, T. (1996). Peer reputation among inner-city adolescents: Structure and correlates. *Journal of Research on Adolescence, 6*, 581–603.

Lytton, H., & Romney, D. M. (1991). Parents' differential socialization of boys and girls: A meta-analysis. *Psychological Bulletin, 109*, 267–296.

Mac Iver, D., Stipek, D., & Daniels, D. (1991). Explaining within-semester changes in student effort in junior high school and senior high school courses. *Journal of Educational Psychology, 83*, 201–211.

Maccoby, E. (1990). Gender and relationships: A developmental account. *American Psychologist, 45*, 513–520.

Maccoby, E. E. (1999). *The two sexes: Growing up apart, coming together*. Cambridge, MA: Harvard University Press

Maccoby, E. (2003). *The two sexes: Growing up apart, coming together*. Cambridge, MA: Harvard University Press.

Maccoby, E. E., & Martin, J. A. (1983). Socialization in the context of the family: Parent-child interaction. In E. M. Hetherington (Ed.), *Handbook of child psychology: Vol. 4. Socialization, personality and social development* (4th ed., pp. 1–101). New York: Wiley.

MacDorman, M. F., Callaghan, W. M., Mathews, T. J., Hoyert, D. L., & Kochanek, K. D. (2007, May). *Trends in preterm-related infant mortality by race and ethnicity: United States, 1999–2004*. Retrieved from http://www.cdc.gov/nchs/products/pubs/pubd/hestats/infantmort99-04/infantmort99-04.htm#ref01

Macintyre, C., & McVitty, K. (Eds.). (2004). *Movement and learning in the early years: Supporting dyspraxia (DCD) and other difficulties*. London: Paul Chapman.

MacWhinney, B. (2005). Language development. In M. H. Bornstein & M. E. Lamb (Eds.), *Developmental science: An advanced textbook* (pp. 359–387). Mahwah, NJ: Erlbaum.

MacWhinney, B., & Bornstein, M. H. (2003). Language and literacy. In M. H. Bornstein, L. Davidson, C. L. M. Keyes, & K. A. Moore (Eds.), *Well-being: Positive development across the life course* (pp. 331–339). Mahwah, NJ: Erlbaum.

Magkos, F., Manios, Y., Christakis, G., & Kafatos, A. G. (2005). Secular trends in cardiovascular risk factors among school-aged boys from Crete, Greece, 1982–2002. *European Journal of Clinical Nutrition, 59*, 1–7.

Magnusson, D., & Stattin, H. (2006). The person in context: A holistic-interactionistic approach. In W. Damon & R. Lerner (Series Eds.) & R. Lerner (Vol. Ed.), *Handbook of child psychology: Vol. 1. Theoretical models of human development* (6th ed., pp. 400–464). New York: Wiley.

Magnusson, D., Stattin, H., & Allen, V. (1986). Differential maturation among girls and its relation to social adjustment in a longitudinal perspective. In P. Baltes, D. Featherman, & R. Lerner (Eds.), *Life span development and behavior* (Vol. 7, pp. 135–172). Hillsdale, NJ: Erlbaum.

Mahoney, J. L., Lord, H., & Carryl, E. (2005). Afterschool program participation and the development of child obesity and peer acceptance. *Applied Developmental Science, 9*(4), 202–215.

Mahoney, J. L., Lord, H., & Carryl, E. (2005). An ecological analysis of after-school program participation and the development of academic performance and motivational attributes for disadvantaged children. *Child Development, 76*, 811–825.

Mahoney, J. L., & Zigler, E. F. (2006). Translating science to policy under the No Child Left Behind Act of 2001: Lessons from the national evaluation of the 21st-Century Community Learning Centers. *Journal of Applied Developmental Psychology, 27,* 282–294.

Main, M., & Cassidy, J. (1988). Categories of response to reunion with the parent at age 6: Predictable from infant attachment classifications and stable over a 1-month period. *Developmental Psychology, 24,* 415–426.

Main, M., & Solomon, J. (1990). Procedures for identifying infants as disorganized/disoriented during the Ainsworth Strange Situation. In M. T. Greenberg, D. Cicchetti, & E. M. Cummings (Eds.), *Attachment in the preschool years: Theory, research, and intervention* (pp. 121–160). Chicago: University of Chicago Press.

Maital, S. L., Dromi, E., Sagi, A., & Bornstein, M. H. (2000). The Hebrew Communicative Development Inventory: Language specific properties and cross-linguistic generalizations. *Journal of Child Language, 27,* 43–67.

Manlove, J. (1998). The influence of high school dropout and school disengagement on the risk of school-age pregnancy. *Journal of Research on Adolescence, 8,* 187–220.

Manlove, J., Mariner, C., & Papillo, A. (2000). Subsequent fertility among teen mothers: Longitudinal analyses of recent national data. *Journal of Marriage and the Family, 62,* 430–448.

Manning, W., & Landale, N. (1996). Racial and ethnic differences in the role of cohabitation in premarital childbearing. *Journal of Marriage and the Family, 58,* 63–77.

Manning, W., Longmore, M. A., & Giordano, P. C. (2000). The relationship context of contraceptive use at first intercourse. *Family Planning Perspectives, 32,* 104–110.

Mannino, D. M., Homa, D. M., Akinbami, L. J., Moorman, J. E., Gwynn, C., & Redd, S. C. (2002). Surveillance for asthma—United States, 1980–1999. *MMWR Surveillance Summaries, 51*(No. SS01), 1–13.

March of Dimes, Pregnancy & Newborn Health Education Center. (2008). *Your first tests.* Retrieved from http://www.marchofdimes.com/pnhec/159_519.asp

March of Dimes. (2008). *Professionals and researchers, quick reference: Smoking during pregnancy* [Fact sheet]. Retrieved from http://www.marchofdimes.com/professionals/14332_1171.asp

Marcia, J. (1966). Development and validation of ego identity status. *Journal of Personality and Social Psychology, 3,* 551–558.

Mares, M. L., & Woodard, E. (2005). Positive effects of television on children's social interactions: A meta-analysis. *Media Psychology, 7,* 301–322.

Markman, E. M. (1999). Multiple approaches to the study of word learning in children. *Japanese Psychological Research, 41,* 79–81.

Markovits, H., & Valchon, R. (1989). Reasoning with contrary-to-fact propositions. *Journal of Experimental Child Psychology, 47,* 398–412.

Markovits, H., Venet, M., Janveau-Brennan, G., Malfait, N., Pion, N., & Vadeboncoeur, I. (1996). Reasoning in young children: Fantasy and information retrieval. *Child Development, 67,* 2857–2872.

Marriage, K., & Cummins, R. A. (2004). Subjective quality of life and self-esteem in children: The role of primary and secondary control in coping with everyday stress. *Social Indicators Research, 66,* 107–122.

Marsh, H., & Yeung, A. (1997). Coursework selection: Relations to academic self-concept and achievement. *American Educational Research Journal, 34,* 691–720.

Marshall, J. D., & Bouffard, M. (1997). The effects of quality daily physical education on movement competency in obese versus nonobese children. *Adapted Physical Activity Quarterly, 14*(3), 222–237.

Marshall, N. L., Coll, C. G., Marx, F., Mccartney, K., Keefe, N., & Ruh, J. (1997). After-school time and children's behavioral adjustment. *Merrill-Palmer Quarterly, 43,* 497–514.

Marshall, W. (1978). Puberty. In F. Falkner & J. Tanner (Eds.), *Human growth: Vol. 2. Postnatal growth* (pp. 141–181). New York: Plenum.

Martin, A., Ruchkin, V., Caminis, A., Vermeiren, R., Henrich, C. C., & Schwab-Stone, M. (2005). Early to bed: A study of adaptation among sexually active urban adolescent girls younger than age sixteen. *Journal of the American Academy of Child & Adolescent Psychiatry, 44,* 358–367.

Martin, C. L., & Fabes, R. A. (2001). The stability and consequences of young children's same-sex peer interactions. *Developmental Psychology, 37,* 431–446.

Martin, C. L., Ruble, D. N., & Szkrybalo, J. (2002). Cognitive theories of early gender development. *Psychological Bulletin, 128,* 903–933.

Martinez, M. (in press). *Learning and cognition: the design of the mind.* Boston: Allyn & Bacon.

Martinez, M. E., & Kalbfleisch, M. L. (in press). Spanning mathematics education research and cognitive neuroscience: Conceptual and epistemological divergences. In A. E. Kelly, S. Jensen, J. Baek, R. L. Kalbfleisch (Eds.), *Neuroscience and mathematics education.* New York: Cambridge University Press.

Martinez, R., & Dukes, R. (1997). The effects of ethnic identity, ethnicity, and gender on adolescent well-being. *Journal of Youth and Adolescence, 26,* 503–516.

Mash, C., Arterberry, M., & Bornstein, M. H. (2007). Mechanisms of visual object recognition in infancy: 5-month-olds generalize beyond the interpolation of familiar views. *Infancy, 12,* 31–43.

May, J. C., Delgado, M. R., Dahl, R., Fiez, J. A., Stenger, V. A., Ryan, N., & Carter, C. S. (2004). Event-related fMRI of reward related brain activity in children and adolescents. *Biological Psychiatry, 55,* 359–366.

Mayes, L. C., Bornstein, M. H., Chawarska, K., Haynes, O. M., & Granger, R. H. (1996). Impaired regulation of arousal in 3-month-old infants exposed prenatally to cocaine and other drugs. *Development and Psychopathology, 8,* 29–42.

Mayes, L. C., Cicchetti, D., Acharyya, S., & Zhang, H. (2003). Developmental trajectories of cocaine-and-other-drug-exposed and non-cocaine-exposed children. *Developmental and Behavioral Pediatrics, 24,* 323–335.

Mayes, L. C., Feldman, R., Granger, R. H., Haynes, O. M., Bornstein, M. H., & Schottenfeld, R. (1997). The effects of polydrug use with and without cocaine on mother-infant interaction at 3 and 6 months. *Infant Behavior and Development, 20,* 489–502.

Mayes, L. C., Granger, R. H., Frank, M. A., Schottenfeld, R., & Bornstein, M. H. (1993). Neurobehavioral profiles of neonates exposed to cocaine prenatally. *Pediatrics, 91,* 778–783.

Mayes, L. C., & Truman, S. D. (2002). Substance abuse and parenting. In M. H. Bornstein (Ed.), *Handbook of parenting: Vol. 4. Applied parenting* (2nd ed., pp. 329–359). Mahwah, NJ: Erlbaum.

Mayo Clinic. (2006). Growing pains. Retrieved October 2, 2008, from http://www.mayoclinic.com/health/growing-pains/DS00888

McCabe, K. M., Hough, R., Wood, P. A., & Yeh, M. (2001). Childhood and adolescent onset conduct disorder: A test of the developmental taxonomy. *Journal of Abnormal Child Psychology, 29,* 305–316.

McCall, R. B., Appelbaum, M., & Hogarty, P. S. (1973). Developmental changes in mental performance. *Monographs of the Society for Research in Child Development, 38*(3, Serial No. 150).

McClelland, D., Atkinson, J., Clark, R., & Lowell, E. (1953). *The achievement motive.* New York: Appleton-Century-Crofts.

McClintock, M. (1980). Major gaps in menstrual cycle research: Behavioral and physiological controls in a biological context. In P. Komenich, M. McSweeney, J. Noack, & N. Elder (Eds.), *The menstrual cycle* (Vol. 2, pp. 7–23). New York: Springer.

McElwain, N., Cox, M., Burchinal, M., & Macfie, J. (2003). Differentiating among insecure mother-infant attachment classifications: A focus on child-friend interaction and exploration during solitary play at 36 months. *Attachment & Human Development, 5,* 136–164.

McGhee, P. E., & Frueh, T. (1980). Television viewing and the learning of sex-role stereotypes. *Sex Roles, 6,* 179–188.

McGraw, M. (1935). *Growth: A study of Johnny and Jimmy.* New York: Appleton-Century.

McGraw, M. (1939). Later development of children specially trained during infancy: Johnny and Jimmy at school age. *Child Development, 10,* 1–19.

McGrew, W. (2004). *The cultured chimpanzee.* New York: Cambridge University Press.

McGue, J., Bouchard, T. J., Jr., Iacona, W. G., & Lykken, D. T. (1993). Behavioral genetics of cognitive ability: A life-span perspective. In R. Plomin & G. E. McClearn (Eds.), Nature nurture & psychology (pp. 59–76). Washington, DC: American Psychological Association.

McHale, S. M, Crouter, A. C., & Tucker, C. J. (2001). Free time activities in middle childhood Links with adjustment in early adolescence. *Child Development, 72,* 1764–1778.

McHale, S. M., Shanahan, L., Updegraff, K. A., Crouter, A. C., & Booth, A. (2004). Developmental and individual differences in girls' sex-typed activities. *Child Development, 75,* 1575–1593.

McKenna, J., Mosko, S., Richard, C., Drummond, S., Hunt, L., Cetel, M. B., & Arpaia, J. (1994). Experimental studies of infant-parent co-sleeping: Mutual physiological and behavioral influences and their relevance to SIDS (sudden infant death syndrome). *Early Human Development, 38,* 187–201.

McLoyd, V. C. (1990). The impact of economic hardship on Black families and children: Psychological distress, parenting, and socioemotional development. *Child Development, 61,* 311–346.

McLoyd, V. C., Aikens, N. L., & Burton, L. M. (2006). Childhood poverty, policy, and practice. In K. A. Renninger & I. E. Sigel (Ed.), W. Damon (Series Ed.), *Handbook of child psychol-ogy: Vol. 4. Child psychology in practice* (6th ed., pp. 700–775). Hoboken, NJ: Wiley.

McNeely, M. J., & Boyko, E. J. (2004). Type 2 diabetes prevalence in Asian Americans. *Diabetes Care, 27,* 66–69.

McNeil, D.G., Jr. (2007, September 13). Child mortality at record low; further drop seen. *The New York Times.* Retrieved September 12, 2008, from www.nytimes.com/2007/09/13/world/13child.html?_r=1&scp=1&sq=child%20mortality&st=cse&oref=slogin

McNelles, L. R., & Connolly, J. A. (1999). Intimacy between adolescent friends: Age and gender differences in intimate affect and intimate behaviors. *Journal of Research on Adolescence, 9,* 143–159.

McQuaid, E. L., Mitchell, D. K., & Esteban, C. A. (2006). Allergies and asthma. In G. G. Bear & K. M. Minke (Eds.), *Children's needs III: Development, prevention, and intervention* (pp. 909–924). Bethesda, MD: National Association of School Psychologists.

Meaney, M. (2001). Maternal care, gene expression, and the transmission of individual differences in stress reactivity across generations. *Annual Review of Neuroscience, 24,* 1161–1192.

Meeus, W., Iedema, J., Helsen, M., & Vollebergh, W. (1999). Patterns of adolescent identity development: Review of literature and longitudinal analysis. *Developmental Review, 19,* 419–461.

Mei, Z., Grummer-Strawn, L. M., Thompson, D., & Dietz, W. H. (2004). Shifts in percentiles of growth during early childhood: Analysis of longitudinal data from the California Child Health and Development Study. *Pediatrics, 113,* 617–627.

Meier, A. M. (2003). Adolescents' transition to first intercourse, religiosity and attitudes about sex. *Social Forces, 81,* 1031–1052.

Meisels, S. J., & Atkins-Burnett, S. (2006). Evaluating early childhood assessments: A differential analysis. In K. McCartney & D. Phillips (Eds.), *Blackwell handbook of early childhood development* (pp. 533–549). Malden, MA: Blackwell.

Meissner, H. C., Strebel, P. M., & Orenstein, W. A. (2004). Measles vaccines and the potential for worldwide eradication of measles. *Pediatrics, 114,* 1065–1069.

Meltzoff, A. N. (1988). Infant imitation and memory: Nine-month-olds in immediate and deferred tests. *Child Development, 59,* 217–225.

Meltzoff, A. N. (1993). Molyneux's babies: Cross-modal perception, imitation, and the mind of the preverbal infant. In N. Eilan, R. McCarthy, & B. Brewer (Eds.), *Spatial representation: Problems in philosophy and psychology* (pp. 219–235). Oxford, UK: Blackwell.

Meltzoff, A. N., & Moore, M. K. (1999). Persons and representation: Why infant imitation is important for theories of human development. In J. Nadel & G. Butterworth (Eds.), *Imitation in infancy* (pp. 9–35). New York: Cambridge University Press.

Ment, L. R., Vohr, B., Allan, W., Katz, K. H., Schneider, K. C., Westerveld, M., et al. (2003). Change in cognitive function over time in very low-birth-weight infants. *Journal of the American Medical Association, 289,* 705–711.

Mervis, C. B., Pani, J. R., & Pani, A. M. (2003). Transaction of child cognitive-linguistic abilities and adult input in the acquisition of lexical categories at the basic and subordinate levels. In D. H. Rakison & L. M. Oakes (Eds.), *Early category and concept development: Making sense of the blooming, buzzing confusion* (pp. 242–274). New York: Oxford University Press.

Mesquita, B., & Karasawa, M. (2004). Self conscious emotions as dynamic cultural processes. *Psychological Inquiry, 15,* 161–166.

Meyer-Bahlburg, H., Ehrhardt, A., Rosen, L., Gruen, R., Veridiano, N., Vann, F., & Neuwalder, H. (1995). Prenatal estrogens and the development of homosexual orientation. *Developmental Psychology, 31,* 12–21.

Mezulis, A., Hyde, J. S., & Abramson, L. Y. (2007). The developmental origins of cognitive vulnerability to depression: Temperament, parenting, and negative life events in childhood as contributors to negative cognitive style. *Developmental Psychology, 42,* 1012–1025.

Michael, R., Laumann, E., & Kolata, G. (1994). *Sex in America.* New York: Warner Books.

Mickelson, R. (1990). The attitude-achievement paradox among black adolescents. *Sociology of Education, 63,* 44–61.

Midgley, C., Berman, E., & Hicks, L. (1995). Differences between elementary and middle school teachers and students: A goal theory approach. *Journal of Early Adolescence, 15,* 90–113.

Mihalic, S., & Elliot, D. (1997). Short- and long-term consequences of adolescent work. *Youth and Society, 28,* 464–498.

Miles, S. B., & Stipek, D. (2006). Contemporaneous and longitudinal associations between social behavior and literacy achievement in a sample of low-income elementary school children. *Child Development, 77,* 103–117.

Millar, S. (1975). Visual experience or translation rules? Drawing the human figure by blind and sighted children. *Perception, 4,* 363–371.

Miller, B. C., Fan, X., Christensen, M., Grotevant, H. D., & van Dulmen, M. (2000). Comparisons of adopted and nonadopted adolescents in a large, nationally representative sample. *Child Development, 71,* 1458–1473.

Miller, B., & Moore, K. (1990). Adolescent sexual behavior, pregnancy, and parenting: Research through the 1980s. *Journal of Marriage and the Family, 52,* 1025–1044.

Miller, D., & Byrnes, J. (1997). The role of contextual and personal factors in children's risk taking. *Developmental Psychology, 33,* 814–823.

Miller, G. (1956). The magical number seven, plus or minus two: Some limits on our capacity for processing information. *Psychological Review, 63,* 81–97.

Miller, L., Davies, M., & Greenwald, S. (2000). Religiosity and substance use and abuse among adolescents in the National Comorbidity survey. *Journal of the American Academy of Child and Adolescent Psychiatry, 39,* 1190–1197.

Miller, P. H., & Seier, W. L. (1994). Strategy utilization deficiencies in children: When, where, and why? In H. W. Reese (Ed.), *Advances in child development and behavior* (Vol. 25, pp. 107–156). New York: Academic Press.

Miller, P., Wiley, A. R., Fung, H., & Liang, C-H. (1997). Personal storytelling as a medium of socialization in Chinese and American families. *Child Development, 68,* 557–568.

Mindell, J. A., & Owens, J. A. (2003). *A clinical guide to pediatric sleep: Diagnosis and management of sleep problems.* Philadelphia: Lippincott, Williams, & Wilkins.

Mindell, J., Owens, J. A., & Carskadon, M. A. (1999). Developmental features of sleep. *Child & Adolescent Psychiatric Clinics of North America, 8,* 695–725.

Minturn, L., & Lambert, W. W. (1964). *Mothers of six cultures: Antecedents of child rearing.* New York: Wiley.

Mitchell, E. (Ed.). (1985). *Anorexia nervosa and bulimia: Diagnosis and treatment.* Minneapolis: University of Minnesota Press.

Mitka, M. (2004). Improvement seen in US immunization rates. *Journal of the American Medical Association, 292,* 1167.

Mittendorf, R., Williams, M. A., Berkey, C. S., & Cotter, P. F. (1990). The length of uncomplicated human gestation. *Obstetrics and Gynecology, 75,* 929–932.

Modell, J., & Goodman, M. (1990). Historical perspectives. In S. Feldman & G. Elliott (Eds.), *At the threshold: The developing adolescent* (pp. 93–122). Cambridge, MA: Harvard University Press.

Moffitt, T. (1993). Adolescence-limited and life-course persistent antisocial behavior: A developmental taxonomy. *Psychological Review, 100,* 674–701.

Moffitt, T. (2006). Life-course persistent versus adolescence-limited antisocial behavior. In D. Cicchetti & D. Cohen (Eds.), *Developmental psychopathology* (2nd ed., pp. 570–598). New York: Wiley.

Moffitt, T. E., Caspi, A., Harrington, H., & Milne, B. J. (2002). Males on the life-course-persistent and adolescence-limited antisocial pathways: Follow-up at age 26 years. *Development and Psychopathology, 14,* 179–207.

Molfese, D. L., & Molfese, V. J. (1994). Short-term and long-term developmental outcomes: The use of behavioral and electrophysiological measures in early infancy as predictors. In G. Dawson and K. W. Fischer (Eds.), *Human behavior and the developing brain* (pp. 493–517). New York: Guilford.

Mondschein, E. R., Adolph, K. E., & Tamis-LeMonda, C. S. (2000). Gender bias in mothers' expectations about infant crawling. *Journal of Experimental Child Psychology, 77,* 304–316.

Monitoring the Future. (2005). The Monitoring the Future Study, University of Michigan. Available from Monitoring the Future Web site: www.monitoringthefuture.org/05data.html

Monroe, S. M., Rohde, P., Seeley, J. R., & Lewinsohn, P. M. (1999). Life events and depression in adolescence: Relationship loss as a prospective risk factor for first onset of major depressive disorder. *Journal of Abnormal Psychology, 108,* 606–614.

Montgomery, M. (1996). "The fruit that hangs highest": Courtship and chaperonage in New York high society, 1880–1920. *Journal of Family History, 21,* 172–191.

Moon, R. Y., Kotch, L., & Aird, L. (2006). State child care regulations regarding infant sleep environment since the Healthy Child Care America-Back to Sleep campaign. *Pediatrics, 118*(1), 73–83.

Moore, G. A., Cohn, J. F., & Campbell, S. B. (2001). Infant affective responses to mother's still face at 6 months differentially predict externalizing and internalizing behaviors at 18 months. *Developmental Psychology, 37,* 706–714.

Moore, K. L. (1998). *The developing human: Clinically oriented embryology* (6th ed.). Philadelphia: Saunders.

Moore, K., Myers, D., Morrison, D., Nord, C., Brown, B., & Edmonston, B. (1993). Age at first childbirth and later poverty. *Journal of Research on Adolescence, 3,* 393–422.

Moore, K. L., & Persaud, T. V. N. (1993). The branchial or pharyngeal apparatus. *The developing human: Clinically oriented embryology* (5th ed., pp. 192–198). Philadelphia: Saunders.

Moore, K. L., & Persaud, T. V. N. (2003). *Before we are born: Essentials of embryology and birth defects* (6th ed.). Philadelphia: Saunders.

Moore, S., & Gullone, E. (1996). Predicting adolescent risk behavior using a personalized cost-benefit analysis. *Journal of Youth and Adolescence, 25,* 343–359.

Moorrees, C. F. A. (1959). *The dentition of the growing child: A longitudinal study of dental development between 3 and 18.* Cambridge, MA: Harvard University Press.

Moos, R. (1978). A typology of junior high and high school classrooms. *American Educational Research Journal, 15,* 53–66.

Morris, B., & Sloutsky, V. (2001). Children's solutions of logical versus empirical problems: What's missing and what develops? *Cognitive Development, 16,* 907–928.

Morrison, F. J., & Connor, C. M. (2002). Understanding schooling effects on early literacy: A working research strategy. *Journal of School Psychology, 40,* 493–500.

Mortimer, J. (2003). *Working and growing up in America.* Cambridge, MA: Harvard University Press.

Mortimer, J., & Johnson, M. (1998). New perspectives on adolescent work and the transition to adulthood. In R. Jessor & M. Chase (Eds.), *New perspectives on adolescent risk behavior* (pp. 425–496). New York: Cambridge University Press.

Mortimer, J., & Lorence, J. (1979). Work experience and occupational value socialization: A longitudinal study. *American Journal of Sociology, 84,* 1361–1385.

Mueller, E. (1972). The maintenance of verbal exchanges between young children. *Child Development, 43,* 930–938.

Mueller, E., & Vandell, D. L. (1979) Infant-infant interaction. In J. Osofsky (Ed.), *Handbook of Infant Development* (pp. 591–622). New York: Wiley.

Muller, P. A., Stage, F. K., & Kinzie, J. (2001). Science achievement growth trajectories: Understanding factors related to gender and racial-ethnic differences in precollege science achievement. *American Educational Research, 3,* 981–1012.

Mulligan, G. M., Brimhall, D., & West, J. (2005). *Child care and early education arrangements of infants, toddlers, and preschoolers: 2001* (NCES 2006–039). U.S. Department of Education, National Center for Education Statistics. Washington, DC: U.S. Government Printing Office.

Munakata, Y. (2006). Information processing approaches to development. In W. Damon & R. M. Lerner (Series Eds.) & D. Kuhn & R. S. Siegler (Vol. Eds.), *Handbook of child psychology: Vol. 2. Cognition, perception, and language* (6th ed., pp. 426–463). Hoboken, NJ: Wiley.

Munakata, Y. (2006). Information processing approaches to development. In D. Kuhn & R. Siegler (Eds.), *Handbook of child psychology: Vol. 2. Cognition, perception, and language* (pp. 426–463). Hoboken, NJ: Wiley.

Munn, P., & Dunn, J. (1989). Temperament and the developing relationship between siblings. *International Journal of Behavioral Development, 12,* 433–451.

Muotri, A. R., & Gage, F. H. (2006). Generation of neuronal variability and complexity. *Nature, 441,* 1087–1093.

Mustanski, B. S., Viken, R. J., Kaprio, J., Pulkkinen, L., & Rose, R. J. (2004). Genetic and environmental influences on pubertal development: Longitudinal data from Finnish twins at ages 11 and 14. *Developmental Psychology, 40,* 1188–1198.

Nader, P. R., O'Brien, M., Houts, R., Bradley, R., Belsky, J., Crosnoe, R., Friedman, S., Mei, Z., Susman, E., & the NICHD Early Child Care Research Network. (2006). Identifying risk for obesity in early childhood. *Pediatrics, 118,* 594–601.

Nagin, D., Farrington, D., & Moffitt, T. (1995). Life-course trajectories of different types of offenders. *Criminology, 33,* 111–139.

Nagin, D., & Tremblay, R. (1999). Trajectories of boys' physical aggression, opposition, and hyperactivity on the path to physically violent and nonviolent juvenile delinquency. *Child Development, 70,* 1181–1196.

Nagin, D., & Tremblay, R. (2005). What has been learned from group-based trajectory modeling?: Examples from physical aggression and other problem behaviors. *Annals of the American Academy of Political and Social Science, 602,* 82–117.

Nagin, D. S., & Tremblay, R. E. (2005). Developmental trajectory groups: Fact or useful statistical fiction? *Criminology, 43,* 873–904.

National Center for Education Statistics. (1999). *The condition of education.* Washington, DC: U.S. Department of Education.

National Center for Education Statistics. (2003). *Trends in international mathematics and science study.* Retrieved September 3, 2008, from http://nces.ed.gov/timss/results03.asp.

National Center for Education Statistics. (2006). *After-school programs and activities: 2005.* Report NCES 2006: 076. Retrieved September 3, 2008, from http://nces.ed.gov/pubs2006/afterschool/index.asp

National Center for Education Statistics. (2006). *Comparing private schools and public schools using hierarchical linear modeling.* Washington, DC: U.S. Department of Education.

National Center for Education Statistics. (2007). *The condition of education.* Retrieved September 3, 2008, from http://nces.ed.gov/pubsearch/pubsinfo.asp?pubid=2007064.

National Center for Education Statistics. (2008). Digest of Education Statistics U.S. Department of Education. Retrieved from September 3, 2008, from http://nces.ed.gov/PUBSEARCH/pubsinfo.asp?pubid=2008022

National Center for Health Statistics. (2000a). 2 to 20 years: Boys stature-for-age and weight-for-age percentiles. Available at http://www.cdc.gov/growthcharts.

National Center for Health Statistics. (2000b). 2 to 20 years: Girls stature-for-age and weight-for-age percentiles. Available at http://www.cdc.gov/growthcharts.

National Center for Health Statistics. (2007). *Prevalence of overweight among children and adolescents: United States, 2003–2004.* Hyattsville, MD: Author. Retrieved March 22, 2007, from http://www.cdc.gov/nchs/products/pubs/pubd/hestats/overweight/overwght_child_03.htm

National Diabetes Education Program. (2006). *Overview of diabetes in children and adolescents: A fact sheet from the National Diabetes Education Program.* Washington, DC: U.S. Department of Health and Human Services. Retrieved September 2, 2008, from www.ndep.nih.gov/diabetes/youth.

National Institute of Allergy and Infectious Diseases. (December 2004). The common cold. Retrieved August 28, 2006, from http://www.niad.nih.gov/factsheets/cold.htm

National Institute of Child Health and Human Development. (2000). *Report of the National Reading Panel. Teaching children to read: An evidence-based assessment of the scientific research literature on reading and its implications for reading instruction* (NIH Publication No. 00-4769). Washington, DC: U.S. Government Printing Office.

National Research Council. (1998). *Prevention reading difficulties in young children.* Washington, DC. National Academy Press.

National Research Council. (1998). *Protecting youth at work.* Washington, DC: National Academy Press.

National Research Council. (2004). *Children's health, the nation's wealth: Assessing and improving child health.* Washington, DC: National Academies Press.

National SAFE KIDS Campaign. (2006). *Childhood injury fact sheet.* Washington, DC.

Natriello, G., & McDill, E. (1986). Performance standards, student effort on homework, and academic achievement. *Sociology of Education, 59,* 18–31.

Neemann, J., Hubbard, J., & Masten, A. (1995). The changing importance of romantic relationship involvement to competence from late childhood to late adolescence. *Development and Psychopathology, 7,* 727–750.

Nelson, C. A., Thomas, K., & deHaan, M. (2006). Neural bases of cognitive development. In W. Damon & R. Lerner (Series Eds.) & D. Kuhn & R. S. Siegler (Vol. Eds.), *Handbook of child psychology: Vol. 2. Cognition, perception, and language* (6th ed., pp. 3–57). Hoboken, NJ: Wiley.

Nelson, C., Bloom, F., Cameron, J., Amaral, D., Dahl, R., & Pine, D. (2002). An integrative, multidisciplinary approach to the study of brain-behavior relations in the context of typical and atypical development. *Development and Psychopathology, 14,* 499–520.

Nelson, E., Leibenluft E., McClure E., & Pine D. (2005). The social re-orientation of adolescence: A neuroscience perspective on the process and its relation to psychopathology. *Psychological Medicine, 35,* 163–174.

Nelson, E., McClure, E., Parrish, J., Leibenluft, E., Ernst, M., Fox, N., & Pine, D. (2008). *Brain systems underlying peer social acceptance in adolescents.* Unpublished manuscript, Mood and Anxiety Disorders Program, National Institute of Mental Health, Washington.

Nelson, K. (1993). Events, narratives, memory: What develops. In C. A. Nelson (Ed.), *Minnesota Symposium on Child Psychology: Vol. 26. Memory and affect* (pp. 1–24). Hillsdale, NJ: Erlbaum.

Nelson, K. (2006). *Young minds in social worlds: Experience, meaning and memory.* Cambridge, MA: Harvard University Press.

Nelson, K., & Fivush, R. (2004). The emergence of autobiographical memory: A social cultural developmental theory. *Psychological Review, 111,* 485–511.

Nettles, S. M., Caughy, M. O., & O'Campo, P. J. (2008). School adjustment in the early grades: Toward an integrated model of neighborhood, parental, and child processes. *Review of Educational Research, 78,* 3–32.

Neville, H. J., & Lawson, D. (1987). Attention to central and peripheral visual space in a movement detection task. III. Separate effects of auditory deprivation and acquisition of a visual language. *Brain Research, 405,* 284–294.

Newcomb, A. F., & Bagwell, C. (1995). Children's friendship relations: A meta-analytic review. *Psychological Bulletin, 117,* 306–347.

Newcomb, A. F., Bukowski, W. M., & Pattee, L. (1993). Children's peer relations: A meta-analytic review of popular, rejected, neglected, controversial, and average sociometric status. *Psychological Bulletin, 113,* 99–128.

Newcomb, M., & Bentler, P. (1989). Substance use and abuse among children and teenagers. *American Psychologist, 44,* 242–248.

Newman, C. G. (1985). Teratogen update: Clinical aspects of thalidomide embryopathy—a continuing preoccupation. *Teratology, 32*(1), 133–144.

Newman, D. L. (2005). Ego development and ethnic identity formation in rural American Indian adolescents. *Child Development, 76,* 734–746.

NICHD Early Child Care Research Network. (1996). Characteristics of infant child care: Factors contributing to positive caregiving. *Early Childhood Research Quarterly, 11*(3), 269–306.

NICHD Early Child Care Research Network. (1997). The effects of infant child care on infant-mother attachment security: Results of the NICHD Study of Early Child Care. *Child Development, 68,* 860–879.

NICHD Early Child Care Research Network. (1999). Child outcomes when child care center classes meet recommended standards for quality. *American Journal of Public Health, 89,* 1072–1077.

NICHD Early Child Care Research Network. (2000a). Characteristics and quality of child care for toddlers and preschoolers. *Applied Developmental Science, 4*(3), 116–135.

NICHD Early Child Care Research Network. (2000b). The relation of child care to cognitive and language development. *Child Development, 71,* 960–980.

NICHD Early Child Care Research Network. (2001). A new guide for evaluating child care quality. *Zero to Three, 21*(5), 40–47.

NICHD Early Child Care Research Network. (2001). Child care and children's peer interaction at 24 and 36 months: The NICHD Study of Early Child Care. *Child Development, 72,* 1478–1500.

NICHD Early Child Care Research Network. (2002). Early child care and children's development prior to school entry: Results from the NICHD Study of Early Child Care. *American Educational Research Journal, 39*(1), 133–164.

NICHD Early Child Care Research Network. (2003). Child care and common communicable illnesses in children aged 37 to 54 months. *Archives of Pediatrics and Adolescent Medicine, 157*(2), 196–200.

NICHD Early Child Care Research Network. (2003). Do children's attention processes mediate the link between family predictors and school readiness? *Developmental Psychology, 39,* 581–593.

NICHD Early Child Care Research Network. (2003). Frequency and intensity of activity of third-grade children in physical education. *Archives of Pediatrics & Adolescent Medicine, 157,* 185–190.

NICHD Early Child Care Research Network. (2004a). Are child developmental outcomes related to before- and after-school care arrangements? Results from the NICHD Study of Early Child Care. *Child Development, 75,* 280–295.

NICHD Early Child Care Research Network. (2004). Does class size in first grade relate to children's academic and social performance or observed classroom processes? *Developmental Psychology, 40,* 651–664.

NICHD Early Child Care Research Network. (2004b). Trajectories of physical aggression from toddlerhood to middle childhood: Predictors, correlates and outcomes. *Monograph of the Society for Research in Child Development, 69*(4, Serial No. 278).

NICHD Early Child Care Research Network. (2005a). *Child care and child development: Results for the NICHD Study of Early Child Care and Youth Development.* New York: Guilford Press.

NICHD Early Child Care Research Network. (2005b). Early child care and children's development in the primary grades: Follow–up results from the NICHD Study of Early Child Care. *American Educational Research Journal, 42,* 537–570.

NICHD Early Child Care Research Network. (2005c). Pathways to reading: The role of oral language in the transition to reading. *Developmental Psychology, 41,* 428–441.

NICHD Early Child Care Research Network. (2006). Child-care effect sizes for the NICHD study of early child care and youth development. *American Psychologist, 61,* 99–116.

NICHD Early Child Care Research Network. (2008). Mothers' and fathers' support for child autonomy and early school achievement. *Developmental Psychology, 44,* 895–907.

NICHD Early Child Care Research Network. (in press). Social competence with peers in third grade: Associations with earlier peer experiences in child care. *Social Development.*

Nichols, S. L., & Berliner, D. C. (2007). *Collateral damage: How high-stakes testing corrupts America's schools.* Cambridge MA: Harvard University Press.

Nicklas, T. A., Baranowski, T., Cullen, K. W., & Berenson, G. (2001). Eating patterns, dietary quality, and obesity. *Journal of the American College of Nutrition, 20,* 599–608.

Nolen-Hoeksema, S., Girgus, J., & Seligman, M. (1992). Predictors and consequences of childhood depressive symptoms: A 5–year longitudinal study. *Journal of Abnormal Psychology, 101,* 405–422.

Nosek, B. A., & Banaji, M. R. (2001). The go/no-go association task. *Social Cognition, 19*(6), 161–176.

Nowakowski, Richard S. (2006). Stable neuron numbers from cradle to grave. *Proceedings of the National Academy of Sciences, 103,* 12219–12220.

Nunes, T., Schliemann, A-L., & Carraher, D. (1993). *Street mathematics and school mathematics.* New York: Cambridge University Press.

O'Brien, M., & Huston, A. C. (1985a). Activity level and sex-stereotyped toy choice in toddler boys and girls. *Journal of Genetic Psychology, 146,* 527–533.

O'Brien, M., & Huston, A. C. (1985b). Development of sex-typed play behavior in toddlers. *Developmental Psychology, 21,* 866–871.

O'Brien, M., Nader, P. R., Houts, R. M., Bradley, R., Friedman, S. L., Belsky, J., Susman, E., & NICHD Early Child Care Research Network. (2007). The ecology of childhood overweight: A 12-year longitudinal analysis. *International Journal of Obesity, 31*(9), 1469-1478.

O'Connor, T. G., Rutter, M., Beckett, C., Kreppner, J. M., & Keaveney, L. and the English and Romanian Adoptees Study Team. (2000). The effects of global severe privation on cognitive competence: Extension and Longitudinal Follow-up. *Child Development, 71,* 376–390.

O'Malley, J. (2006, July 31). Love, in translation: Lao couple found ears and voice in daughter. *Anchorage Daily News.*

O'Malley, P., & Johnston, L. (1999). Drinking and driving among US high school seniors, 1984–1997. *American Journal of Public Health, 89,* 678–684.

O'Neil, R., Parke, R. D., & McDowell, D. J. (2001). Objective and subjective features of children's neighborhoods: Relations to parental regulatory strategies and children's social competence. *Journal of Applied Developmental Psychology, 22,* 135–155.

Oakley, D., & Bogue, E. (1995). Quality of condom use as reported by female clients of a family planning clinic. *American Journal of Public Health, 85,* 1526–1530.

Oettinger, G. (1999). Does high school employment affect high school academic performance? *Industrial and Labor Relations Review, 53,* 136–151.

Ogbu, J. (1974). *The next generation: An ethnography of education in an urban neighborhood.* New York: Academic Press.

Ogburn, W. F., & Nimkoff, M. F. (1955). *Technology and the changing family.* Boston: Houghton Mifflin.

Ogden, C. L., Carroll, M. D., Curtin, L. R., McDowell, M. A., Tabak, C. J., & Flegal, K. M. (2006). Prevalence of overweight and obesity in the United States, 1999–2004. *Journal of the American Medical Association, 295,* 1549–1555.

Oller, D. K. (2000). *The emergence of the speech capacity.* Mahwah, NJ: Erlbaum.

Olney, R.S., Moore, C.A., Khoury, M.J., Erickson, J.D., Edmonds, L.D, & Botto, L.D. (1995). Chorionic villus sampling and amniocentesis: Recommendations for prenatal counseling. *Morbidity and Mortality Weekly Report, 44,* 1–12.

Olweus, D. (1993). *Bullying at school: What we know and what we can do.* Cambridge, MA: Blackwell.

Oppenheim, D., Sagi, A., & Lamb, M. E. (1988). Infant-adult attachments on the kibbutz and their relation to socioemotional development 4 years later. *Developmental Psychology, 24,* 427–433.

Orellana, M. F., Reynolds, J., Dorner, L., & Meza, M. (2003). In other words: Translating or "para-phrasing" as a family literacy practice in immigrant households. *The Reading Research Quarterly, 38,* 12–34.

Orenstein, P. (2006, December 24). What's wrong with Cinderella? *The New York Times.*

Orlando, M., Tucker, J. S., Ellickson, P., & Klein, D. (2004). Developmental trajectories of cigarette smoking and their correlates from early adolescence to young adulthood. *Journal of Consulting and Clinical Psychology, 72,* 400–410.

Oster, H. (2005). The repertoire of infant facial expressions: An ontogenetic perspective. In J. Nadel & D. Muir (Eds), *Emotional development* (pp. 261–292). New York: Oxford University Press.

Otero, G. A. Pliego-Rivero, F. B. Fernandez, T. & Ricardo, J. (2003). EEG development in children with sociocultural disadvantages: A follow-up study. *Clinical Neurophysiology, 114,* 1918–1925.

Otterblad Olausson, P., Haglund, B., Ringback Weitoft, G., & Cnattingius, S. (2001). Teenage childbearing and long-term socioeconomic consequences: A case study in Sweden. *Family Planning Perspectives, 33,* 70–74.

Overton, W. (1990). Competence and procedures: Constraints on the development of logical reasoning. In W. Overton (Ed.), *Reasoning, necessity, and logic: Developmental perspectives* (pp. 1–32). Hillsdale, NJ: Erlbaum.

Overton, W. (2006). Developmental psychology: Philosophy, concepts, methodology. In W. Damon & R. Lerner (Series Eds.) & R. Lerner (Vol. Ed.), *Handbook of child psychology: Vol. 1. Theoretical models of human development* (6th ed., pp. 18–88). New York: Wiley.

Ozer, E., Macdonald, T., & Irwin, C., Jr. (2002). Adolescent health: Implications and projections for the new millennium. In J. Mortimer & R. Larson (Eds.), *The changing adolescent experience: Societal trends and the transition to adulthood* (pp. 129–174). New York: Cambridge University Press.

Padilla, A. M., & Gonzalez, R. (2001). Academic performance of immigrant and U.S.-born Mexican heritage students: Effects of schooling in Mexico and bilingual/English language instruction. *American Educational Research Journal, 38,* 727–742.

Pakaslahti, L., Karjalainen, A., & Keltikangas-Jarvinen, L. (2002). Relationships between adolescent prosocial problem-solving strategies, prosocial behavior, and social acceptance. *International Journal of Behavioral Development, 26,* 137–144.

Papoušek, H., & Papoušek, M. (1978). Interdisciplinary parallels in studies of early human behavior: From physical to cognitive needs, from attachment to dyadic education. *International Journal of Behavioral Development, 1,* 37–49.

Papoušek, H., & Papoušek, M. (2002). Intuitive parenting. In M. H. Bornstein (Ed.), *Handbook of parenting: Vol. 2. Biology and ecology of parenting* (2nd ed., pp. 183–203). Mahwah, NJ: Erlbaum.

Papoušek, M. (1996). Origins of reciprocity and mutuality in prelinguistic parent-infant "dialogues." In I. Markova, C. F. Graumann, & K. Foppa (Eds.), *Mutualities in dialogue* (pp. 58–81). New York: Cambridge University Press.

Papoušek, M., Papoušek, H., & Bornstein, M. H. (1985). The naturalistic vocal environment of young infants: On the significance of homogeneity and variability in parental speech. In T. M. Field & N. Fox (Eds.), *Social perception in infants* (pp. 269–297). Norwood, NJ: Ablex.

Paquette, J. A., & Underwood, M. K. (1999). Gender differences in young adolescents' experiences of peer victimization: Social and physical aggression. *Merrill-Palmer Quarterly, 45,* 242–266.

Parke, R. D. (2002). Fathers and families. In M. H. Bornstein (Ed.), *Handbook of parenting: Vol. 3. Being and becoming a parent* (2nd ed., pp. 27–73). Mahwah, NJ: Erlbaum.

Parke, R. D., & Buriel, R. (2006). Socialization in the family: Ethnic and ecological perspectives. In N. Eisenberg (Vol. Ed.), *Handbook of child psychology: Vol. 3. Social, emotional, and personality development* (pp. 429–504). Hoboken, NJ: Wiley.

Parke, R. D., Simpkins, S. D., McDowell, D. J., Kim, M., Killian, C., Dennis, J., et al. (2002). Relative contributions of families and peers to children's social development. In P. K. Smith & C. H. Hart (Eds.), *Blackwell handbook of child development* (pp. 156–177). Oxford: Blackwell.

Parker, J. G., Low, C. M., Walker, A. R., & Gamm, B. K. (2005). Friendship jealousy in young adolescents: Individual dif-

ferences and links to sex, self-esteem, aggression, and social adjustment. *Developmental Psychology, 41,* 235–250.

Parker, S. W., Nelson, C. A., Zeanah, C. H., Smyke, A. T., Koga, S. F., Nelson, C. A., et al. (2005). The impact of early institutional rearing on the ability to discriminate facial expressions of emotion: An event-related potential study. *Child Development, 76,* 54–72.

Parkhurst, J., & Asher, S. (1992). Peer rejection in middle school: Subgroup differences in behavior, loneliness, and interpersonal concerns. *Developmental Psychology, 28,* 231–241.

Parsons, T., & Bales, R. (1956). *Family, socialization and interaction process.* London: Routledge & Kegan Paul.

Paschall, M. J., Flewelling, R. L., & Russell, T. (2004). Why is work intensity associated with heavy alcohol use among adolescents? *Journal of Adolescent Health, 34,* 79–87.

Pastereski, V. L., Geffner, M. E., Brain, C. Hindmarsh, P., Brook, C., & Hines, M. (2005). Prenatal hormones and postnatal socialization by parents as determinants of male-typical toy play in girls with congenital adrenal hyperplasia. *Child Development, 76,* 264–278.

Paternoster, R., Bushway, S., Brame, R. & Apel, R. (2003). The effect of teenage employment on delinquency and problem behaviors. *Social Forces, 82,* 297–335.

Patterson, C. J. (2006). Children of lesbian and gay parents. *Current Directions in Psychological Science, 15,* 241–244.

Patterson, G. R. (1986). *Development of antisocial and prosocial behavior.* New York: Academic Press.

Patterson, G. R., Capaldi, D., & Bank, L. (1991). An early starter model for predicting delinquency. In D. J. Pepler & K. H. Rubin (Eds.), *The development and treatment of childhood aggression* (pp. 139–168). Hillsdale, NJ: Erlbaum.

Paus, T., Zijdenbos, A., Worsley, K., Collins, D. L., Blumenthal, J., Giedd, J. N., et al. (1999). Structural maturation of neural pathways in children and adolescents: in vivo study. *Science, 283,* 1908–1911.

Pearce, M. J., Jones, S. M., Schwab-Stone, M. E., & Ruchkin, V. (2003). The protective effects of religiousness and parent involvement on the development of conduct problems among youth exposed to violence. *Child Development, 74,* 1682–1696.

Pennington, H. (2003). Accelerating advancement in school and work. In D. Ravitch (Ed.), *Brookings papers on education policy* (pp. 339–376). Washington, DC: Brookings Institution Press.

Pereira, A. C., Huddletson, D. E., Brickman, A. M., Sosunov, A. A., Hen, R., McKhann, G. M., et al. (2007). An *in vivo* correlate of exercise-induced neurogenesis in the adult denate gyrus. *Proceedings of the National Academy of Sciences, 104,* 5638–5643.

Perera, F. P., Rauh, V., Whyatt, R. M., Tsai, W. Y., Tang, D., Diaz, D., et al. (2006). Effect of prenatal exposure to airborne polycyclic aromatic hydrocarbons on neurodevelopment in the first 3 years of life among inner-city children. *Environmental Health Perspectives, 114,* 1287–1292.

Perry, C., Williams, C., Veblen-Mortenson, S., Toomey, T., Komro, K., Anstine, P., et al. (1996). Project Northland: Outcomes of a communitywide alcohol use prevention program during early adolescence. *American Journal of Public Health, 86,* 956–965.

Perry, D. G., Perry, L., & Kennedy, E. (1992). Conflict and the development of antisocial behavior. In C. Shantz & W. W.

Hartup (Eds.), *Conflict in child and adolescent development* (pp. 301–329). New York: Cambridge University Press.

Petersen, A. (1988). Adolescent development. *Annual Review of Psychology, 39,* 583–607.

Peterson, R. R. (1996). A re-evaluation of the economic consequences of divorce. *American Sociological Review, 61*(3), 528–536.

Petitto, L. A., Holowka, S., Sergio, L. E., & Ostry, D. (2001). Language rhythms in baby hand movements. *Nature, 413,* 35–36.

Petitto, L. A., Zatorre, R. J., Gauna, K. Nikeiski, E. J., Dostie, d., & Evands, A. C. (2000). Speech-like cerebral activity in profoundly deaf people processing signed languages: Implications for the neural basis of human lauguage. *Proceedings of the National Academy of Sciences, 97,* 13961–13966.

Petraitis, J., Flay, B., & Miller, T. (1995). Reviewing theories of adolescent substance use: Organizing pieces in the puzzle. *Psychological Bulletin, 117,* 67–86.

Petrill, S. A., Hewitt, J. K., Cherny, S. S., Lipton, P. A., Plomin, R., Corley, R., & DeFries, J. C. (2004). Genetic and environmental contributions to general cognitive ability through the first 16 years of life. *Developmental Psychology, 40,* 805–812.

Petrill, S., Kovas, Y., Hart, S. A., Thompson, L. A., & Plomin, R. (in press). The genetic and environmental etiology of high math performance in 10-year-olds. *Developmental Science.*

Pettine A., & Rosén, L. A. (1998). Self-care and deviance in elementary school-age children. *Journal of Clinical Psychology, 54,* 629–643.

Pettit, G. S., Laird, R. D., Bates, J. E., & Dodge, K. A. (1997). Patterns of after-school care in middle childhood: Risk factors and developmental outcomes. *Merrill-Palmer Quarterly, 43,* 515–538.

Pettit, G. S., Laird, R. D., Dodge, K. A., Bates, J. E., & Criss, M. M. (2001). Antecedents and behavior-problem outcomes of parental monitoring and psychological control in early adolescence. *Child Development, 72,* 583–598.

Pexman, P., & Glenwright, M. (2007). How do typically developing children grasp the meaning of verbal irony? *Journal of Neurolinguistics, 20,* 178–196.

Phillipsen, L. C. (1999). Associations between age, gender, and group acceptance and three components of friendship quality. *Journal of Early Adolescence, 19,* 438–464.

Phinney, J., & Alipuria, L. (1987). *Ethnic identity in older adolescents from four ethnic groups.* Paper presented at the biennial meetings of the Society for Research in Child Development, Baltimore.

Phinney, J., Devich-Navarro, M., DuPont, S., Estrada, A., & Onwughala, M. (1994, February). *Bicultural identity orientations of African American and Mexican American adolescents.* Paper presented at the biennial meetings of the Society for Research on Adolescence, San Diego.

Phinney, J., DuPont, S., Espinosa, Revill, J., & Sanders, K. (1994). Ethnic identity and American identification among ethnic minority adolescents. In F. van de Vijver (Ed.), *Proceedings of 1992 conference of the international association for cross-cultural psychology.* Tilburg, The Netherlands: Tilburg University Press.

Piaget, J. (1932). *The moral judgment of the child.* New York: Free Press.

Piaget, J. (1952). *The origins of intelligence in children.* New York: International Universities Press. (Original work published 1936).

Piaget, J. (1954). *The construction of reality in the child* (M. Cook, Trans.). New York: Ballantine. (Original work published 1937).

Piaget, J. (1955a). *The child's conception of the world.* London: Routledge & Kegan Paul. (Originally published in 1929)

Piaget, J. (1955b). *The language and thought of the child.* New York: Meridian Books. (Originally published in 1923)

Piaget, J. (1962). *Play, dreams, and imitation in childhood.* New York: W.W. Norton & Co. (Originally published in 1951).

Piaget, J. (1964). Development and learning. In T. Ripple & V. Rockcastle (Eds.), *Piaget rediscovered* (pp. 7–20). Ithaca, NY: Cornell University Press.

Piaget, J. (1965). *The child's conception of number.* New York: The Norton Library. (Originally published in 1941).

Piaget, J. (1970). Piaget's theory. In P. H. Mussen (Ed.), *Carmichael's manual of child psychology* (Vol. 1, pp. 703–732). New York: Wiley.

Piaget, J. (1972). *To understand is to invent: The future of education.* New York: Grossman Publishers. (Originally published in 1948)

Piaget, J. (1973). *The psychology of intelligence.* Totowa, NJ: Littlefield, Adams & Co. (Originally published in 1947 in France)

Piaget, J. (1983). Piaget's theory. In P. Mussen (Ed.), *Handbook of child psychology* (Vol. 1, 4th ed.). New York: Wiley.

Piaget, J., & Inhelder, B. (1967). *The psychology of the child.* New York: Basic Books.

Pianta, R. C., Belsky, J., Houts, R., Morrison, F., & The National Institute of Child Health and Human Development (NICHD) Early Child Care Research Network. (2007). Opportunities to learn in America's elementary classrooms. *Science, 315,* 1795–1796.

Pianta, R. C., Belsky, J., Vandergrift, N., Houts, R., Morrison, F., & NICHD Early Child Care Research Network. (2008). Classroom effects on children's achievement trajectories in elementary school. *American Educational Research Journal, 45,* 365–397.

Pierce, K. M., Bolt, D. M., & Vandell, D. L. (in press). Specific features of after-school program quality: Differential associations with children's functioning in middle childhood. *American Journal of Community Psychology.*

Pillow, B. H., & Henrichon, A. J. (1996). There's more to the picture than meets the eye: Young children's difficulty understanding biased interpretation. *Child Development, 67,* 803–819.

Pine, D., Cohen, P., Gurley, D., Brook, J., & Ma, Y. (1998). The risk for early-adulthood anxiety and depressive disorders in adolescents with anxiety and depressive disorders. *Archives of General Psychiatry, 55,* 56–64.

Pinhas-Hamiel, O., & Zeitler, P. (2005). The global spread of type 2 diabetes mellitus in children and adolescents. *The Journal of Pediatrics, 146,* 693–700.

Pinker, C. (2008, January 13). The moral instinct. *The New York Times Magazine.*

Pinker, S. (1994). *The Language Instinct: The New Science of Language and Mind.* New York: Penguin

Pintrich, P., Roeser, R., & De Groot, E. (1994). Classroom and individual differences in early adolescents' motivation and self-regulated learning. *Journal of Early Adolescence, 14,* 139–161.

Pipp-Siegel, S., Robinson, J. L., Bridges, D., & Bartholomew, S. (1997). Sources of individual differences in infant social cognition: Cognitive and affective aspects of self and other. In R. J. Sternberg & E. L. Grigorenko (Eds.), *Intelligence, heredity, and environment* (pp. 505–528). New York: Cambridge University Press.

Piquero, A. R., & Chung, H. L. (2001). On the relationship between gender, early onset, and the seriousness of offending. *Journal of Criminal Justice, 29,* 189–206.

Plomin, R. (2004). *Nature and nurture: An introduction to human behavioral genetics.* London: Wadsworth.

Plomin, R. (2007). Genetics and developmental psychology. In G. W. Ladd (Ed.), *Appraising the human developmental sciences: Essays in honor of Merrill-Palmer Quarterly* (pp. 250–261). Detroit: Wayne State University Press.

Plomin, R., & Daniels, D. (1987). Why are children in the same family so different from one another? *Behavioral and Brain Sciences, 10,* 1–60.

Plomin, R., DeFries, J. C., & Loeblin, J. C. (1977). Genotype–environment interaction and correlation in the analysis of human behaviour. *Psychological Bulletin, 85,* 309–322.

Plomin, R., DeFries, J. C., McClearn, G. E., & McGuffin, P. (2001). *Behavioral genetics* (4th ed.). New York: Worth.

Plomin, R., & Petrill, S. A. (1997). Genetics and intelligence: What's new? *Intelligence, 24,* 53–77.

Pollak, S. D. (2005). Early adversity and mechanisms of plasticity: Integrating affective neuroscience with developmental approaches to psychopathology. *Development and Psychopathology, 17,* 735–752.

Pollak, S. D., & Kistler, D. J. (2002). Early experience is associated with the development of categorical representations for facial expressions of emotion. *Proceedings of the National Academy of Sciences, USA, 99,* 9072–9076.

Pollak, S. D., Klorman, R., Brumaghim, J., & Cicchetti, D. (2001). P3b reflects maltreated children's reactions to facial displays of emotion. *Psychophysiology, 38,* 267–274.

Pollak, S. D., Vardi, S., Bechner, A. M. B., & Curtin, J. J. (2005). Physically abused children's regulation of attention in response to hostility. *Child Development, 76,* 968–977.

Polygenis, D., Wharton, S., Malmberg, C., Sherman, N., Kennedy, D., Koren, G., et al. (1998). Moderate alcohol consumption during pregnancy and the incidence of fetal malformations a meta-analysis. *Neurotoxicology and Teratology, 20,* 61–67.

Pong, S. (1998). The school compositional effect of single parenthood on 10th-grade achievement. *Sociology of Education, 71,* 23–42.

Porter, R. H., Makin, J. W., Davis, L. B., & Christensen, K. M. (1992). Breast-fed infants respond to olfactory cues from their own mother and unfamiliar lactating females. *Infant Behavior & Development, 15,* 85–93.

Porter, R. H., & Winberg, J. (1999). Unique salience of maternal breast odors for newborn infants. *Neuroscience and Biobehavioral Reviews, 23,* 439–449.

Posner, J. K., & Vandell, D. L. (1999). After-school activities and the development of low-income urban children: A longitudinal study. *Developmental Psychology, 35,* 868–879.

Prader, A., Tanner, J. M., & von Harnack, G. A. (1963). Catch-up growth following illness or starvation. *Journal of Pediatrics, 62,* 646–659.

Pressley, M., & Hilden, K. (2006). Cognitive strategies. In W. Damon & R. M. Lerner (Series Eds.) & D. Kuhn & R. S. Siegler (Vol. Eds.), *Handbook of child psychology: Vol. 2. Cognition, perception, and language* (6th ed., pp. 511–556). Hoboken, NJ: Wiley.

Prinstein, M. J., & Aikins, J. W. (2004). Cognitive moderators of the longitudinal association between peer rejection and adolescent depressive symptoms. *Journal of Abnormal Child Psychology, 32,* 147–158.

Prinstein, M. J., & La Greca, A. M. (2002). Peer crowd affiliation and internalizing distress in childhood and adolescence: A longitudinal follow-back study. *Journal of Research on Adolescence, 12,* 325–351.

Pruden, S. M., Hirsh-Pasek, K., Golinkoff, R. M., & Hennon, E. A. (2006). The birth of words: Ten-month-olds learn words through perceptual salience. *Child Development, 77,* 266–280.

Pulsifer, M .B., & Aylward, E. H. (2000). Human immunodeficiency virus. In K. Yeates, D. Ris, & G. Taylor (Eds.), *Pediatric neuropsychology: Research, theory, and practice* (pp. 381–402). New York: Guilford.

Putnam, S. P., Sanson, A. V., & Rothbart, M. K. (2002). Child temperament and parenting. In M. H. Bornstein (Ed.), *Handbook of parenting: Vol. 1. Children and parenting* (2nd ed., pp. 255–277). Mahwah, NJ: Erlbaum.

Quadrel, M., Fischhoff, B., & Davis, W. (1993). Adolescent (in)vulnerability. *American Psychologist, 48,* 102–116.

Quas, J. A., Malloy, L. C., Melinder, A., Goodman, G. S., D'Mello, M., & Schaaf, J. (2007). Developmental differences in the effects of repeated interviews and interviewer bias on young children's event memory and false reports. *Developmental Psychology, 43,* 823–837.

Raffaelli, M. (1997). Young adolescents' conflicts with siblings and friends. *Journal of Youth and Adolescence, 26,* 539–558.

Raffaelli, M., & Larson, R. (1987). *Sibling interactions in late childhood and early adolescence.* Paper presented at the biennial meetings of the Society for Research in Child Development, Baltimore.

Raine, A., Loeber, R., Stouthamer-Loeber, M., Moffitt, T. E., Caspi, A., & Lynam, D. (2005). Neurocognitive impairments in boys on the life-course persistent antisocial path. *Journal of Abnormal Psychology, 114,* 38–49.

Rakison, D. H., & Oakes, L. M. (2003). Issues in the early development of concepts and categories. In D. H. Rakison & L. M. Oakes (Eds.), *Early category and concept development: Making sense of the blooming, buzzing confusion* (pp. 3–23). Oxford, England: University Press.

Ramey, C. T., Campbell, F. A., & Blair, C. (1998). The Abecedarian Project: Long-term effectiveness of educational day care beginning at birth. In J. Crane (Ed.), *Social programs that work* (pp. 163–183). New York: Russell Sage.

Ramey, C. T., & Ramey, S. L. (2004). Early learning and school readiness. *Merrill-Palmer Quarterly, 50,* 471–491.

Randel, B., Stevenson, H. W., & Witruk, E. (2000). Attitudes, beliefs, and mathematics achievement of German and Japanese high school students. *International Journal of Behavioral Development, 24,* 190–198.

Rao, N., & Stewart, S. M. (1999). Cultural influences on sharer and recipient behavior: Sharing in Chinese and Indian preschool children. *Journal of Cross-Cultural Psychology, 30,* 219–241.

Rauh, H., Ziegenhain, U., Müller, B., & Wijnroks, L. (2000). Stability and change in infant-mother attachment in the second year of life: Relations to parenting quality and varying degrees of day-care experience. In P. M. Crittenden & A. H. Claussen (Eds.), *The organization of attachment relationships: Maturation, culture, and context* (pp. 251–276). New York: Cambridge University Press.

Reich, K., Oser, F., & Valentin, P. (1994). Knowing why I now know better: Children's and youth's explanations of their worldview changes. *Journal of Research on Adolescence, 4,* 151–173.

Reimer, M. (1996). "Sinking into the ground": The development and consequences of shame in adolescence. *Developmental Review, 16,* 321–363.

Renzulli, J. S. (1986). The three-ring conception of giftedness: A developmental model for creative productivity. In R. J. Sternberg & J. E. Davidson (Eds.), *Conceptions of giftedness* (pp. 53–92). New York: Cambridge University Press.

Reynolds, A. J., Temple, J. A., Robertson, D. L., & Mann, E. A. (2001). Long-term effects of an early childhood intervention on educational achievement and juvenile arrest: A 15-year follow-up of low-income children in public schools. *Journal of the American Medical Association, 285,* 2339–2346.

Rich, L. M., & Kim, S.-B. (2002). Employment and the sexual and reproductive behavior of female adolescents. *Perspectives on Sexual and Reproductive Health, 34*(3), 127–134.

Richard, J. F., Normandeau, J., Brun, V., & Maillet, M. (2004). Attracting and maintaining infant attention during habituation: Further evidence of the importance of stimulus complexity. *Infant and Child Development, 13,* 277–286.

Richards, M. H., & Larson, R. (1989). The life space and socialization of the self: Sex Differences in the Young Adolescent. *Journal of Youth and Adolescence, 18,* 617–626.

Richards, M., & Larson, R. (1993). Pubertal development and the daily subjective states of young adolescents. *Journal of Research on Adolescence, 3,* 145–169.

Rickford, J. R., & Rickford, R. J. (2000). *Spoken soul: The story of Black English.* Hoboken, NJ: Wiley.

Ridgeway, D., Waters, E., & Kuczaj, S. A. (1985). Acquisition of emotional-descriptive language: Receptive and productive norms for ages 18 months to 6 years. *Developmental Psychology, 21,* 901–908.

Ridley, M. (2003). *Nature via nurture: Genes, experience, and what makes us human.* HarperCollins.

Rigby, K. (2002). Bullying in childhood. In P. K. Smith & C. H. Hart (Eds.), *Blackwell handbook of childhood social development* (pp. 549–568). Malden, MA: Blackwell.

Rimm-Kaufman, S. E., Pianta, R. C., & Cox, M. J. (2000). Teachers' judgments of success in the transition to kindergarten. *Early Childhood Research Quarterly, 15,* 147–166.

Ritter, K. (1978). The development of knowledge of an external retrieval cue strategy. *Child Development, 49,* 1227–1230.

Rivkees, Scott A. (2004). Developing circadian rhythmicity in infants. *Pediatrics, 112,* 373–381.

Rizzo, T. A. (1989). *Friendship development among children in school.* Norwood, NJ: Ablex.

Rizzolatti, G., & Arbib, M. (1998). Language within our grasp. *Trends in Neuroscience, 21,* 188–194.

Rizzolatti, G., Fadiga L., Gallese, V., & Fogassi, L. (1996). Premotor cortex and the recognition of motor actions. *Cognitive Brain Research, 3,* 131–141.

Roberts, B., O'Donnell, M., & Robins, R.. (2004). Goal and personality trait development in emerging adulthood. *Journal of Personality and Social Psychology, 87,* 541–550.

Roberts, D. F., & Foehr, U. G. (2004). *Kids and media in America.* New York: Cambridge University Press.

Roberts, D. F., & Foehr, U. G. (2008). Trends in media use. *The Future of Children, 18,* 1–37.

Roberts, D., Henriksen, L., & Foehr, U. (2004). Adolescents and media. In R. Lerner & L. Steinberg (Eds.), *Handbook of adolescent psychology* (2nd ed., pp. 487–521). New York: Wiley.

Roberts, J. E., Burchinal, M. R., Jackson, S. C., Hooper, S. R., Roush, J., Mundy, M., Neebe, E., & Zeisel, S. A. (2000). Otitis media in early childhood in relation to preschool language and school readiness skills among African American children. *Pediatrics, 106*(4), 1–11.

Roberts, R., Phinney, J., Masse, L., Chen, Y., Roberts, C., & Romero, A. (1999). The structure of ethnic identity of young adolescents from diverse ethnocultural groups. *Journal of Early Adolescence, 19,* 301–322.

Robertson, S. S., & Bacher, L. F. (1995). Oscillation and chaos in fetal motor activity. *Fetal Development: A Psychobiological Perspective, 10,* 20.

Robinson, G. E., & Wisner, K. L. (1993). Fetal anomalies. In D. E. Stewart & N. L. Statland (Eds.), *Psychological aspects of women's health care: The interface between psychiatry and obstetrics and gynecology* (pp. 37–54). Washington, DC: American Psychiatric Association.

Robinson, N., Garber, J., & Hilsman, R. (1995). Cognitions and stress: Direct and moderating effects on depressive versus externalizing symptoms during the junior high school transition. *Journal of Abnormal Psychology, 104,* 453–463.

Robinson, T. N. (1999). Reducing children's television viewing to prevent obesity: A randomized controlled trial. *Journal of the American Medical Association, 282,* 1561–1567.

Rochat, P. (1997). Early development of the ecological self. In C. Dent-Read & P. Zukow-Goldring (Eds.), *Evolving explanations of development* (pp. 91–121). Washington, DC: American Psychological Association.

Roebuck, T. M., Mattson, S. N., & Riley, E. P. (1999). Behavioral and psychosocial profiles of alcohol-exposed children. *Alcoholism: Clinical and Experimental Research, 23,* 1070–1076.

Roediger, H. L., III, & McDermott, K. B. (1995) Creating false memories: Remembering words not presented on lists. *Journal of Experimental Psychology: Learning, Memory, and Cognition, 21,* 803–814.

Roeser, R., Eccles, J., & Freedman-Doan, C. (1999). Academic functioning and mental health in adolescence: Patterns, progressions, and routes from childhood. *Journal of Adolescent Research, 14,* 135–174.

Rogoff, B. (2003). *The cultural nature of human development.* Oxford: Oxford University Press.

Roisman, G. I. (2002). Beyond main effect models of adolescent work intensity, family closeness and school disengagement:

Mediational and conditional hypotheses. *Journal of Adolescent Research, 17,* 331–345.

Roisman, G. I., & Fraley, C. R. (2006). The limits of genetic influence: A behavior-genetic analysis of infant-caregiver relationship quality and temperament. *Child Development, 77,* 1656–1667.

Roschelle, J. M., Pea, R. D., Hoadley, C. M., Gordon, D. N., & Means, B. M. (2000). Changing how and what children learn in school with computer-based technologies. *Children and Computer Technology, 10,* 76–101.

Rosen, B., & D'Andrade, R. (1959). The psychosocial origins of achievement motivation. *Sociometry, 22,* 185–218.

Rosenblum, G., & Lewis, M. (1999). The relations among body image, physical attractiveness, and body mass in adolescence. *Child Development, 70,* 50–64.

Rosvold, H. E., Mirsky, A. F., Saranson, I., Bransome, E. D., & Beck, L. H. (1956). A continuous performance test of brain damage. *Journal of Consulting Psychology, 20,* 343–350.

Rothbart, M. K. (2005). Early temperament and psychosocial development. In R. E. Tremblay, R. G. Barr, & R. deV. Peters (Eds.), *Encyclopedia on early childhood development* [online], Montreal, Quebec: Centre of Excellence for Early Childhood Development.

Rothbart, M. K., & Bates, J. (2006). Temperament. In W. Damon & R. M. Lerner (Series Eds.) & N. Eisenberg (Vol. Ed.), *Handbook of child psychology: Vol. 3. Social, emotional, and personality development* (6th ed., pp. 99–166). Hoboken NJ: Wiley.

Rothbart, M. K., Posner, M. I., & Kieras, J. (2006). Temperament, attention, and the development of self-regulation. In K. McCartney & D. Phillips (Eds.), *Blackwell handbook of early childhood development* (pp. 338–357). Malden, MA: Blackwell.

Rotheram-Borus, M. (1990). Adolescents' reference group choices, self-esteem, and adjustment. *Journal of Personality and Social Psychology, 59,* 1075–1081.

Rotheram-Borus, M., Koopman, C., & Ehrhardt, A. (1991). Homeless youths and HIV infection. *American Psychologist, 46,* 1188–1197.

Rousseau, J. (1911). *Emile* (B. Foxley, trans.). London: Dent. (Original work published 1762)

Rovee-Collier, C., & Barr, R. (2001). Infant learning and memory. In J. G. Bremner & A. Fogel (Eds.), *Blackwell handbook of infant development* (pp. 139–168). Malden, MA: Blackwell.

Rowe, D., Rodgers, J., Meseck-Bushey S., & St. John, C. (1989). Sexual behavior and nonsexual deviance: A sibling study of their relationship. *Developmental Psychology, 25,* 61–69.

Rozin, P., Bauer, R., & Catanese, D. (2003). Food and life, pleasure and worry, among American college students: Gender differences and regional similarities. *Journal of Personality and Social Psychology, 85,* 132–141.

Rubin, K. H., Bukowski, W. M., & Parker, J. G. (2006). Peer interactions, relationships, and groups. In W. Damon & R. M. Lerner (Series Eds.), & N. Eisenberg (Vol. Ed.), *Handbook of child psychology: Vol. 3. Social, emotional, and personality development* (6th ed., pp. 571–645). Hoboken, NJ: Wiley.

Rubin, K. H., Burgess, K. B., Dwyer, K. M., & Hastings, P. D. (2003). Predicting preschoolers' externalizing behaviors from toddler temperament, conflict, and maternal negativity. *Developmental Psychology, 39,* 164–176.

Ruble, D. N., & Martin, C. L. (1998). Gender development. In W. Damon (Series Ed.) & N. Eisenberg (Vol. Ed.), *Handbook of child psychology: Vol. 3. Personality and social Development* (5th ed., pp. 933–1016). New York: Wiley.

Ruble, D. N., Martin, C. L., & Berenbaum, S. A. (2006). Gender development. In W. Damon & R. Lerner (Series Eds.) & N. Eisenberg (Vol. Ed.), *Handbook of child psychology: Vol. 3. Social, emotional, and personality development* (6th ed., pp. 858–932). Hoboken, NJ: Wiley.

Rudolph, K., & Hammen, C. (1999). Age and gender as determinants of stress exposure, generation, & reactions in youngsters: A transactional perspective. *Child Development, 70,* 660–677.

Rueter, M., & Conger, R. (1995a). Interaction style, problem-solving behavior, and family problem-solving effectiveness. *Child Development, 66,* 98–115.

Rueter, M., & Conger, R. (1995b). Antecedents of parent-adolescent disagreements. *Journal of Marriage and the Family, 57,* 435–448.

Rueter, M. A., & Kwon, H. (2005). Developmental trends in adolescent suicidal ideation. *Journal of Research on Adolescence, 15,* 205–222.

Ruff, C., (2003). Growth in bone strength, body size, and muscle size in a juvenile longitudinal sample. *Bone, 33,* 317–329.

Ruff, H. A. (1982). Infants' exploration of objects. *Infant Behavior and Development, 5,* 207.

Ruff, H. A. (1985). Detection of information specifying the motion of objects by 3- and 5-month-old infants. *Developmental Psychology, 21,* 295–305.

Ruff, H. A., & Capozzoli, M. C. (2003). Development of attention and distractibility in the first four years of life. *Developmental Psychology, 39,* 877–890.

Ruggiero, M., Greenberger, E., & Steinberg, L. (1982). Occupational deviance among first-time workers. *Youth and Society, 13,* 423–448.

Rumberger, R. (1995). Dropping out of middle school: A Multilevel analysis of students and schools. *American Educational Research Journal, 32,* 583–625.

Rumberger, R., & Larson, K. (1998). Student mobility and the increased risk of high school dropout. *American Journal of Education, 107,* 1–35.

Russell, A., Mize, J., & Bissaker, K. (2002). Parent-child relationships. In P. K. Smith & C. H. Hart (Eds.), *Blackwell handbook of childhood social development* (pp. 205–222). Malden, MA: Blackwell.

Rutstein, R. M., Conlon, C. J., & Batshaw, M. L. (1998). HIV and AIDS: From mother to child. In M. L. Batshaw (Ed.), *Children with disabilities* (4th ed., pp. 163–181). Baltimore, MD: Brookes Publishing.

Rutter, M. (1983). School effects on pupil progress: Research findings and policy implications. *Child Development, 54,* 1–29.

Rutter, M. (2006). *Genes and behaviour: Nature-nurture interplay explained.* London: Blackwell.

Rutter, M., & Garmezy, N. (1983). Developmental psychopathology. In E. M. Hetherington (Ed.), *Handbook of child psychology: Vol. 4. Socialization, personality, and social development* (pp. 775–911). New York: Wiley.

Saarni, C. (2000). Emotional competence: A developmental perspective. In R. Bar-On & J. D. A. Parker (Eds.), *The handbook of emotional intelligence: Theory, development, assessment, and application at home, school, and in the workplace* (pp. 68–91). San Francisco: Jossey-Bass.

Saarni, C., Campos, J. J., Camras, L, A., & Witherington, D. (2006). Emotional development: Action, communication, and understanding. In W. Damon & R. M. Lerner (Series Eds.) & N. Eisenberg (Vol. Ed.), *Handbook of child psychology: Vol. 3. Social, emotional, and personality development* (6th ed., pp. 226–229). Hoboken, NJ: Wiley.

Saarni, C., Mumme, D. L., & Campos, J. J. (1998). Emotional development: Action, communication, and understanding. In W. Damon & N. Eisenberg (Eds.), *Handbook of child psychology: Vol 3. Social, emotional, and personality development* (5th ed., pp. 237–309). Hoboken, NJ: Wiley.

Sabatini, M., Ebert, P., Lewis, D., Levitt, P., Cameron, J., & Mirnics, K. (2007). Amygdala gene expression correlates of social behavior in monkeys experiencing maternal separation. *Journal of Neuroscience, 27,* 3295–3304.

Sadeh, A., Gruber, R., & Raviv, A. (2002). Sleep, neurobehavioral functioning, and behavior problems in school-age children. *Child Development, 73,* 405–417.

Sadeh, A., Gruber, R., & Raviv, A. (2003). The effects of sleep restriction and extension on school-age children: What a difference an hour makes. *Child Development, 74,* 444–455.

Sadeh, A., Raviv, A., & Gruber, R. (2000). Sleep patterns and sleep disruptions in school-age children. *Developmental Psychology, 36,* 291–301.

Saffran, J. R., Werker, J. F., & Werner, L. A. (2006). The infant's auditory world: Hearing, speech, and the beginnings of language. In W. Damon & R. Lerner (Series Eds.) & D. Kuhn & R. Siegler (Vol. Eds.), *Handbook of child psychology: Vol. 2. Cognition, Perception, and language* (6th ed., pp. 58–108). Hoboken, NJ: Wiley.

Safron, J., Sy, S., & Schulenberg, J. (2003). Wishing to work: New perspectives on how adolescents' part-time work intensity is linked to educational disengagement, substance use, and other problem behaviours. *International Journal of Behavioral Development, 27,* 301–315.

Sagi, A. (1981). Mothers' and non-mothers' identification of infant cries. *Infant Behavior & Development, 4,* 37–40.

Sagi, A., Koren-Karie, N., Gini, M., Ziv, Y., & Joels, T. (2002). Shedding further light on the effects of various types and quality of early child care on infant-mother attachment relationship: The Haifa Study of Early Child Care. *Child Development, 73,* 1166–1186.

Sakai, K. L. (2005). Language acquisition and brain development. *Science, 310,* 815–819.

Sale, E., Sambrano, S., Springer, J. F., Peña, C., Pan, W., & Kasim, R. (2005). Family protection and prevention of alcohol use among Hispanic youth at high risk. *American Journal of Community Psychology, 36,* 195–205.

Salovey, P., & Mayer, J. D. (1990). Emotional intelligence. *Imagination, Cognition, and Personality, 9,* 185–211.

Sandstrom, M. J. (2004). Pitfalls of the peer world: How children cope with common rejection experiences. *Journal of Abnormal Child Psychology, 32,* 67–81.

Sandstrom, M. J., & Coie, J. D. (1999). A developmental perspective on peer rejection: Mechanisms of stability and change. *Child Development, 70,* 955–966.

Santelli, J. S., Lindberg, L., Abma, J., McNeely, C., & Resnick, M. (2000). Adolescent sexual behavior: Estimates and trends from four nationally representative surveys. *Family Planning Perspectives, 32,* 156–165.

Santelli, J., Warren, C., Lowry, R., Sogolow, E., Collins, J., Kann, L., et al. (1997). The use of condoms with other contraceptive methods among young men and women. *Family Planning Perspectives, 29,* 261–267.

Santora, M. (2006, January 12). East meets west, adding pounds and peril. *New York Times.*

Savin-Williams, R. (1988). Theoretical perspectives accounting for adolescent homosexuality. *Journal of Adolescent Health Care, 9,* 95–104.

Savin-Williams, R., & Diamond, L. (2004). Sex. In R. Lermer & L. Steinberg (Eds.), *Handbook of adolescent psychology* (pp. 189–231). New York: Wiley.

Saw, S-M, Chua, W-H, Hong, C-Y, Wu, H-M, Chan, W-Y, Chia, K-S, et al. (2002). Nearwork in early-onset myopia. *Investigative Ophthalmology and Visual Science, 43,* 332–339.

Saxe, G. B. (1991). *Culture and cognitive development: Studies in mathematical understanding.* Hillsdale, NJ: Erlbaum.

Scarr, S., & McCartney, K. (1983). How people make their own environments: A theory of genotype-environment effects. *Child Development, 54,* 424–435.

Scarr, S., & Weinberg, R. (1983). The Minnesota adoption studies: Genetic differences and malleability. *Child Development, 54,* 260–267.

Scarr, S., Weinberg, R., & Levine, A. (1986). *Understanding development.* San Diego: Harcourt.

Schagmuller, M., & Schneider, W. (2002). The development of organizational strategies in children: Evidence from a microgenetic longitudinal study. *Journal of Experimental Child Psychology, 81,* 298–319.

Schama, K. F., Howell, L. L., & Byrd, L. D. (1998). Prenatal exposure to cocaine. In S. T. Higgins & J. L. Katz (Eds.), *Cocaine abuse, behavior, pharmacology, and clinical applications* (pp. 159–179). New York: Academic Press.

Scharf, M., Shulman, S., & Avigad-Spitz, L. (2005). Sibling relationships in emerging adulthood and in adolescence. *Journal of Adolescent Research, 20,* 64–90.

Schellenbach, C., Whitman, T., & Borkowski, J. (1992). Toward an integrative model of adolescent parenting. *Human Development, 35,* 81–99.

Scher, A., Epstein, R., & Tirosh, E. (2004). Stability and changes in sleep regulation: A longitudinal study from 3 months to 3 years. *International Journal of Behavioral Development, 28,* 268–274.

Scherling, D. (1994). Prenatal cocaine exposure and childhood psychopathology: a developmental analysis. *American Journal of Orthopsychiatry, 64,* 9–19.

Schiller, K. (1999). Effects of feeder patterns on students' transition to high school. *Sociology of Education, 72,* 216–233.

Schlegel, A., & Barry, H. (1991). *Adolescence: An anthropological inquiry.* New York: Free Press.

Schmidt, M. E., & Vandewater, E. W. (2008). Electronic media and learning and achievement. *The Future of Children, 18,* 63–86.

Schneider, B. H. (2000). *Friends and enemies: Peer relations in childhood.* London: Oxford University Press.

Schneider, B. H., Atkinson, L., & Tardif, C. (2001). Child-parent attachment and children's peer relations: A quantitative review. *Developmental Psychology, 37,* 86–100.

Schneider, B., & Stevenson, D. (1999). *The ambitious generations: America's teenagers, motivated but directionless.* New Haven: Yale University Press.

Schneider, W. (2004). Memory development in children. In U. Goswami (Ed.), *Blackwell handbook of cognitive development* (pp. 236–256). Malden, MA: Blackwell Publishing.

Schneider, W., Gruber, H., Gold, A., & Opwis, K. (1993). Chess expertise and memory for chess positions in children and adults. *Journal of Experimental Child Psychology, 56,* 328–349.

Schochet, T., Kelley, A., & Landry, C. (2004). Differential behavioral effects of nicotine exposure in adolescent and adult rats. *Psychopharmacology, 175,* 265–273.

Schochet, T., Kelley, A., & Landry, C. (2005). Differential expression of arc mRNA and other plasticity-related genes induced by nicotine in adolescent rat forebrain. *Neuroscience, 135,* 285–297.

Schoenhals, M., Tienda, M., & Schneider, B. (1998). The educational and personal consequences of adolescent employment. *Social Forces, 77,* 723–762.

Schroeder, D. B., Martorell, R., Rivera, J. A., Ruel, M. T., & Habicht, J. (1995). Age differences in the impact of nutritional supplementation on growth. *Journal of Nutrition, 125,* 1051S–1059S.

Schuetze, P., & Eiden, R. D. (2005). The association between maternal smoking and secondhand exposure and autonomic functioning at 2–4 weeks of age. *Infant Behavior & Development, 29,* 32–43.

Schwartz, C. E., Wright, C. I., Shin, L. M., Kagan, J., & Rauch, S. L. (2003). Inhibited and uninhibited infants "grown up": Adult amygdalar response to novelty. *Science, 300,* 1952–1953.

Schwartz, D., Farver, J. M., Chang, L., & Lee-Shin, Y. (2002). Victimization in South Korean children's peer groups. *Journal of Abnormal Child Psychology, 30,* 113–125.

Schweinhart, L. J., Barnes, H. V., & Weikart, D. P. (1993). *Significant benefits: The Perry Preschool Study Through Age 27.* Ypsilanti, MI: High/Scope Press.

Schweinhart, L. J., Montie, J., Xiang, Z., Barnett, W. S., Belfield, C. R., & Nores, M. (2005). Lifetime effects: The High/Scope Perry Preschool study through age 40. *(Monographs of the High/Scope Educational Research Foundation, 14).* Ypsilanti, MI: High/Scope Press.

Schwimmer, J. B., Burwinkle, T. M., & Varni, J. W. (2003). Health-related quality of life of severely obese children and adolescents. *Journal of the American Medical Association, 289,* 1813–1819.

Sebat, J., Lakshmi, B., Malhotra, D., Troge, J., Lese-Martin, C., Walsh, T., Yamrom, B., Yoon, S., et al. (2007, April 20). Strong association of de novo copy number mutations with autism. *Science, 316,* 445–449.

Segalowitz, S. J., & Davies, P. L. (2004). Charting the maturation of the frontal lobe: An electrophysiological strategy. *Brain and Cognition, 55,* 116–133.

Sellers, R. M., Copeland-Linder, N., Martin, P. P., & Lewis, R. L. (2006). Racial identity matters: The relationship between racial discrimination and psychological functioning in African American Adolescents. *Journal of Research on Adolescence, 16,* 187–216.

Selman, R. (1980). *The growth of interpersonal understanding: Developmental and clinical analyses.* New York: Academic Press.

Serbin, L. A., Poulin-Dubois, D., & Eichstedt, J. A. (2002). Infant's response to gender inconsistent events. *Journal of Infancy, 3,* 531–542.

Sethi, S., & Nolen-Hoeksema, S. (1997). Gender differences in internal and external focusing among adolescents. *Sex Roles, 37,* 687–700.

Sewell, W., & Hauser, R. (1972). Causes and consequences of higher education: Models of the status attainment process. *American Journal of Agricultural Economics, 54,* 851–861.

Sharpee, T. O., Sugihara, H., Kurgansky, A. V., Rebrik, S. P., Stryker, M. P., & Miller, K. D. (2006). Adaptive filtering enhances information transmission in visual cortex. *Nature, 439,* 936–942.

Shatz, M., & Gelman, R. (1973). The development of communication skills: Modifications in the speech of young children as a function of listener. *Monographs of the Society for Research in Child Development, 38(5),* 1–38.

Shaw, M., & White, D. (1965). The relationship between child-parent identification and academic underachievement. *Journal of Clinical Psychology, 21,* 10–13.

Shaw, P., Eckstrand, K., Sharp, W., Blumenthal, J., Lerch, J. P., Greenstein, D., et al. (2007). Attention-deficit/hyperactivity disorder is characterized by a delay in cortical maturation. *Proceedings of the National Academy of Sciences, 104,* 19649–19654.

Shaw, P., Greenstein, D., Lerch, J., Clasen, L., Lenroot, R., Gogtay, N., Evans, A., et al. (2006). Intellectual ability and cortical development in children and adolescents. *Nature, 440,* 676–679.

Shedler, J., & Block, J. (1990). Adolescent drug use and psychological health: A longitudinal inquiry. *American Psychologist, 45,* 612–630.

Sheffield, E. G., & Hudson, J. A. (2006). You must remember this: Effects of video and photograph reminders on 18-month-olds' event memory. *Journal of Cognition and Development, 7,* 73–93.

Shevell, T., Malone, F. D., Vidaver, J., Porter, T. F., Luthy, D. A., Comstock, C. H., et al. (2005). Assisted reproductive technology and pregnancy outcome. *Obstetrics and Gynecology, 106,* 1039–1045.

Shumow, L., & Miller, J. D. (2001). Parents' at-home and at-school academic involvement with youth adolescents. *Journal of Early Adolescence, 21,* 68–91.

Shumow, L., Vandell, D. L., & Posner, J. (1998). Perceptions of danger: A psychological mediator of neighborhood demographic characteristics. *American Journal of Orthopsychiatry, 68,* 468–478.

Shumow, L., Vandell, D. L., & Posner, J. (1999). Risk and resilience in the urban neighborhood: Predictors of academic performance among low-income elementary school children. *Merrill-Palmer Quarterly, 45,* 309–331.

Shweder, R., Goodnow, J., Hatano, G., LeVine, R., Markus, H., & Miller, P. (2006). The cultural psychology of development: One mind, many mentalities. In W. Damon & R. Lerner (Series Eds.) & R. Lerner (Vol. Ed.), *Handbook of child psychology: Vol. 1. Theoretical models of human development* (6th ed., pp. 716–782). New York: Wiley.

Siegel, J., Aneshensel, C., Taub, B., Cantwell, D., & Driscoll, A. (1998). Adolescent depressed mood in a multiethnic sample. *Journal of Youth and Adolescence, 27,* 413–427.

Siegel, J., Yancey, A., Aneshensel, C., & Schuler, R. (1999). Body image, perceived pubertal timing, and adolescent mental health. *Journal of Adolescent Health, 25,* 155–165.

Siegler, R. S. (1995). How does change occur? A microgenetic study of number conservation. *Cognitive Psychology, 25,* 225–273.

Siegler, R. S. (1996). *Emerging minds: The process of change in children's thinking.* New York: Oxford University Press.

Siegler, R. S. (2002). Variability and infant development. *Infant Behavior & Development, 25,* 550–557.

Siegler, R. S. (2006). Microgenetic analyses of learning. In W. Damon & R. M. Lerner (Series Eds.) & D. Kuhn & R. S. Siegler (Eds.), *Handbook of child psychology: Vol. 2. Cognition, perception, and language* (6th ed., pp. 464–510). Hoboken, NJ: Wiley.

Siegler, R. S. (2007). Cognitive variability. *Developmental Science, 10,* 104–109.

Siegler, R. S., & Stern, E. (1998). A microgenetic analysis of conscious and unconscious strategy discoveries. *Journal of Experimental Psychology: General, 127,* 377–397.

Siegler, R. S., & Svetina, M. (2006). What leads children to adopt new strategies? A microgenetic/cross-sectional study of class inclusion. *Child Development, 77,* 997–1015.

Silverberg, S., & Samuel, A. G. (2004). The effect of age of second language acquisition on the representation and processing of second language words. *Journal of Memory and Language, 51,* 381–398.

Simmons, R., & Blyth, D. (1987). *Moving into adolescence.* New York: Aldine de Gruyter.

Simmons, R., Blyth, D., & McKinney, K. (1983). The social and psychological effects of puberty on white females. In J. Brooks-Gunn & A. Petersen (Eds.), *Girls at puberty* (pp. 229–272). New York: Plenum.

Simmons, R., Rosenberg, F., & Rosenberg, M. (1973). Disturbance in the self-image at adolescence. *American Sociological Review, 38,* 553–568.

Simpson, R. (1962). Parental influence, anticipatory socialization, and social mobility. *American Sociological Review, 27,* 517–522.

Singer, L. T., Arendt, R., Fagan, J., Minnes, S., Salvator, A., Bolek, T., & Becker, M. (1999). Neonatal visual information processing in cocaine-exposed and non-exposed infants. *Infant Behavior & Development, 22,* 1–15.

Singer, L. T., Eisengart, L. J., Minnes, S., Noland, J., Jey, A., Lane, C., & Min, M. O. (2005). Prenatal cocaine exposure and infant cognition. *Infant Behavior & Development, 28,* 431–444.

Singh, S., & Darroch, J. (1999). Trends in sexual activity among adolescent American women: 1982–1995. *Family Planning Perspectives, 31,* 212–219.

Sirois, S., & Mareschal, D. (2002). Models of habituation in infancy. *Trends in Cognitive Sciences, 6,* 293–298.

Sisk, C., & Foster, D. (2004). The neural basis of puberty and adolescence. *Nature Neuroscience, 7,* 1040–1047.

Skenkin, S. D., Starr, J. M., & Deary, I. J. (2004). Birth weight and cognitive ability in childhood: systematic review. *Psychological Bulletin, 130,* 989–1013.

Skinner, B. F. (1953). *Science and human behavior.* New York: MacMillan Company

Skinner, B. F. (1957). *Verbal behavior.* East Norwalk, CT: Appleton-Century-Crofts.

Skinner, R. A., & Piek, J. P. (2001). Psychosocial implications of poor motor coordination in children and adolescents. *Human Movement Science, 20,* 73–94.

Slap, G., & Jablow, M. (1994). *Teenage health care.* New York: Pocket Books.

Slomkowski, C., Rende, R., Conger, K. J., Simons, R. L., & Conger, R. D. (2001). Sisters, brothers, and delinquency: Evaluating social influence during early and middle adolescence. *Child Development, 72,* 271–283.

Smetana, J. (2006). Social domain theory: Consistencies and variations in children's moral and social judgments. In M. Killen & J. G. Smetana (Eds.), *Handbook of moral development* (pp. 119–154). Mahwah, NJ: Erlbaum.

Smetana, J, & Metzger, A. (2005). Family and religious antecedents of civic involvement in middle class African American late adolescents. *Journal of Research on Adolescence, 15,* 325–352.

Smith, C., Denton, M., Faris, R., & Regnerus, M. (2002). Mapping American adolescent religious participation. *Journal for the Scientific Study of Religion, 41,* 597–612.

Smith, R. E., Smoll, F. L., & Curtis, B. (1978). Coaching behaviors in Little League Baseball. In F. L. Smoll & R. E. Smith (Eds.), *Psychological perspectives in youth sports* (pp. 173–201). Washington, DC: Hemisphere.

Smoll, F. L., & Smith, R. E. (2002). Coaching behavior research and intervention in youth sports. In F. L. Smoll & R. E. Smith (Eds.), *Children and youth in sport: A biopsychosocial perspective* (pp. 211–233). Iowa: Kendall/Hunt Publishing Company.

Snow, C. E. (2006). What counts as literacy in early childhood? In K. McCartney & D. Phillips (Eds.), *Blackwell handbook on early childhood development* (pp. 274–294). Malden, MA: Blackwell.

Snow, C. E., Burns, M. S., & Griffin, P. (1998). *Preventing reading difficulties in young children.* Washington DC: National Academy Press.

Snow, C. E., & Kang, J. Y. (2006). Becoming bilingual, biliterate, and bicultural. In K. A. Renninger & I. E. Sigel (Eds.), *Handbook of child psychology: Vol. 4. Child psychology research in practice* (pp. 75–102). Hoboken NJ: Wiley.

Snowling, M. J. (2004). Reading development and dyslexia. In U. Goswami (Ed.), *Blackwell handbook of childhood cognitive development* (pp. 394–411). Malden, MA: Blackwell Publishing.

Snyder, J., Bank, L., & Burraston, B. (2005). The consequences of antisocial behavior in older male siblings for younger brothers and sisters. *Journal of Family Psychology, 19,* 643–653.

Society for Research in Child Development. (1993). *Ethical Standards for Research with Children.* Ann Arbor: Author.

Sokol, R. J., Delaney-Black, V., & Nordstrom, B. (2003). Fetal alcohol spectrum disorder. *The Journal of the American Medical Association, 290,* 2996–2999.

Sorkhabi, N. (2005). Applicability of Baumrind's parent typology to collective cultures: Analysis of cultural explanations of parent socialization effects. *International Journal of Behavioral Development, 29,* 552–563.

Sousa, D. A. (2006). *How the brain learns* (3rd ed.). Thousand Oaks, CA: Corwin Press.

South, S. J., Baumer, E. P., & Lutz, A. (2003). Interpreting community effects on youth educational attainment. *Youth and Society, 35,* 3–36.

Sowell, E. R., Trauner, D. A., Gamst, A., & Jernigan, T. L. (2002). Development of cortical and subcortical brain structures in childhood and adolescence: A structural MRI study. *Developmental Medicine and Child Neurology, 44,* 4–16.

Spearman, C. (1904). "General intelligence," objectively determined and measured. *American Journal of Psychology, 15,* 201–293.

Spelke, E., & Newport, E. (1998). Nativism, empiricism, and the development of knowledge. In W. Damon & R. Lerner (Series Eds.) & R. Lerner (Vol. Ed.), *Handbook of child psychology: Vol. 1: Theoretical models of human development* (5th ed., pp. 275–340). New York: Wiley.

Spencer, M. (2005). Crafting identities and accessing opportunities post-Brown. *American Psychologist, 60,* 821–830.

Spencer, M. B., & Markstrom-Adams, C. (1990). Identity processes among racial and ethnic minority children in America. *Child Development, 61,* 290–310.

Spencer, M., & Dornbusch, S. (1990). Challenges in studying minority youth. In S. Feldman & G. Elliott (Eds.), *At the threshold: The developing adolescent* (pp. 123–146). Cambridge, MA: Harvard University Press.

Spira, E. G., Bracken, S. S., & Fischel, J. E. (2005). Predicting improvement after first-grade reading difficulties: The effects of oral language, emergent literacy, and behavior skills. *Developmental Psychology, 41,* 225–234.

Spock, B. (1946). *The common sense book of baby and child care.* New York: Duell, Sloan and Pearce.

Sroufe, L. A., Egeland, B., Carlson, E. A., & Collins, W. A. (2005). *The development of the person: The Minnesota study of risk and adaptation from birth to adulthood.* New York: Guilford Publications.

St. James-Roberts, I. (2007). Infant crying and sleeping: Helping parents to prevent and manage problems. *Sleep Medicine Clinics, 2,* 363–375.

St. Louis, M., Conway, M., Hayman, C., Miller, C., Petersen, L., & Dondero, T. (1991). Human immunodeficiency virus infection in disadvantaged adolescents. *Journal of the American Medical Association, 266,* 2387–2391.

Stack, D. M. (2001). The salience of touch and physical contact during infancy: Unraveling some of the mysteries of the somesthetic sense. In J. G. Bremner, & A. Fogel (Eds.), *Blackwell handbook of infant development* (pp. 351–378). Malden, MA: Blackwell.

Staff, J., Messersmith, E., & Schulenberg, J. (in press). Work and leisure in adolescence. In R. Lerner & L. Steinberg (Eds.), *Handbook of adolescent psychology* (3rd ed.). New York: Wiley.

Stams, G. J., Juffer, F., & van IJzendoorn, M.H. (2002). Maternal sensitivity, infant attachment, and temperament in early childhood predict adjustment in middle childhood: The case of adopted children and their biologically unrelated parents. *Developmental Psychology, 38,* 806–821.

Stanton-Salazar, R., & Dornbusch, S. (1995). Social capital and the reproduction of inequality: Information networks among Mexican-origin high school students. *Sociology of Education, 68,* 116–135.

Starkey, P., & Gelman, R. (1982). The development of addition and subtraction abilities prior to formal schooling in arithmetic. In T. P. Carpenter, J. M. Moser, & T. A. Romberg (Eds.), *Addition and subtraction: A cognitive perspective* (pp. 99–116). Hillsdale, NJ: Erlbaum.

Stearn, W. B. (1995). Youth sports contexts: Coaches' perceptions and implications for intervention. *Journal of Applied Sport Psychology, 7,* 23–37.

Stein, Z. (1975). *Famine and human development: The dutch hunger winter of 1944–1945.* New York: Oxford University Press.

Steinberg, L. (1996). *Beyond the classroom: Why school reform has failed and what parents need to do.* New York: Simon & Schuster.

Steinberg, L. (2005). Cognitive and affective development in adolescence. *Trends in Cognitive Sciences, 9,* 69–74.

Steinberg, L. (2007). Risk-taking in adolescence: New perspectives from brain and behavioral science. *Current Directions in Psychological Science, 16,* 55–59.

Steinberg, L. (2008). *Adolescence* (8th ed.). New York: McGraw-Hill.

Steinberg, L. (2008). A social neuroscience perspective on adolescent risk-taking. *Developmental Review, 28,* 78–106.

Steinberg, L., & Cauffman, E. (1995). The impact of employment on adolescent development. In R. Vasta (Ed.), *Annals of Child Development* (Vol. 11, pp. 131–166). London: Jessica Kingsley Publishers.

Steinberg, L., Dahl, R., Keating, D., Kupfer, D., Masten, A., & Pine, D. (2006). Psychopathology in adolescence: Integrating affective neuroscience with the study of context. In D. Cicchetti & D. Cohen (Eds.), *Developmental psychopathology: Vol. 2. Developmental neuroscience* (pp. 710–741). New York: Wiley.

Steinberg, L., & Dornbusch, S. (1991). Negative correlates of part-time work in adolescence: Replication and elaboration. *Developmental Psychology, 17,* 304–313.

Steinberg, L., Dornbusch, S., & Brown, B. (1992). Ethnic differences in adolescent achievement: An ecological perspective. *American Psychologist, 47,* 723–729.

Steinberg, L., Fegley, S., & Dornbusch, S. (1993). Negative impact of part-time work on adolescent adjustment: Evidence from a longitudinal study. *Developmental Psychology, 29,* 171–180.

Steinberg, L., Greenberger, E., Garduque, L., Ruggiero, M., & Vaux, A. (1982). Effects of working on adolescent development. *Developmental Psychology, 18,* 385–395.

Steinberg, L., & Monahan, K. (2007). Age differences in resistance to peer influence. *Developmental Psychology, 43,* 1531–1543.

Steinberg, L., & Silverberg, S. (1986). The vicissitudes of autonomy in early adolescence. *Child Development, 57,* 841–851.

Steinberg, L., & Steinberg, W. (1994). *Crossing paths: How your child's adolescence triggers your own crisis.* New York: Simon & Schuster.

Steiner, J. E. (1979). Human facial expressions in response to taste and smell stimulation. In H. Reese and L. Lipsitt (Eds.), *Advances in child development and behavior* (Vol. 13). New York: Academic Press.

Steinman, K. J. & Zimmerman, M. A. (2004). Religious activity and risk behavior among African American adolescents:

Concurrent and developmental effects. *American Journal of Community Psychology, 33,* 151–161.

Sternberg, R. (1994). Commentary: Reforming school reform: Comments on Multiple Intelligences. *Teachers College Record, 95,* 561–569.

Sternberg, R. J. (1988). *The triarchic mind: A theory of human intelligence.* New York: Viking.

Sternberg, R. J. (1999). The theory of successful intelligence. *Review of General Psychology, 3,* 292–316.

Sternberg, R. J. (2004). Individual differences in cognitive development. In U. Goswami (Ed.), *Blackwell handbook of childhood cognitive development* (pp. 600–619). Malden, MA: Blackwell Publishing.

Stetsenko, A., Little, T. D., Gordeeva, T., Grasshof, J., & Oettingen, G. (2000). Gender effects in children's beliefs about school performance: A cross-cultural study. *Child Development, 71,* 517–527.

Stevenson, H., & Stigler, J. (1992). *The learning gap: Why our schools are failing and what we can learn from Japanese and Chinese education.* New York: Simon & Schuster.

Stewart, S. M., & McBride-Chang, C. (2000). Influences on children's sharing in a multicultural setting. *Journal of Cross-Cultural Psychology, 31,* 333–348.

Stice, E., Presnell, K., & Bearman, S. (2001). Relation of early menarche to depression, eating disorders, substance abuse, and comorbid psychopathology among adolescent girls. *Developmental Psychology, 37,* 608–619.

Stickgold, R. (2005). Sleep-dependent memory consolidation. *Nature, 437,* 1272–1278.

Stilson, S. R., & Harding, C. G. (1997). Early social context as it relates to symbolic play: a longitudinal investigation. *Merrill-Palmer Quarterly, 43,* 682–693.

Stipek, D. (1995). The development of pride and shame in toddlers. In J. Tangney & K. Fischer (Eds.), *Self conscious emotions: The psychology of shame, guilt, embarrassment, and pride* (pp. 237–252). New York: Guilford.

Stocker, C. M., Burwell, R. A., & Briggs, M. L. (2002). Sibling conflict in middle childhood predicts children's adjustment in early adolescence. *Journal of Family Psychology, 16,* 50–57.

Stoolmiller, M., Kim, H. K., & Capaldi, D. M. (2005). The course of depressive symptoms in men from early adolescence to young adulthood: Identifying latent trajectories and early predictors. *Journal of Abnormal Psychology, 114,* 331–345.

Strayer, F. F., & Strayer, J. (1976). An ethological analysis of agonism and dominance relations among preschool children. *Child Development, 47,* 980–989.

Strege, J. (1997) *Tiger: A biography of Tiger Woods.* New York: Broadway Books.

Streissguth, A. P., Bookstein, F. L., Barr, H. M., Sampson, P. D., O'Malley, K., & Young, J. K. (2004). Risk factors for adverse life outcomes in fetal alcohol syndrome and fetal alcohol effects. *Developmental and Behavioral Pediatrics, 25,* 228–238.

Strid, K., Tjus, T., Smith, L., Meltzoff, A. N., & Heimann, M. (2006). Infant recall memory and communication predicts later cognitive development. *Infant Behavior & Development, 29,* 545–553.

Sturmhöfel, S., & Swartzwelder, H. (2004). Alcohol's effects on the adolescent brain: what can be learned from animal models. *Alcohol Research and Health, 28,* 213–221.

Suárez-Orozco, C., & Suárez-Orozco, M. (2001). *Children of immigration.* Cambridge: Harvard University Press.

Sugarman, A. (2001). *Peer influences on adolescent girls' eating behavior and attitudes: A grounded theory approach.* Unpublished doctoral dissertation, Temple University.

Sui-Chu, E., & Willms, J. (1996). *Effects of parental involvement on eighth-grade achievement. Sociology of Education, 69,* 126–141.

Suizzo, M.-A., & Bornstein, M. H. (2006). French and European American child-mother play: Culture and gender considerations. *International Journal of Behavioral Development, 30,* 498–508.

Sullivan, S. A., & Birch, L. L. (1990). Pass the sugar, pass the salt: Experience dictates preference. *Developmental Psychology, 26,* 546–551.

Sun, Y., & Li, Y. (2001). Marital disruptions, parental investment, and children's academic achievement: A longitudinal analysis. *Journal of Family Issues, 22,* 27–62.

Sun, Y., & Li, Y. (2002). Children's well-being during parents' marital disruption process: A pooled time-series analysis. *Journal of Marriage and the Family, 64,* 472–488.

Sur, M., & Rubenstein, J. L. R. (2005). Patterning and plasticity of the cerebral cortex. *Science, 310,* 805–810.

Susman, E. (1997). Modeling developmental complexity in adolescence: Hormones and behavior in context. *Journal of Research on Adolescence, 7,* 283–306.

Susman, E., & Dorn, L. (in press). Puberty: Its role in development. In R. Lerner & L. Steinberg (Eds.), *Handbook of adolescent psychology* (3rd ed.). New York: Wiley.

Susman, E., & Rogol, A. (2004). Puberty and psychological development. In R. M. Lerner & L. D. Steinberg (Eds.), *Handbook of adolescent psychology* (pp. 15–44). Hoboken, NJ: Wiley.

Talan, J. (2007, February 5). Low-level toxicants can harm brain. *Newsday.* Retrieved February 6, 2007, from http://www.newsday.com/news/health/ny-hslead0206,0,3014503.story?coll=ny-lea.

Tamis-Lemonda, C. S., & Bornstein, M. H. (1990). Language, play, and attention at one year. *Infant Behavior & Development, 13,* 85–98.

Tamis-LeMonda, C. S., & Bornstein, M. H. (1991). Individual variation, correspondence, stability, and change in mother and toddler play. *Infant Behavior & Development, 14,* 143–162.

Tamis-LeMonda, C. S., & Bornstein, M. H. (2002). Maternal responsiveness and early language acquisition. In R. V. Kail & H. W. Reese (Eds.), *Advances in child development and behavior* (Vol. 29, pp. 89–127). New York: Academic Press.

Tannen, D. (1994). *Gender and discourse.* New York: Oxford University Press.

Tanner, J. (1972). Sequence, tempo, and individual variation in growth and development of boys and girls aged twelve to sixteen. In J. Kagan & R. Coles (Eds.), *Twelve to sixteen: Early adolescence* (pp. 1–23). New York: Norton.

Tanner, J. M. (1981). Menarcheal age. *Science, 214,* 604.

Tanner, J. M. (1990). *Foetus into man* (2nd ed.). Cambridge: Harvard University Press.

Tasbihsazan, R., Nettelbeck, T., & Kirby, N. (2003). Predictive validity of the Fagan Test of Infant Intelligence. *British Journal of Developmental Psychology, 21,* 585–597.

Taylor, R., Casten, R., Flickinger, S., Roberts, D., & Fulmore, C. (1994). Explaining the school performance of African-American adolescents. *Journal of Research on Adolescence, 4,* 21–44.

Teachman, J., & Paasch, K. (1998). The family and educational aspirations. *Journal of Marriage and the Family, 60,* 704–714.

Terman, L. M. (1916). *The measurement of intelligence.* Boston: Houghton Mifflin.

Terman, L. M. (1947). *Genetic studies of genius: The gifted child grows up* (Vol. 4).

Stanford, CA: Stanford University Press.

Terry, R., & Coie, J. D. (1991). A comparison of methods for defining sociometric status among children. *Developmental Psychology, 27,* 867–880.

Teti, D., & Lamb, M. (1989). Socioeconomic and marital outcomes of adolescent marriage, adolescent childbirth, and their co-occurrence. *Journal of Marriage and the Family, 51,* 203–212.

Thelen, E., & Smith, L. (2006). Dynamic systems theories. In W. Damon & R. Lerner (Series Eds.) & R. Lerner (Vol. Ed.), *Handbook of child psychology: Vol. 1. Theoretical models of human development* (6th ed., pp. 258–312). New York: Wiley.

Thomas, A., Chess, S., & Birch, H. G. (1970). The origin of personality. *Scientific American, 223*(2), 102–109.

Thomas, J. R., & French, K. E. (1985). Gender differences across age in motor performance: A meta-analysis. *Psychological Bulletin, 98*(2), 260–282.

Thompson, P., Giedd, J., Woods, R., MacDonald, D., Evans, A., & Toga, A. (2000). Growth patterns in the developing brain detected using continuum mechanical tensor maps. *Nature, 404,* 190–193.

Thompson, R. A. (2006). The development of the person: Social understanding, relationships, conscience, and self. In W. Damon & R. M. Lerner (Series Eds.) & N. Eisenberg (Vol. Ed.), *Handbook of child psychology: Vol. 3. Social, emotional, and personality development* (6th ed., pp. 24–98). Hoboken, NJ: Wiley.

Thompson, R. A., & Goodvin, R. (2005). The individual child: Temperament, emotion, self, and personality. In M. H. Bornstein & M. E. Lamb (Eds.), *Developmental science: An advanced textbook* (pp. 391–428). Mahwah, NJ: Erlbaum.

Thurstone, L. L. (1938). *Primary mental abilities.* Chicago: University of Chicago Press.

Tiezzi, L., Lipshutz, J., Wrobleski, N., Vaughan, R., & McCarthy, J. (1997). pregnancy prevention among urban adolescents younger than 15: Results of the 'In Your Face' program. *Family Planning Perspectives, 29,* 173–176, 197.

Tomasello, M. (2006). Acquiring linguistic constructions. In W. Damon & R. M. Lerner (Series Eds.) & D. Kuhn & R. S. Siegler (Vol. Eds.), *Handbook of child psychology: Vol. 2. Cognition, perception, and language* (6th ed., pp. 255–298). Hoboken, NJ: Wiley.

Toth, S. L. Cicchetti, D., Macfie, J., Maughan, A., & Vanmeenen, K. (2000). Narrative representations of caregivers and self in male preschoolers. *Attachment and Human Development, 2,* 271–305.

Trehub, S. E., Trainor, L. J., & Unyk, A. M. (1993). Music and speech processing in the first year of life. *Advances in Child Development and Behavior, 24,* 1–35.

Trommsdorff, G. (2006). Development of emotions as organized by culture. *International Society for the Study of Behavioural Development Newsletter, 49,* 1–4.

True, M. M., Pisani, L., & Oumar, F. (2001). Infant-mother attachment among the Dogon of Mali. *Child Development, 72,* 1451–1466.

Trussell, J. (1989). Teenage pregnancy in the United States. *Family Planning Perspectives, 21,* 262–269.

Trusty, J., Plata, M., & Salazar, C.F. (2003). Modeling Mexican Americans' educational expectations: Longitudinal effects of variables across adolescence. *Journal of Adolescent Research, 18,* 131–153.

Tsao, F., Liu, H., & Kuhl, P. K. (2004). Speech perception in infancy predicts language development in the second year of life: A longitudinal study. *Child Development, 75,* 1067–1084.

Tucker, C. J., McHale, S. M., & Crouter, A. C. (2001). Conditions of sibling support in adolescence. *Journal of Family Psychology, 15,* 254–271.

Tucker, C. J., McHale, S. M., & Crouter, A. C. (2003). Dimensions of mothers' and fathers' differential treatment of siblings: Links with adolescents' sex-typed personal qualities. *Family Relations, 52,* 82–89.

Turati, C., Cassia, V. M., Simion, F., & Leo, I. (2006). Newborns' face recognition: Role of inner and outer facial features. *Child Development, 77,* 297–311.

Turiel, E. (2006). The development of morality. In N. Eisenberg (Vol. Ed.), *Handbook of child psychology: Vol. 3. Social, emotional, and personality development* (pp. 789–857). Hoboken, NJ: Wiley.

Turkheimer, E. (1998). Heritability and biological explanation. *Psychological Review, 105,* 782–791.

U.S. Census Bureau. (2004, March). *Children and the households they live in: 2000.* Retrieved October 7, 2008, http://www.census.gov/population/www/socdemo/hh-fam.html

U.S. Census Bureau. (2006). *Current population survey.* Washington, DC: Author.

U.S. Department of Agriculture. (2006, March). *WIC: The special supplemental nutrition program for women, infants and children* [Fact sheet]. Retrieved from http://www.fns.usda.gov/wic/factsheets.htm

U.S. Department of Health and Human Services. (2005, February 21). *U.S. Surgeon General releases advisory on alcohol use in pregnancy.* Retrieved August 13, 2008, from http://www.surgeongeneral.gov/pressreleases/sg02222005.html

Umaña-Taylor, A.J. (2004). Ethnic identity and self-esteem: Examining the role of social context. *Journal of Adolescence, 27,* 139–146.

Underwood, M. (2003). *Social aggression among girls.* New York: Guilford Press.

Underwood, M. K. (2002). Sticks and stones and social exclusion: Aggression among girls and boys. In P. K. Smith & C. H. Hart (Eds.), *Blackwell handbook of childhood social development* (pp. 533–548). Malden, MA: Blackwell.

Underwood, M. K., Beron, K. & Gentsch, J. J. (2007). *Girls' and boys' aggression in middle childhood and adolescence: Forms, contexts, and social processes.* Paper presented at the biennial meeting of the Society for Research in Child Development, Boston, MA.

UNICEF. (2007). *Annual report 2007.* Retrieved October 14, 2008, from http://www.unicef.org/publications/files/Annual_Report_2007.pdf

UNICEF. (2007). *The state of the world's children 2008.* New York: UNICEF.

UNICEF and the World Health Organization. (2008). *State of the world's children.* Retrieved July 27, 2008, from http://www.unicef.org.nz/speaking-out/publications-multimedia/publications/sowc/index.html

Upchurch, D., Aneshensel, C. S., Mudgal, J., & McNeely, C. (2001). Sociocultural contexts of time to first sex among Hispanic adolescents. *Journal of Marriage and the Family, 63,* 1158–1169.

Upchurch, D., Levy-Storms, L., Sucoff, C., & Aneshensel, C. (1998). Gender and ethnic differences in the timing of first sexual intercourse. *Family Planning Perspectives, 30,* 121–127.

Updegraff, K., McHale, S. M., & Crouter, A. C. (2000). Adolescents' sex-typed friendship experiences: Does having a sister versus and brother matter? *Child Development, 71,* 1597–1610.

Valdes, G. (1996). Con respecto: *Bridging the distances between culturally diverse families and schools: An ethnographic portrait.* New York: Teachers College Press.

Valsiner, J. (2006). Developmental epistemology and implications for methodology. In W. Damon & R. Lerner (Series Eds.) & R. Lerner (Vol. Ed.), *Handbook of child psychology: Vol. 1. Theoretical models of human development* (6th ed., pp. 166–209). New York: Wiley.

Van de Walle, G. A., Carey, S., & Pervor, M. (2000). Bases for object individuation in infancy: Evidence from manual search. *Journal of Cognition and Development, 1,* 249–280.

van den Boom, D. C. (1991). The influence of infant irritability on the development of the mother-infant relationship in the first 6 months of life. In J. K. Nugent, B. M. Lester & T. B. Brazelton (Eds.), *The cultural context of infancy: Vol. 2. Multicultural and interdisciplinary approaches to parent-infant relations* (pp. 63–89). Westport, CT: Ablex.

van den Boom, D. C. (2001). First attachments: Theory and research. In J. G. Bremner, & A. Fogel (Eds.), *Blackwell handbook of infant development* (pp. 296–325). Malden, MA: Blackwell.

Van Geert, P. & Steenbeek, H. (2005). Explaining after by before: Basic aspects of a dynamic systems approach to the study of development. *Developmental Review, 25,* 408–442.

van Ijzendoorn, M. H. (1997). Attachment, emergent morality, and aggression: Toward a developmental socioemotional model of antisocial behaviour. *Child Development, 68,* 571–591.

van IJzendoorn, M. (2005). Attachment at an early age (0–5) and its impact on children's development. In R. E. Tremblay, R. G. Barr,, & R. deV Peters (Eds.), *Encyclopedia on early childhood development* [online], Montreal, Quebec: Centre of Excellence for Early Childhood Development.

van IJzendoorn, M., & Bakermans-Kranenburg, M. (2006). DRD4 7-repeat polymorphism moderates the association between maternal unresolved loss or trauma and infant disorganization. *Attachment & Human Development, 8,* 291–307.

van Ijzendoorn, M. H., Bakermans-Kranenburg, M. J., & Sagi-Schwartz, A. (2006). Attachment across diverse sociocultural contexts: The limits of universality. In K. H. Rubin & O. B. Chung (Eds.), *Parenting beliefs, behaviors, and parent-child relations: A cross-cultural perspective* (pp. 107–142). New York: Psychology Press.

van IJzendoorn, M., & Juffer, F. (2005). Adoption is a successful natural intervention enhancing adopted children's IQ and school performance. *Current Directions in Psychological Science, 14,* 326–330.

Vandell, D. L. (2000). Parents, peer groups, and other socializing influences. *Developmental Psychology, 36,* 699–710.

Vandell, D. L. (2007). Early child care: The known and the unknown. In G. Ladd (Ed.), *Appraising the human development sciences essays in honor of* Merrill-Palmer Quarterly (pp. 300–328). Detroit, MI: Wayne State University Press.

Vandell, D. L., & Bailey, M. D. (1992). Conflicts between siblings. In C. Shantz & W. W. Hartup (Eds.), *Conflict in child and adolescent development* (pp. 242–269). Cambridge: Cambridge University Press.

Vandell, D. L., Nenide, L., & Van Winkle, S. J. (2006). Peer relationships in early childhood. In K. McCartney & D. Phillips (Eds.), *The Blackwell handbook of early childhood development* (pp. 455–470). Oxford, UK: Blackwell Publishing.

Vandell, D. L., Pierce, K. M., & Dadisman, K. (2005). Out-of-school settings as a developmental context for children and youth. In R. V. Kail (Ed.), *Advances in child development and behavior* (Vol. 33, pp. 43–77). New York: Academic.

Vandell, D. L., & Ramanan, J. (1991). Children of the National Longitudinal Survey of Youth: Choices in after-school care and child development. *Developmental Psychology, 27,* 637–643.

Vandell, D. L., & Wolfe, B. (2000) *Child care quality: Does it matter and does it need to be improved?* Report prepared for the United States Department of Health and Human Services, Office for Planning and Evaluation. http://www.wcer.wisc.edu/childcare/publication.html#pdf

Vanhatalo, A. M., Ekblad, H., Kero, P., & Erkkola, R. (1994). Incidence of bronchopulmonary dysplasia during an 11-year period in infants weighing less than 1500 g at birth. *Annales Chirurgiae et Gynaecologiae. Supplementum, 208,* 113–116.

Vaughn, B. E., Egeland, B. R., Sroufe, L. A., & Waters, E. (1979). Individual differences in infant-mother attachment at twelve and eighteen months: Stability and change in families under stress. *Child Development, 50,* 971–975.

Vaughn, B. E., Kopp, C. B., & Krakow, J. B. (1984). The emergence and consolidation of self-control from eighteen to thirty months of age: Normative trends and individual differences. *Child Development, 55,* 990–1004 .

Vega, W., Khoury, E., Zimmerman, R., Gil, A., & Warheit, G. (1995). Cultural conflicts and problem behaviors of Latino adolescents in home and school environments. *Journal of Community Psychology, 23,* 167–179.

Venter, J., Adams, M., Myers, E., Li, P., Mural, R., Sutton, G., et al. (2001). The sequence of the human genome. *Science, 291,* 1304–1351.

Venuti, P., Giusti, Z., Gini, M., & Bornstein, M. H. (2008). La disponibilità emotiva madre-gemelli in bambini italiani nel secondo anno di vita [Emotional availability in mothers and twins in the second year of life]. *Psicologia Clinica dello Sviluppo, 12,* 41–67.

Vieno, A., Perkins, D. D., Smith, T. M. & Santinello, M. (2005). Democratic school climate and sense of community in the school: A multilevel analysis. *American Journal of Community Psychology, 36,* 327–341.

Vitaro, F., Brendgen, M., & Barker, E. D. (2006). Subtypes of aggressive behaviors: A developmental perspective. *International Journal of Behavioral Development, 30,* 12–19.

Voelkl, K. (1997). Identification with school. *American Journal of Education, 105,* 294–318.

Volkow, N., & Li, T.-K. (2005). The neuroscience of addiction. *Nature Neuroscience, 8,* 1429–1430.

Volling, B. L. (2003). Sibling relationships. In M. H. Bornstein, L. Davidson, C. L. M. Keyes, & K. A. Moore (Eds.), *Well-being: Positive development across the life course* (pp. 205–220). Mahwah, NJ: Erlbaum.

Von Hofsten, C. (2007). Action in development. *Developmental Science, 10,* 54–60.

Vygotsky, L. S. (1967). Play and its role in the mental development of the child. *Soviet Psychology, 5,* 6–18.

Vygotsky, L. S. (1978). *Mind in society: The development of higher psychological processes.* Cambridge, MA: Harvard University Press.

Vygotsky, L. S. (1986). *Thought and language.* Cambridge, MA: MIT Press.

Wachs, T. D. (1987). Specificity of environmental action as manifest in environmental correlates of infant's mastery motivation. *Developmental Psychology, 23,* 782–790.

Wachs, T. D., & Gandour, M. J. (1983). Temperament, environment, and six-month cognitive-intellectual development: A test of the organismic specificity hypothesis. *International Journal of Behavioral Development, 6*(2), 135–152.

Waddington, C. H. (1940). *Organisers and genes.* Cambridge: Cambridge University Press.

Wagner, S. H., & Walters, J. (1982). A longitudinal analysis of early number concepts: From numbers to number. In G. E. Forman (Ed.), *Action and thought: From sensorimotor schemes to symbolic operations* (pp. 137–161). New York: Academic Press.

Wainright, J. L., Russell, S. T., & Patterson, C. J. (2004). Psychosocial adjustment and school outcomes of adolescents with same-sex parents. *Child Development, 75,* 1886–1898.

Wakschlag, L. S., Gordon, R. A., Lahey, B. B., Loeber, R., Green, S. M., & Leventhal, B. L. (2000). Maternal age at first birth and boys' risk for conduct disorder. *Journal of Research on Adolescence, 10,* 417–441.

Wald, M. (2005). Foreword. In Osgood, D., Foster, M., Flanagan, C., & Ruth, G. (Eds.), *On your own without a net: The transition to adulthood for vulnerable populations* (pp. vii–xi). Chicago: University of Chicago Press.

Walden, T., & Knieps, L. (1996). Reading and responding to social signals. In. M. Lewis & M. W. Sullivan (Eds.), *Emotional development in atypical children* (pp. 29–42). Hillsdale, NJ: Erlbaum.

Walden, T., Lemerise, E., & Smith, M. C. (1999). Friendship and popularity in preschool classrooms. *Early Education and Development, 10,* 351–371.

Walker, E. F., Sabuwalla, Z., & Huot, R. (2004). Pubertal neuromaturation, stress sensitivity, and psychopathology. *Development and Psychopathology, 16,* 807–824.

Wallace, J. M., Forman, T. A., Caldwell, C. H., & Willis, D. S. (2003). Religion and U.S. secondary school students current patterns, recent trends, and sociodemographic correlates. *Youth and Society, 35,* 98–125.

Wallen, K. (2005). Hormonal influences on sexually differentiated behaviors in nonhuman primates. *Frontiers in Neuroendocrinology, 26,* 7–26.

Wallis, C. (2008, February 25). How to make great teachers. *Time Magazine,* 28–34.

Wallis, C., & Steptoe, S. (2006, December 18). How to bring our schools out of the 20th century. *Time Magazine.*

Wang, Q. (2006). Developing emotion knowledge in cultural contexts. *International Journal of Behavioral Development, 30*(Suppl. 1), 8–12.

Wang, Q., & Fivush, R. (2005). Mother-child conversations of emotionally salient events: Exploring the functions of emotional reminiscing in European American and Chinese families. *Social Development, 14,* 473–495.

Warren, C., Santelli, J., Everett, S., Kann, L., Collins, J., Cassell, C., et al. (1998). Sexual Behavior Among U.S. High School Students, 1990–1995. *Family Planning Perspectives, 30,* 170–172, 200.

Warren, J. (2002). Reconsidering the relationship between student employment and academic outcomes: A new theory and better data. *Youth and Society, 33,* 366–393.

Warschauer, M. (2003). *Technology and social inclusion: Rethinking the digital divide.* Cambridge, MA: MIT Press.

Watamura, S. E., Donzella, B., Alwin, J., & Gunnar, M. R. (2003). Morning-to-afternoon increases in cortisol concentrations for infants and toddlers at child care: Age differences and behavioral correlates. *Child Development, 74,* 1006–1020.

Waters, E. (1978). The reliability and stability of individual differences in infant-mother attachment. *Child Development, 49,* 483–494.

Waters, E., Hay, D., & Richters, J. (1986). Infant-parent attachment and the origins of prosocial and antisocial behavior. In D. Olweus, J. Block, & M. Radke-Yarrow (Eds.), *Development of antisocial and prosocial behavior: Research, theories, and issues* (pp. 97–125). New York: Academic Press.

Waters, E., Merrick, S., Treboux, D., Crowell, J., & Albersheim, L. (2000). Attachment stability in infancy and early adulthood: A 20-year longitudinal study. *Child Development, 71,* 684–689.

Watson, J. B. (1929). *Behavior: An introduction to comparative psychology.* New York: H. Holt and Company.

Watson, J. B. (1930). *Behaviorism* (rev. ed.). Chicago: University of Chicago Press.

Watson, J., & Rayner, R. (1920). Conditioned emotional reactions. *Journal of Experimental Psychology, 3,* 1–14.

Watson, K. (1924). *Behaviorism.* New York: People's Institute Publishing Company.

Waxman, S. R., & Lidz, J. L. (2006). Early word learning. In W. Damon & R. Lerner (Series Eds.) & D. Kuhn & R. S. Siegler (Vol. Eds.), *Handbook of child psychology: Vol. 2. Cognition, perception, and language* (6th ed., pp. 299–335). Hoboken, NJ: Wiley.

Way, N. & Greene, M. L. (2006). Trajectories of perceived friendship quality during adolescence: The patterns and contextual predictors. *Journal of Research on Adolescence, 16,* 293–320.

Weaver, I., Cervoni, N., Champagne, F., D'Alessio, A., Sharma, S., Seckl, J., et al. (2004). Epigenetic programming by maternal behavior. *Nature Neuroscience, 7,* 847–854.

Webb, S. J., Monk, C. S., & Nelson, C. A. (2001). Mechanisms of postnatal neurobiological development: Implications for human development. *Developmental Neuropsychology, 19,* 147–171.

Wechsler, D. (1991). *Manual for the Wechsler Intelligence Scales for Children (WISC III)* (3rd ed.). San Antonio, TX: Psychological Corp.

Weir, L. A., Etelson, D., & Brand, D. A. (2006). Parents' perceptions of neighborhood safety and children's physical activity, *Preventive Medicine, 43,* 212–217.

Weir, R. H. (1962). *Language in the crib.* The Hague: Mouton.

Weisner, T. S., & Gallimore, R. (1977). My brother's keeper: Child and sibling caretaking. *Current Anthropology, 18,* 169–190.

Weizman, Z. O., & Snow, C. E. (2001). Lexical input as related to children's vocabulary acquisition: Effects of sophisticated exposure and support for meaning. *Developmental Psychology, 37,* 265–279.

Wellman, H. M. (2002). Understanding the psychological world: Developing a theory of mind. In C. Goswami (Ed.), *Blackwell handbook of childhood cognitive development* (pp. 167–187). Malden, MA: Blackwell.

Wentzel, K. (2002). Are effective teachers like good parents? Teaching styles and student adjustment in early adolescence. *Child Development, 73,* 287–301.

Wentzel, K., & Asher, S. (1995). The academic lives of neglected, rejected, popular, and controversial children. *Child Development, 66,* 754–763.

Wentzel, K., Barry, C., & Caldwell, K. (2004). Friendships in middle school: Influences on motivation and school adjustment. *Journal of Educational Psychology, 96,* 195–203.

Weyer, M., & Sandler, I. N. (1998). Stress and coping as predictors of children's divorce-related ruminations. *Journal of Clinical Child Psychology, 27,* 78–86.

Whalen, C. K. (2000). Attention-deficit/hyperactivity disorder. In A. E. Kazdin (Ed.), *Encyclopedia of psychology* (Vol. 1, pp. 299–303). New York: Oxford University Press/American Psychological Association.

White, B. L., Castle, R., & Held, R. (1964). Observations on the development of visually directed reaching. *Child Development, 35,* 349–364.

Whiting, B. B., & Whiting, J. W. M. (1975). *Children of six cultures: A psycho-cultural analysis.* Cambridge, MA: Harvard University Press

Wichstrøm, L. (1999). The emergence of gender difference in depressed mood during adolescence: The role of intensified gender socialization. *Developmental Psychology, 35,* 232–245.

Wiebe, S. A., Cheatham, C. L., Lukowski, A. F., Haight, J. C., Muehleck, A. J., & Bauer, P. J. (2006). Infants' ERP response to novel and familiar stimuli change over time: implications for novelty detection and memory. *Infancy, 9,* 21–44.

Wiesel, T. N., & Hubel, D. H. (1974). Ordered arrangement of orientation columns in monkeys lacking visual experience. *Journal of Comparative Neurology, 158,* 307–318.

Wiesner, M., & Ittel, A. (2002). Relations of pubertal timing and depressive symptoms to substance use in early adolescence. *Journal of Early Adolescence, 22*(1), 5–23.

Wight, R. G., Sepúlveda, J. E., & Aneshensel, C. S. (2004). Depressive symptoms: How do adolescents compare with adults? *Journal of Adolescent Health, 34,* 314–323.

William T. Grant Foundation Commission on Work, Family, and Citizenship. (1988). *The forgotten half: Non-college youth in America.* Washington, DC: Author.

Wilson, B. J. (2008). Media and children's aggression, fear, and altruism. *The Future of Children, 18,* 87–118.

Wilson, P., & Wilson, J. (1992). Environmental influences on adolescent educational aspirations: A logistic transform model. *Youth and Society, 24,* 52–70.

Wilson, R. S. (1978). Synchronies in menatal development: An epigenetic perspective. *Science, 202,* 939–938.

Wilton, M., Craig, W., & Pepler, D. (2000). Emotion regulation and display is classroom victims of bullying: Characteristic expressions of affect, coping styles, and relevant contextual factors. *Social Development, 9,* 226–245.

Winerman, L. (2005). The mind's mirror. *Monitor on Psychology, 36,* 49–50.

Wintemute, G., Kraus, J., Teret, S., & Wright, M. (1987). Drowning in childhood and adolescence: A population-based study. *American Journal of Public Health, 77,* 830–832.

Winterbottom, M. (1958). The relation of need for achievement to learning experiences in independence and mastery. In J. Atkinson (Ed.), *Motives in fantasy, action, and society* (pp. 453–478). Princeton, NJ: Van Nostrand.

Wismer Fries, A. B., & Pollak, S. (2004). Emotion understanding in postinstitutionalized Eastern European Children. *Development and Psychopathology, 16,* 355–369.

Wojslawowicz, J. C., Rubin, K. H., Burgess, K. B., Booth-LaForce, C., & Rose-Krasnor, L. R. (2006). Behavioral characteristics associated with stable and fluid best friendship patterns in middle childhood. *Merrill-Palmer Quarterly, 52,* 671–693.

Wolf, D., & Perry, M. (1988). From endpoints to repertoires: New conclusions about drawing development. *Journal of Aesthetic Education, 22,* 17–35.

Wolf, S. A., & Heath, S. B. (1992). *The braid of literature: Children's world of reading.* Cambridge MA: Harvard University Press.

World Bank (2006). Repositioning Nutrition as Central to Development. Retrieved October 14, 2006, from http://siteresources.worldbank.org/NUTRITION/Resources/281846–1131636806329/NutritionStrategy.pdf

World Health Organization. (2008, August). *Priority interventions: HIV/AIDS prevention, treatment and care in the health sector.* Retrieved from http://www.who.int/hiv/pub/priority_interventions_web.pdf

Wright, J., Cullen, F., & Williams, N. (1997). Working while in school and delinquent involvement: Implications for social policy. *Crime and Delinquency, 43,* 203–221.

Wrobel, G. M., Hendrickson, Z., & Grotevant, H. D. (2006). Adoption. In G. Bear & K. M. Minke (Eds.), *Children's needs: Vol. 3. Development, prevention, and intervention* (pp. 675–688). Bethesda, MD: National Association of School Psychologists.

Wu, L., & Anthony, J. (1999). Tobacco smoking and depressed mood in late childhood and early adolescence. *American Journal of Public Health, 89,* 1837–1840.

Wu, L., Schlenger, W. E., & Galvin, D. M. (2003). The relationship between employment and substance use among students aged 12 to 17. *Journal of Adolescent Health, 32,* 5–15.

Xu, F. (2003). The development of object individuation in infancy. In H. Hayne (Ed.), *Progress in infancy research* (pp. 159–192). Mahwah, NJ: Erlbaum.

Xue, Y., Leventhal, T., Brooks-Gunn, J., & Earls, F. (2005). Neighborhood of residence and mental health problems of 5- to 11-year-olds. *Archives of General Psychiatry, 62,* 554–563.

Yamaguchi, R., Johnston, L., & O'Malley, P. (2003). Relationship between student illicit drug use and school drug-testing policies. *Journal of School Health, 73,* 159–164.

Yankelovich, D. (1974). *The new morality: A profile of American youth in the 1970s.* New York: McGraw-Hill.

Yasui, M., Dorham, C. L., & Dishion, T. J. (2004). Ethnic identity and psychological adjustment: A validity analysis for European American and African American adolescents. *Journal of Adolescent Research, 19,* 807–825.

Yeh, H., & Lempers, J. D. (2004). Perceived sibling relationships and adolescent development. *Journal of Youth and Adolescence, 33,* 133–147.

Yehuda, R., Mulherin Engel, S. R., Seckl, J., Marcus, S. M., & Berkowitz, G. S. (2005). Transgenerational effects of posttraumatic stress disorder in babies of mothers exposed to the World Trade Center attacks during pregnancy. *Journal of Clinical Endocrinology & Metabolism, 20,* 1–15.

Youngblade, L. M., & Dunn, J. (1995). Individual differences in young children's pretend play with mother and sibling: Links to relationships and understanding of other people's feelings and beliefs. *Child Development, 66,* 1472–1492.

Zahn-Waxler, C., & Radke-Yarrow, M. (1990). The origins of empathic concern. *Motivation and Emotion, 14,* 107–129.

Zaskind, P. S., & Gingras, J. L. (2006). Maternal cigarette-smoking during pregnancy disrupts rhythms in fetal heart rate. *Journal of Pediatric Psychology, 31,* 5–14.

Zaslavsky, C. (1973). *Africa counts: Number and pattern in African culture.* Boston, MA: Prindle, Weber & Schmidt, Inc.

Zhen-Wang, B., & Cheng-Ye, J. (2005). Secular growth changes in body height and weight in children and adolescents in Shandong, China between 1939 and 2000. *Annals of Human Biology, 32,* 650–665.

Zhou, Q., Eisenberg, N., Wang, Y., & Reiser, M. (2004). Chinese children's effortful control and dispositional anger/frustration: Relations to parenting styles and children's social functioning. *Developmental Psychology, 40,* 352–366.

Zigler, E. (1998). School should begin at age 3 years for American children. *Journal of Developmental and Behavioral Pediatrics, 19*(1), 38–40.

Zito, J. M., Safer, D. J., DosReis, S., Gardner, J. F., Soeken, K., Boles, M., et al. (2002). Rising prevalence of antidepressants among U.S. youths. *Pediatrics, 109,* 721–727.

Zucker, K. J. (2004). Gender identity disorder in children and adolescents. *Annual Review of Clinical Psychology, 1,* 467–492.

Zuckerman, B., Stevens, G. D., Inkelas, M., & Halfon, N. (2004). Prevalence and correlates of high-quality basic pediatric preventive care. *Pediatrics, 114,* 1522–1529.

Name Index

Subject Index/Glossary

Bold entries indicate definitions in the margin glossary. Entries followed by "f" indicate figures. Entries followed by "t" indicate tables.

S-1

TO THE OWNER OF THIS BOOK:

I hope that you have found *Development: Infancy Through Adolescence* useful. So that this book can be improved in a future edition, would you take the time to complete this sheet and return it? Thank you.

School and address: _____

_____

Department: _____

Instructor's name: _____

1. What I like most about this book is: _____

_____

_____

2. What I like least about this book is: _____

_____

_____

3. My general reaction to this book is: _____

_____

_____

4. The name of the course in which I used this book is:

_____

5. Were all of the chapters of the book assigned for you to read? _____

   If not, which ones weren't?_____

6. In the space below, or on a separate sheet of paper, please write specific suggestions for improving this book and anything else you'd care to share about your experience in using this book.

_____

_____

_____

_____

_____

_____

WADSWORTH
CENGAGE Learning™

BUSINESS REPLY MAIL
FIRST-CLASS MAIL   PERMIT NO. 34   BELMONT CA

POSTAGE WILL BE PAID BY ADDRESSEE

Attn: Psychology Editor

Wadsworth Cengage Learning
20 Davis Drive
Belmont, CA   94002-9801

FOLD HERE

OPTIONAL:

Your name:_____ Date: _____

May we quote you, either in promotion for *Development: Infancy Through Adolescence*, or in future publishing ventures?

Yes: _____ No: _____

Sincerely yours,

Laurence Steinberg, Deborah Lowe Vandell, and Marc H. Burnstein